SOCIAL POLICY FIRST HAND

An international introduction to participatory welfare

Edited by Peter Beresford and Sarah Carr

First published in Great Britain in 2018 by

Policy Press
University of Bristol
1-9 Old Park Hill
Bristol
BS2 8BB
UK
t: +44 (0)117 954 5940
pp-info@bristol.ac.uk
www.policypress.co.uk

North America office:
Policy Press
c/o The University of Chicago Press
1427 East 60th Street
Chicago, IL 60637, USA
t: +1 773 702 7700
f: +1 773-702-9756
sales@press.uchicago.edu
www.press.uchicago.edu

British Library Cataloguing in Publication Data
A catalogue record for this book is available from the British Library

Library of Congress Cataloging-in-Publication Data
A catalog record for this book has been requested

ISBN 978-1-4473-3236-7 paperback
ISBN 978-1-4473-3235-0 hardcover
ISBN 978-1-4473-3237-4 ePub
ISBN 978-1-4473-3238-1 Mobi
ISBN 978-1-4473-3255-8 ePdf

The right of Peter Beresford and Sarah Carr to be identified as editors of this work has been asserted by them in accordance with the Copyright, Designs and Patents Act 1988.

The statements and opinions contained within this publication are solely those of the editors and contributors and not of the University of Bristol or Policy Press. The University of Bristol and Policy Press disclaim responsibility for any injury to persons or property resulting from any material published in this publication.

Policy Press works to counter discrimination on grounds of gender, race, disability, age and sexuality.

Cover design by Clifford Hayes
Front cover image: Brian Barnes
Printed and bound in Great Britain by TJ International, Padstow
Policy Press uses environmentally responsible print partners

Contents

List of figures and tables   vii
Foreword by Baroness Ruth Lister   viii

Introduction   1
     Peter Beresford and Sarah Carr

Part I: Service users and social policy: an introduction   **12**
1   Challenging injustice: the importance of collective ownership of   14
     social policy
     Danny Dorling
2   Participation and solidarity in a changing welfare state   22
     Peter Taylor-Gooby
3   Social policy in developing countries: a post-colonial critique and   33
     participatory inquiry
     Sweta Rajan-Rankin
4   Advancing sustainability: developing participatory social policy in   43
     the context of environmental disasters
     Margaret Alston
5   Social policy and disability   51
     Colin Cameron
6   A case study of children's participation in health policy and practice   62
     Louca-Mai Brady, Felicity Hathway and Emily Roberts
7   Who owns co-production?   74
     Sarah Carr

Part II: Critiquing and reconceiving Beveridge's 'five giant evils': key areas of   **84**
British post-war social policy from a lived experience perspective
8   Rethinking disabled people's rights to work and contribute   86
     Jane Young
9   Talking policy as a patient   95
     Anya de Iongh
10   'We don't deal with people, we deal with bricks and mortar': a lived   98
     experience perspective on UK health and housing policy
     Alison Cameron
11   Education (ignorance) addressing inclusive education: the issues and   103
     its importance from a participatory perspective
     Tara Flood and Navin Kikabhai
12   "For work, we came here to find work": migrant Roma employment   107
     and the labour of language
     Colin Clark

Part III: The contribution of service user knowledges   118

13   Disability policy and lived experience: reflections from   120
regional Australia
Kathy Boxall, Adam Johnson, Lawrence Mitting, Suzanne Simpson,
Stefan Zwickl, Judith Zwickl, Shae Kermit, Luke and Caroline

14   Renewing epistemologies: service user knowledge   132
Diana Rose

15   Pornography, feminist epistemology and changing public policy   142
Ruth Beresford

16   Making social policy internationally: a participatory research   147
perspective
Nicola Yeates and Ana B. Amaya

Part IV: An inclusive life course and developmental approach to social policy 161

17   Disabled children's lives: an inclusive life course and developmental   163
approach to social policy
Mary Wickenden

18   Troubled youth and troubling social policy: mental health from a   172
Mad Studies perspective
Lucy Costa

19   Disability: an inclusive life course and developmental approach to   181
social policy
Emmeline Burdett

20   Independent living from a Black Disabled Woman's perspective   188
Michelle Daley

21   Food poverty and the policy context in Ireland   195
Deirdre O'Connor

22   Implementing race equality policies in British health and social care: 205
a perspective from experience
Hári Sewell

23   Participatory approaches to social policy in relation to ageing   211
Sarah Lonbay

24   Death, dying and digital stories   223
Lisa Williams, Merryn Gott, Tess Moeke-Maxwell, Stella Black,
Shuchi Kothari, Sarina Pearson, Peter James Simpson, Tessa Morgan,
Marianne Grbin, Matua Rawiri Wharemate and Whaea Whio Hansen

Part V: Transforming social policy   231

25   People acting collectively can be powerful   233
Jennie Fleming

26   Their participation and ours: competing visions of empowerment   243
Iain Ferguson

27   A participatory approach to professional practice   251
Suzy Croft

Contents

28   Dreams of justice   257
      Tina Minkowitz
29   Sustainable-participatory social policy   262
      Marilyn Palmer
30   Participatory social policy in a large EU research project   277
      Joe Greener and Michael Lavalette, with Rose Devereaux and members
      of SUGAH

Part VI: Campaigning and change   289

Section One: Approaches to activism

31   'What is strong, not what is wrong'   292
      An interview with Clenton Farquharson, MBE
32   Participatory social policy and social change: exploring the role of 297
      social entrepreneurship linked to forms of social and micro enterprises
      in the field of social care
      Barbara Fawcett
33   Public duty, whistleblowing and scandal: influences on public policy 306
      Kay Sheldon
34   'Informed gender practice in acute mental health': when policy   311
      makes sense
      Nicky Lambert
35   Making the case for single sex wards   314
      Jolie Goodman
36   #JusticeforLB: in search of truth, accountability and justice   319
      George Julian and Sara Ryan

Section Two: The role of online platforms and social media

37   Guerilla policy: new platforms for making policy from below   323
      Michael Harris
38   A Magna Carta for learning disabled people   327
      Kaliya Franklin and Gary Bourlet
39   Pat's Petition: The emerging role of social media and the internet   332
      Pat Onions and others

Part VII: Breaking down barriers   336

Section One: Inclusion and difference in the formulation and operation of social policy

40   "LGBT History Month is a thing!" The story of an equal rights   338
      campaign
      Sue Sanders
41   Progressing gender recognition and trans rights in the UK   343
      Christine Burns

v

Section Two: User-led approaches to social policy

42   Transforming professional training and education – a gap mending   349
      approach: the PowerUs European partnership
      Helen Casey
43   Grassroots tackling policy: the making of the 'Spartacus Report'   355
      Sam Barnett-Cormack
44   Involvement for influence: developing the 4Pi Involvement Standards   362
      Sarah Yiannoullou and Alison Faulkner

Part VIII: Participatory research and evaluation   **367**
45   From expert to service user: challenging how lived experience   369
      is demeaned
      Michele Moore
46   Participatory methodologies involving marginalised perspectives   376
      Charlotte Williams
47   Developing the evidence to challenge 'welfare reform': the road to   389
      'Cash Not Care'
      Mo Stewart
48   Service user-controlled research for evidence-based policymaking   394
      Alison Faulkner
49   Participatory citizenship, gender and human trafficking in Nepal   406
      *Diane Richardson, Nina Laurie, Meena Poudel, Shakti Samuha and Janet
      Townsend*
50   Experiential knowledge in mental health policy and legislation: 418
      can we ever change the agenda?
      Jasna Russo

Conclusion   427
Peter Beresford and Sarah Carr

Notes on contributors   435

Index   447

List of figures and tables

Figures

2.1	Public spending as a percentage of GDP, 2000–2020	23
2.2	Spending on the core of the welfare: health and pension spending as a percentage of GDP, 1980–2011	26
2.3	Spending on new welfare as percentage of old, 1980–2011	29

Tables

1.1	Household income inequality, most affluent countries of the world, 2004–13	16
16.1	Participatory and conventional research: a comparison	149
16.2	Continua of participation in research projects	151

Foreword

Nearly 30 years ago, at a meeting I'd spoken at, Peter Beresford challenged me about the involvement of people with experience of poverty in research and action on poverty. This led to a collaboration around such involvement, which taught me a lot – about both the experience of poverty and the importance of participation. Some years later I reflected on what I'd learned from this and subsequent involvement in the Commission on Participation and Power from within a framework of citizenship and human rights (Lister, 2002).

The right to participation has been promoted as both a citizenship and a human right. Indeed, it has been theorised as pivotal to a human rights-based approach because it underpins the effective realisation of other rights. It is a right that both recognises and strengthens the agency (including the democratic agency) of people living in poverty and other marginalised groups. It represents recognition of and respect for the dignity of 'the voiceless', referred to in the quotation opening the introduction to this book, by enabling their voices to be heard. As such it helps to strengthen social justice understood as requiring recognition as well as a just (re)distribution of resources. This is reflected in an ongoing ATD Fourth World participatory project involving people with experience of poverty in the training of social workers – an illuminating example of how service users' experience and knowledge can inform the training of service providers (Gupta et al, 2017).

This volume, initiated and edited by Peter and Sarah Carr, isn't about the participation of people with experience of poverty as such but its central themes are as relevant to them as to other 'voiceless' service users. It also underscores the diversity of service users and that, as the first book in this series by Peter illuminates, users are not a separate group (Beresford, 2016). We all experience social policy in various ways – to our advantage or our detriment. Nevertheless, the voices of some users are less likely to be heard than others and this book is an attempt to provide a space for the voices of some of the traditionally voiceless to be heard. It does not just 'talk the talk' of participation but begins to 'walk the walk'.

In doing so, it raises some salient questions, most fundamentally that of the nature of knowledge and expertise, which is a central theme – both explicit and implicit – running through the book. It has become politically fashionable on the Right to dismiss traditional 'experts' – think the Conservative minister Michael Gove's infamous observation during the EU referendum campaign that people 'have had enough of experts' (3 June 2016) and Donald Trump's rejection of the scientific evidence on climate change. While such attitudes have been justly castigated, participatory approaches to social policy do create a challenge for those of us considered 'experts' on the subjects it addresses. There is an important debate to be had about the contribution to be made by the expertise borne of experience and its relationship to more traditional forms of expertise. A report of a remarkable experimental ATD Fourth World project in France, which brought together traditional experts and people with experience of poverty, contended that

> the knowledge that people who have experienced poverty can bring to the table is uniquely valuable ... as long as they have the opportunity to think about what they and those around them experience. This does not exclude other types of knowledge, but these ... can never replace what is contributed and expressed by the poor themselves (Fourth World-University Research Group, 2007: 4).

Social Policy First Hand makes an important contribution to this debate. It does not privilege one form of knowledge and expertise over another and also acknowledges the dangers of over-simplifying the idea of service users' 'experiential knowledge', not least in view of the diversity of service users. Chapters by non-academic service users and activists sit side by side with those by researchers whose expertise is recognised in more traditional ways by the academy and policymakers (for the most part).

The conclusion deals with some of the challenges faced by participatory approaches to social policy (explored also from a research perspective by my colleague Jo Aldridge (2015) in her invaluable account of participatory research). These challenges have implications not just for social policy researchers but also for research funders and for service providers. Some of the challenges are practical (see also Lister, 2007); some raise more fundamental questions of philosophy and principle. But, as the editors observe in the conclusion, underlying these challenges is the even more fundamental issue of inequalities of power. It is worth heeding the warning of Griet Roets and colleagues (2012), based on a critical evaluation of user participation in Belgium: this is not primarily a question of the 'empowerment' of individual service users but of transforming organisational power structures. Otherwise participation runs the risk of tokenism, which can leave people feeling more exploited than empowered. Indeed, one of the loudest messages heard by the Commission on Poverty, Participation and Power was that 'phony participation without the power to bring about change [represents] the ultimate disrespect' (CoPPP, 2000: 18).

Of course, this book is not just about a participatory approach to social policy. It's also about the nature of social policy itself and the perspectives to be gained on it from a participatory approach. It ends with a call to advance 'truly *social* policy, based on and capable of securing the rights and needs of all'. All who care about social policy and the wellbeing of our fellow citizens – as policymakers, service providers, service users, researchers, commentators – should take heed.

Baroness Ruth Lister of Burtersett
Emeritus Professor of Social Policy, Loughborough University and Member of the
House of Lords.
April 2017

References

Aldridge, J. (2015) *Participatory Research*, Bristol: Policy Press.

Beresford, P. (2016) *All Our Welfare: Towards participatory social policy*, Bristol: Policy Press.

Commission on Poverty, Participation and Power (CoPPP) (2000) *Listen Hear. The Right to be Heard*, Bristol: Policy Press.

Fourth World-University Research Group (2007) *The Merging of Knowledge. People in Poverty and Academics Thinking Together*, Lanham, MD and Plymouth: University Press of America.

Gupta, A., Blumhardt, H. and ATD Fourth World (2017) 'Poverty, exclusion and child protection practice: the contribution of "the politics of recognition & respect"', *European Journal of Social Work*, DOI: 10.1080/13691457.2017.1287669.

Lister, R. (2002) 'A politics of recognition and respect: involving people with experience of poverty in decision making that affects their lives', *Social Policy & Society*, 1(1), 37–46.

Lister, R. (2007) 'From object to subject: including marginalised citizens in decision-making', *Policy & Politics*, 35(3), 437–55.

Roets, G., Roose, R., De Bie, M., Claes, L. and van Hove, G. (2012) 'Pawns or pioneers? The logic of user participation in anti-poverty policy-making in public policy units in Belgium', *Social Policy & Administration*, 46(7), 807–22.

Introduction

Peter Beresford and Sarah Carr

I'm grateful that, after an early life of being silenced, sometimes violently, I grew up to have a voice, circumstances that will always bind me to the rights of the voiceless. (Solnit, 2014)

A different approach to social policy

For years there have been growing calls for a different approach to social policy; one that is truly participatory and democratic, rather than paternalistic and controlling. This book is a response to that demand. It is the first exploration of participatory social policy internationally, critiquing its nature, origins and possibilities, as well as the issues and problems it faces.

The promise of participatory social policy is that where people need help or support, or for their rights to be safeguarded, they have a real say in that process, instead of having someone else's moral, ideological, economic, policy or social solutions imposed on them, as has so long been the case. Yet despite the popular support for participatory social policy, it has so far made very limited progress globally. Perhaps this is not surprising. Social policy continues to be a battleground between contending political and ideological forces; each with its policy prescriptions and agendas to pursue. Meanwhile, the subjects of social policy, especially of its more 'heavy end', have had little role in shaping it, often serving only as a stage army that is either patronised or stigmatised, frequently marginalised and excluded from mainstream society. In addition they have largely been excluded from debates, discussions and the formulation of social policy as both an area of policymaking and an academic discipline.

This book is part of a much broader movement to challenge and change this. We need to be realistic about the scope and magnitude of change needed. Moving to participatory social policy represents a paradigm shift. Such a different kind of social policy is not only based on a different set of values and principles to its predecessors, demanding a different approach to implementation. It also requires a radically different approach to understanding, studying, analysing and researching social policy. It calls for a participatory approach in these domains too.

Participatory social policy demands a different approach to analysis and discussion

That is where this book comes in. For the first time it offers a global exploration of the nature, potential and problems of such social policy. Because a fundamentally participatory approach is essentially different to what has come before, we should expect that the 'who, how and what' of examining it will also be different. Thus, if historically the analysis of social policy was the restricted province of the policymakers, politicians, bureaucrats, academics and researchers who were also centrally involved in its construction, participatory social policy demands the involvement of a much wider range of stakeholders, notably those who are the subjects of, receive, work in and pay for social policy. If the 'knowledge' that shaped traditional social policy was the technical knowledge associated with the perceived 'expertise' of planners, researchers, bureaucrats and political leaders, now it also extends to the first hand or 'experiential knowledge', based on direct experience of service users, carers, ordinary citizens, workers and those denied citizenship. And if the ideas, values, goals and priorities that traditionally underpinned social policy were largely owed to the narrow group that owned it, by definition, this will radically change with participatory social policy. As we shall shortly see, such positive disruptions and changes can raise fundamental theoretical, philosophical, practical, ethical and emotional issues.

They can also present challenges to the assumptions and expectations of all of us. The reality is that participatory critiques of social policy, beginning with the pioneering efforts of the disabled people's movement almost half a century ago, have encountered enormous resistance. Few commentators tend to attack participatory social policy explicitly; it could seem like attacking 'Mom' and 'Apple Pie'. However, there is a long hidden history of intellectual and practical objections being raised against it.

We need to be clear about this from the start and readers need to be prepared for something different. If this book does not read like a traditional social policy text, it is because it is not concerned with traditional social policy. This does not mean that it is any less rigorous or research based than any conventional text, but rather that participatory social policy requires we revisit our understandings of such concepts. Participatory social policy grows out of different traditions and, as we shall explain, cannot be judged in the same terms as conventional social policy. However, as we shall argue, that does not make it any less theory or 'evidence' based. Instead, we suggest, because it aspires to involve all stakeholders, participatory social policy has a unique capacity to show the whole picture, rather than just traditional 'expert' takes on it.

The context for change

All Our Welfare, the first text in this series (Beresford, 2016), which focused on the UK welfare state, as a lens through which to explore participatory social policy, raised two key questions. These were:

- How should people look after each other in the 21st century society?

and

- Why and when did taking care of each other as human beings become contentious?

The questions raised by *All Our Welfare* continue to reverberate, yet social policy seems no closer to addressing, let alone answering them. Instead, policymakers appear preoccupied with other problems, many of which seem of their own making. We have witnessed the 'Brexit' decision to leave the EU in the UK, which has increased economic and political uncertainty as well as anti-immigrant feeling; the election of President Trump in the US and his attack on 'Obamacare'; and massive ongoing conflict and enforced population movement globally. All of these have enormous regressive implications for social policy and the many millions affected by it. While the Brexit and US presidential votes have been seen to signify the alienation of many people, particularly disadvantaged people, from both the democratic and policy process, there has been little fundamental reconceptualising of social policy. The unexpectedly high vote received by the UK Labour Party, led by the left-wing Jeremy Corbyn, and political re-engagement of many young people in the June 2017 UK general election can be seen as a political shift in the opposite direction. But it still leaves the political left having to find a way of reconciling itself to participatory approaches to social policy, rather than simply perpetuating its own policy prescriptions. Whether we are talking about neoliberal, traditional Fabian or socialist/communist social policy, it is still largely characterised by being top-down, non-participatory and essentially economistic; that is to say subordinating social issues to narrowly economic ones.

The problems of prevailing social policy

While social policy has often been presented by mainstream commentators as unproblematic, as essentially benign and positive, as if it is simply intended to 'meet people's needs for welfare and wellbeing' (Alcock, 2008: 2), the reality is much more complex and at least ambiguous. From service user perspectives, it is frequently experienced as serving strongly anti-social purposes. Yet this critical perspective has tended to be underplayed in the literature. Thus, for instance, the latest fifth edition of the *Student Companion to Social Policy* (Alcock et al, 2016), current standard work in the teaching of students, includes chapters on service users (written by a non-service user) and disabled people (written by a non-disabled person) with little other discussion of the role of service users, disabled and marginalised people in modern social policy.

There is no question that the pioneering post-war UK welfare state was intended to secure the social rights of citizens and reverse the impoverishing effects of the market. Nonetheless, it perpetuated the subordination of many marginalised groups, including disabled and older people, mental health service users and children in state care. Such groups had little if any say over the policies and services that shaped their lives. Subsequent neoliberal social policies, despite their consumerist gloss, have tended to offer no more say or accountability. Instead they show strong similarities with pre-welfare poor law regimes, as well as placing an emphasis on policing and pathologising welfare user groups (Stewart, 2016).

The historical foundations of social policy in the UK Poor Law are again strongly evident in current policymaking internationally. It is also possible to detect ideological traces of negative quasi-religious moral attitudes to poverty and disability in contemporary policy making. These attitudes can be related to Weber's theories about the 'Protestant work ethic', grace and 'idleness' (Weber, 1905). While Nazi social policy and its euthanasia programme Aktion T4 have become symbolic, the wider destructive effects of social policy, from sterilisation of people with learning difficulties to the forcible 'treatment' of mental health service users, have tended to be marginalised in mainstream discussion. Eugenics policies were not confined to fascist Germany and continued in parts of Northern Europe and some Canadian provinces and US states during the immediate post-war period.

Whether the rationale and aim of social policy is to improve and protect (the post-war UK welfare state) or to regulate and control (Thatcherite welfare), both have more often been imposed than agreed. This explains accounts of 1950s council tenants being reprimanded for not looking after their gardens or stereotyped as 'using the bath to store their coal'. It explains why neoliberal welfare, despite its rhetoric of choice and control, has increasingly meant more surveillance and bureaucracy, more stigma, more institutionalisation and less support to service users. In *All Our Welfare*, three particular characteristics were associated with the post-war UK welfare state, all of which also have had international equivalents. These were its:

- lack of provisions for participation
- frequent failure to treat diversity with equality
- over-reliance on medicalised pathologising models of explanation, diagnosis and treatment.

None of these disappeared with the ascendancy of right-wing welfare ideology. Conventional social policy has transcended political and ideological divisions. Its defining characteristic has been that it has been non-participatory, that is to say, it is social policy whose politics, ideology, policy and practice people on the receiving end do not have an effective opportunity to develop, influence or change.

Thus traditional social policy has been associated with:

- identifying and subordinating those it sees as undesirable and/or pathological;
- restricting the human and civil rights of such groups;
- subjecting them to particular control, which can include institutionalisation, incarceration and enforced 'treatment', extending to sterilisation and in some cases euthanasia;
- exploiting people's labour by using them to undertake no pay or very low pay work; and
- supporting sub-poverty level wages tax credit systems and restricting access to and levels of welfare benefit and housing to force people into such work.

It is difficult to see how such non-participatory social policy can escape being repressive; at least paternalistic, at worst destructive and demeaning. Indeed it can be seen as a system of domination, however benign its intentions or its provisions might sometimes be. We can see how historically it has been used to impose ideological control over those who have come within its orbit, constraining their lives and cultures, restricting their human and civil rights. It has been strongly linked with pseudo-science and racism, as well as other dominant discriminations, corrections and exclusions. It has restricted agency, exposing people to abuse and encouraged internalised oppression.

Unfortunately all these features are still widely to be found in the children's and old people's homes, institutions for disabled people, segregated schools, assessment and welfare-to-work schemes and psychiatric facilities that continue to operate as part of social policy structures. Thus the irony that while traditional Fabian social policy was predicated on equalising social rights, securing social inclusion and social justice, those most closely affected by it may actually instead be separated from their fellow citizens and denied the same political, economic, social and human rights as them. If social policy is ultimately concerned with addressing fundamental human, political, philosophical, moral and ethical concerns with concepts like freedom, agency and power, we may wonder how well it can do this so long as it is non-participatory and this is treated as unproblematic.

The restricted response of academic social policy

Yet there seems to have been a reluctance to challenge such non-participatory approaches to social policy. What attempts there have been within the discipline, as we have already indicated, also seem limited and hesitant. From our experience, social policy as a discipline seems to have found it particularly difficult to address issues of participation – in its operation, its focus and its discussions. The old Fabian approach of having non-user 'experts' offering their findings and interpretations seems still to be powerful. While proponents of neoliberal social policy have attacked traditional left-of-centre approaches as dirigist, centrist and dependency-inducing, they have themselves been subject to similar failings.

As we have already seen, academic social policy does not seem to have mounted much of a challenge to non-participatory social policy, however inconsistent it might be seen to its traditional commitment to social justice, equality and human rights. The increasingly limited influence and impact of academic social policy may perhaps be related to this failure to explore more participatory approaches and engage with service users and their ideas and experience, as well as with wider publics. Certainly if social policy as a practical policy has generally failed to include service users in its construction, it seems no less a problem for the discipline of social policy to mirror this. No wonder that early disabled theoreticians like Mike Oliver and Vic Finkelstein tended to see social policy as a system of oppression rather than liberation (Finkelstein, 1980; Oliver, 1983).

This relates to one of the major changes internationally affecting social policy over the past 30 years or more. This has been the emergence of 'service user' movements and organisations. Service users, including disabled people, mental health service users/survivors, older people, people living with HIV and others with long-term conditions have increasingly developed their own ideas and discourses about themselves and public policy. Sadly this has not yet been properly reflected in the social policy literature, which largely continues to ignore it. Moreover, there is little sense of how problematic doing this may be, leaving out key knowledges and perspectives and perpetuating traditional imposed and paternalistic approaches to public policy.

While service user movements have generally been supportive of the principles of much progressive social policy – its commitment to social justice, empowerment, equality and full citizenship – they have also often been highly critical of the degree to which its practice has made them possible, highlighting instead tendencies to segregate, disempower, impoverish and pathologise.

This contradiction may also help in understanding the relatively limited broader resistance that there has been to the right-wing whittling away of welfare provision and regressive restructuring of social policy in modern times. Without a sense of ownership, people are less likely to defend it. So long as they see it as oppressive, they are unlikely to challenge attacks made on it. Thus while right-wing attacks on welfare have been determined, efforts to defend it have often been weak and narrowly based.

These two problems, the frequent lack of public support for progressive redistributive social policy and the failure of academic social policy to engage with service user discourses, seem to have conspired to make it seem that a significant shift from its neoliberal direction of travel is not possible. This is of course encouraged by neoliberals themselves, their associated mass media and supporters. The conventional wisdom is increasingly that we are inevitably set on a road to less and less public/collective spending to 'look after each other' and we (other than the rich and powerful) must instead make the best arrangements we can on our own. There is a sense that there is no alternative; that there cannot be enough money for anything different and that the old arrangements either did not work or are now outmoded. While subject to local differences, this trend increasingly seems to be global, linked with the ascendancy of globalisation and neoliberalism.

This makes it a time of radical and, for many, regressive change internationally in social policy. What is now needed more than ever is a seismic shift in both its analysis and implementation. Such a changed paradigm needs to be one that fully and equally includes people on the receiving end, particularly those at its 'heavy end'. There is a strong case for social policy books that focus on the need for participatory and inclusive approaches to social policy and the use of experiential knowledge in its construction.

Our aim in this book is to take forward this task and break the current log-jam resulting from polarised thinking narrowly posited between traditional state and market-led approaches to welfare. We hope that this book can help fill a serious gap in social policy literature and discussion. We see at the heart of such a change a need to take seriously issues of participation and sustainability as well as their relationship with each other.

Introducing new voices: challenging old assumptions

We have tried to introduce coherently new voices into the discussion – people and citizens as service users, starting from and being firmly informed by their lived experience and the 'user knowledges' developing from that. We can learn more about:

- what the reality of existing social policies is from their experience;
- how they feel we might challenge current major trends;
- what theories and ideas they have and are developing; and
- how we can bring about change in social policy.

When we were conceiving this book, we were clear that we wanted to pay particular attention to the contributions of people with first hand experience and 'experiential knowledge' of social policy outcomes, who could draw on a wide range of expertise, perspectives and direct experience to explore participatory social policy from the frontline. We believe that one of the distinctive aspects of this book is the inclusion of first hand accounts by grassroots activists; social justice, equality and human rights campaigners; service users, practitioners and citizens, who have influenced or been involved in social policy in various ways. These accounts offer critiques of social policy, its processes and implementation directly from those who live with the consequences – in their own voices. Taken together they form a unique collection of perspectives from people often conceptualised as 'policy problems' or whose lives are the focus for 'policy implementation and outcomes', and give insight into how forms of participatory social policy have already been working in Britain and internationally.

Service users in the book offer a wide range of contributions. They contribute as researchers, academics, activists and educators, united by direct and first hand experience of being on the receiving end of social policy. Some have overlapping identities as academics and researchers and their contributions may be readily recognised as such. Others offer short accounts of their own experience and their involvement in campaigns, as well as their ideas about policy, provision and practice. Such first hand voices are sometimes still dismissed as testimonies, anecdotal or just 'bearing witness'. They are demeaned as descriptive, unsubstantiated and atheoretical. In the conventional hierarchy of knowledge, they tend to be placed at the bottom (Glasby and Beresford, 2006). But service users and citizens are not just here to 'tell their stories'. Such an interpretation ignores the theoretical underpinnings of such contributions as well as the growing theoretical and philosophical discussions they are prompting about their value and validity. The reliability and validity of different kinds of knowledge are now coming in for reassessment (Beresford, 2003). There are now large and growing bodies of Feminist, Black, Queer, Disability and Mad Studies literature exploring the role and significance of subjective and standpoint knowledge. Such accounts are increasingly being recognised as having a valuable role in complementing and critiquing traditionally valued knowledge and evidence sources. One of the issues we explore in this book is their implications for theory, research and analysis.

Many of these voices are new to the formal, published social policy literature, but without them the discussion is not complete. The voice concept is a common trope in discourse about service user involvement, but authentic and uncompromised voices that say challenging or difficult things are not always heard or listened to, and in some cases are marginalised or silenced altogether. As Cook has argued in a paper on engaging service users and communities in the policy process:

> while government does indeed "talk the talk" on consultation, it has yet to "walk the walk". If the objects of social policy – service users, the poor, powerless and disaffected – were to find their voice, the talk itself may become unpalatable' (Cook, 2002: 529).

The range of contributors to this book makes it possible to highlight that 'service users' are not a separate or monolithic group and that major questions are raised by issues of diversity, identity and experience. At the same time we have not sought to privilege any one perspective or set of knowledges. We have been fortunate to recruit many different contributors, including strongly established mainstream social policy academics, as well as service users and user activists and researchers. This offers a reminder that while social policy generally may have been slow to address participation, its ranks certainly include academics who recognise its importance and have been taking forward both analysis and action.

The importance of an international and inclusive approach

We have also given particular priority to the book including and highlighting international perspectives and contributions because of the wider international interest we know there is in more participatory approaches to social policy and practice and because of the different issues that can arise internationally. Such an international overview has been developed as both a theme and a specific element of the book. We have recruited international contributors as well as contributions with an international focus. We have encouraged all contributors to address diversity and to consider international ramifications, even where they may be offering local case studies.

Like an earlier book we co-edited (Beresford and Carr, 2012), *Social Policy First Hand* is strongly research and evidence based. We should also stress again that we have sought to include all kinds of evidence and research, including user controlled research and experiential knowledge. The contents are heavily committed to addressing issues of inclusion, diversity and equality, which we believe was a real strength of our earlier book. This book addresses historical and ideological issues, contemporary social policy debates as well as implications for theory, change, practice, policy, planning, research and education, and training.

Thus the book explores theory, policy, practice and research. Different kinds and lengths of contribution are included, offering readers access to both first hand accounts and also research based academic texts. It should not be assumed that one is offered as having more value or authority than another, or that short first-person accounts are atheoretical. Instead, as we seek to highlight in the book, a participatory approach generates new theoretical discussions and approaches. We have employed different formats deliberately, drawing on an increasing range of texts and materials, including diverse and marginalised perspectives. We also know that not everybody writes in a conventional academic way, and that the first-person voice is the clearest form of expression for some of the contributors. Nor indeed is everyone able or wanting to read conventional academic writing.

We do not believe that there is one legitimate way to write about social policy or accept as unproblematic traditional positivist research assumptions about principles of 'neutrality', 'objectivity' and 'distance', or about what makes for 'rigour', 'reliability' and 'replicability'. From our experience, such variation also encourages the wider use of such texts as a key resource, enabling people to dip in as well as to read sequentially. We have tried to ensure that contributions are as accessible as possible, as well as addressing the key concerns and goals of the book, offering detailed guidance to contributors. In a number of cases, we have also provided direct support to help contributors to write their chapters, so that people less used to writing would not be discouraged. Similarly we have supported more experienced authors to write as accessibly and inclusively as possible.

The structure of the book

Conventional social policy texts tend to be organised according to the history, definition, ideologies, concepts and economics of social policy, examining its different sectors and areas, exploring current debates and developments, as well as issues like who it should be for and how it is delivered.

Participatory social policy demands a different approach that starts with the service users it is primary concerned with, considers how social policy has traditionally related to them, addresses their ideas and proposals for the future and how to bring about change in a participatory way. Not surprisingly, a key issue for service users and others who have been calling for the democratisation of social policy is how to achieve it. Thus, unlike many conventional social policy texts, which are concerned with analysing and describing social policy's past and its present trials and tribulations, as becomes clear in this book, the primary concern of people on the receiving end is how they can bring about change.

While we as editors had some ideas from our own experience as service users and activists, we did not start with a framework of our own for organising the book. Rather this emerged from the process of identifying, collecting and editing the contributions our subject invited. We drew on discussions with contributors and other service users as well as the help of our initial reviewers. As a result we have organised the contents of the book into eight parts. The first four focus on the need for and knowledge base of participatory social policy; the last four on making it happen.

The first part introduces readers to some of the emerging and possible relations between social policy and its end users. It considers some of the threats; the issues for different groups of service users in different parts of the world and the radical potential of participatory social policy, especially in relation to concerns about the sustainability of the planet. In Part II, we return to the founder of the UK welfare state, William Beveridge's 'five giant evils'. The UK welfare state is crucial to understanding modern social policy, but here we now explore Beveridge's 'evils' from the perspectives of groups and issues that tend to have been overlooked or problematised in such typologies. Part III explores the potential and growing contribution of 'service users' knowledges' to social policy, as well as some of the potential problems and difficulties. Service users primarily conceive of issues in terms of their lives, not policies. Part IV offers a participatory and inclusive take on a traditional 'life course and developmental approach to social policy'. Contributors trace the life course from childhood through to death and dying, prioritising people's own perspectives on these and paying particular attention to issues of equality, ethnicity, as well as to indigenous populations and cultural difference.

In Part V, contributors explore the theory and practice of transforming social policy to make it more participatory. They offer macro and micro examples of such change-making, from the perspectives of practitioners, service users, researchers and educators, connecting them with broader concerns with social change. Part VI develops this discussion exploring campaigning to achieve change. It is divided into two sections; the first focusing on different issues and forms for engagement, ranging from becoming involved in formal government bodies to initiating a national campaign after the wrongful death of a disabled son. The second section focuses on the use of social networking and media; exploring the issues raised, problems and potential.

Part VII focuses on ways in which social policy can be truly participatory by breaking down barriers and ensuring the inclusion of groups that face particular discrimination, barriers and exclusion. It is again organised in two sections. The first section reports campaigns concerned with highlighting and achieving equal rights. The second highlights ways of ensuring inclusion and setting standards to achieve it, as well as overcoming barriers to build trust and understanding. Part VII explores research in relation to participatory social policy. It critiques the role and nature of participatory research, provides case studies of such research and offers insights into 'getting involved in research' and the transformative role that participatory research can play.

The book ends with a conclusion by the editors, intended to bring together the overall lessons, messages and recommendations that come from the book's contributors. As well as setting out alternatives to current social policy approaches, it makes the case for participatory approaches and possible ways to achieve them.

References

Alcock, P. (2008) *Social Policy in Britain*, third edition, Basingstoke: Palgrave/ Macmillan.

Alcock, P., Haux, T., May, M. and Wright, S. (eds) (2016) *The Student's Companion to Social Policy*, fifth edition, Oxford: Wiley-Blackwell.

Beresford, P. (2003) *It's Our Lives: A short theory of knowledge, distance and experience*, London: Citizen Press in association with Shaping Our Lives.

Beresford, P. (2016) *All Our Welfare: Towards participatory social policy*, Bristol: The Policy Press.

Beresford, P. and Carr, S. (eds) (2012) *Service Users, Social Care and User Involvement*, Research Highlights Series, London: Jessica Kingsley Publishers.

Cook, D. (2002) 'Consultation, For A Change?: Engaging users and communities in the policy process', *Social Policy and Administration*, 36 (5), 516–31.

Finkelstein, V. (1980) *Attitudes and Disabled People: Issues for disabled people*, Monograph Number 5, New York: World Rehabilitation Fund, http://pf7d7vi404s1dxh27mla5569.wpengine.netdna-cdn.com/files/library/finkelstein-attitudes.pdf

Glasby, J. and Beresford, P. (2006) 'Who Knows Best?: Evidence based practice and the service user contribution, Commentary and Issues', *Critical Social Policy*, 26 (1), 268–84.

Oliver, M. (1983) *Social Work and Disabled People*, Basingstoke: Macmillan.

Solnit, R. (2014) *Men Explain Things To Me and Other Essays*, London: Granta.

Stewart, M. (2016) *Cash Not Care: the planned demolition of the UK welfare state*, London: New Generation Publishing.

Weber, M. (1905) *The Protestant Ethic and the Spirit of Capitalism*, London and Boston: Unwin Hyman.

Part I
Service users and social policy:
an introduction

We start, as any focus on participatory social policy must, with service users. Historically the relationship between social policy and people on the receiving end – 'service users' – has predominantly been a prescriptive one. People as service users have been permitted to play little part in social policy's intellectual or practical development. Instead it has been an essentially unequal non-participatory relationship, with them getting whatever others think is needed. What unifies contributions in Part I is that from diverse perspectives of ethnicity and discipline, as academics and service users, they challenge this tradition and explore different, more equal and inclusive relationships.

Danny Dorling, the social geographer, begins by highlighting the centrality of injustice and exclusion to our world, and their origins in inequality. He suggests that if we want to challenge this, then how we work for solutions will be central. He highlights the importance of social policy being truly social if we want to achieve just and inclusive policies and societies. We are unlikely to end exclusion by seeing ourselves as special and acting or intellectualising in exclusionary ways. Social policy academic Peter Taylor-Gooby focuses on the relationship between participation and solidarity in European welfare states. He highlights the shift in social policy to neoliberalism and individual responsibility, undermining solidarity and increasing social divisions. Equally he warns that, with widening inequality, ostensibly participative and grassroots movement can be used to have damaging consequences for the inclusiveness of the welfare state.

Academic Sweta Rajan-Rankin focuses on the Global South in her chapter, paying particular attention to 'ontology' (the nature of social reality) and 'epistemology' (the theory of knowledge) in doing so. She challenges taken-for-granted assumptions around what social policy is, and how it can be understood in developing world contexts. She draws on post-colonial frameworks as an alternate lens to reimagine social policy from a participatory perspective. She leaves the reader with key questions to help shape a post-colonial theory of social policy in developing countries.

Margaret Alston of Monash University considers the growing phenomenon of environmental disasters, offering two contrasting case studies. She concludes that many social policies are being developed on the basis of neoliberal market-based rather than social justice principles. She argues that social policies based on bottom-up, gender-equitable, participatory processes are necessary if we are to build adaptive capacity and resilience in the face of such mounting environmental disasters.

This is followed by two chapters about the relationship between social policy and particular groups of people as service users. First the activist and academic Colin Campbell explores the relationship between social policy (as political policy) and the experience of disability, using the UK as a case study. He argues that disabled people globally have been marginalised economically and experienced marginalisation and exclusion as a result of social policy, which has largely constructed disability as dependence. He argues that policymakers and professionals must listen more seriously to the voices of those whose lives are shaped by the policies they develop and implement, stressing the continuing struggle disabled people face to achieve this. Then researchers and person with lived experience, Louca-Mai Brady, Felicity Hathway and Emily Roberts, consider children and young people's participation in the development of health policy and service delivery. They explore a systemic approach to 'embedding' their views in health policy and services, based on a UK case study. They offer the lessons for this work from both young people's and professionals' perspectives. While the idea of children's participation may be increasingly popular among policymakers, children are rarely involved in decision making processes and often occupy a marginalised position in healthcare encounters. Children and young people's experience of participation highlights the importance of rethinking how it is frequently actually done.

Finally, Sarah Carr, co-editor of the book and survivor researcher, offers a critical discussion of 'co-production', a key concept emerging in debates about participation. Her chapter addresses some of the fundamental questions; who owns co-production, and the potential of co-production to facilitate radical power shifts towards service users and citizens, for example, in health and social care. She offers an investigation into the origins of the concept and an exploration of how it has functioned in the context of UK social policy rhetoric, where it has been pioneered.

1

Challenging injustice: the importance of collective ownership of social policy

Danny Dorling

Beveridge's former 'five giant evils' – Disease, Idleness, Ignorance, Squalor and Want – are different now (Stephens et al, 2008: 7–8). With the new five modern evils of elitism, exclusion, prejudice, greed and despair, injustice begins to propagate itself more strongly. Writers like me find it easy to say what is so very wrong, but usually struggle to make suggestions as to what could and should be done.

Some say that it is easy to criticise but hard to find solutions. The central argument here is that it is beliefs that matter most – the beliefs that enough of us still hold – the beliefs that underlie most injustice in the world today. To ask what you should do after you dispel enough of those beliefs is rather like asking how to run plantations after abolishing slavery, or how to run society after giving women the vote, or how to run factories without child labour. Elitism, exclusion, prejudice, greed and despair will not end just by being recognised more clearly as unjust, but that recognition is a necessary precursor.

All the five faces of social inequality that currently contribute to injustice are clearly and closely linked. Elitism in Britain suggests that educational divisions are natural. Educational divisions are reflected both in the misfortunes of those usually poorer children who are excluded from life choices because they are seen as not having enough qualifications, and also through the supposed achievements of those able to exclude themselves, often by opting into private or otherwise segregated education.

Elitism is the incubation chamber within which prejudice is fostered. It provides a defence for greed. It increases anxiety and despair as endless school examinations are taken, as people are ranked, ordered and sorted. Those who reach the top are mostly those with most early advantages, mixed up with a few who are unusually pliant and conform to what they are told to do when young. This perpetuates an enforced and inefficient hierarchy in our most unequal of affluent societies, such as the UK, the USA and Israel. Elitism is a profound injustice.

Just as elitism is integral to all the other forms of injustice, so is exclusion. The exclusion that rises with elitism makes 'the poor' appear different, exacerbates inequalities between ethnic groups and causes the racial differences we identify so easily and do not realise are so temporary – racism and wider prejudice always shifts to new targets over time but a minority are often excluded simply because they are said to be racially different.

Similarly, rising greed could not be satisfied without the exclusion of so many, and so many would not now be excluded were it not for extreme greed. But the damaging consequences of exclusion caused by the greed of the rich spread upwards to the rich. They even reach up to those who appear most successfully greedy: rates of despair might be highest for those who are most excluded, but even the wealthy in rich countries are now showing many more signs of despair, as are their children.

Growing despair has become symptomatic of our more unequal affluent societies as a whole. The prejudice that rises with exclusion allows the successfully greedy to try to justify their greed as apparent reward for some superiority, and makes many others think they deserve little. The divisions and ostracism that such prejudice engenders further raise depression and anxiety in those made to look different, the apparent failures, 'the losers'.

When inequalities rise, those who feel that they have succeeded in life usually begin to behave more callously towards others. As elitism incubates exclusion, exclusion exacerbates prejudice, prejudice fosters greed, and greed – because wealth is simultaneously no ultimate reward and makes many without wealth feel more worthless – causes despair. In turn, despair brings us into a state of apathy and prevents us from effectively tackling injustice.

Removing one symptom of the disease of inequality is no cure, but recognising inequality as the disease behind injustice, and seeing how all the manifestations of injustice which it creates, and which continuously recreate it, are intertwined is the first step that is so often advocated in the search for a solution to injustice (Dorling, 2015). Each route to that solution only differs in style, not substance.

In 2014, Janet Yellen, the new chair of the US Federal Reserve, described growing inequality as un-American (Gongloff, 2014). Public surveys, however, showed how far US public opinion still had to go (Da Costa, 2014). The American public could still be sold the American dream even as inequalities rose and rose ever higher in the USA and the dream became a fantasy even more removed from reality. Shortly after securing control of the presidency, in October 2017, Donald Trump sacked Janet Yellen.

It is in the most unequal affluent states of the rich world – the USA, the UK and Israel – that injustices are most commonly presented to the public as fair, right and proper, where walls are built the highest and minorities are excluded most vigorously. It is in these places that the worse of politics is found (Dorling, 2016), and where the environmental damage from behaving so badly is usually greatest (Dorling, 2017).

The table below shows the 20 richest countries for which comparable data on inequality exists from before and after 2004. In ten of the twenty, inequalities have been rising. In the other ten they have been static or falling. There is no inevitability that inequality always rises. Since 2015 it has been falling in more nations than rising (Dorling, 2018). There are huge differences between otherwise similarly rich nations. The degree of inequality and injustice you live under is a choice that is made and which is constantly changing.

Table 1.1: Household income inequality, most affluent countries of the world, 2004–13

Quintile ratio 2005–2013	Ratio from 2004 or earlier	Change 2004–05 to 2013	County	Rank
10.3	6.4	3.9	Israel	1
9.8	8.4	1.4	United States	2
7.6	7.2	0.4	United Kingdom	3
7.6	5.4	2.2	Spain	4
6.9	6.5	0.4	Italy	5
6.4	6.2	0.2	Greece	6
5.8	7.0	-1.2	Australia	7
5.8	5.8	0.0	Canada	8
5.4	3.4	2.0	Japan	9
5.3	6.1	-0.8	Ireland	10
5.2	5.8	-0.6	Switzerland	11
5.1	5.6	-0.5	France	12
5	4.5	0.5	Belgium	13
4.7	4.3	0.4	Germany	14
4.6	4.7	-0.1	Austria	15
4.5	5.5	-1.0	Netherlands	16
4	4.3	-0.3	Denmark	17
4	3.9	0.1	Norway	18
4	3.8	0.2	Finland	19
3.7	4	-0.3	Sweden	20

Note: The table shows the ratio of mean incomes of the best-off 20% of households to the worst-off 20%. The 20 most affluent countries in the United Nations Development Programme's 'highest affluence group' are included.

Source: UNDP, *Human Development Reports* for 2015 (Table 3) and 2005 (Table 14).

The power of crowds

Almost every time there is a victory for humanity against greed, it has been the result of millions of small actions mostly undertaken by people not in government. Examples include: votes for women, Indian independence, civil rights in America, or that earlier freedom won just to be able to say that the earth goes around the sun, a victory against the power of those holding most of the riches of those times and their prejudices.[1]

People can choose between falling into line, becoming both creatures and victims of markets, or they can resist and look back for other ways, other arguments, different thinking. When they have resisted in the past, resistance has been most effective if exercised by those thought to be the most powerless. But we quickly forget this. We need to be constantly reminded.

Almost anyone who gets near the top of any institution is self-selected by a desire for superiority – unless there is evidence of some other strong and intrinsic motivation. That is part of the reason why the harmful effects of inequality go all the way to the top. More inequality means we are all more obsessed with status, and those who get furthest up are the most obsessed; the main exception is those who are born to assume superiority (Wilkinson and Pickett, 2015).

The antidote to being dominated is to act collectively, otherwise all that results is a new aristocracy. It is true that some people genuinely want to get to the top to help others. The quote 'Never underestimate the power of persistence' is usually attributed to Nelson Mandela, but Mandela's power was a movement outside of his prison. It was a movement of millions.

It is also often said that: 'The struggle of people against power is the struggle of memory against forgetting.'[2] Thinking that you have to do all your thinking anew and alone is the wrong place to start. To remember earlier times, times before you were born, you need stories, stories that tell you it need not be like this, because it has not always been like this.

Overcoming the power of kings

The latest era of growing inequalities is coming to an end. It is something that cannot go on forever, and so it will not. But it will not end without the millions of tiny acts required to no longer tolerate the greed, prejudice, exclusion and elitism that foster inequality and despair. Above all else, these acts will require teaching and understanding, remembering what is fundamental about being human, remembering compassion:

> The human condition is fundamentally social – every aspect of human function and behaviour is rooted in social life. The modern preoccupation with individuality – individual expression, individual achievement and individual freedom – is really just a fantasy, a form of self-delusion … (Burns, 2007: 182)

Accept that individuality is an illusion – we all have and are both kith and kin. Start to behave differently, and even the most apocalyptic of writers will agree that every act of defiance, no matter how small, makes a difference; whatever '… we do or desist from doing will make a difference …' (Bauman, 2008: 39). We can never know precisely what difference, and have no reason to expect our influence to be disproportionately large, but nor should we expect it to be especially small.

It is equally vital to recognise that none of us is superhuman (Dorling, 2012). Seeing yourself as special can lead to loathing others you see as lazy or feeble and below you. This contempt can often be hard to disguise, and is clear to see in the expressions of some right-wing politicians when they talk of 'the poor'; they appear to feel dirty just talking about 'them'. At its extreme, for those who hold this disgust for others, social cleansing is attractive – removing the poor because you think they are dirty. This is how fascism begins, and it always ends in death. A fascist is someone who believes it is right to kill. Fascists differ in how dirty they get their hands. They range from the small town doctor slowly dispatching his elderly female patients, to the planner creating the new clean city designed to hold only the chosen few.

Because none of us are that special, trusting a small coterie is dangerous. It makes no sense to expect others to do great deeds and lead us to promised lands, at least not with any reliability. We are slowly, collectively, recognising this, learning not to forget that, although we can learn without limits, we may not get that far when we each try to learn on our own; our minds were not made to live as we now live:

> The world is indeed a strange and mysterious place, but not because of any hidden causal order or deeper purpose. The mystery is largely in the operations of the human mind, a strange organ capable of creating its own vision of reality with little regard to how the world really is. (Baggini, 2008: 181)

We need each other because we have evolved not to be loners. Without tolerance and understanding of each other we are all capable of causing great harm through persecution.

In our minds we can either despair or celebrate our stories. Sometimes we can see absolute immiseration as food prices soar and barbarism takes place in wars on terrorism that repeat older histories of persecution. From other moments of our histories we can tell numerous celebratory stories where injustices have been progressively defeated, the power of kings overcome, principles of equality in law secured, slavery abolished, voting franchises extended, free education introduced, health services or health insurance nationalised, minimum incomes guaranteed (including for unemployment, sickness, old age and childcare). In these celebratory tales, legislation is won to:

> protect the rights of employees and tenants, and ... to prevent racial discrimination. It includes the decline of forms of class deference. The abolition of capital and corporal punishment is also part of it. So too is the growing agitation for greater equality of opportunity – regardless of race, class, gender, sexual orientation, and religion. We see it also

in the increasing attention paid by lobby groups, social research and government statistical agencies to poverty and inequality over the last 50 years; and most recently we see it in the attempt to create a culture of mutual respect for each other. (Wilkinson and Pickett, 2009: 260–61)

We see hope in a redistributive budget in the USA under Obama that could not have easily been imagined as possible a year earlier than it was created. We see despair in the votes for Trump by the millions who did not see change coming quickly enough for them and who were taught to be fearful of others. We see hope in the contempt in which many of those who have taken most are now held, the tax avoiders and art hoarders; but we can also see the danger of a return to business and misery as usual.

'The tradition of all dead generations weighs like a nightmare on the brains of the living' (Marx, 1907). We see our history, our future, our nightmares and our dreams first in our fickle imaginations. That is where we first make our present, in minds which each mix the same ingredients so differently. How we come to live is not predetermined. Across Europe we see change: in a narrow majority of European countries Table 1.1 above shows *equalities* to be rising. Political parties that once would never have made it near the sidelines came to power in Greece in 2015, and are now contenders for power elsewhere. In Britain in 2016, 52% of those that voted in the referendum[3] decided to leave the EU because they were told it was the only way things could get better. They were fooled but still they showed they would act. In France in 2017 the Front National threatened to take power. They did not even come close. Everywhere the masses can now threaten the power of modern political kings and dynasties.

Geographically all it takes is a little imagination, a little 'wishful thinking', to see that a collection of movements will achieve the change so many wish to see in the world; these are movements that need only to exist in our imaginations in order to work. If we have and spread enough faith that they will work, then they will work. These are movements to '... make our own world from below [where we] are the people we have been waiting for' (Shah and Goss, 2007: 17). These are the opposite of movements towards world government: too many of those have been proposed '... in which the best stocks could rule the earth' (Connelly, 2008: 380). These are, instead, movements where it is proclaimed that '... the future will be amazing, and after that the whole world will become a better place. [Because] if we cannot make that happen, then no one can' (Magnason, 2008: 279). And these are movements about which people who advocate them repeatedly tell us that: 'It can happen – so long as everyone does not leave it for somebody else to do ...' (Kelsey, 1997).

The words above were written before the most recent wave of protests; before the Arab spring that began with the death of Tarek al-Tayeb Mohamed Bouazizi in Tunisia on 17 December 2010; before Los Indignados was created in Spain in 2011 (BBC News, 2012); before Syriza became the second largest party in the Greek Parliament in 2012; before the Occupy movement swept around the world, reaching Australia in 2013; before the Podemos Party was formed in Spain in 2014; before, as I wrote in 2014: '*all the events of 2015, 2016 and 2017 which – whatever they are – are unlikely to be predictable, minor, or unrelated to the change that is now upon us*'. The dawning of a fairer world is in front of us as the old order that René Descartes saw take form on the dockside in Amsterdam in 1631 abates (Stott, 2010). In 1631, when still a young man, René Descartes noticed that all around him people had stopped thinking about much beyond earning money. He said: 'In this great city where I am living, with no man apart from myself not being involved in trade, everyone is so intent on his profits that I could spend my whole life without being seen by anyone.' Dany-Robert Dufour, who first pointed out what Descartes was really seeing, goes on to explain: 'Descartes's capitalist Amsterdam has now conquered the world. It is not just that everyone in this planetary city is now involved in trade; trade is now involved in everyone in the sense that it shapes us all' (Dufour, 2008: 168-9).

Change is never simple. It takes a wider geographical perspective: the kind of perspective that Descartes and then Dufour – almost four centuries afterwards – were both grasping for. This short chapter has only just touched on the changes within the wealthiest of nations. Look further afield and a far more optimistic picture begins to take form. Elsewhere in the less rich world are billions of people about to learn from our mistakes. Social policy has to be the product of millions of minds, thousands of books, hundreds of manifestos. When a small group tell you they have all the answers – beware. But also beware pessimism. Even if you live in one of the most unequal and pitiful of affluent nations by the mistakes of your leaders you send a message around the world: Do not act like we have acted, do not follow us, because there lies folly. Social policy learns as much from the mistakes as from the successes.

Notes

[1]   This list is taken from Steel (2008: 247) and Kelsey (1997: 370–71).

[2]   This itself is, of course, just another of those lessons so easily forgotten by humans, given that our brains have not evolved to cope with having to remember so much. The original quote replaced 'people' by 'man', but that has now changed in the telling. For four versions of the chant being remembered and repeated see Field (1999: 74). Patrick Field quotes Milan Kundera, as recorded in turn by Neil Goodwin in *Life in the Fast Lane* on the M11 road protests. See also Bauman (2007: 84), also referring to Milan Kundera's novel *Slowness*. Milan Kundera originally wrote these words in *The book of laughter and forgetting* in 1979. For a much fuller quote and explanation, see http://vannevar.blogspot.co.uk/2009/03/struggle-man-power-memory-forgetting.html

[3]   The 52% majority in the referendum was about 30% of the whole UK population, so it is best to avoid saying 'the majority of the population'.

References

Baggini, J. (2008) *Welcome to Everytown: A journey into the English mind*, 2nd edn, London: Granta.

Bauman, Z. (2007) *Consuming Life*, Cambridge: Polity Press.

Bauman, Z. (2008) *The Art of Life*, Cambridge: Polity Press.

BBC News (2012) 'Spain's Indignados protest here to stay', 15 May, www.bbc.co.uk/news/world-europe-18070246

Burns, J. (2007) *The Descent of Madness: Evolutionary origins of psychosis and the social brain*, Hove: Routledge.

Connelly, M. (2008) *Fatal Misconception: The struggle to control world population*, Cambridge, MA: Harvard University Press.

Da Costa, P.N. (2014) 'Janet Yellen decries widening income inequality', *Wall Street Journal*, 17 October, https://www.wsj.com/articles/feds-yellen-says-extreme-inequality-could-be-un-american-1413549684

Dorling, D. (2012) *The No-Nonsense Guide to Equality*, Oxford: New Internationalist.

Dorling, D. (2015) 'The mother of underlying causes – economic ranking and health inequality', *Social Science & Medicine*, 128, 327–30, https://doi.org/10.1016/j.socscimed.2015.01.008

Dorling, D. (2016) *A Better Politics: How government can makes us happier and healthier*, London: London Publishing Partnership.

Dorling, D. (2017) *The Equality Effect*, Oxford: New Internationalist.

Dorling, D. (2018) *Do We Need Economic Inequality?*, Cambridge: Polity.

Dufour, D.-R. (2008) *The Art of Shrinking Heads: On the new servitude of the liberated in the age of total capitalism* (translation), Cambridge: Polity Press.

Field, P. (1999) 'The anti-roads movement: the struggle of memory against forgetting', in T. Jordan and A. Lent (eds) *Storming the Millennium: The new politics of change*, London: Lawrence & Wishart, pp 68–79.

Kelsey, J. (1997) *The New Zealand Experiment: A world model for structural adjustment?*, Auckland: Auckland University Press.

Magnason, A.S. (2008) *Dreamland: A self-help manual for a frightened nation*, London: Citizen Press Ltd.

Marx, K. (1907 [1852]) *The Eighteenth Brumaire of Louis Bonaparte*, Chicago, IL: Charles H. Kerr.

Shah, H. and Goss, S. (2007) *Democracy and the Public Realm: Compass Programme for Renewal*, London: Lawrence & Wishart.

Steel, M. (2008) *What's Going On*, London: Simon & Schuster.

Stephens, L., Ryan-Collins, J. and Boyle, D. (2008) *Co-production: A manifesto for growing the core economy*, London: New Economics Foundation.

Stott, R. (2010) 'Review of "Injustice" and Tony Judt's "Ill fares the land": a treatise on our present discontents: how can we rediscover the magic of more equal societies?', *British Medical Journal*, 4 August.

Wilkinson, R.G. and Pickett, K. (2009) *The Spirit Level: Why more equal societies almost always do better*, London: Allen Lane.

Wilkinson, R. and Pickett, K. (2015) Personal communication, 31 January.

2

Participation and solidarity in a changing welfare state

Peter Taylor-Gooby

This chapter considers participation and solidarity in the development of the European welfare state. Participation requires that the less powerful groups succeed in making their voices heard. Such groups often have few resources other than their numbers, so that concerted action within a democratic framework is essential. The various welfare states that emerged during the past century rested in different ways on traditions of national male breadwinner working class solidarity, often in class-coalition with middle class groups and supported by an active trade union movement. Welfare policies in the post-war heyday of corporate capitalism reinforced this solidarity. More recently the post-war settlement has been eroded by globalisation, the shift from manufacturing to a service economy, the decline of the nation state, insistent pressures from women's groups and others for greater equality and the emergence of new social risks. The new welfare state settlement is market liberal rather than neo-Keynesian. These shifts disempower the groups that were able to influence the traditional welfare state but empowers new groups affected by new social risks and by globalisation. The key question for a politics of participation is whether these groups can form solidarities that enable them to exert real influence.

The emergence of the current settlement

The Great Recession of 2007–08 and subsequent stagnation had a major effect on European welfare states: in the short term social spending increased, and then in most cases trended back towards previous levels, most swiftly in the case of Germany among the larger economies (Figure 2.1).

Most commentators point out that the main regime differences between European welfare states persist (for example Hemerijck, 2012). However, the commitment across Europe to austerity and balanced budgets (summed up in the 2013 Treaty on Stability, Coordination and Governance which provides for legal enforcement in the Eurozone of a 0.5 per cent cap on deficits, with similar legislation in the UK) suggests a new approach to welfare spending. This perception is reinforced by the stringent conditions attached to joint European Central Bank (ECB), International Monetary Fund (IMF) and European Union (EU) loan packages, including profound cuts in public spending and restructuring of the public sector, privatisation and tax reforms, most evident in Greece, and affecting Ireland, Italy, Spain and Portugal (Hay and Wincott, 2012; Armingeon, 2012; van Kersbergen et al, 2014; Starke et al, 2013).

Figure 2.1: Public spending as a percentage of GDP, 2000–2020

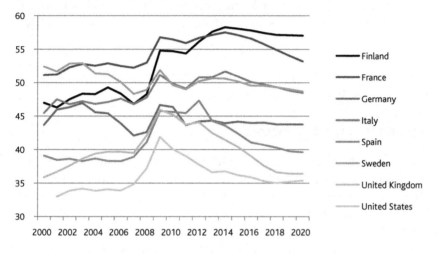

Note: Figures for 2014–20 are predictions by the IMF.

Source: IMF (2017).

The shift in budgetary stances in the context of recognition of severe and increasing pressures on state spending from a globalised economic context, slower growth, the ascendancy of a more neo-liberal economic paradigm and population ageing point to the question: does the crisis and the policy responses to it mark a watershed in the development of European welfare states?

Factors leading to stability and change in welfare state settlements

Factors that influence the development of state welfare (using a modified version of the '5i's' framework; Gough, 2011) include:

- *industrialisation*, the process of production, the use of capital and the relationships within which productive labour was carried out;
- the *international* economic context and the response of national governments to the requirements of competitive trade;

23

- *interests* most notably in the class and family system but also emerging among those who see themselves as net recipients of or as paying for social provision;
- *ideologies*, both at the level of the dominant political economy, the liberalism that rested on the notion of a self-regulating market in the 19th century, increasingly challenged in the 20th century (Keynes, 1936), and at the level of popular understanding and ideology concerning entitlement, the sphere of state provision and the morality of work, family, gender and the male breadwinner (Thane, 1982); and
- the *institutional* framework, including the rise of the nation state and the expansion of its capacity to monitor and regulate the lives of its citizens (Dean, 2010).

All these factors shape the context in which participation and solidarities can influence the direction of the welfare state.

Recent shifts in the five factors

The modern welfare state emerged in established industrial societies with high manufacturing employment and opportunities for skilled working class jobs in which neo-Keynesian interventions could achieve consistent economic growth, contain unemployment and provide tax or social insurance financed social services (Jessop, 2002). The outcome was stability, resting on industrial capitalism, the neo-Keynesian nation state, and ideas and institutions that supported social provision within that structure as part of a compromise of class interests.

In relation to international context, the development of a more globalised international system, in commodity trade, in finance and in attempts at cross-national regulation (OECD, 2013), continues to influence state welfare. New technology reduces the cost of trade (Held, 2000) and makes possible the global integration of knowledge and communication-based industries, from banking to call centres. At the same time, technological changes associated with the use of micro-processors together with new techniques of management are restructuring employment and further individualising labour market experiences (Archibugi and Mitchie, 1997).

In relation to class interests the industrial basis of solidarity is weakened. For some groups in the labour force, employment is low skilled and less well-paid or less secure; for others secure, well-paid but more individualised employment predominates, leading to a growing structural division between the two groups often referred to as dualisation (Rueda, 2005; Emmenegger et al, 2012). At the same time, the structure of capital becomes more complex with large and small capitals competing in a less structured way, reducing the capacity for corporatist bargaining. Finance and business capital, which is more mobile than manufacturing sector capital, expands and gains in influence with government.

The demands for greater competitiveness have coincided with a breakdown of the male breadwinner structure and more vigorous demands for greater equality in education, training, employment and opportunities from women and disabled people. This has led to equal opportunities and anti-discrimination legislation at national and European levels and a gradual improvement in the formal rights of women and disabled people. Women are still over-represented among the poorest groups, under-represented in the highest skilled and best-paid employment and still undertake the largest share of care tasks, spending about two and a half times as long on care and over twice as long on housework as men in OECD countries (OECD, 2014: Figure 2). Disabled people are about half as likely again as the rest of the population to experience poverty and fare badly in employment (Eurostat, 2015: Figure 4). Developed countries are increasingly cutting back on benefits for disabled people and seeking to mobilise them into paid work.

The increased commitment of most governments to neo-liberal free trade strategies, coupled with austerity programmes that seem to benefit a distant multi-national elite but do little for the mass of the population, has led to fightback from left and right. New popular-led left parties are challenging governments across Europe (Podemos in Spain, Syriza in Greece); new Eurosceptic movements are also emerging on the right. Anti-immigrant chauvinism is a powerful force, particularly among lower skilled groups who lose out from the process of globalisation and blame immigrants for taking jobs and opportunities (Kriesi et al, 2012).

The outcome has been enhanced capital flows, the growth of footloose multi-national capitals, a further weakening of labour movements and the development of the women's and disabled people's movements, and anti-immigrant populist movement in developed economies. This has fed through into the third factor, changes in institutional frameworks. As trade union membership declined, legislation shifted against labour movement interests, for example in the right to strike, especially in the weaker economies of Southern Europe but also in the Netherlands, Hungary and the UK (Cuppage, 2013). Employment protection has also grown weaker. Anti-discrimination and equal opportunity legislation has, however, been strengthened. Conversely, capital has grown stronger as opportunities for exit multiply, strengthening bargaining power and enabling more effective lobbying of national governments and international agencies and the emergence of 'winner-takes-all' politics (Hacker and Pierson, 2010). Figure 2.2 uses OECD data to show how incomes more broadly across society diverged between 1990 and 2010 particularly in the US, Germany and France.

The shifts in the pattern of social interests and institutional structure are not confined to the level of class conflict and the weakening of working class pressure for state welfare that meets the interests of male industrial workers. On the one hand, higher employment among married women, population ageing and the greater pressure on employment and the tightening link between skill level and life chances, in a context of increasing budgetary pressure, lead to the emergence of new social risks (Taylor-Gooby, 2001; Bonoli, 2005). Access to childcare and parental support, especially for women, social care to help with disabled people and frail elderly relatives, education and training opportunities and access to sustainable employment especially for young people and increasingly access to provision for those of working age (social housing, support for low paid workers, unemployment benefits) – especially as state provision becomes more tightly targeted – are recognised as risks that people face during their life course. On the other hand, the interests supporting the traditional life-stage risks of pensions and healthcare, at the heart of the welfare state, remain strong as these needs retain their importance.

Figure 2.2: Spending on the core of the welfare: health and pension spending as a percentage of GDP, 1980–2011

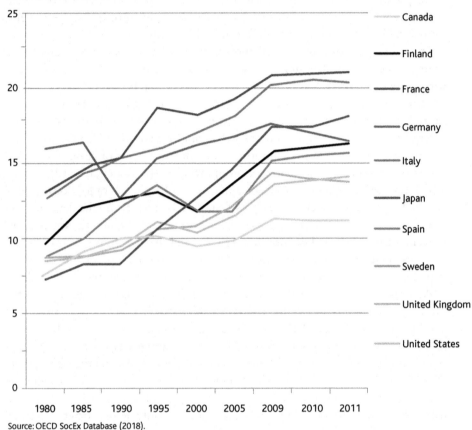

Source: OECD SocEx Database (2018).

New social risks do not reduce the importance of these risks but cut across them. They focus attention on earlier life stages than does the traditional welfare state. Attitude survey data indicates that the traditional areas of state provision receive the highest support from the mass public as areas of state responsibility but that childcare is also endorsed, at a lower level, especially in southern and central and eastern EU countries, while provision for unemployed people receives less support. The new social risks contribute a further dimension to welfare state politics and generate opportunities for political parties to link the interests of social groups across generations in a 'new politics' of welfare (Bonoli and Natali, 2012).

These changes are also reflected in shifts at the level of ideas. The dominant paradigm in political economy has moved from neo-Keynesianism through monetarism, in which the state pays less attention to interventions to maintain demand and confines itself to removing constraints on the supply of capital, labour and materials by freeing up the market, towards a more neo-liberal stance that valorises market freedoms, promoting privatisation and holding tax down.

Popular ideologies have also shifted. Support for the main welfare state services for those outside the labour market (pensions and healthcare, mainly used by older people) remains strong. The decline in class solidarity undermines support for provision for the low-waged and unemployed and there is more emphasis on desert justified by labour market contribution, as against need in the discourse about entitlement (Mau, 2004; Baumberg et al, 2012; van Oorschot, 2000). At the same time, new movements resting on nationhood and resisting the pressures of globalisation have emerged, as the UK referendum debate shows (Hobolt, 2016).

Welfare state outcomes

Shifts in welfare state policy do not undermine welfare state spending but imply substantial changes particularly in provision for those of working age and in entitlement and structuring of welfare. State spending on social provision continued to rise through the period, although the rate of increase has declined, and much of the rise since the 1980s has been in the Mediterranean and some central and eastern European states, catching up with levels of provision elsewhere in Europe. Despite some concerns (Strange, 1996), more intense international competition does not seem to lead directly to welfare state cutbacks, following the logic of a race to the bottom (Swank, 2010: 328). Scharpf and Schmidt (2000) show that the impact of globalisation has been to confirm rather than erode the differences between welfare state regimes across Europe, a finding supported also in a detailed analysis by Hemerijck (2012). Recent changes do not seem to have generated competitive tax cutting (Genschel and Schwarz, 2011). The main changes in patterns of provision lie in three areas: austerity, activation and accountability – or responsibility.

The first includes radical and far-reaching pension reform (Hinrichs, 2000), privatisation and the introduction of quasi-market systems and a whole host of detailed cuts, cost savings and efficiency measures (for example, Baird et al, 2010; Jurd, 2011). These measures have been strengthened in many countries as part of deficit reduction policies, but the move towards spending constraint originated much earlier.

Second, labour market policies and related social security policies have been restructured in order to control costs and also to mobilise more people into paid work and to improve the quality of the labour force. These cut back workers' rights to make labour markets more flexible (Casey, 2004) and pursued the expansion of education at all levels. Of particular importance is the expansion of job opportunities for women (Palier, 2010).

The commitment to activation is apparent in a range of developments including social security reforms to push unemployed people into jobs and support for lower-paid workers. In general, this process directs spending towards new social risks including labour market insecurity and growing need for childcare and support services for disabled and older people. Expenditure increased through the period from the early 1980s up to the late 1990s, but then, tended to slow, reaching a plateau after the recession as in the case of old welfare spending discussed earlier. Finland and Sweden experienced sharp falls in spending in response to the recession of the late 1990s and thereafter resumed a pattern similar to, but rather more generous than, other European countries. The electoral strength of older age groups is indicated by the numbers involved and reflected in the much greater spending in these areas.

Third, a large number of policies directly promote ideologies of individual responsibility. These include restrictions on the right to sickness and disability benefits and to encourage paid employment among these groups, much more stringent policing of benefit rights among unemployed people, and the expansion of individual retirement pensions and similar schemes (Palier, 2010).

Neither popular nor elite ideas about policy challenge the neo-liberal logic of individual rather than collective responsibility for meeting need. Responses to the crisis across Europe endorse the austerity packages favoured by the ECB and supported by IMF and most national governments, the rolling back of short-term interventions to maintain employment in most countries and the continued endorsement of optional contributory pensions. The only major country to adopt a more interventionist stance has been France since 2012. In 2015 the government led by President Hollande nevertheless imposed a sharp VAT increase, reduced taxes on business and presented a strategy (criticised by the German finance minister as too slow) to bring the deficit within Stability and Growth Pact limits by 2017 (Reuters, 2014). Spending cuts have been finally accepted by Ireland, Spain, Italy, Portugal and, after initial resistance, Greece. Anti-austerity politics, both in radical movements (such as 99%) and in more formal parties (Podemos; Syriza; die Linke) have not achieved major changes.

Government concern with activation and responses to new social risks has promoted new welfare, but austerity policies continue to squeeze social spending. The more enthusiastically supported services for older people tend to win out over the services directed at new social risks and at younger groups. Figure 2.3 plots new welfare spending as a percentage of old welfare. The relative size of the new welfare budget varies between 5% and 35% of old welfare, averaging about 20%. There are considerable national variations, and a tendency for new welfare to grow slightly faster in the early phase but this comes to an end by 2000. The prospects for a transition to a new social risk welfare state look bleak. Conversely, despite the transition to post-industrialism and the new austerity, the core of the welfare state in healthcare and pensions directed mainly at older age groups shows no sign of diminishing, although there is every indication that pressures on spending have grown and will grow more severe.

A further indication of the continuing process of shifting spending away from the labour market is that policies are failing to reduce poverty for this group, but are

Figure 2.3: Spending on new welfare as percentage of old, 1980–2011

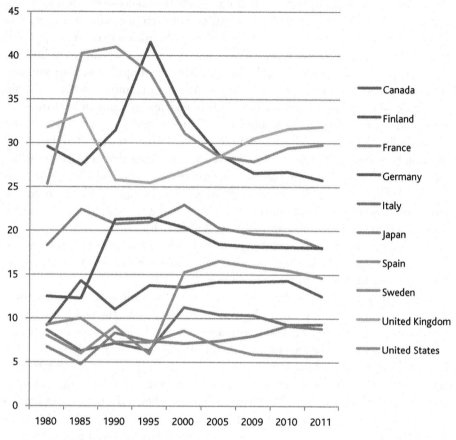

Source: OECD SocEx Database (2018).

succeeding for older people. The combined effect of the tax and benefit system was to reduce poverty levels among 16 to 64 year olds in 2005 by 58 per cent. Cuts and other changes meant that tax and benefits together only cut povery among this age group by 51 per cent in 2014, a rather weaker impact. Among those over pension age, tax and benefits cut poverty by 81 per cent in 2005. The poverty reduction effect had risen to 84% by 2014 (Eurostat, 2018). Policy penalised the young and favoured the old.

Conclusion

The Great Recession did not produce a radical new departure in social policy, but provided an opportunity for existing trends towards neo-liberalism to be taken much further much more rapidly. Popular ideas are also shifting towards individual responsibility and against welfare for those of working age, but support for the traditional welfare state, mainly directed at older people and centring on healthcare and pensions, remains strong. In short we are shifting towards a new settlement, dominated by neo-liberalism rather than neo-Keynesianism in which social policy undermines cohesive solidarities and strengthens divisions between old and young. In this context opportunities for participation to exert real political pressures that generate new and positive directions in state welfare seem limited.

Where do we go next? Globalisation divides the population into winners (the wealthy and/or highly skilled who see their opportunities widen in a more international marketplace) and losers, the less skilled, less rich and/or less fortunate, who find their living standards stagnate and their lives become tougher as the increasingly compete against others in lower income countries. The losers are fighting back but the problem is that fightback can be positive or negative. What has happened is that popular pressures against globalisation and liberal openness have strengthened across Europe both on the left and the right (Podemos in Spain, Syriza in Greece and Momentum in the UK; and the Front National in France, ADF in Germany and UKIP in the UK). The UK EU referendum outcome is arguably the result of these movements. It shows how an ostensibly participative and grassroots movement among more vulnerable groups can have damaging consequences for the inclusiveness of the welfare state.

Three outcomes are possible: victory by the left leading to more inclusive societies and social policy as social investment; victory on the right, leading to isolationism, fewer resources and a contraction of the welfare states; or the status quo – the slow development of neo-liberalism and decline of welfare states led by centrist parties, but shifted in different directions by the influence of extremist movements. The first seems unlikely in Europe at present and the second possible, with the strongest movements in Hungary, France and the UK, but the third seems to present the central direction of most European welfare states. Mass movement participation does have realm influence on national policies but it is only halfway there: the new populism recognises that the elite in global liberalism does not serve their interests, but is vulnerable to a divisiveness that undermines the goal of a welfare society. That is what those who wish to see a new participative and inclusive world must address.

References

Archibugi, D. and Michie J. (eds) (1997) *Technology, Globalisation and Economic Performance*, Cambridge: Cambridge University Press.

Armingeon, K. (2012) The Politics of Fiscal Responses to the Crisis of 2008–2009', *Governance*, 25 (4), 543–65.

Baird, A., Haynes, J., Massey, F. and Wild R. (2010) *Public Service Output, Input and Productivity: Education*, London: ONS.

Baumberg, B., Bell, K. and Gaffney, D. (2012) *Benefits Stigma in Britain*, TurnToUs, London.

Bonoli, G. (2005) 'The Politics of the New Social Policies', *Policy and Politics*, 33 (3).

Bonoli, G. and Natali, D. (2012) *The Politics of the New Welfare State*, Oxford: Oxford University Press.

Casey, B. (2004) 'The OECD Jobs Strategy and the European Employment Strategy', *EJIR*, 10 (3), 329–52.

Cuppage, J. (2013) 'Liberalising Trends in European Labour Regulation', iGlobal Law: Global Labour Law, www.igloballaw.com/liberalising-trends-in-european-labour-regulation/

Dean, M. (2010) *Governmentality*, London: Sage.

Emmenegger, P., Häusermann, S., Palier, B. and Seeleib-Kaiser, M. (eds) (2012) *The Age of Dualization*. Oxford: Oxford University Press.

Eurostat (2018) EU-SILC database, http://ec.europa.eu/eurostat/web/income-and-living-conditions/data/database

Eurostat (2015) Disability statistics – financial situation, http://ec.europa.eu/eurostat/statistics-explained/index.php/Disability_statistics_-_financial_situation

Genschel, P. and Schwarz, P. (2011) 'Tax competition' *Socio-Economic Review*, 9 (2), 339–70.

Gough, I. (2011) 'From financial crisis to fiscal crisis', in K. Farnsworth and Z.M. Irving (eds), *Social Policy in Challenging Times*, Bristol: Policy Press.

Hacker, J. and Pierson, P. (2010). *Winner-Take-All Politics*, New York: Simon & Schuster.

Hay, C. and Wincott, D. (2012) *The Political Economy of European Welfare Capitalism*. Basingstoke: Palgrave Macmillan.

Held, D. (2000). *A Globalizing World?* London New York.

Hemerijck, A. (2012) *Changing Welfare States*, Oxford: Oxford University Press.

Hinrichs, K. (2000) 'Elephants on the move', *European Review* 8 (3), 353–78.

Hobolt, S. (2016) 'The Brexit Vote: a divided nation, a divided continent', *Journal of European Public Policy*, 23 (9), 1259–77.

IMF (International Monetary Fund (2017) World Economic Outlook: database, Washington, DC: IMF, https://www.imf.org/external/pubs/ft/weo/2017/02/weodata/index.aspx

Jessop, R. (2002) *The Future of the Capitalist State*, Cambridge: Polity.

Jurd, A. (2011) *Public Service Labour Productivity*, London: ONS.

Keynes, J. (1936) *The General Theory of Employment, Interest and Money*, London: Macmillan.

Kriesi, H., Grande, E., Dolezal, M., Helbling, M., Hoglinger, D., Hutter, S. and Wuest, B. (2012) *Political Conflict in Western Europe*, Cambridge: Cambridge University Press.

Mau, S. (2004) 'Welfare Regimes and the Norms of Social Exchange', *Current Sociology*, 52 (1), 53–74.

OECD (2013) *Economic Globalisation*, Paris: OECD.

OECD (2014) *Balancing Paid Work, Unpaid Work and Leisure*, Paris: OECD.

OECD (2018) SocEx database, https://stats.oecd.org/Index. aspx?DataSetCode=SOCX_AGG

Palier, B. (2010) *A Long Good Bye to Bismarck?*, Amsterdam: Amsterdam University Press.

Reuters (2014) 'France defies partners with 'no austerity' budget', 1 October, https://uk.reuters.com/article/uk-france-budget/france-defies-eu-partners-with-no-austerity-budget-idUKKCN0HQ36D20141001

Rueda, D. (2005) 'Insider-Outsider Politics in Industrialized Democracies', *American Political Science Review*, 99, 61–74.

Scharpf, F.W. and Schmidt, V.A. (2000) *Welfare and Work in the Open Economy*, Oxford: Oxford University Press.

Strange, S. (1996) *The Retreat of the State*, Cambridge: Cambridge University Press.

Starke, P., Kaasch, A. and van Hooren, F. (2013) *The Welfare State as Crisis Manager*, Basingstoke: Palgrave.

Swank, D. (2010) 'Globalisation', in F.G. Castles, S. Leibfried, J. Lewis, H. Obinger and C. Pierson (eds), *The Oxford Handbook of the Welfare State*, Oxford, Oxford University Press, pp 318-30.

Taylor-Gooby, P. (2001) *New Risks, New Welfare,* Oxford: Oxford University Press.

Thane, P. (1982) *The Foundations of the Welfare State,* London: Longman.

Van Kersbergen, K., Vis, B. and Hemerijck, A. (2014) 'The Great Recession and Welfare State Reform' *Social Policy & Administration*, 48 (7), 883–904.

Van Oorschot, W. (2000) 'Who Should Get What, and Why?', *Policy & Politics*, 28 (1), 33–48.

3

Social policy in developing countries: a post-colonial critique and participatory inquiry

Sweta Rajan-Rankin

Introduction

This chapter resonates with the main tenet of this edited collection book, seeking to examine *first hand* what social policy formulations may look like as told from the perspective of the Global South. Mainstream social policy discourses have focused on post-war welfare provision in rich industrialised countries (Baldock et al, 2011). Economic development was identified as a key driver for welfare state emergence in wealthy countries (Flora and Heidenheimer, 1981). Welfare typology classifications (Esping-Anderson,1990), though criticised for scope and lack of attention to gender (Daly and Rake, 2003), have become established frameworks by which welfare states can be studied in comparative perspective. Original typologies have expanded to include Southern models of welfare (Martin, 1996), transition economies in Eastern Europe (Myant and Drahokoupil, 2011) and, to a very limited extent, Eastern social policy and 'Tiger economies' (Haggard and Kaufman, 2008).

Despite this, I argue that current social policy literature has not grappled sufficiently in terms of world views with the nature of social reality (ontology) or the theories around investigating social reality (epistemology) of developing country contexts. At best social policy initiatives only become visible when developing countries play 'catch up' and achieve rapid economic development, thereby abiding by the criteria for state based welfare. By drawing on emerging social policy literature from the Global South (Mares and Carnes, 2009; Razavi et al, 2004; Surrender and Walker, 2013), this chapter challenges taken-for-granted assumptions around what social policy is, and how it can be understood in developing world contexts. Post-colonial frameworks (Bhabha, 1994; Spivak, 1999) are used as an alternate lens through which we can reimagine social policy from a participatory perspective.

This chapter is a critical conversation inviting anyone interested in social policy in developing countries to engage with its politics. Such an activity – of challenging dominant discourse and considering voices that are hidden, silent or on the margins – is an act of transformative social action (Freire, 1970).

Social policy in developing countries: whose voice matters?

While there is a vast literature on social policy and welfare provision in OECD countries, far less is known about the policy regimes, underpinning ideologies and policy implementation in developing countries. Social policy as a largely Anglocentric project has classified and explored welfare provision in specific ways that often ignore the historical and political oppression of developing countries. I argue that it is not so much that developing countries have been laggard in the development of social protection systems, as they have been *arrested* by the harmful effects of colonialism, trade liberalisation and unequal global development that were pivotal in the *wealth accumulation* of developing countries. In crude terms, social policy emergence in the developed world was made possible through the *welfare state dis-emergence* based on the arresting of economic (and therefore state and welfare) potential of developing countries.

Failure to develop a coherent discourse around social policy in developing countries is linked to the classificatory politics of how 'developing countries' are defined and clustered together. UN classification of developing countries into low income, middle income and high income countries have been widely used to funnel donor aid to these countries. Alonso et al (2014) suggest that the developing world is far more heterogenous and with rapid economic development countries (like India) once classified as part of the developing world have now been re-classified as BRICS (Brazil, Russia, India, China and South Africa) countries or emerging markets, and have impact in real terms in relation to cutting off donor aid. Classificatory politics are essentially a non-participatory exercise and countries in the Global South have little say in how they are labelled, defined or understood.

Mares and Carnes (2009) suggest that the focus on economic classification has meant that other equally important factors, such as social and political context, are often ignored. In their analysis of social insurance policies introduced across Latin America, Africa, Middle East, Asia, Eastern Europe and advanced industrialised countries, they found that authoritarian regimes were much more likely to introduce old age pensions, disability insurance, and sickness and unemployment benefits. These unusual findings highlight the need to examine political influences as well as economic approaches to social policy. These attempts are complicated by the very limited data available on cross-national and temporal differences in social protection across countries, and within-country variations as well. In an ESRC funded project I was involved in (Smith et al, 2008), this gap was addressed by going beyond 'big data' and exploring the potential of micro-data based on case study evidence from India. This involved examining not just policies themselves, but also the actors, institutions and policy logics that underpin policy development. Such exercises demonstrate the fine-grained analysis needed to explore social policy within specific developing country contexts.

Wider political and global factors shaping social policy development in the Global South also need careful consideration. Mishra (1999) contends that globalisation has weakened the nation state, through a shift from national to supranational policy frameworks, which are often much more influential in shaping policy discourse at the local level. Surrender and Walker (2013) highlight some of the problematics of understanding the development of social policy in developing countries, including the increasing importance of social dimensions of welfare, and possible emergence of a 'South-South' model (the emergence of Global South countries and welfare emergence in its own right) in contrast to the traditional 'North-South' frameworks. In the context of developing countries, globalisation has played a pivotal role in shaping social policy and deepening social inequalities.

Following the 1970s OPEC oil crises, the World Bank and IMF instituted structural adjustment programmes in most of the developing world with conditionalities to 'open their doors' and liberalise their economies. Razavi et al (2004) suggest that we need to broaden our thinking around what constitutes social policy in developing countries, by exploring the inter-relationships between economic policies and their social consequences. In my study in Sirsila district in Andhra Pradesh (Rajan, 2005), I encountered farmer suicides and 'communities of widows' that directly resulted from global policy directives. Export-oriented employment meant that farmers were forced to shift from food-crop cultivation to cash-crop cultivation. As subsistence farmers, this meant that many of these families were starving and were forced to enter into severe debt with local money lenders at exorbitant interest rates. Unable to pay off the debt, many of these farmers committed suicide, leaving their families to a life of indentured labour, paying off the debt over many generations. These are not isolated cases, but daily realities of those in extreme poverty for whom globalisation and macroeconomic policies have had dire consequences.

Ghosh (2004) argues that trade liberalisation and increase in export-oriented employment had a significant impact in shaping social policy in developing countries. Drawing on the 'nimble fingered hypothesis', which relates to the preference for docile workers who were less likely to unionise, global export-oriented employment specifically targeted women workers. In my participatory action research study in Bhalaswa, New Delhi (Rajan, 2002), I examined demolitions and forcible evictions of slum dwellers as part of a 'clean city' drive to build the Delhi Metro, an important infrastructural activity to usher in global business. I was involved in local urban housing movements (with local organisations such as *Ankur*[1] and Action Aid, India), with strong participation from community women who conducted *morchas* (marches and sit-ins) and strapped themselves to bulldozers to resist slum resettlement. While the evictions continued unabated, these social movements were able to put pressure on local government to review the impact of evictions and slum dwellers' rights to housing and livelihood. Community action and social movements can hence play a pivotal role in resisting and shaping social policy.

State policy provision and actual implementation on the ground may also differ markedly. In his study of social protection in Nigeria, Makinde (2005) observed a significant 'implementation gap' in the rolling out of family support programmes due to contextual factors such as corruption, political instability and inadequate human and material resources. Similar findings emerge from case study evidence in India. The Mid-day Meal Scheme, aimed at addressing child poverty by providing a hot meal at school, had translated into a different reality on the ground. During my social work training in Dharavi (infamously known as the largest slum in Asia), pre-school children would often be given sacks of grain and rice to take back home, thus addressing the family's food needs rather than addressing child nutrition. These examples illustrate the divergent ways state based policies can be interpreted on the ground. Social policies are often negotiated through complex layers of school, neighbourhood poverty and the micro-level politics of the family before these schemes can reach vulnerable children. In contrast, innovative schemes such as Mobile Crèches in New Delhi (a charity organisation providing a transitory crèche for construction workers near building sites), originally intended to address barriers to maternal employment, have been very beneficial in ensuring child safety and wellbeing. Case study evidence then suggests that state policy provision alone is insufficient to bring about social change, and that a myriad of socio-cultural, economic and political factors play a role as well. In the next section, I explore an alternate discourse to social policy from a post-colonial and participatory perspective.

A post-colonial critique of social policy: towards a participatory ontology

Given that social policy discourse has been framed mainly through the lens and language of the Global North, a participatory approach necessitates a re-examination of what social policy can mean for, and with, people from the Global South. Post-colonial theories, while by no means uncontested, provide an opportunity to do this. Post-colonial perspectives emerge from a commitment to explore the impacts of cultural imperialism (Said, 1993), colonisation and racial oppression (Ashcroft et al, 2006), blackness and internalising oppression (Fanon, 1967) in framing culture, identity and development in the Global South. In his classic work, Bhabha (1994) reminds us of the importance to consider the 'location of culture' in discursive terms, and unpack the ambivalent relationship between the coloniser and the colonised. This 'ambivalence' born of racial subjugation and longing for acceptance eventually disturbs and unsettles dominant discourse.

This ambivalence also characterises the relationship between 'race' and 'nation'. Gilroy (2001, 2002) suggests that the state often serves as an institutionalising process through which racism can be reproduced. Current formulations of 'race' are based on their historical derivation as a bio-political construct (racial superiority of Caucasoid people, inferiority of Negroid, Mongoloid and Australoid groups). This provided a substantial moral basis for the colonial project, which was in its end an economic activity of wealth accumulation for western countries, by plundering the resources of the 'barbaric colonies' (Bhabha, 1994). These biopolitics of race are often viewed as limited to specific timescapes of colonisation which is now historically a 'dead subject'. But the 'ghost of colonialism' is alive and well in contemporary policy. Amin (2010) suggests that there is 'racial debris' that has accumulated over time, space and place, which finds manifestation in current discourse. He suggests that

> ... the intensity of race in a given present (persists) in terms of the play between vernacular legacies of race-coded reception of visible difference and the conjectural mobilization of race by bio-political regimes. (Amin, 2010: 1)

In this sense, 'race' is imagined as a classificatory tool to create the Other based on categories of visible difference and these are influential in shaping the role of the state in constructing its subjects. Spivak (1999) suggests that there is a problem of the 'vanishing present' when we consider race, as linking racialised bodies to their colonial and oppressive pasts visible their historical location, but also ties them to a disempowered future. Strategic essentialism (the deployment of essentialist discourse to energise and bring political attention to specific aspects of colonialism and its human consequences) then bridges these weaknesses by allowing bodies of colour to become visible through engaging with race (even though it brings bio-political tensions), to enable a situated narrative of alternate histories to emerge. This then takes us to a shift away from examining the Global South in terms of structural inequality (which is equally important) to an examination of difference.

Drawing on post-structuralist critiques of Althusser (whose main contribution was the shift from structural analysis to the study of difference), Foucault (who challenges the notion of the 'state' as a single object), and Derrida (who observes subtleties between 'difference' – individual – and '*difference*' – difference within unity), Stuart Hall (1985) makes an important theoretical step, in shifting the focus from redistribution to politics of representation.

> The state condenses very different social practices and transforms them into the operation of rule and domination over particular classes and other social groups. The way to reach such a conceptualization is not to substitute difference for its mirror opposite, unity, but to rethink both in terms of a new concept – articulation. (Hall, 1985: 93)

Hall is reflecting on the importance of not just adapting to a problematic dominant discourse from within, but considering its weaknesses and exploring new forms of conceptualising social policy. Discerning the difference between state as unitary and social practices as discursive 'fact', Hall is making an important observation: that underpinning structuration (the process of stratifying social categories) and inequality is another parallel process – one of signification and representation which the dominant discourse rarely attends to. The 'politics of representation' then speak to the signs, symbols and language by which the 'Other' is created. In his later work, Hall (1997) examines the politics of representation as both ideological and social practice, reproduced through ideas 'in our head' around good/bad, deserving/undeserving, black/white constructions. As de Saussure (2013) observes, these constructions are institutionalised through systems of representations, codes and images (*signifiers*) which relate to normative formulations of objects of difference (*the signified*). Our social location is hence pre-codified in terms of the signifier-signified process and can form the basis for oppression. Thus, Hall is suggesting that the concept of difference or the 'Other' is socially constructed based on proximity or distance from dominant normative frameworks, which are inherently gendered and racialised.

The link between social location and oppression is powerfully articulated by Paulo Freire (1970) who suggests that, while structure plays a role in signifying who has social power, oppression is a separate entity. He suggests that unequal social location is translated to oppression through the dehumanising process by which the marginalised human subject is distanced from their humanity. This is a distinct move away from structures as unitary concepts, rigid and unchanging – to oppression as a historically located, socially constructed (and hence intentional) process of power accumulation, which robs the oppressed of their humanity, their skin, their name, dignity, self-recognition and their history.

Weheliye's (2014) notion of 'bare flesh' brings to sharp relief the embodied nature of how oppression leads to the creation of a 'non-being' through the process of Othering. It suggests that the body is inscribed with signs and symbols (gender, race, sexuality), which combine to create the image of the 'stranger', the 'Other', through a state of non-being. Ahmed observes that

> Stranger fetishism is a fetishism of figures: *it invests the figure of a stranger with a life of its own insofar as it cuts 'the stranger' off from the histories of its determination.* (Ahmed, 2000: 5, original emphasis)

In their work on the politics of Othering, Ploesser and Mecheril (2011) suggest that social policy and direct work with vulnerable people is often shaped by an uncomfortable relationship with difference. It can involve neglect of the Other[2] (through race neutral, gender neutral policy formulations), recognition of the Other (by emphasising and making visible their difference), and deconstructing the difference between the Other and the non-Other (thus challenging power structures). It is very important to note that this process of Othering is by no means limited to developing countries, but to any subject whose embodied identity deviates from the normative dominant discourse. Indeed, skin Othering based on visible difference can both highlight and obscure the politics of difference (Alcoff,

2006). Othering is hence not limited to the raced, colonised and barbaric other (Bhabha, 1994); it has reverberations that are present and alive in contemporary times across the globe.

Current policy discourses could be said to largely operate within the 'neglect of the Other' discourse by failing to engage with the politics of representation, *both* within developing countries *and* in the western world. By focusing on structural analysis of economic development, and ignoring social location, difference and identity, social policy has sowed the seeds of its own discontent by distancing itself from its gendered, racialised and embodied articulations. In this sense, social policy still colours within lines (pun completely intended) – in that the Other – especially the racialised stranger/Other – dances between visibility and invisibility. When the racialised Other residing in western countries achieves social status, they threaten western jobs. When they reside in developing countries, they are non-beings, invisible until they achieve global recognition as having 'emerged' in terms of western conceptions of welfare.

Conclusions

So how can we develop a participatory ontology for social policy in developing countries? This chapter presents a critique of existing social policy frameworks by drawing on a wealth of case study experience from the ground both in India, and from other developing countries. The post-colonial perspective challenges many unspoken policy assumptions including: pre-occupation with state as a basis for welfare (through examination of race and nation); lack of social welfare in developing countries (by reframing as welfare state *dis-emergence*); focus on structural inequality devoid of historical or social context (by refocusing on politics of representation); and the lack of connection between global, national and individual experiences (through embodied politics of race and oppression).

This chapter does not offer a 'new' classificatory framework to replace old formulations. Indeed, to do so would be to once again fall into the trap of classificatory politics, which restricts a more fluid and complex understanding of social policy in developing countries. Instead it presents an alternate lens – a critical, deconstructivist and post-colonial lens – as a tentative framework through which a participatory articulation can emerge that is sensitive to the voices from the Global South.

In conclusion, I leave the reader with the following critical questions which can help shape a post-colonial theory of social policy in developing countries:

1. How does a historically situated analysis of colonialism and post-colonial state development shape contemporary social policy in developing countries?
2. Do World Bank and IMF classifications of developing countries lead to a politics of Othering? In what way can a departure from these classificatory frameworks enable a participatory ontology to emerge?

3. What are the diverse political frameworks (democratic, authoritarian) that explain state based welfare provision?
4. How have unequal global development and rapid economic growth influenced poverty and social exclusion in developing countries?
5. Do state-based policies address or reproduce social inequalities?
6. Does social policy in developing countries operate through a position of neglect of the Other, recognition of the Other or deconstructing of the Other and non-Other? Does this make a difference in terms of outcomes?
7. How does an embodied understanding of gendered and racialised Othering shed light on the macro-politics of social policy construction? How can it explain individual level difference?
8. Could a post-colonial perspective to social policy be useful for explaining both social policy in developing countries and the developed world?

Acknowledgements
My thanks to the editors Peter Beresford and Sarah Carr for their gentle guidance and support in writing this chapter. I am grateful for the Tata Institute for Social Sciences for their rigorous training and helping me become a critical social worker, and to the University of Oxford for helping me gain the tools to understand (and challenge) social policy discourses. To Jana, Pranita, Keith, Dylan and Leela for supporting this venture and helping me find my 'voice'.

Notes
[1] Ankur is a local non-governmental organisation (NGO) in New Delhi dedicated to supporting slum dwellers and urban poor communities to fight for their rights of livelihood and dwelling within the city premises where they contribute so much in terms of economic and social capital.
[2] In post-colonial scholarship, a distinction is made between the Other (constructed by the dominant discourse) and the other (a critical imagination of what such Othering does to the identity of the marginalised) (Ashcroft et al, 2006).

References
Ahmed, S. (2000) *Strange Encounters: Embodied others in post-coloniality*, London: Routledge.
Ahmed, S. (2004) *The Cultural Politics of Emotion*, Edinburgh: Edinburgh University Press.
Alcoff, L.M. (2006) *Visible Identities: Race, gender and the self*, Oxford: Oxford University Press.
Alonso, J.A., Cortez, A.L. and Klasen, S. (2014) *LDC and other country groupings: How useful are these approaches to classify countries in a more heterogeneous developing world*, CDP Background Paper 21. UN, Department of Economic and Social Affairs, www.un.org/en/development/desa/policy/cdp/cdp_background_papers/bp2014_21.pdf
Amin, A. (2010) 'The remainders of race', *Theory Culture & Society*, 27(1), 1–23.
Ashcroft, B., Griffiths, G. and Tiffin, H. (2006) *The Post-Colonial Reader*, second edition, London: Routledge.

Baldock, J., Mitton, L., Manning, N. and Vickerstaff, S. (eds) (2011) *Social Policy*, fourth edition, Oxford: Oxford University Press.

Bhabha, H. (1994) *The Location of Culture*, London: Routledge.

Daly, M. and Rake, K. (2003) *Gender and the Welfare State: Care, Work and Welfare in Europe and the USA*, Oxford: Wiley.

de Saussure, F. (2013) *Course in General Linguistics*, reprint edition, Bloomsbury: London.

Esping-Anderson, G. (1990) *Three Worlds of Welfare Capitalism*, Cambridge: Polity Press.

Fanon, F. (1967) *Black Skin White Masks: Get Political*, New York: Grove Press.

Flora, P. and Heidenheimer, A.J. (1981) *The Development of Welfare States in Europe and America*, New Brunswick: Transaction Publishers.

Freire, P. (1970) *Pedagogy of the Oppressed*, London: Penguin.

Ghosh, J. (2004). 'Globalization, export-oriented employment for women and social policy: A case study of India', in S. Razavi, R. Pearson and C. Danloy (eds) *Globalization, Export-Oriented Employment and Social Policy*, Basingstoke: Palgrave Macmillan, pp 91–125.

Gilroy, P. (2001) *Against Race: Imagining Political Culture Beyond the Color Line*, Boston, MA: Harvard University Press.

Gilroy, P. (2002) *There Ain't No Black in the Union Jack: The Cultural Politics of Race and Nation*, second edition, London: Routledge.

Haggard, S. and Kaufman, R.R. (2008) *Development, Democracy and Welfare States: Latin-America, East Asia and Eastern Europe*, Princeton: Princeton University Press.

Hall, S. (1985) 'Signification, representation, ideology: Althusser and the post-structuralist debates', *Critical Studies in Mass Communications*, 2 (2), 91–114.

Hall, S. (1997) *Representation: Cultural Representations and Signifying Practices*, second edition, London: Sage.

Makinde, T. (2005) 'Problems of policy implementation in developing nations: The Nigerian experience', *Journal of Social Sciences*, 11 (1), 63–9.

Mares, I. and Carnes, M.E. (2009). 'Social policy in developing countries', *Annual Review of Political Science*, 12, 93–113.

Martin, C. (1996) 'Social Welfare and the Family in Southern Europe', *South European Society & Politics*, Special Issue on Southern European Welfare States, 1 (3), 23–41.

Mishra, R. (1999) *Globalization and the Welfare State*, Cheltenham: Edward Elgar.

Myant, M.R. and Drahokoupil, J. (2011) *Transition Economies: Political Economy in Russia, Eastern Europe and Central Asia*, NJ: Wiley.

Ploesser, M. and Mecheril, P. (2011). 'Neglect – recognition – deconstruction: Approaches to otherness in social work', *International Social Work*, 55 (6), 794–808.

Rajan, S. (2002) 'Women's Empowerment in Slum Resettlement: A Case Study of Bhalaswa, New Delhi', Master's thesis, Tata Institute of Social Sciences, Mumbai, India.

Rajan, S. (2005) 'Gendered Impacts of Structural Adjustment: A Study of Three Indian States', MPhil thesis, Department of Social Policy and Social Work, University of Oxford.

Razavi, S., Pearson, D. and Danloy, C. (eds) (2004) *Globalization, Export-Oriented Employment and Social Policy*, Basingstoke: Palgrave Macmillan.

Said, E.W. (1993) *Culture and Imperialism*, New York: Vintage Books.

Smith, G., Pellissiary, S., Rajan, S. and Dubuc, S. (2008) *ESRC Micro-data Scoping Study*, London: Economic and Social Research Council, www.esrc.ac.uk/files/about-us/policies-and-standards/national-data-strategy/international-microdata-scoping-studies-project-india/

Spivak, G.C. (1999) *A Critique of Post-Colonial Reasoning: Towards a History of the Vanishing Present*, Cambridge, MA: Harvard University Press.

Surrender, R. and Walker, R. (2013) *Social Policy in a Developing World*, London: Edward Elgar.

Weheliye, A.G. (2014) *Habeas Viscus: Racializing Assemblages, Biopolitics, and Black Feminist Theories of the Human*, Durham, NC: Duke University Press.

4

Advancing sustainability: developing participatory social policy in the context of environmental disasters

Margaret Alston

Disasters affecting the landscapes in which people live are becoming more frequent and more intense, threatening the sustainability of physical environments, place based economies and social structures. People and communities across the world are experiencing significant upheavals in their lives as a result of the impact of disasters on their sense of 'place', belonging and wellbeing. The destruction of taken-for-granted landscapes significantly affects lives and livelihoods, wellbeing and health as the familiar becomes unfamiliar and the safety of the known becomes destabilised. While the sustainability of environments is challenged, so too is the social sustainability – or the capacity of people to maintain social systems.

When disasters occur, everybody living in the affected area is vulnerable. Nonetheless, the adaptive capacity of individuals, and their ability to absorb and move on, is shaped by a number of factors including gender, poverty, ethnicity, access to resources and input to decision making. Critically, and for the purposes of this chapter, the vulnerability of individuals, and the ongoing social sustainability of communities, can be mitigated somewhat through social policies that acknowledge and support those with limited resources to address and adapt to the critical changes in their lives. However, there are a number of factors that act to prevent policies being sufficiently nuanced to assist people and communities in crisis – chief among these are the underpinning principles upon which social policies are based and the lack of participatory processes that block those affected, including the more marginalised, from having their voices heard. In this chapter I touch briefly on the social impacts of disasters, on vulnerability and on the way social policies can enhance or reduce social sustainability and people's adaptive capacity and resilience in the face of often extraordinary changes in their lives.

Disasters

Critically the increase in environmental disasters is the result of climate changes resulting both from the build-up of greenhouse gases and from the destruction of the environment by other forms of human interventions. For example, actions such as land clearing and deforestation can cause mudslides and erosion, and can deplete ecosystems and destabilise agricultural production. Chemical overuse in agricultural areas, chemical spills in waterways and mining are other examples of human induced disasters that have a critical effect on the health of people and ecosystems. Thus environmental disasters are occurring as a result of both perceptible changes in climate and other human activities and the resulting environmental events and the changes caused to landscapes have a major impact on the people and communities most affected.

These disasters are creating significant upheaval to seasonal weather patterns, to food production and hence to food and water security across the world and are irrevocably changing lives and livelihoods and the social systems that underpin them. At the Gender, Leadership and Social Sustainability (GLASS) Research Unit at Monash University, we have been researching the social and gendered impacts of climate changes across areas of Australia and the Asia-Pacific region for over two decades. During this period there has been a rise in the frequency and intensity of slow onset events such as droughts across the region and an increase in the frequency and fury of extreme weather events such as cyclones, bushfires and floods. Storm surges are increasing along coastal regions, sea levels rises affecting island nations are slowly eroding coastal villages, temperature rises are impacting on health and food production cycles, and these changed seasonal patterns are having significant impacts on food and water security. The uneven global impacts of these changes are reflected in the concerns of small island nations across the Pacific Ocean in the global south. For example, following the climate meeting – Committee of the Parties, COP21 in Paris in 2015 – the president of the small Pacific Island nation of Kiribati warned that the commitment to limit temperature rises to 1.5 degrees would not save his country (Smith, 2015). Thus despite the fact that island nations and others contribute least to global warming they are disproportionately impacted by climate changes.

Vulnerability and sustainability

Definitions of vulnerability to climate changes emanating from international bodies such as the Intergovernmental Panel on Climate Changes (IPCC) usually refer to the capacity of an ecosystem to adapt. *Social vulnerability*, on the other hand, has emerged as a term used by social scientists to refer to the exposure of people in affected areas and their capacity to cope with the impacts of climate changes in their particular circumstances (see for example Kelly and Adger, 2000). Social vulnerability is defined by poverty, inequality and marginalisation (Brooks, 2003) and one of the most critical factors in shaping social vulnerability is gender.

Social sustainability on the other hand is about the capacity of the community to continue to provide basic needs for food, shelter, work, education and health services and to preserve cultural heritage and diversity, as well as the governance structures and participatory processes that facilitate wellbeing. The impacts of environmental disasters on social sustainability and social vulnerability vary depending on the scale of the event, the resources available to mitigate impacts, the vulnerability of people and therefore their capacity to adapt. Critically, loss of life and ongoing morbidity are the most significant impacts experienced in a range of disasters and research suggests that gender is a critical factor, with women being far more likely to die in disasters. For example, up to four times as many women died in the 2004 tsunami (Aglionby, 2005) and Neumayer and Pluemper (2007) suggest women are 14 times as likely to die in a disaster. The reasons are complex but include women protecting their children and not attending shelters because of concerns they may have about their safety.

A range of studies from across the world indicate that women's vulnerability in post-disaster sites, including to increased violence (Alston, 2015; Whittenbury, 2012), results from their unequal access to resources and the wide range of constraints imposed by hegemonic masculinity, including the ongoing provision of care services, health factors, lack of access to family planning in the immediate post-disaster phase, and exposure to increased violence and abuse (Neumayer and Pluemper, 2007; Enarson, 2012; Alston et al, 2014). Gender remains a critical factor in shaping vulnerability and yet it is rarely the focus of social policies aimed at building social sustainability and addressing the impacts of disasters.

Displacement is another significant factor caused by disasters, and one that affects millions of people across the world. Depending on the scale of the disaster, the impact on people's homes and livelihoods can be devastating and this creates the imperative to move if houses are destroyed and water sources are unsafe and to seek safety and income generating activity elsewhere. There are significant movements of people out of areas affected by environmental disasters including from many parts of Africa where desertification has had a significant impact on food production (Nampinga, 2008), across South Asia where droughts, floods, unseasonal weather patterns and water security issues are forcing one or more members of families to migrate away in order to earn remittance income (income earned by the family member that is 'remitted' or sent back to the family) (Alston, 2015), and in the Pacific Island nations where similar patterns of outmigration are evident. There is some suggestion that several hundreds of millions will be forced to migrate in the 21st century (Sachs, 2007).

Other factors that exacerbate vulnerability and deplete social sustainability include poverty, isolation, rurality, class, ethnicity, and life cycle stage with the aged and young people being particularly affected.

Australian example

One example of a major disaster arising from Australia is the long-running drought in the late 1990s and early 2000s. The 'millennium drought', as it has come to be known, affected the entire continent over a period of several years. This slow onset event affected agricultural production and the families and communities dependent on agricultural productivity. Our research suggested that many agricultural families slipped into poverty, and that this had flow on effects to rural communities and the businesses and services that provide the backbone of community viability and sustainability. In several studies we observed the hardship and poverty experienced in rural communities and noted the impacts on women and men, the old and the young (Alston and Kent, 2001, 2006; Alston et al, 2004). Particularly evident were issues relating to mental health, increased violence and drug and alcohol dependency as a form of self-medication and small business closures. Despite this evidence, policies were not nuanced to reflect social vulnerability, or to build social sustainability and access to financial support for farm families was restricted. At the time, Australia's conservative government changed policy drivers from those framed around socially just welfare support to a harsher economic model underpinned by neoliberal policies. Thus drought came to be viewed not as a social catastrophe but as a business risk to be managed by farm families and businesses (Botterill and Fisher, 2003: ii). As a consequence, hardship and poverty increased in rural areas, leading the Deputy Prime Minister and Leader of the National Party (the party that traditionally supported rural people) to note the possibility of Australia becoming two nations:

> The sense of alienation, of being left behind, of no longer being recognised and respected for the contribution to the nation being made, is deep and palpable in much of rural and regional Australia today. ... This issue must be addressed by all of us who collectively make up Australia, if we are to be a whole nation ... (Anderson, 1999)

This view was shared by community organisations left to pick up the pieces including the Australian Catholic Social Welfare Commission. Its 2000 report noted:

> There is now such a deep, almost pathological, cynicism amongst rural Australians about the nature of government interest in them. (ACSWC, 2000)

The drought policy indicated the harsh shift from a gentler polity to one based on economic drivers that were curiously depopulated (or lacking in a focus on people) and lacked critical attention to social vulnerability and sustainability.

Bangladesh example

A second example concerns the impacts of climate changes occurring in Bangladesh, which was the basis for a three-year study undertaken with Oxfam (Alston, 2015; Alston et al, 2014). Our study, which took place in several areas of the country, subject to a diverse range of disasters including floods, storm surges, cyclones, river erosion and drought, revealed the hardships experienced by people in the affected areas. Critically Bangladesh has a high proportion of people living in extreme poverty, and many areas of the country are difficult to access. Services may be cut off during a disaster and aid may be a long time reaching various areas. Our study revealed that the government of Bangladesh has worked hard to reduce poverty with some real success, that there is now a well-developed emergency response process and that significant attention had been paid to developing shelters and supporting communities to prepare for disasters.

Indicators of progress can be found in mortality rates. In 1970, when there had been limited attention given to mitigation, the devastating cyclone Bhola killed more than half a million Bangladeshis. The 1991 cyclone, known as cyclone 2B, resulted in the deaths of more than 130,000 people, 90% of whom were women and children (Schmuck, 2002). This hastened the building of shelters and early warning systems. Cyclone Sidr in 2009, one of the worst on record, resulted in approximately 10,000 people losing their lives. Despite this enormous tragedy and the untold devastation to families and communities, attention to shelters and early warning systems has had an impact on the scale of the devastation over time. Community-based bodies are also being called on to provide advice. Nonetheless, our research reveals that women are particularly vulnerable during and after disasters, are more likely to experience violence, are less financially secure, have more difficulty accessing water and food for the family, have greater caring responsibilities, have reduced access to family planning, have more limited access to early warnings, are not equitably represented on decision making bodies and therefore have more limited opportunities to provide policy advice that would assist gender equality and build social sustainability in the small village communities. Further, girls are more likely to experience forced child marriages and may be forced to drop out of school to assist with household tasks (Alston, 2015).

These two examples, albeit outlined briefly, indicate the significant social and gendered impacts of disasters. They provide contrasting policy responses to extreme situations. The Australian example indicates a policy platform based on neoliberal principles with little input from those most affected and very limited if any attention to building the social sustainability of communities. The second example indicates a country struggling with increased climate disasters making progress on reducing the more extreme impacts. However, there is still a way to go in facilitating the input of village people in general and women in particular. Both examples indicate the need for more comprehensive, gender-equitable, bottom-up participatory processes that will facilitate socially just policy solutions to the emerging environmental crises.

Social policy

My discipline of social work continues to engage with social policy processes and solutions as a critical factor in assisting people and communities. A pertinent definition of social policy emerging from social work is that it involves 'systematic interventions relating to social needs and values' (Fawcett et al, 2009: 5). A more jaundiced definition, and one that appears relevant to the disaster space is that provided by Cheers et al (2007: 26), who define social policy as 'a socially constructed response to a socially constructed problem that involves taking ideological positions, making decisions based on social beliefs and values, and prioritising goals and objectives according to these.' This is more clarifying in highlighting the way politicians adopt ideological positions that impact citizenship rights and values and reduce the social sustainability of affected communities. Thus governments of the day can redefine 'the problem' based on their vision for society through the use of language, legislation, surveillance and regulation, and resource distribution.

This is quite clear in the Australian example above where drought was redefined as a 'managed risk' and redeployed as the responsibility of individual farm businesses. The 'problem' of drought was therefore given limited attention because of the economic ideology underpinning the government response. By contrast the Bangladesh example indicates a commitment to social support, but where limited resources constrain the capacity to act quickly. Thus it is possible to note that, as Fawcett et al (2009) do, that social policy can assist or diminish people, it can strengthen families and communities or divide them, it can reduce inequalities or cement them. I would argue that social policy that assists and strengthens families and communities is based on critical attention to social vulnerability and sustainability. It is also based on comprehensive bottom-up participatory processes that bring together the voices of people most affected to assist in shaping policies that build adaptive capacity and resilience and empower people to face the future.

Social workers are increasingly engaging in policy debates, particularly as is demonstrated in the Australian case, as a more punitive environment surrounds the policy process. My discipline is developing expertise in policy practice (Jansson, 1984; Gal and Weiss-Gal, 2014: 4–5) notwithstanding that the involvement of social workers is highly dependent on the socio-political context of a country and their capacity to engage. These efforts are bolstered by disciplinary developments in theoretical approaches to environmental disasters. This includes our work on ecological social work (McKinnon and Alston, 2016).

Summing up

We know that environmental disasters are increasing and that they are having a devastating impact on people and communities across the world. Yet in many cases social policies are developed on the basis of neoliberal market based principles rather than socially just endeavours aimed at supporting people and communities in crisis. I have argued that social policies based on bottom–up, gender-equitable, participatory processes are necessary if we are to build adaptive capacity and resilience in the face of mounting environmental disasters. Further, there is an urgent need for those engaged in disaster spaces such as social workers to address policy implications as part of their critical role in assisting people in crisis.

References

Aglionby, J. (2005) 'Four times as many women died in the tsunami', *Guardian*, 26 March, www.theguardian.com/society/2005/mar/26/internationalaidanddevelopment.indianoceantsunamidecember2004

Alston, M. (2015) *Women and Climate Change in Bangladesh*, Abingdon: Routledge.

Alston, M. and Kent, J. (2001) *Generation X-pendable: Young, rural and looking for work*, A Report to Woolworths Ltd on funded research, Wagga Wagga: Centre for Rural Social Research, Charles Sturt University.

Alston, M. and Kent, J. (2006) *Impact of Drought on Rural and Remote Education Access: A Report to DEST and Rural Education Fund of FRRR*, Wagga Wagga: Centre for Rural Social Research.

Alston, M., Kent, J. and Kent, A. (2004) *Social Impacts of Drought: Report to NSW Agriculture*, Wagga Wagga: Centre for Rural Social Research, Charles Sturt University.

Alston, M., Whittenbury, K. and Haynes, A. (2014) 'Gender and Climate Change in Bangladesh. A Report to Monash-Oxfam', Melbourne: Monash University, Department of Social Work.

Anderson, J. (1999) 'One Nation or Two? Securing a Future for Rural and Regional Australia', Address to the National Press Club, Canberra, 19 February.

Australian Catholic Social Welfare Commission (ACSWC) (2000) *A Litany of Disadvantage: Rural Communities of Australia*, ACSWC.

Botterill, L.C. and Fisher, M. (eds) (2003) *Beyond Drought: People, policy and perspectives*, Collingwood, Victoria: CSIRO Publishing.

Brooks, N. (2003) *Vulnerability, Risk and Adaptation: A conceptual framework*, Tyndall Centre for Climate Change Research, Working paper 38.

Enarson, E. (2012) *Women confronting Natural Disaster: From vulnerability to resilience*, Boulder, CO: Lynne Reinner Publishers.

Fawcett, B., Goodwin, S., Meagher, G. and Phillips, R. (2009) *Social Policy for Social Change*, Melbourne: Palgrave Macmillan.

Gal, J. and Weiss-Gal, I. (2014) 'Policy practice in social work: an introduction', in J. Gal and I. Weiss-Gal (eds) *Social Workers Affecting Social Policy: An International Perspective*, Bristol: Policy Press.

Jansson, B.S. (1984) *Social Welfare Policy: Analysis, process and current issues*, Belmont, CA: Wadsworth.

Kelly, P.M. and Adger, W.N. (2000) 'Theory and practice in assessing vulnerability to climate change and facilitating adaptation', *Climatic Change*, 47, 325–52.

McKinnon, J. and Alston, M. (eds) (2016) *Ecological Social Work*, London: Palgrave Macmillan.

Nampinga, R. (2008) 'Gender perspectives on climate change', paper presented at the Emerging Issues Panel, UN Commission for the Status of Women meeting, New York, February.

Neumayer, E. and Pluemper, T. (2007) 'The gendered nature of natural disasters: the impact of catastrophic events on the gender gap in life expectancy 1981–2002', *Annals of the Association of American Geographers*, 97 (3), 551–66.

Sachs, J. (2007) 'Climate Change Refugees', *Scientific American* (June 2007), 296, 43 doi:10.1038/scientificamerican0607-43

Schmuck, H. (2002) 'Empowering Women in Bangladesh – report from International Federation of Red Cross and Red Crescent Societies', Reliefweb, 25 February, http://reliefweb.int/node/96333

Smith, L. (2015) 'COP21: Paris deal won't save low-lying island nations from rising sea levels, Kiribati President warns', *Independent*, 15 December, www.independent.co.uk/environment/climate-change/cop21-paris-deal-wont-save-low-lying-island-nations-from-rising-sea-levels-kiribati-president-warns-a6773311.html

Whittenbury, K. (2012) 'Climate change, women's health, wellbeing and experiences of gender based violence in Australia', in M. Alston and K. Whittenbury (eds) *Research, Action and Policy: Addressing the gendered impacts of climate change*, New York: Springer.

5

Social policy and disability

Colin Cameron

In this chapter I will explore the relationship between social policy and the experience of disability, drawing on perspectives developed by disabled people and using the UK as a case study. I will look at contested meanings of both terms, social policy and disability, and develop an argument suggesting that social policy has largely constructed disability as dependency. I conclude that the aspiration to equality for disabled people remains one which requires continued struggle and that progressive intentions do not always take into account ideological and historical contradictions inherent in the situation. While I focus on the UK, it is to be understood that disabled people globally have, as a result of social policies in many separate countries, experienced marginalisation and exclusion from participation in economic production and community life. Rachel Kachaje (2016), Chair of Disabled People's International, states that 'most governments all over the world' fail to invest sufficiently in the economic inclusion of disabled people, arguing that when such a large population in any country is rendered non-productive the eradication of poverty 'becomes a failure'.

A traditional view would state that social policy deals with things like health, education, income maintenance, housing, and personal social services; with the measures required to secure the human wellbeing of a society. It is also, however, wider than this in its significance. Social policy reflects and enables social change, influences the way we communicate with each other, the way we see each other, and gets to the core of our identities: whether we regard ourselves, for example, as citizens with rights or primarily as consumers (Cahill, 1994). By regulating the things we are obliged to do and the things we are allowed to do, it shapes the way we act in the world (Dean, 2012).

It needs to be remembered, importantly, that social policy does not just emerge in a vacuum (Dean, 2012). It is not something imposed *on* society from outside, but is to do with the way society maintains and organises itself. Those who shape social policy do not do so from some outside vantage point, but as members of society. Social policy is always shaped by the concerns, interests, ideas and material conditions amid which policymakers find themselves. It draws on prevailing discourses and available narratives. Because it builds on previous legislation and policy in a piecemeal way, attempting to address current concerns through continuous reform of the existing system, it is important to keep in mind that it has a past and that this past continues to make itself felt in the present. In that it constructs roles, identities and circumstances experienced by diverse social groups – children, older people, women, workers, unemployed people, members of ethnic minorities, disabled people, LGBTQ people, for example – there is a requirement for social policy to be approached with a critical view. The view that human wellbeing is its object must be regarded as contestable. It is necessary to remember the role of social construction in the way we perceive and relate to difference.

Defining disability is a contentious issue. There are two *fundamentally opposed* approaches to identifying disability, known as the medical and social models (Drake, 1999: 14). Used in this sense, models are 'frameworks which not only structure the thoughts, ideas and concepts we hold in our heads and give order to what we know (or think we know) about the world, but also suggest ways of acting upon the world' (Cameron, 2015: 111). The medical model is the dominant model within contemporary society, reflecting a view of disability that has been developed by non-disabled people, and is expressed most clearly in the World Health Organisation's 1980 International Classification of Impairments, Disabilities and Handicaps (ICIDH). This defined disability as:

> any restriction or lack (resulting from impairment) of ability to perform
> an activity in the manner or within the range considered normal for
> a human being. (WHO, 1980, in Barnes and Mercer, 2010: 20)

Within this definition, disability is identified as an individual problem, the direct result of impairment, and has to do with the way some people's bodies are made and experienced, insofar as they differ from the way the majority of bodies are made and experienced. Identified as restriction or lack of ability, disability is conceived as something that can only be understood as a negative personal characteristic. Implied within such a definition is an understanding that the resolution to the problem lies in changing individuals with impairments. Such descriptions are carried forward within WHO's more recent definitions which identify 'disabilities' as *impairments, activity limitations* and *participation restrictions* (WHO, 2012, in Mallett and Slater, 2014).

The social model, which has been developed by disabled people themselves, offers a different view, defining disability as:

> The loss or limitation of opportunities to take part in the normal life of
> the community on an equal level with others due to physical and social
> barriers. (Disabled People's International, 1981, in Barnes, 1992: 2)

Within this view, the focus of the problem is shifted from individuals' impairments to the way that society is organised. Disability is not regarded here as a problem to do with bodies identified as abnormal, but to do with society's unwillingness to value and include physical difference. Relating this to social policy, Roulstone and Prideaux (2012: 3) have commented that:

> to have been disabled for much of (the last 200 years) is to have failed to have lived up to standards or stereotypes of what are held to be 'normal' measures of success, with containment and segregation a key impulse behind disability provision.

In arguing from a social model perspective in this chapter, my aim is to make it clear that the relationship between disabled people and social policy has not always been a very positive one. I would suggest that social policy has played a major part in the construction of disability as deficit, and that there has been a structural purpose served by this construction. What I am suggesting is that much of the disadvantage experienced by disabled people is not the natural outcome of the experience of impairment, but the outcome of the way that – through the social policies, systems and services which have emerged – society has decided to deal with people with impairments.

Hahn (1985: 294) has argued that 'Fundamentally, disability is defined by public policy. In other words, disability is whatever policy says it is'. Hahn makes the point that, rather than being some natural, unchanging *fact*, which will be experienced in much the same way across very different social and historical contexts, what we understand by the word disability is subject to change according to what we are told it means. The UK 2010 Equality Act, for example, identifies someone as disabled 'if you have a physical or mental impairment that has a "substantial" and "long-term" negative effect on your ability to do normal daily activities' (gov.uk, undated). This is a medical model definition in that it identifies being disabled as the direct outcome of being impaired and as a limiting characteristic of individuals. This definition is regarded as carrying authority because it is enshrined in law, however, and is taken as having common sense, obvious validity. What is paradoxical is that it is enshrined in a law that has been established with an ostensibly benign aim: that of protecting disabled people, among others, from discrimination. It establishes disability as a negative experience and at the same time establishes legal codes to prevent people from treating disabled people unequally. This meaning is conveyed to both disabled and non-disabled people. As part of a dominant disability discourse, it 'both opens up and closes down possibilities for action; it constitutes ways of acting in the world at the same time as it posits a description of it' (Abberley, 2002: 122). If we believe that disability is an individual problem, signifying unfortunate limitation, this will influence the way we relate to and respond to the appearance of what we name disability, both at social and individual levels. As Oliver and Barnes (2012: 14) remark:

> If we define situations as real, they are real in their consequences … As far as disability is concerned, if it is seen as a tragedy then

disabled people will be treated as if they are the victims of some tragic happening or circumstance.

I would argue that this contemporary paradox is largely the outcome of a line of thinking about disability which can be strongly associated with the development of social policy in industrialised capitalism.

Barton (2001: 169) has pointed out that 'insofar as disability is thought of socially, culturally, or historically, it is usually represented in terms of improvement'. The days of long-stay, remote institutions are past, disabled children often now receive school education alongside their non-disabled peers, and high street shops, restaurants and places of leisure are commonly more accessible than they were a couple of decades ago. However, Barton continues:

> I would argue that disability also must be defined as a more complex social construct, one which reflects not a benign evolution of acceptance but a dynamic set of representations that are deeply embedded in historical and cultural contexts (Barton, 2001: 169).

While undoubtedly the past few decades may have seen progress in some areas, disabled people are still significantly more likely to be unemployed than non-disabled people; more likely to hold fewer educational qualifications; more likely to experience unfair treatment at work; more likely to live in poverty; more likely to live in unsuitable housing; more likely to find it difficult to access public transport; and significantly less likely to participate in cultural, leisure or sporting activities (DWP, 2014). There has been recent controversy in the UK about the large numbers of disabled people who have died shortly after the termination of their claim for employment and support allowance (ESA) following a finding by a work capability assessment that they were fit for work (DWP, 2015). There is great concern about and active resistance to the possibility of the legalisation of assisted suicide because of well-founded arguments that this will lead to pressure on many disabled people to end their lives (Armer, 2014). Parents of unborn children identified through pre-natal screening as impaired are routinely expected to terminate pregnancies (Maynard, 2014). There is increasing recording of hate crime against disabled people (Sherry, 2010). The story of disability is, then, hardly one of ever-widening emancipation and acceptance. Rather, it is one of contradiction.

Medical model thinking has its origins in the processes of industrialisation which transformed British society during the 19th and 20th centuries and in the social policy measures that emerged both as a response to and as a means of trying to manage this transformation. While there is much evidence that people with impairments have been on the receiving end of prejudice throughout the history of western civilisation (Barnes, 1997), there is a consensus among Disability Studies theorists that 'prior to the Industrial Revolution of the late eighteenth century, disabled people were part of an undifferentiated mass poor, and hence clustered at the lower reaches of society, but not excluded from it' (Borsay, 2002: 103). The 1601 Poor Law recognised people whose impairments meant they were unable to work as deserving of 'outdoor relief' in terms of financial or in kind support. Roulstone and Prideaux (2012: 4) have noted that:

> The recognition of the unmet needs of sick, infirm and disabled people, although very basic and locally haphazard, did afford basic protection for disabled people to at least survive among their non-disabled counterparts.

Impairment was commonplace, regarded as inevitable and ordinary rather than as something separate from everyday life or requiring normalisation. The shift in the circumstances of people with impairments came with the emergence of the factory system of production, the establishment of new production norms, and the requirement for an army of able-bodied workers who could operate the new machines that would generate profit for capitalist manufacturers. The appearance of normality as a principle underpinning social organisation coincided with the struggle during the 19th century to find ways of controlling the rapidly increasing scale of human movement that accompanied industrialisation (Garland-Thomson, 2009). The word 'normal', as used to mean 'conforming to, not deviating or differing from, the common type, standard, regular, usual', only enters the English language around 1840 (Davis, 1995: 24).

The Poor Law Amendment Act 1834, which has been identified by many as the first modern piece of UK social policy legislation, had as its object the assurance of the operation of a 'free' labour market 'by ensuring that all who were sane and able-bodied should work – never mind where or upon what terms such work might be found' (Dean, 2012: 18). A distinction continued to be made between 'the deserving' and 'the undeserving' poor, with relief being dependent on admission to one of the newly built local workhouses. Conditions within these workhouses were made as miserable as possible, a deliberate policy intended to deter any from seeking public support and to ensure that this would always be regarded as a last option. Moral values of self-sufficiency and industriousness were preached, exhorted and inculcated through the Church and through popular culture, exemplified by Samuel Smiles' 1859 book *Self Help*. People with impairments, identified as 'idiots, lunatics and cripples', were herded into asylums and workhouses where they first came under the gaze of medical professionals who saw it as their task to cure or restore these inmates to health (Barnes, 1997). From a social model perspective, it was this historic removal from society that established disablement and stigmatised and medicalised impairment (Oliver and Barnes, 2012). A role was created for disabled people as objects of pity and horror. A terror of the same fate became a concern of the able-bodied. To be in want of charity became regarded as a mark of shame and personal inadequacy. Dickens' character Betty Higden in *Our Mutual Friend* depicts this well (Dickens, 2008).

The migration of labour from the land to the expanding centres of production, the towns and cities, led to chronic overcrowding as large numbers of people lived in closer proximity to each other than ever before. As Dean (2012) has noted, social policy measures in terms of public health and factory legislation were introduced to safeguard the health of the industrial middle class and to maximise the efficiency of industrial production. Accompanying new social policy measures there was a requirement for individuals to focus increasingly on self-surveillance and the exercise of bodily self-control. Ferguson has remarked that:

> appropriate dress, appearance, polite modes of eating and drinking, acceptable means of coughing, sneezing, urination and defecation, the proper restraint in gesture and forms of interaction, and the provision and protection of personal space all featured in the new corporeal pedagogy (Ferguson, 2006: 106).

Economic survival in industrialised Victorian Britain required ever closer attention to the presentation of self as normal. The introduction of compulsory elementary education after 1870 was 'not so much for the benefit of the working classes as to fit them for the requirements of the new economic and social order' (Dean, 2012: 18). School education was primarily a disciplinary process through which children could be transformed into 'docile bodies' (Foucault, 1984), and learn how to become the people they were required to be: the next generation of producers within capitalism. The Elementary Education (Blind and Deaf Children) Act 1893, was premised on the assumption that disabled children would be educated separately from non-disabled children. The impact of early social policy, then, in relation to disability, is to wedge an increasing distance between disabled and non-disabled people. When conformity to the requirements of industrial society is required, the 'normal' self-consciousness must be that of:

> people who have been compelled to adopt a very high degree of restraint, affect, control, renunciation and transformation of instinct, and who are accustomed to relegating a large number of functions, instinct-expressions and wishes to private enclaves of secrecy withdrawn from the gaze of the 'outside world' (Elias, 2001: 28).

The uncivilised, rebellious bodies of the impaired were removed from the public sphere because they acted as a reminder of the indiscipline of the natural body, an unsettling threat that might undermine perceptions about the naturalness of the new social order. At the same time, within the institutions they had been removed to, disabled people were made to understand the ugliness and wrongness of their own embodied physicality. They learned that the only hope for anything better in life was dependent on becoming more like 'normal' people.

The Liberal Reforms made between 1906 and 1911 extended the sphere of government intervention into areas including housing, health and social services, education and national pension provision that had not previously been considered its responsibility. Rather than being the outcome of a humanitarian interest in the welfare of its citizens, however, these reforms were made in response to the discovery during the Boer War of the extent of unfitness and ill health among recruits (Alcock, 2008). They were not so much about the welfare of individuals as about ensuring the defence of the interests of capital against external threat.

Many of the architects of emerging social policy were strongly committed eugenicists. Eugenicists applied Darwin's theory of natural selection to human beings, arguing that while those with strong, healthy genes should be encouraged to breed and extend the population, others with 'unhealthy genes' should be strongly discouraged from reproducing. Social problems including crime, vagrancy, alcoholism, prostitution and unemployment were linked with physical and intellectual impairment (Brignell, 2010). Eugenicists questioned the idea of providing medical support and social services to disabled people, arguing that this would enable those to survive who were not meant to survive and lead to the degeneration of the national gene stock. In 1903 Parliament established a committee on 'national deterioration' and set up the Eugenics Record Office in London. The 1913 Mental Deficiency Act introduced IQ tests to identify 'feeble-minded' children who were sent to segregated schools (Burdett, 2014). Key left wing thinkers prominent in the development of social policy, including the founders of the Fabian Society, Beatrice and Sidney Webb, and the architects of the post-1945 British welfare state, William Beveridge and John Maynard Keynes, were fervent advocates of eugenics. As Beresford (2016: 142) has noted:

> many social reformers are better understood as committed to moral and utilitarian rather than humanistic concerns ... Interest was less to do with the personal welfare of the people and groups involved and more to do with what they saw as the ugliness, inefficiency, immorality, evil and wider damage that they associated with them.

Fabianism, which became the dominant strand in the study of social policy in the early 20th century, was characterised by a reformist approach, seeking 'change within the system rather than a change of systems' (Walker, 2013: 39). It supported the ideas of state intervention and the planned redistribution of resources, but involved a very elitist, 'top-down' approach (Croft and Beresford, 1992). It was identified as being the province of 'experts' to identify, investigate, research and prescribe resolutions to what they defined as 'social problems', regarding this as an administrative task rather than as one involving power. This has led to a problematic history within social policy that has involved experts identifying their own solutions to people's problems and imposing them on them, rather than listening to people's views about themselves and their own experiences (Dean, 2007). As Walker (2013: 40) points out, the constructions informing social policy do not stand in isolation: 'They do not arise spontaneously nor are they sustained "naturally". They are linked to wider ideologies and as such can be seen to support different and competing interests.' The development of disability policy has been based on problematic historical constructions involving the medicalisation of disabled people and their being viewed through the prism of eugenics.

Abberley (2002: 132) has argued that, while the expansion of the post-1945 British welfare state was the outcome of working class strength, it retained a controlling function. 'The dual function of the welfare state, which takes place within a set of class (and other) forces continuously in struggle, consists in services provided with an inextricably dominating character and function.' This domination is to be found in the unequal power relationships between professionals, who had the authority to define situations as real, and service users. The welfare state was also characterised by values of paternalism which failed to recognise disability as a rights issue, instead identifying it primarily as an issue of individual need (Oliver, 1996). The compensatory approach within the welfare state, which included compensatory benefits schemes and specialist domiciliary and residential care services for disabled people, still rested on the assumption that disability was to be addressed as personal deficit. As Dean (2012: 88) notes, 'compensatory approaches tend to perpetuate and consolidate rather than confront the implications of difference'. Rather than valuing diversity as part of human experience to be included and affirmed, difference – not just in terms of disability, but in terms of age, ethnicity, gender, sexuality culture, for example – has been typically treated as a problem to be managed and contained. A presumption of the value of normality – of 'right' and 'wrong' ways of being and doing in a culture where the subject position of the white, straight, middle class, non-disabled male is considered universally valid – has further entrenched oppression among those disabled people who possess more than one group characteristic defined by dominant culture as discreditable difference, such as Black disabled women.

The 1960s was a period of social change during which different social groups including feminists and the Black civil rights movement staked claims for equality and recognition on their own terms, leading to the establishment of the Sex Discrimination Act 1975 and the Race Relations Act 1976. The Disabled People's Movement, organising around the social model, gained momentum in the 1970s and 1980s and, in the face of prolonged opposition from the then Conservative government, campaigned to get anti-discrimination legislation enacted. This resulted finally in the Disability Discrimination Act 1995, which, although it established the first anti-discrimination legislation in relation to disability in Britain, was identified by many campaigners as weak legislation (Swain et al, 2003). It contained numerous exemptions and loopholes, omitted key areas that had been called for, and failed to define such key terms as 'reasonable adjustments', giving employers and service providers room to dispute their responsibilities. Finally, and significantly, it retained the medical model definition of disability, which was passed into its successor, the 2010 Equality Act.

As Dean (2012: 83) has noted:

Equal opportunities approaches can fail to address the fundamental causes of disadvantage and underlying relations of power. They work from the implicit premise that it is discriminatory attitudes and prejudices that are the problem. It is a premise that neglects the extent to which attitudes are no more and no less than reflections or consequences of the institutional processes by which differences are socially constituted.

In terms of social policy, neither compensatory provision nor equal opportunities legislation, such as the DDA and the Equality Act, have successfully addressed the inequality and oppression experienced by disabled people. The most that current UK legislation will do is modify some existing arrangements and leave others untouched. Where examples of good policy and practice do exist – the development of opportunities for self-directed support, the increased requirements for local authorities to engage in co-production, and the increasing recognition of the importance of participatory, user-led and emancipatory disability research, for example – it needs to be recognised that the aspiration to equality for disabled people remains a struggle. While arrangements vary in different parts of the UK, the Independent Living Fund in England was closed in 2015, with ring-fenced money being transferred to individual local authorities, which are having to make ever deeper spending cuts in a time of fiscal austerity (Disability Rights UK, 2012). Current social policy measures in terms of welfare to work programmes have disciplinary and punitive functions compelling disabled people to conform to work practices often incompatible with their impairments (Harrison and Hemingway, 2016). It is not that policymakers or professionals are necessarily bad people who even begin to consider their role in the continued marginalisation of disabled people. As Iris Young has observed:

> The conscious actions of many individuals daily contribute to maintaining and reproducing oppression, but these people are usually simply doing their jobs or living their lives and do not understand themselves as agents of oppression (Young, 1990: 42).

What is probably more accurate to say is that social policy as it relates to disability is a very complex business that requires a broader understanding of the historical and ideological contexts in which it is made and experienced. There is a clear need for policymakers and professionals to listen more seriously to the voices of those whose lives are shaped by the policies they develop and implement.

References

Abberley, P. (2002) 'Work, Disability and European Social Theory', in C. Barnes, M. Oliver and L. Barton (eds) *Disability Studies Today*, Cambridge: Polity.

Alcock, P. (2008) *Social Policy in Britain*, third edition, Basingstoke: Palgrave Macmillan.

Armer, B. (2014) 'Disability, Death and Dying: A Rights-Based Discussion of the Ultimate Barrier Facing Disabled People', in J. Swain, S. French, C. Barnes and C. Thomas (eds) *Disabling Barriers: Enabling Environments*, third edition, London: Sage

Barnes, C. (1997) 'A legacy of oppression: a history of disability in Western culture', in L. Barton and M. Oliver (eds) *Disability Studies: Past, Present and Future*, Leeds: The Disability Press, pp 1–24.

Barnes, C. and Mercer, G. (2010) *Exploring Disability*, second edition, Cambridge: Polity.

Barton, E.L. (2001) 'Textual Practices of Erasure: Representations of Disability and the Founding of the United Way', in J.C. Wilson and C. Lewiecki-Wilson (eds) *Embodied Rhetorics: Disability in language and culture*, Carbondale, IL: Southern Illinois University Press.

Beresford, P. (2016) *All Our Welfare: Towards participatory social policy*, Bristol: Policy Press.

Borsay, A. (2002) 'History, power and identity', in C. Barnes, M. Oliver and L. Barton (eds) *Disability Studies Today*, Cambridge: Polity, pp 98–119.

Brignell, V. (2010) 'The eugenics movement Britain wants to forget', *New Statesman*, 9 December, www.newstatesman.com/society/2010/12/british-eugenics-disabled

Burdett, E. (2014) 'Eugenics', in C. Cameron (ed) *Disability Studies: A Student's Guide*, London: Sage, pp 53–6.

Cahill, M. (1994) *The New Social Policy*, Oxford: Blackwell

Cameron, C. (2015) 'Turning experience into theory: The affirmation model as a tool for critical Praxis', *Social Work and Social Sciences Review*, 17 (3), 108–21.

Croft, S. and Beresford, P. (1992) 'The Politics of Participation', *Critical Social Policy*, 12 (35), 20–44.

Davis, L.J. (1995) *Enforcing Normalcy: Disability, deafness and the body*, London: Verso.

Dean, H. (2007) 'Welfare, Identity and the Life Course', in J. Baldock, N. Manning and S. Vickerstaff (eds) *Social Policy*, third edition, Oxford: Oxford University Press.

Dean, H. (2012) *Social Policy*, second edition, Cambridge: Polity Press.

Department of Work and Pensions (DWP) (2014) 'Disability facts and figures', 16 January, www.gov.uk/government/publications/disability-facts-and-figures/disability-facts-and-figures

Department of Work and Pensions (DWP) (2015) *Mortality Statistics: Employment and Support Allowance, Incapacity Benefit and Severe Disablement Allowance*, www.gov.uk/government/uploads/system/uploads/attachment_data/file/459106/mortality-statistics-esa-ib-sda.pdf

Dickens, C. (2008) *Our Mutual Friend*, Oxford: Oxford World Classics.

Disability Rights UK (2012) 'Independent Living Fund replacement schemes', www.disabilityrightsuk.org/independent-living-fund

Drake, R.F. (1999) *Understanding Disability Policies*, Basingstoke: Macmillan.

Elias, N. (2001) *The Society of Individuals*, London: Continuum.

Ferguson, H. (2006) *Phenomenological Sociology: Experience and Insight in Modern Society*, London: Sage.

Foucault, M. (1984) *Discipline and Punish*, London: Penguin.

Garland-Thomson, R. (2009) *Staring: The Way We Look*, Oxford: Oxford University Press.

gov.uk (undated) 'Definition of disability under the Equality Act 2010', https://www.gov.uk/definition-of-disability-under-equality-act-2010

Harrison, M. and Hemingway, L. (2016) 'Social policy and the new behaviourism: towards a more excluding society', in M. Harrison and T. Sanders (eds) *Social Policies and Social Control: New perspectives on the 'not-so-big society'*, Bristol: Policy Press.

Kachaje, R. (2016) 'Achieving 17 goals for the future', Disabled People's International, www.dpi.org/statements/achieving-17-goals-for-the.html

Mallett, R. and Slater, J. (2014) 'Language', in C. Cameron (ed) *Disability Studies: A Student's Guide*, London: Sage, pp 91–4.

Maynard, A. (2014) Genetics, Disability and Bioethics', in J. Swain, S. French, C. Barnes and C. Thomas (eds) *Disabling Barriers: Enabling Environments*, third edition, London: Sage.

Oliver, M. (1996) *Understanding Disability: From Theory to Practice*, Basingstoke: Macmillan.

Oliver, M. and Barnes, C. (eds) (1998) *Disabled People and Social Policy: From Exclusion to Inclusion*, Harlow: Longman.

Oliver, M. and Barnes, C. (2012) *The New Politics of Disablement*, Basingstoke: Palgrave Macmillan.

Sherry, M. (2010) *Disability Hate Crimes: Does Anyone Really Hate Disabled People?* Farnham: Ashgate.

Swain, J., French, S. and Cameron, C. (2003) *Controversial Issues in a Disabling Society*, Buckingham: Open University Press.

Walker, M. (2013) 'Difference and Diversity', in P. Dwyer and S. Shaw (eds) *An Introduction to Social Policy*, London: Sage, pp 38–50.

Young, I.M. (1990) *Justice and the Politics of Difference*, Princeton, NJ: Princeton University Press.

6

A case study of children's participation in health policy and practice

Louca-Mai Brady, Felicity Hathway and Emily Roberts

Introduction

This chapter considers children and young people's participation in the development of health policy and service delivery. The chapter was written by Louca-Mai, at the time a postgraduate researcher at the University of the West of England, in collaboration with Emily (Barnardo's Participation Manager) and Felicity[1] and draws on our experience of a project in the Bristol Community Children's Health Partnership (CCHP). The project involved health professionals, young people and Barnardo's participation service working collaboratively to develop a strategy and framework to support children's participation in the organisation. The chapter considers the lessons from this work for the involvement of children and young people[2] in health policy and services from both professional and young people's perspectives.

Children's participation and children's rights

The United Nations Convention on the Rights of the Child (CRC: UN, 1989) established international recognition that all children have a right to the highest possible standards of both healthcare and participation (Alderson, 2014). The CRC encompasses social, economic, civil and political rights, and 'asserts children's right to have a voice in decision-making, as well as rights to freedom of thought and expression' (Percy-Smith and Thomas, 2010: 1). The understanding that children should be involved in decisions which affect them has been increasingly reflected in law, policy, guidance and regulation (Franklin and Sloper, 2005). But participation is a multi-layered (Sinclair, 2004) and sometimes contested concept (Lansdown, 2006; Shaw et al, 2011). There are also concerns about when and whether participation is meaningful for all those involved, effective in terms of impacts on service decision making and outcomes for children, and sustained (Crowley, 2015).

Children's participation is an increasingly popular concept in many healthcare organisations (Percy-Smith, 2007; Weil et al, 2015). There have also been repeated calls to involve patients and members of the public in healthcare improvement in response to serious clinical and service failings in the UK and internationally (Ocloo and Matthews, 2016). The global evidence for children's participation in health services is growing rapidly and international examples of children's voices informing healthcare decision making and services include the Youth Friendly Hospital Programme in Australia, Give Youth a Voice in Canada (Weil et al, 2015) and the World Health Organization's *Adolescent Friendly Health Services: an Agenda for Change* (WHO, 2002). Council of Europe Guidelines for Child Friendly Healthcare set out three levels at which children should be provided with opportunities for participation: individual decision making, providing feedback on their experience of services, and in the policymaking and planning processes of the health services they use (CoE, 2011). But, despite the CRC and the Council of Europe guidelines, children in Europe are still 'generally excluded and not sufficiently involved' in clinical decision making, service improvement and policymaking (Ehrich et al, 2015). In the UK austerity measures have reduced the range of health services that protect and fulfil children's rights (Children's Commissioners, 2015) and mean that many children are not receiving appropriate healthcare when they need it (CRAE, 2015). Furthermore, public involvement in health policy tends to focus on adult input, and services for children are seen as the 'poor relation' to adult services within the National Health Service (NHS; Evans, 2016).

Children's rights apply to children as individuals and as a constituency, for example when a group of children are involved the development of health services or policy (Franklin and Sloper, 2005). A rights-based approach to children's participation in health services requires consideration of the involvement at the level of individual decision making (participation in decisions that affect their own lives) and at a more strategic level (participation in policy and service development) (for example, Kirby et al, 2003; Wright et al, 2006). This chapter is primarily concerned with the latter, strategic participation, although we found that the boundaries between the two levels were not clear cut. Any consideration of children's participation in health policy and practice also requires an understanding of 'the dynamics of power and control which operate in their relations with adults' (Devine, 2002: 303). Both parents and health professionals also often 'take a protective stance towards children to act in their best interest' (Coyne and Harder, 2011: 12), based on ideas about children's competence or the view that children's participation in decision making processes is potentially disruptive to their wellbeing (Vis et al, 2011).

Children's participation in health policy and practice

There is an expectation inherent in the UK NHS Constitution 'that patients, service users and the public participate nationally and locally in the development, implementation and accountability processes of health and social care policy and services' (DH, 2013a, Chapter 4: 2). The Chief Medical Officer's report emphasises the importance of the CRC to these participation processes and says that:

> This expectation for patient and public participation has no age limit. Children and young people ... should be encouraged and facilitated to participate in decisions about their own care and, more broadly, about the health and social care services and policies that affect them (DH, 2013a, Chapter 4: 2).

There has been increasing awareness of the importance of developing children's participation in health services in a strategic and systematic way (AYPH, 2010; DH, 2013b). Developments in England have included NHS England establishing a Youth Forum,[3] the introduction of new children's experience measures within the NHS, the Care Quality Commission involving children in their inspection activities,[4] and the involvement of children on the board of Healthwatch England and within local Healthwatch bodies (DH, 2013a). But there is a lack of evidence on if and how these rights are enabled in local practice, and whether this has necessarily led to improved outcomes for children (Ferguson, 2013), or on policymaking and service delivery (Byrne and Lundy, 2015; Crowley, 2015). Participation in health services has been limited and patchy (Blades et al, 2013; RCPCH, 2010) and children have often been 'generally excluded and not sufficiently involved in individual healthcare decisions ... service improvement and policy-making' (Ehrich et al, 2015: 783). Participation in healthcare often relies on individual professionals and this can mean a focus on consultation with children about their individual health needs rather than collaboration in the commissioning, delivery or evaluation of health services (Blades et al, 2013; Ocloo and Matthews, 2016), or in the development of health policy. This chapter outlines how we sought to address these issues in the CCHP and embed children's participation in the development of health policy and practice.

Children's participation in the CCHP

The CCHP was a partnership between North Bristol National Health Service Trust (the NHS Trust) and the children's charity Barnardo's.[5] From 2009 to 2016 the CCHP was responsible for the delivery of children's community health services in Bristol and South Gloucestershire including child and adolescent mental health services (CAMHS), health visiting, school nursing, physiotherapy, speech and language therapy, occupational therapy, community paediatricians and seven specialist services, including an inpatient adolescent unit. These services had over 800 staff and were previously managed by four separate organisations. The ambition was to provide equitable and integrated care with a focus on participation and the voice of the child from the outset. The commissioning of

CCHP included a dedicated participation service called HYPE (Helping Young People to Engage) delivered by Barnardo's. Following interim recommissioning since 2016 the CCHP has been delivered as an interim partnership between three healthcare organisations and Barnardo's.[6] At the time of writing this new partnership was the preferred provider to deliver the new substantive contract from 2017.

But, while there was a commitment to give children's views and experiences a stronger platform in CCHP, this was a challenge to a hierarchical healthcare culture where the power to make decisions is held by professionals. Barnardo's HYPE service found that prioritising cultural change was a huge part of making room for the impact of participation to be enabled. After a slow and difficult start, by 2013, children's participation in CCHP had gathered momentum. There was a cohort of engaged and active children, young people and parents and an increasing number of signed up professionals and services. The relationship between the Barnardo's service and CCHP staff was cementing in pockets but was still fragile at other points. At the time at which the authors began working together, CCHP was therefore looking for a ways to improve and consolidate practice so that children's participation would be understood and owned by staff and children across the organisation.

Between September 2013 and June 2015 the CCHP was a case study for Louca-Mai's doctoral research on 'embedding children and young people's participation in health services and research'. CCHP were identified as providing a unique opportunity to explore what it means to embed children's participation in health services given the organisation's commitment to children's participation from the outset, as well as the multi-disciplinary and multi-agency nature of the organisation. Louca-Mai worked with CCHP managers and staff, young people and other stakeholders through a series of collaborative workshops. These sought to explore what it meant to embed children's participation within and across the health partnership, and develop and pilot a participation strategy[7] and framework which could be used to do this.

A young person's perspective

I used health services for a long period before CCHP was formed and for a short while after. I then remained involved in the capacity of an ex-service user for five years. The width and breadth of my experience has enabled me to witness the changing ethos of participation in health services. Due to the inherent barriers and challenges discussed above there was some initial resistance, but over time this was replaced in CCHP by a passion for children's participation at both individual and strategic level.

As a group of young people with a collective experience of ten different services within CCHP we knew first hand that pockets of excellent participation were happening in the organisation, but also that the journey was not complete. We wanted to help develop a strategy to embed participation on every level so that all children and young people using CCHP services were having a consistently positive experience. We wanted to give participation the same importance as every other policy and provide a standard and formal tool for professionals to work to.

We met on several occasions with staff from CCHP and this partnership seemed to ignite a lot of enthusiasm and discussion. We tried to work creatively, which was somewhat novel for some staff, but really facilitated expression and cohesion and dissolved the disparity between young people and staff. The development of an authentic and meaningful strategy could only have been achieved through authentic and meaningful collaboration – as that was the very essence of what we were aspiring to embed.

Key findings on children's involvement in policy

Understanding participation in practice

We began by exploring how participation was understood by the practitioners and young people involved in the workshops, so that we could agree a shared understanding from which to build. This process highlighted how individual level participation in health services can help to develop children's capacity for more participation in strategy and policy:

> 'People needed to be empowered and feel empowered ... whether that is in their day to day care, so they are feeling empowered towards making decisions ... or whether that is acquiring knowledge and experience and skills to take place in other forms of decision making ... it is about building people's capacity to be included.' (Participation worker, staff workshop)

Individual participation can also inform the development of services and policy more directly. For example, Barnardo's had worked with parents to gather stories from families of children with particular health conditions, which were then used in work on care pathways in order to give clinicians an understanding of people's journey through accessing services, receiving a diagnosis and further involvement from the relevant professional teams, as well as new insights into the 'patient journey' beyond their services.[8]

Children's participation in the development of policy and services tends to focus on adult-initiated, context-specific participation within a formal setting (Davis and Hill, 2006; Malone and Hartung, 2010) often in formal groups such as forums and advisory groups (Crowley, 2015). But we found that *how* children were involved in the development of policy and practice was as important as *what* they were involved in. Children are not a homogenous group: age and other aspects of social background such as race and ethnicity, disability, social class, family background and use of services 'intersect as aspects of who children are, their social position, and what researchers [and policymakers] need to consider' in designing approaches appropriate to the children they wish to involve (Clavering and McLaughlin, 2010: 604). The mechanisms of formal participation may privilege the already privileged (Crowley, 2015), and this is reflected in uncertainty about 'how to involve a diversity of patients and the public, rather than a few selected individuals' in healthcare (Ocloo and Matthews, 2016: 2). We found that formal participation groups did not work for everyone and also assume a model of participation in which children have ongoing involvement with an organisation. But many children using a health service such as CAMHS, physiotherapy or school nursing would not necessarily identify themselves as a service user of the larger organisation of which the service is a part. We sought to address this through the creation of opportunities for shared learning and tools and practical support to develop both practitioners' and children's confidence. Young people involved in the project spoke about the benefits of participation for their wider peer group, as well as personal benefits including being able to use difficult personal experiences to create positive change. However, doing this safely required building relationships of trust with the adults supporting their participation.

We found that good participation, especially in the development of services and policy required expertise and the identification or appointment of specific members of staff 'dedicated to the development of participation' (Wright et al, 2006: 24). As Barnardo's were not responsible for delivering clinical services they were in a more neutral role and able to be a critical friend, as well as championing participation and taking the lead in developing practice and evaluating participation. But this needed to be balanced with the need to make participation 'everyone's business' and acknowledge children as 'experts by experience'. Young people involved in the workshops talked about how participation should be empowering and have benefits for both children and young people involved and their wider peers (for example several talked about it helping their recovery), but also about the importance of participation needing to be meaningful and lead to change.

A young person's perspective

Professionals and young people need to develop a shared understanding of what is meant by participation and what this will look like when done well. In order to work collaboratively you need to be heading towards the same destination. For me, meaningful participation needs to extend far beyond tokenism in a way that is relevant and meaningful to young people as well as improving services. I wanted to feel that my input would contribute to other young people receiving all of the good parts of my experience and none of the bad.

Involving young people in the development of a strategy

The process of involving young people in the development of the CCHP participation strategy and framework highlighted some interesting issues around implementing ideas of participation in the development of policy. The intention was that the strategy and associated framework would be both a starting point both for the development of participation in CCHP services and, hopefully, a vision and statement of intent for commissioners and potential new contract holders. An associated film and other materials developed by young people[9] would similarly raise awareness of participation amongst current and potential users of CCHP services. The collaborative nature of the project was seen as really important:

'We wouldn't have been able to create [the strategy] without the different types of people who are in this room [and] some people who are not in this room ... there's no way Barnardo's or young people or [CCHP] staff could have done this on their own. It's quite a powerful demonstration to me of how much better things are when you [create] them from different type of perspectives.' (Participation worker, CCHP staff workshop)

But the original plan for a 'one size fits all' strategy for staff and young people changed when it became clear that what was needed for the development of organisational practice would not work for children and vice versa:

'[I]t's really difficult to enthuse young people about strategies and policies ... that's been a bit of a challenge for us, the fact that the whole process is trying to actually make the strategy come alive, to make it interesting and relevant [to children]. It only comes alive when they can relate it to their own experiences and then they ... understand what it's about more. Especially from the children's rights angle, a lot of young people get passionate about 'oh we need to make it better for other young people, they don't want to go through the same thing that I went through and we need to change that'. If you frame it in that sort of way then [young] people seem to have an interest in what is actually in the words of a strategy.' (Participation worker, meeting with staff and young people)

'We [group of young people involved in the workshop] had quite a hard time trying to read through [the draft strategy] ... because we felt [it] was too wordy and that the meaning was sort of lost because it was taking so much energy to read all the words ... we all thought that maybe the idea of having a poster of the values ... re-writing them in a more simple way [would be better], we couldn't ... understand how you can only have one version of [the strategy] really, how one version could meet all the needs of staff, parents and young people and we thought a poster would be good and we would have a cool time designing it.' (Young person. workshop with staff and young people)

A young person's perspective

When the strategy was written, we worked together with staff to make it come alive, be truly meaningful and become more than words on paper. We also thought about how we communicate to young people what they can expect from good health care and what 'good' looks like in relation to both experience of services and participation. Another young person and I worked with Barnardo's to produce a film of our participation journey.[10] The past few years of our lives have been quite a difficult journey. We both agreed that a big part of the progress we have made can be attributed to the participation we have been involved in. We made the film to convey the impact and difference good participation makes to individuals on a more personal level.

Having started out in participation as a service user I am now working as a healthcare professional, and it seems that it is also pretty difficult to enthuse staff about policies from that perspective! If there is a more accessible version hanging around, I find that staff make a beeline for it. I think that the process we went through to create the strategy made it come alive for staff as well as young people. Narratives are a really powerful way to get staff on board, especially when the people who those narratives belong to are sitting right there in the room with you.

CCHP staff having a clear, organisation-wide vision and standards for participation for all staff across the organisation was central to embedding participation – hence the strategy and framework. But, as discussed earlier in this chapter, children using health services may come and go, and talk about seeing a physiotherapist or going to CAMHS rather than identifying themselves as a user of CCHP services. Perhaps this model may work for the children who work with the Barnardo's HYPE service in strategic or service development related participation activity, but we wanted something that would be relevant to every child coming into CCHP services. Therefore, the materials developed by young people focused on informing children about their right to have a say in the services they used, rather than being something to which they needed to 'sign up'. So what we ended up with was separate but linked documents: the participation strategy and framework alongside the young people's film and poster. Furthermore, this work and events associated with it created a significant breakthrough in CCHP being able to reach other services and as a result more children and families. CCHP also started more diverse informal group opportunities to enable a wider range of children to meet, and give their participation more flexibility as well as structure.

Discussion

Children's participation is an increasingly popular concept in many healthcare organisations and in health policy. However, there is limited evidence on how this apparent commitment to participation and its reflection in legislation, guidance and policy translates into practice and children's experience of participation. Children's views are still not consistently sought or acknowledged within healthcare settings or in health policy; they are rarely involved in decision making processes and often occupy a marginalised position in healthcare encounters.

Although the CCHP was unique in the way a health and a voluntary sector organisation had come together to deliver a service underpinned by children's participation, it has lessons for health services and policy development in the UK and more widely. We found that for participation to be meaningful and effective for both services and children, and embedded in service delivery and policy, children, and children's rights, needed to be at the centre of plans to involve them in the development of health policy and practice. This included a focus on working in child-centred ways and a commitment to developing policy in collaboration with children. Furthermore, it was important to consider who needed to be included for the participation to be meaningful and relevant to the service or policy area under consideration, that different ways of working may work for different children and indeed that not all children may want be able to participate. Children's participation often also involves parents, carers and other professionals who may act as gatekeepers and can both enable and constrain children's participation and the potential outcomes and impact of their participation.

Realistic participation in policy and service development requires honest consideration of the boundaries and limits such as wider organisational policies and procedures, requirements of commissioners and regulatory bodies and available resources. Children's participation and the systems and processes that support this are interdependent, and these internal and external influences can both support and limit children's participation in policy and service development. At the same time it is important to acknowledge and seek to address issues of power and control, and consider what say children have in what they were participating in, and how, when and where they participate. In order to be effective children's participation in health needs to measure both the quality of children's engagement in participation and the impact of this process on service quality, improvement and policy. Children need to see that they are part of an evolving and improving process for them and services and mechanisms need to be in place to prioritise this alongside other work commitments. While our work to develop the participation strategy was exciting and innovative, the current climate of austerity and increasing privatisation has implications for children's participation in health services and policy, and learning from participation needs to be much more routinely captured or shared in order that good or innovative practice is not lost.

Acknowledgements

With thanks to all the staff and young people from the CCHP who collaborated on this work, and without whom it would not have happened, and to North Bristol NHS Trust and the University of the West of England for supporting it.

Notes

[1] At the time of the project Felicity was involved with the service as a young service user but is now a young adult training as a healthcare professional, so her contributions here were made from this dual perspective as well as reflecting discussions with other young people involved in the project.

[2] The term 'children' is used throughout this chapter to refer to children and young people under the age of 18. However, we have used 'young people' when referring to the young people involved in this work, as although they were involved because of their experience of using health services when under the age of 18, they were aged between 15 and 22 at the time of our work together.

[3] https://www.england.nhs.uk/participation/get-involved/how/forums/nhs-youth-forum/

[4] www.cqc.org.uk/content/how-we-involve-you

[5] http://cchp.nhs.uk/cchp/what-cchp/barnardos-hype

[6] http://cchp.nhs.uk/cchp/what-cchp

[7] http://cchp.nhs.uk/cchp/what-cchp/young-peoples-participation

[8] http://cchp.nhs.uk/cchp/your-say/cchp-family-stories

[9] http://cchp.nhs.uk/cchp/visiting-cchp/what-goes-there

[10] See note 4.

References

Alderson, P. (2014) 'Children as Patients', in G. Melton, A. Ben-Arieh, J. Cashmore, G. Goodman and N. Worlet (eds) *The Sage Handbook of Child Research*, London: Sage, pp 100–17.

AYPH (2010) *Involving young people in the development of health services*, Making Health Services Work for Young People: Sharing the learning from the Teenage Health Demonstration Sites, London: Association for Young People's Health, www.ayph.org.uk/publications/50_BriefingPaperI.pdf

Blades, R., Renton, Z., La Valle, I., Clements, K., Gibb, J. and Lea, J (2013) *We Would Like to Make a Change: children and young people's participation in strategic health decision-making*, London: Office of the Children's Commissioner.

Byrne, B. and Lundy, L. (2015) 'Reconciling Children's Policy and Children's Rights: Barriers to Effective Government Delivery', *Children and Society*, 29 (4), 266–76.

Children's Commissioners (2015) *Report of the UK Children's Commissioners: UN Committee on the Rights of the Child Examination of the Fifth Periodic Report of the United Kingdom of Great Britain and Northern Ireland*, Children's Commissioners for Wales, England, Scotland and NICCY.

Children's Rights Alliance for England (CRAE) (2015) *UK implementation of the UN Convention on the Rights of the Child: Civil society alternative report 2015 to the UN Committee – England*, London: CRAE.

Clavering, E.K. and McLaughlin, J. (2010) 'Children's participation in health research: from objects to agents?' *Child: Care, Health and Development*, 36 (5), 603–11.

Council of Europe (CoE) Committee of Ministers (2011) *Council of Europe guidelines on child-friendly health care*, www.coe.int/en/web/children/child-friendly-healthcare

Coyne, I. and Harder, M. (2011) 'Children's participation in decision-making: balancing protection with shared decision-making using a situational perspective', *Journal of Child Health Care*, 15 (4), 312–19.

Crowley, A. (2015) 'Is Anyone Listening? The Impact of Children's Participation on Public Policy', *International Journal of Children's Rights*, 23 (3), 602–21.

Davis, J.M. and Hill, M. (2006) 'Introduction', in E.K.M. Tisdall, J.M. Davis, M. Hill and A. Prout (2006) *Children, Young People and Social Inclusion: participation for what?* Bristol: Policy Press, pp 1–22.

DH (Department of Health) (2013a) *Annual Report of the Chief Medical Officer 2012: Our Children Deserve Better: Prevention Pays*, www.gov.uk/government/publications/chief-medical-officers-annual-report-2012-our-children-deserve-better-prevention-pays

DH (2013b) *Improving Children and Young People's Health Outcomes: a system wide response*, www.gov.uk/government/uploads/system/uploads/attachment_data/file/214928/9328-TSO-2900598-DH-SystemWideResponse.pdf

Devine, D. (2002) 'Children's Citizenship and the Structuring of Adult-Child Relations in the Primary School', *Childhood*, 9 (3), 303–20.

Ehrich, J., Pettoello-Mantovani, M., Lenton, S., Damm, L. and Goldhagen, J. (2015) 'Participation of Children and Young People in Their Health Care: Understanding the Potential and Limitations', *The Journal of Pediatrics*, 167 (3), 783–4.

Evans, K. (2016) 'Listen and learn', *Journal of Family Health*, 26 (3), 44–6.

Ferguson, L. (2013) 'Not merely rights for children but children's rights: the theory gap and the assumption of the importance of children's rights', *International Journal of Children's Rights*, 21, 177–208.

Franklin, A. and Sloper, P. (2005) 'Listening and responding? Children's participation in health care within England', *International Journal of Children's Rights*, 13, 11–29.

Kirby, P., Lanyon, C., Cronin, K. and Sinclair, R. (2003) *Building a Culture of Participation: Involving children and young people in policy, service planning, delivery and evaluation*, London: DfES.

Lansdown, G. (2006) 'International developments in children's participation: lessons and challenges', in E.K.M. Tisdall, J. Davis, M. Hill and A. Prout (eds) *Children, young people and social inclusion: Participation for what?*, Bristol: Policy Press, pp 139–58.

Malone, K. and Hartung, C. (2010) 'Challenges of participatory practice with children', in B. Percy-Smith and N. Thomas (eds) *A Handbook of Children and Young People's Participation: Perspectives from theory and practice*, London: Routledge, pp 24–38.

Ocloo, J. and Matthews, R. (2016) 'From tokenism to empowerment: progressing patient and public involvement in healthcare improvement', *BMJ Quality and Safety* (March), 1–7.

Percy-Smith, B. (2007) '"You think you know? ... You have no idea": youth participation in health policy development', *Health Education Research*, 22 (6), 879–94.

Percy-Smith, B. and Thomas, N. (eds) (2010) *A Handbook of Children's Participation: Perspectives from Theory and Practice*, London: Routledge.

RCPCH (2010) *Not just a phase: A guide to the participation of children and young people in health services*, London: Royal College of Paediatrics and Child Health.

Sinclair, R. (2004) 'Participation in Practice: Making It Meaningful, Effective and Sustainable', *Children and Society*, 18 (2), 106–18.

Shaw, C., Brady, L.M. and Davey, C. (2011) *Guidelines for Research with Children and Young People*, London: National Children's Bureau, www.participationworks.org.uk/resources/guidelines-for-research-with-children-and-young-people

Vis, S.A., Strandbu, A., Holtan, A. and Thomas, N. (2011) 'Participation and health – a research review of child participation in planning and decision-making', *Child and Family Social Work*, 16 (3), 325–35.

Weil, L.G., Lemer, C., Webb, E. and Hargreaves, D.S. (2015) 'The voices of children and young people in health: where are we now?', *Archives of Disease in Childhood*, 100 (10), 915–19.

World Health Organization (WHO) (2002) *Adolescent friendly health services: An agenda for change*, Geneva: WHO, www.who.int/maternal_child_adolescent/documents/fch_cah_02_14/en/

Wright, P., Turner, C., Clay, D. and Mills, H. (2006). *The participation of children and young people in developing social care*, Participation Practice Guide 06, SCIE: London, www.scie.org.uk/publications/guides/guide11/

UN(United Nations) (1989) *Convention on the Rights of the Child*, www.ohchr.org/EN/ProfessionalInterest/Pages/CRC.aspx

7

Who owns co-production?

Sarah Carr

Introduction

In order to answer the question in the title, this chapter presents a brief investigation into the origins of the concept of 'co-production' and an exploration of how it has functioned in UK social policy rhetoric since the mid-2000s. In doing so, it traces what could be termed its 'ownership records', to examine how the policy concept is being, or can be, implemented in practice. Critical questions, informed by international literature on the topic, are asked about the true potential of 'co-production' to facilitate radical power shifts towards disenfranchised or marginalised service users and citizens, and to fundamentally change how policy decision making and public service provision is done.

The origins of the co-production idea

The origins and meaning of co-production as a way of facilitating power sharing and decision making with citizens and/or service users as equals in social policy and public service provision are somewhat confused or at least contested (Scourfield, 2015). It appears to be a policy idea that has gradually become 'lost in translation', even at early stages of conceptualisation, and as a result co-production can be as difficult to define as it is to do. Bovaird suggests that co-production comes in a variety of forms, and is often specific to particular contexts (Bovaird, 2007), while Ewert and Evers argued: 'in a changed welfare environment, there is no dominant, coherent narrative for co-production ... co-production refers to a fragmented set of activities, expectations and rationales' (Ewert and Evers, 2014: 427).

Despite this, it is generally agreed that the first individuals to use the term were Elinor and Victor Ostrom, who developed the concept to describe relationships between citizens and public institutions, in the context of US public management research (Ostrom and Ostrom, 1977). The most well-known example of their work concerned the relationship of distanced and bureaucratised approaches to policing and its impact on local citizens and crime rates. In summary, Elinor

Ostrom's research suggested that the quality of relationships between service providers and citizens were or primary importance, as citizens were valuable sources of unique knowledge to inform service development and improvement. Ostrom wrote:

> We developed the term 'co-production' to describe the potential relationships that could exist between the 'regular' producer (street-level police officers, school teachers, or health workers) and 'clients' who want to be transformed by the service into safer, better educated, or healthier persons' (Ostrom, 1996: 1079).

'By the 1980s, the limitations of traditional "provider-centric" models of the welfare state had become obvious' (Bovaird, 2007: 846), and a policy drive towards the privatisation of public services had begun. Accounts from US local government and public management literature from the 1980s define 'citizen co-production [as] the productive involvement of urban residents can supply to the provision of city services', and located in 'a variety of participatory roles that citizens can perform in local government' (Percy, 1984: 431). In a 1985 *Administration and Society* paper, US scholar Brudney notes an early confusion with the concept of 'participation' and maintains that

> consensus obtains that as distinguished from citizen participation, co-production refers to the involvement of service consumers in the actual delivery of services (rather than in policy formulation and legitimation activities), normally in concert with public agencies ... A growing literature links the model to key goals of urban governance, including effectiveness and efficiency of service delivery and a resurgence of citizenship among the populace (Brudney, 1985: 244).

So, in its original conception in the US, co-production appeared to be a new approach to public service delivery, which made it clear that welfare 'outcomes' are not the same as 'goods' and therefore require relationships and certain behaviours between the various human actors if public service delivery is to be effective (Garn, 1973). Much of the initial co-production discourse therefore remained contained within the field of public management and service delivery, where 'the role given to service users and communities varied greatly in these initiatives but continued to be decided by managers and professionals' (Bovaird, 2007: 846).

A change in the direction and tone of co-production discourse came in 2000, when US legal academic and citizen advocacy pioneer Edgar Cahn made the explicit link between co-production and wider social justice aims. Cahn's (re) conceptualisation was debatably more radical than that provided by the field of public administration. His vision for societal (not just service) co-production was as a way to fundamentally challenge administration and service delivery, locating power and worth with the citizen, rather than using them to improve the 'system' or service delivery and effectiveness. Cahn believed in co-production for developing what he called 'the core economy'. By this he meant using the resources embedded in people's everyday lives and relationships, such as loyalty, vigilance, empathy, love, trust, knowledge, experience and skills. Productivity is therefore also defined by social contributions.

In his book *No More Throw-away People* (2000), Cahn situates co-production within the broader field of social justice, social economy and community development. He set out four universal co-production values:

- An asset perspective: no more throw-away people;
- Redefining work: no more taking the social contribution of people for granted;
- Reciprocity: stop creating dependencies and devaluing those whom you help whilst you profit from their troubles;
- Social capital: no more disinvesting in families, neighbourhoods and communities. (Cahn, 2008: 31)

Instead of citizens and service users being invited by officials to participate in the administration, delivery or performance of public services, Cahn argues that co-production should disrupt 'the conventional distinctions between producers and consumers, professionals and clients, providers and recipients, givers and takers' and move from 'subordination and dependency to parity ...' (Cahn, 2008: 35). The type of co-production Cahn offered was later defined as 'a potentially transformative way of thinking about power, resources, partnerships, risks and outcomes, not an off-the-shelf model of service provision or a single magic solution' (Needham and Carr, 2009: 1).

Cahn's version did not take a technocratic approach to making public services more effective and efficient, perhaps because he had personally experienced the loss of identity, powerlessness and altered social perceptions of worth associated with illness or disability when he became a 'dependent' hospital patient, following a massive coronary at 45:

> I didn't like feeling useless. My idea of who I was – the 'me' that I valued – was someone who could be special for others, who could do something they needed. And here I was, a passive recipient of everyone else's help. That was when it struck me: All of those people I had read about in the newspapers were being declared useless, too. And it occurred to me, I'll bet they don't like it any more than I do. And in that moment, I realized that a new fight had begun. It was a fight over being declared useless. (Cahn, 2000: 5)

Unlike some of his predecessors who developed co-production within an intellectual problem solving paradigm, Cahn's conceptualisation was informed by his experiential knowledge of being rendered 'useless' by the way health and care services function. While Ostrom envisaged co-production as a management means for 'clients' to be transformed into 'safer ... healthier persons' by services, Cahn turned his sights on transforming the services themselves through societal co-production, questioning a culture that requires people to be passive and perform deficits, rather than be active and use their assets.

The emergence of co-production as an idea in UK social policy

By 2007 'co-production' terminology was permeating UK health and social care policy in the 'modernisation' and 'transformation' agendas, specifically 'personalisation' in adult social care (Newman et al, 2008; Needham and Glasby, 2014). It was promoted as being 'transformational' for health and social care services towards the end of the UK New Labour government (1997–2010; Needham, 2008). One of the earliest appearances of the term in central government policy came in the 2007 Putting People First Concordat, which asserted that the proposed transformation of adult social care sought 'to be the first public service reform programme which is co-produced, co-developed, co-evaluated and recognises that real change will only be achieved through the participation of users and carers at every stage' (HM Government, 2007: 2). Did this mean Ostrom's expanded notion of public administration and service delivery 'participation' or the 'Cahnian' social justice and power redistribution vision of co-production? It was unclear from the Concordat policy document how government understanding of the new thing called 'co-production' differed from established and existing types of service user and carer involvement in health and social care, which had had varying and often limited impact on change and power realignment (Carr, 2007).

What was clear was the popularity of co-production concepts with UK left-leaning think tanks as means for promoting social and public service transformation, with a proliferation of discussion reports during 2008–09 (Stephens et al, 2008; Gannon and Lawson, 2008; Boyle and Harris, 2009). Bovaird and Loeffler, leading British co-production advocates, called it a radical innovation in policymaking with 'the public sector and citizens making better use of each other's assets and resources to achieve better outcomes and improved efficiency' (Bovaird and Loeffler, 2012). Co-production was the subject of a New Economics Foundation 'manifesto', largely redefining Cahn's core social economy approach for a type of public service reform that recognised 'public service clients as assets who have skills that are vital to the delivery of services' (Stephens et al, 2008: 16). Organisations like the National Endowment for Science Technology and the Arts (NESTA) promoted and invested in co-production public service and health demonstration and development programmes, using the language of 'people power', and showcasing existing community organisations and pioneering care and support initiatives that identified as doing co-production (Boyle and Harris, 2009; Boyle et al, 2010; NESTA, 2012). Therefore, in UK social policy co-production rapidly became associated with the language of 'innovation', 'modernisation' and 'transformation'. This is perhaps most clearly illustrated when it was championed by the 'Innovation Unit', a former unit of the British government Department for Education and Skills, which then became an independent not-for-profit social enterprise and worked with NESTA on co-productive approaches for 'radical efficiency' and 'system change' in health and public services (Nesta Lab Innovation Unit, 2010).

The influence of 'epochalist' policy making

In his paper, 'The Tyranny of the Epochal' (2003), Du Gay explores 'epochalism in public administrative reform', which he argues is infused with the discourse of innovation, transformation and momentous change. He cites the think tank policy architects of the New Labour government health and social care transformation as examples:

> In the life-order of government across the liberal democratic world, for instance, regimes of many different political hues are home to prestigious exponents of the 'epochal arts'. Epochal theorists such as … Geoff Mulgan [NESTA think tank: co-production] and Charles Leadbeater [Demos think tank: personalisation (Carr, 2014)], for example, have all been involved, either implicitly or explicitly, with the development of public policy in Britain's New Labour government, and the epochal formulations and designations … can be seen to structure reforms in many areas of governance—not least in the field of public administration. (Du Gay, 2003: 670)

Using Du Gay's critical framework, co-production can be seen as something formulated to serve the interests of policymakers intent on creating a new historical era of 'entrepreneurial government' (Du Gay, 2003: 607). Such government is based on entrepreneurial management principles where 'they empower those working on the frontline to make more of their own decisions and to take responsibility for solving their own problems … entrepreneurial managements constantly seek to do more for less, through "re-engineering" their work systems and processes' (Du Gay, 2003: 672). It is not hard to see how a version of co-production fitted with these ambitions.

It appears that co-production was owned by think tanks taking a top-down, intellectual approach to public sector reform, using the language of radical power sharing to promote 'epochal change' and 'entrepreneurial government'. So, were Cahn's radical social justice intentions diminished by what Pigliucci calls 'think tankery', which he criticises for 'spin-doctoring rather than rigorous analysis of the problem at hand' (Pigliucci, 2010: 130)? Findings from a Scottish study into co-production with diverse, disadvantaged communities reveals the effect of such top-down 'think tankery': 'the range of views gathered throughout this research underscores the perceived gap between policy prose and "real practice on the ground" when applying asset-based approaches to health inequalities' (de Andrade, 2016: 136).

The problems of power and control in health and social care

A hybrid version of co-production finally coalesced as a core health and social care reform policy concept when the National Health Service (NHS) associated it with their 'patient leadership and experience' programme (McNally, 2016). This hybrid version fused the Cahnian language of 'sharing power, value, community and citizenship' with that of health managerialism and 'leadership', and was introduced into NHS hierarchical systems, seemingly without a serious assessment of whether the desired culture change and power redistribution is at all possible using this top-down approach or within the present system itself (Coalition for Collaborative Care, 2016). Again, an 'epochalist' tendency can be detected here, and ownership remains firmly with professionals and leaders with the power to control the momentous change; to design how co-production works and to determine what it should achieve. While there is a stated aim to 'improve patient experience', there is no real analysis of how and why the health (particularly mental health) system 'declares people useless'. In UK health think tank reports there is talk of 'patient leaders' having 'collaborative relationships' with clinical or managerial leaders (Seale, 2016), but without close consideration of the fundamental power realignment, preparation, facilitated personal reflection and individual role renegotiation that needs to occur before this is possible (Carr and Patel, 2016). As early as the 1980s, it was noted that 'a potential source of manipulation arises from the power imbalance between citizens and the service bureaucracy in the design of co-production programmes' (Brudney, 1985: 252).

In this hybrid co-production discourse, to gain power or influence the patient or service user is required to be a type of management consultant, in a similar way to their construction as a 'social entrepreneur' in the associated UK social care personalisation policy (Scourfield, 2007; Carr, 2014). But as with personalisation, 'current system configurations, eligibility criteria and processes can actively prevent them [service users and patients] from exercising their 'citizenship' [power]' (Carr, 2014). In reality, the individuals who are expected to participate in the management consultancy model of co-production are precisely those for whom health and social care 'institutions and powers ... create and maintain inequitable circumstances' (de Andrade, 2016: 138). This point is further exemplified by German research on role expectations on services users as mainstream system 'change agents':

> the twin demands simultaneously being agents of change in a system that many see as being on the wrong track *and* acting as service providers that help consumer-citizens to get along as well as possible within the system as it stands, are challenging user organisations in many respects (Ewert and Evers, 2014: 437).

Here Du Gay's critique of epochalist policymaking is useful for pinpointing one of the key problems of transformation policy-driven models of co-production: 'it is precisely the individual circumstances that epochal approaches make invisible or render insignificant, and herein lies their practical danger' (Du Gay, 2003: 671). Bovaird's analysis of the practical feasibility of 'greater co-production' reveals one of these practical dangers 'essentially politicians would need to support users in co-constructing their own identity rather than accepting one constructed by experts' (Bovaird, 2007: 858).

There are in fact long-established ways of doing such 'identity construction' work, independently developed by the service user/survivor, disability and self-advocacy movements over decades (Beresford and Carr, 2012; Barnes and Cotterell, 2012). Autonomous user-led and self-advocacy organisations play a vital role in providing the collective, independent power base from which service users can self-define, self-determine and become politically active. However, the fundamental social and political groundwork done by service user and disability movements, as well as learning from what has and has not worked for health and social care involvement, has not been adequately factored into versions of co-production crafted and owned by political think tanks (Carr, 2014). Pestoff, a critical exponent of co-production, is clear that small user-led and community groups 'can prove very important for facilitating the participation of persons with serious physical, mental, or social problems and for retaining their participation over time' (Pestoff, 2013: 12). Further he argues that:

> if governments intend to facilitate greater citizen co-production in the provision of enduring welfare services, they need to devise ways of promoting self-help groups, social service co-ops, and other forms of third sector provision of such services that tend to be small scale and facilitate formal, collective interaction among well-defined groups of service users in a democratic fashion (Pestoff, 2013: 11).

Pestoff's proposals imply more than making existing public services more efficient and effective – they are about creating a separate platform and power base from which service users can work. As such they fit more closely with Cahn's ideas of co-production being about social justice and developing the core social economy, and more importantly, with some key values and principles of service user, survivor and disability movements (Sayce, 2015; Campbell and Oliver, 1996).

Conclusion: 'The fight over being declared useless'

This chapter has traced some of the 'ownership records' of co-production to explore who owns the concept, with early literature coming from US public administration disciplines, then being reconceived as a more radical understanding of the social economy by Cahn in 2000 who used his personal experiences to inform his thinking. In UK health and social care policy, co-production appears to have become a fusion between Cahn's core social economy ideas and public service management ambitions through the work of think tanks promoting 'epochalist' or momentous change in health and social policy. Arguably, co-production came to be owned by non-user policy think tanks and government policymakers. Service users, their ideas and organisations can have a fractured, highly compromising relationship to service-driven co-productive approaches that require them to be management consultants, and many service users say they do not feel they own what is promoted in policy. However, service user organisations are crucial for realigning power and providing a strong base from which service users can collectively determine how co-production works, but 'the reluctance of autonomous user-led organisations to enter into 'co' relationships with branches of the state is understandable if they believe ... that it may compromise their ability to tackle wider issues beyond service delivery' (Scourfield, 2015: 552).

This exploration has revealed a fault line of mutual incompatibility between the think tank policy formulation of co-production, built on persuasive argument about momentous entrepreneurial public service reform, and the lived reality of the users of the health and social care services that need reform – in Cahn's terms those who have been 'declared useless' by those services. Here, a final question arises about 'use' and 'ownership': if social policy and services can declare people 'useless', can they also declare people 'useful'? As early as 1985, a public management paper examining the potential of co-production warned that:

> It may lead to service delivery arrangements in which citizens undertake activities that fit administrators' preferences for citizen involvement and/or the convenience of their present positions – rather than those that might augment service effectiveness or contribute to a restoration of communitarian values and citizenship' (Brudney, 1985: 252–3).

Therefore, perhaps the most fundamental question to ask is not 'who owns co-production?', but 'who owns service users and citizens?'

References

Barnes, M. and Cotterell, P. (eds) (2012) *Critical Perspectives on User Involvement*, Bristol: Policy Press.

Beresford, P. and Carr, S. (2012) *Social care, service users and user involvement*, London: Jessica Kingsley Publishers

Bovaird, T. and Loeffler, E. (2012) 'From Engagement to Co-production: How Users and Communities Contribute to Public Services', in T. Brandsen and V. Pestoff (eds) *New Public Governance, the Third Sector and Co-Production*, London: Routledge.

Bovaird, T. (2007) 'Beyond Engagement and Participation: User and Community Coproduction of Public Services', *Public Administration Review*, September/October, 846–60.

Boyle, D. and Harris, M. (2009) *The challenge of co-production: How equal partnerships between professionals and the public are crucial to improving public services*, London: NESTA.

Boyle, D., Coote, A., Sherwood, C. and Slay, J. (2010) *Right here, right now: Taking co-production into the mainstream*, London: NESTA.

Brudney, J.L. (1985) 'Coproduction: Issues in implementation', *Administration and Society*, 17 (4), 243–56.

Cahn, E. (2000) *No more throw-away people: the co-production imperative*, Washington: Essential Books.

Cahn, E. (2008) 'Foreword: A commentary from the United States', in L. Stephens, J. Ryan-Collins and D. Boyle, *Co-production: A manifesto for growing the core economy*, London: New Economics Foundation.

Campbell, J. and Oliver, M. (1996) *Disability Politics: Understanding Our Past, Changing Our Future*, London: Routledge.

Carr, S. and Patel, M. (2016) *Practical guide: progressing transformative co-production in mental health*, Bath: National Development Team for Inclusion.

Carr, S. (2007) 'Participation, power, conflict and change: theorising dynamics of service user participation in the social care system of England and Wales', *Critical Social Policy*, 27 (2), 266–76.

Carr, S. (2014) 'Personalisation, participation and policy construction: a critique of influences and understandings', in P. Beresford (ed) *Critical and radical debates in social work: Personalisation*, Bristol: Policy Press, pp 27–32.

Coalition for Collaborative Care (2016) *A Co-production Model*, London: NHS England.

de Andrade, M. (2016) 'Tackling health inequalities through asset-based approaches, co-production and empowerment: ticking consultation boxes or meaningful engagement with diverse, disadvantaged communities?' *Journal of Poverty and Social Justice*, 24 (1), 127–41.

Du Gay, P. (2003) 'The Tyranny of the Epochal: Change, epochalism and organizational reform', *Organization*, 10 (4), 663–84.

Ewert, B. and Evers, A. (2014) 'An Ambiguous Concept: On the meanings of co-production for health care users and user organisations', *Voluntas*, 25, 425–42.

Gannon, Z. and Lawson, N. (2008) *Co-production: The modernisation of public services by staff and users*, London: Compass.

Garn, H.A. (1973) 'Public services on the assembly line', *Evaluation*, 1 (36), 41–2.

HM Government (2007) *Putting People First: A shared vision and commitment to the transformation of adult social care*, London: HM Government.

McNally, D. (2016) 'Joining up 'co-production' and 'patient leadership' for a new relationship with people who use services', NHS England Blog, 27 September, www.england.nhs.uk/2016/09/david-mcnally/

Needham, C. and Carr, S. (2009) *Co-production: an emerging evidence base for adult social care transformation*, London: SCIE.

Needham, C. and Glasby, J. (eds) (2014) *Debates in Personalisation*, Bristol: Policy Press.

Needham, C (2008) 'Realising the potential of co-production: Negotiating improvements in public services', *Social Policy and Society*, 7 (2), 221–31.

NESTA (2012) *People Powered Health Co-production Catalogue*, London: NESTA.

Nesta Lab Innovation Unit (2010) *Radical Efficiency: Different, better, lower cost public services*, London: NESTA.

Newman, J., Glendinning, C. and Hughes, M. (2008) 'Beyond modernisation? Social care and the transformation of welfare governance', *Journal of Social Policy*, 37 (4), 531–57.

Ostrom, V. and Ostrom, E. (1977) 'Public goods and public choices', in E.S. Savas (ed) *Alternatives for delivering public services: Toward improved performance*, Boulder, CO: Westview, pp 7–49.

Ostrom, E. (1996) 'Crossing the Great Divide: Coproduction, Synergy, and Development', *World Development*, 24 (6), 1073–87.

Percy, S. (1984) 'Citizen participation in the coproduction of urban services', *Urban Affairs Quarterly*, 19 (4), 431–46.

Pestoff, V. (2013) 'Collective action and the sustainability of co-production', *Public Management Review*, 16 (3), 383–401.

Pigliucci, M. (2010) *Nonsense on Stilts: How to tell science from bunk*, Chicago: University of Chicago Press.

Sayce, L. (2015) *From Psychiatric Patient to Citizen Revisited*, Basingstoke: Palgrave Macmillan.

Scourfield, P. (2007) 'Social care and the modern citizen: client, consumer, service user, manager and entrepreneur', *British Journal of Social Work*, 37 (1), 107–22.

Scourfield, P. (2015) 'Implementing co-production in adult social care: An example of meta-governance failure?' *Social Policy and Society*, 14 (4), 541–54.

Seale, B. (2016) *Patients as Partners: Building collaborative relationships among professionals, patients, carers and communities*, London: The King's Fund.

Stephens, L., Ryan-Collins, J. and Boyle, D. (2008) *Co-production: A manifesto for growing the core economy*, London: New Economics Foundation.

Part II
Critiquing and reconceiving Beveridge's 'five giant evils': key areas of British post-war social policy from a lived experience perspective

The post-war UK Beveridgean welfare state has provided a key reference point for contemporary discussion of social policy. But arguably it has also limited such discussion by tying it to its own logic, to be accepted or attacked. Here we try to move beyond this. In his famous report, William Beveridge identified what he saw as 'five giant evils' in society. He framed these in terms of personal ills, but addressed them as social problems that he sought to remedy – thus:

- Want – poverty and lack of social security
- Disease – lack of access to healthcare
- Squalor – poor housing
- Ignorance – inadequate education
- Idleness – unemployment

These five issues have long been strongly associated with the UK post-war welfare state as the major challenges it sought to resolve. In Part II of the book we take a radically different look at them. We have done this by reference to particular groups, which have often been ill-served by conventional social policy and which were certainly poorly understood by post-war Western welfare state policymakers, beginning with Beveridge. They offer much broader and deeper insights for understanding and critiquing his giant evils and for more participatory approaches to overcome them. Most combine direct experience with the expertise that comes from direct engagement in challenging them.

Disability activist Jane Young focuses on social security in her opening contribution, rethinking ideas of rights and responsibilities through the lens of the experience of disabled people. She explores the underpinning values and effects of welfare reform policies directed at disabled people which have been pioneered in the UK. While framed in terms of getting disabled people into employment and reducing dependence, the reforms actually increase their impoverishment, personal and social insecurity. Instead of truly rethinking employment policy and challenging want and disablist inequality, they are making them worse.

Anya de Iongh identifies as a patient leader with long-term health conditions. In her chapter she focuses on health policy from the perspective of her lived experience. There has long been a tension in the UK and other health services between excellence and innovation in the context of acute conditions and its more limited success in addressing and managing long-term ones. This inequality can be traced to the post-war labour reforms. Anya highlights the transformative role that service users can play in health policy as well as in their own lives by bringing their experience to bear and the way that this can be achieved in inclusive and accessible ways.

Alison Cameron's chapter gives a forensic, critical account of the impact of housing policy, 'squalor' and health from the perspective of someone who has been homeless. As such she offers some first hand truths for those who have made and implemented social policy that was forged from Beveridge's five giant evils, but also clear advice on how things could be different. She takes us beyond a 'bricks and mortar' understanding of housing to remind us of its importance as part of wider structures and networks of psychological and social support and how it can help us rebuild our lives and find ourselves again, to the extent of playing a helpful role in improving policy and practice for ourselves and others.

Tara Flood and Navin Kikabhai of the UK Alliance for Inclusive Education (ALLFIE) focus on the global marginalisation of disabled people in education. They draw a distinction between 'locational, social or functional integration' and inclusion, which they see as: 'the wholesale restructuring of education' to secure disabled people's human rights, social justice and principally about the politics of recognition. They argue that education policy has rarely included the voices of disabled people, see the shift to neoliberal ideology as worsening the situation, and see hope in more unified resistance internationally building on alliances with disabled people.

Finally, at a time when economic and forced migration have come to dominate political and public policy discussions, with rising numbers of refugees fleeing conflict and harassment, academic Colin Clark focuses on employment issues as experienced by Roma people who have come to the UK from central and eastern Europe. Drawing on their lived experience, he contrasts the 'often racist' media representations of them as 'idle', with their determined efforts to secure a place in the labour market. He explores the barriers they face under prevailing social and economic policy, the complexity of such diverse communities and the continuing need to listen to them to develop appropriate training and employment policy.

8

Rethinking disabled people's rights to work and contribute

Jane Young

Introduction

When considering the extent to which the evil of want has been tackled and overcome since Beveridge's time, there are good reasons to focus on the experience of disabled people,[1] whose needs were poorly recognised in the post-war period. Under the Disabled Persons (Employment) Act 1944, employment for disabled people was characterised by segregation, marginalisation and low pay, with employment support mainly focused on servicemen disabled in the two world wars. In addition, for those disabled people who were unable to work, the financial support available from the welfare state was inadequate, confusing to claim and stigmatising (Borsay, 2005). This chapter therefore seeks to explore the impact of employment and social security policies on the economic wellbeing of disabled people today, using the UK as a case study.

Changing attitudes to disability

Society's understanding of disability and attitudes to disabled people have changed significantly since the immediate post-war period. According to the social model of disability, developed by disabled people from the 1960s/1970s onwards (Campbell and Oliver, 1996), people with impairments are disabled by the physical, organisational, financial, and most importantly attitudinal barriers in a society organised by and for non-disabled people. These barriers need to be dismantled or overcome to enable disabled people to participate in paid work and enjoy a reasonable standard of living. In practice, this very often necessitates the provision of assistance to overcome the impact of impairment, such as social care support to enable a disabled person to get ready for work in the morning or disability benefits to fund mobility.

While governments have increasingly purported to frame their policies with reference to the social model, evidence shows that the 2008 recession and the years of economic austerity since 2010 have increased barriers to participation in countries like the UK, with reductions in social care and social security (Young and Nolan, 2014). In addition, some disabled people with long-term, debilitating health conditions have highlighted the perceived failure of the social model to give adequate recognition to the functional impact of symptoms, or impairment effects,[2] such as pain, fatigue and mental distress, which is much harder to overcome by external adjustments such as the provision of equipment (Benstead and Nock, 2016).

In recent decades there has also been an increased focus, in both international and domestic law, on equality and human rights. Under international law, obligations in relation to social and economic rights (including the right to work and the right to an adequate standard of living) date back to the mid-1970s,[3] and in 2009 the UK government ratified the UN Convention on the Rights of Persons with Disabilities (UNCRPD), which focuses specifically on disabled people's human rights, including their economic and social rights. Although UN human rights conventions are binding on State signatories, they are not justiciable in British courts, and recent evidence appears to show that the UK government, for example, barely acknowledges the obligations they confer.[4] On the other hand, domestic equality legislation, namely the Equality Act 2010, has been more effective. A central feature of this legislation is the duty on employers and service providers to make 'reasonable adjustments' to overcome barriers and to provide a more level playing field for disabled people. However, inadequate enforcement mechanisms, coupled with a certain lack of political will, have reduced the Act's effectiveness (Select Committee on the Equality Act 2010 and Disability, 2016).

Disability as a driver of poverty

Despite this shift in attitude and policy, research in the UK shows that disability remains a significant driver of poverty, with almost half of households in poverty including a disabled person (Tinson et al, 2016). In 2012 just over 30% of all disabled people, and nearly 45% of BME (black and minority ethnic) disabled people, were living in household poverty, with disabled women experiencing even lower incomes (Trotter, 2012). Reducing disability poverty, especially among women and minority groups, must therefore be an essential part of tackling the continuing evil of want in the UK and indeed globally.

The reasons why disabled people are more likely to be poor are complex, but in the UK they include:

- the considerable gap in employment rates and earnings between disabled people and their non-disabled peers (Tinson et al, 2016), a gap that is even greater for BME disabled people (Trotter, 2012);
- higher living expenses than non-disabled people (Brawn, 2014), which are not fully covered by benefits like personal independence payment (the UK benefit intended to help meet these additional costs);

- the lack of accessible, affordable housing (Leonard Cheshire Disability, 2014);
- the failure of housing benefit to cover rent (Work and Pensions Select Committee, 2014a);
- the 'manifestly inadequate' level of income-replacement benefits in the UK (European Committee of Social Rights, 2014).

The focus of this chapter is on the ability of disabled people to find and keep paid employment and, for those unable to work or to find suitable employment, the availability and security of income-replacement benefits. Many consider that policies in this area are driven as much by ideology and rhetoric as by research and evidence.

A 'right to work' versus 'welfare to work'

Under international human rights law (UNCRPD Article 27) disabled people have a right to work that is freely chosen, with fair conditions of employment and an expectation of state intervention to ensure a fair and inclusive labour market and non-discriminatory employment practices. It is also implicit in Article 27 that work should be sufficiently well paid to enable disabled people to meet their living expenses. UNCRPD Article 28 provides a right to social protection and to an adequate standard of living, in which income-replacement benefits for disabled people who are unable to work or have significant labour market barriers play an important part.

In contrast to the rights-based approach adopted in UN human rights law, the overwhelming emphasis of the UK government over the past 20 years, but especially since the 2010 general election, has been on 'welfare to work' policies, which compel benefit claimants to apply for and accept almost any job, regardless of suitability or aspiration. To some extent this reflects an international trend, although the UK offers an advanced example of it. Failure to take a job, or to comply with compulsory work preparation activities, may lead to stopping payment of out of work benefits (Dean and Patrick, 2011). This approach undermines work as a positive good, characterising it instead as an unpleasant activity, in which people have to be forced to participate.

A 'welfare to work' approach to social security policy assumes that disabled benefit claimants lack motivation and need the threat of acute financial hardship, through benefit 'sanctions' (stopping or reducing benefits), to ensure compliance with work preparation activities and the obligation to accept work. However, recent research by and with disabled benefit claimants suggests that the majority of disabled people do want to work, but their impairments, such as mental health difficulties or symptoms such as pain or fatigue, make it difficult to function reliably in the workplace or even to comply with the conditions of benefit receipt (Hale, 2014; Benstead and Nock, 2016). Disabled people are also more likely than non-disabled people to lack the education and skills to compete successfully in the labour market (Trotter, 2013).

Income-replacement benefits for disabled people

Disabled people generally receive a higher level of out of work benefits than non-disabled jobseekers, principally because it typically takes them much longer to get back to work because of disabling barriers to employment (Low et al, 2015). However, in an attempt to reduce public spending and increase disabled people's participation in employment, successive governments have made it increasingly difficult to qualify for the higher rate of benefit. At the time of writing, the higher level of benefit in the UK is Employment and Support Allowance (ESA), eligibility for which is determined by the controversial Work Capability Assessment (WCA). ESA claimants deemed able to participate in back to work activities with a view to re-entering paid employment in the future are assigned to the work-related activity group (WRAG), while those deemed unable to undertake any form of work-related activity are assigned to the Support Group. Claimants assigned to the WRAG, as well as disabled people claiming Jobseeker's Allowance (JSA) – including those claiming JSA because they have been found to be fit for work through the WCA – may have their benefits sanctioned for failing to comply with mandatory work-related obligations.

The challenge of assessing fitness for work

There is widespread acknowledgement, including among some parliamentarians (Work and Pensions Select Committee, 2014b) that the WCA is deeply flawed and needs to be replaced. Disabled people and academic researchers have argued that one of the reasons the WCA does a poor job of assessing genuine fitness for work, or the support a claimant would need to enable them to work, is its irrelevance to the demands of paid employment in the 21st century. It also takes no account of factors affecting employability, such as the claimant's age, education or work experience, despite evidence from other Western countries showing that taking such factors into account is often the norm (Baumberg et al, 2015).

In addition, many disabled people, especially those with long-term physical or mental health conditions, argue that there is a considerable mismatch between the functional impairments assessed by the WCA and the disability or health-related factors that actually prevent disabled people from working (Benstead and Nock, 2016). They point out that a mechanistic, points-based system cannot accurately assess disabled people who are chronically sick (Benstead et al, 2014). For example, people with ME/CFS (myalgic encephalomyelitis /chronic fatigue syndrome) may be assessed as well enough to work or prepare for work because they can undertake specific, one-off activities during the assessment itself, but due to post-exertional malaise may be bedridden for the following few days, due to the effort required to travel to and participate in the assessment itself.

Although the WCA purports to take account of other medical evidence, people with long-term health conditions and others argue that one of the main reasons the assessment is poor at assessing health-related barriers to work is that little

89

account is taken of the views of their own doctors and consultants, who know them, their conditions and treatment the best. Many disabled people therefore consider that a reformed assessment process should include a greater role for their own doctors, although NHS doctors have expressed good reasons for not wanting to actually make decisions on fitness for work themselves (Benstead et al, 2014).

Making out of work benefits safer for disabled people

Any worthwhile changes to the WCA will realistically take a long time to achieve. However, in the meantime it is arguable that JSA and ESA (WRAG) could be made 'safer' benefits for disabled claimants, by minimising the use of benefit sanctions and ensuring they are not applied unreasonably. This would go a long way towards mitigating some of the worst hardship resulting from the failings of the WCA (Baumberg et al, 2015).

This view is supported by research undertaken in 2014 into the experiences of disabled people in the ESA WRAG (Hale, 2014). The research found that failure by Job Centre Plus and their contracted Work Programme providers to comply with their duties under the Equality Act 2010, including by making reasonable adjustments to take account of the impact of impairment, was one reason why claimants were exposed to the risk of benefit sanctions. Of 500 respondents to the research, 60% said no adjustments were discussed or implemented to enable them to take part in mandatory work-related activity. In all, 86% of respondents were fearful and anxious that they would be sanctioned for not being able to meet their work-related activity requirements (Hale, 2014). The author of the research, who has ME/CFS, was unable to walk more than 200 metres or sit upright for more than 30 minutes, as documented in her WCA report. Her benefit was sanctioned for failing to undertake mandatory work-related activity that necessitated travelling to a venue more than a mile from public transport and sitting in a work preparation course for four hours (Pring, 2014). Overall, the evidence suggests that even a process predicated on a 'welfare to work' approach could be made safer if those with the power to sanction disabled people's benefits were to comply fully with both the letter and the spirit of the Equality Act 2010 (Hale, 2014).

'Welfare to work' employment policies

UK government-commissioned employment support programmes have traditionally been underpinned by the assumption that a poor work ethic and 'culture of dependency' are major barriers to employment and that disabled people need to be made to understand the supposed benefits of paid work (Hale, 2014). The focus is therefore on cajoling and coercing disabled people into work preparation activities. Such programmes focus almost exclusively on the 'supply side' of the labour market (disabled benefit claimants) rather than on the 'demand side' (employers), so there is little support for employers to provide job and career opportunities and to meet the access needs of disabled employees (Young and Nolan, 2014).

Government programmes typically consist of mandatory, generic activities, such as CV writing, interview technique and online job search. The aim is to get the claimant into any job, since the primary purpose is to stop people claiming benefits rather than to secure sustainable employment (Public Accounts Committee, 2013). This 'one size fits all' approach to employment support often fails to address disabled people's need for education or skills training or to take into account their existing qualifications (Young and Nolan, 2014).

> 'They looked at my CV and laughed because I have a Masters and all they had was shelf stacking.' (Hale, 2014: 19)

There is also a failure to take account of disabled people's access and support needs. In commenting on published statistics, which have generally shown very poor outcomes for ESA claimants on the Work Programme, the mental health charity Mind has suggested that a significant reason for such poor outcomes is the failure to tailor support for individuals' specific needs:

> This scheme is failing people with mental health problems because they aren't given the right support. If you have a mental health problem, CV-writing workshops will not help you overcome crippling anxiety or suicidal thoughts, and the threat of losing your benefits if you don't comply is highly likely to make you far more unwell, not more motivated. This flawed, punitive approach is backfiring, making thousands more unwell and pushing them further away from work. (Mind, 2015)

Respecting disabled people's 'right to work'

In contrast with the ideology underpinning current government policy, disabled people contest that their principal barrier to employment is not a poor work ethic but a complex combination of external and impairment-related barriers (Benstead et al, 2014). These include symptoms such as pain and fatigue, the fluctuating nature of health conditions, lack of education and skills, social and family circumstances, lack of support (both employment-specific and general support such as healthcare or adult social care) and many other individual factors (Benstead and Nock, 2016). They argue that it would be more effective to provide personalised support that builds on most disabled people's tenacious commitment to paid work and their right to a good job that pays well, uses their education and skills and provides dignity and purpose.

> Work is considered desirable because it provides an earned income, not charity, and the desire to earn one's own income is strong. People

need neither a reduction in out-of-work benefits nor an increase in in-work benefits to incentivise them to work; work has enough value in and of itself. The commitment to work is tenacious.' (Benstead and Nock, 2016: 7)

Several well-known disability organisations have produced useful, evidence-based material on the most helpful policies to support disabled people into good jobs. They recommend a focus on voluntary participation in personalised support based on their education, skills, experience and interests, investment in additional skills training, an accurate assessment of access and support needs and, crucially, active engagement with local employers (Sayce and Crowther, 2013; Trotter, 2013). Importantly, such an approach provides employers with the encouragement and targeted support they need, to benefit from what disabled people have to offer. Two programmes in particular, 'supported employment' and 'individual placement and support', have been shown to be particularly successful in helping people with learning difficulties and those with mental health problems into sustainable employment (Sayce and Crowther, 2013).

Many disabled people with long-term, often fluctuating health conditions have raised considerable concerns about their ability to compete in the labour market and the amount and nature of the support they would need to do so. They point out that their needs, often for a highly flexible, personalised routine, go far beyond the usual type of workplace adjustment such as adaptive software or wheelchair access. Despite their desire to work, they find that their health interferes significantly with their ability to enter employment (Hale, 2014; Benstead and Nock, 2016).

> 'Employers do not understand and can't make jobs available for someone who can work one day OK but not for two weeks, then maybe manage three days and be off for a month. It just doesn't work like that!' – survey response (Hale, 2014: 16)

While working mainly at home, totally flexibly and at times when they feel able to, may be feasible, rewarding and productive for highly motivated individuals with chronic, fluctuating conditions, working in this way would not be practical or acceptable to most employers. Disabled researchers therefore argue that it is unrealistic to expect them to sustain paid employment without significant government support for the employer (Benstead and Nock, 2016). In the meantime, out of work benefits for disabled people should be sufficient and secure, to support them to make a contribution in other ways, such as volunteering, undertaking user-led research or caring for a child or adult dependent (Benstead et al, 2014).

Conclusion

As a society we need to choose whether we value and believe in disabled people, their commitment to making a contribution and their rights to work and support, or whether we continue with punitive 'welfare to work' policies founded on low expectations and begrudging, inadequate and insecure support. Since disability employment rates remain stubbornly low and disability remains a significant driver of poverty, it is at least arguable that 'welfare to work' is failing to achieve its aim and a change of approach would be appropriate. Disabled people have a tenacious commitment to work and to making a contribution in other ways, but they cannot to do so without a commitment from government to provide the support they need to do so. Only then may we start to banish the evil of want from the lives of disabled people and their families, for the lasting benefit of our society and our economy.

Notes

[1] In this chapter, the term 'disabled people' should be taken to include people with long-term health conditions.

[2] There is an interesting academic debate over the consideration of impairment effects under a social model of disability (Thomas, 1999), which falls outside the scope of this chapter.

[3] The UK ratified the International Covenant on Economic, Social and Cultural Rights (ICESCR) in 1976 but has failed to incorporate the majority of its provisions into domestic law.

[4] The UK government was severely criticised by the United Nations Committee on Economic, Social and Cultural Rights in its Concluding Observations published in 2016. The committee had a number of concerns, including the failure to bring into force those elements of the Equality Act 2010 that enhance protection of economic and social rights (United Nations Committee on Economic, Social and Cultural Rights, 2016).

References

Baumberg, B., Warren, J., Garthwaite, K. and Bambra, C. (2015) 'Incapacity needs to be assessed in the real world': Rethinking the work capability assessment, London: Demos.

Benstead, S., Marsh, S., Richardson, C., Cartwright, J., Hale, C., Barnet-Cormack, S. and Smith, R. (2014) Beyond the Barriers: a Spartacus Network report into employment support allowance, the work programme and recommendations for a new system of support, Spartacus Network in collaboration with Ekklesia.

Benstead, S. and Nock, E. (2016) Replacing Employment and Support Allowance Part One: Support needs of people with chronic illness, Ekklesia.

Borsay, A. (2005) Disability and Social Policy in Britain since 1750, Palgrave Macmillan.

Brawn, E. (2014) Priced out: Ending the financial penalty of disability by 2020, Scope.

Campbell, J. and Oliver, M. (1996) Disability Politics: Understanding our past, changing our future, London: Routledge.

Dean, A. and Patrick, R. (2011) 'A New Welfare Settlement? The Coalition Government and welfare to work', in H.M. Bochel (ed) *The Conservative Party and Social Policy*, Bristol: Policy Press.

European Committee of Social Rights (2014) *Conclusions XX-2 (2013) (Great Britain) Articles 3, 11. 12. 13 and 14 of the 1961 Charter.*

Hale, C. (2014) *Fulfilling Potential? ESA and the fate of the work-related activity group*, Mind.

Leonard Cheshire Disability (2014) *No Place Like Home*, www.leonardcheshire. org/sites/default/files/no-place-like-home-leonard-cheshire-disabiltiy.pdf

Low, C., Meacher, M. and Grey-Thompson, T. (2015) *Halving The Gap? A review into the Government's proposed reduction to employment and support allowance and its impact on halving the disability employment gap*, Mencap.

Mind (2015) 'Government back-to-work scheme failing thousands with mental health problems', 17 September, www.mind.org.uk/news-campaigns/news/ government-back-to-work-scheme-failing-thousands-with-mental-health-problems

Pring, J. (2014) 'No DWP apology for Work Programme "discrimination and punishment"', *Disability News Service*, 3 October, www.disabilitynewsservice. com/no-dwp-apology-for-work-programme-discrimination-and-punishment/

Public Accounts Committee (2013) *Department for Work and Pensions: Responding to change in Jobcentres, 5th report of 2013–14*, House of Commons.

Sayce, L. and Crowther, N. (2013) *Taking control of employment support*, Disability Rights UK.

Select Committee on the Equality Act 2010 and Disability (2016) *The Equality Act 2010: The impact on disabled people*, House of Lords.

Thomas, C. (1999) Female Forms, Open University Press.

Tinson, A., Aldridge, H., Born, T.B. and Hughes, C. (2016) *Disability and poverty: Why disability must be at the centre of poverty reduction*, The New Policy Institute, supported by the Joseph Rowntree Foundation.

Trotter, R. (2012) *Over-looked communities, over-due change: How services can better support BME disabled people*, Scope.

Trotter, R. (2013) *Work in progress: Rethinking employment support for disabled people*, Action on Hearing Loss, Mencap, Mind, RNIB, Scope.

United Nations Committee on Economic, Social and Cultural Rights (2016) *Concluding observations on the sixth periodic report of the United Kingdom of Great Britain and Northern Ireland.*

Work and Pensions Select Committee (2014a) *Support for housing costs in the reformed welfare system, 4th report of 2013–14*, House of Commons.

Work and Pensions Select Committee (2014b) *Employment and Support Allowance and Work Capability Assessments, 1st report of 2014–15*, House of Commons.

Young, J. and Nolan, A. (2014) *Dignity and Opportunity for All: Securing the rights of disabled people in the austerity era*, London: Just Fair.

9

Talking policy as a patient

Anya de Iongh

As someone with long-term health conditions, health policy is important to me, because it can affect which services I access and how. On paper, at least, that is reflected in UK policy, with phrases such as 'nothing about us without us'[1] and the NHS Constitution[2] placing great important on people like me getting involved as patient leaders.

My lived experience began when I was 19 and still studying at university. After the initial shock and disruption of getting diagnosed with long-term health conditions, it quickly became clear to me that this was a far more informative experience than information I was trying to learn in my studies. It is hard to describe the lived experience I am accumulating as each day goes by, since it varies from good to bad, acute to chronic, specialist care and the 'get on and cope with it yourself' approaches as well as the almost inevitable mental health challenges caused by the physical health.

Combining that with a hunger for a new identity since my old identity had been robbed by the health conditions motivated me to want to make this experience of some value for somebody somewhere – although at first, I really wasn't sure who or where that would be. I think the sentiment of 'wanting to improve things for others', or 'make sure others don't have to go through the same experience' is a common motivator for people, and I am certainly no exception. The challenge for me came in finding something that fitted that bill, and enabled me to use my lived experience.

Communication and collective approaches online with social media

Social media was the key to overcoming those challenges. The common criticism of Twitter as an echo chamber does mean that it is a great forum for peer support and to find (and then interact with) role models from the UK and further afield across the world. When I was finding my feet, this proved invaluable. As my confidence started to grow, I joined in conversations and interacted with professionals who, due to the traditional hierarchy of the NHS and institutions, were out of my reach in real life. Yet on Twitter, that hierarchy is swallowed up and senior medical directors, policymakers, clinical staff and patients can come together as equals.

For an area as complex as health, sometimes 140 characters doesn't suffice so I also use a blog (hosted by Google's Blogger). At first, this was a space for reflection that I didn't share and just used to chart the experiences I was gaining, but as my confidence grew along with my desire to contribute my ideas, experiences and thoughts to the debate, I made it public.

In my work, it's a valuable tool to connect me to others, acting as my office water-cooler, when working from home. In order to manage my health conditions, it is important to avoid too much travelling and so I find myself working from home, which suits me very well. One of the down sides of working from home, the social isolation, has been erased by social media. Other social media platforms such as Skype, Facetime and YouTube have enabled me to deliver lectures and talks from home as well. When fatigue and other symptoms are exacerbated by travel, social media has meant I can still work, contribute and engage. When one's legs are not working, the power of having a world at one's fingertips becomes even more pertinent.

In roles when I can feel like an outsider, it is reassuring to share challenges and collect ideas and solutions from others. I used it in this way very recently, after chairing a patient, carer and public engagement group meeting that didn't go to plan. Reflecting with others enabled me to find two or three specific things to do for next time, because I heard a range of perspectives on the matter. If people involved in policymaking at all levels had this opportunity to reflect in a safe area, it would enable us all to learn some important lessons.

The actions that can influence

Since starting out of this journey, my eyes have been opened to the full spectrum of ways that people with lived experience can have a role. Before entering this world, it is a very invisible one to outsiders. Dividing health into a number of discrete areas, I've had some very positive experiences:

- delivering education to healthcare professionals as a lecturer at universities and supporting groups of patients to develop policies for involvement in university faculties
- supporting research as a lay contributor, and specifically with a research team to develop a person-centred culture through a long-term relationship
- informing commissioning of self-management services and strategic commissioning and implementation of policy direction through chairing patient, carer and public engagement group
- contributing to the national self-management support agenda through authorship of key publications and peer reviewing others, and
- speaking at regional and national conferences from a patient's perspective and championing participation in policy development.

Conclusion

With an institution as complex as the UK National Health Service, I feel it is hard to really quantify the impact, but I am optimistic that these activities and the brilliant work of other patient leaders and experts by experience, or whatever name they choose to go by, adds up to be so much more than the sum of its parts. Again, social media gives us a platform to share that, to build a critical mass of people who are thinking in this way. Without it, I have no idea how I would find out about other work that is going on.

If we are able to promote and mobilise people to be patient leaders, and co-develop social policy, then that momentum can help participative social policy and patient leadership fulfil their potential.

Notes

[1] Department of Health (2010) *Equity and excellence: Liberating the NHS*, www.gov.uk/government/uploads/system/uploads/attachment_data/file/213823/dh_117794.pdf

[2] NHS (2015) *The NHS Constitution: The NHS belongs to us all*, www.gov.uk/government/uploads/system/uploads/attachment_data/file/480482/NHS_Constitution_WEB.pdf

10

'We don't deal with people, we deal with bricks and mortar': a lived experience perspective on UK health and housing policy

Alison Cameron

Introduction

The statement in the title by a Housing Officer in my local borough said so much. The focus on the provision of at best a *house* rather than a *home* ignores the impact lack of suitable housing can have on the human beings who are so often the recipients of the results of decisions made about them without them.

Having made the transition from homelessness to now having a social housing tenancy and a further transition from long-term dependency on benefits, I have come to redefine my understanding of Squalor – one of the 'giant evils' Beveridge defined in his then groundbreaking report.

I believe he meant it in a 'bricks and mortar' sense. Having people living in squalid conditions was clearly the key challenge in those times. I have come to see it these days as having deeper connotations.

An archaic definition of 'stigma' is a brand on the skin. I see squalor as also being about mud that sticks. People forced to rely on benefits, and if lucky housed in social housing, are increasingly viewed as being of lesser worth – the 'undeserving poor', the 'feckless', and so on. I noted with horror the building of so-called 'affordable housing' in private developments with separate entrances for those lesser mortals. The creation of 'poor doors' with markedly less attractive fixtures and fittings and even segregated bins to make sure even the rubbish of the lesser is kept away from the throwaways of the privileged.

The UK Care Act 2014 defines housing as one of nine areas of 'wellbeing' which local authorities must promote and give proper attention to 'the suitability of living accommodation' (HM Government, 2014)

In 2015 the Building Research Establishment more than doubled its 2010 estimate of cost to the UK National Health Service (NHS) of poor housing from £600 million to £1.5 billion. It also talks of other 'other losses to society of leaving people in poor housing such as the impact on educational attainment and economic performance' (Simon et al, 2015: 9). This is an ever-worsening picture with cuts to welfare, particularly targeted at society's most vulnerable, and to services, leading to denial of basic support to an increasing number of people (Tinson et al, 2016).

In this chapter I have opted to move away from academic discussion and policy rhetoric. There is enough out there in 'Think Tank Land' to satisfy those for whom that floats a boat (with or without an iceberg on the horizon). I have chosen instead for the first time to talk in detail about my personal experiences of housing in a way that might have more impact than that glossy policy document gathering dust on the shelf. This is not meant to be yet another 'inspirational story' but to show in stark detail what the data often used in policy can only partly convey – a story of waste of assets the system can ill afford and of immeasurable cost in human terms.

'Revolving doors'

I estimate that lack of safe housing delayed my recovery from a combination of post-traumatic stress disorder (PTSD) and related substance misuse by some 15 years. It actually added layers of trauma. I was diagnosed after the death of my colleagues in the course of my job in international relations and in order to try to cope I self-medicated with alcohol. That, in combination with an unsupportive working culture, led to my retirement on ill health grounds at the age of 32. I lost my home, as after sick pay came to an end I was unable to keep up mortgage payments.

I moved back in with my parents and with their support I appeared to be on the mend. I somehow succeeded in getting a job as a Political Administrator to a Member of the European Parliament. Away from my family, I quickly disintegrated and started on what became a dehumanising process in which what remained of my identity and my mental and physical health were shattered. Very soon I had no job, no home and was adrift in London. I managed somehow to get myself to my borough town hall to declare myself homeless and they agreed to house me. I stepped that day onto a joyless merry-go-round that was to spin on for more than a decade.

Life for me became entirely about trying desperately to get help and find ways of getting my fragmented self safely across a sinkhole-ridden service landscape. My mental health and alcoholism were worsening and I became even more of a challenge to the system. I was too mad for substance misuse services, and too drunk for the mental health services. There seemed to be a chasm between health and social services in Britain, with housing seeming to exist in isolation on some other planet.

Over and over again I appeared in hospital Accident and Emergency departments only to be patched up and packed off to another dingy room in some other bed and breakfast or hostel well away from where my support, such as it was, was situated. Every time I would be discharged back into these unsafe squalid places where my visible vulnerability led to me to be preyed upon, leading to physical and sexual assault and rape.

My response was to drink even more to cut myself off from my reality, and had I not done so I believe I would have taken my own life. The drinking would inevitably lead to yet another admission and a few days later another exit again back into oblivion.

I felt totally disconnected from the person I was before I became unwell, the person who ran international projects and was commended for her work in the Chernobyl zone. I knew she existed but was cryogenically suspended in another room in some other part of the building to which someone else with all the power had the key.

Turning points

I was eventually given a place in a Turning Point supported housing project. For the first time in years I had a safe roof over my head. Turning Point clearly understood the importance to their client group often battered into oblivion by mental health and substance misuse issues of an environment in which it might just be possible to regain some dignity and start to heal. I cried with joy that I actually had a kettle and a toaster. I recall my first night there. I was so unused to being in comfortable surroundings that I thought I might not be 'allowed' to sit on my bed so I sat totally motionless on an armchair not quite believing I had the right to be there.

I felt devoid of any rights by this stage. I had been stripped down to nothing and re-labelled as 'vulnerable', 'complex' and 'hard to reach'. I absorbed and became what was written on my labels.

It was to be a long and hard process of pushing the rock up the hill from then on but at least the rock started coming to rest a little further up each time.

I recovered sufficiently to move on from Turning Point to a social housing tenancy. This brought with it a whole new range of problems. I was simply plonked in the nearest available space with no consideration for my mental health or precarious recovery from alcoholism in this case under a very well-known crack den. Under such conditions I stepped back again on the merry-go-round of relapse and hospital admissions during which every time 'unsafe housing' was writ large on my notes.

I became trapped as a so-called 'bed blocker' for just under a year at a cost per night of more than the Dorchester on an acute mental health ward. The police had deemed where I was living too dangerous. I could have told them that years before if I had ever been asked.

The fact is with my illness triggered by noise and chaos I would have happily compromised on being housed out of area in a tiny cupboard as long as it was a safe and quiet one. The problem was I was never asked.

I was eventually rehoused in another property where I have managed to recover despite struggling with periods of antisocial behaviour and being on the receiving end of hate crime. My mental health labels have been used as an excuse not to listen to me on a whole range of issues from repairs to subletting. I have lived in squalor with damp so bad that I had crops of mushrooms invading my bedroom through the electric sockets and through the ceiling. That was finally resolved two years after I first reported the problem after my tweets under hashtag #mushroomwatch attracted national attention.

Finding a voice and a choice

This was another turning point. Largely due to the levelling power of social media, I was finding my voice. Power was gradually shifting back to me. My increasingly public profile led to a miraculous shift in how I was viewed from irritating tenant/service user/patient with several axes to grind to someone worth listening to in case of potential reputation damage if nothing else. I was saying what I had always said but people in high places were, it seems, viewing me through a different lens. I was speaking at conferences and invited to healthcare leaders' summits where I was able to observe first hand the disconnection from the realities people like me face the higher people climb up the career ladder. Finally, two years ago, after a 17-year career break, I was able to start my own consultancy advising health, social care and housing organisations how to work in genuine co-production with citizens.

We even succeeded in bringing a level of co-production to our building. Residents were given funds to redesign the entrance hall of our beautiful Victorian building, which had been allowed to decay to the extent it was open house to drug dealers and street drinkers. The resulting changes have transformed the appearance of the communal areas of our home at far lower cost and more sustainably. It is an environment not usually associated with social housing. With the improvement in the appearance of our building the perceptions of other residents in our street started to change. A well-heeled gent living opposite stated that "all the really dreadful people have been moved by the government to Manchester and replaced with respectable people who now look after the building properly". In fact the residents had been there for years. Now, however, they lived in a building that was safe, attractive and to which they felt a sense of belonging. As for myself I finally have a flat of a decent standard in which I can live safely as I am seen and heard by my landlord. Getting to that stage has taken some 15 years.

From 'stock' to assets

This story says so much about assumptions that are made. People living in social housing must by definition be incapable and unworthy of living in anything other than the Squalor Beveridge named as one of his giant evils. This is fuelled in our times by the other giant evil of Ignorance manifesting itself in the scapegoating of the so-called 'Benefit Scrounger'.

Undoubtedly the Beveridge Report was revolutionary in its day but it nevertheless focused on delivery by the state to passive recipients rather than shifting power in order to enable shared solutions. It failed to recognise that there are strengths in people and communities if the right conditions are created for them to flourish.

The work of the US social justice activist Professor Edgar Cahn on time banking and co-production really resonates with me. In the introduction to *Manifesto for the Core Economy* he says

> It will take massive labour of all kinds to build the core economy of the future – an economy based on relationships and mutuality, on trust and engagement, on speaking and listening and caring – and above all on authentic respect. We will not get there simply by expanding an entitlement system which apportions public benefits based on negatives and deficiencies, what one lacks, what disability one has, what misfortune one has suffered. (NEF, 2008: 3)

Housing providers and policymakers need to concentrate less on 'asset management' of bricks and mortar 'stock' and more on the building and proper utilisation and valuing of 'human assets'. A mindset shift is needed away from the deficit model that sees people like myself solely in terms of 'needs' that are all but impossible to meet due to ever dwindling resources. They need a clearer understanding of how people and communities, including those considered the most 'vulnerable' can contribute to the design and running of services, a shift from formal largely tokenistic consultation to transformative co-production – an 'equal and reciprocal relationship between professionals, people using services, their families and their neighbours. Where activities are co-produced in this way, both services and neighbourhoods become far more effective agents of change' (Boyle and Harris, 2009: 9).

References

Boyle, D. and Harris, H. (2009) *The challenge of co-production*, London: NESTA.

HM Government (2014) Care Act 2014, www.legislation.gov.uk/ukpga/2014/23/contents/enacted

NEF (New Economics Foundation) (2008) *Co-production: A manifesto for growing the core economy*, London: NEF.

Simon, N., Roys, M., Garrett, H. and BRE (2015) *The Cost of Poor Housing to the NHS*, Watford: BRE.

Tinson, A., Ayrton, C. Barker, K., Born, T.B., Aldridge, H. and Kenway, P. (2016) *Monitoring Poverty and Social Exclusion 2016*, York: Joseph Rowntree Foundation.

11

Education (ignorance) addressing inclusive education: the issues and its importance from a participatory perspective

Tara Flood and Navin Kikabhai

So far the approach of UK social policy to addressing inclusive education has been a pick-and-mix affair. It has primarily been related to notions of locational, social or functional integration (DES, 1978) rather than inclusion; that is, the wholesale restructuring of education in its totality, relating to human rights, social justice and principally about the politics of recognition (Barton, 2003). Indeed this can be seen as the global situation with few exceptions. As regards a participatory approach, educational state policy rarely includes the 'voice' of disabled people, a point raised by Oliver (1996), although in relation to welfare policy. Oliver's comment is worth repeating (with amendment) in this context of inclusive education, that:

> I have watched in dismay as [*segregated educational services*] continue to be reorganised on the basis of advice from people who have little or no experience of them and how the advice of [*disabled people who have attended such provision*] continues to be ignored. (Oliver, 1996: 43–44; emphasis added)

The concept of *inclusive* education, rather than 'integration', emerged during the early 1990s, primarily through a series of conferences initiated and facilitated by a group of individuals but principally by Joe Whittaker (who was then situated at the University of Bolton, previously Bolton Institute of Higher Education, and currently a trustee of the Alliance for Inclusive Education). Among other initiatives, these conferences set the tone for change, and centrally involved disabled people at the forefront of sharing knowledge, drawing upon their own lived experiences.

Even the movement for education inclusion, led by disabled people, began life in 1990 as the *Integration* Alliance (emphasis added) with a name change to the Alliance for Inclusive Education (ALLFIE) in the mid-1990s. The term integration was rejected as ALLFIE became clearer about the need for systemic and fundamental change as the only way to ensure all disabled pupils and students (including those with labels of so-called 'special educational needs') would be welcomed and supported in a single inclusive education system.

ALLFIE built a movement for inclusive education based on an alliance that included parents seeking something new, different and inclusive for their disabled children. That desire for change was helped along by the opportunities that ALLFIE created for disabled adults to share their stories of segregated 'special' schooling with parents of young children, to dispel the myths that exist about the so-called specialness of 'special' education.

ALLFIE's inclusive education movement focused on the right of disabled people to be equal members of society and an essential element of this right being realised is the ending of segregated education and the creation of an education system that welcomes all pupils and students irrespective of difference or background – an education system that is based on a core principle that all pupils and students have a right to be there, without the struggle for support.

This marked shift in thinking about inclusive education, in part, was mirrored globally, in the publication of the Salamanca Statement (UNESCO, 1994), which fed into a UK New Labour policy; for example, *Excellence for All Children* (DfES, 1997) and *Removing Barriers to Achievement* (DfES, 2004). Interestingly, in 1996 the post-16 sector published *Inclusive Learning* (Tomlinson, 1996), which also began to address the problem of post-16 segregated discrete provision.

In the last 30 years consecutive governments have failed to adopt a social model of disability approach in terms of re-visioning education and instead have continued to policy and law which may have skilfully adopted inclusive language, but in reality remains entrenched in an medialised individual approach that seeks to make interventions based on perceived learning deficits. Further, the educational (ignorance) gaze has begun to focus much more on individual impairment, mainly around issues of so-called 'challenging behaviour' and 'autism', as justifications as to why such individuals cannot be included in mainstream provision. This narrowing of education (ignorance) for pupils and students that can and should be part of mainstream is at odds with successive governments' apparent commitment to greater parental choice. There is evidence to show that instead current notions of 'choice' are masking issues of control and exclusion (Foucault, 1998; Ballard, 2004; Thomas, 2007).

Since 2006 and the elaboration of the UN Convention on the Rights of Persons with Disabilities (CRPD), the UK has become increasingly out of step with a global commitment to the development of inclusive education practice. The UK government ratified the CRPD in 2009 and with it created caveats that have restricted its implementation, particularly with regard to Article 24: the Right to Inclusive Education. The UK is the only northern hemisphere country that has taken such a retrograde step and despite text in the Interpretative Declaration committing to 'building the capacity of mainstream to be more inclusive', the

UK government has sought to introduce policy and law that is systematically undermining its CRPD obligations.[1]

Since 2010, and given neoliberal agendas, the educational policy context and provision has radically changed. Despite former Prime Minister David Cameron's apparent personal crusade, based on his experience as a parent of a disabled child, his pursuit of small state politics and private sector interventions in the delivery of education had the effect of sabotaging decades of work to develop inclusive education practice.

In the UK, neoliberal social policy, the welfare reform legislative assault on disabled people, has fuelled violence and hostility towards disabled people, including disabled pupils and students. This signals a return to political ignorance with little political opposition to slow its pace or indeed challenge its misconceptions about who disabled people are and the value we bring to society.

In such a hostile political climate, disabled people's organisations (DPOs) such as ALLFIE are finding greater strength and clarity in our thinking about building broader alliances with fellow DPOs, but also mainstream allies who share our fears for the future of education, but also our hope that a more unified resistance to the current political ideology will burst the bubble of poisonous rhetoric of an 'education marketplace'.

In any movement for change there are good times and times that are more challenging; ALLFIE, as with so many other disabled people-led organisations, has a clear vision for equality and inclusion and we have the blueprint for how to get there. For ALLFIE there is an acute awareness of the evils of education shaped by political ignorance and that only a truly transformative and inclusive educational experience will create opportunities for change. Indeed, this sense of struggle is encapsulated by Nelson Mandela, who reminds us that:

> As long as poverty, injustice and gross inequality persist in our world, none of us can truly rest.

Note
[1] www.allfie.org.uk/pages/work/article24.html

References

Ballard, K. (2004) 'Ideology and the Origin of Exclusion: A case study' in L. Ware (ed) *Ideology and the Politics of (In)Exclusion*, New York: Peter Lang Publishing, Inc.

Barton, L. (2003) *Inclusive Education: A basis of hope or a discourse of delusion* (Professorial lecture), London: IOE.

DES (1978) *Report of the Committee of Enquiry into the Education of Handicapped Children and Young People* (The Warnock Report), London: HMSO.

DfES (1997) *Excellence for All Children: Meeting special educational needs*, London: DfES.

DfES (2004) *Removing Barriers to Achievement: The Government's Strategy for SEN*, London: DfES.

Foucault, M. (1998) *Politics, Philosophy, Culture: Interviews with other writings 1977–1984*, London: Routledge.

Oliver, M. (1996) *Understanding Disability: From theory to practice*, Basingstoke: Palgrave.

Thomas, C. (2007) *Sociologies of Disability and Illness: Contested ideas in disability studies and medical sociology*, Basingstoke: Palgrave Macmillan.

Tomlinson, J. (1996) *Inclusive Learning*, London: DfEE.

UNESCO (1994) *Salamanca Statement*, Paris: UNESCO.

12

"For work, we came here to find work": migrant Roma employment and the labour of language

Colin Clark

Introduction

'I came here for job. It was not easy. It was hard before because I didn't speak English … it was difficult to go to job centre and apply for job. Now is easier because I speak English and I have job. Now is all right.' Marek (M, 28, Slovakia)

'To give people work. It's very hard if people do not speak language … this is very big question.' Kornelie (F, 47, Romania)

This chapter explores the Beveridge 'giant' of 'idleness' – and its presumed slayer, a political commitment to achieving full employment – via the lens of 'first hand' experiences of Central and Eastern European (CEE) migrant Roma ('Gypsy') communities who have moved to the UK in the past decade or so from countries such as Slovakia and Romania. To do this, a few words will first be said about how we both understand and interpret 'idleness' and employment in the historical and contemporary age. This section will necessarily investigate the specific Beveridge approach to combatting 'idleness' and look at some of the fundamental diversity and equality issues that it raises, including racism, classism, xenophobia and sexism. Likewise, from an international or at least trans-European perspective, the chapter will locate and analyse what might be termed the 'labour of language'. What is meant by this? In a later section it is argued that for many CEE Roma workers in the UK – such as Marek from Slovakia and Kornelie from Romania, who are quoted above – one of the first issues to be confronted is a 'working language' barrier, in addition to many other challenges in seeking even basic service provision in key social policy areas such as housing, social security, health and education. It is evident that notions and experiences of employment are crucially shaped by the issue of language and assumptions that are often made regarding both its acquisition and practice by individuals who are deemed by employers, and others, to be 'not British'. The chapter actively employs a 'first hand' approach by drawing on empirical data from a recent study in Glasgow and it privileges these 'Roma voices' while also offering some critical commentary on the wider, structural factors that are at play in determining the 'life chances' of such workers and the extended families they often support both in the UK and back in Central and Eastern Europe.[1] Before moving to this empirical data, it is first necessary to provide comment on the giant of 'idleness' and how this has been understood both in the time of Beveridge and more recently in the 21st century.

'Idleness'

> Any proposals for the future, while they should use to the full the experience gathered in the past, should not be restricted by consideration of sectional interests established in the obtaining of that experience. Now, when the war is abolishing landmarks of every kind, is the opportunity for using experience in a clear field. A revolutionary moment in the world's history is a time for revolutions, not for patching. (Beveridge, 1942, Part 1: 7)

It was the famous Beveridge Report of 1942, formally entitled *Social Insurance and Allied Services* (Beveridge, 1942), that boldly declared a post-war social justice campaign against a related set of 'giants' that were identified as being barriers to achieving the 'good society' (Galbraith, 1996). In 1945, following their convincing election victory, the Labour Party set about establishing what we now refer to as the welfare state via a series of Acts and accompanying social policies that included the Family Allowances Act (1945), the National Health Service Act (1946) and the Landlord and Tenant (Rent Control) Act (1949) (Hill, 1993). This progressive legislative programme of social change and protection – which was certainly not a form of 'patching' as Beveridge notes above – has remained pivotal to government agendas across the 20th and 21st centuries although, as we shall see, there have been continuous efforts to prune and dismantle entire sections of the welfare state, starting not long after its foundations were built. Indeed, progress has been far less linear and more a series of backwards and forwards moves depending on the government of the day and its political and ideological leanings. What is clear is that the Beveridge 'five giants' – Want, Disease, Ignorance, Squalor and Idleness – have shifted and mutated throughout the years and have taken on new forms and realities for changed circumstances. It is undoubtedly the case that a 21st century Beveridge Report would look quite different from the 1942 version, in form, content and language, but some of the original post-war struggles are still very real, not least in terms of the challenges of employment and unemployment ('idleness'). Nonetheless, as Larry Elliot (2014) writing in the *Observer* has suggested, it is evident when examining various 'cradle-to-grave' indicators, that progress has been made and a 'new' Beveridge Report would recognise this:

> It would start by recognising that great progress that has been made. Britain is a richer, healthier, better educated and more tolerant country than it was 70-odd years ago. Life expectancy has risen by well over a decade; university education is no longer for a tiny elite; incomes adjusted for inflation are four times higher than they were at the end of the second world war; the number of people in owner-occupation has more than doubled; people no longer live in sub-standard homes without baths and inside toilets.

It can be asserted that the assorted giants have been tackled and weakened, if not slain for good, and significant progress has been made since the post-war years in the areas of poverty, health, education, housing and work. For example, although 'idleness' certainly remains a rather belligerent and defiant giant, the UK unemployment rate as of November 2016 was 4.9% (BBC, 2016). It is worth recalling that in mid-1980s, under conditions of Thatcherism, the unemployment rate was around the 12% mark quite consistently – that is, over 3 million people (Nunns, 2013). One point raised by Larry Elliot in his piece for the *Observer* could be queried though: is Britain really a 'more tolerant' country now? Certainly, when examining the empirical evidence that follows below, this is an open question and one that needs to be reflected on. Certain excluded and marginalised groups in society would argue that it is actually less tolerant, not more tolerant – including Romani families from Central and Eastern Europe.

However, what is also evident is that since the 1980s the five giants have become rather more selective in the groups they choose to do battle with. Inequalities in the UK and beyond are sharply rising in areas such as income, housing, employment among various socially excluded groups, including women, young people, those on low incomes, minority ethnic groups, LGBT+ individuals, migrants, refugees and disabled people. Such groups of people are increasingly enduring sustained attacks on welfare provision that were designed to guarantee basic, minimum standards in times of need (Stone, 2015). For example, in relation to 'idleness', it is evident that various UK governments since the post-war period have used aspects of the social security system as a means to regulate, control and govern the unemployed population (Squires, 1990). It is also the case that conditionality has been a longstanding feature of the welfare state – conditionality of category, circumstance as well as conduct as Clasen and Clegg (2007) have argued.

At the heart of such approaches to welfare is a high degree of focus on individualised and often pathologised behaviour – that is, in order to have access to, take up and receive welfare payments, individuals must meet strict, imposed, pre-defined behavioural conditions (for example, to attend appointments at the job centre on time, to be judged to be 'actively seeking work', to dress for and attend job interviews in a 'work ready' fashion, and so on). If such behaviours are not noted by agents of the state, such as Jobcentre Plus employment advisors, then penalties and sanctions are often applied which can have a severe impact on entitlement including reducing, suspending or ending payments (Wright, 2016). Interestingly, and perhaps not entirely coincidently, this focus on behaviour (as well as 'culture') has also been noted within the political arena. Two contributions to recent debates stand out here where senior politicians felt the need to speak out about the need to 'change the behaviour and culture' of Roma migrants as well as the fact that such behaviours are, it was argued, judged to be 'intimidating' and 'offensive'. Witness the remarks of the former Labour Home Secretary David Blunkett MP and the former Deputy Prime Minister of the Coalition Government, Liberal Democrat Nick Clegg MP:

> 'We have got to change the behaviour and the culture of the incoming community, the Roma community, because there's going to be an explosion otherwise. We all know that.' David Blunkett (quoted in Engineer, 2013)

> 'There is a real dilemma ... when they [Roma] behave in a way that people find sometimes intimidating, sometimes offensive.' Nick Clegg (quoted in Bennett, 2013)

Within these parameters, there are revived debates on the overall ethics and efficacy of such conditional forms of welfare and how such measures are being enacted to govern and police assumed 'idleness' (Joseph Rowntree Foundation, 2014). Indeed, it is notable that the Department for Work and Pensions (DWP) has even been criticised by the usually quite staid National Audit Office (NAO) in relation to its use of benefits sanctions and the serious impact such measures have on people in receipt of benefits (National Audit Office, 2016). Moving forwards, the impact and consequences of such disciplinary regimes will be discussed in the following 'case study' section, which examines the situation and circumstances of migrant Roma workers from Central and Eastern Europe who stay in Glasgow. The agency and voices of such individuals are given focus and prominence as well as critical commentary to better contextualise the issues and matters raised.

Labour of language

> 'I work first as I came to this country for Big Issue. One job, very good one, is not possible to find. Because when you don't speak English it is not possible to find. There is better for Romania, they help you ... for Big Issue, they help you to manage, to pay little by little. But to find work ... you don't understand English ... it is not possible to find work.' Galina (F, 30, Romania)

As Galina is acutely aware, austerity and insecurity are weapons being increasingly used to tackle the giant of 'idleness' by an invariably pernicious and damaging neoliberal state (Varoufakis, 2017). The regulation of her day-to-day (working) life is governed by a climate of precarity, fear and uncertainty over rights of residence. It is also, as we shall see, a 'labour of language' where access to English language support and related resources are deemed crucial to securing progress within a highly regimented labour market that privileges people who 'look and sound British' and have a strong and fluent working command of English. For Roma migrants, such as Galina, this is a tall order given that literacy in even basic Romanian cannot be assumed as approximately a quarter of the Romanian Roma population is judged to be illiterate (Tarnovschi, 2012).

With regards to employment and tackling the 'giant' of idleness, it is evident from the preceding sections that even though the stated Beveridge goal of full employment in Britain was abandoned during the aftermath of the post-war period, the regulation and control of the 'reserve army of labour' was an important matter to attend to. This subjugation and surveillance took on new forms with the emergence of Windrush-era immigration in the post-war period and the wider incorporation of migrant labour into the UK economy (Castles and Kosack, 1973). Similarly, although Roma migration from Central and Eastern Europe to the UK has taken place for a number of years now, it is the case that following European Union (EU) accession in 2004 (the 'A8' countries of the Czech Republic, Estonia, Hungary, Latvia, Lithuania, Poland, Slovakia and Slovenia), and then again in 2007 (the 'A2' countries of Romania and Bulgaria), there was increasing evidence of cross-border Roma movement from East to West for reasons of work and employment as well as to ensure family safety in the face of discrimination and neo-Nazi attacks in Central and Eastern Europe (Clark, 2014, 2015).

In response to such mobility from both across and outside the EU, as well as inflamed media rhetoric on 'numbers', concerns regarding border security and public expenditure, UK immigration and asylum policies have been subjected to increased strengthening and enforcement – not least in relation to movement from Central and Eastern Europe (Balch and Balabanova, 2016). Although there have always been both explicit and implicit connections between the legal position of migrants and associated rights of residence, work and welfare in Britain, it is apparent that recent narrowing of eligibility is going some way to impose a culture and practice of economic self-reliance and the removal of various entitlements, such as child benefit and housing benefit, as well as a much-thinner welfare 'safety net'. As an example, the Immigration Act 2016 has introduced new sanctions on what it identifies as 'illegal working' as well as preventing 'illegal migrants' – the term used within the Act – from accessing public services. As the Migrants' Rights Network has argued, the recent Act is largely designed to target irregular migrants and to assist the government in meeting their ambitious, if not impossible, 'tens of thousands' net migration manifesto commitments (Müller, 2016).

In terms of actual lived experience, it is prudent to consider some of the views on employment, settlement and integration that have been shared directly by Roma women and men from Central and Eastern Europe who are currently living and working in Glasgow. Such sentiments give an insight into how matters of employment and unemployment ('idleness') can be viewed through an intersectional lens that recognises the importance of language and migration as well as ethnicity and nationality. The southside of Glasgow, especially the area of Govanhill, has witnessed the growth of a sizeable Roma community – numbering some 3,000–4,000 people –in the last few years from various parts of Central and Eastern Europe (Clark, 2014, 2015). Such Roma movement and settlement is also noted in major cities such as London, Sheffield, Manchester and Belfast. The case of Milan, noted below, is a case in point – he is someone who has moved to, and stayed in, Glasgow by choice for over a decade and he has benefited from *not* being located in London as well as relying on a series of peer networks and informal contacts from *within* the Slovak Roma community itself – almost a type of informal social security in the absence of state assistance. As he says himself:

> 'I have been here for 12 years. I chose for Glasgow because when I came, I came to London, but London – it is big, but I did not find any work. And my friends came to Glasgow and immediately after one week found work, so I came here for work. It was difficult from the start without money, no English, but friends helped me a lot to get my head around English, finding work and everything.' Milan (M, 39, Slovakia)

Milan is by no means alone. Other interviewees, such as Galina, stressed the importance of family and extended peer group support, as well as reasons for movement and why it was deemed necessary and prudent to leave their home country and relocate, often at some expense both financial and emotional. Such reasoning underlines the neoclassical 'push' and 'pull' model of migration – that there are distinct reasons to 'leave' one's home country but also explicit reasons to 'come to' the new territory (Banulescu-Bogdan and Fratzke, 2015). That is, such mobility is regarded as a logical solution to structural, racist unemployment patterns at home in Romania where poverty is deep-rooted and discrimination is rife against Roma (as noted by the European Commission, 2015), but it was also spoken about in terms of a reasoned and rational investment in the future via, unsurprisingly, her children:

> 'This country is better than my country, one question is for work, Romania is not good for working and for the … problem is, you don't have work, it's not possible to have life for children. This is the problem why I came to this country. To have a good life, my family…

to find work. And it is better for doctor, for everything.' Galina (F, 30, Romania)

Indeed, such processes are also clear in the following response from Juraj. Based in Glasgow for over a decade now, he has made Scotland his home and has a strong family around him now, all moving over from Slovakia. He has spoken of a search for a 'better life', acknowledging that 'back home' his children and grandchildren were subjected to racial discrimination within the education system, as well as the labour market, because of their Roma ethnicity which classified them as 'Blacks' in Slovak discourse (Rorke, 2016). Further, there is a non-apologetic recognition of rights to mobility as EU citizens – something that is often denied or ignored in popular representations of Roma movement in the mainstream tabloid media where they are invariably portrayed as 'illegal immigrants' who are in Britain due to the perceived 'failures' of the EU (Hardman, 2016). Juraj suggests, when presented with the reality, the decision to leave Slovakia was an easy one:

'I have been here since 2007, I came for better life. Is it a good answer? I saw people were coming here, so I earn money for the bus ride here and I came. I do not have where to live back home, so ... Yes we left, we have the right to go anywhere. Yes it was easy to decide.' Juraj (M, 57, Slovakia)

Echoing Juraj's thought processes are the words of Valeria, who came to Glasgow from the Czech Republic. However, she speaks of the decision to leave home being 'hard' to make but also, again, the importance of pre-existing networks and contacts from within the family and wider community to ease the transition process. Of those interviewed, Valeria was possibly the most settled and integrated within the local area, to the extent of being in a position to buy property and improving her English to such an extent that she was able to secure what she considered to be a 'good' job. The importance of regular hours and a fixed wage, with prospects of promotion, were vital to securing the means to afford her house:

'It was hard but I decided because I liked to live better than home. So this why I came. It was okay because my brother [and his wife] were here so they took me beside them, to live with them. They found job for me then I started to work. It was easy because I was getting my wages and I bought a house. They applied for everything I needed and I live my life.' Valeria (F, 47, Czech Republic)

On a different level, the experiences of Ladislav were a lot more mixed and perhaps reflect what happens when there are sudden changes in terms of life situation and how this shift and reality can cause severe difficulties. In many ways, the experiences of Ladislav are not that far removed from what happens to the central character in the Ken Loach film *I, Daniel Blake* (Loach, 2016), which illustrates the inhumanity of recent changes in UK welfare provision and how 'blaming the victim' has become normalised via policy and practice:

> 'For work, we came here to find work. Yes I knew … I have here my son and my daughter, so it was easy to come here … they were already here. But work … I found work myself. I worked at a potato farm. It was okay. I worked for few months and then I had a heart attack, so I cannot work now, I am on leave 'til after New Year … [I hope for] better work, better work conditions. For example, where we go to search for a job, one needs to speak well English. But if you don't "no English – no work."' Ladislav (M, 59, Slovakia)

At the time of writing, in early 2017, it is insecurity and worries about the future that abound within the diverse and heterogeneous Roma communities across the UK, including Glasgow. This fear is largely driven by the outcome of the EU referendum in June 2016. A recent study by the Institute for Public Policy Research concluded that such communities faced a 'triple whammy of risks' because of Brexit, including 'uncertainty over their future legal status, rising concerns about hate crime, and a potential loss of EU funding for integration and support services.' (Morris, 2016: 28). The report further suggests that in order to best mitigate against some of these risks, certain measures at a national and local level can be enacted, including local authorities taking more pro-active measures to develop and nurture progressive forms of integration that ease pressure on services, ensure value for money and enhance community relations. Such integration efforts must be determined, engaging and transparent, including direct assistance with factors such as language acquisition and employment initiatives. How this will actually play out within Roma communities themselves depends, to a large extent, on how Brexit is taken forward by the UK government now that Article 50 has been triggered. Continuing uncertainty regarding what life will look like after March 29, 2019, the date when the UK formally leaves the European Union, means that some commentators, such as Professor Danny Blanchflower of Stirling University, have predicted that a second independence referendum could be triggered in Scotland (Sheeden, 2016).

Conclusion

> 'First time I worked in potatoes factory. It was easy because I send application from Slovakia to work here. Now it is a big problem to find job. Now I am working delivery job … is hard work.' Marek (M, 28, Slovakia)

This chapter has examined the everyday situations and circumstances of migrant Roma individuals and families from Central and Eastern Europe via the 'lens' of work and employment. As Marek from Slovakia notes above, the current economic climate makes securing decent work a hard task in itself and what work is available is often insecure, temporary and does not offer many protections in terms of sick pay, holiday pay and other in-work benefits. The chapter has illustrated that, despite popular and often racist representations to the contrary by the tabloid press, commentators and certain politicians, 'idleness' is not something that is especially noted within the communities, certainly not as a deliberate or conscious 'lifestyle choice'. In fact, the day-to-day life of Roma migrants in Britain is often one that is plagued by fear, worry and trying to plan, for themselves and their families, for an uncertain future. Indeed, if anything it is these experiences of insecurity, austerity and the likely fallout of Brexit that ensure a determined engagement with the labour market and trying to earn an income and secure a 'good' job. Drawing on the empirical data has assisted in keeping the focus on experiences of service users and it has foregrounded their experiential knowledge. Such 'real life' perspectives have helped to inform earlier discussion around the 'five giants' and the continued place and presence of 'idleness' among the other Beveridge giants. Furthermore, the discussion has noted that reducing such experiences to an 'ethnic' or 'migrant' dimension is simplistic as intersectional approaches help demonstrate the fact that there are classed, aged and gendered aspects at work that serve to isolate and exclude CEE Roma individuals from formal labour markets. A key argument of the chapter has been the 'labour of language' aspect – that is, to try and properly account for the importance of English language skills in negotiating a demanding labour market for migrants, especially where semi-skilled and professional jobs are being sought. Moving forwards, it is clear that one of the main foundations of migrant integration remains education, training and employment. This is as true for the diverse Roma communities in the UK as it is for any other migrant group.

Note

1 The project ran in 2015–16 under the Fundamental Rights Agency's 'Local Engagement for Roma Inclusion' (LERI) programme. Glasgow was one of the 'case study' locations. Further details about this work can be found at http://fra.europa.eu/en/project/2015/local-engagement-roma-inclusion-leri-multi-annual-roma-programme

References

Balch, A. and Balabanova, E. (2016) 'Ethics, Politics and Migration: Public Debates on the Free Movement of Romanians and Bulgarians in the UK, 2006–2013', *Politics*, 36 (1), 19–35.

Banulescu-Bogdan, N. and Fratzke, S. (2015) 'Europe's Migration Crisis in Context: Why Now and What Next?', Migration Policy Institute, 24 September, www.migrationpolicy.org/article/europe-migration-crisis-context-why-now-and-what-next

BBC News (2016) 'UK unemployment rate holds steady', 19 October, www.bbc.co.uk/news/business-37701672

Bennett, O. (2013) 'Thousands call Nick Clegg's LBC radio show to back Daily Express petition on EU migration', *Daily Express*, 31 October, www.express.co.uk/news/uk/440366/Thousands-call-Nick-Clegg-s-LBC-radio-show-to-back-Daily-Express-petition-on-EU-migration

Beveridge, W. (1942) *Social Insurance and Allied Services* (the Beveridge Report), Cmd 6404, London: HMSO.

Castles, S. and Kosack, G. (1973) *Immigrant Workers and Class Structure in Western Europe*, Oxford: Oxford University Press.

Clark, C. (2014). 'Glasgow's Ellis Island? The integration and stigmatisation of Govanhill's Roma population', *People, Place and Policy*, 8 (1), 34–50.

Clark, C. (2015) 'Integration, exclusion and the moral "othering' of Roma migrant communities in Britain', in M. Smith (ed) *Moral Regulation*, Bristol: Policy Press.

Clasen, J. and Clegg, D. (2007) 'Levels and levers of conditionality: measuring change within welfare states', in J. Clasen and N.A. Siegel (eds), *Investigating Welfare State Change: The 'dependent variable problem' in comparative analysis*, Cheltenham: Edward Elgar, pp 166–97.

Elliot, L. (2014) 'What would a 2014 Beveridge report say?', *Observer*, 20 April, www.theguardian.com/society/2014/apr/20/what-would-2014-beveridge-report-say

Engineer, C. (2013) 'David Blunkett issues riot warning over Roma migrants', *Daily Star*, 13 November, www.dailystar.co.uk/news/latest-news/350447/David-Blunkett-issues-riot-warning-over-Roma-migrants

European Commission (2015) *Assessment of Romania's National Strategy for Roma Integration*, Brussels: European Commission, http://ec.europa.eu/justice/discrimination/files/roma_country_factsheets_2015/romania2015_en.pdf

Galbraith, J.K. (1996) *The Good Society: The Humane Agenda*, New York: Houghton Mifflin.

Hardman, R. (2016) 'The town where even immigrants are fed up with migration: Failing schools, filthy streets and benefit fraud', *Daily Mail*, 9 December, www.dailymail.co.uk/news/article-4018946/The-town-immigrants-fed-migration-Failing-schools-filthy-streets-benefit-fraud-ROBERT-HARDMAN-dispatch-accuse-Brexiteers-racist-read.html

Hill, M. (1993) *The Welfare State in Britain: A political history since 1945*, Aldershot: Edward Elgar.

Joseph Rowntree Foundation (2014) *Welfare Sanctions and Conditionality in the UK*, York: Joseph Rowntree Foundation, www.jrf.org.uk/sites/default/files/jrf/migrated/files/Welfare-conditionality-UK-Summary.pdf

Loach, K. (2016) *I, Daniel Blake* [motion picture], UK: BBC Films.

Morris, M. (2016) *Roma Communities and Brexit: Integrating and empowering Roma in the UK*, London: Institute for Public Policy Research, www.ippr.org/files/publications/pdf/Roma-communties-and-Brexit_Oct2016.pdf

Müller, A. (2016) 'The Immigration Act 2016 – What's next for migrants' rights?', *Migrants' Rights Network*, 16 May, www.migrantsrights.org.uk

National Audit Office (2016) *Benefit Sanctions*, HC 628 30 November, London: National Audit Office, www.nao.org.uk/wp-content/uploads/2016/11/Benefit-sanctions.pdf

Nunns, A. (2013) 'Dispelling the Thatcher Myths', Red Pepper, 9 April, www.redpepper.org.uk/dispelling-the-thatcher-myths/

Rorke, B. (2016) 'Slovakia: Roma exclusion and the dark side of democracy', Open Democracy, 29 April, www.opendemocracy.net/can-europe-make-it/bernard-rorke/slovakia-roma-exclusion-and-dark-side-of-democracy

Sheeden, S. (2016) 'Lack of Brexit plan will drive Scots to indyref2, warns economist', *Scotsman*, 22 November, www.scotsman.com/news/lack-of-brexit-plan-will-drive-scots-to-indyref2-warns-economist-1-4296046

Stone, J. (2015) 'The five most controversial welfare cuts the Government is making', *Independent*, 20 July, www.independent.co.uk/news/uk/politics/the-five-most-controversial-welfare-cuts-the-government-is-making-10401191.html

Squires, P. (1990) *Anti-Social Policy: Welfare, ideology and the disciplinary state*, London: Harvester Wheatsheaf.

Tarnovschi, D. (ed) (2012) *Roma from Romania, Bulgaria, Italy and Spain between Social Inclusion and Migration*, Bucharest: Soros Foundation, www.fundatia.ro/sites/default/files/Comparative%20Study_0.pdf

Varoufakis, Y. (2017) *And the Weak Suffer What They Must? Europe, austerity and the threat to global stability*, London: Vintage.

Wright, S. (2016) 'Conceptualising the active welfare subject: welfare reform in discourse, policy and lived experience.' *Policy & Politics*, 44 (2), 235–52.

Part III
The contribution of service
user knowledges

The knowledge base of social policy has tended to be treated as unproblematic, yet it is far from that. Historically it has been narrow and excluding. Part III of the book focuses on the role that service users' 'experiential' knowledges can play in social policy across a wide range of policy areas and user groups. This is a new and contentious field of study and activity. There has tended to be a hierarchy of knowledge in social policy and other academic disciplines and the knowledge(s) of people on the receiving end of policy and theory have often been excluded and given the least value. Here we can explore the contribution such user knowledge can play, as well as hearing directly from people about their own.

Supported by Kathy Boxall, a group of people, including people often labelled as having learning difficulties or disabilities, offer their own take on their lives and public policy. They write in their own words what their lives are like in a small town in Australia; how support works, what is good and bad, showing how their realities and experience connect with the rationales of policymakers from a whole life perspective and what say they feel they do and do not have in what happens to them and how this could be improved. They also tell us what they feel about the experience of writing this chapter.

In her chapter, mental health service user Diana Rose, the world's first professor of user-led research, offers a critical consideration of the role of service user knowledges in underpinning a participatory approach to social policy. She highlights problems as well as opportunities, both in relation to experiential knowledge and the emerging field of 'mad studies', from both a practical and theoretical perspective. While her view may not be the only one, it offers some helpful warnings to take note of for the future, and pitfalls to avoid from the history and experiences of others in developing social policy's knowledge base.

Ruth Beresford draws on feminist epistemology to look at the role women's lived experience of pornography could play in developing policy. While pornography tends not to be considered as a subject for social policy, she argues that recognising 'lived experience' as a type of expertise on pornography could be crucial in developing more relevant and sustainable public policy on pornography. She concludes that 'drawing upon the experiential expertise of victims, professionals and practitioners could be crucial in formulating policy that actually works, and works in a way that is helpful'.

Diane Richardson, Nina Laurie, Meena Poudel, Shakti Samuha, and Janet Townsend explore how a new agenda on post-trafficking in Nepal is gaining momentum through anti-trafficking collaborations based on co-producing knowledge with women who have returned from trafficking situations. They describe a collaborative research and policy partnership to change the way human trafficking is understood and addressed in Nepal with Shakti Samuha, an anti-trafficking campaigning and advocacy organisation founded in 1996 by women with experience of being trafficked.

Finally, academics and researchers Nicola Yeates and Ana Amaya offer a case study of the use of participatory action research (PAR) with its aim of producing knowledge for action that is of direct benefit and use, most of all to people experiencing social vulnerability, disadvantage and oppression. They check out its strength and weaknesses in relation to social policy change, working with policymaking groups in Southern regional contexts. As they say, advocates of PAR argue that valuing otherwise marginalised knowledge and experiences through active participation of research 'subjects' in the research process democratises knowledge production, secures ownership of research and improves research quality, leading to a greater likelihood that results will be put into practice.

13

Disability policy and lived experience: reflections from regional Australia

*Kathy Boxall, Adam Johnson, Lawrence Mitting, Suzanne Simpson,
Stefan Zwickl, Judith Zwickl, Shae Kermit, Luke and Caroline*

Introduction

This chapter is about what it's like to live in Bunbury, Western Australia (WA) and the things that the government does for people with disabilities. The City of Bunbury is 180 kilometres south of Perth, in the south west corner of WA. About 32,000 people live in the City of Bunbury. There are also other shires near Bunbury – for example, the Shire of Harvey, where some of us live. A shire is a local government area. The Greater Bunbury Region includes the Shires of Harvey, Dardanup and Capel. Altogether, about 80,000 people live in Greater Bunbury. There are a lot of kangaroos in Bunbury too; you see them all the time on the golf course in Australind, at the Bird Park, and at the University. Edith Cowan University has a regional campus in Bunbury, which is where Adam and Kathy work.

Adam and Kathy organised meetings and helped us write this chapter. We met five times – each time we met, we had lunch first and then we had a group discussion for two hours. We made recordings of our discussions and Kathy typed up what we said in the recordings and used our words to write the chapter. We talked about whether we would use our real names in the chapter, or just our first name, or choose another name – we all did what we wanted to do. We have used real names for most of the organisations we talk about in the chapter – but in a few places, we have used a false name and put it in inverted commas. We have written the chapter as a group and when one person is speaking for themselves, their words are indented.

We know each other from going to the same schools or day centres, or from Advocacy South West. Some of us would say we have learning difficulties, others prefer to say we have special needs – and the rest of us don't say anything! We don't think we should be separated out from other people, the important thing is to mix in with everyone else and Bunbury and Australind are good places to live if you want to be part of the community.

Living in Bunbury

Bunbury isn't in the country – well technically it is, but it doesn't look like it! Bunbury's a regional city and it's big enough to have two hospitals – a public hospital, and the St John of God private hospital. Both hospitals are on the same site, next door to each other. Australind is a country town in the Shire of Harvey. Three of us live in Australind and people are very friendly there – you can go into town and get things done because people help you. Australind is a really great spot and a great community. People are also very helpful in Bunbury, where the rest of us live. You can go to the Post Office in Bunbury and people will help you. And they help you in the street as well, if you need some help.

There's a very beautiful spot near Bunbury and Australind – it's called Buffalo Beach and it's in the Leschenault Conservation Park – there's a lovely beach and lots of bush walks. Bunbury has lots of beaches as well. The beaches we like are Koombana Bay and Jetty Baths – you can see a beautiful water scene at Jetty Baths and there used to be an old wooden jetty there, but it's gone now. Bunbury is a good place to come for a holiday – it has a Taffy shop which sells handmade toffees, ten pin bowling and the Grand Cinema. There's a Dome café and lots of other cafés as well. Bunbury is famous for a building called the Milk Carton, which looks just like a milk carton! The weather here is about average for Australia – not too hot and not too cold, most of the time. But it can get very hot in summer!

Bunbury is not quite as modern as Perth – it's a little bit old fashioned. We go to Perth sometimes on the train or the coach, but not that often. We like living in Bunbury because it's not as fast as Perth and it's easier to get around. Some of us drive our own cars – it's easier to drive in Bunbury than in Perth. Perth is a lot busier and there are a lot more accidents – and more coppers! There are accidents in Bunbury, but not so many.

People from different cultures live in Bunbury and there's a Multicultural Festival – one of us helps with the Multicultural Festival every year.

> I'm interested in multicultural things and I have friends from church who are from countries in Africa and the Pacific Islands too.

One of us used to come to Bunbury for respite and then moved into Bunbury because there are more opportunities. You can go on excursions if you live in Bunbury, on a coach to places like Pemberton. But if you live outside Bunbury you can't really go on excursions because they start from Bunbury.

Bunbury's a great place to live with beautiful sunsets all year round!

The government

Before we explain what the government does for people with disabilities we're going to say something about voting. All Australian citizens have to vote in the elections. If you don't vote, you get a fine. They send a letter to your house – we know people who've been fined! You also get fined if you don't fill in the Census. The Australian Census happens every five years. We just had the 2016 Census. Some of us don't have to fill in our own Census because we live with our family and our house is behind their house, like a granny flat. It counts as the same household, so they fill it in for us. The government does the Census to make the country a better place, to plan for the future. The Census has questions about disability, so they can make plans for people with disabilities for the future.

In Australia, there's the Federal Government (also called the Government of the Commonwealth of Australia), State government and local government and there's also the Indigenous Land Corporation, NGOs (Non-Governmental Organisations), church groups and charities. The Federal Government in Canberra decides some things for Western Australia and Bunbury. The State government for Western Australia is in Perth, they decide some things for Bunbury as well. The City of Bunbury is local government.

These days, a lot of the government in Australia works by computers, laptops, tablets and even mobile phones. If you want to do something to do with the government you can find their website and get the information. But if you live in Bunbury or Australind, it's easy to meet the politicians. We know John Castrilli (Member of the Western Australian Legislative Assembly) and Nola Marino (Federal Member of Parliament). One of us meets up with John Castrilli once a year for a coffee and a catch up. Most of us have seen Nola Marino – she's interested in disability and always talks to us when we see her.

Help you get from the government

If you have a disability you get the Disability Pension from the Federal Government. They pay you the money straight into your bank account. Everyone who gets the pension gets a Pensioner Concession card, that's everyone in the Australian states and territories, including the Australian Capital Territory (which is surrounded by New South Wales). You get the Pensioner Concession card from the Australian Government Department of Human Services – from the Federal Government, that's the same as the Commonwealth Government – they send it to you in the post. You can use it to get discounts:

> When I go to my local swimming pool I get a discount when I show my Pension card – the pool's run by the Shire.

If you get the Disability Pension, you can get other cards too. If you live in a regional area, you can get a Fuel card, which you can use for taxis or to buy petrol. You get $575 a year on your Fuel card, and they send you another card in June or July, for the next year. Some people with disabilities can get taxi vouchers as well – in a voucher book. They're called TUSS vouchers (taxi users' subsidy scheme) and you get them from the Department of Transport. Not everyone can get taxi vouchers – you have to see the doctor first and they sign a form. When you show the Fuel card to the taxi driver they give you a discount. You can use your Fuel card to discount your taxi voucher book too.

And if you have a car you can get a discount on the rego (motor vehicle registration) for your car.

Once a year, near your birthday you get a free pass from TransWA to go on a journey and you can go as far as Kalgoorlie. It comes in the post and arrives in your mailbox, just before your birthday.

Another card you can get is the National Disability Service Companion card. This means that you can take a companion with you to lots of things and they can get in for free. You have to pay, but your companion doesn't have to pay, not a cent! They can get in free at the cinema and if you go to the Medieval Festival in Balingup – your companion can get in free there as well.

If you are new to Bunbury and you want to find out about the cards and discounts for people with disabilities, you can go to Centrelink which is run by the Australian Government Department of Human Services. Lots of towns have a Centrelink. If you go there, they tell you what you are entitled to. The government doesn't send someone from Centrelink to sort it out for you, you have to go and see them. Or you could go to the Post Office and they would help you fill in some forms. Or you can look it up on a computer and find out that way.

Disability Services Commission

The WA Disability Services Commission helps people with disabilities. They have Local Area Co-ordinators (LACs) who can come to your home and help you with any problems that you have. If there's problems where you live, or if your hot water system gets stolen (which happened to one of us), your LAC can help you get transferred to a new unit (a 'unit' is a unit of accommodation, like a flat). They can arrange for you to be transferred out of the unit that you're in now, to another unit in another area. They can get money for things too, like getting you going to the gym or the pool. And they can get money for a carer for you, and help you find the carer as well. There are disability organisations (NGOs) in Bunbury which provide support and carers for people with disabilities.

LACs can help you find work experience as well, or help you find a job. And they can arrange for you to go for an appointment at a Special Needs Centre up in Perth.

> My LAC helps me do things for myself as much as I can, helps enable
> and support me in the things I like doing – like going to football,
> going to the pub on St Patrick's Day, and helping me look at my

family tree. I've actually found my ancestors who came from County Clare in Ireland to Australia 200 years ago!

But there's some things that the government doesn't help you with and then you need your family, or your friends or your church to help you.

> I've got cockroaches and mice. I got the spray guy come in and he sprayed the whole house and I got the bill and it was $179 and I had to pay that. If you've got cockroaches or mice you don't get any help from the government sorting it out!

Medicare and doctors

Every Australian citizen gets a Medicare card from the government to use when they go to the doctor. Sometimes when you go to the doctor, Medicare pays half of the bill and you have to pay the other half. You have to pay from your own pocket – how much you pay depends on how long the appointment is. If it's for 5 or 10 minutes it's about $50 or $60, but if they bulk bill, you pay nothing! That means the government pays for you. But some doctors won't do it, they won't do bulk billing and that means you have to pay to see the doctor. You have to ask them if they do bulk billing before you make an appointment. If a doctor does bulk billing and if you show your Medicare card and show your Pensioner Concession card, then it costs you nothing. Once you're in their system, you don't have to keep showing your cards.

If you know the right doctors to go to you can see the doctor and get everything completely free. If you have to go to hospital it's free, if you go to the public hospital – but you have to pay at the private hospital. Some people pay for a Health Insurance card which they can use to pay for the private hospital.

Housing

You can apply for housing from the Western Australian government or from housing associations like Homes West, or Access Housing. It can take a long time to get a house or unit and you don't always get what you want. You might want two bedrooms so you can find a friend to share with you, but if you are on your own they will only give you a one bedroom unit. Sometimes there are problems with the unit they give you. Sometimes the walls are very thin between you and next door and you can hear noise through the walls. And sometimes you can smell the cigarette smoke if the person next door is smoking – if they want to smoke they should go outside!

You can apply to move but you might have to wait quite a while to get a new unit and it would be difficult to get one with two bedrooms. You can apply to other housing providers at the same time if you want to move, everyone can do that – you don't have to stay with the same one. If you have problems with your housing, your LAC can help you sort it out.

Employment

Some of us have had paid work and some of us have done work experience. If you're on the pension, and you get paid for work, you have to report your earnings to Centrelink – you can do it on the internet. If you work part-time, and someone helps you to report your earnings on the Tuesday (on the internet) then you get paid on the Thursday (into your bank account).

We've done different kinds of work. Two of us have worked at Woolies (Woolworths supermarket), collecting trollies and baskets. We liked working there and we'd like to go back. It isn't easy to get a job. There's lots of people with disabilities who want a job but they can't get one. Some people just don't want people who've got disabilities in their business. It's not all of them, but some employers are prejudiced against people with disabilities.

All of us keep busy and work when we can. Here are some of the things we've been doing.

> If I wasn't working with my family's business, it would be harder for me, because I'd be stuck at home doing nothing. 'Jobs4U' got me a job before, picking flowers, but it wasn't for long. The most help I've had is from my family and if they didn't help me I'd just be at home.

> I work with my family's building business. I'm a house re-stumper. I go underneath the house (old wooden house) and get the old stumps out and put new ones in. You have to dig holes underneath the house to take out the old stumps. You put jacks next to the old wooden stump and then take it out, dig it right out and make sure the old foot plate is out. Then you get your new sole plate and put that down and make it level and get the new stump and put a tin end cap (to stop white ants) on top of it, then you bang the new stump in with a hammer and make sure it's level. Then you fill in the hole and bang nails in at the top.

> I also do house removing – that's taking away a whole house, not taking away the furniture. You saw the house in half and drive half the house away and put it somewhere else. Then you drive back and get the other half. But we don't do house removing much these days.

> My social worker from the 'Out and About Club' got me work experience at Coles New World (supermarket) in Collie when I lived there – collecting up the trollies outside. I work in the bakery at Woolies now, they call me the Bakery Assistant. I usually work

from 8 to 12 Monday, Wednesday and Thursday. I have to report my earnings to Centrelink as well.

I drive into Bunbury to look for work. I go to different businesses and to 'Jobs4U' and they help me. They say if I do courses I can get a job, but I don't want to do any more courses because I've done them over and over again – how to dress for a job, how you should present yourself, that sort of thing. I've done all the courses, now I want a job!

I work at Kindy (Kindergarten) one day a week. I started working there more than 10 years ago. I do a lot at home for them as well – cutting circles out, cutting rabbits out. They keep saying come back next year – they don't want to lose me!

I work at Good Sammy's (Good Samaritan Industries) in retail. I serve the customers. I take their money and fold up the clothes. I like working there – there isn't anything I don't like about it.

I used to work at Hungry Jack's. I worked there for 21 years. Washing-up, serving cool drinks and wiping the tables as well. It was paid work, my money was paid straight into the bank.

I used to work at Hungry Jack's too.

I did work experience out at the Environmental Centre last year but I didn't like it! I didn't like working outside and I didn't like the flies or the heat – but I stuck it out for a couple of months and they were very proud of me. I would like to go back to the workforce, not rush it but find something that suits me – I want to be part of the workforce again, but I don't want to work outside.

Transport

The government provides cheap bus fares for people with disabilities. It's not completely free – you have to pay a bit sometimes. But from 9am to 3pm on weekdays it's completely free and it's completely free at the weekends.

My unit's just round the corner from the bus stop. It only costs me $1.20 to get into town in the week.

In my area, no buses come past us, so we have to walk about a kilometre to the nearest bus stop. We both drive a car but I'd rather catch the bus because it's cheaper.

Because I've got a car, I can keep in touch with my family and friends. I drive into town two or three days a week.

I don't drive and where I live, there's no buses on a Sunday. If there's no buses, then you have to get a taxi and it's expensive! With your Fuel card you only get a certain amount of taxis. I'd come into Bunbury and go to the beach if there was buses on Sunday.

Spare time

We do lots of things in our spare time. Some of us go to dance classes at Bunbury Dance Studio – we do ballroom dancing, rock and roll, all different sorts of dancing – everything! We've been going for a long time. Some of us have passed all the different levels and even won medals. We also like to meet our friends for coffee and go to the movies and out for meals. Some of us have other hobbies too.

Two of us grow vegetables – so far, we've grown parsley and spring onions, but we want to try growing other vegetables and strawberries.

I do umpiring for HBL (Harvey Brunswick Lions). I do the kids matches – I go all over the place doing umpiring for all the different matches.

I'm getting things organised for my 50th birthday party – I've been planning it for a long time! And I've been doing a history of my birth mum.

Some of us would like to do cooking classes in our spare time. You can do cooking classes at 'Day Activities Incorporated' – they do other activities there as well but it's expensive because you have to pay a HACC fee (Home and Community Care fee). If you go on an excursion with them, they charge you the full cost of the excursion and a HACC fee of $8 on top!

Questions from Adam and Kathy

Adam asked us if we had ever made a complaint or if we knew how to make a complaint or who to complain to if we were unhappy with disability services. None of us had ever made a complaint – but people have made complaints about us!

One of us has just heard that their support hours have been cut from 20 hours a week to 16 hours a week and they don't know why. They are upset about it and thinking about maybe making a complaint.

Kathy asked us if we had heard of the NDIS – the National Disability Insurance Scheme. Only one of us had heard of the NDIS – they saw it on television, on the ABC (Australian Broadcasting Commission) news.

It means people with disability decide for themselves. Ourselves, we decide.

But if someone else is choosing how many hours of support you get, you can't choose then. That's not fair is it?

Questions from the editors

The editors of this book asked if things were staying the same, getting better or getting worse for people with disabilities like us, who live in Bunbury. Some of us think things are getting worse, and some of us think things are getting better – but there's still a long way to go! We talked about what things were like ten years ago and what things are like now.

It's better for me now, I've got my own unit.

Things are better for me now. Ten years ago I was trying to get help because I couldn't write and I couldn't do things. I had no money and I didn't know what to do. I had a couple of jobs but they weren't full-time ones. I started out working for my Dad but he decided to retire. Then I was working with my brother, but we were getting less work – and what could I do? And then I found out from 'Jobs4U' that I could get the Disability Pension. Things are better now, because I've got more money and I've still got some work with my family, but the times are changing, everything's changing. There's not many houses that need re-stumping now and they're not moving houses – the houses are different now, they're not made of wood and you can't move them.

It's a lot different now. Ten years ago, I'd just left school and I was trying to look for jobs. It was hard but it's more difficult for people leaving school now who are trying to look for jobs. It was easier for me ten years ago. Now people have to use a computer for everything – even to get your driver's licence! When I got my licence it was so easy, you didn't have to use the computer.

Ten years ago, when you went to the cash registers in the supermarket, you used to be able to talk to a real person – but that's changing. At first they put in five self-service machines with one person to help you. Now they've put in ten machines and one person to help. That's cutting people's jobs and it's more difficult to do. Sometimes I put my money in and it spits it back out at me!

There is help for people like us who want to get a job or get their driving licence but it's getting harder and harder to get jobs now.[1] We should have the right to work but it's hard to get a job here now.

Aboriginal people with disabilities

The editors also asked what things are like for Indigenous or Aboriginal people with disabilities. We don't really know because none of us are from Aboriginal families and we're not in touch with any Aboriginal people with disabilities.[2] When one of us was at special school for children with disabilities, there were three children from an Aboriginal family there, but that was in another town. One of us is interested in multiculturalism and wanted to meet Indigenous people, and then they got a new support worker who is Indigenous.

> One of my back-up support workers is Indigenous – her daughter is Indigenous too – that's the only people I know. Her daughter's a Dockers (football team) supporter like me, and she gives me a half price haircut at the Hairdressers where she works!

What we would like to be different

Most of us are very happy living in Bunbury and Australind – one of us said:

> I just want to say that I'm very happy here, I've got great workers and my church group and my family are very supportive, all of them!

But there are a few things we would like to be different:

> I want buses on Sundays.

> It's expensive to run a car – if we can't have buses near us, it would be good to have a new car!

> A social club with excursions and meeting for coffee and pizza. We had a social club before. I'm proud of what we had in the past and I know how it was set up. I would like to get something like that up and running again. I'm going to organise a Halloween pizza night at our place and ask everyone to bring $5 to pay for the pizza.

> More jobs and more work experience.

What it was like writing this chapter

We enjoyed meeting to write this chapter. We've never done anything like this before – never!

It's been excellent!

I like telling my story.

I want to thank my sister who has done a lot for me. I want to say thank you to my sister Theresia.

I'd like a copy of the chapter for two politicians I know, John Castrilli and Nola Marino, who are interested in disability.

It will be good to hear what people think – I hope they get in touch.

We'd like to know what it is like in other places and countries for people with disabilities.

We'd like them to see our chapter, so they can read it and see what life is like in Bunbury.

We hope you have enjoyed reading our chapter. If you would like to get in touch with us, please email Kathy Boxall (k.boxall@ecu.edu.au).

Acknowledgements

We would like to acknowledge the support of the City of Bunbury Library and use of their Activity Room for meetings to write this chapter.

Notes

[1] In July 2006, the unemployment rate for Western Australia (for people aged 15+ years) was 2.9%; and in July 2016 it was 6.3% (ABS, 2016).
[2] The prevalence of disability in the Indigenous population is higher than for the Australian population as a whole, but Indigenous people with disability are less likely to access services. Research by John Gilroy et al (2016) identified 12 factors that that influence the participation of Aboriginal people in disability services – for example, colonisation and trauma, racism, trustworthiness of services, and community connections.

References

ABS (2016) *Labour Market Data: Unemployment Rate, Participation Rate and Employment Rate Time Series for States/Territories*, Australian Bureau of Statistics.

Gilroy, J., Donelly, M., Colmar, S. and Parmenter, T. (2016) 'Twelve factors that can influence the participation of Aboriginal people in disability services', *Australian Indigenous Health Bulletin*, 16 (1), http://healthbulletin.org.au/wp-content/uploads/2016/03/bulletin_original_articles_Gilroy.pdf

14

Renewing epistemologies: service user knowledge

Diana Rose

Introduction

This chapter will focus on mental health service users and survivors with attention not only to health systems but to housing, welfare benefits and poverty. In terms of disability more generally I shall also have something to say about deaf people particularly as regards education policy. The main object of the chapter is to contest privileged knowledge in social policy and associated practices by exposing its nature and to counterpose this with 'knowledge from below'. I will argue that this knowledge is collective at two levels: in the discourses produced by organisations of users of welfare services; and then in the development of this by new forms of theoretical and empirical knowledge taking shape in the academy and other spaces by service user researchers engaged in transforming how we think about the welfare state and social policy. It is important to state at the outset that these forms of knowledge are not uniform. This is partly because different groups of service users are positioned differently both by the welfare state and also in how they respond to it, a set of differences captured by the term 'intersectionality'. However, epistemological responses themselves are not homogenous and there is increasing debate on just how the situation of users of the welfare state should be understood.

Links with feminism

Looking back at the rise of the mental health survivor movement, Judi Chamberlin made explicit links with the feminist practice of consciousness raising (Chamberlin, 1990). Writing in an Indian context, Davar shows how the survivor movement grew out of the Indian feminist movement (Davar, 2013), which exposed the detrimental effects of patriarchy on women's emotional health. Elsewhere, I have argued that feminist epistemology holds lessons for survivor epistemology (Rose, 2009). However, there is a problem when it is a question of the contemporary welfare state. There is a voluminous feminist literature on women as informal carers of older and disabled people and this is seen as an emotional labour that is part of the difficult oppression of the politics of the personal (Ungerson, 1987). Often the word 'burden' is used and in the case of carers of people with diagnoses of severe mental health conditions there is even a scale to measure 'carers' burden' (Scazufca and Kuipers, 1996). Again, even when it is a case of formal care delivered from within a state apparatus, feminists may assume that disability is unproblematically a matter of welfare responsibility (Fraser, 2013). I do not argue that caring is a simple matter, materially or emotionally, quite the reverse. However, these arguments position welfare users as people who cannot have a voice of their own. I make these points because later I will argue that renewing epistemologies around welfare and social policy can learn much from critical theory, including feminist theory. But as long as welfare recipients are understood as sources of burden or the evident responsibility of a welfare state that goes uncriticised, there may be difficulties in effecting a theoretical rapprochement.

Service users and their organisations

Service user organisations offer spaces where experiences can be shared, validated and, critically, reframed. These organisations require both structural and cultural conditions to emerge and be sustained. For people with sensory or physical impairments, people with learning disabilities and mental health system survivors, one of these conditions was an end to segregation in institutions. To be sure, little acts of resistance are commonplace in institutions and there is theoretical writing about this (Vinthagen and Johansson, 2013). But such is the level of regimentation that the organisation of residents to effect change is prohibited, even unthinkable (Goffman, 1968). At the same time, there is a culture of inmates in such places commonly characterised by solidarity and the sharing of information and this can sow the seeds for later developments.

Across the Western world, deinstitutionalisation began in the last quarter of the 20th century. The reasons are fiercely debated (Scull, 2015; Porter, 1987). However, the closure of the institutions was one condition for the emergence of independent user organisations. In the early days, these were not user-led but included carers and often social workers committed to community forms of provision. Nurses were less conspicuously present (Campbell, 1996). There could also be real tensions between such groups and social policy academics seeking to support them as witnessed in the debate between the Union of the Physically Impaired Against Segregation and Peter Townsend, Professor of Social Policy at the London School of Economics (UPIaS and Disability Alliance, 1975). Key to this debate was the distinction between organisations 'for' disabled people and organisations 'of' disabled people. The distinction first emerged in the thinking of activists with physical and sensory impairments but spread rapidly. This shows that the relation between deinstitutionalisation and activism is neither causal nor one-way. The forms of solidarity present in institutions are reinvented and reframed in activist organisations and changing policy meant residents were active in the transformation. Neither are these organisations a result of radical new thinking by academics or professionals. In respect of psychiatry, the Survivors History Group argues that Nick Crossley is quite wrong in his assessment that the users' movement grew out of anti-psychiatry. They see psychiatric survivor activism as an autonomous, grassroots development with a complex relation to institutions (Crossley, 2005; The Survivors History Group, 2012).

Structural and systemic change is insufficient as a condition for the emergence of user organisations. Cultural and political change is also important. In the 1970s and 1980s the civil rights movement was at its height and many left wing groups were becoming disenchanted with Marxism's exclusively class-based analysis. So new social movements emerged which residual Marxists termed 'superstructural' and others called liberation. There were movements of women, people of colour, post-colonial peoples and LGBTQ groups. Disability organisations can be situated here as can their focus on the social determinants of disability and the development of a social model (Finkelstein, 2001). It is worth noting that this model has long come in for development and reassessment (Shakespeare and Watson, 2001). For many years, organisations of people with learning disabilities or mental health diagnoses were somewhat marginalised from this cultural and political shift. This may be related to my earlier comments about feminist positions on disability but there are probably deeper reasons to which I shall return. However, debate concerning the links between physical disability and distress is now well-established (Spandler et al, 2015; Beresford et al, 2010).

Finally, institutional and cultural and political change can take other forms. The education of children with sensory impairments is becoming mainstreamed. Parents worry about bullying. But 'integration' may dilute the potential for activism. When deaf or blind children are educated together, a distinct culture emerges and when certain conditions pertain, the impairment can be reframed in cultural minority terms. Hence deaf activists distinguish themselves from other disabled groups by capitalising Deaf and campaign for their rights on the grounds of being a linguistic minority (Lane et al, 1996; Lane, 2005).

I do not wish to imply that large sections of welfare recipients are now engaged in action for change or in a human rights struggle. Most are not. However, I would argue that these movements are now part of the cultural and political landscape, at least in the industrialised West. They may come in many forms and they may be resisted to the point of ridicule but they can no longer be ignored.

The movements just described themselves have created new knowledge by reframing what it means to be a disabled person, someone with a mental health diagnosis, a deaf person and so on as well as being a welfare recipient. This knowledge contests mainstream privileged knowledge. As this chapter concerns epistemology, the next step is to try to elaborate this knowledge and locate it in a broader literature. The appropriate literature is a critical one which has already contested mainstream knowledge from the perspectives of marginalised groups.

Renewing epistemologies: drawing on critical theory

If part of the goal of social movements is to reimagine members' social position and to press for change, the role of theorists is to introduce and elaborate the knowledge and practices thus generated into academic and other spaces that formalise knowledge either theoretical or empirical. Mainstream social policy thinking positions welfare recipients as a social problem and as passive vesicles for state benevolence. Some are positioned as not even deserving benevolence – the age-old distinction between the deserving and the undeserving poor. This has been well documented by Beresford (Beresford, 2016a). I propose then to draw on the critical literature developed in feminist, post-colonial, queer and disability studies with my earlier caveat about caring by women.

A primary means through which mainstream academic knowledge is contested is by appeal to the experience of people about whom theories are being developed and towards whom interventions are intended. Experiential knowledge is argued to be a specific form of expertise that should be incorporated in research and theory-building (Gillard et al, 2010; Slade et al, 2010; Faulkner and Thomas, 2002). Some go further in arguing that experiential knowledge is superior to knowledge that proclaims itself 'objective' and value-free (Beresford, 2003). This is an epistemological claim concerning how to ground credible knowledge.

There are, however, problems with appeals to experience if that is conceived as the experience of individuals. Scott has argued, in the context of critical history, that 'experience' has become a foundational category and is assumed to inhere in individual psychology (Scott, 1991). For Scott, as a post-structuralist, all experience is conditioned by discourse and the power relations which characterise the institutions involved. While this argument has been very influential in critical theory, it has also been held to homogenise marginalised social groups. Within feminism this problem of what came to be termed 'intersectionality' was recognised very early, particularly with regard to racialised groups (McCall, 2005; Crenshaw, 1991; Hooks, 1982). Within the emerging field of Mad Studies considerable attention is also being paid to issues of ethnicity, gender, sexuality and disability (Spandler et al, 2015; Tien, 2015; Kalathil, 2008). One response has been to emphasise the multiple differences and identities that characterise any socially marginalised group (Voronka, forthcoming) but this runs the risk of returning to a conceptual focus on individuals and a political focus on what divides rather than connects us. It is not unknown for fierce arguments to break out that take the form 'you can't know my experience'.

There would seem to be a difficult tension when experience is used as a central epistemological category between emphasising its socially constructed character and a turn to phenomenology and individual difference. Peter Beresford seems to have recently firmed up his position on experience as a collective phenomenon inhering in disabled people's organisations (Beresford, 2016b).

It is here that I would argue lessons can be learned from feminism. Early on in second wave feminism and especially among radical feminists there were arguments that women's experience was fundamentally different to that of men (Echols, 1989). However, feminist theorists later came to question this essentialism. Sandra Harding argues that a feminist standpoint is achieved and not assigned by nature and it is achieved through political and theoretical struggle (Harding, 2004). She later argued that the role of feminist scholars is to systematically 'study up' what women bring to activism and indeed the lives of women in general (Harding, 2008). Harding's arguments hinge on the insistence that 'experience' is collectively grounded but located in a particular politics that affects many more than declared activists.

Standpoint epistemology as developed by writers such as Harding has been critiqued as 'relativist' on the basis that the position of women varies so considerably across the world and that multiple interpretations of these positionings are possible. The epistemology itself contains no criteria for adjudicating between different positions and so we have not just epistemological but also ontological and moral relativism. Harding does in fact offer a theory of 'strong objectivity' (Harding, 1991) but for reasons of space I will deal with this issue by addressing the work of Donna Haraway.

In my view, the best counter to the charge of relativism has been provided by Donna Haraway (Haraway, 1988; Haraway and Goodeve, 2013). Haraway is a biologist and primatologist making her unusual in this field where social science and the humanities dominate. She describes mainstream science as playing 'the God trick'. This means that such science and its underlying epistemology hold that science can be universal, applicable across all time and place, and that the scientist is the value-free, objective, universal knower. Of course, social scientists have done much work on differences between social groups, domestically and internationally, but the methods used are believed to be universally applicable and there has always been an assumption, explicit or tacit, that all should aspire to the image of the Western white middle-class family. Haraway takes Thomas Kuhn's critique of 'normal science' to its logical conclusion (Kuhn, 2012). If contemporary normal social science rests on an epistemology of universal knowledge and the universal knower, critical theory promises a paradigm shift. Haraway argues that *all* knowledge is partial because it is situated in the beliefs and values of social groups – mainstream groups no less than those denied access to privileged knowledge. Knowledge for Haraway is doubly situated – it springs from the lives and values of particular social groups but it is also situated in its nature as it can never be universal. It follows that an epistemology that is explicit about its social and political grounding is more transparent than one that denies its location in particular social configurations. This does mean that knowledge in general would be the sum and interaction of particular situated knowledges and they would be multiple. But mainstream knowledge is no longer privileged and so knowledge generation has the potential to be more democratic. For Harding and Haraway and other critical theorists the knowledge of marginalised groups is to be privileged also on political and ethical grounds because they have always been the object of knowledge and now can be its subjects. Gayatri Spivak, writing from a post-colonial perspective, put the question nicely when she asked 'Can the subaltern speak?' (Spivak, 1988). I would contend also that this approach goes some way to address the intersectionality issue. In the next section I shall consider how far these briefly sketched ideas may help to develop a theoretical framework for understanding and contesting the situation of welfare recipients. For reasons of space, the focus will be on the UK.

Renewing epistemologies for social welfare practices

The above arguments suggest that service user knowledge has a double nature. First is the knowledge generated in organisations of disabled people, those with sensory impairments or users or survivors of psychiatry and this knowledge is generated as they validate and re-frame their traditionally allocated place in welfare structures. Second is the knowledge that starts with this but elaborates it in relation to other theoretical and empirical discourses, in the above argument by locating it in critical theory. The crucial point, however, is that this knowledge contests what has always been privileged – the universalist theories of social policy and the practices that (supposedly) derive from them. These are seen to be no longer tenable and so there is a theoretical and political struggle to displace privileged knowledge and foreground the understandings of those who previously were silenced so that new forms of practice can emerge. It is these that are important. Those of us who develop theory work in the foothills and the ultimate test of the kinds of argument that I have developed above is whether they are useful in changing practice. I would argue that there is also a role for intervening in mainstream discourse itself because privileged knowledge is powerful and needs to be challenged.

At this point I would like to consider the politics of working in the academy and make what may seem a surprising argument. This concerns mental health research in England so it is a particular argument but may have more general applicability. England's main health research funder, the National Institute for Health Research (NIHR), has made a strong commitment to 'Patient and Public Involvement (PPI)' in research. Mental health has been the domain where this has been most developed. A recent paper estimated that 800 persons in England identified as 'service user researchers' and the authors called this a 'hidden workforce' (Patterson et al, 2014). However, the same year that this article was published, the network lost its infrastructure and the 800 service user researchers no longer had a coherent voice (Rose, 2015). It is important to point out that this network was very constrained in what it could do. It could make little difference to standard methodologies and it was driven by a 'clinical' agenda (Jones and Brown, 2012). It certainly did not broach questions of epistemology because it worked in a framework that denies it has any underlying theoretical principles – usually termed positivism. It could be argued to be only 'tinkering at the edges'. However, activity was substantial and certainly research questions shifted. Most of the individuals involved in this network had left school early because of mental distress and had no formal qualifications. I venture then that, whatever else it was, this network was an exercise in the democratisation of science. The new orthodoxy in mental health research is Mad Studies emanating from Canada (Burstow et al, 2014; Menzies et al, 2013) but rapidly growing in Europe especially England (McWade et al, 2015; Beresford and Russo, 2016; Russo and Sweeney, 2016). It is an exciting development but I think it runs a risk. The concepts and theories being developed are sophisticated and most of the prominent writers have PhDs or are candidates (this is not entirely so with the Russo and Sweeney collection). The discourse is actually alien to representatives of the 'hidden workforce' to whom I have spoken. So despite its avowed and best intentions I would argue that Mad Studies runs the risk of being elitist and leaving behind people who put enormous effort into PPI in mental health research. Of course by writing this chapter I may be running the self-same risk. It is a perennial problem for any theoretical work on marginalised groups and was certainly a problem in early second wave feminism where people building theory were labelled 'theoreticist'. The dilemma is that the academy and other spaces can open their doors but not much changes in terms of the means of knowledge production or real change is promised but those doors remain closed to large sections of the community. I do not have an answer but just lay the dilemma on the table in light of what seems to be the current rush to embrace Mad Studies.

Participatory social policy

Peter Beresford has argued cogently for a new form of welfare provision based on participatory principles (Beresford, 2016a). This would seem to be the logical form of practice that aligns with the arguments I have made here. Knowledge is power. If social policy theory and practice are found wanting in their knowledge base and if welfare recipients are generating practical and formal knowledge that challenges this then power relations should shift in favour of those who previously were seen only as needy, troublesome or irrational. The argument is not that the welfare state should be dismantled because the structures and personnel base their practice on flawed premises. Flawed premises are neither determinant nor do they embrace all theory of practice. It is more a call for dialogue and the shifting of power relations because recipients now have something fundamental to teach practitioners. Doubtless they always had but were never listened to or were pathologised.

I would just like to conclude on a note of caution. This shift to a more equal and participatory welfare state is not going to be easy. While for Beresford, it is a question of opening up spaces for previously silenced groups to find their own analyses and alternative arrangements, in other texts this move self-consciously advocates utopia – or 'eutopia', almost a return to primitive communism (Burstow, 2015). In current conditions of hate crime and austerity, this seems very naïve as it underestimates the strength and reach of conditions that need to be overturned before change will be possible. Pre-figurative struggle is important but it is not enough. This is not meant to be a counsel of despair nor to undermine the changes that have and can be brought about. It is simply to draw attention to the overwhelming power of the structural forces, including economic forces, in which these are situated. The same applies to shifting understandings.

References

Beresford, P. (2003) *It's Our Lives: A short theory of knowledge, distance and experience*, London: OSP.

Beresford, P. (2016a) *All Our Welfare: Towards participatory social policy*, Bristol: Policy Press.

Beresford, P. (2016b) 'The role of survivor knowledge in creating alternatives to psychiatry', in J. Russo and A. Sweeney (eds) *Searching for a Rose Garden: Challenging Psychiatry, Fostering Mad Studies*, Monmouth: PCCS Books.

Beresford, P. and Russo, J. (2016) 'Supporting the sustainability of Mad Studies and preventing its co-option', *Disability & Society*, 1–5.

Beresford, P., Nettle, M. and Perring, E. (2010) *Towards a Social Model of Madness and Distress*, Londo:, Joseph Rowntree Foundation.

Burstow, B. (2015) *Psychiatry and the Business of Madness: An Ethical and Epistemological Accounting*. London and New York: Palgrave Macmillan.

Burstow, B., Lefrançois, B.A. and Diamond, S. (2014) *Psychiatry Disrupted: Theorizing Resistance and Crafting the (R) evolution*, Montreal and Kingston, Canada: McGill-Queen's Press-MQUP.

Campbell, P. (1996) 'The history of the user movement in the United Kingdom', in *Mental health matters: A reader*. London and New York: Springer.

Chamberlin, J. (1990) 'The ex-patients' movement: Where we've been and where we're going', *Journal of Mind and Behavior*, 11, 323–36.

Crenshaw, K. (1991) 'Mapping the margins: Intersectionality, identity politics, and violence against women of color', *Stanford Law Review*, 1241–99.

Crossley, N. (2005) *Contesting psychiatry: Social movements in mental health*, London: Routledge.

Davar, B. (2013) 'From mental illness to disability: choices for women users / survivors of psychiatry in self and identity constructions', in R. Addlakha (ed) *Disability Studies in India: Global Discourses, Local Realities*, New Dehli, Abingdon: Routledge.

Echols, A. (1989) *Daring to be bad: Radical feminism in America, 1967–1975*, Minneapolis: University of Minnesota Press.

Faulkner, A. and Thomas, P. (2002) 'User-led research and evidence-based medicine', *The British Journal of Psychiatry*, 180, 1–3.

Finkelstein, V. (2001) 'The social model of disability repossessed', *Manchester Coalition of Disabled People*, 1.

Fraser, N. (2013) *Fortunes of feminism: From state-managed capitalism to neoliberal crisis*, London: Verso Books.

Gillard, S., Borschmann, R., Turner, K., Goodrich-Purnell, N., Lovell, K. and Chambers, M. (2010) '"What difference does it make?" Finding evidence of the impact of mental health service user researchers on research into the experiences of detained psychiatric patients', *Health Expectations*, 13, 185–94.

Goffman, E. (1968) *Asylums: Essays on the social situation of mental patients and other inmates*, New Jersey: AldineTransaction.

Haraway, D. (1988) 'Situated knowledges: The science question in feminism and the privilege of partial perspective', *Feminist Studies*, 14, 575–99.

Haraway, D. and Goodeve, T. (2013) *How like a leaf: An interview with Donna Haraway*, London and New York: Routledge.

Harding, S. (1991) '"Strong objectivity" and socially situated knowledge', in S. Harding (ed) *Whose Science? Whose Knowledge?*, New York: Cornell University Press.

Harding, S. (2004) 'Introduction: Standpoint Theory as a Site of Political, Philosophic, and Scientific Debate', in S. Harding (ed) *The Feminist Standpoint Theory Reader: Intellectual and political controversies*, London and New York: Routledge.

Harding, S. (2008) *Sciences from below: Feminisms, postcolonialities, and modernities*, Durham, NC: Duke University Press.

Hooks, B. (1982) *Ain't I a Woman? Black Women and Feminism*, Boston: South End.

Jones, N. and Brown, R. (2012) 'The absence of psychiatric C/S/X perspectives in academic discourse: Consequences and implications', *Disability Studies Quarterly*, 33.

Kalathil, J. (2008) *Dancing to our own Tunes: Reassessing black and minority ethnic mental health service user involvement*, London, UK: National Survivor User Network in collaboration with Catch-a-Fiya.

Kuhn, T.S. (2012) *The structure of scientific revolutions*, Chicago: University of Chicago Press.

Lane, H. (2005) 'Ethnicity, ethics, and the deaf-world', *Journal of Deaf Studies and Deaf Education,* 10, 291–310.

Lane, H.L., Hoffmeister, R. and Bahan, B.J. (1996) *A Journey into the Deaf-world*, San Diego, CA: DawnSignPress.

Mccall, L. (2005) 'The complexity of intersectionality', *Signs*, 30, 1771–800.

Mcwade, B., Milton, D. and Beresford, P. (2015) 'Mad studies and neurodiversity: a dialogue', *Disability & Society*, 30, 305–09.

Menzies, R.J., Lefrançois, B.A. and Reaume, G. (2013) *Mad Matters: A Critical reader in Canadian Mad Studies*, Canadian Scholars Press.

Patterson, S., Trite, J. and Weaver, T. (2014) 'Activity and views of service users involved in mental health research: UK survey', *The British Journal of Psychiatry*, 205, 68–75.

Porter, R. (1987) *Mind-forg'd Manacles: A history of madness in England from the Restoration to the Regency*, Harvard University Press.

Rose, D. (2009) 'Survivor produced knowledge', in S. Sweeney, P. Beresford, A. Faulkner, M. Nettle and D. Rose (eds) *This is Survivor Research*, Ross-on-Wye: PCCS Books.

Rose, D. (2015) 'The contemporary state of service-user-led research', *The Lancet. Psychiatry*, 2, 959–60.

Russo, J. and Sweeney, A. (eds) (2016) *Searching for a Rose Garden: Challenging Psychiatry, Fostering Mad Studies*, Monmouth: PCCS Books.

Scazufca, M. and Kuipers, E. (1996) 'Links between expressed emotion and burden of care in relatives of patients with schizophrenia', *The British Journal of Psychiatry*, 168, 580–7.

Scott, J.W. (1991) 'The evidence of experience', *Critical Inquiry*, 17, 773–97.

Scull, A. (2015) *Madness in civilization: A cultural history of insanity, from the Bible to Freud, from the madhouse to modern medicine*, Princeton: Princeton University Press.

Shakespeare, T. and Watson, N. (2001) 'The social model of disability: an outdated ideology?' in S.N. Barnartt and B.M. Altman (eds) *Exploring theories and expanding methodologies: Where we are and where we need to go*, JAI Press, pp 9–28.

Slade, M., Bird, V., Chandler, R., Fox, J., Larsen, J., Tew, J. and Leamy, M. (2010) 'The contribution of advisory committees and public involvement to large studies: case study', *BMC Health Service Research*, 10, 323.

Spandler, H., Anderson, J. and Sapey, B. (2015) *Madness, Distress and the Politics of Disablement*, Bristol: Policy Press.

Spivak, G.C. (1988) 'Can the subaltern speak?' in C. Nelson and L. Grossberg (eds) *Marxism and the Interpretation of Culture*, London: Macmillan Education.

The Survivors History Group (2012) 'The Survivors History Group takes a critical look at historians', in M. Barnes and P. Cotterell (eds) *Critical Perspectives on User Involvement*, Bristol: Policy Press.

Tien, S. (2015) 'Book Review: Mad Matters: A Critical Reader in Canadian Mad Studies', *Review of Disability Studies: An International Journal*, 10.

Ungerson, C. (1987) *Policy is personal: Sex, gender and informal care*, London: Tavistock.

UPIaS and Disability Alliance (1975) *Fundamental Principles of Disability*, London: Leeds University.

Vinthagen, S. and Johansson, A. (2013) 'Everyday Resistance; Exploration of a concept and its theories', *Resistance Studies Magazine*, 1, 1–46.

Voronka, J. (forthcoming) 'The politics of 'people with lived experience': Experiential authority and the risks of strategic essentialism', *Philosophy, Psychiatry & Psychology*.

15

Pornography, feminist epistemology and changing public policy

Ruth Beresford

I am currently undertaking research for my PhD into women's experiences of pornography. I have researched pornography twice before: once for a short undergraduate project and once for my Master's dissertation. Each time the research has been conducted with women living in the UK and so primarily is located within the British context; however, not all who participated were British nationals. Additionally, pornography does not necessarily have national boundaries and I have drawn upon international (though primarily Western) research and examples. This research may therefore have some international relevance, though I recognise the limitations to this given that the position of pornography within societies varies greatly globally. Pornography is a subject I have always had a political and feminist interest in, and now also an epistemological and methodological one. My interactions with it have largely been academic and pornography is not something I use or am personally interested in. It is, however, something I would consider myself to have a lived experience of, and it is this experience that has been formative in shaping my political opinions on it. As I have learned more about pornography, had new life experiences, and learned about other women's experiences, the ways in which I have sought to research pornography, and subsequently understand it as a phenomena, have changed.

In this chapter, I am going to outline why I think a feminist epistemological approach and participatory methodology to researching pornography could have innovative implications for how we seek to formulate policy and law on pornography. Put simply, I will explore why taking a feminist approach to how we develop knowledge on pornography could change how we seek to regulate it within our society. I will argue that recognising 'lived experience' as a type of expertise on pornography could be crucial in developing more relevant and sustainable public policy on pornography.

I would like to invite you read this chapter actively, and to reflect on your own experiences of pornography as you do so. By reflecting on your own lived experience, you can be the judge of my argument, and consider whether lived experience of pornography is a knowledge source missing from policy formulation and debate. What does it mean to 'experience' pornography? This is a difficult question and one that I am trying to address in my research. Try to reflect on times where you have come across or interacted with pornography in your life or in your interactions with others. I would encourage you to think broadly about ways in which you may have interacted with pornography: have you seen it? Have you used it? Have you made it? Have you shared it? Have you talked about it? Do you know somebody else who has done any of the above? Have you worried about it? Have you felt interested in it? Reflect on these questions as you read this chapter and come to your own conclusions about research on pornography.

Pornography has been cast as one of the great social problems of our time. New technologies and the internet have facilitated an availability, accessibility and diversity of materials on an unprecedented scale. Media discussions, government policy, academic research and charity reports concerned with the potentially destructive, corrupting, corrosive power of pornography are plentiful. Within these, there is a worry that it is a threat to healthy sexual practice, the welfare of women, and of young people. Pornography, we are told, has the power to shape how we understand and practise sex. There is an abundance of research and literature on pornography to support these claims. Feminist theory which is anti-pornography has long condemned pornography as patriarchal (see Andrea Dworkin, Catherine MacKinnon, Gail Dines) and there are vast psychology and criminology studies investigating the negative 'effects' of pornography on users' attitudes and behaviour (or example Malamuth et al, 1980; 2012). In the past decade in the UK we have seen significant legislative changes on pornography; for example possession of 'extreme pornography' has been criminalised and tighter regulations on online pornography have been and are being implemented. Government policy and discourse has focused on censorship, control and regulation.

However, in stark contrast to these fears are the casual and mundane ways in which pornography is referenced in everyday media and culture. There are playful references to it in films and TV, and there is a growing normalisation around pornography. In addition, we are seeing an ever growing discussion around the positive potentials of pornography. There is a growing social media presence of pornography performers who candidly discuss and promote their work. There is also a growing body of academic literature seeking to research pornography in a more diverse and critical way (for example, see *Porn Studies* journal). This research criticises the polarised nature of feminist debates on pornography and the 'cause and effect' research which has been so popular. This academic research is largely unacknowledged in government inquiries and policy documents (see Papadopolous, 2010; DfE, 2011; DfCMS, 2016).

Making sense of pornography, in our personal lives and within society, is somewhat difficult in the face of such competing and polarised narratives. If pornography is so dangerous, why is it so popular? Are we so consumed by our own desires that we use it without restraint or consideration of its effects? If pornography is so exciting, why does so much research warn us of the dangers surrounding it? Is it not a part of normalising unhealthy attitudes towards women and sex? How do we learn about the realities of pornography and what its effects or influence are? Finally, what government policy is best suited to regulating pornography within society and helping people make informed decisions around it – and how is this to be achieved?

When I first conducted research into pornography, my own opinions largely mirrored and were informed by anti-pornography standpoints and research. I conducted a small project as an undergraduate student into young women's perceptions of the male consumption of pornography. I was inspired by a conversation with a female friend who had visited Spearmint Rhinos (the lap dancing club) with a group of male friends. When I asked why she had gone, she told me that it was on her 'bucket list' and she was intrigued by the idea. This got me thinking about how women perceive the use of what I assumed were male orientated heterosexual entertainment services. I began to wonder how women felt about men using pornography given that it seemed to me to be so widespread. I was interested in how all women felt about this, not just heterosexual women, as I assumed it impacted on gender relations more broadly than just within heterosexual relationships. Personally, I found the idea of men using pornography politically troubling but felt unable to talk about this to many of my peers. I was curious about how other women felt about it and what they might tell me in the private environment of an all-female interview.

Although the project was small, I had hit upon an interesting topic area. Although much of the discussion on pornography focuses on its impact on women, there is little research that asks women how they experience it for themselves. The women I interviewed shared a diverse range of opinions on the male consumption of pornography: positive, negative, indifferent and a mix of good and bad. I decided to expand the project for my Master's dissertation and I incorporated a feminist epistemological approach and a participatory inspired methodology, having just learned about these approaches to research.

I interviewed 11 women about their perceptions of men using pornography, asking them how widespread they thought it was, and what influence they thought it had on both male and female perceptions of sex, the body and attitudes towards women. The epistemological and methodological approach I chose meant that I asked the women to play a greater role in the research process. As well as listening to their experiences, I shared my own which enabled us to reflect critically on our own opinions and experiences together. I also asked them to validate my interpretations of their responses and they were part of analysing the main themes from our interviews.

I came to realise that I had framed the research questions assuming that other women disliked the male use of pornography and that they did not use it themselves, much the same as me. I realised it narrowed the discussion to limit the research to perceptions of male use, as it did not provide the space to discuss their own or other women's use of pornography. Instead, their opinions were much more complex than this. The types of experiences they had with pornography were broader than is given credit for by much existing research. They were not just 'victims' or 'consumers' but had a much more complex range of interactions with or exposure to pornography. Their experiences were instrumental in shaping how they perceived pornography, what they believed about it and how they lived accordingly. Despite this wide array of opinions and values, they were all to a varying degree wary of governmental policies which censor pornography.

The feminist epistemological approach I used was crucial in getting at the experiential expertise of these women, and enabling me to reflect on my experiences. There is no single feminist epistemology but rather different and diverse approaches (see Hesse-Biber, 2012). However, there are commonalities among them. They are about challenging traditional research paradigms and producing knowledge that includes and accounts for women's experiences. The emphasis is on recognising lived experience as a form of expertise, being subjective and including the emotional and the personal, building equitable research relationships, being reflexive, and research being political and action orientated. We developed new knowledge on pornography through turning to our own experiences.

Such a critical analysis of my own experience of pornography meant I had to readdress some of my views on it. I realised that ome of my concerns about pornography did not stem from direct experiences with men or from any pornography I had seen myself. Rather, it was from what I had read in women's magazines, or seen on TV, or heard from conversations with friends. In the year between my Master's and my PhD, I had new relationships and new interactions with men, all of which made me reconsider the way sex, sexuality and sexual practice an be discussed in anti-pornography discourses – sometimes in very narrow, heteronormative, moralistic tones. I also realise that these discourses can deny the agency people exercise if and when they use pornography, and how they choose to do so. This is not to say there are no negative implications around pornography but rather we need to broaden the discussion around it.

A second reflection is that a feminist epistemological approach is not enough in itself. It enables the inclusion of women's experiences but ultimately the knowledge produced is through the interpretations and viewpoints of the researcher. The different pieces of research I conducted into pornography made me realise how many uncritical assumptions I held about it, which framed how I researched it. A participatory approach helps mitigate this unacknowledged bias through including the diverse expertise and experience of many, facilitating critical reflection and having a more democratic research process. Historically, I universalised my own viewpoint as I was not aware of other experiences and opinions around pornography; a participatory approach inhibits this.

Research into pornography that uses a feminist epistemology and a participatory methodology could have radical implications for policy on pornography. It would recognise that women have a diverse range of experiences of pornography, good and bad, and that policy needs to be responsive to this. It has the potential to be receptive to diversity, and ensure that the experiences of women from different social backgrounds are heard. All of the women I interviewed felt that better sex and relationship education (SRE) is key to helping people navigate pornography within their lives. The censoring and control of pornographic content was thought to be inadequate at dealing with the negative issues that can arise from pornography. Drawing upon their own experiences, the women felt that there was not enough open discussion around sex, sexuality, our bodies and relationships. The British government has very recently committed to making SRE compulsory within schools, though it remains to be seen what will be included in the curriculum. Putting experience at the heart of pornography-related policy could have radical implications elsewhere. In 2014, welcome legislative changes were introduced criminalising pornography revenge. But preliminary reports suggest that these have been largely ineffective at preventing offences or punishing offenders. Drawing upon the experiential expertise of victims, professionals and practitioners could be crucial in formulating policy that actually works, and works in a way that is helpful.

References

DfCMS(Department for Culture, Media and Sport) (2016) *Child Safety Online: Age Verification for Pornography*, www.gov.uk/government/uploads/system/uploads/attachment_data/file/541366/AV_ConsultationDCMS_20160216_Final__4_.pdf

DfE (Department for Education) (2011) *Letting Children be Children: Report of an Independent Review of the Commercialisation and Sexualisation of Childhood*, London: The Stationery Office.

Hesse-Biber, S.N. (ed) (2012) *The Handbook of Feminist Research Theory and Praxis*, London: Sage Publications.

Papadopolous, L. (2010) *Sexualisation of Young People Review*, http://webarchive.nationalarchives.gov.uk/+/http:/www.homeoffice.gov.uk/documents/sexualisation-of-young-people.pdf

16

Making social policy internationally: a participatory research perspective

Nicola Yeates and Ana Amaya

Introduction

The relevance of participatory action research (PAR) within policy-facing social sciences is increasingly recognised due to the growing emphasis on research uptake and impact. This is because participatory research affirms stakeholders as agents bringing diverse knowledge and techniques, and a commitment to and ownership of research findings and outputs in ways that are deemed more likely to be translated into action and achieve policy change. Indeed, PAR is used widely as a research strategy across the social and health sciences wherein it is strongly associated with the production of knowledge for action that is of direct benefit and use, most of all to people experiencing social vulnerability, disadvantage and oppression.

PAR is distinguished from 'conventional' research less by the specific methods it uses than by the methodological contexts in which particular methods are used, and by its overarching emancipatory orientation towards participants who take ownership of the research and apply its results to improve living conditions or effect other localised social change. Advocates of PAR argue that valuing otherwise marginalised knowledge and experiences through active participation of research 'subjects' in the research process democratises knowledge production, secures ownership of research and improves research quality, leading to a greater likelihood that results will be put into practice (Greenwood et al, 1993; Cornwall and Jewkes, 1995; van Niekerk and van Niekerk, 2009).

Given its emancipatory project, PAR tends to be used in a range of contexts directly involving conditions of social disadvantage and/or oppression. In health, for example, PAR is frequently associated with community-based projects in low-income settings where it is used for needs assessment and planning for health services evaluation (De Koning and Martin, 1996; Baum et al, 2006) and work with indigenous populations (Hecker, 1997; Pyett, 2002); and in high-income settings primarily used to empower patients in decision making about forms of treatment (Weaver and Nicholls, 2001). There is little documented evidence of this research approach being used with other kinds of populations, such as policymakers and other social 'elites'.

This chapter examines arguments for, opportunities and limits of PAR in relation to social *policy* change. Its main concern lies with PAR in relation to 'non-standard' PAR populations – policymakers and public officials – in international development contexts. It draws on insights from the ESRC-funded Open University Poverty Reduction and Regional Integration (PRARI) project (see Yeates, 2014, and www.open.ac.uk/socialsciences/prari for an overview), which used collaborative modes of PAR to work with policymaking groups to design region-wide indicators-based health poverty monitoring 'toolkits' in Southern regional contexts (specifically in Southern African and South America).[1] Practice of PAR methodology has in this context a potential to generate focused, intensive and action-oriented collaboration with public officials, civil society actors and policymakers from the two regional groupings in the project (the Southern African Development Community and the Union of South American Nations) who are most able to influence regional level policy affecting key social issues – in this case poverty-related health issues.

The chapter emphasises that, contrary to the surface appeal of PAR in eliciting policy change, there is no intrinsic synergy or automatic relationship between the adoption of participatory methods and policy change. Rather, how PAR is applied, together with the conditions under which it is practised, significantly influences the extent to which opportunities for policy change are successfully 'captured' and/or generated. The chapter concludes on the considerable potential to develop the field of PAR in relation to social policymaking as a subject of research in its own right, an area in which there is currently little scholarship.

On participatory policy research

Participation is as widely applied to a range of research approaches and methods as it is to modes of policy development. As Cornwall and Jewkes (1995) point out, all research involves participation of some kind at some stage. Some projects involve only limited interactions with people outside the research team but can be termed participatory, whereas others involve in-depth participation at certain stages without being considered participatory.

> What is distinctive about PR is not the method, but the methodological contexts of the application of methods ... Locating debate about PR within the controversies about the qualitative-quantitative divide obscures issues of agency, representation and power which lie at the core of the methodological critiques from which the development of participatory approaches stem ... The key difference between participatory and other research methodologies lies in the location

of power in the various stages of the research process. (Cornwall and Jewkes, 1995: 1667–8)

Participatory research is, then, not a specific research method but an *orientation* or *approach* to research based on a commitment to egalitarianism, pluralism and interconnectedness in the research process. It is distinguished from 'conventional' research by virtue of the purpose of research and the process by which it is carried out (Table 16.1).

Table 16.1. Participatory and conventional research: a comparison

	Participatory research	Conventional research
What is the research for?	Action	Understanding with perhaps action later.
Who is the research for?	Local people	Institutional, personal and professional interests.
Whose knowledge counts?	Local people's	Scientists'
Topic choice influenced by?	Local priorities	Funding priorities, institutional agendas, professional interests.
Role of researcher	Facilitator, catalyst	Director.
Methodology chosen for?	Empowerment, mutual learning	Disciplinary conventions, 'objectivity' and 'truth'
Who takes part in the stages of research process?		
Problem identification	Local people	Researcher.
Data collection	Local people	Researcher, enumerator.
Interpretation	Local concepts and frameworks	Disciplinary concepts and frameworks
Analysis	Local people	Researcher
Presentation of findings	Locally accessible and useful	By researcher to other academics or funding body
Action on findings	Integral to the process	Separate and may not happen
Who takes action?	Local people, with/without external support	External agencies
Who owns the results?	Shared	The researcher
What is emphasised?	Process	Outcomes

Source: Adapted from Cornwall and Jewkes (1995, Table 1, p 1669)

The discussion now explores three interlinked themes within the participatory research literature (empowerment and social learning; power and ownership; and knowledge for action) before moving to examine PAR from the perspective of its practice.

Inquiry as empowerment and social learning

PAR is a methodology for surfacing alternative sources and kinds of knowledge (Reason, 1994). Transcending the distinctions between activism and research, it achieves 'common sense' understanding and academic expertise through its double objective: to produce knowledge and action of direct use to people, and to empower people through the process of involving them directly in using their own knowledge. The emphasis on inquiry as empowerment emerges from a critical social science that serves emancipatory interests.

The emphasis on inquiry as empowerment means that for participatory action researchers:

> the methodologies that in orthodox research would be called research design, data gathering, data analysis and so on are secondary to the emergent processes of collaboration and dialogue that empower, motivate, increase self-esteem and develop community solidarity (Reason, 1994 p 329)

In PAR, then, the research process – and its political nature – are emphasised. Outcomes of research are defined through the collaborative process, which is responsive to all partners, and the context in which research is undertaken. Iterative participation is achieved as stakeholders are continually involved in planning, testing, reflecting and generating mechanisms for action. It is a flexible process of *social learning*:

> PAR is a reflective and collaborative process of problem-solving. It is generally applied within social learning contexts, where multiple actors collectively define the problem and objectives, and work towards solutions. Iterative cycles of action and reflection make change processes more robust by ensuring that learning and sharing take place, that actions are adjusted to align with objectives, and that the actors themselves learn and adapt. (IDRC/CRDI/DfiD, 2012: 2)

Power, control and ownership

A range of modes of participation are possible under the broad PAR rubric. Following Biggs (1989, cited in Cornwall and Jewkes, 1995: 1669), modes of participation range from 'shallow' 'contractual' modes at one end of the spectrum – involving the retention of maximal ownership and control by researchers over the research process – to 'deep' 'collegiate' modes at the other, whereby ownership of research is devolved to the extent that it is controlled by participants rather than researchers (Table 16.2).

These four modes of participation suggest less defined models for action than a participation-control nexus. For example, 'shallow' modes of participation with the objective of including and empowering participants through professional relations of collegiality may – to many eyes – bear more than a passing resemblance to conventional research approaches. At the same time, it is important to recognise that there may be movement between modes at different stages of research and for different purposes (Cornwall and Jewkes, 1995: 1669). In PRARI we used collaborative modes of PAR.

Table 16.2: Continua of participation in research projects

Contractual	People are contracted into projects directed by researchers to take part in their enquiries or experiments	
Consultative	People are asked for their opinions and consulted by researchers before interventions are made	
Collaborative	Researchers and local people work together on projects designed, initiated and managed by researchers	
Collegiate	Researchers and local people work together as colleagues with different skills to offer, in a process of mutual learning where local people have full control over the process	

The right-hand column shows a vertical arrow: at the top "→ Shallow / Ownership devolved ----researcher controlled" and at the bottom "Deep ← / Ownership devolved ----researcher controlled".

Source: Cornwall and Jewkes (1995: 1669), following Biggs

As Table 16.2 suggests, defining features of participatory research are the relinquishing of full control and ownership of the research process.

> Arguably, 'participatory research' consists less of modes of research which merely involve participation in data collection than of those which address issues of the setting of agendas, ownership of results, power and control. (Cornwall and Jewkes, 1995: 1669)

At the same time, beyond the markedly different research dynamics that these diverse modes engender, participatory research signals a critical role for and influence of the researcher while also carrying risks as well as benefits. In relation to the latter, research projects involving participatory research (especially collaborative and collegiate modes) are susceptible to levels of uncertainty and risk to a degree that are not normally encountered by projects using conventional methods.

Knowledge – action

In theory, PAR offers significant advantages over 'conventional' research models. Conventionally, research is developed by researchers in a process defined and controlled by researchers, and the completed findings are distributed to research subjects and/or other research users. Arguments in favour of PAR, in contrast, hinge on the 'virtuous' relationship between knowledge, ownership and action. PAR affirms stakeholders in the research process as agents bringing diverse knowledge and techniques, and this affirmation brings a commitment to and ownership of research findings and outputs more likely be translated into action and effect social change (Bergold and Thomas, 2012; Loewenson et al, 2014). Pro-PAR advocacy arguments centre on the intrinsic and instrumental value of interaction and collaboration between the researchers in terms of understanding and local practice: whether because they lead to clearer or new understandings of concepts (for example, of vulnerability), coherent application of known techniques in new contexts (sustainable, field-tested solutions), or to new techniques themselves (for example, approaches to adaptation; Mapfumo et al, 2013: 3).

The PAR approach can lead to more informed policy by:

- *enhancing mutual learning*: by facilitating interaction, learning and collaboration, gaining deeper insights and understandings of the complexities of a given issue;
- *enhancing policy dialogue and coordination*: by acting as a broker or dialogic platform for participant stakeholders; helping to build partnerships that in turn facilitate institutional collaboration and policy coordination or innovation;
- *promoting research uptake*: by stimulating demand for the research among research users/policymakers (depending on prior levels of awareness of issues); where policymakers are already aware of the need or where teams have established institutional links with research users, projects may inform the development of new plans and policies;
- *generating a better understanding of the policy process*: by bringing new perspectives into the political process of policymaking, generating learning among participants about effective working with the policy process and policymakers (Loewenson et al, 2014).

Practising PAR

We now consider some challenges and tensions navigated in the course of practising PAR in international contexts and with 'non-standard' PAR populations. The discussion draws from the experiences of using PAR in an international research project spanning three continents. PAR was central in the PRARI project's development of pro-poor health policy monitoring systems in the Southern African Development Community (SADC) and Union of South American Nations (UNASUR) regions (Amaya et al, 2015a, b, c, d, e; Amaya and Yeates, 2015). Our analysis of previous attempts to develop regional monitoring toolkits to track policy change in the context of regional integration had highlighted the potential of metrics and indicators in monitoring to provide additional precision, transparency and policy relevance. And in a context where all too often progress in regional integration is restricted to measures of economic (market) integration, the use of social indicators-based policy monitoring instruments can be useful to capture the characteristics and effects of 'positive' regional integration policies, such as health and social protection policies and the extent to which such regional level policies are promoting social equity. Absolutely crucial to the success in developing *durable* regional monitoring policies and instruments is local and regional ownership. Previous efforts funded and developed by donors and actors external to the regions concernedusing conventiona research methods had tended not to take hold, and we concuded full participation in the development of such monitoring instruments from the start and throughout are vital in efforts to improve monitoring systems and optimising their chances of institutional embeddedness (De Lombaerde et al, 2008, 2011; www.open.ac.uk/socialsciences/prari).

Querying assumptions that the relationship between PAR research and policy change is 'seamless', the experience of PRARI nevertheless suggests that how PAR is used in practice and the contexts in which it is practised are vital to whether and how PAR research translates into policy. Echoing Carden (2007), we find that PAR's 'pathways to impact' are context specific and multiform. In what follows, we look at different specific challenges encountered in translating participatory research theory into practice of collective international research – challenges that are at once methodological and logistical. Collaborative research of this kind work surfaced distinctive issues around the distribution of risks, benefits and power during the research process, around the skills and capabilities of professional researchers, and around the extent to which a common international (regional) policy framework that is 'owned' by key actors within the region can be obtained and sustained.

McDonald (2009) distinguishes between individual and community level risks and benefits of participatory research:

1. Tensions between those directly involved in the issues and those less directly involved and their relative power in the process
2. Bias in who represents communities
3. Tensions over whose interests are driving the process
4. Managing privacy and protecting information that communities or individuals do not want widely disclosed
5. Tensions over how the evidence and analysis is documented and reported
6. How unfavourable or negative information will be managed
7. Social harms, for example when a marginal group becomes more aware of their disadvantaged position, and become more stressed or unhappy
8. Risks from participating in the action phase, which may lead to unfavourable consequences from those taking action from people in higher positions of power.

These tensions are also evident when working with PAR in an international context. As might be expected, the ways in which these tensions manifest themselves depends on the setting, nature and purposes of the research. Nevertheless, it is clear that power imbalances are unavoidable when involving a varied group of stakeholders, particularly when they are drawn from different countries or regions. This is not a necessarily negative feature: there are clear benefits of a well-respected member encouraging the participation of others, especially if this brings in new perspectives (Christopher et al, 2008). At the same time, it is important to recognise that the research process can be more easily facilitated if organised through the medium of dominant groups – such as those who are professionally proximate to institutional research, most able to mobilise resources (in particular time), and to articulate issues and concerns using common conceptual or political 'grammar'.

The cyclical nature of a research project that uses PAR methodologies requires a stable group of stakeholders, preferably involved throughout the span of the research project. Ensuring that commitment and momentum is sustained is crucial for this but maintaining group cohesiveness over time can be challenging. These challenges are related to both the nature of the collaborators (for example, policymakers may be unable to fully engage in time-consuming processes) and the alignment of interests.

The core of the participatory approach is the generation of collective knowledge through partnerships between professional researchers and 'local' experts, in order to enhance research outcomes beyond what can be achieved by an individual or team of professional researchers. However, partnerships are not intrinsically synergistic and require the alignment of purpose, values and goals (Jagosh et al, 2012). In an international context, this requires reaching consensus among individuals from different cultural, social and political backgrounds. Working with stakeholders from different countries inevitably uncovers power imbalances and tensions that may result from structures of international political economy – namely, the geo-strategic (regional or global) position of the countries that these individuals represent. This uncovers another layer of negotiation that requires the researcher be aware of, in terms of cultural or political sensitivities, so that all participants' voices are heard and treated equitably and respectfully.

Carefully balancing competing priorities and negotiating common positions are key tenets of participatory research, and the skills of the professional researcher are vital in negotiating among different parties and interests in the process of arriving at a common position. These challenges become all the more pronounced and acute in relation to political topics such as health and other social inequalities, especially where they concern countries and socio-cultural systems other than the researcher's own.

In PRARI the opportunities for interaction and capacity building were not only between stakeholders from different countries of the region (from state and non-state sectors), some with divergent characteristics, but also with regional level officials working within secretariats of the regional organisations concerned. Identifying perspectives, building trust, bridging understandings, strengthening bonds, facilitating information sharing and interactivity, and negotiating participation and a common 'platform' were among the many key tasks and skills involved (Amaya et al, 2015c; Amaya and Yeates, 2015).

The alignment of the varied interests towards a common goal may lead to sharing of experiences and expanding partnerships to other areas of work beyond the research project, generating not just momentum but also capacity. The importance of generating capacity becomes even more relevant when working with stakeholders from countries with varying levels of development or limited access to data or other resources (Amaya et al, 2015a, b, c). The aperture of channels of communication through partnerships offers greater possibility for mechanisms to respond to unexpected challenges. Where policy or institutional change is the objective, fostering sustained and engaged collaborative inputs is vital for championing the process and outputs, and the longer-term realisation of policy change.

As noted, the researcher occupies an equal but distinct role within the research partnership as a key facilitator of change, bringing specialist knowledge, working closely with the collaborators throughout, to arrive at the agreed outcome. This inevitably requires the researcher to work beyond the boundaries of what would conventionally fall within the scope of a research project, juggling competing and complex national, intra-regional and international agendas. Researchers' interpersonal and facilitation skills alongside their research skills are critical to the successful conclusion of participatory research as much as is their understanding of the theoretical and political impetuses behind PAR (Meyer, 2000; Loewenson et al, 2014).

Positive outcomes require time to build trust (Cornwall and Jewkes, 1995), and funders' expectations of outcomes over often-condensed time frames sit uneasily with the reflexive and long-term nature of such an approach (Springett and Wallerstein, 2008). This means that the researcher sometimes struggles between academic goals and the more 'distant' project deliverables and outcomes (Loewenson et al, 2014). This is a clear tension, considering pressures arising from finite project funding, lines of responsibility and accountability, and project targets and deliverables.

These issues escalate when working in international context where the researcher may be located far from the PAR collaborators, with limited face-to-face interactions. This has implications for trust-building and can translate into significant financial investment. During the PRARI project (which spanned three continents), we found the supplementary use of ICT essential in this regard, likewise working with committed partners within the region who can support the process locally. Unpredictable as the process may be, it may also lead to opportunities for unanticipated different or greater impacts that originally envisaged (Viswanathan et al, 2004). The pursuit of these can have significant resource implications and it is in this respect that mobilising the communities of interest and stakeholders can prove challenging in the face of finite project funding and timelines.

Finally, the researcher's affiliation (institution or project funding source) and social background may also generate responses from collaborators who may believe that there are a priori expectations about what results, findings and solutions are acceptable. Zemelmann (2000), for example, describes this potential issue where the normative perspective of the researchers and practitioners may lead to them interpreting information in a particular way, or looking for clues and signs of what they expect to see or would like to see. There is scope for such misunderstandings to arise and affect the responses of the team, especially if the project is funded by an international donor, as participant researchers may bring preconceptions about the aims and expected outcomes of donor-funded projects to the research. Concretely, although PRARI was funded by the UK Economic and Social Research Council (in collaboration with the UK Department for International Development), there was a great deal of scope for misunderstanding the nature of the project because of its association with UK DfID, which has a significant presence in Southern Africa as a bilateral donor of country-level development aid. Such aid is accompanied by conditionalities, and we needed to reiterate that in PRARI no such conditions were present and that outcomes from it were not linked to future DfID funding.

Conclusion

The impulses towards participatory approaches frequently derive from perceived limitations of 'conventional' research for embedding priorities of research impact beyond the academy. Engagement with participatory agendas encounters a different set of impulses and priorities: emancipation, empowerment, interconnectedness, social learning and a commitment to problem-led, action-led policy research. These encounters are not unproductive – though the different logics governing conventional and participatory research give rise to challenges which those working within and outside the academy must navigate. These are all the more complicated when working across extensive geographical, cultural, social and political spaces.

This chapter has discussed challenges and considerations when undertaking participatory research – professional, political, logistical – in collaboration with policy stakeholders and in an extended international context. Our use of PAR in an international development and policy context needed to contend with external forces related to the professional and institutional agendas of those involved (local, regionally and internationally), and a perception that participatory research is a donor-driven agenda (Casaburi et al, 2000). The 'ideal' of participation has a long and contested history in development contexts and our use of PAR proved more contentious among some than we anticipated. Ideals of democracy and democratic development used to advocate participation in research resonate strongly with donors but may encounter resistance unless the research process is fully owned and controlled by 'local' stakeholders. This suggests that a collegiate mode of PAR may be more suitable than a collaborative mode in certain contexts.

The skills and quality of interpersonal interactions among the research collaborators are paramount. The skillset of the successful PAR collaborators extends beyond research design and practice to advanced leadership skills of diplomacy and negotiation. This applies as much to the researcher as to other participants, especially where the project brings together individuals from diverse institutions, countries and continents. At the same time, it is important to recognise that the 'participants' from member states and pan-regional organisations (as was the case in PRARI) are participating in a multi-institutional process over which they relinquish full control. In this sense, they bear significant risks, notably those of a time-consuming process combined with uncertain outcomes. This is complicated when, as in the case of PRARI, the research process includes policy actors from several countries regionally in a pan-regional collaborative research project.

Using PAR to generate meaningful partnerships with policymakers and engaging with processes of social change and sources of social oppression has the potential to reframe traditional understandings of empowerment. In the context of PRARI, the ultimate goal of PAR is to mobilise 'local' actors in two regional formations in the global south to facilitate more concerted regional policymaking from within the region itself. From working with Southern policymakers within an international development context in ways that give an international 'voice' to marginalised perspectives in global and regional policymaking, we conclude that PAR is capable of enabling social learning among diverse stakeholders. Introducing markedly different viewpoints strengthens the potential for positive change by raising awareness of the extent and nature of profound social inequalities in other countries of the region, and by mobilising key actors in a cross-regional community of interest revolving around the development of a tangible regional policy instrument capable of addressing entrenched social problems profoundly affecting the life chances of significant proportions of the population. At the same time, the prospects of a common *regional* instrument (applicable to many different countries) being progressed into further stages of development relies on institutional sponsorship and regional political leadership over the longer term. Given the limits of donor funding, sponsorship and ongoing support by the region concerned is vital in the determination of whether the policy instrument is taken forward through the policymaking process or whether it stalls. If navigating the context specific regional policy structures, politics, programmes and processes is critical, then so too is the power of a transnational coalition of partners committed to the achievement of inclusive and participatory social policy as means of addressing entrenched social inequalities.

Finally, the relationship between PAR and policy development is a relatively under-developed focus of methods research. There remains ample scope for better understanding whether and how PAR influences policymakers' approach to problem solving. Greater attention to PAR as an ongoing area of research enquiry in its own right could help further this. Questions for ongoing research may usefully include:

- How does including research participants from diverse social fields who occupy disparate power positions mediate the process and research outcomes?
- What difference does it make to the objective of social change to practise participatory approaches that democratise knowledge, compared with more instrumental participatory methods of policy development?
- Is PAR more effective than 'conventional' research methodologies for effecting institutional (re)design and policy change and, if so, what are the key determinants in specific conditions and contexts?

In the quest for participatory and inclusive approaches to social policy research and analysis, a stronger understanding of the strengths, limits and challenges of PAR as a way of ensuring the maximal input into national and transnational policy design from those with experiential knowledge must be a priority of the first order.

Note

[1] PRARI was funded by the joint programme on poverty reduction of the Economic and Social Research Council and the UK Department for International Development (grant reference ES/L005336/L). It does not necessarily reflect the opinions of the ESRC. Further information about PRARI and project materials are available from Nicola Yeates (Principal Investigator) at The Open University: www.open.ac.uk/socialsciences/prari/about/participatory-action. php. The regional monitoring toolkits (Amaya et al, 2015a, b) together with Policy Briefs and Working Papers (Amaya et al, 2015c, d; Amaya and Yeates, 2015) are freely available from this Open University website.

References

Amaya, A.B. and Yeates, N. (2015) Participatory Action Research: new uses, new contexts, new challenges', PRARI Working Paper 15-6, Milton Keynes: The Open University.

Amaya, A.B., Choge, I,. De Lombaerde, P., Kingah, S., Longwe, S., Mhehe, E.A., Moeti, T., Mookodi, L., Luwabelwa, M., Nyika, P. and Phirinyane, M. (2015a) *Measuring Regional Policy Change and Pro-Poor Health Policy Success: a PRARI Toolkit of Indicators for the Southern African Development Community (SADC)*, Milton Keynes: The Open University, www.open.ac.uk/socialsciences/prari

Amaya, A.B., Cabral, C.R., Clavell, E., Coitiño, A., De Lombaerde, P., Giler, G., Faria, M., Herrero, M.B., Kingah, S., López Ramos, S., Luna, C., Rigirozzi, P., Rojas Mattos, M., Pippo, T., Tobar, K. and Ueleres, J. (2015b) *Measuring the Progress and Success of Regional Health Policies: PRARI Toolkit of Indicators for the Union of South American Nations (UNASUR)*, Milton Keynes: The Open University, www.open.ac.uk/socialsciences/prari

Amaya, A.B., Bagapi, K., Choge, I., De Lombaerde, P., Kingah, S., Kwape, I., Luwabelwa, M., Mathala, O., Mhehe, E., Moeti, T., Mookodi, L., Ngware, Z. and Phirinyane, M. (2015c) 'Monitoring Pro-Poor Health Policy Success in the SADC Region', PRARI Policy Brief No 7, Milton Keynes: The Open University, www.open.ac.uk/socialsciences/prari

Amaya, A.B., Kingah, S. and De Lombaerde, P. (2015d) *Multi-level Pro-Poor Health Governance, Statistical Information Flows, and the Role of Regional Organisations in South America and Southern Africa*, PRARI Working Paper 15/1, Milton Keynes: The Open University-United Nations University Institute on Comparative Regional Integration Studies.

Amaya, A.B., Yeates, N. and Moeti, T. (2015e) 'Participatory Action Research: a methodology for Impact?' ALARA World Congress, 4–7 November, Centurion, South Africa.

Baum, F., MacDougall, C. and Smith, D. (2006) 'Glossary: Participatory action research', *Journal of Epidemiology and Community Health*, 60, 854–7.

Bergold, J. and Thomas, S. (2012) 'Participatory Research Methods: a methodological approach in motion', *Forum: Qualitative Social Research*, 13 (1) Art. 30, January, www.qualitative-research.net/index.php/fqs/article/view/1801

Carden, F. (2007) 'Context matters: The influence of IDRC-supported research on policy processes', in E.T. Ayuk and M.A. Marouani (eds) *The policy paradox in Africa: Strengthening links between economic research and policymaking*, Trenton, NJ and Ottawa: Africa World Press and IDRC, pp 93–116.

Casaburi, G., Rigirozzi, M., Tuozzo, M. and Tussie, D. (2000) 'Multilateral development banks, governments and civil society: Chiaroscuros in a triangular relationship', *Global Governance*, 6 (4), 493–517.

Cornwall, A. and Jewkes, R. (1995) 'What is participatory research?', *Social Science and Medicine*, 41 (12), 1667–76.

Christopher, S., Watts, V., McCormick, A.K. and Young, S. (2008) 'Building and maintaining trust in a community-based participatory research partnership', *American Journal of Public Health*, 98, 1398–406.

De Koning, K. and Martin, M. (1996) *Participatory Research in Health: Issues and experiences*, London: Zed Books.

De Lombaerde, P., Estevadeordal, A., and Suominen, K. (2008) *Governing Regional Integration for Development. Monitoring experiences, methods and prospects.* Ashgate: London.

De Lombaerde, P., Flores, R.G., Lapadre, P.L. and Schulz, M. (eds) (2011) *The Regional Integration Manual. Quantitative and Qualitative Methods*, Routledge: London.

Greenwood, D., Whyte, W.F. and Harkavy, I. (1993) 'Participatory Action Research as a Process and as a Goal', *Human Relations*, 46 (2), 177–89.

Hecker, R. (1997) 'Participatory action research as a strategy for empowering Aboriginal health workers', *Australian and New Zealand Journal of Public Health*, 21, 784–8.

IDRC/CRDI/DfID (2012) *New pathways to resilience: outcomes of the climate change adaptation in Africa research and capacity building program 2006-2012.*

Jagosh, J., Macauley, A.C., Pluye, P., Ssalsberg, J., Bush, P.L., Henderson, J., Sirett, E., Wong, G., Cargo, M., Herbert, C.P., Seifer, S.D., Green, L.W. and Greenhalgh, T. (2012). 'Uncovering the benefits of participatory research: implications of a realist review for health research and practice', *The Milbank Quarterly*, 90, 311–46.

Loewensen, R., Laurell, A.S., Hogstedt, C., D'Ambruoso, L. and Shroff, Z. (2014) *Participatory Action Research in Health Systems: A Methods Reader.* Harare, Zimbabwe: TARSC, AHPSR, WHO, IDRC, EQUINET. Available at: www.equinetafrica.org/sites/default/files/uploads/documents/PAR%20Methods%20Reader2014%20for%20web.pdf

Mapfumo, P., Adjei-Nsiah, S., Mtambanengwe, Chikowo, R. and Giller, K.E. (2013) 'Participatory action research (PAR) as an entry point for supporting climate change adaptation by smallholder farmers in Africa', *Environmental Development*, 5: 6–22.

McDonald, M. (2009) *Ethics and Community-engaged rResearch*, Durham, NC: Duke University Press.

Meyer, J. (2000) 'Using qualitative methods in health related action research', *BMJ*, 320, 178–81.

Pyett, P. (2002) 'Working together to reduce health inequalities: reflections on a collaborative participator approach to health research', *Australian and New Zealand Journal of Public Health*, 26, 332–6.

Reason, P. (1994) 'Three Approaches to Participative Inquiry', in N. Denzin and Y. Lincoln (eds) *Handbook of Qualitative Research*, Thousand Oaks, CA: Sage Publications.

Springett, J. and Wallerstein, N. (2008) 'Issues in participatory evaluation', in M. Minkler and N. Wallerstein (eds) *Community Based Participatory Research in Health*, second edition, San Francisco: Jossey Bass.

van Niekerk, L. and van Niekerk, D. (2009) 'Participatory action research: Addressing social vulnerability of rural women through income-generating activities', *Journal of Disaster Risk Studies*, 2 (2), 127–44.

Viswanathan, M., Ammerman, A., Eng, E., Garlehner, E., Lohr, KN., Griffith, D., Rhodes, S., Samuel-Hodge, C., Maty, S., Lux, L., Webb, L., Sutton, S.F., Swinson, T., Jackman, A. and Whitener, L. (2004) *Community-Based Participatory Research: Assessing the Evidence*, Summary, Evidence Report/Technology Assessment: Number 99. AHRQ Publication Number 04-E022-1, August 2004. Agency for Healthcare Research and Quality, Rockville, MD, www. ahrq.gov/clinic/epcsums/cbprsum.htm

Weaver, Y. and Nicholls, V. (2001) 'The Camden "Alternative choices in mental health"', in R. Winter and C. Munn-Giddings (eds) *A Handbook for Action Research in Health and Social Care*, London: Routledge.

Yeates, N. (2014) *Global Poverty Reduction: What can regional organisations do?*, PRARI Policy Brief No 3, The Open University, Milton Keynes.

Zemelmann, H. (2000) *Conocimientos y sujetos sociales: contribucion al estudio del presente*, second edition, Centro de Estudios Sociologicos, Mexico DF: Colegio de Mexico.

Part IV
An inclusive life course and developmental approach to social policy

Social policy service users have much to say about their lives and the intersection of policy and practice with them. But they come at them from a different perspective to traditional discussions focusing on the life course and a developmental approach. Here we have a chance to explore and develop these.

A series of contributions in Part IV of the book explore an *inclusive* life course and developmental approach to social policy from childhood through to end of life. Focusing on issues of inclusion and participation and paying particular attention to people's own perspectives and experience, they cast fresh light on this approach to understanding and developing social policy by concentrating on groups and situations where people face particular barriers and discriminations.

First, in her chapter, Mary Wickenden shows that disabled children and young people, especially in the Global South, are still particularly disadvantaged as a group, although there are many similarities in experiences and concerns across cultural divides. Despite the growing rhetoric round the involvement and empowerment of young people and their identification as a group in policy, responses to both children and to disability do to some extent transcend specific cultural influences. Despite policies to improve their lives and encourage their involvement, we learn how disabled children are still significantly disadvantaged internationally.

Lucy Costa, as a psychiatric system survivor and advocate in Canada, writes from a 'Mad Studies' perspective about the mental health troubles of young people and the sometimes troubling policy responses made to them. We hear about the experience of three such girls – Mary, Katelynn and Ashley – and learn about the continuing gap between the rhetoric of participation and the often harsh reality of the psychiatric system. Lucy considers both the limitations and transformative possibilities of Mad Studies for these and other mental health service users.

Emmeline Burdett's focus is disability and disabled people. She contrasts the lofty principles associated with the Paralympic Games with the disablist, individualising and sometimes life-limiting ones that operate more generally in social policy. She explores the reality of life for a disabled person like herself under modern Western neoliberal social policy, critiquing the subtle and hidden ways in which paternalism and barriers can still operate in every aspect of disabled people's lives.

161

Activist Michelle Daley writes from the standpoint of being a black disabled woman in her chapter on equality and independent living from a social model of disability perspective. As a case study, she explores the relationship between British social care policy and practice, ethnic diversity, racism, disability and intersectionality.

Deirdre O'Connor, food policy academic, offers an overview of the issue of food poverty in Ireland and how it is defined, understood and measured in the Irish policy context. She considers how it is experienced by those living in food poverty and understood by activists in the food poverty arena concerned with both relieving immediate hunger and pursuing social justice and human rights.

Former London Mental Health NHS Foundation Trust director Hári Sewell contributes from the perspective of a professional responsible for implementing a policy that has implications for him politically and personally. He discusses the ambiguities and challenges for applying race equality policies from within the British health and social care system, including in central government, and how he used his own experiences of racialisation and racism to inform and reflect on his work.

Sarah Lonbay focuses on ageing in her chapter and contrasts the traditional 'expert' development of social policy with people's desire to have more say and involvement in how it affects their lives. She looks at the construction of ageing and older people, different participatory approaches and the activity of participation in relation to the life course and older people and how their participation can be made real and given meaning.

Finally, in their concluding chapter, Lisa Williams and her colleagues introduce us to the reality that the 21st century 'marks the emergence of a new demography of death', marked by longevity and long-term illness. They connect a participatory research approach – digital storytelling – with the culture and ways of doing of an indigenous people and explore how it can work as a basis for participatory social policy that includes and amplifies their voices, rather than excluding or imposing on them.

17

Disabled children's lives: an inclusive life course and developmental approach to social policy

Mary Wickenden

Introduction

This chapter focuses on the structural position of disabled children in diverse contexts worldwide, and the types of global and international policies that help or hinder them in living lives on equal terms with their nondisabled peers. I will draw broadly on my own experiences of working with disabled children and their families in a number of cultural contexts: UK, South Asia and East Africa. Perhaps unsurprisingly because of globalisation, despite the many obvious or more subtle differences between these settings and the vast diversity of children's experiences, there are many similarities in experiences and concerns across cultural divides. These suggest overarching generic trends and influences on policy and practice everywhere. Although we should be wary of generalisations, responses to both children and to disability do to some extent transcend specific cultural influences.

There has been a recent upsurge of recognition and interest in disabled children, a group who have historically been ignored and excluded both from their communities and from the majority of policy initiatives worldwide. Estimates suggest that there are 150–200 million children with disabilities globally, of these 93 million under 14 with moderate/severe impairments (WHO and World Bank, 2011; UNICEF, 2013). Around 5–10% of children have developmental difficulties (UNICEF, 2013); however, often, in many settings they are hidden from view.

Growing evidence, shows that disabled children are at a huge relative disadvantage compared with their nondisabled peers, across all sectors. This is true globally, across all regions and countries. For example they often have poorer access to healthcare and education, and experience increased levels of neglect, abuse and violence (WHO and World Bank, 2011). There is some evidence of a gendered aspect to this as disabled girls are likely to be 'doubly disadvantaged' compared with boys, although data is scarce (UNICEF, 2013). Most disabled children live in the Global South, where the majority of the world's people live and in many countries children are the majority of the population (UNICEF, 2013).

Yet, disabled children are invisible citizens (Sabatello, 2013). They are members of two structural groups (children and disabled) who are often cast as burdensome, vulnerable, helpless and as net receivers rather than contributors in society. They are at risk of and often experience structurally violent treatment. This may be institutionalised and not challenged by policy and practice, and or the level of the family or community. Disabled children's rights as outlined in the two relevant UN Conventions (UNCRC, 1979; UN, 2007) are regularly unrecognised and denied (Lansdown, 2012). Despite the dominant discourse in the Global North that disability is a social, political, relational concept not a purely biomedical one (WHO, 2001; Barnes and Mercer, 2010), this rhetoric has arguably not achieved universal changes in the prevalent notions that disabled people are vulnerable, incompetent and often objects of pity, embarrassment or shame. They remain an excluded minority who have reduced opportunities for active agency.

Disabled adults (notably those with acquired impairments) may have had access to education, healthcare and positive social experiences, in short, considerable social capital, before becoming impaired and then have had to respond to negativity from others (Ghai, 2001). Disabled children in contrast grow up with this status from an early age. They embark on a disabled life course and have the difficult task of negotiating for themselves a positive identity, combatting a myriad of disadvantages. In practice, for many, especially if they are living in poverty, this means a lifetime of exclusion (Singh and Ghai, 2009).

In this chapter I discuss the changing conceptualisations of children as a structural group over recent decades. I consider whether and how disabled children have been included in this movement towards the recognition of young citizens' autonomy and right to a voice. Second, I consider the increasing interest in and sometimes critique of 'developmental' approaches to children globally. There is much discussion about how to 'maximise the potential' of all children, this being an essential part of a 'lifespan' approach to community development. I reflect on whether policies and practices that are supposedly 'child-centred' and resolutely 'developmental' have benefited disabled children as much as their peers. I explore specifically the terms 'inclusion and 'agency', both of which are often used in the policy environment and are arguably problematic and under-theorised. I ask whether the way they are operationalised serves disabled children well. These reflections lead to a conclusion that, despite the positive rhetoric, disabled children remain significantly disadvantaged globally.

Children and childhood: roles, status and categories

It is useful to consider how different children are viewed by societies, how they become categorised. Taking a 'life course' approach is currently popular, and seems to imply paying attention to individuals from 'cradle to the grave'. However, children and young people have only been recognised as an important structural group within society for 30 years or so, since the emergence of the 'new sociology of childhood' (James et al, 1998). This perspective rejects seeing children as vulnerable, incompetent and powerless, regarding them as social actors who can contribute to shaping their worlds. This conceptualisation has precipitated moves towards increased consultations and participatory research with children, asking them about policies and practices of relevance to them (for example, education, health, environment, rights, law, transport) (Kirby et al, 2003; Gallaher and Gallagher, 2008; Ennew et al, 2009) This move towards including children and young people in policymaking and planning is increasingly accepted, although perhaps more in the Global North, than the South. In some cultural contexts the idea of consulting with children and them having autonomy is unusual, unacceptable or even laughable. It is an idea that demands a shift in understandings about children and in expectations about who they should be and what they can do. It necessarily challenges power relations with adults who traditionally in many cultures, control children's lives.

In international development there has been a rise in interest in the wellbeing of children. Particularly there is focus on 'early child care and development' (ECCD) policies and programmes, including surveillance, monitoring children's development and interventions to accelerate these and get children 'school ready' (Engle et al, 2007; Lake, 2011). Increased school attendance has been and is now the target of huge multi-agency international development efforts (such as Sustainable Development Goal 4; UNDP, 2015).

However, a cynic might spot a neoliberal economic agenda here and might be concerned about the fate of any category of children who fail to conform to the agreed and expected developmental norms. Most of the focus is on the cost effectiveness of ECCD inputs. The return on investment in early intervention is the potential contribution children will make to the economy later as adults. The cost in the early years is financially justified on this basis and 'reaching their potential' is the prevailing mantra. Children have always been seen within families as a source of future security and prosperity, but institutionalising this at a policy level is arguably perilous, particularly for those individuals who do not 'tick the developmental boxes', i.e. who 'fail' to conform to developmental expectations. It is thus a very uni-dimensional way of viewing children and young people's role in society.

Notwithstanding these criticisms an increased focus on children's wellbeing is broadly positive, but the question remains: what happens to individuals whose potential is incompatible with future economic productivity, such as disabled children, particularly those who have severe and complex impairments? How can they be included in policies and practice and more importantly in their communities as valued and contributing citizens?

In a target-orientated, normalising world, the child who is different is of little interest or value, beyond the identification of their impairments. Children identified as 'developmentally faltering' regularly fail to attract any further attention. Often there is no plan about how to support them. They are othered and so their lifetime of social exclusion begins. Positive acceptance of difference or indeed support to accommodate and welcome them into the educational or social systems is usually lacking. For disabled children then, dominant developmental approaches that assume and privilege normative development can exacerbate their risk of disadvantage (Garth and Aroni, 2003; Feldman et al, 2013). Often, target driven developmental approaches to children and child development do not take into account varying cultural contexts and the variation between children whether labelled disabled or not (Rogoff, 2003; Burman, 2008). As Goodley and Runswick-Cole (2011: 79) say developmentalism can be tyrannical and sometimes disabled children fall outside or between social policies. In many countries it is common for disabled children not to be considered specifically, or at best only in a segregated pathologising way, although this is now slowly changing (Burman et al, 2015).

Two popular concepts: inclusion and agency

A number of buzzwords currently popular in policy and practice around children and childhoods are potentially problematic and need careful interrogation in relation to disabled children.

Inclusion is a term most commonly linked to educational provision, promoting the idea that all children should ideally be educated together This is enshrined globally in the Salamanca statement (UNESCO, 1994), which mandates signatory states to adopt inclusive education as their policy. Local mainstream schools should adapt to the children rather than vice versa through accommodating difference, acceptance and celebration of diversity. This philosophy is underwritten by human rights treaties which emphasise the right to equality of opportunity (UN, 2007).

The concept of inclusion is increasingly being applied across other sectors, such as inclusive health, sport and leisure, access to justice and so on. Inclusion is seen as the philosophy best promoting a 'rights based' approach to disability across all these sectors. Contrary to the notable lack of mention of disability or inclusion in the MDGs (Groce and Trani, 2009), the Sustainable Development Goals (SDG); (UNDP, 2015), through intensive lobbying by the disability community, endorses a disability inclusive approach (IDA, 2016; UN, 2013).

Despite this increased espousal of the idea of inclusion, I question whether this aspiration and its implications are well understood outside specialist arenas and whether it will really be achieved (Katsui and Kumpuvouri, 2008). Unless there is a sea change in acceptance of, understandings about and celebration of difference, the exclusion of 'abnormal' people is likely to continue blatantly or more subtly. Thomas's (2007) concept of 'psycho-emotional' disablism, exclusion that continues when the more overt forms of discrimination are outlawed, which can be seen in high income countries, signals a strong warning that there may be many barriers to realising inclusion through the SDGs or other means. The evidence suggests that those living in low income settings may continue to be excluded (UNICEF, 2013). The SDGs' strapline and aspiration to 'Leave no one behind' needs to be treated with suspicion.

Globalisation tends to bring with it a shrinking welfare state and privatisation of services, so the rolling out of inclusive policies may not be a priority by governments. However, more positively the nongovernment sector including many 'mainstream' development organisations working with children are including disabled children in their programmes. A good example is PLAN International, which now actively works on disability. These organisations could usefully support governments to develop more inclusive approaches to service planning and provision.

Changes in how children's *agency* is viewed have emerged latterly (Tisdall and Punch, 2012), but there is less consideration of disabled children's agency. Disabled children rarely have the opportunity to express their opinions and make choices. When asked for their views, they often insist that they are 'normal' kids or teenagers – more like others than they are different (Wickenden and Kembhavi, 2014). Furthermore, for their families a disabled child IS 'normal' in a social-relational sense, as they are significant, ordinary members of their household in contrast to their child's status in the outside world, where they may be seen as a lesser citizen (Paget et al, 2016). The way that disabled children express agency echoes Bordonaro and Payne's (2012) notion of 'ambiguous agency' when the type of person the child can be or wants to be threatens conventional expectations. Participation and children's agency as hegemonic ideas need to be ascribed to disabled children, as much as to others, although their enactment of these may be unconventional. So children who cannot speak or understand well may express their opinions and contribute in ways that are difficult to recognise and value.

Tisdall and Punch (2012) drawing on Klocker (2007) and Ansell (2009), suggest that children's agency may be 'thickly' expressed in local situations but is 'thinner' at macro and policy levels. I suggest that this difficulty with recognising agency is amplified greatly for disabled children at any level above the micro (such as within families). In my experience, they want to be asked and heard and have plenty to say. They are natural 'social modellists', rejecting ableist judgements about them and assumptions about their competenciecial and expect ordinary childhoods like other children's, not 'disabled childhoods' (Tisdall, 2012; Curran and Runswick-Cole, 2013). Choice and control are recognised as inalienable rights of disabled adults, but seemingly not yet of disabled children. With a few notable exceptions (LCD, 2014), the disability activists' slogan 'nothing about us without us' is not heard loudly enough in relation to disabled children.

Conclusions

There are an increasing number of global and national policies that could, but have not yet, impact positively on the lives of disabled children. Inclusion, recognition of agency, participation and life course approaches, all hegemonic axioms, are at least superficially incontrovertible. They are driven by equity and rights-based agendas and by the recognition that to reduce poverty and inequality, deliberate efforts to include everyone are needed. Because the SDGs (UNDP, 2015) espouse such principles, disabled activists are beginning to expect and aspire to inclusive development efforts globally.

Further, life course approaches promise an inclusive approach in policies and practices from cradle to grave across all sectors. The crucial question is how and how well this is interpreted and implemented at national and local levels, particular in low income settings where sociocultural, political and financial constraints are huge. At a practical level, practitioners in these contexts may lack the knowledge, skills and confidence to work inclusively. An inclusive approach to training and job preparation of all service providers is vital. Health workers, social workers, judges, teachers, police and the rest all need to expect to work with disabled children and adults alongside their other clients, with the positive attitudes, confidence and resources to do so.

Child specific policies and initiatives are in the ascendant; but truly inclusive approaches have yet to emerge, to counterbalance highly normative approaches to children's development (*Lancet*, 2016). When these are underpinned by narrow economic production-oriented notions of citizenship, they arguably put disabled children at further risk of exclusion. It seems that there is an inexplicable conceptual gap between considering the welfare and development of all children and those labelled disabled. Making sure children identified as 'different' also benefit from these supposed universal programmes would be true inclusion. This is perhaps still too challenging and takes skills, imagination and acceptance of difference, which is often sadly lacking.

There are many international and national disability and general policies promoting inclusion even in the poorest countries, usually precipitated by the state's signing of the UNCRPD. Sadly though, during my field work in East Africa and South Asia I have encountered too many examples of disabled children being excluded and mistreated to be convinced that these policies have changed mindsets about their worth as people. Most disabled children are as yet not regarded as valuable citizens who can make a net contribution to their communities. It is not clear how someone who may never be a financial contributor, and in fact is seen as burdensome, can be valued in an increasingly globalised world narrowly focused on the economic productivity of its citizens.

The latest global policy mantra 'Leave no one behind' espouses inclusive and lifespan approaches, but only time will tell whether these aspirations will really improve the lives of the most excluded group globally and those with the quietest voices: disabled children.

Acknowledgements

Many thanks to Marguerite Schneider for her helpful comments and editing.

References

Ansell, N. (2009) 'Childhood and the politics of scale: descaling children's geographies?' *Progress in Human Geography*, 32 (2), 190–209.

Barnes, C. and Mercer, G. (2010) *Exploring Disability*, Cambridge: Polity Press.

Bordonaro, L. and Payne, R. (2012) 'Ambiguous agency: critical perspectives on social interventions with children and youth in Africa', *Children's Geographies*, 10 (4), 365–72.

Burman, E. (2008) *Deconstructing Developmental Psychology*, London: Routledge.

Burman, E., Greenstein, A. and Kumar, B.M. (2015) 'Editorial: Frames and debates for disability, childhood and the global South: Introducing the Special Issue', *Disability and the Global South*, 2 (2), 563–9.

Campbell, F.K. (2010) 'Crippin' the Flâneur: Cosmopolitanism, and Landscapes of Tolerance', *Journal of Social Inclusion*, 1 (1), 75–89.

Curran, T. and Runswick-Cole, K. (eds) (2013) *Disabled Children's Childhood Studies: Critical approaches in a global context*, Basingstoke. Palgrave Macmillan.

Engle, L.P., Black, M.M., Behrman, J.R., Cabral de Mello, M., Gentler P.J., Kapiriri, L., Martorell, R., Eming Young, M. and the International Child Development Steering Group (2007) 'Child development in developing countries 3: Strategies to avoid the loss of developmental potential in more than 200 million children in the developing world', *The Lancet*, 369.

Ennew, J., Abebe, T., Bangyai, R., Karapituck, P., Kjørholt, A.T., Noonsup, T., Beazley, H., Bessell, S., Daengchart-Kushanoglu, P. and Waterson, R. (2009) *The right to be properly researched: how to do rights-based, scientific research with children*, Bangkok: Black on White Publications.

Feldman, M.A., Battin, S.M., Shaw, O.A. and Luckasson, R. (2013) 'Inclusion of children with disabilities in mainstream child development research', *Disability & Society*, 28 (7), 997–1011.

Gallacher, LA. and Gallagher, M., (2008) 'Methodological iImmaturity in childhood research? Thinking through 'participatory methods', *Childhood*, 15, 499–516.

Garth, B. and Aroni, R. (2003) "I value what you have to say'. Seeking the perspective of children with a disability, not just their parents', *Disability & Society*, 18, 561–76.

Ghai, A. (2001) 'Marginalization and disability: experiences from the Third World', in M. Priestley (ed) *Disability and the Life Course: global perspectives*, Cambridge: Cambridge University Press, pp 26–37.

Goodley, D. and Runswick-Cole, K. (2011) 'Problematising policy: Conceptions of 'child', 'disabled' and 'parents' in social policy in England', *International Journal of Inclusive Education*, 15 (1), 71–85.

Groce, N.E. and Trani, J.F. (2009) 'Millennium development goals and people with disabilities', *The Lancet*, 374 (9704), 1800–01.

IDA (2016) 'High Level Political Forum. Ensuring that no one is left behind: Position paper by Persons with Disabilities', www.internationaldisabilityalliance. org/blog/day-one-high-level-political-forum-2016

James, A., Jenks, C. and Prout, A. (1998) *Theorizing Childhood*, Cambridge: Polity Press.

Katsui, H. and Kumpuvouri, J. (2008) 'Human rights based approach to disability in development in Uganda: a way to fill the gap between political and social spaces', *Scandinavian Journal of Disability Research*. 10 (4), 227–236.

Kirby, P., Lanyon, C., Cronin, K. and Sinclair, R. (2003) *Building a culture of participation: involving children and young people in policy, service planning, delivery and evaluation*, London: Department for Education and Skills, http://dera. ioe.ac.uk/17522/1/Handbook%20-%20Building%20a%20Culture%20of%20 Participation.pdf

Klocker, N. (2007) 'An example of thin agency: child domestic workers in Tanzania', in: R. Panelli, S. Punch and E. Robson (eds) *Global Perspectives on Rural Childhood and Youth: Young rural lives*, London: Routledge, pp 81–148.

Lancet (2016) 'Advancing early childhood development: from science to scale ', *The Lancet*, 389, no 10064, www.thelancet.com/series/ECD2016

Lake, A. (2011) 'Early childhood development – global action is overdue', *The Lancet*, 378 (9799): 1277–78, doi: 10.1016/S0140-6736(11)61450-5.

Lansdown, G. (2012) *Using the Human Rights Framework to Promote the Rights of Children with Disabilities*, New York: UNICEF.

LCD (2014) 'Leonard Cheshire Disability: Young Voices', http://lcdyoungvoices. tumblr.com/ and www.youtube.com/user/YoungVoicesLCD

Paget, A., Mallewa, M., Chinguo, D., Mahebere-Chirambo, C. and Gladstone, M. (2016) '"It means you are grounded" – caregivers' perspectives on the rehabilitation of children with neurodisability in Malawi', *Disability and Rehabilitation*, 38 (3), 223–34, DOI: 10.3109/09638288.2015.1035458

Rogoff, B. (2003) *The Cultural Nature of Human Development*, Oxford: Oxford University Press.

Sabatello, M. (2013) 'Children with Disabilities: A critical appraisal', *International Journal of Children's Rights*, 21 (3), 464–87.

Singh, V. and Ghai, A. (2009) 'Notions of self: Lived realities of children with disabilities', *Disability & Society*, 24 (2), 129–45.

Thomas, C. (2007) *Sociologies of Disability and Illness: Contested Ideas in Disability Studies and Medical Sociology*, Palgrave Macmillan: Basingstoke.

Tisdall, E.K.M. (2012) 'The challenge and challenging of childhood studies? Learning from disability studies and research with disabled children', *Children & Society*, 26 (3), 181–91.

Tisdall, E.K.M. and Punch, S. (2012) 'Not so 'new'? Looking critically at childhood studies', *Children's Geographies*, 10 (3), 249–64.

UN (United Nations) (1989) Convention on the Rights of the Child. Available at: www.unicef.org.uk/Documents/...pdfs/UNCRC_PRESS200910web

UN (2007) UN Convention on the Rights of Persons with Disabilities, www. un.org/development/desa/disabilities/convention-on-the-rights-of-persons-with-disabilities.html

UN (2013) 'Outcome document of the high-level meeting of the General Assembly on the realization of the Millennium Development Goals and other internationally agreed development goals for Persons with disabilities: the way forward, a disability-inclusive development agenda towards 2015 and beyond', UN A/68/L.1

UNDP (2015) 'Sustainable Development Goals', www.undp.org/content/undp/en/home/sustainable-development-goals.html

UNESCO (1994) *The Salamanca Statement on principles, policy and practice in special needs education*, http://unesdoc.unesco.org/images/0009/000984/098427eo.pdf

UNICEF (2013) *State of the World's Children: Children with Disabilities*, New York: UNICEF, www.unicef.org/sowc2013/

WHO (2001) *The international classification of functioning, disability and health (ICF)*, Geneva: WHO.

WHO and World Bank (2011) *World Report on Disability*, www.who.int/disabilities/world_report/2011/report.pdf

Wickenden, M. and Kembhavi, G. (2014) 'Ask us too! Doing participatory research with disabled children in the Global South', *Childhood*, 21, 400.

18

Troubled youth and troubling social policy: mental health from a Mad Studies perspective

Lucy Costa

While there has always been some focus on the mental health of young people, the past 20 years in the province of Ontario and Canada more broadly have specifically heightened professional and policy interest and focus to ensure there are interventions into the lives of 'troubled' youth. Initiatives exist today in order to help with a variety of identified priorities concerning young people – everything from youth homelessness, to various strategies into mental health symptomatology, and of course the crisis of youth suicide.

Strategies include enthusiasm for interventions that target primary and post-secondary students via mental health awareness campaigns such as 'Right By You'1 or others that specifically seek out the inclusion of youth themselves such as the 'Jack Project', an initiative created in 2010 by parents after their son Jack, a first year university white student, died by suicide at Queen's University.[2] There are also efforts by national organisations such as the Mental Health Commission of Canada to develop policy for young people that addresses access to psychiatric services in rural communities, particularly for Black and Indigenous communities who are deemed to be 'at risk'.

I am starting with, and reflecting on, the experiences of younger people who may or may not come in contact with services of various kinds, because they will inevitably inherit the impacts of legislation and social policy we construct today. As such, I am interested in creating a future that *is informed by* the people most affected by government policies, and so on, with the caveat that such future processes think carefully about what meaningful participation and inclusion of young voices looks like. In order to participate, people, but especially youth, need to understand the scope of governmental frameworks, their implications, what they have to gain by offering feedback and what utility projects hold for adolescent interests. As such, future community development must be of a calibre that pushes critical thinking through pedagogy, politics and activism. The knowledge currently being fostered through the emergent discipline of Mad Studies is one hopeful avenue towards providing an alternative to the current rhetorical limitations of inclusion discourse circulating in social policy. I begin my discussion using three stories all of which have been imprinted upon by both policy and death.

Troubled Teens: Mary

At the age of 16, I left home for good and lived in a Toronto group home from 1986 until 1988 with 17 other young women who, for one reason or another, were alone, pregnant or had also left home (or had no home to begin with). In addition to the day staff of social workers, there would also be an occasional visit by a psychiatrist who would work with specific girls who had been identified as having 'complex issues'. After one year, most group home residents were required to transition into independent living, with part of this process of transition requiring setting oneself up with welfare. It was part of group home policy to try to move girls out as soon as feasible. It is important to note that once you left the group home, girls were not afforded follow up assistance from staff. One of the girls who had been identified as having complex issues was Mary; a young South Asian girl who had been in the group home much longer than the time limited one-year mark.

Mary lived in the group home many years longer than other residents. Aside from being funny, and a great storyteller, Mary was a relentless cigarette smoker and drank many cups of coffee on any given day. When I lived in the house, she was eventually prohibited from drinking more than one cup a day. Most unforgettably, Mary had recurrent nightmares often causing her to wake up screaming in the middle of the night, and some occasions causing her to run out of the house and into the street in her night clothes. Most of us (including staff) often assumed she was dealing with a lot of stress and that she drank too much coffee. It was not until about 20 years later that I learned that Mary had committed suicide a few years after leaving the group home, that she was an incest survivor, and that her 'nightmares' were actually flashbacks of her traumatic experiences.

Thinking about this period, and the ways in which the group home focused primarily on social work modalities as opposed to psychiatric ones, raises important questions about how time and context impact the way in which youth were understood. Today it is quite probable that Mary's strange behaviour would be understood as a psychiatric diagnosis, and I am most certain that she would be deemed to be attention seeking, manipulative and 'acting out'. It is likely that today, she would have received a diagnosis of borderline personality disorder. Over the years, increasing public discussion about mental illness and associated 'stigma' talk have simultaneously allowed scientific determinism to influence other disciplines and therapeutic modalities in order to resolve multifaceted social problems, and more importantly, to rehabilitate or cure troubled teens or 'appear to be able' to rehabilitate them. This turn towards biomedicine and psychologisms has led to legitimacy that reinforces neoliberal (management) expectations of the role social service or community agencies should play. In other words, there are virtually no agencies that can operate and offer support to young people without expected outcomes that prioritise metrics of success over quality relationships, unless such agencies are supported through independent fundraising or philanthropic donation. Thus, much of the discourse on youth support is moving, and will continue to move towards emphasising biomedical narratives as cause for concern and remedy. The work of Canada's Mental Health Commission is a case in point.

In 2016, the Mental Health Commission of Canada (MHCC) put forward a proposal for systemic change from the perspective of youth, and in it they state that the document was created via the Youth Council at the MHCC. Replicating similar types of sound bites in respect of the 'stigma of mental illness' and its troubling statistics, there is little evidence thus far that the Youth Council veers away from the very normative narratives that have been circulating through a biomedical lens to understand youth distress. The Youth Council also created a similar and familiar network of speech, reinforcing particular kinds of knowledge which bolster the familiar ways government funded mental health organisations address social problems. Like the MHCC, the Youth Council produced its version of a strategic direction document, mirroring the same template.

The MHCC Youth Perspective document begins by stating that they use a 'critical youth lens to rewrite all six strategic directions, drawing on personal experiences to make sense of a large policy document and turn it into something original' (MHCC, 2016). The main aim, in their words, was to have the report mirror the strategies as created in a previous report entitled *Changing Directions, Changing Lives: The Mental Health Strategy for Canada* (MHCC, 2012). The MHCC reports that 70% of young adults with mental illnesses state that their symptoms first started in childhood (Government of Canada, 2006). Like previous reports and policies, there is an ever present urgency in regards to attending to potential 'crisis' for youth. The report does mention human rights, but only briefly in the context of police interactions, housing rights and the criminal justice system; there are, however, no articulations of rights as important while in hospital. The report is somewhat heavily laden with discussion of prevention as a means to save people from becoming unwell.

While 'prevention' might be useful for some, there is a woeful lack of discussion or strategy on how to help children who are struggling with social factors: poverty, child abuse, and so on. There has never been an awareness campaign to stimulate awareness within our very own households to the same degree as it currently exists for 'stigma' or mental illness awareness. An area that merits further consideration is whether these national initiatives or health policy frameworks even play any useful role in local jurisdictions. How might youth involved in these projects move away from tokenistic performances of inclusion to truly understanding whether such frameworks assist in promoting consistency and coordination of policy, or effective standard setting and evaluation? Policies that are aimed at helping vulnerable young people can betray them. For example, there are a variety of policies that guide workers at various professional sites, such as social services or hospitals, who are obliged to report mistreatment of young people. While this is a helpful policy, it falls flat if aid does not follow through. The story of Katelynn Sampson serves as such a case.

Children's Aid: Katelynn Sampson

Katelynn was a 7-year-old who was beaten to death in the summer of 2008. The forensic pathologist documented 70 brutal injuries across her body, including eight broken ribs, holes in both lips where her teeth had cut through, and a wound in her middle finger so deep it exposed the bone. In a misguided effort to give her daughter a better life, Bernice Sampson, Katelynn's mother, sent her daughter to live with two friends who, like her, had a serious addiction to crack cocaine. During the inquest into the circumstances of Katelynn's death, it became obvious that, despite a number of red flags, two different child protection agencies had failed to follow policy and keep up with Katelynn's file (Porter, 2015). Following the inquest, 173 recommendations into Katelynn's death were made, resulting in the Ontario Legislature passing Bill 51, the Katelynn Principle, which aims at overhauling child protection laws.[3] Included in this Bill are the following principles when making a decision that affects a child:

1. The child must be at the centre of the decision.
2. The child is an individual with rights. The child must always be seen, the child's voice must be heard, and the child must be listened to and respected.
3. The child's heritage must be taken into consideration and respected. Attention must be paid to the broad and diverse communities the child identifies with, including communities defined by matters such as race, ethnicity, religion, language, and sexual orientation.
4. Actions must be taken to ensure that a child who is capable of forming their own views, is able to express those views freely and safely about matters affecting them.
5. The child's views must be given due weight in accordance with the child's age and maturity.
6. In accordance with the child's age and maturity, the child must be given the opportunity to participate before any decisions affecting the child are made, whether the participation is direct or through a support person or representative.
7. In accordance with the child's age and maturity, the child must be engaged through honest and respectful dialogue about how and why decisions affecting them are made.

This Bill attempts to prioritise the child's voice. It is important to consider the voice and rights of children, but how do we centre this inclusion while still paying attention to other systemic issues that impact on why children interface with these various agencies in the first place? We know for instance that, as demonstrated by Katelynn, much of the literature speaks to the overrepresentation of Indigenous or black children in the child welfare system (Dettlaff and Rycraft, 2010). How does the history of colonialism in Canada integrate with the desire to include children's voices – are youth aware and exposed to this history and if not, would that not constitute another form of abuse? Ying Yee, Hackbusch and Wong argue that the future of childcare services must incorporate an anti-oppression approach to help understand why there is a continuous disproportionality of representation of marginalised children and youth in child welfare systems, but most importantly they make the following point:

> While opportunities for institutional change exist, they are hampered by the broad policy context, what Healy (2002) describes as a post-industrial environment whereby welfare state agencies are financially rewarded for their productivity and economic efficiency, rather than for their progress toward meeting social justice imperatives such as reduction of poverty, racism and other inequalities. (Ying Yee et al, 2015: 488)

While the challenges and tension of policy as it rolls out in community spaces are many (for example, standardisation of practices, 'risk management'), they are equally if not more so obstructing in mental health institutions. There are legal and privacy protections which, while very important, also subsequently allow for authorisation to cover up what occurs in these spaces until there is public pressure to expose misconduct or negligence. If Katelynn been subjected to mental health incarceration, her voice might not be centred in the same way, or at all – the Katelynn Principle in this instance would prove irrelevant given a finding of her incapacity. In Ontario, individuals under 12 years old cannot appeal a finding of incapacity. If you are between the ages of 12 and 15, you can't appeal the decision of a parent or substitute decision maker who is admitting you, but you can however apply to the Consent and Capacity Board to determine whether you need, 'observation, care and treatment in a psychiatric facility'. The Consent and Capacity Board is then able to consider a young person's wishes. Once a person reaches 16 years of age, they then follow the same processes as any adult.[4] This is important to keep in mind as psychiatric units are being offered as an alternative to correctional facilities for youth as was argued throughout the Ashley Smith inquest as they tried to determine whether she was 'mad' or 'bad.'

Youth and confinement: Ashley Smith

No other story confused and outraged the country more than the story of the death of 19-year-old Ashley Smith in 2007. While the province, and wider federal system, have since had a decade to advance the recommendations and advice stemming from her death, neither have done so. Ashley's story represents one of the cruellest examples of carceral care for youth – one where institutional policy literally played led to her death.

Ashley Smith died on the prison segregation cell floor of Grand Valley Institution for Women wearing nothing more than a prison gown as correctional staff watched her tie a ligature around her neck choking herself to death. After observing her for 30 minutes lying on the floor, they entered the cell but were too late to revive her. One of the most disturbing facts that emerged throughout the inquest was that senior administrators had ordered frontline staff not to intervene when Ashley tied ligatures around her neck until she lost consciousness:

> The inquest has heard from guards that senior managers ordered them to stay out of Smith's cell as long as she was breathing, because they believed the teen was simply acting out. (*Canadian Press*, 2013

The final verdict in the 2013 inquest into Ashley Smith's death ruled it to be a homicide[5] – that Ashley was a victim of the judicial and correctional processes that excluded her voice and violated her rights. In light of this, there has been ongoing pressure to abolish the use of segregation rooms in prison, and a media story in 2016 reported that since 2014, Corrections Service Canada's use of indefinite solitary confinement was cut in half. In the 2015–16 fiscal year, 247 federal prisoners spent more than 120 days in 'segregation', down from 505 in 2013–14 (Correctional Service Canada, 2016). The claims from Corrections Service Canada that there were too many offenders in need of segregation, did not hold water – the corrections system did not lose control of its prisons and learned that it is possible to curb the overuse of segregation. Yet despite this research and the inquest recommendations, solitary confinement remains a live issue with stories such as that of Adam Capay, a 23-year-old Anishinaabe young man who spent close to 1,600 days over four and a half years locked in a 5-by-10-foot cell, the lights on 24 hours a day (Cole, 2017). This should concern us all as well as some of the assumptions that if troubled youth were placed in a psychiatric facility for care that there would be less abuse. In Ashley Smith's inquest, the Empowerment Council[6] had standing to participate in proceedings and argued against the presumption that the hospital is a safer place for youth with serious mental health distress. While psychiatric facilities employ different policies than correctional facilities, they are still both subject to the restriction of liberties and much work has yet to be done to advocate for recognition that both are sites that impact vulnerable bodies.

The role of Mad Studies

Mad Studies is an interdisciplinary field that stretches across both academic and community based knowledge to produce education, scholarship and analysis about the experiences, history, culture, narratives of a diversity of people who have experienced psychiatry and the mental health system(s).[7] As this field continues to progress it has a significant role to play in future discussions of social policy, particularly as applied to young people moving through these systems and as they 'age out' of support and services. Specifically, it can continue to inform and shift policy as pertinent to issues of access, equity and accommodation. Scholarship in the field is already burgeoning though discussions that examine and analyse how local and international policy and legislation impacts on service users (Russo and Sweeney, 2016). Mad Studies can further collaborate across other disciplines such as queer studies, critical disability studies, critical race studies, and Indigenous studies (to name a few). As this potentially transformative and subversive field takes hold, it is important that our qualitative and quantitative research describes and accounts for the experiences of service users in our current austerity and violence regimes, which, if left to their own devices, will dispose of those who are most vulnerable.

As part of this, future work might further interrogate the opportunities and limitations of current Mad identity politics and the role of activism in enabling change. I say this as Mad Studies itself is a product of the early years of activism, of creating an alternative voice and understanding on experiences of madness. Mad Studies' greatest strength is in organising a variety of perspectives and values, and determining what common thread unites us. Future Mad Studies scholars will also be instrumental in mapping the shifting debates in various sectors and in relationship to broader discussions of disability inclusion. If I reflect on what Mad Studies could have offered Mary, whom I met years ago in the group home, the answer is connection and an understanding of her struggles, not singularly as applied to her individually, but of their importance to others with similar experiences. We have not yet explored our role in understanding histories captured through child protection agencies as in Katelynn's story. But, we did try to intervene from our knowledge base in the inquest of Ashley Smith via the work of a service user organisation.

We have already been challenged to ensure that making Mad Studies work accessible to other jurisdictions whereby people with disability and mental health issues are disproportionally represented among the world poorest, as well as lacking the most basic needs. It is one thing to examine the various limitations of welfare and child protection services in the western world, but it is a whole other thing to look at these problems in communities that have no guidelines at all. Historically and thus far, the response to these challenges is to ensure we are being inclusive and allowing for representation at decision making levels and, while this is an important point, we have also learned that representation itself is not enough – the values and actions put forward are distinctly important and impactful.

Increased access to data and statistics of various kinds will assist us in understanding the scope of problems, but we have yet to ensure knowledge translation and community development is at the place it needs to be to comprehend these technologies of governance. Perhaps the real challenge ahead is to stop arguing for 'inclusion' at all – in some regards that theoretical battle has been won. Instead, our efforts must move towards finding the means to ensure we curb anti-intellectualism and to continuously find new ways to critically engage our young people by supporting their interests and teaching community responsibility, as opposed to continuously simply preparing people for an increasingly ruthless labour market, the conditions of which subsequently relegate individuals to become agents of the state. We see this with the ways in which 'lived experience' and 'peer work' has established and coopted itself so readily in the mental health sector. Mad Studies holds much potential, but only insofar as it links its past with the present with new imaginings to counter the desperate lives of vulnerable young people who become the women and men left behind by uncaring systems.

Notes

[1] For more information, visit http://rightbyyou.ca/en

[2] The project changed its name to jack.org and encourages youth to engage, raise awareness and reduce the stigma around the vital topic of mental health.

[3] Bill 51 has passed two readings and is now being reviewed by the Senate Committee on Justice where it then will be passed back for third reading and vote. If passed, it will receive Royal Assent and become a law.

[4] Justice for Children and Youth (2013) *Legal Rights Wiki*, http://jfcy.org/en/rights/psychiatric-facilities/

[5] It is important to note that a finding of homicide at an inquest does not constitute any charges or trial for correctional staff. Inquests are merely an inquisitorial process designed to explore the circumstances of a death.

[6] The Empowerment Council is an independent advocacy organisation run by current and former service users representing the rights of clients of the Centre for Addiction and Mental Health and others outside the hospital in Toronto, Canada.

[7] For more information, visit the Mad Studies Network: https://madstudies2014.wordpress.com

References

Canadian Press (2013) 'Ashley Smith inquest told guards had call on intervention: Prison official tells inquest she can't recall staff asking for direction', 23 September, www.cbc.ca/news/canada/toronto/ashley-smith-inquest-told-guards-had-call-on-intervention-1.1865051

Cole, D. (2017) 'Abolish solitary confinement for Ontario's children and youth', *Toronto Star*, 5 January, www.thestar.com/opinion/commentary/2017/01/05/abolish-solitary-confinement-for-ontarios-children-and-youth.html

Correctional Service Canada (2016) *Examining Time Spent in Administrative Segregation*, June, www.csc-scc.gc.ca/research/092/rib-16-07-eng.pdf

Dettlaff, A.J. and Rycraft, J.R. (2010) 'Factors contributing to disproportionality in the child welfare system: Views from the legal community', *Social Work*, 55 (3), 213–24.

Government of Canada (2006) *The human face of mental health and mental illness in Canada*, www.phac-aspc.gc.ca/publicat/human-humain06/pdf/human_face_e.pdf

MHCC (Mental Health Commission of Canada) (2012) *Changing Directions, Changing Lives: The Mental Health Strategy for Canada*, http://strategy.mentalhealthcommission.ca/pdf/strategy-images-en.pdf

MHCC (2016) *The Mental Health Strategy for Canada: A Youth Perspective*, www.mentalhealthcommission.ca/English/document/72171/mental-health-strategy-canada-youth-perspective

Porter, C. (2015) 'How can a child protection agency ignore a child: Porter', *Toronto Star*, 27 November, www.thestar.com/news/gta/2015/11/27/how-can-a-child-protection-agency-ignore-a-child-porter.html

Russo, J. and Sweeney, A. (eds) (2016) *Searching for a Rose Garden: challenging psychiatry, fostering mad studies*, Monmouth: PCCS Books.

Ying Yee, J., Hackbusch, C. and Wong, H. (2015) 'An Anti-Oppression (AO) Framework for Child Welfare in Ontario, Canada: Possibilities for Systemic Change', *British Journal of Social Work*, 45 (2), 474–92.

19

Disability: an inclusive life course and developmental approach to social policy

Emmeline Burdett

Introduction

It sometimes seems to get forgotten that impairment and disability are worldwide issues, even though they might be dealt with differently in different parts of the globe. To this end, the International Paralympic Committee has laid down a series of four core principles which demonstrate its values: Courage, Determination, Inspiration and Equality.[1] As Cameron (2013) and very many others have pointed out, the whole issue of the Paralympics and their ethos and image is extremely problematic from a Disability Studies point of view. It is possible that, in terms of the Paralympics' core principles, the focus on the athletes themselves, rather than on problems they experience from the societies in which they live, is intended in part to be unthreatening and to be applicable to as much of the world as possible – while not 'rocking the boat'.

The focus on the Paralympians as 'inspirational individuals' also makes it appear that they – and by extension, disabled people in general – exist outside of any kind of social context, and are effectively not part of society as a whole. An inclusive view of the life course would inevitably have to reject this line of thought and instead realise that a well-functioning society is one in which people differ, and their differences are accepted and responded to in the most appropriate way. One way in which this approach differs from current reality concerns the issue of the abortion of foetuses found to have impairments. The UK actress Sally Phillips has recently challenged the idea that eradicating Down's syndrome constitutes progress.[2] In asking this question, Phillips raised a number of significant ethical questions that make points integral to issues raised in this chapter. Her investigation, and the resulting BBC2 documentary, 'A World Without Down's Syndrome?', makes timely remarks about the causal link between the ease with which impaired foetuses may be aborted and the growth of damaging and prejudicial ideas about existing disabled people – because, apart from anything else, challenges to these ideas are neither sought nor noticed by much of mainstream society. One example of this is Iceland, in which – Phillips discovered – 100% of pregnancies in which the foetus is found to have Down's syndrome end in termination. Clearly, in such a situation, it is impossible for people with Down's syndrome to develop any ideas about how their society might function better and become more inclusive and convinced of their worth – simply because there are no people with Down's syndrome! In this chapter, I am going to look at various initiatives both by individuals and by disabled people and/or their advocates collectively, and argue that they constitute opportunities to think about how to do things differently, and how to create a different and better kind of society than the one we currently have. I contend that this is particularly important in the current climate in many societies, in which a relentless political emphasis on 'work' has helped to foster the idea that to be a mere human being is not enough – it is instead necessary to be a 'human doing' (meaning that such people as corrupt bankers and expenses-dodging politicians can operate free from censure). In addition, current British 'austerity' policies have contributed in no small part to an unleashing of the baser instincts of which human beings are capable, in which the ability to understand someone else's circumstances has been replaced by an ignorant desire to condemn them for perceived failings or supposed fraud. So, in this chapter I will argue that, in order to create a better society, it is not necessary to eradicate impairments, but that it *is* necessary to eradicate many ideas which are gaining currency, with regard to people with impairments. The chapter begins, however, by looking at the somewhat less malignant but still constraining idea that the leisure time of disabled people with support needs is essentially valueless, and at the efforts that are being made to combat this idea.

In July 2016, I rather belatedly left the parental home. As I am a wheelchair user, this meant that I would be having a support worker, initially in the morning for an hour, and in the evening for 30 minutes. While the morning session was and remains absolutely fine, the evening worker's job was to help me get into bed, and the up-shot was that I had to go to bed at 8.30pm, several hours before I actually wanted to do so. There seemed to be little or no awareness that, for a 38-year-old, this situation was far from ideal. I did attempt to get my evening care moved to a later time, but was unsuccessful, as I was told that it would be impossible for the agency to send someone any later. Fortunately, I realised that I could manage by myself, and was thus able to stop my evening visits, but what if this approach is unfeasible or simply not desired? As Cameron (2013: 21) and many others have pointed out, the notion of 'care' is a problematic one. Nevertheless, the aim should surely be that of helping the person to live as full a life as possible. It often seems, however, that the person requiring support is supposed to fit in with the shift patterns/desire to get home early of the support worker. When this happens, the person requiring support is in a sense depersonalised, as his or her individuality – tastes, preferences, personality – are disregarded. This is one area in which disability – as opposed to impairment – impacts strongly upon the life course. After all, if you cannot do the things you want to in the evenings, or you need to be ready by a particular time in the morning so you can go to work or elsewhere, the chances of you living a life which is in any way fulfilled diminishes considerably, and you are left trying to squeeze the things you want or need to do into the time left to you by your care agency. As this section will clearly demonstrate, this is not simply an individual problem experienced by me alone, and as such disabled people have embarked on both campaigning for change, and bringing it about for their own lives.

'We noticed our fans leaving our gigs at 9pm'

The Brighton-based organisation 'Stay Up Late' originated with the members of the punk band 'Heavy Load', who noticed that when they played gigs, there was often a mass exodus of fans at 9pm – when everything was just getting started. After wondering if this was a comment upon the quality of their music, the band realised that – like them – many of their fans had learning difficulties, and were leaving concerts at 9pm not because they were bored or did not like the music, but because their support workers' shifts finished at 10pm, and so they had to get home in time. These aspiring concertgoers were experiencing just what I experienced – because they needed some level of support which was not the norm for adults in society, their personalities and interests had to play second fiddle to the inflexibility of someone else's schedule.

As the members of 'Heavy Load' point out, being free to spend one's leisure hours in the way one wants is not a trivial matter. Quite the reverse, in fact:

> Being able to go out in the evening is vitally important in terms of our informal support networks, friendships, and how we express ourselves. It's also no doubt going to have a significant effect on people's physical and mental health.[3]

To this end, Stay Up Late campaigns for change, but in practical terms has also organised the initiative 'Gig Buddies', which originated in Sussex, but now has branches in Midlothian and in Sydney, Australia.[4] The project describes its four core principles as follows:

- It's about friendships – real friendships
- It's about doing mainstream cultural activities in your community
- It's about people with learning disabilities making real choices about the way they live their lives
- It's about creating a project led by people with learning disabilities.[5]

Potential accusations of paternalism are in some sense avoided by the project's emphasis on the need for volunteers to have a genuine interest in the gigs to which he or she accompanies a disabled person:

> Gig Buddies matches adults who have a learning disability to a volunteer who has similar interests to go to events together that you both love.[6]

In this way Gig Buddies and Stay Up Late do seem to seek to create a genuine connection and meeting of minds between their volunteers and the people who use the service, which might help to break down barriers and might potentially not be replicated even if, for example, the person being supported had his or her own personal assistant rather than a support worker from an agency. The difficulty comes when the organisers describe the benefits of the service, which they do in depressingly familiar terms of 'getting people to see past the disability':

> We know that this [making sure people are socially connected rather than isolated] is not just healthier for individuals, it's also healthier for communities. A community that sees people as individuals with particular interests will see past any disability and get to know the person.[7]

There can be no doubt at all that the first part of this statement is correct. It is indisputably better for people not to be socially isolated, and it is similarly vital that people are viewed as individuals with particular interests, not just as tasks to be completed before support workers can return home. The problem comes with the last sentence, which strongly suggests that Gig Buddies' prospective clients can only hope to be seen as individuals once they reach a point at which others can overlook their impairments. This runs counter to Gig Buddies' stated aim of having their project led by people with learning difficulties, and is something of a 'fly in the ointment' for a clearly much needed initiative which could do much to break down barriers and create societal change. The number of testimonials from happy attendees is testament to the success of the project.[8]

'Stay Up Late' is an interesting initiative, and one which, if taken up more widely, could have many benefits for society as a whole. In terms of 'an inclusive approach to the life course', however, it would have to change its ethos of 'getting people to see past the disability', because it is only by seeing a person's impairment as part of him or her that anything becomes truly inclusive.

'Fit for work'

At the beginning of this chapter I referred to the current relentless emphasis on 'work', and the government's 'austerity' policies, which have seen many people denied the financial support to which they had previously been entitled, and shoehorned into jobs that are completely unsuitable for them. Apart from the problem I referenced, in other words that such things as rising levels of hate crime indicate that these policies are successfully fostering an idea that benefits claimants are lazy, workshy drains upon the rest of society, it is also noteworthy that these expectations place the onus entirely on disabled people to get themselves into employment – with no attention paid to the fact that it is usually necessary to be hired by an employer. In this way, societal bonds are broken, rather than created. This is the exact opposite of what organisations like Gig Buddies are doing.

At a recent Labour Party rally attended by the Labour leader, Jeremy Corbyn, the disabled performer Liz Carr drew attention to the current governmental obsession with 'work' by making a rather controversial reference to 'Arbeit Macht Frei' ('Work Sets You Free') – the sign on the entrance gates to Auschwitz, the Nazi concentration camp. 'Where have we heard this before?' Carr asked those attending the rally. 'Sorry, but it needs to be said'.[9]

Carr's meaning, and the question of whether or not her reference was apposite, could be the subject of a whole other essay, or quite possibly of a whole book. Nevertheless, it does raise the question of how one might both reference current injustices, and point to a different way of doing things. A possible answer to this question is provided by the disabled artist and activist Liz Crow, and her installation 'Figures'. This was an art installation – timed to coincide with the 2015 general election – which saw Crow making 650 individual figures out of Thames river mud, each representing a real individual at the sharp end of the UK government's policy of welfare cuts.[10] Crow spoke about the various ways in which she hoped that the installation would help to bring about societal change. The first and most obvious was clearly that of drawing attention to the devastating effect that austerity policies were having, but beyond that, it was a reflective piece which opened up the possibility of creating dialogue about possibilities for a better, kinder, less judgemental society, and what form this should take.[11] In addition, Crow came to recognise that, although this was not necessarily intentional, the project had to be done in a very collaborative and interdependent way, which really mirrored the change in society that it sought to create:

> 'I hadn't initially seen getting me down the steps as part of the performance, but I realise it is, because it is a space where particular values have to be put into practice for it to work.'[12]

While this is true, and much needed, particularly in the current climate – hostile as it is to the idea of anyone needing help – it is not the only answer. The concept and execution of the Figures project were Crow's, and the organisation Disability Arts Online seeks to raise the profile of disabled artists and provide them with a platform for their work.

This chapter's final investigation into the possibilities of creating societal change takes us to Weersp, in the Netherlands, and to Hogeweyk, a purpose-built village for people with dementia. Conventional thinking tells us that dementia is not only a tragedy, but a growing threat to humanity, given that we have an ageing population. Hogeweyk takes a different approach, with residents living, in groups of six or seven, in 23 houses in different styles which are recognisable from the residents' own histories. The Hogeweyk website stresses that

> the fact that a person [is] handicapped by dementia does not mean that they no longer have a valid opinion on their day-to-day life and surroundings.[13]

In a sense, this emphasis upon the residents' agency and the value of their opinions and personalities links it to 'Stay Up Late', where aspiring concertgoers are regarded as people with an interest in music, not as 'patients' whose support needs should take precedence over every other area of their lives.

One potential problem, however, is the fact that the residents of the Hogeweyk village are still, in a sense, 'lumped together' – something which is anathema to anyone concerned with the social model of disability, essentially because if a group of people are taken outside of mainstream society, they become ghettoised, and both they and their requirements become regarded as 'Other' – something that mainstream society does not have to worry about. On the other hand, the Hogeweyk residents do live in houses which are chosen for their applicability to each resident's former life, which does suggest an element of recognition of the individuality of each resident. In addition, Hogeweyk accepts that its residents can be happier if their mode of living reflects the past, to which they have a stronger connection, rather than the present. This is in marked contrast to the way in which an unhappy and confused person with dementia can often be 'forced' to live solely in the present, as the present is what society as a whole considers important. Speaking about an excursion to Graz in Austria, connected with an exhibition of her work, the disabled artist and academic Ju Gosling recalled how colleagues had told her that Europeans 'do not understand the social model of disability' to which Gosling replied that there was no reason why a US theory taken up and developed in Britain *would* be understood in Austria.[14] Gosling may have meant, for example, that civil rights movements originated in the US, but her assertion that the Social Model is a US theory is incorrect, as it originated in Britain (Cameron, 2013: 137–40). Nevertheless, this takes us back to the point raised at the beginning of this chapter – namely, can we have inclusive ideas and policies about disability which are applicable to the whole world, or at least to a region of it? As the examples I have chosen show, any such policies have to have the active involvement of disabled people, as well as recognition that impairment is part of someone, not something nasty to be overlooked or cured.

Conclusion

This chapter has looked at various initiatives, both collective and individual, to challenge stereotypes, prejudices and dismissive attitudes towards disabled people. The chapter began with a discussion of the organisation Stay Up Late, and how they are challenging the idea that people with support needs have needs, but no personalities or individual interests that need concern anyone – just so long as they were in bed by 10pm. The next section of the chapter focused on Liz Crow, and the ways in which her installation 'Figures' sought to effect societal change, both by drawing attention to the human cost of government policies, and by opening up discussions about how to create a different kind of society. The nature of both the installation and the way in which Crow and her team collaborated to produce it relate back to Sally Phillips' comments at the beginning of this chapter, regarding the view of disabled people as a mere waste of resources, and of taxpayers' money. The final section of the chapter focused on the Dutch 'dementia village' of Hogeweyk. Though it seems that this village is more of a practical response to current problems regarding the ways in which dementia is approached, rather than an overarching attempt to change the ethos of society as a whole, when considered in conjunction with the other two examples given in this chapter, it may constitute another way of changing society for the better. In conclusion, one can say that an inclusive approach to the life course would have to be one which takes account not only of impairment, but of the individuality, talents and experience of disabled people.

Notes

[1] www.paralympic.org/feature/what-are-paralympic-values

[2] Sally Phillips' recent television documentary, 'A World Without Down's Syndrome?', is discussed in the text.

[3] http://stayuplate.org/stay-up-late-at-the-great-escape-part-1

[4] www.gigbuddies.org.uk/other-gig-buddies-projects

[5] www.gigbuddies.org.uk

[6] www.gigbuddies.org.uk

[7] www.gigbuddiesinabox.org

[8] www.gigbuddies.org.uk/review/the-together-the-people – many other testimonials can be found in the same section.

[9] www.mirror.co.uk/news/uk-news/actress-liz-carr-stuns-audience-8911590

[10] http://wearefigures.co.uk

[11] http://wearefigures.co.uk

[12] www.disabilityartsonline.org.uk/Interview-Liz-Crow-on-Figures

[13] https://hogeweyk.dementiavillage.com/en/kenniscentrum/

[14] www.accessmagazine.co.uk/take-ten-interview/ (10 July 2012)

References

Cameron, C. (ed) (2013) *Disability Studies: A Student's Guide*, London: Sage.

20

Independent living from a Black Disabled Woman's perspective

Michelle Daley

Introduction

The discourse pertaining to Black Disabled People is often negative, it manifests itself, resulting in discriminatory practices, and may contribute to the inequality to access of services. It is from this point of view that this chapter will discuss the quality and experience of policy implementation and what it achieves in practice. It will also look at independent living from a personal perspective, as a Black Disabled Woman, as well as drawing on literature for evidence.

Finally, this chapter also argues the need for policymaking to be participatory but also that there is no comparable difference between White and Black Disabled People's ambition and motivation to achieve independent living.

Do Black Disabled People have a different understanding of 'independent living'?

I want to emphasise from the outset that I do not believe that Black Disabled People have a different understanding of independent living or disability issues. Furthermore, our experiences are likely to differ between those born and/or raised in Great Britain, and those that have moved to live here. This is particularly true for those who come from conflict and economically poor countries, where circumstances would have forced them to struggle to achieve freedom, independence politically and personal gain (Driedger,1989). This point sets the premises to further the discussion.

While I believe in one human race, there is a division of races that creates a division of opportunities. For the purpose of this chapter 'Black People' are described as people from African, Caribbean and some Asian descent. Also, I will use the term 'Black Disabled People' to encompass our different intersectionalities. Crenshaw (2015), a prominent American Black Civil Rights advocate and scholar, introduced the intersectionality theory to highlight the complexities and interplay of different identities different experiences of a human life, and underpins the fundamental idea that people are not homogenous and a one size will not fit all. I will elaborate on this concept later in this chapter.

Many of the accomplishments people appreciate today are owed to the work and efforts of the Women's, Black and Independent Living Movement in challenging discrimination. The Independent Living Movement made the concept of 'independent living' (Kudlick, 2003) a reality; it gave Disabled People control and a voice over their lives. Disability Rights UK, a national organisation that works with other Disabled People's organisations to campaign for the rights of Disabled People, advocates independent living as empowering Disabled People

> to have greater choice and control in directing your own life, having the same range of choices as a non-disabled person to make informed decisions about any practical support you require to go about your everyday life. It is living independently without the dependency created by institutions (Disability Rights UK, 2012).

Despite these improvements literature has shown a negative disparity between White and Black Disabled People's take up of support and services, such as direct payment (Commission for Social Care Inspection, 2008). In their book *Reflections*, influential British Black Disabled advocates Nasa Begum, Mildrette Hill and Andy Stevens (1994) make a persuasive argument that 'Black Disabled People are perceived as being part of a problem which can only be resolved by empowered others' (1994: 41). I argue this perpetuates racism, causes inequality to access of services thus hindering our opportunity to achieve independent living (Kudlick, 2003).

Crenshaw (2015) revealed to me how policy and practice create oppression, inequality but also injustice. At this point I direct our attention to the Macpherson Report of the Stephen Lawrence Inquiry (1999), which came about because of the murder of Stephen Lawrence, a young Black British man, by a gang of White youths in South London and the subsequent Metropolitan police inquiry and the UK Criminal Justice System response. It was in this report that the term 'institutional racism' first appeared, and was defined as:

> The collective failure of an organisation to provide an appropriate and professional service to people because of their colour, culture, or ethnic origin. It can be seen or detected in processes, attitudes and behaviour which amount to discrimination through unwitting prejudice, ignorance, thoughtlessness and racist stereotyping which disadvantage minority ethnic people. (Macpherson, 1999: para 6.3)

Essentially the report strengthens the arguments of Crenshaw (2015) and Begum et al (1994) regarding institutions viewing us as the problem, rather than the institution itself. Macpherson (1999) provided strong evidence for the need to address the systemic inequality and to change the way institutions work to discriminate against people.

I would argue that every Black Disabled person is motivated and capable, with support, of achieving independent living (Kudlick, 2003). We are not the problem or intellectually inferior compared to our White Disabled counterparts. And there is no fundamental difference in the way we conceptualise 'independent living' (Kudlick, 2003). We want the same opportunity to live an ordinary life but we need to be part of the decision making processes.

In what way can service providers and the like address oppressive practices if we [Black Disabled People] are absent from the political debates?

Prominent Black Disabled People have written at length on the issue of our absence from within the political debates about disability. For example, Begum and colleagues wrote that Black Disabled People's contributions are seen as 'at best mystifying, at worst ... ignored as irrelevant rhetoric' (1994: 41). They further argue that Disabled People's Movements have failed us by not fully engaging or involving our experiences within its agenda. With great eloquence Mildrette Hill (Begum et al, 1994) creates a positive argument that a Black Disabled People's Movement would give us a political voice to challenge oppressive practice, as well as address our absence from political debate.

Prior to becoming politically aware of disability issues, I had little understanding of disability and intersectionality. I was introduced to the Disabled People's Movement in the late 1990s and the politics through an encounter with a good friend, Jaspal Dhani, the former chief executive officer of United Kingdom Disabled People's Council, then a leading Disabled People's organisation. I soon learnt about positive prominent and influential Black Disabled activists at a local and international level. People of the likes of Dr Ossie Stuart, Saadia Neilson, Jaspal Dhani and Nasa Begum played a significant role in the formative years of my career.

Sadly, Nasa Begum and Mildrette Hill are no longer with us. I connected with them, and this allowed me to better understand my own experiences as a Black Disabled Woman but also knowing society's attitudes to each of these intersectionalities is just as important. Speaking from this point of view Patricia Hill Collins (2008), an American Black feminist, describes intersectionality as the 'Matrix of Dominance'. She looks at the way inequality and oppression are organised based on social constructs and social hierarchy and reveals how segregation and discrimination work in institutions and human lives. The value of her argument has highlighted to me the reason why policy, and service providers and other organisations would find someone like me a challenge, too complicated or a desirable person to tick boxes to fulfil equality and diversity monitoring exercises. This only emphasises to me that, while the concept of policy and practice is to promote equality, what I see is many institutions continuing to be steeped in traditions of oppression in policy and practice that effect the delivery of human services.

In order to address our intersectionality, the division of race and the division of opportunities. I am persuaded by the idea of a Black Disabled People's Movement, because history has taught me that it is movements that have 'taken up the struggle for equality and participation' (Driedger, 1989: 1).

Do you think that Black Disabled People receive a better, worse or the same quality of health and social care service in comparison to their White counterparts?

The passing of the Community Care (Direct Payments) Act 1996 (Jarrett, 2015) and most recently the introduction of personal health budgets (NHS England Patient Participation Team, 2014) was central to the policy of health and social care personalisation (Local Government Association, 2014). The UK government made it legal for social care service provision and funding to be chosen and controlled by those eligible for support, and directed local authorities to relinquish their control. Most commonly, this meant that many individuals chose to receive their support as a cash payment, based on an eligibility and needs assessments. The cash payment is referred to as a direct payment (Jarrett, 2015; NHS England Patient Participation Team, 2014) – this is used to purchase services to meet assessed and agreed support needs.

Unfortunately, despite these policy and practice changes, the idea of independent living (Kudlick, 2003) for many Disabled People remains a figment of their imagination. The UK Conservative government's austerity measures have drastically reduced public sector spending and Disabled People and people on low incomes have been disproportionately affected by these cuts, with health and social care services forced to tighten their eligibility criteria and reduce funding packages (Duffy, 2013; Daley, 2014). This austerity has had a particularly adverse effect on Black Disabled People (Runnymede Trust, 2015).

To help understand the barriers Black Disabled People experience when accessing services, it is worth focusing on a 2008 bulletin from the former English Commission for Social Care Inspection (now the English Care Quality Commission). It highlighted some of the barriers encountered by Black Disabled People in the way they access and receive services, particularly that services made cultural assumptions about requirements rather than consulting with individuals. In my opinion, another contributing factor is related to diversity deficit in health and social care policymaking and the knowledge gap regarding our support needs among professionals. For example, when an assessor presents their client's case to their senior manager requesting support for a Black Disabled Woman to maintain her hair and skin care, there is a risk that this will be rejected because of a lack of understanding about Afro textured hair and skin sensitivity. If this support request is turned down, is the service refusal related to racism, sexism or both? Is it budget driven or simply the result of lack of understanding? Such issues can be understood though the arguments of Mildrette Hill (Begum et al, 1994) and Macpherson (1999) about the failures of institutions to address the barriers that disadvantage Black People and perpetuate discrimination. Patricia Hill Collins (2008) further explains that inequality and oppression will continue to manifest themselves because institutions do not understand intersectionality and administrative systems cannot accommodate difference and complexity. For things to change, society needs to be better informed about who institutions involve in their decision making processes and how policy and practice are used to shape and influence the design and delivery of services. Then people can properly assess how oppression and inequality is being addressed, or not, through participation in decision making.

To illustrate this, I will share a personal account from a social care support assessment following surgery. It was not positive; it created fear and felt invasive. I was infuriated when, after major surgery, a hospital Social Worker informed me that my support requirements were 'too high' for me to return home, and so they were looking to place me in a nursing home. I refused and exerted my power to demonstrate that I had rights. During this time I constantly reminded myself that I am the author of my own future and not at the power of their pen. I successfully returned home. Such institutionalised administrative practice and insensitivity could be one of the reasons why Black People who are in need of support are deterred by the assessment process, and then end up needing to access services at crisis point.

I believe my experience relates to organisational constraints, but it can also to be understood in relation to the functioning of International Development project planning tools such as the Blueprint approach (Dale, 2004; Daley, 2014). The key purpose of national public sector and international aid agencies is to help improve conditions for people in need of support. However, the recipients of support from these sources regard these institutions as bureaucratic, regimented and led by professionals (Daley, 2008; Daley 2014), with help tied to conditions that are in the interests of the institution or organisation. For some Black Disabled People, these institutions remind them of a past where systems and plans were used to exert power and gain dominance during colonial times. Is this another reason why Black Disabled People often delay engaging with services until they are at a crisis point?

Despite the challenges to achieving independent living there are many services available, but in my opinion direct payments (Jarrett, 2015) and personal health budgets (NHS England Patient Participation Team, 2014) are where independent living (Kudlick, 2003) can be appropriately supported and achieved. For Black Disabled People, direct payments and the personal health budget can improve the quality of service and support they receive because they can be creative in how they meet their support requirements, and employ personal assistants that meet their lifestyle and are culturally sensitive.

Conclusion

This chapter discussed independent living from a personal perspective of a Black Disabled Woman; it also drew on literature for evidence. It revealed that simplistic policy assumptions about discrimination and inequality or simple solutions to achieving equality may in fact result in continued social inequality and injustice for Black Disabled People. These factors need to be considered as a reason for inequality to access of appropriate support, low take up of services and inferior support compared to our White Disabled counterparts.

Direct payments can be a positive way to meet different diverse support needs, but there are many challenges to implementing them. So, the time has come for Black Disabled People to strengthen our voice and presence and have Black Disabled People construct and implement policy and change the political discourse on disability to one that promotes equality to independent living.

References

Begum, N., Hill, M. and Stevens, A. (eds) (1994) *Reflections: Views of Black Disabled People on their Lives and Community Care*, London: Central Council for Education and Training in Social Work.

Commission for Social Care Inspection (2008) 'Putting people first: Equality and Diversity Matters 2: Providing appropriate services for black and minority ethnic people', *In Focus: Quality Issues in Social Care*, 8, London: Commission for Social Care Inspection, www.thinklocalactpersonal.org.uk/_assets/Resources/Personalisation/Localmilestones/Putting_people_first_Equality_and_Diversity_Matters_2.pdf

Collins, P.H. (2008) *Black Feminist Thought: Knowledge, Consciousness, and the Politics of Empowerment*, first edition, Oxford: Routledge.

Crenshaw, K. (2015) *On Intersectionality: The Essential Writings of Kimberlé Crenshaw*, New York: The New Press.

Dale, R. (2004) *Developing Planning: Concepts and Tools for Planners, Managers and Facilitators*, London: Zed Books Ltd.

Daley, M. (2014) 'Lived experience as a BME disabled person', presented at the 'Let's Get Personal' Conference on Self-Directed Support and BME Communities, Edinburgh, 14 May.

Daley, M. (2008) 'Project and Programme Design: Critically assess the blueprint approach to project design', MSc dissertation, London: University of East London.

Disability Rights UK (2012) 'Independent Living', Disability Rights UK Factsheet F38, www.disabilityrightsuk.org/independent-living-0

Driedger, D. (1989) *The Last Civil Rights Movement: Disabled Peoples' International*, London: C. Hurst & Co Publishers Ltd.

Duffy, S. (2013) *A Fair Society? How the Cuts Target Disabled People*, Sheffield: The Centre for Welfare Reform, www.centreforwelfarereform.org/uploads/attachment/354/a-fair-society.pdf

Jarrett, J. (2015) *Social Care: Direct Payments from a Local Authority (England)* (Number 03735), London: House of Commons.

Kudlick, C.J. (2003) 'Disability history: Why we need another "Other"', *The American Historical Review*, 108 (3), 763–93, www.jstor.org/stable/3523085

Local Government Association (2014) *Personalisation*, www.local.gov.uk/sites/default/files/documents/must-knows-adults-persona-249.pdf

Macpherson, W. (1999) *The Stephen Lawrence Inquiry: Report of an Inquiry*, Cm 4262-I, Secretary of State for the Home Department, www.gov.uk/government/uploads/system/uploads/attachment_data/file/277111/4262.pdf

NHS England Patient Participation Team (2014) *Guidance on Direct Payments for Healthcare: Understanding the Regulations*, Leeds: NHS England, www.england.nhs.uk/wp-content/uploads/2017/06/guid-dirct-paymnt.pdf

Runnymede Trust (2015) *The 2015 Budget: Effects on Black and Minority Ethnic People*, London: Runnymede Trust.

21

Food poverty and the policy context in Ireland

Deirdre O'Connor

Introduction

The purpose of this chapter is to provide an overview of the issue of food poverty in Ireland, starting with a discussion of how it is defined, understood and measured in the Irish context. We then consider how it is experienced by those who are 'food poor' in Ireland before moving to review the nature and range of interventions that address the issue and identifying the main actors involved. A key argument within this discussion is that the relevant policy context is characterised by inaction, incoherence and ineffectiveness, with the community and voluntary sector stepping in to fill the vacuum left by state and market failure.

How is food poverty defined/understood in Ireland?

In their review of food poverty and policy in Ireland, Friel and Conlon (2004: 120) state that food poverty is the 'inability to access a nutritionally adequate diet and the related impacts on health, culture and social participation'. Using a similar approach, Dowler et al (2001: 12) define food poverty as 'the inability to consume an adequate quality or sufficient quantity of food in socially acceptable ways, or the uncertainty that one will be able to do so'. In their attempts to define this concept, many authors use the concept of *food security* as a starting point, which is articulated by the Food and Agriculture Organization (FAO, 2008: 1) as a situation that exists when '… all people, at all times, have physical, social and economic access to sufficient, safe and nutritious food which meets their dietary needs and food preferences for an active and healthy life'. So, conversely, the concept of 'food insecurity' put forward by Tarasuk (2001: 2) denotes 'the limited, inadequate or insecure access of individuals and households to sufficient, safe, nutritious, personally acceptable food, both in quality and quantity, to meet their dietary requirements for a healthy and productive life'. What these multiple definitions of food poverty/food insecurity share is a reflection of the multi-faceted nature of the issue and the extent to which the debate on food poverty is constantly evolving. Caraher (2003) argues that whereas 'old' food poverty discourses were dominated by themes such as under-nutrition, a lack of food and the non-availability of food, the 'new' food poverty literature emphasises such issues as the over-abundance of processed food; imbalance in the diet; the inability to access food; and social and cultural isolation. Returning specifically to the Irish context, food poverty appears to be a central dimension of people's overall experience of poverty in Ireland (Dowler and O'Connor, 2012). The annual EU Survey on Income and Living Conditions (SILC), which estimates of the proportion of Irish households living in poverty, tracks the proportion of Irish households in 'consistent poverty' by combining an income poverty measure with eleven deprivation indicators capturing exclusion from normal living patterns – three of which are food-related (Department of Social Protection, 2015).

As noted above, the terms food poverty and food security are often used interchangeably in the Irish context. More recently, the closely-related concept of food and nutrition security (FNS) has received some attention in Ireland, notably in the context of an EU-level study, the TRANSMANGO project, which identifies the drivers of change, threats and weaknesses in the European and global food system that are likely to impact on FNS throughout Europe (Carroll et al, 2016). Key factors identified as likely to affect FNS in Ireland include agri-environmental issues (climate change and water quality in particular); power relations within the food system (growing retailer power and its resultant impact on agri-food producers); unhealthy food choices and their impacts on human health; and the long-term consequences of the recent sustained period of economic austerity in Ireland (O'Connor et al, 2015).

The extent, nature and lived experience of food poverty in Ireland

The aforementioned food-related deprivation indicators,[1] which address either food consumption or food-related social participation, have in recent years been used to generate a food poverty indicator for Ireland (Carney and Maître, 2012). Using 2010 data, based on people experiencing two or more of these indicators, the results suggested that food poverty affected 10% of the general population in the Republic of Ireland in that year (Department of Social Protection, 2015). This figure more than doubles to 23% for certain vulnerable households including lone parent and unemployed households, while households where the head is ill or has a disability also have a substantially increased risk (21%) of experiencing food poverty. Using a similar but simplified methodology, more recent sources have estimated that approximately one in eight people – or approximately 13% of the population – in Ireland currently experiences food poverty, while confirming the previously observed trend that rates are higher (up to 23%) among specific vulnerable groups, such as low income households, lone parent families, children and those who are unemployed or have a disability (Department of Social Protection, 2015).

Activists in the arena of food poverty – or in the broader realm of poverty – in Ireland have a long track record in highlighting the inadequacy of income from wages or welfare benefits to meet basic needs for healthy living, including food (Dowler and O'Connor, 2012). Research by the Vincentian Partnership for Social Justice (2000) on low income households in Ireland found that the prevailing social welfare rates and minimum wages rates at that time did not reflect the cost of 'even the most frugal standard of living', while Friel and Conlon (2004) concluded that rates of social welfare or minimum wage were such as to make purchasing a healthy diet 'almost impossible'. More recent work shows the cost of healthy eating for different types of low income households range from 13% (elderly lone adult), to 49% (lone parent with one child) and as high as 58% (two adults, two children) of the weekly Social Welfare Allowance, depending which retail outlet can be accessed – as local convenience stores can be up to twice as expensive as discount stores (Ross et al, 2009). Studies from the Food Safety Authority of Ireland have shown that it is up to ten times cheaper to provide calories in the form of unhealthy foods that are high in fat, salt and sugar than it is in the form of protective foods such as fruit and vegetables and other foods such as lean meat and fish (Conway et al, 2014). Consequently, it is not surprising that there is a social gradient evident in Ireland in terms of the consumption of protective or health-promoting food, with a lower uptake among lower socioeconomic groups in Ireland and resultant impacts in terms of disease and mortality rates (safefood, 2011).

Another dimension of food poverty in Ireland is the extent to which food serves a marker of social exclusion or inclusion. This was portrayed vividly and poignantly in research undertaken by Coakley (2001) who charts how mothers in low income households constantly juggle the constraints of time, inadequate income and lack of physical access to good quality, nutritious food with the desire that their families (particularly children) are not excluded from the norms enjoyed by the rest of society – such as eating 'treats' or 'child-friendly' foods; eating out or entertaining friends and family. More recently, documenting the 'everyday experience' of a number of low income families experiencing food poverty in Ireland, safefood (2011) notes how their experiences around food shopping, cooking and eating were overwhelmingly negative. Recurrent themes included feeling a lack of control over requisite resources and the absence of choice; little room for experimentation with food for fear of wastage; high levels of stress and anxiety related to shopping and cooking; and the need for a 'strategic' approach – such as strict meal planning and budgeting, stockpiling food where possible or targeting particular retailers for specific goods (safefood, 2011). Given that food purchasing and preparation typically falls into the domain of what McLaughlin and Lynch (1995) call women's caring labour or love labour, it is not surprising that many studies report how food poverty is experienced differentially within the household. A longstanding and recurring theme in Irish-based studies is the extent to which women 'go without' in order to safeguard provision for other family members, with the needs of children remaining paramount (Cantillon and Nolan, 1998; Coakley, 2001; Friel and Conlon, 2004; safefood, 2011).

Approaches, actors and interventions addressing food poverty in Ireland

Food poverty literature makes a useful distinction between *downstream* approaches to tackling food poverty (such as direct provision of food; measures to address information/skills deficits; local community-based food projects) and *upstream* approaches, which have a greater focus on influencing the wider policy context. Downstream approaches are frequently underpinned by a view that food poverty is an issue of personal responsibility, with the focus on individuals' poor health and nutrition status, attributable primarily to poor food choices and inadequate levels of the relevant skills and knowledge (Dowler and Caraher, 2003; Caraher and Coveney, 2004; Dowler and O'Connor, 2012). However, there is increasing recognition that food poverty needs to be seen as an issue of human rights and social justice, with a greater focus on the structural barriers facing individuals and households – such as inadequate incomes, poor infrastructural provision, poor housing and retail planning – in their struggle to achieve food security (Dowler, 2003; Watson, 2001).

Food poverty interventions in Ireland can be characterised as predominantly downstream in nature, heavily reliant on the community and voluntary sector, with the state and its agents playing a largely philanthropic role – to use the term coined by Dowler and Caraher (2003). They encompass a wide range of initiatives from food banks to meals-on-wheels services, school breakfast clubs, drop-in centres, community cafes, food co-operatives, community growing schemes/gardens and skills development in cooking, nutrition, budgeting and shopping (O'Connor et al, 2008; Carroll et al, 2016). Authors including Riches (1996) are highly critical of the extent to which civil society organisations have become 'part of the problem' in the sense that they have depoliticised the food poverty issue and allowed governments to 'look the other way'. A more trenchant critique is that the growth of such initiatives is a salient marker of social policy failure with respect to hunger (Lambie-Mumford, 2013) and a failure of governments to meet their right to food obligations (De Schutter, 2012).

At the same time, the dilemma facing those who provide such services is acute, as they are frequently torn between the necessity to provide temporary assistance and the knowledge that their efforts represent short-term solutions that allow society to avoid confronting more comprehensive policy initiatives (O'Connor et al, 2008).

Writing specifically about food assistance measures such as food banks, Poppendieck (1999) identified the 'persistent dilemma' facing them – namely the 'deeply felt tension' between responding to immediate hunger and tackling the myriad ways in which hunger stems from social injustice. Concerns about alienating the political and corporate support (O'Connor et al, 2008; Hebinck et al, 2016) on which many community-based food initiatives depend, compound the difficulties faced by them. Furthermore, a recent review of the rise of food banks in Ireland (Carroll et al, 2016) and in the Netherlands (Hebinck et al, 2016) pointed to the reluctance of many government and private sector interests to publicly support such initiatives, couching it in terms of 'engaging as admitting'. In other words, engaging in support for food redistribution initiatives was acknowledgement of the failure of the food system and of social support systems more generally.

So, the role of community and voluntary interventions in addressing food poverty is a contested one in Ireland, as elsewhere, but arguably represents an attempt to fill the void left by state and market failure. Indeed, as Dreze and Sen (1989) argue, to be overly dismissive of such efforts is to ignore what they call the importance of 'adversarial' public participation in social change processes and the fact that community-based food poverty interventions may serve as a gateway through which people address more fundamental problems of poverty and social exclusion (Carroll et al, 2016). Moreover, while, from an analytical perspective, it is useful to be able to locate food poverty interventions along a spectrum of activity using the upstream/downstream criterion discussed above, many community and faith-based initiatives in Ireland attempt to address the issue on a number of levels simultaneously, defying the neat categorisation or binary interpretation outlined above. For example, Crosscare, the Social Care Agency of the Dublin diocese of the Catholic Church, operates the Dublin Food Bank, which co-ordinates the redistribution of foodstuffs donated by industry to a number of charitable and voluntary organisations. At the same time, it has also commissioned some landmark pieces of research on food poverty in Ireland and was instrumental in establishing Healthy Food for All, a multi-agency initiative set up in 2006, with the aim of promoting access, availability and affordability of good quality food to low income households, addressing both upstream and downstream food poverty concerns (O'Connor et al, 2008).

Food poverty and the policy context

By contrast, state-led policy responses to food poverty in Ireland exhibit what Riches (1996) describes as a sense of 'fractured responsibility' for the issue. As Dowler and O'Connor (2012) note, policy responses related to food draw on a consumerist model that supports 'informed choice', the provision of appropriate dietary guidelines and the regulation of food supply, presiding over an environment where trade and financial rights govern entitlement. Apart from piecemeal funding of NGO-led activities, state involvement in measures directly addressing food poverty is limited to the provision of a restricted and much-critiqued School Meals Scheme and the administration of EU Schemes related to the provision of Aid to the Most Deprived (O'Connor et al, 2015). Furthermore, as Dowler and O'Connor (2012) point out, while food poverty can be seen as a central dimension of the people's overall experience of poverty, the idea that people should be able to get to shops stocking appropriate food, with sufficient money to buy it, is largely left to the market to secure, and the cost of food in relation to wages or welfare payments is not regulated. Food poverty is not at the core of broader poverty alleviation measures in Ireland, nor does it feature significantly on the general social policy landscape or in sectoral issues such as education or health (O'Connor et al, 2008). Furthermore, there are a number of important policy arenas and actors who appear to have no linkage whatsoever with the food poverty agenda. An obvious case in point is the domain of agriculture and food policy and the associated statutory agencies for research, development and food marketing (O'Connor et al, 2008). References to food accessibility in the arena of planning and competition policy tend to be couched in terms of consumer choice, and with the exception of a very small number of community-led responses, there are practically no interventions that address the production aspect of the food system or that seek to identify viable alternative supply chains for food insecure people. Many of the failures articulated above are not unique to the Irish experience. EU-level food system weaknesses are frequently attributed to incoherent, inconsistent and ineffective policies in different domains and at various levels of national and supra-national governance, most recently highlighted within the context of the aforementioned TRANSMANGO project on the drivers of FNS in EU member states (Moragues Faus et al, 2015).

Interventions that attempt to simultaneously address both upstream and downstream issues related to food poverty are rare in Ireland. However, one exception was the multi-agency initiative *Healthy Food for All* (HFFA), established in 2006 in the wake of a landmark report on the relationship between food poverty and policy in Ireland by Friel and Conlon (2004). While an important part of its focus was on supporting community-based initiatives and the identification of best practice in these areas, it also aimed to promote awareness of food poverty across all aspects of public policy with specific reference to availability, access and affordability issues. It gave effect to these objectives by providing networking opportunities for actors involved in community food projects, by commissioning research on best practice for school and community food initiatives, and by making submissions into a range of relevant policy arenas. Funding was a perennial issue for the initiative and was based on short-lived donations from government departments and statutory agencies and, in the face of continuing uncertainty around this issue which compromised its sustainability, HFFA ceased its operations in 2016 (Healthy Food for All, 2016).

While the picture painted by this catalogue of interventions and analysis is a familiar and somewhat pessimistic one, insights from case studies conducted for the aforementioned TRANSMANGO project suggest there are potential 'bright spots' in terms of how food poverty issues are being addressed in Ireland (Carroll et al, 2016). One such initiative is the Cork Food Policy Council (CFPC), the first such council in Ireland, established in 2013 by a range of stakeholder interests in Cork city, and one which has multiple, diverse aims and objectives. These are based around improving access to a nutritious, balanced and affordable diet for all;

encouraging the development of food enterprises that make use of local resources and reducing the size of Cork's ecological footprint. Specific activities include support for a wide range of community growing and other food-related activities; promoting lifelong learning and skills around food issues; organising events that are designed to address the issue of food waste and lobbying policymakers/decision makers on a plethora of issues, ranging from food waste to the siting of fast food outlets near schools (Carroll et al, 2016).

These activities suggest that the CFPC's aims and objectives are very much in line with those of Food Policy Councils elsewhere, which are usually underpinned by the goals of community food and nutrition security. Typically, such councils aim to make local food systems more socially just and conducive to public health goals; to support the livelihoods of producers and to direct local food systems towards greater energy efficiency and biodiversity (Green, 2007; Webb et al, 1998). In pursuit of these goals, fundamental objectives common to Food Policy Councils include highlighting the systemic nature of food and the consequent need to recognise causal links between issues such as diet-related disease, poverty and economic development.

Given the ambitious and broad scope of such objectives, it is not surprising that Food Policy Councils face numerous challenges in attempting to reach their goals. These range from policymakers' reluctance to recognise the complexity and severity of issues related to food security/food poverty (Scherb et al, 2012); the pressure to achieve 'quick, visible wins' in a dynamic and complex political environment which is frequently governed by the electoral cycle (Harper et al, 2009); and their dependence on voluntary effort, which mitigates against the ability to maintain a consistently high level of activity or to work collaboratively across a range of constituencies and interests (Borron, 2003). Limited financial resources, characterised by minimal and inconsistent funding, is the most often cited problem for Food Policy Councils (Dahlberg, 1994). The demise of the aforementioned HFFA organisation for reasons related to financial sustainability – an initiative that shared a similar multi-actor and multi-level perspective to many Food Policy Councils – should serve as a cautionary tale in this respect.

Concluding remarks

The conceptualisation of food poverty in Ireland shares many features with what has been observed in other countries. There has been an evolution in thinking about food poverty, with an increasing focus on the importance of structural factors underpinned by the need to see the problem as one of human rights and social justice. Notwithstanding this development, in Ireland as elsewhere, responses to the issue continue to emanate primarily from the community and voluntary sector with a predominantly 'downstream' focus and remain heavily dependent on a mosaic of intermittent funding sources from both the statutory and non-statutory sectors. This is not intended as a critique of the significant contribution made by the community and voluntary sector. Their presence and profile is the inevitable consequence of state and market failure in this arena and it is to their credit that they have managed to move beyond a 'damage limitation' role. While there is widespread acknowledgement of the importance of civil society engagement and insights from the lived experience of those who are food poor, of paramount importance is the need for concerted state-led action across a wide range of policy domains, at various levels of governance, to address the structural dimensions of this issue.

Note

[1] People that are excluded from consuming/experiencing the following, due to an inability to afford them, are considered to be experiencing deprivation: Eat a meal with meat, chicken, fish (or vegetarian equivalent) every second day; Have a roast joint or its equivalent once a week; Have family or friends for a drink or meal once a month.

References

Borron, S.M. (2003) *Food Policy Councils: Practice and Possibility*, Oregon: Congressional Hunger Center.

Cantillon, S. and Nolan, B. (1998) 'Are married women more deprived than their husbands?', *Journal of Social Policy*, 27 (2), 151–71.

Caraher, M. (2003) 'Food protest and the new activism', in S. John and S. Thomson (eds) *New Activism and the Corporate Response*, Basingstoke: Palgrave, pp 185–205.

Caraher, M. and Coveney, J. (2004) 'Public health nutrition and food policy', *Public Health Nutrition*, 7 (5), 591–8.

Carney, C. and Maître, B. (2012) *Constructing a Food Poverty Indicator for Ireland Using the Survey on Income and Living Conditions*, Social Inclusion Technical Paper No 3, Dublin: Department of Social Protection.

Carroll, B., Kinsella, J., O'Connor, D., Helfgott, A., Foord, W. and Lord, S. (2016) *Dublin TRANSMANGO Scenarios Workshop Report: Towards a fairer, healthier, more secure and sustainable food system in Cork*, TRANSMANGO, www.transmango.eu/userfiles/update%2009112016/local%20case%20studies%20 %C3%A2%E2%82%AC%E2%80%9C%20workshop%20reports/8%20ireland%20 workshop%20cork.pdf

Coakley, A. (2001) 'Healthy eating: food and diet in low income households', *Administration*, 49 (3), 87–103.

Conway, M.C., Wicklow, A.W., Keaveney, E.M. and Flynn, M. (2014) 'Affordability of healthy eating in Ireland 2009 and 2014', *Proceedings of the Nutrition Society*, 73 (OCE2), E75.

Dahlberg, K. (1994) 'Food Policy Councils: the experience of five cities and one county', a paper presented at the Joint Meeting of the Agriculture Food and Human Values Society and the Association for the Study of Food and Society, Tucson, AZ, 11 June.

Department of Social Protection (2015) *Social Inclusion Monitor 2013*, Dublin: Department of Social Protection.

De Schutter, O. (2012) *Report of the Special Rapporteur on the Right to Food on his Mission to Canada (6 to 16 May 2012)*, www.ohchr.org/Documents/HRBodies/HRCouncil/RegularSession/Session22/AHRC2250Add.1_English.PDF

Dowler, E. (2003) 'Food and poverty: insights from the North', *Development Policy Review*, 21 (5-6), 569–80.

Dowler, E. and Caraher, M. (2003) 'Local food projects: the new philanthropy?', *Political Quarterly*, 74 (1), 57–65.

Dowler, E. and O'Connor, D. (2012) 'Rights based approaches to addressing food poverty and food insecurity in Ireland and UK', *Social Science & Medicine*, 74 (1), 44–51.

Dowler, E., Turner, S. and Dobson, B. (2001) *Poverty Bites: Food, Health and Poor Families*, London: Child Poverty Action Group.

Dreze, J. and Sen, A. (1989) *Hunger and Public Action*, Oxford: Clarendon.

FAO (2008) *An Introduction to the Basic Concepts of Food Security*, www.fao.org/docrep/013/al936e/al936e00.pdf

Friel, S. and Conlon, C. (2004) *Food Poverty and Policy*, Dublin: Combat Poverty Agency.

Green, M. (2007) 'Oakland looks towards greener pastures', *Edible East Bay*, Oakland: The Oakland Food Policy Council, pp 36–37

Harper, A., Shattuck, A., Holt-Giménez, E., Alkon, A. and Lambrick, F. (2009) 'Food Policy Councils: Lessons learned', *Journal of the Institute for Food and Development Policy*, 1–63.

Healthy Food for All (2016) *2006–2016: A Legacy to Address Food Poverty in Ireland*, www.oireachtas.ie/parliament/media/.../Presentation---Healthy-Food-for-All.docx

Hebinck, A., Villarreal, G., Oostindie, H., Hebinck, P., Zwart, T.A., Vervoort, J., Rutting, L. and de Vrieze, A. (2016) *Urban Agriculture Policy-making: Proeftuin040 – TRANSMANGO Scenario Workshop Report, The Netherlands*, www.transmango.eu/userfiles/update%2009112016/local%20case%20studies%20%C3%A2%E2%82%AC%E2%80%9C%20workshop%20reports/5%20the%20netherlands%20proeftuin%20040%20workshop.pdf

Lambie-Mumford, H. (2013) 'Every town should have one: emergency food banking in the UK', *Journal of Social Policy*, 42 (1), 73–89.

McLaughlin, E. and Lynch, K. (1995) 'Caring Labour and Love Labour', in P. Clancy (ed) *Irish Society: A Sociological Perspective*, Dublin: Institute of Public Administration, pp 250–92.

Moragues Faus, A., Sonnino, R. and Marsden, T. (2015) *Delphi Report*, TRANSMANGO, www.transmango.eu/userfiles/d5%201%20delphi%20analysis%20report%20correction.pdf

O'Connor, D., Carroll, B. and Kinsella, J. (2015) *National Report: Ireland*, TRANSMANGO, www.transmango.eu/userfiles/project%20reports/d2.2%20p9%20ireland.pdf

O'Connor, D., Walsh, J. and Cantillon, S. (2008) *Rights-Based Approaches to Food Poverty in Ireland*, Combat Poverty Agency Working Paper Series 11/01, Dublin: CPA.

Poppendieck, J. (1999) *Sweet Charity? Emergency Food and the End of Entitlement*, New York: Penguin.

Riches, G. (1996) *First World Hunger: Food Security and Welfare Politics*, London: Macmillan.

Ross, V.M., O'Brien, C.M., Burke, S.J., Faulkner, G.P. and Flynn, M.A. (2009) 'How affordable is healthy eating?' ,*Proceedings of the Nutrition Society*, 68, E107.

safefood (2011) *Food on a Low Income: Four Households tell their Story – Summary Report*, www.safefood.eu/SafeFood/media/SafeFoodLibrary/Documents/Publications/Research%20Reports/Summary-Food-on-a-low-income---four-households-tell-their-story.pdf

Scherb, A., Palmer, A., Frattaroli, S. and Pollack, K. (2012) 'Exploring food system policy: a survey of Food Policy Councils in the United States', *Journal of Agriculture, Food Systems, and Community Development*, 2 (4), 3–14.

Tarasuk, V. (2001) *Discussion Paper on Household and Individual Food Insecurity: Report prepared for Health Canada*, Government of Canada, www.hc-sc.gc.ca/fn-an/nutrition/pol/food_sec_entire-sec_aliments_entier_e.html

Vincentian Partnership for Social Justice (2000) *One Long Struggle: A Study of Low Income Families*, Dublin: VPSJ.

Watson, A. (2001) *Food Poverty: Policy Options for the New Millennium*, London: Sustain.

Webb, K.L., Pelletier, D., Maretzki, A.N. and Wilkins, J. (1998) 'Local food policy coalitions: evaluation issues as seen by academics, project organizers and funders', *Agriculture and Human Values*, 15 (1), 65–75.

22

Implementing race equality policies in British health and social care: a perspective from experience

Hári Sewell

A paradox of implementing race equality policy is that continued use of the term 'race' further embeds the word in language. Race is usually referred to as a set of genetic differences that denote discrete sub-categories of the human race. Alongside this process of categorising is the ascribing of attributes associated with races. Bamshad et al (2004) analysed the genetic basis for race and pointed out that the genetic differences between groups of people are small, around 1%. Sometimes the genetic differences within so called races are wider that those across what are considered to be separate races.

An alternative approach is to focus on the process of racialisation. Garner (2010) described the process by which people are described as being racially different based on a notion that 'White' is the norm and non-white people belong to an 'other' race. Racialisation shifts the focus from an assumption that behaviours and inequalities are biologically or culturally determined to an analysis of social and structural factors that drive inequality.

Experience

I have been involved in implementing race equality policies at the national and local level within the statutory sector and working independently. I will explore three challenges that manifest themselves in three contexts in which I have worked.

Contexts

• National policy implementation
• Local policy implementation
• Supporting race equality policy as an independent consultant

Challenges

- Maintaining integrity in role
- The subordination of system approaches
- The avoidance of racism in implementing race equality

Rationale for the choice of challenges

The three challenges to be explored in this chapter reflect those that have been discussed elsewhere in published literature. As such there is already reference material that expands what is summarised in the following four paragraphs.

One of the biggest challenges, particularly for people from racialised minorities in senior roles implementing race equality policies, is maintaining integrity in the role. There are complex dynamics at work but the salient point is that racialised people with insight into causes of race inequality and potential solutions are sometimes appointed to develop or implement race equality policy but are then required to suppress their criticism of the employer or system of which they are then a part. This has the effect of diminishing their integrity in the eyes of stakeholders who experience their new corporate voice as a sign that they have surrendered their values for personal gain, either financial or status (Sewell, 2014).

System approaches in organisations are largely recognised as more effective solutions to system problems, as was argued in the acclaimed McKinsey 7S model (Waterman et al, 1980). One model that I developed, based on years of experience and secondary research was the Locked Hexagon Model (Sewell, 2009a; CSJ, 2011). The model focused on the challenges of race inequality in mental health and suggested that improvement in outcomes is more likely to be achieved when all aspects of a system are being developed simultaneously. The absence of one component has a disproportionately negative effect on the success of the whole approach.

The avoidance of racism as an explanation for inequalities was seen at the launch of the Delivering Race Equality in Mental Health policy (Department of Health, 2005). The then Secretary of State was reported to have avoided reference to racism despite this being a theme in the inquiry report that was a catalyst for the policy (Sewell, 2009b). Not all race-based variation can be assumed to be as a result of racism within the organisation under scrutiny (Singh and Burns, 2006; Singh et al, 2013). However, the analysis sometimes fails to recognise that agencies operate within a system and become complicit in the failures further upstream if they fail to tackle and challenge the system problems. Additionally, if their responses to the inequities that racialised groups face at the point of referral are not proportionate to the level and complexity of need response, this weakens arguments for denying the challenges of racism.

Implementing national mental health race equality policy

I was involved in supporting the implementation of the Delivering Race Equality (DRE) mental health policy programme in England. My role included supporting community development workers through a national network; supporting national DRE Champions, who were service users and carers; and reviewing, developing and quality assuring a national training module.

Challenges to maintaining integrity in role

The role was delivered through the National Mental Health Development Unit (NMHDU), an executive agency of the Department of Health. In practice this meant that the expectations of delivering the role were not dissimilar to being a government civil servant. This made it a highly politicised context in which the requirement was to be politically neutral, and there was a requirement to endorse national policy. Stakeholders who had known me and my work over several years questioned my motives when I needed to speak in support of a move towards a single equality approach, which had some merit but had supplanted rather an augmented attention given to race. The concept of intersectionality is important; that is the recognition that people have multiple aspects of their identities and face discriminations resulting from this (Walby et al, 2012). However, the ways in which racism operate need to be tackled and specific measures to redress these are needed.

A strategy to maintain integrity in the role was to support critical voices, hearing them in a non-defensive manner and supporting them with information and spaces to articulate their critiques.

The subordination of system approaches

The DRE policy included many elements of a system approach but performance management was of selected aspects. The highest profile monitoring of national implementation was in relation to the appointment of 500 community development workers. Fernando (2009) critiqued an approach to major mental health system reform where the greatest emphasis was on the appointment of junior workers.

Avoidance of racism

One striking aspect of the DRE policy implementation nationally, both in the work of the centre and services across England, was the fact that a policy on delivering race equality did not include any strategy to address racism (Sewell, 2014). This meant that implementation focused largely on what could be done to help racialised communities, with little emphasis on what the system had to do to change itself (apart from the nationally endorsed training module, which was targeted at frontline staff).

Local services

I worked in an inner city integrated mental health and social care trust as an executive director for nearly seven years. Implementing race equality policy as a discrete responsibility was a very small component of my portfolio but by then I had been having work published and my name was known in the field of race and mental health.

Challenges to maintaining integrity in role

In local services, I had freedom to critique national policy but given the seniority of my role I had to exercise caution and avoid direct criticism of the national administration. At a senior level, I had freedom to act within the parameters of organisational policy, using the senior management team to seek investment in areas of development. My integrity within my role was easily demonstrated as stakeholders including service users and carers were part of programmes of improvement that I led, so were able to see the way in which I advocated for improvement based on clear outcomes. A good example was the development of an improvement model called Changing Outcomes (Sewell, 2009b), a system approach that included service-based targets (set by themselves) and six other components which were to be implemented across local area systems within the trust's overall area.

The subordination of system approaches

Implementing DRE in a local trust from a board level position enabled buy-in for the idea of the Changing Outcomes system approach but the practical implementation was affected by top down pressures and changing agendas. There was significant competition for a share of the rapidly shrinking trust budget and the organisation had a desire to see immediate tangible gains. This usually translated into output measures rather than outcomes.

The avoidance of racism

Local services were open to the discussions on subjects such as institutional racism. Following a board seminar that I led a non-executive director said that she now understood very clearly how institutional racism operated and that the organisation could explore it without it being emotive. It was also the case, however, that in solidarity with the wider mental health workforce, the trust found it difficult to embrace the analysis surrounding the David 'Rocky' Bennett case that racism was a factor in the circumstances that led to that patient's death (*Guardian*, 2010). Racism was easier to explore as an idea, or as something that occurs elsewhere.

Independent consultant

I have worked independently since 2008, most of that time running my own training and management consultancy organisation. This usually involves writing projects (books and articles) and supporting delivery of race policy in organisations that commission my services.

Challenges to maintaining integrity in role

An independent role has afforded me more freedom to challenge the approaches to race equality policy, particular in mental health by speaking explicitly about institutional racism as reported by the BBC (BBC News, 2012) and publishing explicit critiques of psychiatry (Vige and Sewell, 2013). Particularly following the BBC article (which took one phrase out of context and used it as a headline), I had many messages from strangers across health and social care expressing pleasure that I had spoken up on a matter over which many feel required to remain silent about; I also had critics.

A major challenge still remains as an independent consultant in that the system being criticised is also the system from which contracts are sought.

The subordination of system approaches

As an independent consultant, proposals are submitted and are then considered in a context of service cuts. Where proposals have offered system approaches, these have been responded to as a carte blanche menu as opposed to a set meal. Arguing for a system approach has required care to avoid it being viewed sceptically as an attempt to artificially inflate costs as a means of making money. I have experienced this in service delivery responses as well as workforce race equality issues.

The avoidance of racism

It is in my role as an independent consultant that I have most frequently heard organisations name the possibility of racism as a factor in the variations and inequalities that they face, both in service delivery and in workforce. A privilege of my independent role is that organisations secure my services because they recognise that there is a problem and are keen that this is explored, and if it includes racism by managers or unintended racism in service approaches, for this to be identified.

Conclusion

At all levels considered in this chapter it appears that the contentious nature of race and racism has an impact on the freedom to honestly appraise what needs to be tackled. This had the potential to affect the integrity of how roles were fulfilled. Use of allies with more freedom by virtue of the role seems to be essential giving voice to stronger critiques but also there needs to be ways of discussing racism that are based on a desire to achieve positive outcomes. Some organisations demonstrated this openness. It can be achieved.

References

Bamshad, M., Wooding, S., Salisbury, B.A. and Stephens, J.C. (2004) 'Deconstructing the relationship between genetics and race', *Nature Reviews Genetics*, 5, 598–609.

BBC News (2012) "Institutional racism is an issue' in NHS says ex-executive', 7 December, www.bbc.co.uk/news/uk-england-london-20210842

CSJ (2011) *Completing the Revolution: Transforming mental health and tackling poverty*, London: Centre for Social Justice.

Department of Health (2005) *Delivering Race Equality in Mental Health Care: An Action Plan for Reform Inside and Outside Services and The Government's Response to the Death of David Bennett*, London: Department of Health.

Fernando, S. (2009) 'Inequalities and the politics of race', in S. Fernando and F. Keating (eds) *Mental Health in a Multi-Ethnic Society*, Sussex: Routledge

Garner, S. (2010) *Racisms: An introduction*, London: Sage.

Guardian (2010) *Too little, too late*, Guardian Online, https://www.theguardian.com/society/2004/feb/11/mentalhealth.comment1

Sewell, H. (2009a) 'Leading race equality in mental health', *International Journal of Leadership in Public Services*, 5 (2), 19–27.

Sewell, H. (2009b) *Working with Ethnicity Race and Culture in Mental Health: A Handbook for Practitioners*, London: Jessica Kingsley Publishers.

Sewell, H. (2014) 'Developing mental health policies that address race and culture', in R. Moodey and M. Ocampo (eds) *Critical Psychiatry and Mental Health*, Sussex: Routledge.

Singh, S. and Burns, T. (2006) 'Race and mental health: there is more to race than racism', *British Medical Journal*, 333, 648–51.

Singh, S.P., Burns, T., Tyrer, P., Islam, Z., Parsons, H. and Crawford, M.J. (2013) 'Ethnicity as a predictor of detention under the Mental Health Act', *Psychological Medicine*, 44, 997–1004.

Vige, M. and Sewell, H. (2013) 'Black people and mental health', in H. Sewell (ed) *The Equality Act 2010 In Mental Health: A Guide to Implementation and Issues for Practice*, London: Jessica Kingsley Publishers.

Walby, S., Armstrong, J. and Strid, S. (2012) 'Intersectionality: multiple inequalities in social theory', *Sociology*, 46, 224–40.

Waterman, R.H., Peters, T.J. and Phillips, J.R. (1980) 'Structure is not organisation', McKinsey Quarterly in-house journal, McKinsey & Co., New York.

23

Participatory approaches to social policy in relation to ageing

Sarah Lonbay

> Changes and progress very rarely are gifts from above. They come out
> of struggles from below. (Chomsky, 2008)

In recent years, there has been considerable focus on the world's 'ageing
population'. Projections from 2014 (UK) estimate that there will be an 89.3%
increase in the number of people aged over 75 by 2039 (Office for National
Statistics, 2015). These projections have resulted in wide discussions around how
to manage the 'rising demands from an ageing population' as well as the need to
adapt the UK welfare system so that it is appropriate. (Cracknell, 2010: 45). Key
challenges also relate to the need to adapt pensions policy and review retirement
ages. Such challenges are a global concern with projections from the United
Nations (UN) estimating that the world's population over the age of 60 will more
than triple by 2100 (UN, 2015).

Historically, the development of social policy has been driven by an 'expert'
agenda, with older people themselves having little choice or control. This chapter
highlights some of the key areas of current knowledge and understanding of
ageing in relation to social policy. In particular, the chapter considers some of
the key challenges and practicalities of a participatory approach to social policy.

Understanding involvement

Current approaches to the development of social policy tend to be underpinned
by a focus on perceived problems in relation to older people. This reinforces a
belief that expertise is needed; older people are viewed as unable to 'contribute
effectively' and therefore it is up to the 'experts' to make decisions and shape the
social policy framework (Cornwall and Gaventa, 2000: 51).

Dissatisfaction with this stance has increasingly been voiced by recipients of
social policy. In relation to health and social care policy, a rejection of the 'poor
quality, paternalism and social control of welfare services' led to the emergence

of new social movements (Croft and Beresford, 1993: 2). Older people began to challenge the right of the state to take control of their lives, arguing that they had the right to make choices about social policy and services that impacted upon them. For example, there have been links between older people and pensions policy in the UK, with welfare payments, education and reproductive rights in the USA, and with the running of older political candidates in Australia (Beresford, 2016: 200). Furthermore, forums such as the Elders Council in Newcastle Upon Tyne (UK) work towards challenging discriminatory views about older people and ageing and actively contribute towards creating 'age friendly' cities (Elders Council, 2016).

Involvement is rooted in the belief that that all people have the right to make choices about their own lives (Cowden and Singh, 2007; Croft and Beresford, 1990, 1993). It is underpinned by values of respect, empowerment, and equality, although questions remain about how to translate these key principles into action. Some of the difficulties associated with this include the number of factors that need to be considered, such as the aims of participation, who (or what) is driving the initiative, and why it is being undertaken. These difficulties have made involvement hard to conceptualise

Current approaches

While some social policy has emphasised the involvement of older people, there is often not a clear directive regarding the 'type' of involvement and thus the prioritisation of 'expert' voices has continued. Indeed, it has been increasingly documented internationally that many 'involvement' agendas may not be allowing people to have choice and control, and rather are more aligned with a consumerist approach which allows organisations to 'legitimate their own ends' (Cornwall and Gaventa, 2000: 52).

The importance of involvement lies not only in the explicit acknowledgement of the value of older people's views and experiences, but also in recognising the differing perspectives that may abound between those developing social policy and those on the receiving end. For example, adult safeguarding policy in England (policy which has been developed to protect and prevent the abuse of older people) has changed considerably over the past decade or so, culminating in this area of work being placed on a statutory footing in 2014. The development of this policy framework has largely occurred without the input of older people, despite the fact that they are the most highly represented group within adult abuse and neglect prevalence figures (NHS Information Centre, 2014). Research undertaken in the UK, South America, Canada, India, Lebanon and Sweden has demonstrated clearly that older people may have different views from policymakers about what constitutes abuse (O'Brien et al, 2011; WHO/INPEA, 2002).

Citizenship and participatory approaches to social policy

Attempts to address imbalances between government and individual perspectives on social policy have drawn on concepts of citizenship. It has been positioned as a 'social right', as a 'form of agency and practice', and as a 'relationship of accountability between service providers and their users' (Barnes, 1999; Cornwall and Gaventa, 2000: 53). Each of these has also been critiqued. For example, considering citizenship as a universal social right raises issues around some people being 'more equal citizens than others' (Cornwall and Gaventa, 2000: 53). This critique has emerged from feminist writers who cite power differentials as underpinning the issue. In relation to older people, such a critique can also be levied, for example, due to unequal power differentials between young and old which may also lead to discrimination and abuse. Additionally, this perspective has been critiqued for 'occluding diversity in experiences, identities and welfare needs' by creating a 'false uniformity' (Cornwall and Gaventa, 2000: 53). This can also be associated with the understanding of older age as a distinct life course category, discussed further below. Such categorisation ignores the diversity of the older population.

Citizenship as a form of agency and practice is about how 'citizenship as rights enables [older] people to act as agents', thus positioning participation itself as a right (Cornwall and Gaventa, 2000: 54). This approach acknowledges the impact that user movements have had and highlights the message that, through this work, older people have challenged the orthodoxy of older age equating to lack of ability to take control and have become more than simply 'passive beneficiaries of abstract rights' (p 54). This further enables people to 'assert their citizenship in the third sense through seeking greater accountability from service providers' (p 54). In order to achieve this, consideration needs to be given to the form that involvement takes, as well as the 'extent to which marginalised groups are able to articulate their concerns' (p 54). Again this underscores the need for considering diversity within all of these discussions; people are not just old, or female, or disabled; we all have multiple elements to our identities that may be more or less salient at different times. Moriarty and Manthorpe (2012) carried out a scoping review of equalities in access to services for older people in the UK, finding that there was a paucity of research that reflects the diversity of the older population. In particular, sexual orientation, gender identity, and religion and belief were 'almost wholly absent' (p 12). Cronin and King also argued that sexuality was often ignored in the older population and that 'older LGB adults [have been] rendered invisible' (2010: 881). Participatory approaches must acknowledge and respect differences by creating inclusive communities within which 'the voices of minorities within communities can also be heard' (Lister, 1998: 233).

Participatory approaches represent a 'major attempt to enable people to speak for themselves, instead of being spoken for' (Beresford, 2016: 173). Shifting the focus away from traditional approaches to social policy requires a move away from the devaluing and lack of attention to the perspectives of service users towards a model that acknowledges the expertise and value of the lived experience of those on the receiving end of social policy (Beresford, 2016). For older people, there has often been a focus on perceived lack of willingness or ability to be involved in shaping social policy and they are often under-represented. The current neoliberal political discourse focuses on personal responsibility and 'active citizenship'; it is the responsibility of the citizen to 'control and manage their own needs, and ... contribute to their communities' (Hudson, 2011: 23). However, many groups, including older people, are often excluded from such active citizenship through societal and structural inequalities. For example, in Ghana and Senegal, where schemes have been established to exempt older people from paying premiums for health and social care services, there is some evidence to suggest that there is inequality in uptake, largely influenced by political, socio-cultural and economic factors. In particular, older people who are at risk of social exclusion are more likely to be disadvantaged in terms of access to the scheme (Parmar et al, 2014). Several authors have also provided evidence that demonstrates that chronological age has been used within health and social care services in the UK to mark out older people and deny them resources and opportunities that other (younger) people would be offered (Kingston, 1999; Lang, 2012; Ward, 2000). Some older people from black and ethnic minority communities may also be doubly disadvantaged due to issues such as the inaccessibility of information and language barriers (Blood and Bamford, 2010). Limited access to health services has also been noted in the USA and in sub-Saharan Africa. These accessibility issues are related to both lower socioeconomic status among some of the older population and the focusing of such services on the needs of younger adults (WHO, 2015). All of these critiques and issues have led to the development of a focus on more radical participation; one where older people have a more active role in the development of social policy (Cornwall and Gaventa, 2000).

Challenges and practicalities of participatory approaches

To move forward with a participatory agenda, there is a need for the promotion of older people's voices, and also for an increase in receptiveness to those voices (Gaventa, 2002). There is otherwise a danger that this agenda will continue to fall into the 'student/teacher trap', whereby existing power dynamics are reinforced, rather than being challenged and reframed (Sakamoto, 2005: 439). Participatory methods, such as August Boal's Theatre of the Oppressed (1979), contest the traditional focus on professional expertise, instead drawing attention to the need to value lived experience and that such experience reinforces individual expertise (Boal, 2000; Friere, 1990; Yoeli et al, forthcoming). For example, Sakamoto (2005), writing about social workers, argued that they needed to challenge traditional power dynamics through critically examining their own role; as Friere would argue, 'the oppressors as well as the oppressed require liberation' (Yoeli et al, forthcoming). All of us are constrained and impacted upon by psychological, societal and structural mechanisms. For participatory social policy to become a reality we need to recognise and respond to these in a holistic manner through consideration of the multiple factors that can impact on involvement. Some of these factors are considered below.

Context

Context is important in a number of ways; for example, societal and economic factors influence the availability of resources to support participation (Houston, 2010). Other contextual elements such as culture and gender constructions are also important. Agarwal (cited by HelpAge, 1999: 7) drew attention to the issue of meeting attendance by older women in India and Nepal being viewed as 'challenging and abnormal', meaning that those women who were under 'fewer social constraints', such as widows and unmarried older women, were more able and likely to be involved in 'collective action'.

The manner in which the category of 'older person' has been constructed is also influenced by wider contextual factors such as ageist stereotyping and in turn influences the development of social policy (through the focus on ageing as a 'social problem' that needs to be solved). Overall at a national level, the impact of a neoliberal agenda on the approach taken to developing social policy is also influential in shaping participation, for example, by shifting the focus to a consumerist perspective whereby offering choice and control is grounded in rhetoric, rather than reality. At a local level, context is also important. For example, the influence of power within decision making spaces. Such spaces have historically been 'closed' (to use Gaventa's, 2007, terminology) to older people. While some may now have opened up as 'invited' (institutionally instigated, but where older people are invited to take part) spaces for consultation, their formal nature may yet remain, causing issues with accessibility for some older people. Inaccessibility can relate to the venue, size and nature of meetings (Lonbay, 2015). This can also relate to the potential to lack the confidence to contribute meaningfully within such a space (Beresford, 2013, Lonbay, 2015).

Gatekeepers' views about participation

Beresford (2013) used the term 'gatekeeper' to refer to those in a position to 'support or obstruct the involvement of service users' (Beresford, 2013: 40), stating that they could be a barrier to involvement. Understanding the personal motives of those involved in policy development for involving older people is therefore a central aspect of understanding participation. As Gaventa has argued, increasing the receptiveness to the voices of service users is an important element of effective participation. I found a predominantly positive view about involving older people at a strategic level in developing local adult safeguarding policy, although the ability to do so was limited by numerous other factors (Lonbay, 2015).

The construction of ageing and older people

I also found that views about older people impacted on the extent to which they might be involved (Lonbay, 2015). Discussions tended to focus on deficits, rather than strengths within this piece of research. Studies across the life course have tended to focus on fixed and somewhat distinct stages from infancy through to old age, fixing a relationship between chronological age and life course categories. Typically, older people are considered as those who are over the age of retirement and are generally depicted as a homogenous group (Harbison and Morrow, 1998). As such, our understanding of who older people are has been largely shaped by economic factors, particularly labour market forces. Social policy has reflected this stance by focusing on 'conceptions of age based categories' (Hockey and James, 2003: 63). However, retirement ages are set to regulate the workforce rather than as 'part of an individual's 'natural' lifecycle' so this construction of older people seems arbitrary (Harbison and Morrow, 1998, p. 694). Additionally, the association of being over the age of retirement with being reliant on state welfare contributes to a discriminatory view of older people as dependent or vulnerable, on the basis of age (see Fealy and McNamara, 2009). This association has also been shown to occur in countries that have a stronger focus on a family support structure, rather than state welfare for older people. In Nigeria, for example, it was found that younger adults perceived older people as dependent, suspicious and conservative (Okoye and Obikeze, 2005). Ageing is also often seen as a time for degeneration, rather than acknowledging the potential for physical, mental and social growth and development across the life course.

This categorisation is a form of 'world-making' (Bourdieu, 1989: 22). It is a conflict between '*symbolic powers that aim at imposing the vision of legitimate divisions*, that is, at constructing groups' (Bourdieu, 1989: 22, emphasis in original). Bourdieu further states that this needs to be challenged in order to make changes. For symbolic power to exist there must be an 'authorized spokesperson' who imposes this recognition of divisions and these divisions must be grounded in some reality (p 23). In relation to older people, therefore, the categorisation as an older person will depend on this 'authorized spokesperson'. In this example, those who are in a position to influence and construct social policy and the gatekeepers of involvement (Beresford, 2013). The manner in which the category of 'older age' is constructed is important for a number of reasons. As Holstein and Miller (2003) discussed (albeit in a different context), the practical work of social policy formulation is conceptualised through assigning people to categories, in this instance to 'old' or 'not old'. As such, decisions about how to respond to an ageing population can be made and justified on the basis of constructions about older people and their circumstances (Holstein and Miller, 2003). Indeed, Phillipson and Baars (2014: 68) wrote that 'ageing is invariably viewed as a "problem" to be solved through certain forms of social regulation and public intervention'. This assertion certainly seems to be reinforced by current discussions on the challenges and issues presented by an ageing population. Such dichotomous thinking also ignores diversity within the older population, further serving to marginalise older people.

More recently, life course perspectives have challenged this viewpoint, advocating instead a focus on the fluidity of transition across the life course and accepting the blurred boundaries that exist between life course stages (Hockey and James, 2003). However, as can be seen by depictions of older age and the strong links between identification as an older person and, for example, leaving employment, such a fixed stage focus still has a hegemonic role within society. The links drawn between ageing and dependency may be reinforced by different perspectives on ageing that have surfaced over the years. For example, the biomedical perspective on ageing has been a dominant paradigm, within which ageing is viewed as a medical and social problem (Phillipson and Baars, 2007). The association of ageing and dementia is an example of this. The medical model has been the dominant approach in understanding and responding to dementia. This model prioritises the voices of medical professionals and reduces the ability of the person to have choice or control over decision making (Harding and Palfrey, 1997). Shifting the focus away from a medical and biological perspective and considering ageing through the lens of a social model allows other perspectives to arise, such as those that question society's role in creating barriers, reducing inclusion and allowing ageism. Importantly, such a shift in perspective also actively encourages the voice of the older person to be heard, allowing them to define themselves, rather than be defined by others.

Older people often are willing and able to be involved in participatory approaches. Doyle and Timonen (2010) considered older people's motivations for engaging within a participatory research project. They found that the core reason for their involvement was related to the perceived benefits of the work, both in relation to the potential impact the project would have on improving local services and benefiting other older people. Some also cited personal benefits as an incentive for being involved, for example, the acquisition of knowledge that could benefit them personally and the development of new friendships within the local community. These older people also welcomed the participatory nature of the project. Similar findings have been documented as incentives for being involved in other elements of work, for example, policy development (Lonbay, 2015).

The activity of participation

The final element to be discussed here is the activity of participation; the 'methods, models, techniques and relational approaches' used to enact a participatory approach to social policy (Blom and Morén, 2009: 12). The development and maintenance of relationships is an integral aspect of this, indeed involvement itself has been conceptualised as 'relationships within social contexts' (Smith et al, 2009: 200). Effective communication is a key aspect of developing stronger relationships. This includes avoiding the use of jargon, which was considered by Tony, an older person involved in local policy decision making, to be an attempt to "flummox" him and "show ... authority" because "maybe [they] are frightened of a power difference" (Lonbay, 2015).

There are numerous ways to promote effective communication, for example, the development and dissemination of accessible information. The use of jargon, however, is frequently documented as a barrier to effective participation (for example, Beresford, 2013). Reed et al (2006: 52) examined the involvement of older people in policy and planning activities and described a 'red card' approach to reducing the use of jargon, whereby a red card is raised if jargon is used. Other flexible and inclusive approaches to sharing knowledge and understanding may also be helpful, such as the use of participatory mapping (a method used within participatory research) (Emmel, 2008). The use of both verbal and non-verbal communication, careful listening, consideration of environmental factors, and using illustrations are also important, particularly when communicating with people with advanced stages of Alzheimer's disease (Goldsmith, 1996). Additionally, translating and interpreting services should be offered when they may be needed (Moriarty and Manthorpe, 2012). The advantages of advocacy in supporting and empowering older people who may not be as readily able to communicate their views has also been extensively documented (Brandon et al, 1995; Lonbay and Brandon, 2016; Stewart and MacIntyre, 2013).

Training can also help to foster relationships and develop communication skills. An example is provided by Wood and Wright (2011), who explored the involvement of older people in policy development. They facilitated, in collaboration with Age Concern, a course designed to help older people with their communication skills. Older people reported that, not only had the course helped them with their communication, it also helped them to develop their confidence. While demonstrating the importance of communication for participation, this also highlights the important role of support and training in encouraging and promoting involvement. Training for participation can also involve the dissemination of information about roles and responsibilities, confidence-building and awareness raising. Overall it is about developing the confidence and the capacity to work effectively and to challenge (Gaventa, 2005; Lonbay, 2015).

Conclusion

Ultimately, participatory approaches are about the need to recognise and value people, regardless of their perceived 'status'. The importance lies not only in the practical benefits, but also in a moral element. Honneth (1996) argued that the basis for human wellbeing and self-actualisation lies in people being recognised in relation to their rights and personal qualities. By closing decision making spaces to older people, or positioning them as 'unable' to contribute, the overarching discourse perpetuates ageist stereotypes and devalues the contributions that older people can and do make.

This chapter has argued that there is a need to challenge top-down approaches to developing social policy, but also the need to challenge deficit based views about older people. To move towards participatory social policy, there is also a need to challenge the hegemony of neoliberalism. Within this meritocracy, the individual is presumed to have the freedom to act, but this freedom is not afforded to all. The shift from traditional, 'expert' led social policy development to a participatory approach is one that seeks to shift it from users as consumers to people as citizens who have a fundamental civil right to active participation in policy development. As Cornwall and Gaventa (2000) stated, it is a shift from being 'users and choosers' to being 'makers and shapers' (p 50). Participatory approaches therefore challenge the concept of 'expertise' and 'lever' open policy space for the 'emergence of alternative interpretation of needs and with this, alternative policy solutions' (Cornwall and Gaventa, 2000: 55). Within this we need participation that not only allows older people to challenge their role as passive recipients of social policy, but that also acknowledges and addresses the diversity of the group.

References

Barnes, M. (1999) 'Users as Citizens: Collective Action and the Local Governance of Welfare', *Social Policy and Administration*, 33 (1), 73–90.

Beresford, P. (2013) *Beyond the Usual Suspects: Research Report*, London: Shaping Our Lives,

Beresford, P. (2016) *All Our Welfare: Towards participatory social policy*, Bristol: Policy Press.

Blom, B. and Morén, S. (2009) 'Explaining social work practice–the CAIMeR theory', *Journal of Social Work*, 24, 586–600.

Blood, I. and Bamford, S. (2010) *Equality and Diversity and Older People with High Support Needs*, York: Joseph Rowntree Foundation.

Boal, A. (2000) *Theatre of the Oppressed*, London: Pluto.

Bourdieu, P. (1989) 'Social Space and Symbolic Power', *Sociological Theory*, 7(1), 14–25.

Brandon, D., Brandon, T. and Brandon, A. (1995) *Advocacy: Power to People with Disabilities*, Birmingham: Venture Press.

Chomsky, N. (2008) 'What Next? The Elections, The Economy and the World', Democracy Now, 24 November, www.democracynow.org/2008/11/24/noam_chomsky_what_next_the_elections

Cornwall, A. and Gaventa, J. (2000) 'From users and choosers to makers and shapers: repositioning participation in social policy', *IDS Bulletin*, 31(4), 50–62.

Cowden, S. and Singh, G. (2007) 'The "User": Friend, Foe or Fetish? A Critical Exploration of User Involvement in Health and Social Care', *Critical Social Policy*, 27(1), 5–23.

Cracknell, R. (2010) 'The Ageing Population', in A. Mellows-Facer (ed) *Key Issues for the New Parliament 2010*, London: House of Commons Library Research.

Croft, S. and Beresford, P. (1990) *From Paternalism to Participation: Involving People in Social Services*, London: Joseph Rowntree.

Croft, S. and Beresford, P. (1993) *Citizen Involvement: A Practical Guide for Change*, London: Palgrave Macmillan.

Cronin, A. and King, A. (2010) 'Power, Inequality and Identification: Exploring Diversity and Intersectionality Amongst Older LGB Adults', *Sociology*, 44 (5), 876–982.

Doyle, M. and Timonen, V. (2010) 'Lessons from a community-based participatory research project: Older participants' and researchers' reflections', *Research on Ageing*, 32(2), 244–63.

Elders Council of Newcastle (2016) 'The Elders Council of Newcastle: A manifesto for growing old well in Newcastle upon Tyne', www.elderscouncil. org.uk/Manifesto

Emmel, N. (2008) *Participatory Mapping: An Innovative Sociological Method*, ECRD National Centre for Research Methods.

Fealy, G. and McNamara, M. (2009) 'Constructing Ageing and Age Identity: A Case Study of Newspaper Discourses', National Centre of the Protection of Older People, Study 1, November.

Friere, P. (1990) *Pedagogy of the Oppressed*, New York: Continuum Press.

Gaventa, J. (2002) 'Exploring Citizenship, Participation and Accountability', *IDS Bulletin*, 33(2).

Gaventa, J. (2005) 'Reflections on the uses of the "power cube" approach for analyzing the spaces, places and dynamics of civil society participation and engagement', prepared for Dutch CFA Evaluation 'Assessing Civil Society Participation and Engagement', Brighton: University of Sussex.

Gaventa, J. (2007) 'Levels, Spaces and Forms of Power. Analysing Opportunities for chance', in F. Berenskoetter and M.J. Williams (eds) *Power in World Politics*, London: Routledge, pp 204–24.

Goldsmith, M. (1996) *Hearing the Voice of People with Dementia: Opportunities and Obstacles*, London: Jessica Kingsley Publishers.

Harbison, J. and Morrow, M. (1998) 'Re-Examining the Social Construction of "Elder Abuse and Neglect": a Canadian Perspective', *Ageing and Society*, 18, 691–711.

Harding, N. and Palfrey, C. (1997) *The Social Construction of Dementia: Confused Professionals?* London: Jessica Kingsley.

HelpAge (1999) 'Older Widows as Leaders', *Ageing and Development*, 3, 7.

Hockey, J. and James, A. (2003) *Social Identities Across the Life Course*, New York: Palgrave Macmillan.

Holstein, J.A. and Miller, G. (2003) 'Introduction: A Fork in the Road: Challenges and Choices in Social Constructionism', in J.A. Holstein and G. Miller (eds) *Challenges and Choices: Constructionist Perspectives on Social Problems*, New York: Walter de Gruyter, Inc., pp 1–16.

Honneth, A. (1996) *The Struggle for Recognition: The Moral Grammar of Social Conflicts*, Bristol: Policy Press.

Houston, S. (2010) 'Prising Open the Black Box: Critical Realism, Action Research and Social Work', *Qualitative Social Work*, 9 (1), 73–91.

Hudson, B. (2011) 'Big society: a concept in pursuit of a definition', *Journal of Integrated Care*, 19 (5), 17–24.

Kingston, P. (1999) *Ageism in History*, London: NT Books, Emap Healthcare.

Lang, I. (2012) 'Ensure Age is no Barrier to Accessing Health Service', in Age UK, *Improving Later Life: Understanding the Oldest Old*, pp 70–71.

Lister, R. (1998) 'Citizenship in Action: Citizenship and Community Development in a Northern Ireland Context', *Community Development Journal*, 33 (3), 226–35.

Lonbay, S. (2015) 'Bridges and Barriers: The Involvement of Older People in Adult Safeguarding', PhD thesis, Northumbria University.

Lonbay, S. and Brandon, T. (2017) 'Renegotiating power in adult safeguarding: The role of advocacy', *The Journal of Adult Protection*, 19 (2), 78-91.

Moriarty, J. and Manthorpe, J. (2012). *Diversity in Older People and Access to Services – An Evidence Review*. London: Age UK.

NHS Information Centre (2014) *Safeguarding Adults Annual Report, England 2014–15 Experimental Statistics*, NHS Information Centre, Social Care Team.

O'Brien, M., Begley, E., Anand, J. C., Killick, C., Taylor, B., Doyle, E., McCarthy, M., McCrossan, S.and Moran, E. (2011) *"A Total Indifference to our Dignity" Older People's Understandings of Elder Abuse*, Dublin: Centre for Ageing Research and Development.

Office for National Statistics (2015) *National Population Projections: 2014-based Statistical Bulletin*, London: Office for National Statistics.

Okoye, U.O.and Obikeze, D.S. (2005) 'Stereotypes and perceptions of the elderly by the youth in Nigeria: implications for social policy', *Journal of Applied Gerontology*, 24 (5), 439-52.

Parmar, D., Williams, G., Dkhimi, F., Ndiaye, A., Asante, F.A., Arhinful, D.K. and Mladovsky, P. (2014) 'Enrolment of Older People in Social Health Protection Programs in West Africa – Does Social Exclusion Play a Part?', *Social Science and Medicine*, 119, 36–44.

Phillipson, C. and Baars, J. (2007) 'Social theory and social ageing', in J. Bond, S. Peace, F. Dittman-Kohli and G. Westerhof (eds) *Ageing in Society*, London: Sage Publications, pp 68–84.

Reed, J., Cook, G., Bolter, V. and Douglas, B. (2006) *Older people ' getting things done': Involvement in policy and planning initiatives*, York: Joseph Rowntree Foundation.

Sakamoto, I. (2005) 'Use of Critical Consciousness in Anti-Oppressive Social Work Practice: Disentangling Power Dynamics at Personal and Structural Levels', *British Journal of Social Work*, 35 (4), 435–52.

Smith, E., Donovan, S., Beresford, P., Manthorpe, J., Brearley, S., Sitzia, J. and Ross, F. (2009) 'Getting ready for user involvement in a systematic review', *Health Expectations: An International Journal of Public Participation in Health Care and Health Policy*, 12 (2), 197–208.

Stewart, A. and MacIntyre, G. (2013) 'Advocacy: Models and Effectiveness', *Insights: evidence summaries to support social services in Scotland*, 20, April, Institute for Research and Innovation in Social Services, www.iriss.org.uk/sites/default/files/iriss-insight-20.pdf

United Nations (UN) (2015) *World Population Prospects: Key Findings and Advance Tables (2015 Revision)*, New York: United Nations.

Ward, D. (2000) 'Ageism and the abuse of older people in health and social care', *British Journal of Nursing*, 9 (9), 560–63.

WHO (2015) *World Report on Ageing and Health*, Luxembourg: World Health Organization.

WHO/ INPEA. (2002) *Missing Voices: Views of older persons on elder abuse*, World Health Organisation: Geneva.

Wood, C. and Wright, M. (2011) 'Promoting Involvement of Older People in Shaping Policy and Practice', *Community Care, Policy and Practice*, 15 (2), 80–86.

Yoeli, H., Lonbay, S., Morey, S. and Pizycki, L. (forthcoming) 'From Realism to Ritual: Using Forum Theatre to Research Lay and Professional Attitudes Towards Adult Safeguarding', *The Journal of Adult Protection*.

24

Death, dying and digital stories

Lisa Williams[1], Merryn Gott[1], Tess Moeke-Maxwell[1], Stella Black[1],
Shuchi Kothari[2], Sarina Pearson[2], Peter James Simpson[2], Tessa Morgan[1],
Marianne Grbin[1], Matua Rawiri Wharemate[3] and Whaea Whio Hansen[3]

The 21st century marks the emergence of a new demography of death, one in which longevity and chronic illness rather than short lives and infant mortality define its parameters (Leeson, 2014). By 2050, lifespans will have risen from 65 years in 1950 to an expected 83 years in developed regions and from 42 years to 75 years in less developed regions (United Nations, 2013). Concurrently, it is expected that by 2050 there will be 434 million people 80 years of age and older with chronic and complex health conditions.

As a result of these shifts in ageing and disease prevalence it is reasonable to assume that palliative care will increasingly become part of the life course as people encounter death and dying in advanced age. (Palliative care may be defined as care and treatment that is meant to improve the quality of life of individuals with a life-limiting illness and their families (World Health Organization, 2016).) Yet despite the existence of policy calling for the 'delivery of high quality [palliative] services in all locations' (National Health Service, 2008: 11), ample evidence exists that older people are at risk of receiving sub-optimal care (Ahmed et al, 2004; Burt and Raine, 2006; Burt et al, 2010). Solutions to the problem often focus on the need for improvement within professional health services (Browne et al, 2014; Keim-Malpass et al, 2015), which suggests an underlying belief that change is best left to the experts in the healthcare profession and the statutory sector.

Emerging discourses in palliative care, however, offer a different perspective. New public health approaches to palliative care, which may be better known by such names as Health Promoting Palliative Care or compassionate communities, make the locus of palliative care the community, rather than professional services (Paul and Sallnow, 2013). The goal of these approaches is to educate, upskill and empower communities to more effectively generate meaningful solutions regarding the handling of death and dying and attendant issues such as ageing, chronic illness and bereavement (Sallnow and Paul, 2014).

Centering palliative care in the community may promote the expression of divergent perspectives, ones rooted in the particulars of locality. Yet many voices remain underrepresented. Writing about the disability sector, Stienstra and

Chochinov (2006) noted that when disabled people arrived for palliative care treatment they were treated as if their 'various needs and vulnerabilities' could be 'accommodated within routine standards of practice' (p 166).

Perhaps not surprisingly, LGBTQ issues in relationship to palliative care have tended to be limited to young men and HIV/AIDS, and little research has focused 'explicitly on LGB end of life care and bereavement' (Almack et al, 2010: 909). Nor has gender received much notice; our own research, published only in the last two years, has been among the first to explore the implications of gender and palliative care (Morgan et al, 2016; Williams et al, 2017). Indigenous populations fare little better; until early in this century very little attention was devoted to the topic (Kitzes and Domer, 2003; McGrath et al, 2006). A distinctively Māori perspective on palliative care, New Zealand's indigenous people, did not appear until 2005 (Reid, 2005).

Digital storytelling as a means for extending life course discourse

As these examples indicate, additional work must be undertaken if palliative care is to be discussed more meaningfully within life course discourse. However, current methods may not always be appropriate for exploring the diverse range of voices that ought to be included. New methods may need to be employed, and digital storytelling (DST) holds promise as one effective means. Digital stories consist of 3–5 minute visual accounts that incorporate combinations of images, videos, voice recordings, music and text to create narratives. They are developed within a workshop setting with usually a small group of no more than eight members. Workshop leaders teach participants how to shape their stories into written scripts after they have first shared them orally within a group story circle session. During the final step participants learn from the workshop leaders how to combine their scripts with images, music, sounds and voice-over using digital editing software (Lambert, 2013).

One reason for the value of digital stories lies in their ability to enable individuals and communities to share their experiences about subjects of deep personal importance to them (Lambert, 2013). Indeed, the implications of DST for social research are significant as gaining a deeper understanding of the meaning people ascribe to their lives is at the heart of any qualitative social research endeavour (Gubrium and Turner, 2009). Moreover, DST enables individuals and communities to exercise ownership over their stories and ensure they are represented accurately (Gubrium and Turner, 2009).

Digital stories have proven effective for a diverse range of voices that have been ignored or misrepresented (Gubrium and Turner, 2009). For example, young African refugees in Australia regarded digital storytelling as a mode for self-representation, which acted as 'a mechanism to speak back to the complex and systematic racialisations of place constructed through the mainstream media' (Salazar, 2010). Similarly, young Latina women in the United States regarded 'truth telling' as a benefit of the digital story workshop they took part in. Recounting their own stories and having their voices heard offered an opportunity to 'revise inaccurate and disparaging representations and perceptions' (DiFulvio et al, 2016: 3).

For Canadian women with eating distress, digital storytelling provided them with a way to resist hegemonic constructions and assert their often-subjugated perspective on the subject (LaMarre and Rice, 2016). Also in Canada, Rice et al (2015) made use of DST to challenge stereotypes associated with disability and difference that foster barriers to healthcare. The authors have archived more than 100 digital stories created by people living with disabilities/differences as well as by healthcare providers.

A second strength of DST as a method of inquiry is its usefulness for projects operating within a Community-Based Participatory Research (CBPR) framework. In a health context, CBPR has been defined as 'a collaborative approach to research that equitably involves all partners in the research process and recognizes the unique strengths that each brings' (Minkler and Wallerstein, 2008: 6). The research topic chosen for exploration holds significance for the community involved and the goal of the project includes the generation of new knowledge, but also extends beyond this to incorporate social change for the community's betterment (Minkler and Wallerstein). Used in such a way, digital stories become a tool for grassroots explorations of social issues as they are expressed in specific localities and circumstances by the people experiencing them.

As an example, Jernigan et al (2012) incorporated digital stories into a three-phase CBPR project designed to address food insecurity affecting a Native American community in rural California. Their ten-member community coalition viewed digital stories as a way to inject 'local relevance' into the project. Some of the stories generated by the 12 community leaders who took part were then used to engender discussion in focus groups designed to pinpoint factors associated with food insecurity.

Māori digital stories

In our own experience, we found DST helpful for exploring Māori whānau [extended family] experiences of providing care at the end of life for their kaumātua [revered elders]. Māori, like indigenous groups elsewhere, experience marginalisation due to the deleterious effects of colonisation (Beltran and Begun, 2014). Their disenfranchisement has led to, among other inequities, ongoing health disparities between Māori and non-Māori in New Zealand (Beltran and Begun, 2014; Reid and Robson, 2006),

We modified the three-day digital story workshop to conform to Māori cultural conventions by incorporating the Māori pōwhiri process of engagement, which refers to a formal welcome by the tangata whenua [Māori hosts] of manuhiri [visitors] (Gott et al, 2016). The pōwhiri process also encompasses underlying practices and protocols present during the pōwhiri (McClintock et al, 2010), such as aroha [love and empathy], manaakitanga [hospitality] and mana [prestige] that are then enacted throughout the research project.

Our eight participants all completed short videos that highlighted aspects of end-of-life care or bereavement, and they responded enthusiastically about the experience in their written evaluations. Creating the stories gave them an opportunity to celebrate their tupuna [deceased relatives/ancestors]. One participant stated, "I believe I honoured my kuia [older female relative] where I was able to uphold her mana".

Yet this is not to suggest our DST project was without its drawbacks. Māori pōwhiri protocol dictates that speakers hold the floor until they are finished, regardless of length of time. As a result, our story circle ran longer than anticipated, thereby contributing to time pressures that affected the prescribed timing of the workshop's activities. Mastering the technology proved to be another challenge. One participant reported on the evaluation that it caused fatigue and "raised issues of incompetence".

Implications for social policy research

The Māori digital stories, which may be viewed online (Wharemate et al, 2015), are now a teaching tool for nursing lecturers at the University of Auckland as well as for healthcare professionals in hospice, district health boards and other tertiary institutions around New Zealand. While the scope of our project did not allow for an official evaluation of impact, we offer this example of how DST can be useful for engaging communities in dialogue about topics relevant for them. An email from a hospice administrator to Stella Black, a member of our research team who also participated in the Māori digital stories project, demonstrates how the stories generated discussion about end-of-life decisions. The administrator wrote:

> 'I wanted to say a really big thank you for allowing us to share your whānau story at the hui [meeting] yesterday. We were talking to them about having conversations with whānau about what they might want towards the end of their life. We had around 140 kaumātua there and they really could relate to your korero [discussion]. It was really moving and very relevant to our message. I think many of us could really identify with what your Dad and you all went through.' (Carroll, 2016)

In a similar way, digital stories could be used to bolster community involvement in social policy issues. Not only does DST offer marginalised groups a means to explore their own views but re-presenting them to wider audiences serves as a political act, one that counters social problem narratives that are often written into policy (Matthews and Sunderland, 2013). Furthermore, digital stories allow those who are unable to personally engage in policy consultation to make a contribution. Included in a digital story collection, their narratives can become part of 'a broader palette of everyday experience from which policy makers and others can draw both wisdom and "data"' (Matthews and Sunderland, 2013). Indeed, the Native American food insecurity project offers an example of just such a use for digital stories. In addition to being an integral tool for the research phase of the project, aspects of the digital stories were incorporated into presentations designed to influence changes in local policies (Jernigan et al, 2011).

Digital stories may also be useful for influencing policy implementation. New domestic violence legislation in Nepal needed effective public education strategies and government accountability to make a difference in the lives of those impacted by violence. To engender support, Saathi Nepal, a non-governmental Nepalese organisation, turned to digital stories as its preferred mode for speaking out. It partnered with Silence Speaks to create digital stories told by abuse survivors and to craft a strategy for their distribution (Silence Speaks, 2016).

If analysed as empirical data, digital stories might lead to an understanding of the deeper implications of people's narratives. Certainly at a fundamental level the stories can raise questions about the shaping and interpreting of reality (Gubrium and Turner, 2009), which LaMarre and Rice (2016) demonstrated in their interrogation of digital stories created by women with eating distress. They concluded that Margot's story challenged common media tropes; for example, that girls who suffer from eating disorders are 'shallow, vain or fragile'. Margot's story also questioned the value of 'striving toward excellence', a prized objective 'for modern Western (neoliberal) society'. Read in this way, narratives such as Margot's offer a counterweight to top-down approaches where 'experts', including policymakers, 'generalize an experience for a targeted community' (Gubrium and Turner, 2009: 486).

Yet creating, analysing and presenting digital stories to diverse audiences does not guarantee changes will be made manifest in policy. Citing Australia's social inclusion framework, which drives the nation's formulation of social policy, Dreher (2012) distinguished between voices that are spoken and voices that are heard. Quoting Couldry (2010), she stated that 'neo-liberalism offers proliferating opportunities for voice, but not necessarily listening – "a system that provides formal voice for its citizens but fails so markedly to listen"' (Dreher, 2012: 158). She also argued that for DST projects to 'ensure voice that matters' (p 163), an effective dissemination strategy must be among the means employed, a viewpoint we share. To increase exposure for our Māori digital stories we developed a distribution plan that included an official launch that gained broadcast news media coverage, placement on internet and social media sites, distribution to health professionals through our email networks, presentations at conferences, and inclusion in the University of Auckland undergraduate and graduate nursing curriculum.

Conclusion

Digital storytelling offers a means for making more visible the viewpoints of groups typically elided from social policy discourse. Positioned within a CBPR framework, in which researchers and communities collaborate to explore issues of concern, DST projects can amplify the voices of those affected by policy decisions that, all too often, they have had little input in shaping.

Notes

[1] School of Nursing, Faculty of Medical and Health Sciences, University of Auckland, Auckland, New Zealand.

[2] Media, Film and Television, Faculty of the Arts, University of Auckland, Auckland, New Zealand.

[3] Kaumātua, Te Ārai: Palliative Care and End of Life Research Group, School of Nursing, Faculty of Medical and Health Sciences, University of Auckland, Auckland, New Zealand.

References

Ahmed, N., Bestali, J.E., Ahmedzai, S.H., Payne, S.A., Clark, D. and Noble, B. (2004) 'Systematic review of the problems and issues of accessing specialist palliative care by patients, carers and health and social care professionals', *Palliative Medicine*, 18, 525–42.

Almack, K., Seymour, J. and Bellamy, G. (2010) 'Exploring the impact of sexual orientation on experiences and concerns about end of life care and on bereavement for lesbian, gay and bisexual older people', *Sociology*, 44, 908–24.

Beltran, R. and Begun, S. (2014) 'It is medicine: narratives of healing from the Aotearoa digital storytelling as indigenous media project (ADSIMP)', *Psychology and Developing Societies*, 26, 155–79.

Browne, S., Macdonald, S., May, C., Macleod, U. and Mair, F. (2014) 'Patient, carer and professional perspectives on barriers and facilitators to quality care in advanced heart failure', *PLoS One*, 9, e93288.

Burt, J. and Raine, R. (2006) 'The effect of age on referral to and use of specialist palliative care services in adult cancer patients: a systematic review', *Age and Ageing*, 35, 469–76.

Burt, J., Shipman, C., Richardson, A., Ream, E. and Addington-Hall, J. (2010) 'The experiences of older adults in the community dying from cancer and non-cancer causes: a national survey of bereaved relatives', *Age and Ageing*, 86–91.

Carroll, N. (2016) 'RE: Query. Type to BLACK, S.', 17 August (personal communication).

Difulvio, G., Gubrium, A., Fiddian-Green, A., Lowe, S. and Del Toro-Mejias, L. (2016) 'Digital storytelling as a narrative health promotion process: evaluation of a pilot study', *International Quarterly of Community Health Education*, 0, 1–8.

Dreher, T. (2012) 'A partial promise of voice: digital storytelling and the limits of listening', *Media International Australia*, 142, 157–66.

Gott, M., Moeke-Maxwell, T., Morgan, T., Black, S., Williams, L., Boyd, M., Frey, R., Robinson, J., Slark, J., Trussardi, G., Waterworth, S., Wharemate, R., Hansen, W., Smith, E., Kaka, K., Henare, K., Henare, E., Poto, M., Tipene-Carter, E. and Hall, D. (2016) 'Working bi-culturally within a palliative care research context: the development of the Te Ārai palliative care and end of life research group', *Mortality*, 22 (4), 291–307, http://dx.doi.org/10.1080/1357 6275.2016.1216955

Gubrium, A. and Turner, K. (2009) 'Digital storytelling as an emergent method for social research and practice', in S. Hesse-Biber (ed) *The handbook of emergent technologies in social research*, Oxford: Oxford University Press.

Jernigan, V., Salvatore, A., Styne, D. and Winkleby, M. (2012) 'Addressing food insecurity in a Native American reservaiton using community-based participatory research', *Health Education Research*, 27 (4): 645–55.

Keim-Malpass, J., Mitchell, E., Blackhall, L. and Deguzman, P. (2015) 'Evaluating stakeholder-identified barriers in accessing palliative care at an NCI-designated cancer center with a rural catchment area', *Journal of Palliative Medicine*, 18, 634–7.

Kitzes, J. and Domer, T. (2003) 'Palliative care: an emerging issue for American Indians and Alaskan natives', *Journal of Pain and Palliative Care Pharmacotherapy*, 17, 201–10.

Lamarre, A. and Rice, C. (2016) 'Embodying critical and corporeal methodology: digital storytelling with young women in eating disorder recovery' *FQS*, 17.

Lambert, J. (2013) *Digital storytelling: Capturing lives, creating community*, New York: Routledge.

Leeson, G. (2014) 'Increasing longevity and the new demography of death', *International Journal of Population Research*, 2014, 1–7.

Matthews, N. and Sunderland, N. (2013) 'Digital life-story narratives as data for policy makers and practitioners: thinking through methodologies for large-scale multimedia qualitative datasets', *Journal of Broadcasting & Electronic Media*, 57, 97–114.

McClintock, K., Mellsop, G., Moeke-Maxwell, T. and Merry, S. (2010) 'Pōwhiri process in mental health research', *International Journal of Social Psychiatry*, 58, 96–7.

Mcgrath, P., Patton, M., Mcgrath, Z., Olgivie, K. and Rayner, R. (2006) "It's very difficult to get respite out here at the moment': Australian findings on end-of-life care for Indigenous people', *Health & Social Care in the Community*, 14, 147–55.

Minkler, M. and Wallerstein, N. (2008) *Community-based participatory research for health: from process to outcome*, San Francisco: Jossey-Bass.

Morgan, T., Williams, L. and Gott, M. (2016) 'Gender and family caregiving at the end-of-life in the context of old age: a systematic review', *Palliative Medicine*, 30, 616–24.

National Health Service (NHS) (2008) *End of life care strategy for England*, London: NHS.

Paul, S. and Sallnow, L. (2013) 'Public health approaches to end-of-life care in the UK: an online survey of palliative care services', *BMJ Supportive and Palliative Care*, 0, 1–4.

Reid, P, (2005) 'Contemporary perspectives', in M. Schwass (ed) *Last words: approaches to death in New Zealand's cultures and faiths*, Wellington: Bridget Williams Books with the Funeral Directors Association of New Zealand.

Reid, P. and Robson, B. (2006) 'The state of Maori health', in M. Mullholland (ed) *State of the Maori nation: twenty-first century issues in Aotearoa*, Auckland: Reid.

Rice, C., Chandler, E., Harrison, E., Liddiard, K. and Ferrari, M. (2015) 'Project Re•Vision: disability at the edge of representation', *Disability & Society*, 30 (4), 513-27.

Salazar, J. (2010) 'Digital stories and emerging citizens' media practices by migrant youth in Western Sydney', *3CMedia: Journal of Community, Citizen's and Third Sector Media*.

Sallnow, L. and Paul, S. (2014) 'Understanding community engagement in end-of-life care: developing conceptual clarity', *Critical Public Health*, 25, 231–8.

Silence Speaks (2016) 'Saathi Nepal: voices for justice – survivors link their personal stories to public policy for ending violence against women in Nepal', StoryCenter, www.storycenter.org/case-studies/saathi-nepal

Stienstra, D. and Chochinov, H. (2006) 'Vulnerability, disability, and palliative end-of-life care', *Journal of Palliative Care*, 22 (3), 166–74.

United Nations (2013) *World Population Ageing 2013*, New York: UN.

Wharemate, D., Smith, E., Kaka, K., Henare, R., Nepia, J., Black, S., Hall, D. and Moeke-Maxwell, T. (2015) 'Maori digital stories about whānau caregiving', www.youtube.com/watch?v=G9zXJOnRuEI

Williams, L., Giddings, L., Bellamy, G. and Gott, M. (2017) "Because it's the wife who has to look after the man': a descriptive qualitative study of older women and the intersection of gender and the provision of family caregiving at the end of life', *Palliative Medicine,* 31 (3), 223–30.

World Health Organization (2016) 'WHO definition of palliative care', www.who.int/cancer/palliative/definition/en/

Part V
Transforming social policy

In Part V, we take forward the theme of how social policy can become more participative and democratic. Contributors coming from a wide range of perspectives – academic, activist, practitioner, service user/disabled person and researcher – draw on first hand experience to show how it is possible in a variety of ways and at different levels to transform social policy. They highlight the issue of bringing about social change, different ways of achieving change and new goals for change.

Jennie Fleming, with a lifetime's international experience supporting a participative approach to social policy, begins by highlighting the importance of doing things together – groupwork – as a means of gaining skills, knowledge, confidence, to bring about change – within yourself, in policy and at a broader level. She offers case studies with young people that demonstrate this and which also show that change *can* be achieved.

Iain Ferguson, the academic and activist, problematises the idea and practice of participation, highlighting its ambiguity and frequent use to advance a consumerist neoliberal agenda. He raises the question of if we can really change social policy and not just get pointlessly involved. He also identifies tensions between participation in narrow identity politics and in broader equality based struggles. At the same time, offering developments in the Scottish city of Glasgow as a case study, he suggests that current struggles to resist the harsh effects of anti-public service policies and ideology may also be giving rise to new movements and alliances offering 'a vision of collective participation that provides an ideological alternative'.

Writing from her experience as a long-term practitioner, Suzy Croft looks at participatory practice. She emphasises that participation starts with how we work with people and that underpinning a participatory approach to social policy is a participatory approach to occupational practice. She illustrates this through two people she worked with, highlighting that working in a participatory way is not necessarily a comfortable or cosy journey to make. She also makes clear that, while she worked as a social worker, what she describes is true for all kinds of occupational and professional practice, working with all groups of people.

American psychiatric survivor and New York attorney, Tina Minkowitz, describes her role at the United Nations, where she represented the World Network of Users and Survivors of Psychiatry in the drafting and negotiation of the Convention on the Rights of Persons with Disabilities. She offers a rare insight into the involvement of social policy service users at the highest level. She was directly involved in making possible the inclusion of the perspectives of mental health service users/survivors in the Convention and reports how this was achieved, the values it rested upon and why it was important.

Next, writing from a feminist perspective, Marilyn Palmer, an Australian academic, takes as her starting point the right wing assault on both welfare states and the environment. She points to the failure of traditional social policies to advance sustainability and suggests that the relationship between participatory and sustainable social policy is one of interdependence. She explores the idea that sustainable-participatory social policy is a pathway to 'eco-justice', a term that 'holds together concerns for the natural world and for human life'.

In the final chapter in this part, academics and activists Joe Greener and Michael Lavalette report on a participatory action research project they co-produced with a service user group, funded by the European Union. This project focused on the impact of 'austerity' policies on marginalised groups and how they could challenge it by influencing academic and policy debates. They report with honesty the constraints the research placed on equal involvement, ways of overcoming them and the contribution such co-produced research can make to achieving more participatory social policy.

25

People acting collectively can be powerful

Jennie Fleming

Groupwork is a powerful means of creating social change. Groups of people with shared experience and common concerns can undertake collective action and, as they become more than a collection of individuals and harness the range of skills, knowledge and experiences of their members, can become extremely powerful entities (Doel and Kelly 2014: 55). Organising collectively can enable people who are regarded as disempowered, vulnerable and socially excluded to organise effectively and they can achieve empowerment through coming together in groups (Beresford and Fleming, 2015: 3).

Groups and groupwork can be defined in many different ways, so providing a definition can be problematic. The groups discussed here all form part of what could be called self-directed groups or mutual aid groups in some way. In these groups the focus is external. Group members come together seeking change in their world. Any personal growth of members is a secondary – not primary – benefit; it is the change in the external world that is sought (Mullender et al, 2013: 8).

This chapter considers the power of groupwork in creating policy change. It looks at examples where groupwork was consciously chosen as the means of organisation. It is not always possible to prove a direct causal connection between the work of groups and policy impact; however, the groups described here can be credited to a large degree for achieving the changes they sought. The examples are not the result of rigorous research, but ones young people I know or colleagues have been part of. I have had conversations with people involved; the quotes are from those conversations. I have also reviewed reports and websites. All the examples are about young people, a marginalised and un-enfranchised group in society, taking action to change things for themselves and others. While there are many examples of groups of young people campaigning for change with unknown or limited impact (Fleming, 2012), I was pleased to also find examples of groups of young people successfully achieving policy changes – locally, nationally and internationally.

Examples range from the Scottish Youth Parliament's involvement in getting the vote for 16 and 17 years olds in the 2014 independence referendum, to young women successfully working to achieve equal pay for apprenticeships, to groups of young carers affecting local and national policy. This chapter, while drawing on all these conversations, focuses primarily on three examples of groups of young people affecting policy locally (Mosquito device ban), nationally (UK youth justice) and internationally (climate change education) – each briefly described in boxed text. Each group had diverse membership – in terms of gender, ethnicity, ability and sexuality. Two of these groups were UK based, one was international; there are however examples of groups of young people taking action for change across the world (see for example Percy-Smith and Thomas, 2010).

Local policy change: mosquito devices

Young people in a UK midlands city objected to the council's use of 'mosquito devices' on council buildings. A mosquito device is an electronic device designed to disperse groups of young people from specific places by emitting high frequency sound that only young people can hear.

A group of young people came together to work to change this policy and for the removal of these devises. There was a core group of about six or seven young people, aged about 16 at the time, who did most of the work and meet face to face. Alongside there was a wider group of around 30 young people with virtual involvement – through email and social media. The core group used social media to attract interest and gauge young people's opinions about the mosquito devises – all were united in their opposition.

The group had no adult involvement and no leader. The young people worked together as equals, took turns in doing things and shared responsibility. They wrote letters to a local newspaper, took part in debates on local radio, were interviewed for local TV news and had articles about the campaign in local and regional media. They made contact with an anti-social behaviour officer, who worked with the group to create the report for the council about the mosquito devices and the opposition to them.

It took the group about 6 months to persuade the council to change its policy. The council also recommended that partners, such as the police, do likewise and refused to endorse the use of mosquito devices.

Further information:
www.education.gov.uk/positiveforyouth
Mullender, Ward and Fleming (2013)
Children and Young People Now (2011)

Common concerns

In a group, personal troubles or individual passions can be translated into common concerns. In the groups discussed here members are the 'knowers' and it is recognised this knowledge counts (Russo and Beresford, 2015). In these groups young people are seen as the experts in their lives, and this is the starting point for conversation (Mullender et al, 2013). The experience of being with other people in the same position can engender strength and new hope, and develop a sense of self-confidence and potency, which individuals on their own could not contemplate. Groupwork can open up new possibilities and opportunities for change (Ward, 2000).

> 'Groupwork creates a conversation and brings up topics, issues, ideas – that you had no idea were coming. The quality and depth of conversations the young people had in the groups, we would not have had this without the group experience. We could never have achieved these insights in a series of one to one conversations, a worker and a young person. The conversations amongst themselves were really powerful and revealing.' (Adult groupworker)

> 'When you are inside you are thinking to yourself this really needs to change, in the group you are coming up with an idea ... and we start to debate how to make it better.' (Young person, in Fleming et al, 2014: 30)

For some groups, such as the young people in the criminal justice system, the realisation that others have similar experiences, helps people move away from self-blame and feelings of inadequacy.

> 'The collective voice is so much stronger than the individual. You could see the light go on as they realised others were in the same situation. It stopped them looking in on their selves and made them want things to change externally.' (Adult groupworker)

The intentional focus on common concerns and collective commitment to change can harness the power of group members as they move from a collection of individuals to the whole – a group is greater than the sum of its parts (Doel and Kelly, 2014). Equally, groupwork allows for different perspectives to be heard. Groupwork enables the pooling of experiences, ideas, knowledge and skills and promotes the potential to learn from each other. Young people spoke of the range and diversity of view there can be in groups, and how the discussion of these is crucial.

'Being a female ex-prisoner is completely different to being a male ex-prisoner – we have had the same sort of experience but in a completely different manner.' (Young person, in Fleming et al, 2014: 31)

National Policy: Youth Justice

U R Boss was a UK project aiming to create attitudinal, policy and practice improvements for young people encountering the penal system. The project was set up by the Howard League for Penal Reform in consultation with young people. Groupwork with young people was key to the work. All the young people had experience of the justice system; many had periods of time in custody; they had experienced disadvantage and faced considerable challenges in their lives.

Groupwork took place in different ways throughout the project. The key groupwork was with the Young Advisors – young people who worked to decide the direction of work and took an active part in its delivery. Groupwork also took place with young people both in custody and the community to gain a wide range of experiences and views that the Young Advisors incorporated into their work.

The Young Advisors group worked for more than three years, albeit with some changes of membership. Throughout, the group was supported by youth participation workers who worked with them to enable them to identify the key areas they wanted to seek policy change, and take action to achieve that change. With the Young Advisors groupwork was open and organic, developing in directions chosen by the young people. At the start there were always two adult workers in the group: one to facilitate and one to note take (keeping records was necessary to create policy documents, and so on). Over time the young people began to take on many of the group process tasks themselves. The Young Advisors developed their skills as groupworkers and towards the end of the project were the main facilitators of many of the groups in custody.

The young people developed *A Young Person's Manifesto* setting out the key issues for change.[1] They were involved in a range of campaigning activities – speaking at political party conferences, lobbying MPs, working with Howard League's policy officer creating briefings. There were a considerable number of policy and legalisation changes as a result of the group's work including the end of routine strip searching of children on arrival at Youth Offending institutions, changes in the Rehabilitation of Offenders Act, and changes to remand legislation.

Further information:
https://howardleague.org/wp-content/uploads/2016/03/use-your-situation_final.pdf
Fleming et al (2014)

Finding voice

Young people are not used to being listened to and influencing or making decisions. This is even more true for some groups than others; the workers who worked with the young women's groups and the young people in the justice system said that it took young people a long time to overcome their 'voicelessness' and how finding their voice and believing people would listen, and feel what they had to say was worth listening to, was a core part of the group work. A first step was for people to find their voice. Not all group members were able to speak out, but those that were used the collective experiences to make their case. A secondary advantage of being part of collective efforts for change is that it can make those involved more articulate, confident and aware.

> 'If it wasn't for U R Boss I wouldn't have been able to use my prison experience to the positive, it would just be a negative hanging around from my past forever. I would not have had that confidence in me.'
> (Young person, in Fleming et al, 2014: 60)

Speaking beyond individual personal experience was an important part of all three groups. Each had a core and active group with a wider group of young people whose experiences they could draw on. In YOUNGO, the young people were all from national climate change groups; the young people seeking the mosquito ban deliberately created a wider group of young people to check out views and opinions with. The core groups were advocates for other young people with similar views or in similar situations. The Young Advisors in the community met face to face, but there were also Young Advisors in custody who contributed to the group in many ways.

> 'Being a Young Advisor in custody you are doing the same thing as outside, but have more time to give it as there are less distractions. It is the same you just don't meet with the others. It gives you the opportunity to do something good even when you are messed up and are inside.' (Young person, in Fleming et al, 2014: 27)

In this situation the workers were the conduit for information sharing between the young people in custody and those outside. This sharing of information and common purpose reduced isolation and created a sense of solidarity.

Young people finding their voice is only part of the solution – adults need to learn to listen. Young people's voices need to be valued and listened to: this is often not the case.

Responsibility for the group process

Many groups of young people do have adult or worker facilitation, like U R Boss. Groups do need someone to take responsibility for group processes and do need do to be able to resolve disagreements, keep to deadlines, stay focused, ensure all voices are heard and make and keep to decisions, but such functions are not the special province of workers or adults. Even when there are adults with responsibility for the group, such tasks are often shared among group members (Mullender et al, 2013: 63); this happens as young people gain confidence in themselves as well as understanding of how the group works. Young Advisors did take on some of the facilitation themselves, and demonstrated that they had felt more ownership and leadership towards the end of the project by having a clear grasp of direction and plans; however, the organisation and administration of the groups remained with staff throughout.

The other two case studies are part of the growing movement of youth-led groups and were entirely youth run. Both adopted equalitarian ways of working. YOUNGO agreed a way of operating based on a clear model groupwork – consensus; when challenging the mosquito devices the core group worked as equals, took turns in doing things and shared responsibility among themselves.

International policy change: climate change education

YOUNGO is the official youth constituency of the UN Framework Convention on Climate Change. It is a group space at global climate change negotiations for young people. YOUNGO does not have a physical base. It organises throughout the year online and meets physically during the annual negotiations; these meetings change location (Cancun, 2010; Durban, 2011; Doha, 2012; Warsaw; 2013; Lima, 2014; Paris, 2015). Attendance is dominated by European, North American, and Australian/New Zealand activities. Great efforts are made to ensure delegates from the global south can also attend, through developing partnerships and providing bursaries. Young people from the region where the meeting is being held are usually a strong contingent.

Climate education, known as Article 6 in the climate movement, is seen as a crucial component in ensuring children and young people can make informed decisions as individuals, as well as understand the global impact of the changing climate. YOUNGO successfully got a decision passed on climate education.

> It's now UN policy that there should be climate change education both in school and out of school and that young people should be involved in decision-making on climate change. Plus, we changed World Bank policy and increased funding for participation and education! (UK Youth Climate Coalition)

YOUNGO is a self run group that works to a consensus model. Consensus decision making is a way of reaching agreement between all members of a group and being committed to finding solutions that everyone actively supports, or at least can live with. This ensures that all opinions, ideas and concerns are taken into account and seeks to weave together everyone's best ideas and key concerns (Seeds for Change, 2010).

During the climate negotiations, decisions are made by those who attend the daily YOUNGO meetings. Throughout the rest of the year, numerous online discussion groups are used to facilitate policy positions and campaign decisions. While at the negotiations the young people meet every day. A group member takes on the role of facilitator – often one of the more experienced group members. Young people become very fluent with the process – both in terms of the practical hand signals as well as the rationale behind consensus: for YOUNGO, consensus decision making fits with its values of equality, equity and participation. People learn by experience and gain knowledge in doing. The facilitator does not take a position, but looks after the process for the group. The group is self monitoring and holds itself to high levels of accountability. The members make the rules and also ensure they are kept – which can be very challenging.

Further information:
http://ukycc.org
https://unfccc.int/cc_inet/cc_inet/youth_portal/items/6795.php
http://ukycc.org/article-6-a-double-win-for-young-people/
www.positive.news/2010/archive/2555/success-for-young-people-at-climate-talks/

Group action

Once they had agreed their priorities and strategy, all of the groups undertook lobbying and campaigning. They produced briefings, spoke on the radio, used social media, attended political meetings and conferences, and had meetings with those in power who could effect the changes they wanted to see.

The group was where the young people prepared for these tasks. Groupwork was how they came up with their plans, set agendas for meetings, and prepared what was to be said and by whom. Some role-played meetings with young people taking on different roles. The YOUNGO daily meetings meant that members were prepared for both the content and the process of what they wanted to achieve.

Once again the strength of the group and the collective experiences was an important factor.

> 'They knew they might be the one standing up there [at a party conference], but they knew they had a whole army of young women behind them and represented them in their story.' (Adult groupworker)

Access to power

To have impact any group needs to gain access and the ear of those with power. This is an opportunity often denied to young people. Marginalised groups often do not have access to decision makers, and have to rely on others to speak for them. In these three examples, young people did gain access to decision makers. The young people campaigning for the removal of mosquito devises made contact with and gained the support of council workers who helped them get their message across to those in power locally. YOUNGO attended the climate change summits alongside adult decision makers, and hence had the opportunities to meet formally and informally with decision makers. There were opportunities for interaction, spaces for conversations; they did not have to fight for access as is so often the case. Importantly, they were ready to take advantage of such opportunities as they arose. U R Boss was part of the Howard League for Penal Reform which has a long record of campaigning for social justice in the criminal justice system. It was able to provide the Young Advisors with access to powerful decision makers to make their case. The Howard League also has a Policy Department which supported the work of the young people.

Conclusion

Why were these examples successful in creating policy change? There are a number of reasons, many of which are set out above – the power of the group, the solidarity, the confidence being part of a group can bring, gaining access to those in power.

> 'From the experiences we have gained from campaigning it's kind of given us the knowledge – you know we can do this – we have all had a taste and now let's get out of the paddling pool and go for a swim.' (Young person, in Fleming et al, 2014: 50)

In addition, it is important that the issues were identified by young people themselves. They were concerns young people themselves knew needed change.

> 'The young people knew their lives, they had lived the things, they had direct knowledge.' (Adult groupworker)

All three groups recognised that groupwork is a practice requiring knowledge and skill. YOUNGO provided workshops on consensus groups for its facilitators and members. The adult facilitators of groups all had considerable experience in groupwork with young people and some had training.

The groups all showed persistence; they were not put off by initial lack of progress, they continued to fight their cause,

'We would not take no for an answer. In the end our persistence paid off. Young people were instrumental in creating stronger and more resilient policy.' (UK Youth Climate Coalition, 2012)

They were passionate and committed to their campaigns and influencing the issues they were concerned with. I leave the last words to the young people.

'Basically, we wrote the text. This was a BIG win. For the first time we can point to actual paragraphs of the text and say 'young people did that.' One of the UN chairs said this was unprecedented and he'd never seen such a well-written, well-thought out brief before. We got a decision passed on climate education when at the beginning of the conference we wouldn't have thought it possible in our wildest dreams.' (UK Youth Climate Coalition, no date)

'I wanted to be part of getting things to change. I want things to be different for young people in prison – not just me, others too. I want to help change things.' (Young person, in Fleming et al, 2014: 61)

Acknowledgements

With thanks to Harrison Carter, Alex Farrow, Paula Jackson-Key, Lucy Russell, Jess Southgate and Ali Thomas for sharing their great knowledge and experience.

Note

1   *A Young Person's Manifesto*, no longer available, but previously accessed at www.urboss.org.uk/ what-were-doing/campaigns/young-peoples-manifesto

References

Beresford, P. and Fleming, J. (2015) 'Groupwork and user involvement: a critical pairing', *Groupwork*, 24 (1), 3–8, DOI:10.1921/8501206

Children and Young People Now (2011) 'Participation in Practice: Mosquito Ban in Sheffield', 21 February, www.cypnow.co.uk/cyp/other/1045129/ participation-in-practice-mosquito-ban-in-sheffield

Doel, M. and Kelly, T. (2014) *A–Z of Groups and Groupwork*, Basingstoke: Palgrave Macmillan.

Fleming, J. (2012) 'Young People's Participation – Where Next?' *Children and Society*, DOI:10.1111/j.1099-0860.2012.00442.x

Fleming, J., Smith, R. and Hine, J. (2014) *Use your situation to change your destination*, http://howardleague.org/publications/use-your-situation-to-change-your-destination/

Mullender, A., Ward, D. and Fleming, J. (2013) *Action for Empowerment: Self-directed groupwork*, London: Palgrave Macmillan

Percy-Smith, B. and Thomas, N. (eds) (2010) *A Handbook of Children's and Young People's Participation*, London: Routledge.

Russo, J. and Beresford, P. (2015) 'Between Exclusion and Colonisation: Seeking a Place for Mad People's Knowledge in Academia', *Disability & Society*, 30 (1), 153–7.

Seeds for Change (2010) 'Consensus Decision Making', www.seedsforchange. org.uk/consensus

UK Youth Climate Coalition (no date) 'Youth Delegation History', http://ukycc. org/uk-youth-delegation-history/

UK Youth Climate Coalition (2012) 'Article 6: A double win for young people', 5 December, http://ukycc.org/article-6-a-double-win-for-young-people/

Ward, D. (2000) 'Totem not Token: Groupwork as a Vehicle for User Participation', in H. Kemshall and R. Littlechild (eds) *User Involvement and Participation in Social Care: Research Informing Practice*, London: Jessica Kingsley, pp 45–6.

26

Their participation and ours: competing visions of empowerment

Iain Ferguson

Introduction: 'Cuts cost lives'

On 12 November 2014, a demonstration of around 200 people – mental health workers, trade union activists, service users and carers – gathered outside the Victorian City Chambers in George Square in Glasgow. Inside the building a full meeting of the Labour-controlled Glasgow City Council was voting on whether to make cuts to social care services of almost £30 million. The cuts included a proposed reduction of 40% to the budget of the Glasgow Association for Mental Health (GAMH), one of the biggest voluntary sector providers of mental health services in the city. The message of the protestors outside to the Labour-controlled council inside the building was a simple but powerful one: 'Cuts cost lives!' This was no empty rhetoric. While not easy to quantify, in Scotland as elsewhere in the UK the politics of austerity have led to an increase both in levels of mental distress and also in the number of suicides (Psychologists against Austerity (Scotland), 2015).

Glasgow, of course, is far from unique. Massive cuts to services, alongside reductions in disability benefits, the application of brutal sanctions and the imposition of a punitive and degrading Work Capability Test have greatly increased the levels of stress experienced by many disabled people across the UK (Gunnell et al, 2015). The picture is a grim one. In this context discussing service user participation can seem either hopelessly naïve or akin to re-arranging the deck chairs on the Titanic: exactly what is it that service users are being invited to 'participate' in? Yet amid the nightmare of 'welfare reform', there is one bright light. For the past decade has also seen the revival of a collective disability movement that had seemed to go into abeyance in the years following the election of a New Labour government in 1997.

In this chapter I shall argue that this renewed movement and the alliances that are being created offer the best hope both of defending the gains that have been made over the past 30 years and of offering a vision of collective participation that provides an ideological alternative to dominant neoliberal individualism.

We shall return to a discussion of that movement in the final part of this chapter. Before then, however, it is necessary to revisit some earlier debates around participation as a basis for critiquing the forms of service user participation which have been dominant in the UK over the past two decades.

Participation: who benefits?

We live in a society where, most of the time, the vast majority of us have very little control over our lives. That lack of control is evident not just in the political or workplace spheres but also in relation to the health and social care services we receive – and it particularly affects those who require these services on a long-term basis. Not surprisingly, then, the demand for a greater degree of control over, and participation in, these services has been a core demand of service user movements since their inception, alongside a call for new and different services more suited to our needs.

The demand for more participation, the right to have a say over decisions affecting our lives was also a central feature of the social movements of the 1960s, a decade when every taken-for-granted assumption, whether it be about the place of women in society, the nature of sexuality or the meaning of mental ill health, was subject to a radical questioning (Harman, 1988; Kurlansky, 2005). Yet that demand was accompanied by a recognition that not all forms of participation were benign, and that at the very least, to use a contemporary term, participation needed to be 'problematised'. Commenting on the notion then popular on the Left of workers' participation in industry, for example, a poster from the 'events' of May 1968 in France, a time when a mass student uprising and the largest general strike in history rocked French society to its foundations, ran (in English) as follows:

> I participate
> You participate
> He/she participates
> We participate
> You participate
> They profit.

A similar scepticism towards participation was evident the following year in the publication of Sherry Arnstein's famous Ladder of Participation, the bottom rung of which was 'manipulation', progressing through 'placation' to the (rather more positive) 'citizen control' at the top (Arnstein, 1969). Reflecting the experience of a decade that had seen the rise of the black civil rights movement in the US, a huge movement of opposition to the Vietnam war, new social movements for women's and gay liberation, and massive workers' struggles across the globe, both Arnstein and the young French radicals were saying two things. First, that while people everywhere were demanding a say in decisions affecting their lives, the invitation from the powerful to oppressed minorities and to those challenging the status quo to 'participate' was not always a benign one. At best it could amount to little more than tokenism; at worst, it was a means of engaging them in their own oppression. Second, the new horizons opened up by the social struggles of these years meant that for many 'participation', 'having a say' – the chance to contribute to the reform of existing social and economic structures – was not enough. Or, in the words of another popular slogan of the time, 'We don't want the crumbs – we want the whole bloody bakery!'

As I shall argue, these discussions are not merely of historical interest: the same ambiguities and contradictions permeate the varieties of participation on offer today and the debates that surround them.

Service user participation: missing the bigger picture?

> The rationale for this reorganization is the empowerment of users and carers ... this redressing of the balance of power is the best guarantee of a continuing improvement in the quality of services. (Department of Health, 1991)

Given a long history during which services for people with physical and mental impairments or disabilities were typically characterised by a complete lack of service user voice and a blanket denial of individuality, it is scarcely surprising that the promise of participation and involvement held out by the guidance quoted above to the 1990 NHS and Community Care Act was greeted with enthusiasm and expectation.

What the language of the 1990 Act and the guidance surrounding it also reflected, however, was an emerging neoliberal vision of welfare which saw 'dependency' as the greatest evil and which had no hesitation in deploying the disability movement's language of choice, control and empowerment to promote individualised forms of welfare in the context of a social care market. As John Harris noted in his study of 'the social work business', far from being a charter for emancipation the 1990 Act was

> the primary vehicle for accomplishing the transformation of social work and the establishing of the social work business. The promotion of a new policy direction in community care, embodying a market framework, was integral to the Conservative Government's radical reform of the welfare state and the reduction of Social Service Departments' role in service provision. (Harris, 2002: 36)

The four key components of that transformation were:

- The introduction of market mechanisms
- The promotion of competition leading to efficiency gains and savings
- The keeping of state provision to a minimum
- The pursuit of individualism and individual choice. (Harris, 2002: 37–8)

In reality, it has been this market-driven agenda, not the collective vision of the disability movement, that has shaped the forms of participation that have developed over the past two decades. Not surprisingly then, much of that early enthusiasm has evaporated, for three main reasons.

First, while there have been some excellent examples of service users, when given the opportunity, shaping new and imaginative services in different areas of health and social care, for many people the overall experience has been one of tokenism, of the appearance of participation rather than its substance, with real power and control remaining in the hands of the state (or increasingly, of large private providers). As Branfield and her colleagues noted in a review of service user involvement for the Joseph Rowntree Foundation in 2006:

> There has been an increasing emphasis in recent years on user involvement in health and social care policy and practice. However, it has come in for growing questioning. Service providers and researchers have begun to ask what evidence there is that it improves services. Service users and their organisations have raised the issue of what they are actually able to achieve by their involvement and to question the usefulness of getting involved. (Branfield and Beresford, 2006)

Second, such service user involvement as has taken place has tended to be confined to voluntary or third sector organisations in the fields of health and social care (Ferguson and Woodward, 2009). Insofar as service user involvement has been promoted within the statutory health and social work sector, it has usually been in the very limited consumerist form of complaints procedures, involvement in case conferences and so on. That disparity has allowed successive UK governments, both Conservative and New Labour, simultaneously to present the third sector as more progressive and inclusive than the state sector while at the same time promoting a funding regime based on competition between voluntary organisations for contracts, the effect of which has been to result in a 'race to the bottom' and poorer quality services (Cunningham et al, 2013).

Third, early concerns that the rhetoric of consumerism and choice would prove to be little more than a smoke screen for the privatisation and wholesale marketisation of health and social services has been amply justified. As White has documented in his recent study of the 'shadow state', the 'secret companies that run Britain', the private sector now runs most areas of social care, including childcare, on a for-profit basis. This, in England, three quarters of the homes housing the 5,000 young people in residential care are privately owned, in many cases by private equity companies, with the top five providers turning over a profit of £30 million (White, 2016). The uncovering of abuse in 2011 of residents at Winterbourne View, a private hospital for adults with learning disabilities, by an undercover team working for the BBC's Panorama, gave the lie to the notion that the quality of care is superior in the private sector. And the collapse of Southern Cross, also in 2011, at that time the biggest provider of residential care for older people in the UK, highlighted the risks involved in handing over the care of some of the most vulnerable people in society to whose existence is subject to the vagaries of the market. There is also no evidence that the degree of service user involvement is any higher in the private sector than the (very low) levels in the state sector.

Nor has that neoliberal reclaiming of the visions and demands of disabled people and people with mental health problems been confined to service user involvement in organisations. In a powerful re-assessment of the experience of direct payments policy and practice, Jenny Morris has argued that:

> One key example of past successes in finding opportunities within prevailing political agendas concerns the campaign for direct payments. The resulting legislation, passed by a Conservative government in 1996, fitted in with an agenda which sought the privatisation of services and an undermining of public sector trade unions. While disabled people's organisations did not support such policies, we did – when making the case for direct payments– use language which fitted well with the individualist political framework which was becoming more and more dominant ... My concern is that – in engaging with the dominant policy agendas – we have lost touch with more fundamental issues concerning the welfare state, and that we have, unintentionally, contributed towards a steady undermining of collective responsibility and redistribution. From my perspective, this matters because I do not believe that the alternative – a small state and a market of private providers – will deliver the opportunities and quality of life which disabled people should expect in the twenty-first century. (Morris, 2011)

Similar criticisms have been made by Peter Beresford and others concerning the experience of one offshoot of direct payments, personalisation (Beresford, 2014: Ferguson, 2007).

Conclusion: what is to be done?

How best then to resist a politics of austerity that would make the poorest sections of society pay for a crisis of capitalism in whose creation they played no part? In conclusion I shall suggest that three responses – ideological, strategic, political – are likely to be of particular importance.

First, a vision of independence that challenges the spurious and stigmatising neoliberal view of independence as total self-sufficiency and replaces it with one which recognises our interdependence and the fact that we all needs services at some points in our lives. In the words of the definition provided by the Independent Living Movement:

> Independent living means all disabled people having the same freedom, choice, dignity and control as other citizens at home, a work and in the community. *It does not necessarily mean living by yourself or fending for yourself. It means rights to practical assistance and support to participate in society and live an ordinary life.* (Independent Living Scotland, no date, emphasis added)

That means challenging the egoistic liberal notion that we are all rivals who can only benefit at the expense of the other. Here we can draw on the tradition of Aristotle, Hegel and Marx which recognises that we are social animals and that, in Marx's words, 'the free development of each is the condition for the free development of all' (Eagleton, 2011). The failure of neoliberalism to recognise our social nature and our human need for interconnectedness has been one factor that has contributed to a global epidemic of social isolation and loneliness, which has been profoundly damaging to mental and physical health (Monbiot, 2016). In its place, we need to assert a vision of individualism (and of collectivism) that combines a recognition of our common social nature with respect for diversity and difference.

Second, the experience of the past two decades has shown the dangers of relying on governments, whether Conservative or Labour, to bring about real change and real participation from above. Only strong collective organisation from below can do that. In a gloomy assessment written in 2006, Mike Oliver and Colin Barnes concluded:

> [W]e no longer have a strong and powerful disabled people's movement. … since the late 1990s the combination of the Government and the big charities have successfully adopted the big ideas of the disabled people's movement, usurped its language, and undertaken further initiatives which promise much but deliver little (cited in Slorach, 2016: 129).

In this respect at least the picture now is a more positive one. The emergence in recent years of organisations such as DPAC (Disabled People Against Cuts) and, in the mental health field, Black Triangle and the Mental Health Resistance Network (MHRN) has given some hope to those of us, disabled and non-disabled, who wish to challenge the politics of austerity. DPAC's policy statement is clear and uncompromising:

DPAC is for everyone who believes that disabled people should have full human rights and equality. It is for everyone that refuses to accept that any country can destroy the lives of people just because they are or become disabled or sick. It is for everyone against government austerity measures which target the poor while leaving the wealthy unscathed. (DPAC, 2016)

The fact that these organisations have formed alliances with trade unions such as the PCS (Public and Civil Servants), as well as with other campaigning organisations, such as Shaping Our Lives and the Social Work Action Network, is also a hopeful sign. For while no one can doubt the courage and determination of their members, the numbers involved are often small and success is more likely to be achieved through linking up with more powerful social forces.

Finally, earlier in this chapter the question was posed as to what 'participation' might mean in the conditions of the long crisis of neoliberal capitalism. In fact, the past few years have seen popular participation taking place on a scale that has not happened for decades. From the inspiring Arab Spring in 2011 to the Scottish referendum campaign in 2014, from the movement around the American socialist senator Bernie Sanders to the magnificent struggles of Greek workers against austerity, millions of so-called ordinary people, usually labelled as apathetic, have marched, voted, struck and organised to challenge poverty, inequality and oppression and in support of the demand that 'another world is possible'. In the US black and white people have protested police violence and brutality through the Black Lives Matter Campaign. And in the squalid conditions of the so-called 'Jungle' camp in Calais in France, refugees from around the globe have fought back against the French and British states and those who would deny them their right to live free from war, torture and oppression. It is through participation in such struggles, rather than through a narrow identity politics which emphasises difference, that all of us can both defend the very real gains that have been made over the past few decades and at the same time help to create the conditions for a different kind of society not based on the scapegoating and oppression of minorities.

References

Arnstein, S.R. (1969) 'A ladder of citizen participation', *Journal of the American Institute of Planners*, 35 (4), 216–24.

Beresford, P. (2014) 'Personalisation: from solution to problem?' in I. Ferguson and M. Lavalette (eds) *Personalisation*, Bristol: Policy Press.

Branfield, F. and Beresford, P. (2006) *Making user involvement work: Supporting service user networking and knowledge*, York: Joseph Rowntree Foundation, www.jrf.org.uk/report/making-user-involvement-work-supporting-service-user-networking-and-knowledge

Cunningham, I., Hearne, G. and James, P. (2013) 'Voluntary organisations and marketisation: a dynamic of employment degradation', *Industrial Relations Journal*, 44, 171–88.

Department of Health (1991) *Care Management and Assessment: Management of Practice*, London: HMSO.

DPAC (Disabled People Against Cuts) (2016) 'About', http://dpac.uk.net/about/

Eagleton, T. (2011) *Why Marx was Right*, New Haven and London: Yale University Press.

Gunnell, D.. Donovan, J., Barnes, M., Davies, R., Hawton, K., Kapur, N., Hollingworth, W. and Metcalfe, C. (2015) *The 2008 Global Financial Crisis: Effects on Mental Health and Suicide*, Policy Bristol, Policy Report 3/2015, www.bris.ac.uk/media-library/sites/policybristol/documents/PolicyReport-3-Suicide-recession.pdf

Ferguson, I. (2007) 'Increasing user choice or privatising risk? The antinomies of personalisation', *British Journal of Social Work*, 37, 387–403.

Ferguson, I. and Woodward, R. (2009) *Radical Social Work in Practice: Making a Difference*, Bristol: Policy Press.

Harman, C. (1988) *The Fire Next Time: 1968 and After*, London: Bookmarks.

Harris, J. (2002) *The Social Work Business*, London: Routledge.

Independent Living Scotland (no date) 'Independent Living', www.ilis.co.uk/independent-living

Kurlansky, M. (2005) *1968: The Year that Rocked the World*, New York: Vintage.

Monbiot, G. (2016) 'Neoliberalism is creating loneliness. That's what's wrenching society apart', *Guardian*, 12 October, www.theguardian.com/commentisfree/2016/oct/12/neoliberalism-creating-loneliness-wrenching-society-apart

Morris, J. (2011) *Rethinking Disability Policy*, York: Joseph Rowntree Foundation, www.jrf.org.uk/report/rethinking-disability-policy

Psychologists against Austerity (Scotland) (2015) 'Austerity measures contribute to mental ill health', Letter, *Herald*, 4 May.

Slorach, R. (2016) *A Very Capitalist Condition: a history and politics of disability*, London: Bookmarks.

White, A. (2016) *Shadow State: Inside the Secret Companies that Run Britain*, London: OneWorld Publications.

27

A participatory approach to professional practice

Suzy Croft

I have worked in a hospice in England – with people with life limiting conditions and those facing bereavement – for over 26 years. Hospice or palliative care, with its origins in St Joseph's London and the pioneering work of Dame Cicely Saunders, is a UK development that has become a worldwide movement. It is from this perspective, as a palliative care social worker, that I write this chapter. As soon as I was invited to do so, I thought of 'Richard'[1] who was referred to the hospice day centre 20 years ago. Richard was a 46-year-old homeless white man with advanced cancer of the kidney. Due to his past problems with alcohol, he had been estranged from his family for several years but his ex-wife had recently been offering support, albeit that she did not want him to move back into the family home. Richard needed support around his medical symptoms, accessing welfare benefits and rehousing. He was very keen to meet with the social work team but found the hospice day centre a bit overwhelming and described it as 'a bit too posh for me'. When we sat down in the rather scruffy social work team office, he said to me 'this is more like it'!

The first time I met 'Richard', he talked about his cancer diagnosis and how for him it had meant that he was able to have contact with his children again. But there were a lot of practical issues to sort out. His living conditions were very precarious and he had been temporarily placed in a hostel. The next time I saw him he was really anxious to talk about the past and his feelings on being reunited with his children. He was thrilled that they wanted to be in touch with him and had welcomed him back into their lives. He wanted to tell me all about them.

However, I felt there really wasn't time to talk about all of that then as Richard had been offered a local authority flat and it was essential to arrange the viewing, sort out the transport to get him there and arrange for someone to go with him. Richard was grateful but appeared unconcerned about this offer of housing. I always remember how keen he was to talk and talk about the renewed relationships with his ex-wife and children. But I persuaded him that we should do that in more detail next time.

To my great regret Richard died unexpectedly two days later. Whether he sensed that he was imminently dying and thus rehousing was irrelevant, or whether he was just so pleased and relieved to finally have someone to talk to I will never know. Obviously I did not know that Richard was going to die so soon, and from a social work point of view it was extremely important that Richard be rehoused, due to his serious illness. But Richard's desire to talk about his feelings and his relationships, which I had cut short, remained with me for a long time afterwards and informed a lot of my thinking in my work. I had not listened to what was most important to him.

A participatory approach to professional/occupational practice is not necessarily a straightforward course to follow. It does not easily lend itself to tick-box exercises or simple solutions and can feel like a challenge to our expertise as professionals. It means a lot of careful thought and hard work. However, I would argue such an approach to practice is essential if, as a social worker, or indeed any other practitioner, you want to be able to offer the most appropriate support to a service user, that is the kind of support that most meets their needs whatever their particular situation.

So what is a participatory approach and why is it important? For me it is based on the model of person-centred support for which service users and their allies have long argued. The Standards We Expect Project, a project funded by the Joseph Rowntree Foundation, examined the ways in which people and services were working in different person-centred ways to enable people to get the support they needed to live their lives. The project culminated in a book, *Supporting People: Towards a person-centred approach* (Beresford et al, 2011). The authors, building on what service users said, stated that person-centred support:

> Means the service user is at the centre of the service and services should work with the service user to help them live the life they want – it's not just about them fitting into an existing service and accepting what is on offer.

The project identified the core values of person-centred support from service users and others as being Inclusion, Respect, Independence and Personal Choice and these, I would argue, are the values that also lie at the heart of a participatory approach to professional practice.

A participatory approach involves working in partnership with service users to build a relationship of trust and mutual respect. It means really listening to what that person has to say, discussing with them what they are most worried about, what they want to happen, what are their hopes, their fears, their practical problems and so on. It is not about a professional telling a service user how things have to be and how they have to be done.

What is important to remember is that each person is unique and has their own thoughts and feelings about what is happening to them. It means taking account of issues of diversity and cultural and social differences. In palliative care you are often meeting people approaching the end of their life and you may have only one chance to get it right with them. It is very important for people to be able to 'tell their story' however long it may take and even if you feel you have heard it all before or it is getting in the way of getting on with the task in hand.

It is important that you, as a professional, and the service user, are able to develop an agenda for future action together. For example, this may be that you will undertake to help with a practical task such as claiming welfare benefits, trying to apply for rehousing or agreeing to meet and talk more about the support that person needs to cope with what is happening to them. At this stage it is crucial to be clear, honest and open about what support you can or cannot offer. For example, if you know that due to local state financial cuts or strict eligibility criteria it would be impossible for someone to be rehoused or to access social care from their local authority, then you need to explain that clearly and be honest from the start that you are unlikely to be able to help them achieve those aims. My experience is that most people can cope with knowing the limits and boundaries of what you can do and will appreciate openness and honesty. A participatory approach means being able to continually discuss and reflect on what work you and the service user are doing together and involving them in that discussion, being prepared to be flexible about what is needed.

It is important, where possible, to go at a service user's own pace whatever you feel the issues to be. When I first met 'Mercy' she was in the inpatient unit at the hospice. Mercy was a black African young woman with an advanced cancer that had spread to her brain. She had had radiotherapy treatment for the brain secondaries, but it hadn't yet taken effect and she was disinhibited in her manner and could appear quite aggressive. I was asked to see her as the hospice staff were puzzled and concerned about Mercy's relationship with her mother with whom she had been living. Her mother spent all day at the hospice with Mercy but they rarely spoke to each other and neither of them were communicative with the staff. When I first met Mercy and her mother they clearly found it hard to think of any kind of support they would want. Mercy's mother, although not unfriendly, was very reticent in her manner and said very little. However it became clear that they were worried about Mercy's welfare benefits and that she did not have enough money to live on and as a starting point it was agreed I would help her with that. This did not prove to be an easy task as a claim for Personal Independence Payment (a UK benefit for disabled people aged 16–64 years) had been previously started and then discontinued and this caused huge problems with the relevant government department – the Department for Work and Pensions (DWP). Necessary telephone conversations with the DWP were difficult as, due to her brain secondaries, Mercy was extremely rude to the call handler! Eventually I was successful in sorting this out and when Mercy went home I kept in touch with her and her mother, sorting out other practical problems as they arose.

For a long time I did not feel I really understood the relationship between Mercy and her mother as they were pleasant and friendly, but not communicative. But

I was sure that things were not good between them. Just as when Mercy was in the hospice they rarely spoke to each other when I saw them on my visits. I felt unsure if once all the practical problems were sorted that either of them would want any further support or reveal anything of how they really felt.

However, one day Mercy phoned me when she was at home on her own. She told me that her mother had told her she should leave as Mercy was quite a lot better at the time and her mother felt she should be 'standing on her own feet again'. Mercy then told me her relationship with her mother had always been difficult and that prior to being ill she had been living independently. We agreed I should help her apply for rehousing with her local authority but I warned this would not be easy due to all the cuts in social housing.

After a lot of hard work Mercy was finally supported by the council to move into a private rented bedsit and I went to see here there. When I first arrived I felt dismayed about how small and dingy the room was. But Mercy was thrilled with it. She was so pleased to have her own home and for the first time she talked and talked about her life, her previous job, her relationship with her mother and her hopes for the future.

Using a participatory approach in my work with Mercy meant that through ensuring she could take the lead in setting the agenda for our work together, she finally felt able to talk about her relationship with her mother and seek support around that issue. After she was able to move into her own home Mercy's relationship with her mother improved and they went on holiday together. After Mercy died her mother commented on how helpful the social work support had been for her daughter and as a result she accepted bereavement support for herself from a colleague.

But of course a participatory approach in palliative care social work, as in any branch of social work or other helping profession, does bring its challenges. Obviously service users are experts in themselves but professionals are also experts. You may have knowledge and expertise which the service user does not have and that can be painful or difficult to share. Mercy often spoke to me about how she would bring up her children when she had them, but I knew she would never have children. Clearly we were not able to have an open discussion about that as Mercy never spoke about dying or acknowledged that she would not live long.

Conflict can still arise between service users and practitioners within a participatory framework. For example, I have worked with mothers who are extremely reluctant to tell their children they are dying or to make plans for a child's future. They, not surprisingly, want to carry on as normal for as long as possible. But there is a clear conflict of interests here as obviously children need to be prepared for such a traumatic event as a parent dying. On those occasions time may be short and going at the pace dictated by the service user may just not be appropriate if the children's interests are to be served.

It is important to recognise the importance of open, honest discussion, being prepared to tackle difficult issues and knowing that a participatory approach means that difficult questions will have to be raised and addressed, and there may be times when the relationship with a service user feels frayed and a lot of anger is expressed. A key point here is that a participatory approach has to be part of team and inter-disciplinary working. It is helpful that when relationships become frayed, another member of the team can be involved in offering support at difficult times and perhaps play a different role. For example, a social work colleague of mine, working with a seriously ill woman, continually raised with her that her three children had to know their mother was dying, especially as it would probably mean having to live with their father whom they hardly knew. This mother resisted all such attempts and would often be out when visits had been arranged and agreed. One morning the clinical nurse specialist from the team called round and recognised immediately that this mother was dying. She persuaded the mother to allow her to collect the children from school there and then and the nurse then spent the whole day with the family, supporting the children to be with their mother as she died.

Similarly a participatory approach does not involve the practitioner in having to have all the answers or being able to solve all problems. It is important to recognise that the values of personal choice and autonomy mean we must recognise that service users will not always make the choices practitioners feel are the best ones – but it is their right to do that. I worked with one man who did not tell me for many months that he was actually sharing a bank account with his son who was systematically taking all his money so that he did not have enough to live on. When he finally told me, he was adamant he did not want to involve the authorities and get his son into trouble but agreed that I could help him open his own bank account.

What is crucial is that as workers, we are not afraid to challenge or confront difficult issues, but offer support to services users to lead their lives in the way they think is best. For example, there have been occasions when I have felt frustrated or disappointed that a service user has not accepted a highly desirable council flat in spite of all my advice, or times when a service user has taken a long time to trust me, as the professional, with some very important information.

Outcomes cannot always be measured in ways that are clear cut and you may not always know what the results of your intervention are. But what is so important is that service users know that there is someone on whom they can rely.

In a survey of service users views carried out by the social work team in 2012 at the hospice we asked the question '*what has been the most helpful thing for you in your contact with the social worker?*' I think some of the responses truly reflect the value of participatory working:

'Honesty, Objectivity, Helping me to be less manipulated when at my most vulnerable ...'

'Being treated with dignity, patience, willing to find out more information'

'Her support giving me confidence'

'Most important is when they showed care, love, offered help that they can give to me that made me stronger to face my illness'

And perhaps the last is the most important – that if we, as professionals, offer support in the right way, that is in a participatory way, then of course we cannot make everything alright and solve all problems but we can play a crucial part in enabling service users to feel stronger in facing their problems and difficulties and to know that they are not alone in their struggles.

Note
[1]   All names have been changed.

Reference
Beresford, P., Fleming, J., Glynn, M., Bewley, C., Croft, S., Branfield, F. and Postle, K. (2011) *Supporting People: Towards a person-centred approach*, Bristol, Policy Press.

28

Dreams of justice

Tina Minkowitz

Introduction

This chapter discusses the drafting and negotiation of the Convention on the Rights of Persons with Disabilities, in which the perspective of users and survivors of psychiatry was successfully incorporated into public policy. I will describe the process and my involvement in it, and explain the factors that contributed to a successful outcome.

Background

From June 2002 through December 2006 a process took place at the United Nations headquarters in New York City to draft and negotiate a human rights treaty that is now known as the Convention on the Rights of Persons with Disabilities (CRPD). This process was the culmination of years of work by the disability community and supportive states. Mexico succeeded in passing a General Assembly resolution to consider treaty proposals by persuading countries of the Global South that social development was enhanced when persons with disabilities are included as contributing members of society. The treaty was to draw on both human rights and social development. The human rights component was to become primary, and CRPD became the first human rights treaty of the 21st century.

Although users and survivors of psychiatry have had diverse and sometimes contentious relationships to the disability community, we were fortunate that the World Network of Users and Survivors of Psychiatry (WNUSP) was a member of the International Disability Alliance (IDA). As such, even though WNUSP was a young organization, it had an assured opportunity to participate in the treaty process. IDA was a forum for cooperation of the leadership of seven global disability organizations, which were mostly organizations of people with disabilities. It included the cross-disability organization Disabled Peoples' International as well as others such as World Blind Union, World Federation of the Deaf, and World Federation of the Deafblind, along with WNUSP, which were single disability. This feature of IDA made it possible for WNUSP to play a distinctive role in the formulation of policy as spokesperson for the rights of users and survivors of psychiatry.

My involvement

I became involved in April 2002 when I wrote a position paper for WNUSP to bring to an expert meeting convened by the Mexican government prior to the first meeting at the UN. I was well prepared for this as I had spent a good deal of time and energy in law school from 1998–2001 developing ideas about how to apply human rights and a disability non-discrimination perspective to the issue of psychiatric abuse and oppression. Karl Bach, WNUSP treasurer and board member, used the paper successfully at the meeting, and our positions were incorporated into a joint NGO paper entitled 'What Rights Should a Treaty Contain?'. This paper not only represented an initial platform of NGOs, but was also used in the Ad Hoc Committee to structure the plenary discussion around particular rights as enumerated by the NGOs.

As I lived in New York and was interested and capable of carrying out the task, WNUSP designated me as its representative in the Ad Hoc Committee meetings. While I was later joined by other WNUSP members and members of other user/survivor organizations, I retained overall responsibility and initiative regarding the user/survivor input into the process and the text of the Convention. One key stage in the process was the Working Group met in 2004 to produce a draft text for negotiation from the contributions that had been received from states and civil society, including text that I prepared on behalf of WNUSP. I represented WNUSP in the Working Group and participated as an equal member in a consensus-based process with other NGOs chosen by the disability community together with state delegations and a national human rights institution. In addition to drafting text, I established working principles for a general approach to the treaty: there should be nothing in the text contrary to our human rights, the entire treaty should be relevant to users and survivors, and our key issues should be incorporated. The Mexico paper had earlier asserted that we define our human rights and do not allow anyone to speak for us.

I represented WNUSP in the steering committee of the International Disability Caucus (IDC), the platform of disabled people's organizations and allies that we created at the Ad Hoc Committee. I informally contributed to coordinating the work of the IDC together with Maria Veronica Reina and Stefan Tromel, and also led topic workgroups on Articles 12, 14, 15 and 17.

Key advocacy issues

The key advocacy issues shifted slightly during the course of the process but focused on physical and mental integrity, liberty, and equal legal status or legal capacity. I will trace the development of issues from the Mexico paper to the adopted treaty and beyond.

We argued that forced interventions aimed at correcting or improving an actual or perceived impairment should be prohibited, as they met the criteria for torture established in Article 1 of the Convention against Torture. While this language was cut from the final text of the CRPD, it was later adopted by the Special Rapporteur on Torture and applied to forced or non-consensual administration of electroshock, psychosurgery and mind-altering drugs such as neuroleptics, as I had proposed.[1] Meanwhile, I also made sure that the treaty included a right to free and informed consent in the article on health, so that we retained a textual basis for the right to refuse treatment.

We argued that disability-based detention should be prohibited as it is discriminatory, and this was adopted into Article 14 on liberty and security of the person. Some states attempted to add the word 'solely' so as to allow detention based on disability plus some other factor, other states disagreed and no such change was made. The CRPD Committee interprets this provision to prohibit involuntary commitment in mental health facilities, as we intended.

With respect to legal capacity, we began by asserting a right to equal legal status, only indirectly referencing guardianship, which had been raised by other WNUSP members. When we needed to develop this further in light of the incorporation of guardianship issues in the 'What Rights?' paper, I consulted WNUSP members and found uniform support for an absolute right to legal capacity with no exceptions. Working with survivor Sherry Darrow and ally attorney Kim Darrow, I developed a position on the right to full legal capacity without exception, while providing for assistance in understanding information and other aspects of making and expressing decisions. At the Working Group I found that Inclusion International, the organization advocating for people with intellectual disabilities, had developed a similar concept they called supported decision making, and the two constituencies were able to join forces.

The Working Group text on legal capacity captured WNUSP's perspective but we were open to improvements in order to both obtain greater collective ownership of the text and to streamline and strengthen its connection with other human rights instruments. WNUSP member and law professor Amita Dhanda contributed significantly to streamlining the text and to explaining the reasoning for the paradigm shift from substitution to support.

The profile of legal capacity as a pivotal human rights issue was raised due to conflict over insertion of a footnote in the last hours of negotiations that would have restricted the meaning of legal capacity in three UN languages to 'capacity to hold rights' and not 'capacity to act'. I led a successful lobbying effort to remove the footnote, which preserved the core meaning of legal capacity as autonomy and decision making.

Factors in success

The following factors led to our success with the CRPD, which changed international law to prohibit practices that degrade people in situations of serious distress and violate our physical and mental integrity and personal freedoms.

The nature of the process dovetailed with my framing of the rights needed to stop commitment and forced treatment in terms of non-discrimination, which is a core value of human rights. Our paradigm of legal capacity as freedom plus enabling support elaborated and drew strength from core values of the independent living movement as part of disability rights.

States were open to disabled people's expertise and leadership. This, together with our significantly grassroots character, our ability to self-organize in a rational way that gave voice to diverse constituencies and promoted a win–win outcome in case of disagreement among ourselves, gave us significant power as de facto partners in the negotiations, which we exercised.

A high level of trust and cooperation was built among all concerned, including between state delegations and Disabled People's Organizations, partly as a result of the Working Group in which we participated as peers. The aim of producing a treaty sharpened everyone's focus and allowed us to concentrate on what we cared most about while dropping issues that were of less concern. The text gave an objective focus to debates and questions of interpretation, ambiguity and compromise. I was able to support the text based on assessment of the legal merits regarding the weight of possible arguments for and against the interpretation that would uphold our rights. At different points in the negotiations I made strategic decisions based on assessments that certain text would be harmful to our rights, or that another text might be weaker than desired but still functional and viable.

Finally, it made a difference that I had a conceptual framework and understanding of the initiative as valuable irrespective of the outcome, and was able to devote full-time work during the four years of the treaty process and for almost a decade afterwards to secure the interpretation. Asserting our human rights on the world stage, and every victory along the way, meant that there was no turning back. At the same time, it became a responsibility to not squander the opportunity and to bring the potential to life.

Dissolution, and moving on

Perhaps it was inevitable that after a sustained period of intense work focused on preparation of a negotiated text, accompanied by development of a community and emotional ties around that process, there would be a letdown as we came back to reality in which the text remained an aspiration to be achieved. Breakdown occurred in relations at all levels, with power plays emerging and conflicts of interests re-emerging. I had to focus on interpretation of the text until the CRPD Committee issued its definitive General Comment on Article 12 (legal capacity) in 2014 and its Guidelines on Article 14 (liberty) in 2015. Others were more involved with implementation and monitoring, having started to envision during the negotiations how it could happen in different national contexts and how to work with funders.

Since 2015, I have moved on from WNUSP and work on CRPD-related issues through the Center for the Human Rights of Users and Survivors of Psychiatry (CHRUSP), a non-profit that I founded in 2009. At the present time CHRUSP priorities are to support the development of jurisprudence on forced psychiatry under the CRPD Optional Protocol by writing amicus briefs or bringing individual cases, to develop an online course on the CRPD, to contribute to implementation and monitoring and advise others in relevant projects, and to participate in relevant UN consultative processes developing and extending the CRPD standards.

Like any single thread in a fabric of justice, CRPD raises additional questions. Does the legal construct of personhood as an individual subject of a state limit our freedom as well as protecting it? How does the differential experience of being a woman, rather than a man, inform perspectives on legal capacity? Is there an underlying coherence relating legal capacity, liberty and integrity as the rights needed to abolish forced psychiatry, or were they just pragmatic and strategic choices? These questions have led me into new areas of work, just as forced psychiatry led me to the survivor movement and motivated my work on CRPD.

Note

[1] See UN Doc. A/63/175.

29

Sustainable-participatory social policy

Marilyn Palmer

Preamble

My grandparents arrived in Australia from England in the early part of the last century. I am from the colonising or settler culture, more accurately understood as the invading culture. One set of grandparents took up (occupied or stole depending on your perspective) land which belonged to the Noongar people in what is now known as Western Australia. When I visited my extended farming family as a child, Aboriginal workers who provided casual labour were camped opposite the house. At that time, there was no requirement to pay Aboriginal people the basic wage. Two years later, in my first vacation job, I was shocked to learn that boys got paid more than girls; the explanation that boys would eventually be breadwinners seemed ridiculous. I was ignorant of the discrimination against Aboriginal people and even when discrimination impacted on me (mildly by comparison), I failed to see these things as systemic injustices, preferring to see them as just old-fashioned, fast-fading ideas and values.

At university, drawn to feminist and radical social work, I was excited to be part of an Australian society which was *making progress*. Then in 1981 the documentary *Eight Minutes to Midnight* (Benjamin, 1981) was my epiphany; a wake-up call about something seriously wrong with the social, economic and political fabric of my world. That the human species would willingly take itself to the brink of nuclear war rather than resolve Cold War territorial and ideological differences seemed astonishing. Nothing was quite the same for me after that, although it was several years before I made connections between the nuclear arms race, logging ancient forests near where I lived in the south west of Western Australia and my work as a social worker. Eventually I came to understand that policies which tolerated our allies' nuclear weapons, clear-felled forests and removed Aboriginal children from their families and communities might somehow be connected.[1] However, by then, there were few signs the values underpinning these policies were fading.

Introduction

Social policy is generally understood as a process by which the state (mainly through its legislative and executive functions) identifies what counts as a social issue, responds to it with a promise or a plan and then makes an effort to implement the plan through legislation, directives to government departments and/or funded programs (Graycar and Jamrozik, 1989). *Sustainable* social policy establishes the natural realm as the space within which all life and therefore policymaking takes place. The natural realm provides a reason and a shape to policymaking; it also sets the material limits on what is possible. *Participatory* social policy facilitates the advancement of social justice and human rights by privileging the voices of those most affected by policy decisions and practices, in particular service users and their advocates (Beresford, 2016). The aim of this chapter is to explore the idea that sustainable-participatory social policy is a pathway to *ecojustice*, a term which 'holds together concerns for the natural world and for human life, that recognizes that devastation of the environment and economic injustice go hand in hand, and that affirms that environmental and human rights are indivisible' (Pedersen, 1998: 254).

The chapter begins by describing the contemporary macro socio-political context with a brief account of how neoliberalism has become the nemesis of ecojustice. Tony Benn's (2010) contention that there is no final victory or defeat in the struggle for peace and justice frames the rest of the chapter and I explore how ecological collapse, as a consequence of unsustainability, may be a defeat, albeit temporary, for humankind. However, ecojustice proffers a victory and this idea is illustrated through an account of how sustainable-participatory policymaking begins with resistance; it is local activism which has stalled, successfully so far, the contentious policy announced by the Western Australian state government in 2015 to close 150 remote Aboriginal communities. The chapter concludes by proposing that policymakers engage in prefigurative politics, making the goals of their policies explicit, and recognising the extent to which community members will increasingly self-organise to counter the insidiousness of neoliberalism (Springer, 2016, Hopkins, 2013).

From environmentalism to the neoliberal plague

The idea the world faces a significant ecological crisis has been developing since Carson's (1962) *Silent Spring* warned the indiscriminate use of pesticides would cause irreparable harm to natural ecosystems. Ten years later, Meadows et al (1972) published their modelling on global ecological limits to growth. They concluded that a sustainable ecological system would not be possible unless humans recognised the Earth as a finite system and radically changed their relationship to it. Despite the irrefutable science, simplicity and logic of Carson (1962) and Meadows et al (1972), their warnings about the fragility of the biosphere were met with dismissal or derision (Turner, 2014; Hamilton, 2010). A further decade along, Capra (1982: 1) started his book, *The Turning Point*, with the following statement:

> At the beginning of the last two decades of our century, we find ourselves in a state of profound, world-wide crisis. It is a complex, multi-dimensional crisis whose facets touch every aspect of our lives – our health and livelihood, the quality of our environment and our social relationships, our economy, technology, and politics. ... For the first time we have to face the very real threat of extinction of the human race and of all life on the planet.

Critiquing the worldview of Cartesian-Newtonian science, Capra promoted ecological systems theory as an approach that could help western cultures navigate their way through the crisis. He finished his 1982 book with a diagram of two intersecting arcs, showing that in the context of cultural evolution, before the dominant civilisation disintegrates, a new culture emerges and begins its rise, concluding that:

> While the transformation is taking place, the declining culture refuses to change, clinging ever more rigidly to its outdated ideas; nor will the dominant social institutions hand over their leading roles to the new cultural forces. ... As the turning point approaches, the realization that evolutionary changes of this magnitude cannot be prevented by short-term political activities provides our strongest hope for the future. (Capra, 1982: 466)

However, it was not going to be anything 'short-term' that would thwart cultural, social and economic change across western countries. By 1984 Margaret Thatcher and Ronald Reagan had won second terms as the leaders of their respective countries and were already removing Keynesian economics from its post-war dominance. In its place, they were privileging economic theory and practices variously known as economic rationalism, monetarism or neoliberalism, the latter an anti-collectivist economic and political ideology which establishes a powerful hegemonic discourse of market fundamentalism. Referred to as a kind of hyper-capitalism, neoliberalism valorises and promotes a globalised free market for money, goods and services (Fox Piven, 2015). Adherents promote minimalist government intervention in the lives of individuals while advancing policy interventions to create the right environment for corporate and private capital to thrive. These include regressive taxation policies; unfettered economic growth; the contracting out of public goods (such as health, education and welfare); the privatisation of essential services such as power, water and public transport; and the deregulation of laws originally established to protect labour, consumer rights and the natural environment (Springer et al, 2016).

By the mid-1990s, centrist left political leaders were in place in Britain, the United States and Australia. Tony Blair's New Labour, Bill Clinton's New Democrats and the pragmatic economics of Paul Keating in Australia acted as unwitting incubators for the rampant neoliberalism that was to come. In the context of social policy, these governments sought to build on and sustain welfare state structures which had developed in western democracies as part of the post-war social democratic contract. However, their attempts at a new consensus rapidly came under challenge and leftist discourses of egalitarianism, collectivism and community were easily subsumed by the discourses of individualism, personal responsibility and free choice, the latter to be exercised within an unsustainable, perpetual-growth-oriented market economy. Now, over 35 years since Capra's optimistic description of how a 'rising culture' would take us to the Solar Age, people across the globe are trying to find meaningful responses to what Labonte (2014) refers to as the 'neoliberal plague'.

There is no simple explanation of how neoliberal imperatives have come to dominate public and private life, undermine the health of the biosphere, and determine the role and purpose of nation states and the relationships between them (Springer et al, 2016). Brown (2006: 694; emphasis in original) notes that neoliberalism 'depicts free markets, free trade, and entrepreneurial rationality as *achieved and normative*'. Ife (2016) makes a similar point, that neoliberalism presents as natural and inevitable; 'it is assumed that indeed there is no practical alternative' (p 22). Neoliberalism's unflinching acceptance by the fiscally conservative political right and collusion by the centrist political left in western countries has entrenched its dominance (Brown, 2006; Beresford, 2016). For others, such as hooks (2010), we need to look beyond simple economics to understand how an industrialised, globalised, militarised and corporatised hyper-capitalist system has come to dominate the planet. She laments 'there is no place in the existing structure of imperialist white-supremacist capitalist patriarchy where we are truly safe, individually or collectively' (p 171). However, as a call to action, Benn (2010) holds that:

> Every generation has to fight the same battles as their ancestors had to fight, again and again, for there is no final victory and no final defeat. Two flames have burned from the beginning of time – the flame of anger against injustice and the flame of hope.

Ecological collapse: a defeat

Simply put, a sustainable global ecological system functions when we extract resources from the natural environment at the pace at which they can be replaced and discharge pollutants at a pace at which they can be successfully absorbed. In addition, effective feedback loops provide data for monitoring human impact (such as atmospheric temperature or ocean acidification), and suggest timely, effective responses to adverse data to ensure we do not exceed the Earth's carrying capacity

(Atkisson, 2011; Moran et al, 2008; Meadows et al, 2005). However, the human species' relationship with the 20 kilometre-wide, life-sustaining biosphere that hugs the Earth's surface looks nothing like this. Our current relationship with the ecological system is one of *overshoot* with the number of humans expanding at an exponential rate while globally extracting and polluting well beyond replacement or absorption rates. At the same time, our feedback loops operate very slowly and our responses to adverse data are neither timely nor adequate (Atkisson, 2011; Meadows et al, 2005).

The Ecological Footprint calculates human demand on the Earth's biosphere based on trends in human population growth and consumption patterns, wild spaces and arable land (Moran et al, 2008). The Global Footprint Network translates ecological overshoot into the number of planet Earths it takes to support humanity's demand on the biosphere. In 2010, we were overshooting the Earth's carrying capacity by 50% each year; we would have needed 1.5 Earth equivalents to be sustainable (Ewing et al, 2010: 18). On current projections, there will be a 100% overshoot by the 2030s, or two Earth equivalents.[2]

Significantly, the responsibility for this overshoot is not evenly distributed; on a per capita basis, people living in wealthy, overdeveloped countries contribute to overshoot much more than those living elsewhere. In 2003, Western Europe had an Earth equivalent measure of three and the United States a measure of five; if everyone on the planet consumed and polluted to the extent of North Americans, we would have overshot our global carrying capacity to five Earth equivalents (Moran et al, 2008). Also, the consequences of ecological overshoot impact disproportionately on the most disadvantaged within and between countries (Agyeman et al, 2002). For example, industrial disasters such as the 1984 gas leak in Bhopal create localised collapse events and impact disproportionally on workers and others, often desperately poor, who live adjacent to industrial sites, while company managers and investors rarely experience the same level of injury, death or loss of income. Similarly, at the 2009 Copenhagen climate change conference, Pacific island nations Kiribati and Tuvalu warned that sea level rise and salt water inundation would force their populations to settle elsewhere in the coming decades. Australia and New Zealand, two wealthy neighbours with ecological footprints far in excess of the island nations, rejected approaches to be part of a resettlement plan (Bedford and Bedford, 2010).

As noted above, unsustainability leads to expanding overshoot and eventual collapse. Randers, who worked on the original limits to growth study, defines ecological collapse as 'a sudden, unwanted, and unstoppable decline in the average welfare of a number of global citizens' (Randers, 2008: 857). Specifically (although he acknowledges arbitrarily), Randers defines a collapse as global 'if it affects at least 1 billion people, who lose at least 50% of something they hold dear, within a period of 20 years' (2008: 859). He suggests crises likely to precipitate a global ecological collapse (and likely triggered by climate change) would be epidemics, war, famine or a global economic depression. These could manifest locally as inadequate responses to extreme weather events, mass migrations, internecine conflicts over scarce resources, food insecurity, unemployment and failing governments (Randers, 2008: 864).

The post-ecologist turn

Blühdorn (2013) refers to a 'post-ecologist turn' to explain western societies' exhaustion and lack of interest in eco-politics despite scientists, politicians, public servants, non-government organisations and campaigners providing unprecedented information about threats to the environment, particularly in relation to climate change. He suggests this weariness with ecological concerns and a normalisation of the environmental crisis within post-industrial consumer societies is due to value and cultural shifts away from sustainability ideals. Sugarman (2015) notes how neoliberalism creates ideals of personhood (such as the resilient, entrepreneurial self) which align neatly with the values and interests of capitalism. Discursive constructions of the person as fundamentally individual, independent, competitive and enterprising subjugate notions of people as interdependent, community oriented and caring (Sugarman, 2015: 104). Blühdorn similarly describes how neoliberal ideology devalues eco-political values of cooperation and care, valorising instead identity, self-determination and self-realisation, ideals which are:

> profoundly incompatible with the norms underpinning ecologist thinking in that they are: to an unprecedented extent based on ever accelerated consumption; highly complex, flexible and open to internal contradiction in way [sic] that is incompatible with any notion of *ecological virtues* or an *ethics of ecological duty or responsibility*; and inherently anti-egalitarian and exclusive, and therefore represent a permanent source of social conflict (Blühdorn, 2013: 19, emphasis in original).

In addition, according to Blühdorn (2013), post-ecologist politics uses the strategies of *simulation*, promoting green consumerism to produce and maintain an appearance of care and concern for the environment while masking unsustainability. The language of adaptation and resilience is used to 'provide reassurance that the problem [of unsustainability] is taken seriously, that it is being researched and addressed with all available expertise, and that appropriate counter-strategies are being pursed with undivided determination' (Blühdorn, 2013: 21).

Strategies of simulation are also at play in relation to social sustainability, where governments hide policies which abrogate their social justice and human rights responsibilities behind self-satisfying narratives of care and concern for the vulnerable. For example, in Australia, asylum seekers are incarcerated indefinitely on the pretext of disrupting 'the people smugglers' business model' to prevent deaths at sea (Murphy, 2015). Austerity measures limit eligibility for benefits for disabled people and their carers to *incentivise* them to join the paid workforce, on the pretext of preventing long-term unemployment (Barlow, 2016).

Similarly, in 2015, when the Western Australian state government announced its policy decision to withdraw essential services (water and power) from Aboriginal people living on their traditional lands, it cited high rates of alcohol abuse, domestic violence and child sexual abuse as one of the reasons, though the state government policy was first considered only when the Federal government indicated it no longer intended to fund essential services to remote Western Australian communities (O'Connor, 2015). If implemented, the policy would force many Aboriginal people to abandon their communities and spiritual obligations, and its announcement provoked a sustained campaign of resistance from Aboriginal people and their allies. The policy is viewed by some as a de facto land grab with several aims: to diminish Aboriginal peoples' claims to continuous occupation of their lands, weakening their native title claims; to pave the way for unfettered access to resource-rich land for agriculture, mining and gas extraction; to relocate Aboriginal people to regional centres where they can be better assimilated into the capitalist economy; and to reduce the cost of service provision to selected remote locations within Western Australia (Gregoire, 2015; McQuire, 2015; Woodley, 2015; Wahlquist, 2015).

The struggling welfare state

The egalitarian and redistributive policies of what is left of the welfare state in Australia and elsewhere are vulnerable once the status and apparatus of the neoliberal, globalised market begins to dominate. Ife (2016) notes that it has been difficult to defend a welfare state often viewed (and experienced by some) as overly bureaucratic, ineffective, inefficient and alienating. In Australia, Aboriginal people have had an uneasy and often unproductive relationship with state agencies which ignore Aboriginal cultural traditions and often reinforce a history of colonisation and domination (Briskman, 2014). The idea that the government can emancipate the subjugated other through the welfare state is also inherently paternalistic, adding to its vulnerability:

> Critically, the founders of the welfare state didn't engage or involve the population in their reforms as workers, citizens or service users. In no way could the latter be said to set the agenda. Instead they were there as a stage army. The founders of the welfare state did not adequately educate them about the welfare state or give them a sense of ownership that would either lead them to identify with it, or encourage them to defend it. (Beresford, 2016: 117)

Furthermore, attempts so far to preserve the welfare state continue to rely on a business-as-usual, growth-oriented economic system, which, as noted earlier, is unsustainable. Thus, for Ife, 'it is inappropriate to put too much energy into defending or strengthening the welfare state. A more useful direction is to ask what might be an alternative form of social provision that would be consistent with the newly emerging social and economic order' (Beresford, 2016: 23). In a similar vein, Purcell rounds off Springer et al's (2016) critique of neoliberalism by suggesting we stop giving neoliberalism oxygen, and get on to address the following: 'What do we want to create? What are we capable of producing? Who are we capable of becoming, together? What worlds, what ways of life have we already started to build, and how can we help them grow, spread and flourish?' (Purcell, 2016: 616).

Ecojustice: a victory

If social policy is a process by which the nation state identifies, defines and addresses social needs (Fawcett et al, 2010), then sustainable-participatory social policies will be difficult to achieve within an obdurate neoliberal orthodoxy which promotes unsustainability and inequality (Macleavy, 2016). In this context, Purcell's (2016) and Hopkins' (2013) suggestion to 'just get on with it' has value, whether through generating renewable energy at the neighbourhood level or engaging with the grassroots activism of social movements, progressive political parties or supra-national structures such as the European Union or the International Women's League for Peace and Freedom. Regardless of the structures or systems from which we act for change, it is important to have some vision of what we want to achieve and how we can intervene most effectively.

Meadows (1997) proposed an order of effectiveness for places to intervene in a system. She noted that the paradigm or mindset of a system is the most effective point of intervention while measures such as subsidies, taxes and standards are the least effective. Unfortunately, it is these least effective measures that form the mainstay of business-as-usual politics and policy. In the rest of this chapter, strategies for developing sustainable-participatory social policies are explored through Meadows' top three places to intervene in a system: the social and cultural paradigm; working with the goals of the system; and working with the power of self-organisation.

At the level of paradigm or mindset, poststructural ecofeminism supports sustainable-participatory social policy. The extent to which humans rely on the exploitation of other species and the natural realm for sustenance, shelter, infrastructure, consumer goods and entertainment is self-evident. By challenging the right of humans to exploit other animal species and the natural realm for wealth creation (rather than just co-existence), ecofeminism opens the door to a moral attack on modern capitalism and the scientific, religious and economic justifications that non-human species are fair game for exploitation, even to the point of extinction. Gaard (2011) illustrates how ecofeminism, over many decades, has highlighted 'the intersectional analysis of oppression' (p 38), and in doing so, has rejected the idea that humans are somehow separate from non-human species, the natural realm and by extension, from one another. Mary Lane, an elder in Australian social work, explains her attraction to ecofeminism informed by postmodernism:

> ecofeminism offers a synthesis of social and ecocentric purposes and values as a basis for tackling inequalities, while postmodern feminists enlighten our understanding of difference and encourage us to renounce certainty and last proofs. (Lane, 1997: 319)

Poststructural ecofeminism aligns with an affirmative (rather than nihilistic) postmodernism (Rosenau, 1992); unsettling simplistic binaries and embracing the idea of fluid subjectivities, using a power analysis and critical reflexivity to better understand how humans can interact with other humans and the natural realm in ways which promote ecojustice.

Working with the 'goals of the system' is Meadows' (1997) second most effective level of intervention; policy analysis and policy formulation only make sense if the goals of the policy (and thereby the vision for the state) are made clear. Bacchi (2009) promotes a poststructural approach to policy analysis by placing the question *What's the problem represented to be?* (WPR) at the centre of the policy analysis process. This question demands that the implicit purpose, vision and goals of proposed policies be revealed by policymakers: important because:

> among the many competing constructions of a 'problem' that are possible, governments play a privileged role because their understandings 'stick' – their versions of 'problems' are formed or constituted in the legislation, reports and technologies used to govern (Bacchi, 2009: 33).

In 2015 in Western Australia, Indigenous community leaders, their allies and advocates (trade unions, academics and social justice organisations) established a program of resistance to a state government policy which would deny services to remote Aboriginal communities and force their closure. In doing so, community leaders challenged the government's privileged version of what the problem was represented to be. Describing the communities as dysfunctional, with references to child sexual abuse and endemic poverty, the Barnett Liberal Government had sought to garner electoral support for the closures. However, the obvious gap between the problem representation (dysfunctional community) and the proposed policy solution (remove to towns) meant government statements were unconvincing. Forcing Aboriginal people to abandon their spiritual connection to the land to live in poorly resourced regional centres with others traumatised by poverty and dispossession would not address poverty or child abuse. Bacchi (2009: xix) notes that 'the task [of WPR] is to identify *deep conceptual premises* operating within problem representations'. As the government continued to try and convince the electorate to support forced closures, it exposed its 'deep conceptual premise' that Aboriginal culture and continuing connection to the land *had no value*, or that it had *less value* than the money that would flow from mining and pastoral pursuits on Aboriginal land.

Goal setting for sustainable-participatory social policy formulation can be facilitated by identifying principles consistent with a poststructural ecofeminist paradigm. Holmgren's (2002) three maxims of permaculture (care for the Earth, care for people and fair share) is one possible goals framework; those outlined in The Earth Charter (2010) another. In Australia it is possible to look to the cultures of First Nations people for guidance about setting sustainable-participatory policy goals (Ife, 2016; Pascoe, 2014). For example, Michael Woodley (2015), responding to questions about a mining company's intrusion onto Aboriginal land and the inevitable damage, shares the meaning of the old people's phrase 'ask the baby':

> We have to realise there is life beyond us, in the same way there was life beyond our old people. Our old people never missed a beat in terms of what was their responsibility – giving over the Yindjibarndi knowledge in the country to the next Yindjibarndi generation. Like the old people say ... old Mayaringbungu, Ned Cheedy ... when they asked him who is the owner of the country, he said, "Ask the baby". ... When that baby get big he got to listen, he has to go through the Birdarra Law, he then got to be a man, get married and have kids, and when he get old, 80 or 90 years old, then you ask him [who is the owner of the country?], and if that man been taught the right way, that baby, he'll say, 'ask the baby'. ... It's a generational thing. Until we know that there are no more Yindjibarndi coming you got no right to give this country away.

These words illustrate how sustainable-participatory policy goals can be achieved by articulating a future focus that embeds a deep conceptual premise of intergenerational equity, an idea which came to prominence in western countries through the Bruntland Report's definition of sustainable development (World Commission on Environment and Development, 1990),

Finally, Meadow's third level of intervention is the recognition of the power of self-organisation. As Beresford has observed:

> The key way ... in which the subjects of social policy have been able to engage with it and speak for themselves, has been through the emergence of their own welfare movements and organisations. (Beresford, 2016: 176)

Aboriginal people in Western Australia have organised to resist the closure of remote communities and to demand the government, a signatory to the UN Declaration on Human Rights, respect their right to live on Country.[3] A key feature of their organisation was a national and international campaign protesting the closure policy and, closer to home, establishing a cultural code of conduct for urban-based activists who wanted to participate. One of the points in the code ('Be firm, yet non-violent') exemplifies the idea of self-organisation with an explanation of why non-violence is important to the campaign:

> We understand the importance of keeping our actions safe from harm, so that our children, disabled and Elders who are marching with us remain protected and respected. Acts of violence lose our message in the community – and to lose our message will mean all our marches will have been in vain. (sosblakaustralia, 2015)

Another organising strategy of the campaign coordinators from the West Kimberley was speaking the truth to power, specifically to the Premier of Western Australia at the time, Colin Barnett. In preparation for a major protest against the closure policy in 2015, Daisy Ward and Elizabeth Marrkilyi Ellis from Wingellina in remote Western Australia recorded their demands on a YouTube video:

> 'We don't want to move from our smaller communities into bigger communities … and towns because in larger communities and towns there are big problems and if we take our young people there will be problems. Young people be going to jail. … Government looking at us as if we are uncivilized people who don't know how to look after ourselves and treating us like little kids. … We're not children. We're grandmothers, we're great-grandmothers. We have obligations, we have responsibilities. We do hard work looking after our families, and our lands, our sacred lands. This is our land, always was and will be and we still live here. We're not refugees in our own country. … We demand that the West Australian Premier Colin Barnet retract his decision to close that 150 Aboriginal communities and to say sorry to us, apologise publicly for putting us in a state of extreme worry, stress and concern and we don't know what is going to happen to us, where we're going to end up. This is not fair. Do your job West Australian government and provide power and water services to all towns and communities in Western Australia.' (Ward and Ellis, 2015)

West Australians did not know if there would be a victory for ecojustice in relation to Indigenous people being able to determine their own future until the outcome of the 2017 Western Australian state election. As it turned out, in 2017 the government of Colin Barnett was defeated; the incoming McGowan Labor Government gave a reassurance in its campaign materials that it would not forcibly close remote Aboriginal communities, stating:

> WA Labor supports tenure reform to ensure that Aboriginal people have certainty over land to ensure that they can never again be

vulnerable to the Government of the day threatening the closure of communities and the removal off country. (McGowan, 2017, p 25)

Conclusion

The aim of this chapter has been to establish the nexus between sustainable and participatory social policy as one of interdependence; neither on their own will achieve ecojustice. There are a number of value frameworks that can guide policymakers towards policy goals to achieve something close to social, economic and ecological sustainability (Holmgren, 2002; Eckersley, 1992; Atkisson, 2011). There are many impediments to this but so far little consensus about precisely what they are, how to tackle them, in what order or who is best to lead the process. If there is anything like a consensus it may be to just get on and do stuff (Hopkins, 2013; Purcell, 2016). This has been the way of the women of the Pilbara and Kimberley in Western Australia, angry and hopeful that they can continue to live on Country to fulfil their obligations to their ancestors, those alive today and the babies to come.

Notes

[1] The *Bringing them Home* report (HREOC, 1997) and the apology to Indigenous Australians made in the Parliament by Prime Minister Kevin Rudd in February 2008 formally acknowledged that there had been policies in Australia to forcibly or coercively remove Aboriginal children from their families and place them for adoption or in state care. The impact of these policies had been to exacerbate the intergenerational trauma which had begun with invasion and colonisation.

[2] www.footprintnetwork.org

[3] Aboriginal people live on Country in order to care for the land and one another, through caring for the culture, undertaking important ceremonies and fulfilling traditional obligations.

References

Agyeman, J., Bullard, R.D. and Evans, B. (2002) 'Exploring the nexus: Bringing together sustainability, environmental justice and equity', *Space & Polity*, 6, 77–90.

Atkisson, A. (2011) *Believing Cassandra: How to be an optimist in a pessimist's world*, London: Earthscan.

Bacchi, C. (2009) *Analysing policy: What's the problem represented to be?*, Frenchs Forest, Australia: Pearson Australia.

Barlow, K. (2016) 'A new 'investment approach' to breaking the welfare cycle: Young carers, parents and students are the target', Huffington Post, www.huffingtonpost.com.au/2016/09/19/a-new-investment-approach-to-breaking-the-welfare-cycle/

Bedford, R. and Bedford, C. (2010) 'International migration and climate change: A post-Copenhagen Perspective on options for Kiribati and Tuvalu', in B. Burson (ed) *Climate Change and Migration: South Pacific Perspectives*, Wellington, NZ: Institute of Policy Studies, Victoria University of Wellington.

Benjamin, M. (1981) *Eight minutes to midnight: A portrait of Dr. Helen Caldicott*.

Benn, T. (2010) *Letters to my grandchildren: Thoughts on the future*, London: Arrow.

Beresford, P. (2016) *All Our Welfare: Towards Participatory Social Policy*, Bristol: Policy Press.

Blühdorn, I. (2013) 'The governance of unsustainability: ecology and democracy after the post-democratic turn', *Environmental Politics*, 22, 16–36.

Briskman, L. (2014) *Social work with Indigenous communities: A human rights perspective*, Leichhardt, Australia: The Federation Press.

Brown, W. (2006) 'American nightmare: Neoliberalism, neoconservatism and de-democratization', *Political Theory*, 34, 690–714.

Capra, F. (1982) *The turning point: Science, society and the rising culture*, London: Fontana.

Carson, R. (1962) *Silent Spring*, New York: Houghton Mifflin.

Eckersley, R. (1992) *Environmentalism and political theory: Toward an ecocentric approach*, London: UCL Press.

Ewing, B., Moore, D., Goldfinger, S., Oursler, A., Reed, A. and Wackernagel, M. (2010) *The Ecological Footprint Atlas 2010*, Oakland, CA: Global Footprint Network.

Fawcett, B., Goodwin, S., Meagher, G. and Phillips, R. (2010) *Social policy for social change*, South Yarra, Australia: Palgrave Macmillan.

Fox Piven, F. (2015) 'Neoliberalism and the welfare state', *Journal of International and Comparative Social Policy*, 31, 2–9.

Gaard, G. (2011) 'Ecofeminism revisited: Rejecting essentialism and re-placing species in a material feminist environmentalism', *Feminist Formations*, 23, 26–53.

Graycar, A. and Jamrozik, A. (1989) *How Australians live : Social policy in theory and practice*, South Melbourne: Macmillan Australia.

Gregoire, P. (2015) 'Are mining interests behind Western Australian remote Aboriginal community closures?' VICE, www.vice.com/read/are-mining-interests-behind-western-australian-remote-aboriginal-community-closures

Hamilton, C. (2010) *Requiem for a species: Why we resist the truth about climate change*, Crows Nest, Australia: Allen & Unwin.

Holmgren, D. (2002) *Permaculture: Principles and pathways beyond sustainability*, Hepburn, Victoria: Holmgren Design Services.

hooks, B. (2010) *Teaching critical thinking: Practical wisdom*, New York: Routledge.

Hopkins, R. (2013) *The power of just doing stuff*, Cambridge: UIT/Green Books.

Human Rights and Equal Opportunity Commission (HREOC) (1997) *Bringing Them Home: Report of the National Inquiry into the Separation of Aboriginal and Islander Children from their Families*, Sydney, Australia: HREOC.

Ife, J. (2016) *Community development in an uncertain world: Vision, analysis and practice*, Port Melbourne, Australia: Cambridge University Press.

Labonte, R. (2014) "But they just can't kill the beast': The ongoing neoliberal plague', Global Health Watch: Mobilizing Civil Society around an Alternative World Health Report, 2 December, www.ghwatch.org/node/45473

Lane, M. (1997) 'Community work, social work: Green and postmodern?' *British Journal of Social Work*, 27, 319–41.

Macleavy, J. (2016) 'Neoliberalism and welfare', in S. Springer, K. Birch and J. Macleavy (eds) *Handbook of neoliberalism*, New York: Routledge.

McGowan, M. (2017) *WA Labor Plan for the Kimberley: A Fresh Approach for WA*, WA Labor Policy, Perth, Australia.

McQuire, A. (2015) 'Unions slam closure of remote Aboriginal communities in WA', newmatilda.com, https://newmatilda.com/2015/04/17/unions-slam-closure-remote-aboriginal-communities-wa/

Meadows, D., Randers, J. and Meadows, D. (2005) *Limits to growth: The 30-year update*, London: Earthscan.

Meadows, D.H. (1997) 'Places to intervene in a system (in increasing order of effectiveness)', *Whole Earth*, Winter, 91, 78–84.

Meadows, D.H., Meadows, D.L., Randers, J. and Behrens, W.B. (1972) *The Limits to Growth*, New York: Universe Books.

Moran, D., Wackernagel, M., Kitzes, J., Goldfinger, S. and Boutaud, A. (2008) 'Measuring sustainable development: Nation by nation', *Ecological Economics*, 64, 470–74.

Murphy, K. (2015) 'The problematic 'saving lives at sea' argument', *Eureka Street*, 25.

O'Connor, A. (2015) 'Leaked document reveals 192 WA Aboriginal communities deemed unsustainable in 2010', ABC News, 24 March, www.abc.net.au/news/2015-03-24/federal-review-reveals-192-communities-deemed-unsustainable/6343570

Pascoe, B. (2014) *Dark emu: Black seeds, agriculture or accident?*, Broome, Australia: Magabala Books.

Pedersen, K. (1998) 'Environmental ethics in interreligious perspective: Comparative religious ethics and interreligious dialogue', in S. Twiss and B. Grelle (eds) *Explorations in global ethics*, Boulder, CO: Westview Press.

Purcell, M. (2016) 'Our new arms', in S. Springer, K. Birch and J. Macleavy (eds) *Handbook of neoliberalism*, New York: Routledge.

Randers, J. (2008) 'Global collapse – fact or fiction?' *Futures*, 40, 853–64.

Rosenau, P. (1992) *Post-modernism and the social sciences: Insights, inroads and intrusions*, Princeton, NJ: Princeton University Press.

sosblakaustralia (2015) 'Information pack: 10 points to a cultural code of conduct', www.sosblakaustralia.com/media

Springer, S. (2016) 'Fuck neoliberalism', *ACME: An International E-Journal for Critical Geographies*, 15, 285–92.

Springer, S., Birch, K. and Macleavy, J. (eds) (2016) *Handbook of neoliberalism*, New York: Routledge.

Sugarman, J. (2015) 'Neoliberalism and psychological ethics', *Journal of Theoretical and Philosophical Psychology*, 35, 103–16.

The Earth Charter (2010) 'The Earth Charter', *Journal of Education for Sustainable Development,* 4, 317–24.

Turner, G. (2014) *Is Global Collapse Imminent? An Updated Comparison of The Limits to Growth with Historical Data*, Melbourne, Australia: Melbourne Sustainable Society Institute, The University of Melbourne.

Wahlquist, C. (2015) 'Kimberley landowner stands guard as oil company prepares for fracking', *Guardian*, 1 May.

Ward, D. and Ellis, E.M. (2015) 'Daisy and Elisabeth talk about the Wingellina protest, 2015', Centre for Indigenous Story, http://indigenousstory.com.au/now/2015/daisy-and-elizabeth-talk-about-the-wingellina-protest-2015-108/

Woodley, M. (2015) *Ask the baby*, Yindjibarndi Aboriginal Corporation.

World Commission on Environment and Development (1990) *Our common future: Report of the World Commission on Environment and Development*, Melbourne: Oxford University Press.

30

Participatory social policy in a large EU research project

*Joe Greener and Michael Lavalette, with Rose Devereaux
and members of SUGAH[1]*

Introduction

This chapter draws on participative action research (PAR) undertaken by academics at Liverpool Hope University and members of SUGAH ('Service User Group At Hope', a mental health service user and self-advocacy group). The project was funded by the European Union (EU) as part of its Horizon 2020 agenda and the group are part of the *Rebuilding an Inclusive, Value based Europe of Solidarity and Trust through Social Investments* (RE-InVEST) programme, which is looking at the impact of austerity on marginalised communities. The research has been framed in terms of the coproduction of knowledge, the active participation of academics and service users as equal partners in research and knowledge production, with engaged action as one of the outcomes.

The overall aim of RE-InVEST is to influence political and academic debates on the nature and impact of austerity and, in particular, to invigorate reinvestment in welfare, social policy and the economy. Strategically, the project puts the 'voices of vulnerable groups and civil society organisations' at the centre of the programme (RE-InVEST, 2017a). It aims to establish research designed to meet the needs of the people it serves; and, through active participation, the coproduction of new knowledge to develop political demands for change.

The project has been funded for four years (2015–19). The first element of the research, conducted between September 2015 and October 2016, was tasked with addressing the 'social impacts of the present crisis' and this element of the overall project is discussed here.

Coproduction and the RE-InVEST project

The RE-InVEST programme is committed to the involvement of 'vulnerable groups' in the research process (RE-InVEST, 2017a). This has presented some issues. First, the definition of 'vulnerability' is inexact but broadly considers groups who are subject to a range of labour market activation programmes in various EU countries. In practice, it refers to those marginalised by the processes of austerity. The project in its entirety has so far engaged with refugees and migrants, young unemployed people, older unemployed groups, lone parents, homeless people and users of mental health services. This final grouping is represented by SUGAH and is the subject of the present chapter. The focus on engagement with these groups sets the present project apart from many other similar EU-funded programmes investigating social policy across the region.

As the project webpage states, RE-InVEST 'adopts a participative approach that gives voice to vulnerable groups and civil society organisations' (RE-InVEST, 2017b). The project puts the voices of people who use public services at the centre of both its data collection and its wider political aims:

> For the academic researchers, this will be an opportunity to be confronted with the lived experience of vulnerable groups who will have the chance to reflect on their experience and co-construct the conceptual framework (human rights, capabilities, social investment etc.) to be used in the next stages of the research (RE-InVEST, 2017c)

However, as we will discuss later, there are some legitimate questions to be raised about the extent to which service users have been fully involved in all aspects of the research process.

The major theoretical tools driving the project are rooted in the capabilities approach with a focus on human rights. The capabilities approach attempts to put the focus on the ways that socioeconomic contexts either promote or hinder people's attempts to realise their ambitions and life plans (Sen, 2001). The rights aspect requires researchers to consider how austerity has impacted on individual and collective access to human rights. The project goal is to ascertain the ways these approaches can inform a more robust investment in social policy across Europe that is framed by its commitment to a 'social Europe'.

The initial phase of the research has been concerned to establish the 'social damage' caused by the current crisis of 'austerity'.

The initial project in Liverpool brought two established research activists together with the service user and self-advocacy group SUGAH, which is facilitated by Rose Devereaux from the Liverpool-based voluntary sector organisation Person Shaped Support (PSS). SUGAH has been in existence for five years. Its members have a wide range of experiences of the mental health system in England. A number of the members have been through the work capability test (WCA or 'ATOS assessment' as it is often commonly known), many have been active in the recent campaign to save Liverpool day centres (Moth et al, 2015).

Coproduction, as an approach, places value on the active engagement of a range of people in the production of knowledge. It recognises the importance of knowledge through experience which, for example, service users and activists have, and attempts to combine this, in a symbiotic relationship, with the training, knowledge and experience of professional researchers (Moran and Lavalette, 2016). The purpose is to challenge and scrutinise existing knowledge and perspectives. It can also allow for greater user voice throughout the process, in particular, the opportunity for service users to influence the priorities, objectives and design of projects (Telford and Faulkner, 2009). Finally, this mode of social science, if done effectively, allows participants to develop critical understandings of their own experiences and life biographies.

Theoretical framing

Within the coproduction framework, the researcher activists have a particular role. Their responsibility is to bring one type of expertise and knowledge, derived from their position within the academy, into a symbiotic relationship with another type of 'expert knowledge' derived from service user direct experiences. The purpose of coproduction is not to *prioritise* lived experience, or knowledge from experience, but rather it is to recognise that such knowledge and experience can further enhance and enrich our research findings and challenge our theoretical and policy frameworks (on this see Moran and Lavalette, 2016; Ferguson et al, 2018; Rees, 1998).

In order to realise the wider RE-InVEST aims of merging the knowledge of academics with vulnerable groups, the research has drawn broadly from the work of Freire (1970) and Vygotsky (1986).

One of the attractions of coproduction within participatory action research is that it addresses two concepts which appear most clearly in the work of Paulo Freire: *anti-assistentialism* and *conscientisation*.

Freire (1970) argued that education should allow the oppressed to regain their sense of humanity, which, in turn, can be the starting point for their political intervention to tackle (and perhaps even overcome) their condition. But for this to occur, the oppressed individual must play a role in their liberation. As he argues:

> No pedagogy which is truly liberating can remain distant from the oppressed by treating them as unfortunates and by presenting for their emulation models from among the oppressors. The oppressed must be their own example in the struggle for their redemption. (Freire, 1970: 54)

Anti-assistentialism appears in the work of Freire as the conscious rejection of dependency; the tendency, in some social policy frameworks, to treat service users as passive recipients of top-down aid, charity or welfare. Anti-assistentialism re-asserts the vitality of service user voice and active, engaged participation in society and in all decisions about their lives, perhaps best captured in the slogan of the Disability Movement 'nothing about us, without us'.

Conscientisation is a more widely used and understood concept derived from Freire. It relates to the transformative learning processes that take place within the participatory action research model. In other words, the vision that, through the research process, participants become more aware of the broader social, political and economic structures that shape their experiences, and helps them to challenge individualising discourse about the causes of social problems.

Neither anti-assistentialism nor conscientisation are inevitable outcomes of the research process. For these goals to be achieved the facilitator role must be acknowledged. Here the work of Vygotsky (1986) is important.

Lev Vygotsky was a Russian educationalist and theorist of cognitive development. He developed his ideas during the intellectual flourishing that took place in the aftermath of the Russian revolution and claimed that he wanted to bring the Marxist method to the study of mind. Simply stated, Vygotsky argues that to develop our learning we have to work in what he called the 'Zone of Proximal Development' (ZPD), that is the difference between what a learner can do without help and what (s)he can do with support. Working in the ZPD requires appropriate 'scaffolding' (support and mental tools) that are provided by teachers, mentors and peers to support new learning. For Vygotsky, interaction with peers is a particularly effective way of developing skills, strategies and new learning.

Here the researcher's role is one of providing the scaffolding – the setting, the support, the framework and the intellectual problem solving challenges – that allow participants to reflect on their experiences in ways that allow them to reject notions of dependency (anti-assistentialism) and see their marginalised position as part of a broader system of oppression (conscientisation).

The PAR process

The detailed research activity took place over five focus group sessions, carried out during 2016. The first session involved all participants (including the research facilitators) creating 'austerity snakes'. The austerity snakes allowed participants to locate significant personal events within particular timeframes. One of the initial problems to address for the British participants in the RE-InVEST programme was that the EU and RE-InVEST were concerned with welfare changes that were a result of the austerity regimes established across Europe in the aftermath of the banking crisis on 2007/08. However, in Britain 'welfare transformation' has a longer history with significant changes to welfare provision being dated to the 1980s. The austerity snakes, therefore, were a device to locate experiences within the EU programme time framework. They also worked as a mental tool to remind participants of key events and markers both in their life and in the recent history of broad 'welfare developments' in Britain.

The following three sessions addressed issues of human rights, capabilities and stigma. These terms were not part of the 'normal' language or conceptual framework utilised by participants and required introduction and explanation by facilitators. A variety of different group exercises and tasks were developed to provoke understanding and discussion. This included, for instance, short seminar teaching on the Human Rights Act of 1998, the use of visual stimuli such as tabloid headlines about welfare users, and the completion of worksheets to encourage participants to think about the different aspects of their life which helped them to manage mental distress.

The final session was devoted to the group's 'action' output. The participants decided to use photographs to highlight what austerity had meant to them and part of the action output involved photographs of important symbols, buildings and networks that had been lost or threatened by austerity cuts.

Key findings

There were two key sets of findings. First, findings emerged in relation to the forms of injustice and oppression that people had experienced as a direct result of welfare transformation and austerity. A second set of findings focused on how mentally distressed people were able to survive and challenge these transformations.

Everyone in the group described the intensification of economic hardship as a consequence of austerity. The reductions in benefits payments, disentitling forms of financial support and increased labour market flexibilisation all made it more difficult to meet daily subsistence. The introduction of the Under Occupancy Charge (the 'bedroom tax') had hit a number of the co-researchers who lived in social housing. Declining personal finances were linked to social isolation and feelings of insecurity.

Just as social, political and economic change under austerity impacted on the financial situation of individuals and households, cuts to important services due to National Health Service (NHS) and Local Authority budget reductions also meant that the available support for people with mental health problems had been reduced. This was perhaps best exemplified in the reductions to day centre care. The network of mental health day centres across Liverpool had been slowly reduced for some time but the intensity and level of support had decreased rapidly since Local Authority budgets came under attack (Moth et al, 2015). For instance, the largest centre in the area had changed its focus to 'reablement', meaning that services were no longer designed to offer sustained support; people were supposed to come to terms with often lifelong mental health problems in a matter of six weeks (Carter, 2016).

Similarly, SUGAH members emphasised the difficulties accessing talking therapies, despite NHS England's 2008 policy commitment to widening access through the Increasing Access to Talking Therapies programme. Agnes described how she was referred to a Recovery College as a form of assistance. Recovery Colleges attempt to deliver group therapy to a large number of people within one session. As she said:

'There's 25 of us in a hall and two women who couldn't organise a piss up in a brewery, they've got a computer going onto the big screen and they're just reading stuff out. It takes them ten minutes to set the computer up. We don't get a cup of tea, the place is really, really hot and we're all falling asleep. One man in the first session said 'this is no good to me, aren't we allowed to talk about how we're feeling? Have we just got to sit here and listen to you?' At the end of the session they gave us a 69 page booklet to read.'

This example emphasises the restructuring of services which are increasingly individualised in nature, emphasising personal responsibility and the need to 'embark on a journey of self-recovery': an example of the twin processes of welfare state disinvestment and service restructuring in line with neoliberalisation principles (Beresford, 2012).

As well as a reduction in entitlement to various services and financial assistance, SUGAH members described having to deal with new conditionality mechanisms as fundamentally reinforcing feelings of shame and inadequacy. Jensen and Tyler (2015) have argued that austerity pressures on services and benefits have been blamed on excessive immigration and imagined freeloading welfare dependents. These political narratives are geared towards providing legitimacy for welfare transformation. Co-researchers described the distressing experiences of having to have their credibility checked through new forms of assessment. The most hated and feared of those was the WCA, which was seen as a humiliating and unjust process. Many of the accounts revealed service users being insulted by healthcare professionals, government administrators and other 'welfare' workers.

This reflects the wider stigma associated with being understood as mentally ill or dependent on welfare. A number in the group also felt that increasingly people in the local community were looking down upon them and saw them as 'scroungers'. As Rob said:

'Everybody judges you, why aren't you working? What's wrong with you? You don't want to go into it, you don't want to tell everyone why you're not working.'

Our findings seemed to suggest that the stigma associated with mental distress has intensified under austerity. The views and experiences expressed by the group concerning the changing nature of both mental health support and welfare assistance reflect deeper shifts in the foundations and principles of a changing social policy landscape. Underneath many of the transformations that have been part of austerity is the age-old principle that poverty, and now mental distress, is your own personal responsibility (Brown and Baker, 2012). Here, reductions in mental health support can be reimagined as beneficial, when the assistance and support itself is viewed as counterproductive to 'recovery' (Wiggan, 2012). Removing housing or financial assistance can be seen as favourable if people accept the logic that welfare support promotes and creates dependency and hinders people's ability to 'stand on their own two feet'. The data generated through the study does not suggest that many of these experiences are especially novel, but it does suggest that increasing conditionality and disentitlement is, in many cases, entrenching feelings of indignity, social isolation and inadequacy.

The second set of findings emerged around how people resisted and survived despite the attacks on their character and economic security.

From the discussion, participants identified four sources of hope and help in coping with their mental health. Many of the respondents identified spaces and places in their life where their mental health difficulties were recognised by others. This could include mental health day centres or activist groups where they felt that others understood the nature of mental distress, but it could also be with trained professionals such as in talking therapy sessions. Crucial here was the idea that they were being taken seriously and the severity of their symptoms and experiences was not called into question. Second, opportunities to engage in therapeutic activities were also seen as beneficial to living with mental distress. This, again, transcended formal services and people talked about a whole range of different activities including walking, pet ownership, playing sports, arts and crafts groups and engagement with various different religious or spiritual groups. A further aspect was empowered participation in service user groups, some of which were political in nature and were actively campaigning for better mental health or welfare services. The value of these social spaces was often noted as offering the possibility to challenge the dominant politics of welfare by both actively constructing narratives that challenged welfare users as disingenuous and, in some cases, actively engaging in campaigning. Lastly, social locations offering safety and security were seen as highly advantageous. In this quote Peter discusses the first time he accessed day centre following a number of severe crises in his psychological state. The quote reflects many of the themes just discussed:

'I had always struggled to talk about my illness and events that took place. But through the service, we did bee-keeping, we did gardening, we did eco-world projects, we did interior design projects, we did DIY. It would be with skilled workers and there'd be a small group of people that worked with them and did these activities. It was just a joy, a quiet joy. It was really kind of under the surface all the good it was doing and you know it stopped me from having that cycle of admissions to hospital. It helped me to have better relationships with my family again, it gave me security, it gave me a positive outlook on life, it gave me confidence, it gave me support, and it gave me an understanding of my mental health. And from one of the key workers I had while I was there, I learned things about bee-keeping, I learned things about the allotment, plants and flowers, and I learned things about politics. It was just brilliant, it was like university all over again without the pressure and all the essays to hand in, just the social side, and I'm still supported by it now.'

Overall, our findings revealed the social damage done to those with enduring mental health problems by austerity politics and policy. Economic and social policy transformations have created a toxic environment for mental health in England (Barr et al, 2015). Psychologists Against Austerity (PAA, 2013) showed that depression, suicide and anxiety are all linked to psychological states of distrust. Newly erected policy processes disentitle people of the various forms of support they have relied on, resulting in exacerbating and deteriorating emotional and psychological wellbeing. Government spending cuts and welfare transformation have dismantled many of the resources of hope and help fundamental to the capacity to manage distress.

Action outcomes

1. A central part of PAR is the emphasis on some form of engaged action that arises The group organised a photo exhibition. The team took a range of photos to reflect aspects of their life that they saw as beneficial or as a hindrance for managing mental distress. The photos were then organised to reflect the themes emerging from the qualitative data analysis. A range of local politicians, professional, service user and activist groups attended the event. It generated discussion about how the demands of the group should be taken forward and pressure brought to bear on those in positions of power and authority.
2. The group were involved in organising a one-day conference on the impact of work capability assessments. The group were involved in developing thinking around 'psycho-compulsion', in other words, extending knowledge of how social policy and mental health care use psychological techniques to try to realise 'positive effects' (such as returning people to the labour market) and the impact that this has on the lives of service users. The active involvement of group members at the conference emphasised a deepening 'conscientisation' – a growing, reflective, self-realisation of the socio-political structures impacting on their lives and the need to challenge these oppressive structures to facilitate their wellbeing and their liberation.

Challenges in service user participation in EU research

Our research design offered a social space where participants could reflect on how their own biographies were rooted in larger social, political and economic currents, in the process allowing them to develop a more critical understanding of their experiences with mental distress and associated services. However, a number of challenges presented themselves in the course of managing the research, the most significant being the attempt to elevate service user inclusion or participation to tangible control over the direction and aims of the research.

Perhaps the central shortcoming identified in the literature on service user involvement in social science research is that it can be tokenistic (Bradshaw, 2008; Lowes and Hulatt, 2005). If research is likely to identify and support the emancipatory concerns of the users themselves then 'user controlled' strategies should be fostered, rather than more low level forms of inclusion and participation. However, a number of rigidities, which accompany large-scale social science and social policy research, can serve to prevent moving projects beyond service user involvement, and towards the realms of service user control. Some of these could be implemented through improving the internal operations of projects themselves; however, some would require a change in the way funders organise research.

The inclusion of 'vulnerable voices' was central to RE-InVEST's aim to understand and ultimately improve the situation of excluded and oppressed groups of people across Europe. The bold claims made, however, need to be placed within certain constraints that arose in relation to carrying out the research. First, the co-researchers were not involved in the process of writing the EU bid, setting the RE-InVEST programme aims or setting the appropriate time frame for the research. In many ways this reflects the limits to competitive EU funding rounds, but these facts question, to a degree, the claim to 'coproduction'.

Second, time constraints imposed by the programme funders (the EU) means research teams have to meet certain deliverables by specific times. This puts considerable pressure on all participants to generate the required data within relatively short timeframes. The coproduction of knowledge on a topic such as mental distress requires considerable time to develop a trusting relationship, a safe space, a shared research programme and an agreed method. Wicks and Reason (2009) have argued, for instance, that for action research to create a truly 'communicative space', it has to go through a number of different phases where trust initially is built and deeper forms of data gathering occur later.

Third, a further problem arose with regard to the way that research data, which merged the understandings of both academic and service user researchers, had to fit into the research project's theoretical framework. The emphasis on both human rights and capabilities drove the different research tasks. While it was reasonably simple to get the groups thinking and talking about human rights and how they felt their experiences of using mental health and welfare services had violated or contravened the 1998 Human Rights Act, it proved more difficult to operationalise the capabilities approach. As the research developed it was also clear that the capabilities approach, as a guiding theoretical frame for the project, failed to encapsulate many of the experiences of the group. Capabilities focus on how societies manage to help people realise what they are able 'to do and to be' (Sen, 2001). The benefits of this approach, it has been argued, is its ability to further a human rights analyses from a simplistic focus on what formal rights exist into an investigation of what people are really able to achieve (or otherwise) in a given social, economic and cultural context (Brunner and Watson, 2016). This approach transcends more legalistic analyses of rights, but for social policy analysis, the capabilities approach requires us to analyse whether different forms of welfare services really do help people to turn life plans into a reality.

However, the problem with applying capabilities to social policy is that it tends ignore the structural role of welfare in a capitalist society. Our research uncovered stories of welfare users who are subject to welfare policies that are not shaped by increasing the rights and improving the capabilities of individuals but are more concerned with controlling people's activities and behaviours: social policies are often a double-edged sword of support and coercive control. Despite our belief that the capabilities approach fails to accurately describe and explain social policy transformation under austerity, straying too far away from attempting to operationalise it would have meant not meeting some of the key deliverables at the centre of the projects aims and objectives.

The fact that a role for participatory action research methods is given in a project such as RE-InVEST is something to celebrate even if we have noted some challenges. There are a number of ways in which service user activists and social policy academics could encourage large governmental and policy funders to facilitate the involvement of survivors and service users to be more meaningful and consequential.

First, funders should be made aware of how time consuming, and therefore resource driven, facilitating deeper levels of service user involvement is. For instance, ensuring involvement at either end of the research project could develop participation at points in the research process that is driven by academics and policy framers. Turner and Beresford (2005: x) note that 'most funding has been devoted to supporting user involvement in research and proportionately very little to take forward user controlled research'. Interpreted another way this would mean greater funding for involvement both at the stage of inception of aims, objectives and priorities as well as the actual necessary design of methodological strategies. At the other end, it would mean greater monies spent in ensuring that service user involvement could occur at writing up and dissemination stage.

Lastly, and reflecting Freire's anti-assistentialism, there is often something of an assumption that service users and other oppressed groups are not actively taking their own actions in order to ensure that their voices are heard. Yet, SUGAH members have shown that many were already making sure that professionals, others in their communities and politicians were listening to their experiences. Perhaps a further recommendation for thinking about how EU-driven projects and other large institutionally funded projects could include and extend the power of service users is to think about how user- and survivor-led organisations could be included in research further helping to fuse different forms of knowledge.

Note

1   SUGAH is an acronym for 'Service User Group at Hope'. The group is a mental health service user and self-advocacy group. They are also heavily involved in the design, development, teaching and recruitment for an undergraduate and postgraduate social work programme.

References

Barr, B., Taylor-Robinson, D., Stuckler, D., Loopstra, R., Reeves, A., Wickham, S. and Whitehead, M. (2015) 'Fit-for-work or fit-for-unemployment? Does the reassessment of disability benefit claimants using a tougher work capability assessment help people into work?' *Journal of Epidemiology and Community Health*, 70 (5), 452–8.

Beresford, P. (2012) 'Psychiatric system survivors: an emerging movement', in N. Watson, A. Roulstone and C. Thomas (eds) *Routledge Handbook of Disability Studies*, London: Routledge, pp 151–64.

Bradshaw, P. (2008) 'Service user involvement in the NHS in England: genuine user participation or a dogma-driven folly?' *Journal of Nursing Management*, 16 (6), 673–81.

Brown, B.J. and Baker, S. (2012) *Responsible Citizens: Individuals, Health and Policy under Neoliberalism*, London: Anthem Press.

Brunner, R. and Watson, N. (2016) *What can capabilities approach add to policy analysis in high-income countries?*, What Works Scotland, Working Paper.

Carter, R. (2016) 'Coming face-to-face with the impact of social care cuts you've made: a director's story', *Liverpool Echo*, 11 May.

Ferguson, I., Lavalette, M. and Ioakimidis, V. (2018) *Global Social Work in a Political Context*, Bristol: Policy Press.

Freire, P. (1970) *Pedagogy of the Oppressed*, New York: Herder and Herder.

Jensen, T. and Tyler, I. (2015) ''Benefit Broods': The cultural and political crafting of anti-welfare commonsense', *Critical Social Policy*, 35 (4), 470–91.

Lowes, L. and Hulatt, I. (2005) 'Introduction', in L. Lowes and I. Hulatt (eds) *Involving Service Users in Health and Social Care Research*, London: Routledge.

Moran, R. and Lavalette, M. (2016) 'Co-production: workers, volunteers and people seeking asylum: 'popular social work' in action in Britain', in C. Williams and M.J. Graham (eds) *Social Work in a Diverse Society: Transformative practice with Black and Ethnic Minority individuals and communities*, Bristol: Policy Press, pp 109–26.

Moth, R., Greener, J. and Stoll, T. (2015) 'Crisis and resistance in mental health services in England', *Critical and Radical Social Work*, 3 (1), 89–101.

Psychologists Against Austerity (PAA) (2013) *The Psychological Impact of Austerity: A Briefing Paper*, PAA.

Rees, J. (ed) (1998) *Essays in Historical Materialism*, London: Bookmarks.

Sen, A. (2001) *Development as Freedom*, New York: Anchor Books.

Telford, R. and Faulkner, A. (2009) 'Learning about service user involvement in mental health research', *Journal of Mental Health*, 13 (6), 549–59.

Turner, M. and Beresford, P. (2005) *User Controlled Research: Its meanings and potential, Final Report*, Shaping Our Lives and the Centre for Citizen Participation, Brunel University.

Vygotsky, L (1986) *Thought and Language*, revised and edited by A. Kozulin, Cambridge, MA: MIT.

Wicks, P.G. and Reason, P. (2009) 'Initiating action research: Challenges and paradoxes of opening communicative space', *Action Research*, 7 (3), 243–62.

Wiggan, J. (2012) 'Telling stories of 21st century welfare: The UK Coalition government and the neo-liberal discourse of worklessness and dependency', *Critical Social Policy*, 32, 383–405.

Part VI
Campaigning and change

When we think about making change, we are likely to think about campaigning and collective activism. What we quickly learn, however, when we explore such activities from a participatory perspective, is that there are different kinds of campaigning and activism and that both may be more or less inclusive and engaging. In a discussion of participatory social policy we are rapidly drawn to more participatory approaches and it quickly becomes apparent that these have developed enormously in recent years and that there is now a helpful and significant body of knowledge and experience to be drawn on. Much of this knowledge comes from welfare service users.

While accounts by people on the receiving end of social policy run right through this book, they are as we might expect particularly evident in the next two sections, Parts VI and VII. Both are further divided into two sections. Part VI, which focuses on campaigning and change, begins with a series of chapters looking at different approaches to more inclusive activism. These highlight the different location of pressures for change, the different forms and purposes campaigning may have, as well as the different ways in which they can be reported.

Section One: Approaches to activism

Clenton Farquharson begins with the story of his politicisation after he became disabled, offering a rich account of how the personal and political can become inseparable. His involvement as a disabled black man with national policymakers demonstrates the importance of including service users at the 'top table', repeatedly reminding policymakers of the potential consequences of their decisions for the lives of disabled and older people and those from ethnic minority communities. Social work academic Barbara Fawcett examines the history and concept of 'social entrepreneurship' in health and social care, and the potential role the approach might have for progressing participatory social policy, particularly in the context of the Care Act 2014 for England and Wales. She sketches out the connections between this and the provision of health and social care support by community-based or service user-led 'micro' organisations.

A number of the case study authors convey sometimes unpalatable truths about how social policy can impact on people's lives and their efforts to use these truths to challenge injustice and call those in power to account. Kay Sheldon, mental health service user and activist, details a turning point for English national social care policy reform in her account of high profile 'whistle-blowing' on serious failings at a UK National Health Service Trust while on the Board of the English Care Quality Commission (CQC). She describes how not speaking up would have been 'a neglect of duty'. As an artist, Jolie Goodman chose to use graphics here to tell her story of how she and a number of sister women mental health service users and survivors came together to raise their collective voice to tell the truth to the British government about sexual violence and harassment on mixed-sex psychiatric wards.

Mental health nurse and educator Nicky Lambert gives a feminist practitioner view on implementing the UK National Health Service policy on mental health acute care for women, which was an outcome of the service user and survivor led campaign Jolie Goodman describes in her graphic chapter. She demonstrates how the policy helped her to align her professional, personal and political selves in her work and made sense because it was informed by service users and aimed at practitioners. Sarah Ryan, mother of Connor Sparrowhawk, aka Laughing Boy, and co-campaigner George Julian, write about their international struggle to secure #JusticeforLB. The eventual inquest verdict was that his death was due to neglect with serious failings attributed to the health trust involved, but their campaign was also concerned with the poor treatment of learning disabled people more generally. In their chapter, they set out what happened, look at the problems they faced campaigning, the lessons they learned and how policy and services might be different.

Section Two: The role of online platforms and social media

In the second section, we hear more about the role of social networking and media in progressive campaigning.

In his opening chapter, founder of the Guerilla Policy and Guerilla Wire blog sites, Michael Harris outlines his vision for 'disruptive' participatory social policy based on ideas of co-production and using online and social media platforms. He critiques conventional think tanks as part of the problem in social policy formation, arguing for a different kind, based on co-production and social networking. Longstanding campaigner with learning difficulties Gary Bourlet and Kaliya Franklin, disability rights campaigners, have contributed a chapter adapted from an openDemocracy blog they wrote for the 800th anniversary of the Magna Carta. In it they explore what a Magna Carta for learning disabled people might look like today. Highlighting that people with learning difficulties are modern serfs denied basic rights, they identify priorities for ensuring them basic freedoms and use online publishing as a way to make their case freely and globally available.

Pat Onions and her colleague disabled people and carers discuss a new way in which people previously excluded can be involved in collective campaigning, via the internet, and work effectively to achieve change. But it is not a simple success story and they also discuss its limitations and the need to overcome them.

31

'What is strong, not what is wrong'

An interview with Clenton Farquharson, MBE

What brought you to doing the policy and campaigning work you've done over the years? What's your motivation?

My journey to being active in disability campaigning started with a life-changing event when I got stabbed. It was 16 February 1995 and the date is etched on my mind. A young lady was being raped. I could have ignored the calls but I had to do something. At the time I was a bouncer at a city centre nightclub, but off duty. When I intervened I was stabbed repeatedly and that's how I acquired my disability. I lost three weeks of memory as I was in intensive care and then six months in hospital while health and social care arguing over who would pay for stair lifts as I was living in a flat at the time. That introduced me to the physical and emotional journey of disability.

Later on I was diagnosed with post-traumatic stress disorder (PTSD) as a result of my trauma. I had to do a lot of mental health work too. I went to psychiatrists as I wanted to kill myself. I was angry at people and angry at the situation I found myself in. But the experience I lived through shaped the way I think of the world, and made me who I am. I suppose now you could say I've got a calling to fight for social justice because I hate bullies and I hate inequality, but I had to personally go though it to really understand it. I thought things were in place for disabled people, but on 16 February 1995 I woke up when I became disabled.

I had internal battles with myself when I became disabled. I was frightened. I didn't have a real empowering picture of disability and so I filled in all the blanks to create my own negative story. Then I got to know other disabled people who were going through the same sort of thing. I thought what we were going through just wasn't right.

I met some great friends through going to a clinic and talking through some of my anger and anxiety with others. The funniest thing I remember in the group was an argument over who was the most depressed. I realised I had been doing this for nearly three years and I thought I've got to do something! I moved on and tried to start locally. I got involved in the Coalition of Disabled People in Birmingham and in the black and minority ethnic disability partnership that I started up. Some of this was for selfish reasons, to give me a purpose.

So that's where I started. I was fed up of the culture of people doing things to me and I wanted a culture of doing with. But there wasn't any recognition of the skills and talents I and other disabled people have. I saw one of the biggest stumbling blocks were labels, especially in health and social care, to describe you. I had loads of labels and people thought they knew me because of those labels.

The person I most look up to and who motivated me is my Mum. I was bought up with my sisters and my Mum had three or four different jobs and she cares about people. She said to us caring about people isn't just saying it, you have to do it. And that's why I get involved, because like my Mum I don't like unfairness. That's my motivation.

What difference do you think your contribution based on your lived experience made to social policy?

My involvement with national policy started in 2006 with the British New Labour government when they created the Equality 2025 and Better Life Chances for Disabled People policies. I ended up being the West Midlands representative. I always felt I was in the wrong place because people were always talking about the theory and I would have to remind them that the theory in practice means this or that for disabled people. I would always say 'when you talk about that policy, how might that look at the local level, what does it mean for people's lives?' I tried to get a pen picture of how that policy might work or not work in practice. I always try to be practical when I get into policy. I ask things like 'for example how would that work for Freda, down the road?' and that's how I try to work.

I got involved in campaigning because I believe in the right to self-determination in care and support. If there's a change in the mindset of the people delivering social care and health services, it absolutely can make a difference. So for example, for the personalisation policy to happen in England it's about creating the right behaviours and creating the right support system to make that happen. That means the policies, procedures and practice to enable professionals and the people who use services and their communities to influence and feel real change.

What's the most significant policy issue you've been involved with and why was it so important to you?

It was the personalisation health and social care policy in England because I saw it going alongside social justice. For me the cornerstone of social justice should be ensuring that everyone no matter who we are or where we live has the opportunity to develop, nurture and grow. But inequality can stop all of that, and inequality isn't just about the process, the policies and procedure, it's about the attitudes and behaviours. Personalisation is actually quite simple, but services have made it very complex. We've forgotten it's about creating better relationships in services to help people have better lives. It's about the structures, systems, policies and procedures that you put in place to make that happen. Do they efficiently support the goal of people having better lives – not just services – lives? Some people might need a helping hand, so how do we do that with them?

One problem is the inconsistency around how personalisation has been adopted and understood by councils and care providers in England. The right to a better life shouldn't be distorted through inequality of practice. For some personalisation works really well, but there's not enough to embrace the complex elements that lead to better lives. Disabled people need choice and control, but you have to be supported and well informed. Individuals and communities now don't trust personalisation because they've experienced it as a cover for funding cuts. We should be reclaiming it and not letting personalisation be determined by service providers. The ownership has to sit with individuals and communities.

When things don't work, it's so often about battles between the local authority and the NHS. We need to keep reminding them to stop doing the wrong thing and that's where co-production and disabled people's skills and assets should be working. I've known some really, really intelligent, clever people who the system just doesn't listen to because of the label that they have been given. That can stop real innovation and creativity. A whole section of society is missing who've experienced the issues and who know at face value some of the solutions because they've had to work them out. We have to present ourselves as being powerful individuals and communities who can create change.

Sometimes I feel we end up measuring the wrong things, and there's so much we don't know that's really important for policy and practice. Personalisation is often talked about in terms of personal budgets and direct payments, but they're just the vehicle that services have used. Councils say 'we've got so and so many people on personal budgets now', and I say 'great, but what's the quality of their lives like? Are they happier?' What are we measuring? Data should also be about understanding things we need to reflect on to empathise with people. It should allow for thoughtful decision-making.

Based on your own experience in working on national policy, do you think people at the grassroots and with lived experience can really make a difference to social policy? If so, how?

The difference seems to be reminding policymakers that social policy has massive implications for people and communities. I know that people say 'well that's obvious', but so many forget the connection. They think in a vacuum and don't understand how policy interacts with people and where they're at in any given situation in their lives. How do we encourage and empower people who use public services to change that relationship? Service users should be the cornerstone of policy discussions and really defining and testing the purpose of a policy like personalisation.

We're supposed to be creating a stronger idea about seeing people's talents and strengths to help shape their own destiny. But you need tools and support to do that. Co-production is a must, for policy too. If you're going to do anything about public services, people and communities have to be at the core in designing and delivering the services. They have to have ownership. That's what we should be talking about at policy level. We've been having loads of conversations that have gone around and around and kept the status quo. We should be having constructive, equal conversations with service users, families, friends and communities where everyone understands that we now have to do something different.

There needs to be a willingness to change and for some that will mean letting go of power. And that's scary, especially if you've been in the position of determining what an individual or community should or shouldn't get. Then someone comes along and says 'we've now got to support individual and communities to decide for themselves', well that is quite scary for some. So how do we manage that?

Cormac Russell of the Asset Based Community Development (ABCD) Institute at Northwestern University, Chicago said 'we tend to focus on what is wrong, not what is strong'. I think labels encourage a focus on what is wrong. Taking them away means we can have a new type of constructive conversation as you then see the whole person. We all have experiences, ideas and skills to bring to the discussion – this is what's strong – and empowerment works both ways.

Professionals have to feel that they're empowered too. So many of them feel they have to seek permission to do the right thing. When I've asked professionals how they go about doing the right thing, they say they usually have to go under the radar. If they don't feel empowered, how can they do the same for people who use services?

This is why creating the culture, conditions and environment for that to happen is so important – the engagement is person to person. That needs to start at policy level. There's an assumption that we can send a policy document out, everyone looks at it and everyone is on the same page, but this can create confusion. In that confusion we tend to create our own interpretations and stories, so how do we find common ground and consistency?

How would you like to conclude?

Have you ever seen the film 'High Noon'? It's a movie about a courageous sheriff who was facing off four bad guys who'd come to town on the noon train and none of the town folks would stand with the sheriff to confront them, except one brave woman who turned out the make the difference.

The message is clear: 'Will you stand with me?' All the faint-hearted men of the town drew the blinds closed. People can't keep on drawing the blinds down. But we need more than one exceptional, brave woman who turns out to be the difference. We need a social movement to improve the way social policy is done to make sure people have better lives and more hopeful futures as a result – this is High Noon for me.

32

Participatory social policy and social change: exploring the role of social entrepreneurship linked to forms of social and micro enterprises in the field of social care

Barbara Fawcett

Introduction

The relationship between social policy and social change can be dynamic and can bring about significant transformation. However, this relationship is not linear and is affected by political climate, by context, by those who are either involved or excluded and by the extent of media attention. On the one hand there can be blocks, revisions and retractions, but, on the other, there can be breakthroughs and significant movement. There are many ways in which social policy can contribute to participatory social policy and social change and in this chapter we look how social entrepreneurship linked to forms of social and micro enterprise can operate as a major change element, particularly when opportunities, such as those contained in the Care Act 2014, are utilised by those whom the policy most affects.

When links are made between social policy and social change, a pivotal area relates to the extent of involvement of those who utilise services. Involvement can take many different forms and operate at many different levels. It can be deep and meaningful or superficial and meaningless (Fawcett et al, 2010). Recently, co-production is a term that has been coined to clarify what involvement can and arguably should incorporate. The Social Care Institute for Excellence (SCIE, 2015) maintain that co-production should be regarded as a number of principles rather than as a singular entity. They point to the importance of power imbalances being addressed and to attention being paid to reciprocity and to acknowledging and working with diversity. Accordingly, there is a strong emphasis on assets, rather than on deficits and on negotiation, mutuality and exchange. In terms of a working example, the Care Act 2014 can be regarded as an area where policy can be used as a catalyst for social change by the utilisation of forms of support provisions that draw on service user and community assets.

Social entrepreneurship

The concept of entrepreneurship has featured in the field of business for many years. However, over the past 20 years or so, it has gained relevance in a number of non-business arenas, particularly in those of education and health and has been reframed in a variety of ways, with these including both top down and bottom up influences. Until recently, relatively little attention has been paid to its utility in the arena of social care and this is despite initial pioneering work being undertaken by the Settlement Movement in the 19th century.

The Settlement Movement interpreted social entrepreneurship as a fusion of vision, campaigning and practical action. They drew in all who could help and extended their social reach in vertical as well as in horizontal directions. The key precepts they used are still evident in current versions of social entrepreneurship and it is useful to consider these in more detail. De Leeuw (1999), for example, defines social entrepreneurs as those who work proactively to utilise and draw from a range of perspectives in order to bring about innovation, transformation and change. De Leeuw clearly separates social entrepreneurs from those operating in the field of business. She emphasises the importance of collaboration and communality, with social entrepreneurs flexibly applying skills, knowledge and expertise in fluid and unpredictable situations and actively learning by doing as a means of critically reflecting and engaging. Dabbs (2002) makes it clear that social entrepreneurship is about avoiding 'quick fix' solutions and involves 'thinking outside the box' in order to explore opportunities, build on strengths, make connections, and generate and maximise transformational potential.

Fawcett and South draw attention to social entrepreneurship being used as a 'pragmatic, innovative means of attending to process issues' (2005: 198). They maintain that 'it offers a flexible approach, emphasizing negotiation and management which can be employed in different settings to overcome resistance and barriers to change' (Fawcett and South, 2005: 198).

In the USA, Nandan, London and Bent-Goodley (2015) view social entrepreneurship as a means of both addressing complexity and responding to shrinking resources. They maintain that as the nature and complexity of the problems and challenges experienced by individuals and communities continue to grow, with this taking place in an economic, social, and political climate where resources have to be utilised as creatively as possible, there is a call for social entrepreneurs to lead and facilitate social change, to create social value and to ensure social impact and financial sustainability. Writing from a social work perspective, they differentiate between social entrepreneurship, social intrapreneurship and social innovation. They regard social entrepreneurship broadly as 'the establishment of initiatives to implement social innovations' (Nandan et al, 2015: 38). They go on to say that what characterises social entrepreneurs is the use of innovation to create social value and bring about social change in the public, private, citizen or non-profit sector. Social intrapreneurship is viewed as the application and integration of social innovations within organisations, such as social service agencies. Social intrapreneurs are employees such as social workers, who focus on innovation and creativity in ways that transform how organisations 'do business and create social solutions' (Nandan et al, 2015: 39). Social Innovation, they maintain, is about 'accomplishing more with less, working together, leveraging resources, sharing data, and creating models for change that are sustainable' (Nandan et al, 2015: 39). Nandan, London and Blum (2014) regard social innovations that emerge from community-based collaborations as being particularly effective as they build on the strengths of the community and partner with those that understand social issues and social problems. They insist that involving 'clients' in all stages of the development and delivery of a new idea, not only strengthens social innovation, but also creates sustainability for implementation. In particular, they maintain that involving members of marginalised communities in designing and developing new ideas is a very effective means of building capacity.

Germak and Singh (2010) regard social entrepreneurship as a hybrid of macro social work practices and business skills and activities. Depending on the scope of change either envisaged or in train, they see social entrepreneurs operating as social bricoleurs (addressing small scale social issues); social constructionists (filling the gaps created by market failures that affect disenfranchised populations); or social engineers (addressing social problems by changing larger social systems). In each of these instances, they assert, social entrepreneurs are tuned into recognising opportunities in their environments, although the level of risks they are able to take is directly related to the scale of change they hope to create.

Cho (2006) is more guarded in his analysis of what social entrepreneurship can offer. He acknowledges that social entrepreneurship appears to speak 'a compelling language of pragmatism, cooperation and hope' (Cho, 2006: 53), that it has achieved successes, and that it is broadly embraced by a diverse range of stakeholders. Yet, he highlights that these opportunities also contain constraints in that these can all too easily be viewed as a panacea for current inadequacies, and that proclamations of success can mask conflicts of interest. He emphasises that, as a motivational and operational construct, social entrepreneurship can be set against existing ways of operating in a binary manner. He draws attention to definitions of what constitutes 'the social' inevitably containing political influences, with some issues and concerns being included and some excluded. Building on his recommendations, social entrepreneurship can be regarded as having a lot to offer, but there are provisos. These are that it has to be seen as a means of complimenting what is currently in place and that inclusive and participatory forms of partnership working have to be foregrounded. This includes defining what 'partnership working' actually means in specific situations to ensure that rhetorical forms are not substituted for other forms of governance and ways of operating. Last but not least, social entrepreneurial activity has to be sustainable, taking on board structural as well symptomatic issues.

A discussion of what social entrepreneurship is and what it can do draws attention to both the constraints and the opportunities. However, one big leap forward is to pluralise social entrepreneurship so that we do not appear to be referring to a single individual, the social entrepreneur, but to all those involved in an endeavour. This brings to the fore the importance of co-production between service users, carers and practitioners and highlights the central role of negotiation in bringing about social change. It is important to highlight that this interpretation does not rule out individual social entrepreneurs recruiting others, or roles, responsibilities and the overall contribution towards the change process being agreed according to situation, time available and the goals agreed. What it does do is to socialise the activity at the outset and put in place the ground rules for the cooperation required to make a difference and bring about meaningful social change. It is also about including those so often marginalised and excluded.

Application to practice: The Care Act 2014

The Care Act 2014 is influenced by marketisation, by neoliberal versions of consumerism and by aspects of third way thinking. Nevertheless, it is also informed by disability rights and social model orientations. and within the Act the active promotion of wellbeing is prioritised. As a result, it brings to the fore opportunities as well as constraints. With regard to the constraints, Fawcett et al (2017) maintain that the provision of financial support/services remain linked to assessments of the level of deficit, that is what an individual cannot do, and to professional decisions about the legitimacy of the needs presented. This, they argue, preserves a significant functionalist orientation. The perpetuation of an individualising element can also be seen in that relatively little emphasis is placed on the organisational involvement of 'carers' and those who use services, in the planning and operationalising of social care.

Scourfield (2007) argues that the direct payments scheme, which is embedded in the Care Act 2014 as part of the personalisation process, requires welfare consumers or service users to become managers and entrepreneurs. He argues that responsibilities not rights are transferred and that 'for the individual citizen, personhood is expressed through being entrepreneurial, managing, risk taking and innovating' (Scourfield, 2007: 119). He asks the question about what then happens to those 'who are unable to manage (in all senses of the word), or who are not innovators or who are insufficiently enterprising' (Scourfield, 2007: 119).

Operating principles drawn from consumerism, marketisation and 'third way' modernism can influence interpretation towards the shifting of responsibilities, the downplaying of rights and the cutting of resources. Notwithstanding these aspects, the opportunities within the Care Act 2014 can be used to bring about change; change that has the potential to move away from the ongoing links to deficit and individualisation. This is particularly the case in relation to the requirement for

Local Authorities to both prevent and delay the provision of individualised care and support packages by actively promoting community initiatives. Accordingly, it is argued that social entrepreneurship, defined as a means of pluralising and promoting co-production and involvement and linked to forms of social and micro enterprises, can utilise the spaces opened up to make a constructive difference and address the potentially divisive aspects highlighted by Scourfield (2007).

Social enterprise and micro enterprise

Social enterprise and micro enterprise clearly have roots in the promotion of the mixed economy of welfare, but the Localism Act (2011) and the Social Value Act (2013) not only enable community groups to take over and run local services, but the 2013 Act requires service commissioners to look at how the services they commission can work to enhance the economic, social and environmental wellbeing of the area, adding social value and promoting community engagement (Hall, 2016). Within these developments, there is clearly a driver to improve efficiency and cut costs, but in terms of involvement and co-production, there is much more that can be seen to be on offer.

The Social Enterprise Unit was established in 2001 and defined social enterprise as 'business(es) with primarily social objectives whose surpluses are principally reinvested for that purpose in the business or in the community, rather than being driven by the need to maximize profit for shareholders and owners' (DTI, 2002). This is a wide-ranging definition, which as Miller and Millar (2011) state can refer to social enterprises operated by co-operative and voluntary organisations as well as for profit business with social purposes. It also does not just focus on innovation and Miller and Millar (2011) point out that a social enterprise can contract to deliver an existing public sector service which can include the need to work to detailed and possibly constraining specifications.

Miller and Millar (2011) have focused on the establishment of social enterprises in the health field, with this having been particularly promoted by the Right to Request programme introduced in 'High Quality Care for All – NHS Next Stage Review Final Report' (DH, 2008). This enabled staff in the NHS to develop social enterprises by externalising NHS services. Miller and Millar (2011) identify both negative and positive aspects in this significant policy move. The constraints include the underpinning marketisation ethos and the consequences of the social enterprise no longer having direct NHS branding. This results in the social enterprise rather than the NHS taking responsibility for the service with a concomitant fudging of legislative responsibility. Pay and conditions also become external to the remit of a large organisation. However, they identified gains, which include increased flexibility, the provision of flatter management structures, the potential for greater community engagement and, overall, increased capacity for inclusive innovation. These findings, as can be seen from research carried out by Needham et al (2014) and discussed below, have considerable relevance for the social care sector.

With the rolling out of the Care Act 2014, there are increasing examples coming to the fore of social enterprises, particularly those linked to community-based and collective support making a difference in terms of what is on offer. In the arts, there are a range of contemporary dance courses being provided for adults with learning disabilities funded through direct payments. These ventures, although having a specific focus, also have a wider brief of looking at how wellbeing, with regard to health and social care, can be met in a more inclusive and asset orientated manner. There are also social enterprises, which look to engaging older adults and adults with learning disabilities in arts projects, where in addition to the opportunity to do something new, social aspects and the need to reduce social isolation are emphasised. In the major shift in policy and practice brought about by the Care Act 2014, some Local Authorities are also turning social work into freestanding social enterprises and an example here is North East Lincolnshire. The stated drivers behind this particular move are to increase flexibility, which is seen as being increasingly difficult to find within the public sector, and to promote and sustain community involvement. It is also promoted as signalling a move away from individually orientated forms of social work practice towards social workers taking on the role of a community broker. This involves facilitating the full use of community assets, enabling people to take control, and prioritising the building of community capacity. The longevity and success of these enterprises has yet to be determined, as has the relationship between rhetoric and practice and austerity and resourcing but there can be seen to be real opportunities in these developments with regard to innovation, change and participation.

Hall (2016) looks at the micro enterprise response to the personalisation agenda, which, as highlighted, is re-emphasised in the Care Act 2014. Micro enterprises are much smaller entities than social enterprises and tend to have fewer than five workers. As a result, they are generally flexible, can be related to the provision of personal and social assistance and can employ family members. Hall (2016) quotes Lockwood (2013):

> Micro-providers are simply local people using their gifts and skills creatively to deliver support and services that benefit other local people and their community ... They blur the distinction between service provider and service user – many people delivering micro-services themselves use social care and health services (Lockwood, 2013: 27).

Hall (2016) emphasises that microenterprises often provide employment for disabled and excluded people, and enhance social capital within a community, however that community may be defined. They also are able to work in ways that are personalised, responsive and flexible and generally have low overheads and a non-hierarchical management structure. There are constraints, which include limited or uncertain incomes, job security and pensions and the need to develop on-the-job business skills. Micro enterprises can also fall under the radar with regard to public funding. However, in terms of involvement and co-production they can be seen to have a wide-ranging relevance in terms of promoting flexibility and change in the social care sector.

Needham et al (2014) carried out research looking at how micro enterprises compare to larger providers with regard to delivering services that are 'personalized, valued, innovative and cost effective' (Needham et al, 2014: 1). The team looked at micro domiciliary services, micro accommodation, micro day support and micro support in the home. All of the micro services focused on building relationships and enabling people to make connections and engage with activities in the local community.

Needham et al (2014) found that micro enterprises did facilitate more personalised approaches, particularly with regard to more flexibly orientated micro domiciliary services. They linked this to the autonomy of the staff to alter what they offered according to what was wanted at any given time, to greater continuity of staff and to the high level of accessibility of managers to staff and people using the service. With regard to day-to-day activities, the differences between what micro providers and larger providers could offer was more mixed with micro providers being able to offer a more personalised service, with larger providers having a wider range of activities to choose from.

Overall, they concluded that micro providers appeared able to deliver more personalised and valued support for lower sums without any compromise on quality as a result of lower overheads, although the services provided did not appear to be more innovative than larger-scale providers. They also found that although micro providers were good at how they operated and the emphasis on relationships was valued, there could be issues relating to over attachment and burnout. Micro providers also generally lacked access to local authority referrals and tended to operate by means of local networks rather than by supporting people on personalised budgets. These findings highlight that micro enterprises have a valuable role to play and significantly add to the social care mix, but that sustainability is an issue that has to be addressed. It also draws attention to how social entrepreneurship more directly linked to micro enterprises could play a part in fostering greater co-production, innovation and partnership working.

Concluding remarks

The concept of wellbeing is not a straightforward one and a number of varying interpretations can be applied. This can be perceived as a drawback but also viewed as strength in that there are now opportunities to change how social care is both viewed and taken forward. As part of this project, social entrepreneurship, linked to forms of social and micro enterprise can be seen to have a great deal to offer. Spaces have been created for social workers, service users, carers and communities to work together on small scale projects, as well as larger-scale enterprises that are more responsive and inclusive, particularly with regard to involving people from marginalised and underserved groups. As a result, there is a very real possibility that better outcomes for wide range of individuals and groups can be both created and sustained.

Social entrepreneurship linked to inclusively orientated forms of social and micro enterprise is clearly not a global solution. There are provisos and context is important. However, there are significant opportunities to shape social policy in different ways and, as part of this process, to bring about meaningful social change in the arena of social care.

References

Cho, A.E. (2006) 'Politics, Values and Social Entrepreneurship: A Critical Appraisal', in J. Mair, J. Robinson and K. Hockerts (eds) *Social Entrepreneurship*, Basingstoke: Macmillan.

Dabbs, S.C. (2002) 'Taking the risk to blossom: the Salford Social Entrepreneurs Programme', in L. Bauld and K. Judge (eds) *Learning from Health Action Zones*, Chichester: Aeneas Press.

De Leeuw, E. (1999) 'Healthy Cities: Urban Social Entrepreneurship for Health', *Medicine and Health*, 14 (3), 261–70.

DH (Department of Health) (2008) *High Quality Care for All – NHS Next Stage Review Final report*, London: Stationery Office.

DTI (Department of Trade and Industry) (2002) *Strategy for Social Enterprise*, London: HM Treasury.

Fawcett, B. and South, J. (2005) 'Community Involvement and Primary Care Trusts', *Critical Public Health*, June, 15 (2), 1–14.

Fawcett, B., Goodwin, S., Meagher, G. and Phillips., R. (2010) *Social Policy for Social Change*, Melbourne/Basingstoke: Palgrave/Macmillan.

Fawcett, B., Fillingham, J., River, D. and Ward, N. (2017) *Service User and Carer Involvement in Health and Social Care: A Retrospective and Prospective Analysis*, Basingstoke: Palgrave.

Germak, A.J. and Singh, K.K. (2010) 'Social entrepreneurship: changing the way social workers do business', *Administration in Social Work*, 34 (1), 79–95.

Hall, K. (2016) 'Using Social Entrepreneurship and Social Enterprise to Tackle Social Problems', Lecture for the British Council, Seoul, 18 March.

Lockwood, S. (2013) 'Community Assets Helping to Deliver Health and Well-Being and Tackle Health Inequalities', *Journal of Integrated Care*, 21 (1), 26–37.

Miller, R. and Millar, R. (2011) *Social Enterprise Spin Outs from the English Health Service: A Right to Request But Was Anyone Listening?*, Birmingham: HSMC/University of Birmingham.

Nandan, M., London, M. and Bent-Goodley, T. (2015) 'Social Workers as Social Change Agents: Social Innovation, Social Intrapreneurship, and Social Entrepreneurship', *Human Service Organizations: Management, Leadership and Governance*, 39 (1), 38–56, DOI: 10.1080/23303131.2014.955236.

Nandan, M., London, M. and Blum, T.C. (2014) 'Community Practice Social Entrepreneurship: An Interdisciplinary Approach to Graduate Education', *International Journal of Social Entrepreneurship*, 3 (1).

Needham, C., Allen, K., Hall, K., McKay, S., Glasby, J., Carr, S., Littlechild, R., Tanner, D. and the Micro Enterprise Project Co-Researchers (2014) *Micro Enterprises: Small Enough to Care?*, Birmingham: University of Birmingham/ ESRC.

Perrini, F. and Vurro, C. (2006) 'Social Entrepreneurship: Innovation and Social Change Across Theory and Practice' in J. Mair, J. Robinson and K. Hockerts (eds) *Social Entrepreneurship*, Basingstoke: Palgrave.

SCIE (2015) *Co-production in social care: What it is and how to do it*, London: SCIE

Scourfield, P. (2007) 'Social Care and the Modern Citizen: Client, Consumer, Service User, Manager and Entrepreneur', *British Journal of Social Work*, 37, 107–22.

The Stationery Office (2011) *The Localism Act 2011*, London: TSO.

The Stationery Office (2013) *The Social Value Act 2013*, London: TSO.

The Stationery Office (2014) *The Care Act 2014*, London: TSO.

33

Public duty, whistleblowing and scandal: influences on public policy

Kay Sheldon

Introduction

From time to time a 'scandal' or wrongdoing is exposed – often through the dogged persistence of individuals – which has a substantial influence on public policy, especially in health and social care. The relationship is a complex one as Butler and Drakeford (2006) observed: 'Scandal is constructed out of a very particular set of events and processes, inhabited by real people and built on unique experiences' (p 5). In 2011 I made a decision that was to dominate my life for the next two years: I decided to speak up about the serious concerns I had about the leadership and approach of the Care Quality Commission (CQC), the national regulator of health and social care services in England. This was a controversial, and unusual, step as I was a current member of the CQC's board. Such was my concern that I felt the CQC was, or was at risk of, not meeting its statutory duties.

It is fair to say that I am not unaccustomed to raising difficult issues. I pursued successful legal action following years of neglectful care from mental health services. As a result of my experiences I have campaigned on mental health issues and worked with numerous organisations to provide or facilitate the voice of people receiving care services. I have brought three successful legal claims for disability discrimination, including as a litigant-in-person. These previous experiences were helpful when I was faced various behaviours when speaking up: I knew what worked and I was prepared for the emotional rollercoaster.

In this chapter I describe my experiences of 'blowing the whistle', the challenges this presented and how it ultimately helped influence changes to policy and practice, namely more effective regulation of health and social care services, and furthering the development of a more open culture in health and social care.

Experiences: raising concerns from within and outside

The concerns I had about CQC amounted to serious failures of leadership and governance. The organisation had abandoned its agreed strategy without board approval or public consultation and had repeatedly failed to deliver. Radical changes were proposed to the regulatory model which would mean that care services would simply pass or fail; and would be deemed as compliant with essential standards of quality unless there was evidence to the contrary. This raised questions as to how poor care and abuse would be identified and addressed. Furthermore, I was concerned about an oppressive and suppressive organisational culture. I discovered many issues were not reported to the board and I heard numerous accounts of bullying. I felt 'doing nothing' was not an option and that resigning would be a neglect of duty.

As I could not secure an adequate response from my board colleagues, I decided I had to go outside of the organisation. I discovered that the National Audit Office (NAO) had a whistleblowing remit so I met with the head of the NAO to explain my concerns. Regrettably his advice was merely to keep my head down so I would not be associated with anything.

In late 2011 I approached the ongoing Public Inquiry that was investigating the serious failures of care at the Mid Staffordshire NHS Foundation Trust and the systemic and cultural problems that had allowed the problems to carry on for such a long time. As a result I was called to give evidence alongside a CQC inspector who had also independently blown the whistle. It is significant that Public Inquiry came about as a result of extensive campaigning by a small group of relatives who had been affected by the neglectful care there. The publication of the report in 2013 validated their concerns. As well as detailing shockingly poor care and failures at every level, the report made 290 recommendations for the UK health system (Francis, 2013).

Response, retaliation and resilience

I received a great deal of positive feedback after I had spoken up. This was not the case for those who held power, who responded with anger, denial and exclusion. Sadly I found out that Ministers and those in other very senior positions are not willing to lead by example when it comes to honesty, openness and accountability. Somewhat ironically, at the same time as I was trying to be heard and agonising whether to go further, Andrew Lansley, the Secretary of State for Health in 2011, announced that NHS staff would be expected to raise concerns at the earliest opportunity and NHS organisations should support staff in doing this. He also promised clarity on existing legal rights to protect people from detriment when they do speak up.

Previous life experiences had shown me that organisations with the weight of power and money behind them are much better placed to engineer favourable outcomes than lone, self-funding individuals. As the retaliation kicked in, I became very familiar with the prevailing culture characterised by attempts to silence those raising concerns rather than listen and respond.

On the day I gave evidence to the inquiry my board colleagues issued a public statement refuting the issues I raised. I did not know at this point that the CQC chair at the time had written to the Secretary of State, requesting my removal from the board. I was asked not to attend board meetings (which I politely declined) while an 'independent review' was undertaken. Alarm bells were already sounding and I sensed an intention to quietly dispose of me, and so the issues I had raised.

My first meeting with the board was – unsurprisingly – one of anger. I suggested mediation but there was no appetite for this. I was asked not to raise any more issues in the public interest as this would be a breach of confidentiality. I suggested it was inappropriate to ask someone not to make public interest disclosures and pointed out that there were many instances when I could have breached confidentiality but had not. Another board member (a doctor) wrote down that I had said I would not maintain confidentiality and, despite me remonstrating this is not what I said, would not correct her note. More alarm bells – and sure enough my 'refusal' to maintain confidentiality was used to support the case for my removal from the board.

Throughout 2012 and 2013, I faced numerous attempts to discredit me. In March 2012 the 'independent' review – undertaken by Gill Rider, the former head of human resources for the UK's Civil Service – concluded, saying I should leave the board. I instructed lawyers who made it clear that the review was unfair, unlawful and illegal. Andrew Lansley backed down immediately, agreed to pay my legal costs and I stayed on the board.

One particularly shocking revelation was that Dame Jo Williams, supported by other board members, tried to get me removed by saying I was mentally unwell. When I received my personal data I found a report from the owner of a private occupational health company, Medigold, saying that I was suffering from a serious paranoid illness (believing the rest of the board was against me – which of course they were!) and that I needed to be removed as soon as possible. This was based on a short phone call where I had said that I did not need to see a doctor but a supporter in board meetings particularly given the nature of the behaviour I was being subjected to.

Going a bit further

In an attempt to further demonstrate my concerns I used the example of University of Morecambe Bay Hospitals NHS Trust (UHMBT). I felt that not only had regulation been largely inadequate – as far back as 2010 when the Trust was registered by CQC as compliant with all standards – but that some directors at CQC had sought to minimise – even suppress – these failings. When I raised these issues in 2012, I was met with denial and obfuscation, and told it had been a robust piece of work. The Department of Health also refused to look at these concerns.

In 2013, after critical media coverage, the new CQC chief executive commissioned an independent review into the concerns I had raised about the regulation of UHMBT. The investigation confirmed that the regulation had been inadequate and also identified a specific act of passive cover up – the suppression of an internal report into the regulation of UHMBT. While I had no specific knowledge of this report, it was indicative of the organisational culture that I had heard about and experienced. Unfortunately the executives implicated were allowed to leave, some with significant financial pay offs, before the report was published despite the fact disciplinary action was pending.

Through my focus on UHMBT I came across another group of bereaved families pushing for an independent investigation into the serious concerns they had about a maternity unit at the Trust. After great persistence, the Morecambe Bay Action Group secured the investigation which reported in 2015 detailing serious failings at the maternity unit and by organisations responsible for scrutiny and oversight (Kirkup, 2015).

Winds of change: policy, practice and promises

In 2014 a review into raising concerns in the NHS was announced. The final report, *Freedom to Speak Up* (Francis, 2015) described whistleblowers as 'crushed' and was solution-focused aimed at developing a culture where raising concerns is seen as the norm. The establishment of a 'Freedom to Speak' National Guardian and local guardians in NHS organisations was recommended to champion culture change and offer support and guidance. The report also contained recommendations to enhance legal protections for whistleblowers as well as proposals for better handling of concerns, greater use of mediation and dispute resolution. It takes time for attitudes and behaviour to change. However, the seeds have been sown.

CQC has changed beyond recognition. A new board was appointed and a more thorough, expert approach to regulation has been developed. Inspections are carried out by people with experience of relevant services, either using or providing them. A key feature has been co-production – working in partnership. Quality regulation is still at an early stage as is research into what helps organisations improve in a sustainable way. However, CQC has demonstrated its renewed willingness to listen, learn and collaborate. It has also shown it is not afraid to take action if circumstances warrant this. The CQC's *State of Health Care and Adult Social Care in England in 2015/16* report (2016) shows the impact it is having directly on the quality of care as well as through an authoritative commentary on the national picture. There is more to do and perhaps always will be, given the fast-changing landscape of health and social care.

I was re-appointed to the CQC board for a further term of office which was important to me as I wanted to be part of the solution. I retain a sense of disappointment that neither the Secretary of State nor very senior managers and civil servants have been willing to address their part in what happened, which is in direct contrast to the expectations they have set for those working in the health and social care services.

In 'scandal' scenarios there's a tendency to put people into the 'good' or 'bad' category, the victim–hero or the perpetrator–bully. But that is too simplistic, too easy. Emotive issues polarise opinion, an effect significantly magnified if associated with media coverage. Social media is increasingly being used by people who have been affected by poor care. Narratives build up to support particular perspectives, bias infuses the 'truth'. There can be uneasy tension between a bereaved family wanting justice and a system wanting to improve and move on. This does not mean poor behaviour or performance should not be challenged, or subject to sanctions, but there is a need to understand different perspectives, to respond earlier and differently, in a way that is fair and sensitive to all involved. Not only could this mean earlier intervention in a deteriorating situation, it would also provide the best chance of learning, changing and healing.

References

Butler, I. and Drakeford, M. (2006) *Scandal, Social Work and Social Welfare*, Bristol: Policy Press.

Care Quality Commission (2016) *The State of Health Care and Social Care in England 2015/2016*, www.cqc.org.uk/sites/default/files/20161019_stateofcare1516_web.pdf

Francis, R. (2013) *Report of Public Inquiry into Mid Staffordshire NHS Foundation Trust, 2013*, http://webarchive.nationalarchives.gov.uk/20150407084003/http://www.midstaffspublicinquiry.com/report

Francis, R. (2015) *Freedom To Speak Up*, http://webarchive.nationalarchives.gov.uk/20150407084003/http://www.midstaffspublicinquiry.com/report

Kirkup, B. (2015) *Report of the Morecambe Bay Investigation*, www.gov.uk/government/uploads/system/uploads/attachment_data/file/408480/47487_MBI_Accessible_v0.1.pdf

34

'Informed gender practice in acute mental health': when policy makes sense

Nicky Lambert

I am a born mental health nurse and while I recognise the issues inherent in the system, it is still core to my identity – I love it! One of the things I am less enthused by are the rafts of mental health policy seemingly written by people with no understanding of what helps mental health workers do their jobs. However, there is a notable exception to this. I was working across two roles in the National Health Service (NHS) as a Mental Health Ward Manager and Practice Development Nurse when the UK policy document *Informed Gender Practice: Mental health acute care that works for women* came out (NiMHE, 2008). I am not normally *moved* by policy documents but this one changed the scope of my practice and what I thought was possible.

The explicit articulation of four core principles – equality, knowledge, commitment and relationships – made the power dynamics that are frequently left unspoken in mental health care, very clear. It also positioned the importance of therapeutic relationships centrally. The foreword noted the importance of coproduction and partnership at all levels of services and the guidance was developed using a wide range of sources which gave voice to the experience and concerns of a diverse group of women using and providing services. The combination of an evidence base drawn from research and personal narrative with practical advice on how to provide the best possible care was a potent departure from the 'wish lists' I had seen up to that point.

The personal is political

I was happy in my work but knew that we could do better; I felt there was something missing from the care offered. It was when I read this document that I understood that what was missing was a commitment to social justice – that my professional and personal selves were misaligned.

Nursing sometimes clings to the belief that to be professional is to remain neutral and some nurses think that the source of their societal influence is their apolitical stance. As a student I looked at the impact of inequalities in society on vulnerable people and I felt differently – I just did not know what to do about it. *Informed Gender Practice* spoke directly to me about the kind of person I wanted to be at work and the kind of nursing care I wanted to give. It was the first policy document I had seen that was written to be read and implemented by practitioners; it addressed thorny issues such as good practice in terms of language with 'better ways of speaking'. It offered clear guidance on supporting black and minority ethnic (BME) populations and working respectfully with women across a spectrum of sexuality and gender identity.

Most importantly it was explicitly political and it was a call to arms; as the UK mental health service user activist Anne Beales said in her introduction, 'Doing nothing is not an option'.

Turning ideas into practice

When I went on to open and manage single gender wards (both Female and Male) the guidance *Informed Gender Practice* offered around Clinical Governance, policy and staffing proved invaluable. The messages around the importance for women to have access to female support workers, both as positive role models and to facilitate compassionate and gender-specific responses were central to how we recruited and countered criticism. It addressed the impact of gender inequality on women's mental health; and it drew on feminist ideas to underpin good practice. I recognised the importance of having a choice of single gender mental health services – women's wards in particular are key to providing a safe environment (especially for people who have experienced sexual trauma). I was lucky that many of my colleagues from lesbian, gay, bisexual and transgender (LGBT) communities supported the idea of gendered care provision, as not everyone welcomed the changes. Concerns ranged from anxieties that we would be establishing an 'un-staffable' self-harmers ward, to charges of sexism. I even had to respond to the statement that female service users acted as a 'civilising' influence on the male patients and we would be exposing staff to violence if they were removed!

Language is used carefully in this document and one of the most valuable tools proved to be a glossary. While that seems a very simple thing, it enabled people who were instinctively committed to promoting women's mental health – all of whom were coming from different backgrounds and levels of awareness – to develop shared language and understanding of how to move forward. Being able to draw on an evidence base and to use theory to give clear rationales for decisions helped us not only to widen the debate on single sex services throughout the trust but enabled us to articulate their purpose and clarify what made them different to what had gone before. This is simply expressed in the document as: 'A move from "what's wrong with this woman?" to "what happened to this woman".'

Conclusion

The lessons I learned from working with this policy and the knowledge that came from nursing in alignment with my personal, professional, political and social ethics have lead me into teaching, practice development, writing, research, management and re-reading it today I can still see its formative influence on the work I do now. This guidance supported staff and service users together to articulate a vital gap in service provision and enact a more successful way to move towards recovery – acknowledging the systemic as well as the personal difficulties people were facing.

It is a high water mark in terms of coproduced, compassionate and socially aware mental health support. It helped place women's services on the map and its withdrawal left a gaping hole in terms of underpinning theory, which (in conjunction with underfunding) has impacted on quality. Successful gendered care provision is not merely putting everyone with a vagina in one place. It is a way of understanding and working with others in mutual respect with an understanding that the determinants of health can be both internal and external.

The Girls' Attitude survey from Girlguiding (2016) shows a picture of British girls experiencing sexism from a young age and having their confidence and self-image undermined. The report *No Country for Young Women* (Young Women's Trust, 2016) presents a picture of young women as anxious, in debt and pessimistic about their futures, which is echoed by the Adult Psychiatric Morbidity study (NHS Digital, 2016) finding higher rates of mental health issues in women. Work by Agenda (2016) found only one of the Mental Health Trusts they approached with a Freedom of Information request still had a strategy for providing gender-specific services to women. In the current climate it would be timely to revisit this document and the possibilities it offers.

References

Agenda (2016) 'Agenda mental health gender responsiveness briefing', September, http://weareagenda.org/policy-research/agendas-reports/

Girlguiding (2016) *Girls' Attitude Study 2016*, www.girlguiding.org.uk/globalassets/docs-and-resources/research-and-campaigns/girls-attitudes-survey-2016.pdf

NiMHE(National Institute for Mental Health in England) (2008) *Informed Gender Practice: Mental Health Acute Care That Works for Women*, http://webarchive.nationalarchives.gov.uk/20110512085708/http://www.nmhdu.org.uk/silo/files/informedgenderpractice.pdf

NHS Digital (2016) *Adult Psychiatric Morbidity Survey: Survey of Mental Health and Wellbeing, England, 2014*, London: NHS Digital.

Young Women's Trust (2016) *No Country for Young Women*, www.youngwomenstrust.org/assets/0000/4258/No_country_for_young_women__final_report.pdf

35

Making the case for single sex wards

Jolie Goodman

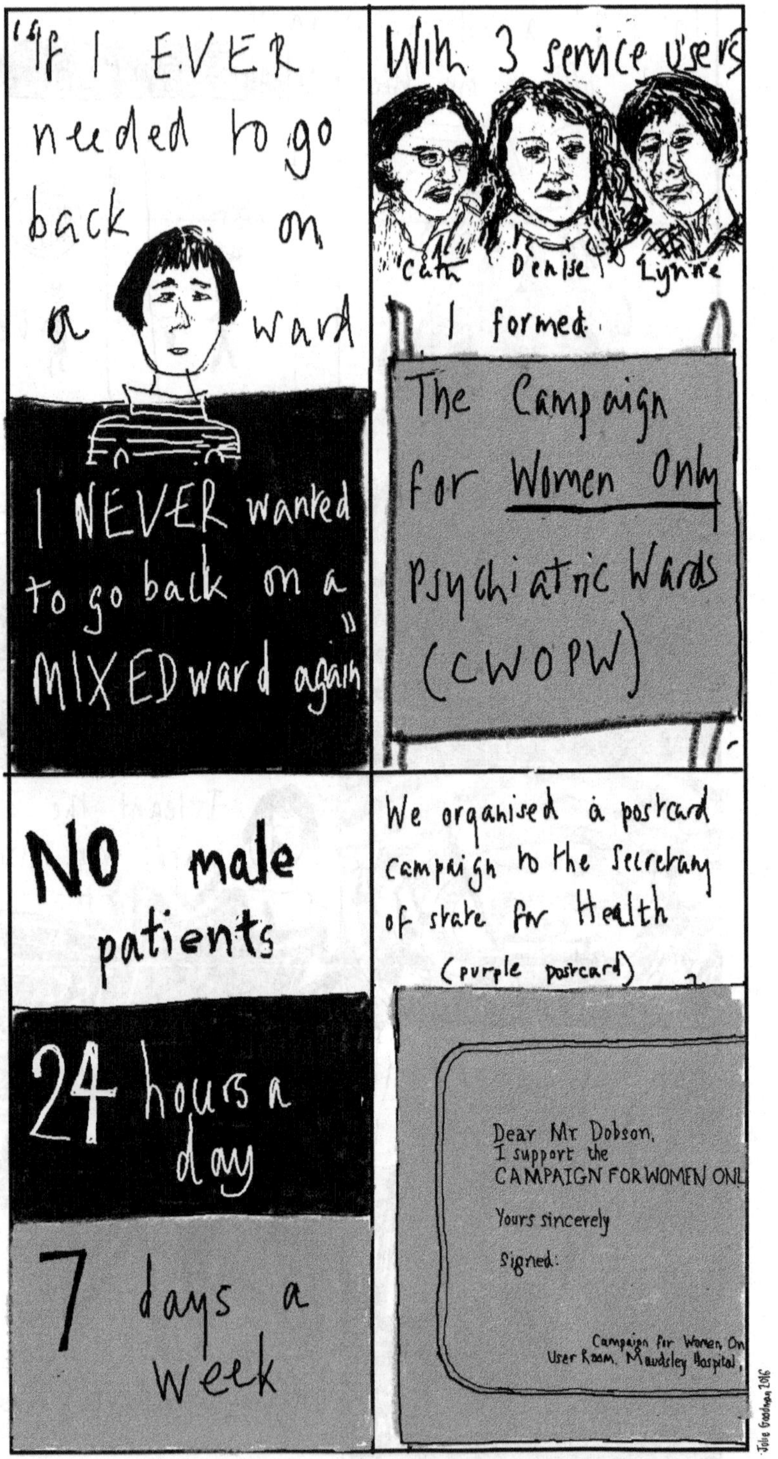

At the 1998 National Mind Conference we spoke of the **rape** and **abuse**, experienced in mixed psychiatric wards, women had written letters to the Campaign about

100s of postcards were received by the Department of Health

At a meeting with the health under-secretary, John Hutton, he told us

The Government can't guarantee women's safety anywhere ....

Dr Julian Lewis MP raised a parliamentary question about mixed psychiatric wards;

so our experiences were heard in the House of Commons and recorded in Hansard.

Entering the games room I tripped over the legs of a man masturbating

Julie Goodman 2016

The national picture was too BIG so we campaigned LOCALLY
South London
Isabel Morris, Borough Director of Southwark Mental Health Services said;
"Women only Wards are a MORAL ISSUE"
In 4 S. London boroughs wards were segregated:
RIVER THAMES
SOUTHWARK 2002
LAMBETH 2002
LEWISHAM 2003/4
CROYDON 2003/4
In Southwark women from the campaign were involved in the planning process for the segregation of the Acute Wards
Women Only Psychiatric Ward
This campaign is important:
It was led by women service users
It was a feminist campaign
It was successful.
Julie Goodman 2016

36

#JusticeforLB: in search of truth, accountability and justice

George Julian and Sara Ryan

What happened?

In March 2013, 18-year-old Connor Sparrowhawk, diagnosed with autism and epilepsy, was admitted to an assessment and treatment unit after becoming intensely agitated and unhappy. He was subsequently sectioned and drowned in the bath there on 4 July. Southern Health NHS Foundation Trust (SHFT) who ran the unit said Connor (known as Laughing Boy or LB) died of natural causes. His mother (Sara Ryan, SR) wrote a blog, mydaftlife, about family life and this became a diary of Connor's time in the unit. This public writing of Connor's story enabled the family to access human rights support when he died and generated outrage among blog followers who came together on social media to create the #JusticeforLB campaign. George Julian (GJ) was a core contributor to the setting up and running of this organic and innovative social media based social movement. The campaign drew on joy, colour and creativity including running a #107daysofaction event which invited people, a year on, to adopt each of the days Connor was in the unit to raise awareness or funds (for legal representation at his inquest).

The 107 days ended up over-subscribed and an extraordinary range of activities happened in Connor's memory. These included sporting events, songs and laments by several choirs, an evening of comedy, dedicated talks and lectures, and arts and crafts activities to raise awareness, including drawing buses, stitching patches for a justice quilt and other craftivism. A further outcome of #107daysofaction was the #LBBill, a crowd sourced private members' bill, focusing on changing the law around the 'placement' of learning disabled people. While so far unsuccessful in securing an MP to adopt the bill, the content is still under deliberation and the draft serves as a reminder of how it is possible to work collaboratively in an open and transparent way.

The campaign reached Canada, the US, New Zealand, Spain, the Philippines and Australia. Mark Sherry, an academic in the US, put forward a motion to the Society for the Study of Social Problems that scholars would examine what happened to Connor further. This was passed unanimously. Disability Studies academics and activists Katherine Runswick Cole and Dan Goodley took a #JusticeforLB flag to Australia and New Zealand, meeting self-advocacy groups, the New Zealand Disability Commissioner and various academic audiences. In 2016, the campaign went to Northern Spain, raising awareness by walking part of the Camino de Santiago and meeting local people and politicians who expressed horror and outrage about what had happened. This activity underlines the awful and continued acceptability of the poor treatment of learning disabled people in the UK.

The campaign was meticulous in scrutinising the public board minutes of SHFT and other, relevant organisations, lobbying, meeting ministers and politicians and continuing to make visible poor practice. We persuaded NHS England to commission a review into patient deaths in SHFT learning disability and mental health provision. This review found that only two out of 337 unexpected deaths in learning disability provision were investigated, less than 1% of older people's deaths in mental health services and 30% of the deaths of people with mental ill health, laying bare the barbaric dismissal of the lives (and deaths) of certain people in the UK.

The campaign has used social media as a tool to raise awareness, create a public record and to provide transparency. We have live tweeted from events and meetings, from SHFT Board meetings, throughout the two-week inquest into Connor's death and most recently while walking the Camino. We have used blogs to share thoughts and pictures, and a number of campaigners have produced videos and films including *The Tale of Laughing Boy*, a 15-minute film produced by professional filmmakers and a self-advocacy group, My Life My Choice, and various animations including *Far Beyond the Pale* by David Harling.

In 2015 a jury at Connor's inquest found his death was due to neglect with serious failings attributed to the Trust.

What does it say to you about conventional services?

What happened to Connor and the subsequent fight for accountability demonstrates how conventional services are inadequate for learning disabled people. There was no appropriate support available to prevent Connor's admission to the unit and, once admitted, there was no understanding of him (or the other patients) as humans with aspirations, hopes and lives to live. In short, we argue that much of conventional services simply miss the point.

Furthermore, the campaign has highlighted how there are no clear lines for accountability in these circumstances. NHS Trusts, and other care providers, typically go on the defensive and try to close down attempts by families to gain answers and the rights of the person who died. Many families have told us they are not allowed to access records or are not allowed to say anything publicly about their experiences. Families are not often aware of their rights and so many have been easily directed down complaints routes that appear to be designed to exhaust a family rather than provide answers or closure. Many families report lengthy processes with little help or clarity from the care providers, Patient Advice and Liaison Services (PALS), or the Public Health Services Ombudsman (PHSO). There can be no doubt that the typical response of private and NHS services is to deny or cover up any wrong doing rather than a quest for answers and improvement.

The campaign also revealed the gulf between the archaic practices of trusts and their lack of understanding of the power and reach of social media; their probably longstanding techniques of telling families whatever they want to tell them, riding roughshod over families and the person who died, are beginning to fray as social media allows a reaching of people, transparency and focus on the tactics used and a democratising of the process.

What problems in campaigning/getting involved have you faced?

The campaign has been run on a voluntary basis with remarkable contributions from a range of people including learning disabled people, self-advocacy groups, politicians, health and social care professionals, human and information rights specialists, disability activists and academics. It has taken a considerable amount of time, particularly for GJ and SR. It has been challenging at times to remain upbeat in the face of relentless and seemingly impermeable obstruction and a refusal to listen. We have tried to keep the campaign positive and lively as well as hard hitting and the balance has sometimes strayed.

Early on we took a leap of faith in actively engaging with print, TV and radio journalists and media. There were concerns about the extent to which our message would be altered or misunderstood; however, the media have been one of our biggest allies. The initial challenge of reaching the general public, especially local to Oxford, was helped by local journalists such as Serena Martin and Phil Gayle who attempted to hold Trust spokespeople to account and shared publicly incredulity at what had happened. Another challenge has been to keep on top of media coverage of the campaign and we benefitted enormously from the skill and commitment of Liz Piercy who archived all mentions of the campaign in the media, Hansard or other publications and made them available on mydaftlife.

An ongoing challenge has been how to effectively keep people's interest. The appalling treatment of learning disabled people is not a good news story, is not a simple story, and is not one that everyone is likely to readily engage with. We have used many different visual hooks and approaches to create conversations and challenge people to take notice of these issues. One problem has been the apathy of large scale charities that dominate the campaigning landscape with their own campaigns and agendas. Often these organisations (who provide services as well as campaign) appear unprepared to go far enough in pushing forward necessary change.

A related challenge has been campaigning about NHS failings at a time when the NHS is under immense pressure and political will looks to be seeking justifications for privatisation. We have faced defensiveness, outrage and accusations of NHS 'bashing'. It appears that, for some, staff morale and a focus on reputation are more important than improving services.

What have you learned from this experience about getting involved/things you might do differently?

The campaign emerged organically as a result of outrage felt by readers of SR's blog, her family and friends. Much of the success of the campaign has been a result of this ongoing organic development. We have not wasted time and energy on formal organisation, strategy or planning meetings (although they may have helped at times), conducting risk assessments or worrying about key performance indicators or targets. The underpinning principle has been that all contributions are welcome. People self-identify as 'JusticeforLBers', there is no membership form or entry criteria. Nearly all our requests for support have been made loosely and publicly, for example 'Would you like to adopt a day for 107days?'; 'Would you like to stitch a gingerbread man?'; 'Would you like to donate to support My Life My Choice to join the Camino?' and we have been repeatedly surprised and delighted at the support generated.

In some respects, our lack of bureaucracy and organisation combined with our social media savviness enable us to respond to issues as they arose in real time in contrast to the typically sanitised responses of large national charities. We are weary of the government being 'called upon' every time there is an unfolding atrocity story involving learning disabled people. At the same time, these organisations can draw on such remarkable resources that they have considerable influence in agenda setting. We're left unsure whether we could have combined #JusticeforLB with existing charities so we could have access to the resources they hold. Ultimately, however, we are left thinking that these organisations have grown too far from their original purposes to offer the necessary forthright, evidence based challenges.

What does your experience say about how social policy and services could be different?

Our experiences demonstrate how the gulf between policy and practice, with a historical backdrop of consistently failing learning disabled people, remains. We have the evidence, there has been too much talking, we now need action to actually improve things. Relentless policy rhetoric has worn thin in this area. The unfunded campaign of committed people prepared to act, revealed further, terrible evidence of inhumane practice. We are encouraged by strong support from those not connected to the learning disability 'arena' that this simply unacceptable. Removing the 'learning disability' goggles and engaging people as human, first and foremost, can only lead to improvements in people's lives.

Section Two: The role of online platforms and social media

37

Guerilla policy: new platforms for making policy from below

Michael Harris

What if that machinery were reversed? What if the habits, problems, actions, and decisions of the wealthy and powerful were daily scrutinized by a thousand systematic researchers, were hourly pried into, analysed, and cross referenced, tabulated and published in a hundred inexpensive mass-circulation journals and written so that even the fifteen-year-old high school drop-outs could understand it ... ? (Martin Nicolaus, 1968)[1]

Introduction

My interest in a new participatory social policy has been inspired by two things: co-production, and the internet. These led me to establish Guerilla Policy – a website platform to argue for a different approach to making policy, and as a (work-in-progress) demonstration of grassroots policy thinking and commentary.

Co-production means designing and delivering services with people, in recognition of their expertise about their own lives. This goes well beyond merely consulting with service users, to designing services around people's (often ignored) capabilities – a fundamental break with seeing people as the passive dependents of professionals in public services (for example, Harris and Boyle, 2009).

The internet has enabled new forms of individual and collective expression, creativity and collaboration across virtually every sector – from websites that allow people to rate everything from hotels to video games, to myriad forms of user-generated content.

One of the areas that seems largely untouched by either of these trends – and how they might be combined – is how we develop policy. Instead, despite widespread public dissatisfaction with the political class and with political institutions, we remain subjects to a closed 'policy priesthood'.[2]

I've seen this close up and been part of it (marginally anyway). I've worked in and around think tanks, central and local government, corporate charities and public services. Not only is how we make policy undemocratic and unrepresentative: because we largely exclude experience and expertise from the frontline, we produce poor quality policy – weakly evidenced, badly designed, and difficult if not impossible to implement. As a result of policy failure, we lurch from one hoped-for 'silver bullet' to the next (which sustains the market for new ideas at least). This is wasteful, ineffective and counter-productive.

The need for a different kind of think tank

To me, think tanks exemplify the problem. In their original inception, they were meant to improve objective and 'scientific' (evidence-based) policy analysis and formulation. With some notable exceptions, many think tanks today are led more by ideology and interests. Those think tanks that are closest to government typically share the same assumptions as many policymakers – for example, about the imperative of outsourcing and privatising public services, often directly on behalf of interests who would benefit commercially.

It is possible though to imagine a different kind of think tank, and a different way of developing policy. We could start by recognising the many people and groups that are already doing this, and how they are using the internet and social media to do it.

In the UK, disability rights groups such as Spartacus and DPAC (Disabled People Against Cuts) have been challenging government 'welfare reforms' and researching alternative approaches. Such groups have been at the forefront of recording the human cost of 'reform' – the hidden deaths, the broken assessment systems, the bureaucracy, and other examples of dysfunctional policy.

Education bloggers have been vigorously debating not only practice but policy, especially around the 'standards agenda' and the government standards regulator in England, Ofsted. They have also developed their own education reform and improvement manifestos, for example the Headteachers' Roundtable group.

Policing also has a very active online presence, through blogs, Facebook and Twitter, and which has been part of an unusually political (for police services) debate about cuts and the effects on policing and community safety. There are many others.

I call these and many others 'guerilla policymakers' – 'guerilla' in the sense of guerilla marketing, which is to say unofficial, unorthodox, reliant on energy rather than privileged position or money, and without having asked anyone for 'permission'.

I've been struck by a number of things about these bloggers. They are often extremely well-informed, critical, committed, passionate, sometimes angry, and don't share the assumptions of the policy priesthood. They are numerous (we publish more than 500 on the site). Some have been blogging for years, others are new. Some are more like personal journals, others have loyal audiences larger than many mainstream media columnists.

Because many of them work at the frontline of public services or are personally affected by policy decisions, they are sceptical of silver bullet ideas and especially large-scale structural reform of services (now often branded as 'innovation'). They are much more interested in the practical complexities of improving services, and how policy often inhibits this. Creating a hub for them has also helped some sector-focused bloggers to take a broader perspective, for example to recognise the similar currents of ideologically-imposed 'reform' across sectoral boundaries.

Of course, there have long been civil society organisations. Many have developed recommendations for policy. The difference now is how they are enabled by cheap and widely-available technologies, and how quickly they can form and mobilise. Among others, the Occupy protests and more recently Black Lives Matter show the revolutionary potential of grassroots movements enabled by social media. There are also platforms such as 38 Degrees (in the UK), Avaaz, Change.org and so on, which promote and aggregate campaigning efforts.

The coming disruption of policymaking

What is noticeable is the absence of conventional political actors and institutions from these discussions. Traditional, limited forms of consultation are largely discredited for their lack of integrity and transparency, but new forms of more meaningful engagement with civil society haven't been developed.

Echoing co-production, government and think tanks could regard frontline workers, independent groups and grassroots campaigns as equal partners in developing policy. What would emerge would be better researched, more credible, more reliable, and more grounded in real life. What we don't yet have is a platform for co-producing policy, one that policymakers, if they wished to, could draw on to develop better policy.

Oddly, the thought is sometimes expressed that opening up policy in this way would be somehow undemocratic, that for example it would raise issues of fair representation (as if our current approaches to policy are representative).

I think the real objection though, mostly unstated for obvious reasons, is that the dominant 'ideology' of policymaking is profoundly anti-participatory. This is the direct outcome of neoliberal arguments about how the state is supposedly captured by 'producer interests' such as professions and trade unions (though there seems to be less concern about the capture of policymaking by elite and corporate interests). It's tragic that the result has been to discount the views and perspectives of service providers and users as 'interested parties', when this is precisely what makes them so valuable for policy development.

I don't think this will hold. Just as traditional media, to take just one example, is being disrupted and reshaped, it's inevitable that traditional means of policymaking will also be overturned. Technological and social change are almost impossible to resist, especially in combination.

We need a new approach to developing policy based on co-production principles, facilitated by technology, and drawing on ideas and energy of the proliferating groups, networks, and individuals who are already engaging in policy and social change in new and diverse ways.

Conclusion

I believe we could create a different type of think tank, based on new 'platforms' for co-producing policy – non-hierarchical, much more open and diverse, and much more expert.

The precise practices and techniques and challenges of engagement and participation are not the focus in the limited space available here. There are many experts, organisations and resources better placed than me on these matters; many of them can be found in this book.

This isn't just about how we make policy. It's about the health of our democracies, and it should be especially important for progressives. A revolution in how we make policy needs to be at the heart of progressive politics. Beyond a tired centre-left managerialism that claims to speak for people, progressivism needs to find new ways to help people represent themselves. Without changing how we make policy, nothing else is possible.

No one can be sure about where these trends will lead, but it feels like we're at a tipping point – one at which, to paraphrase Martin Nicolaus, the machinery of knowledge is being thrown into reverse.

The Guerilla Policy website can be found at www.guerillawire.org

Notes

[1] I came across this quote only recently, in Slater (2016). It comes from Nicolaus (1968).

[2] The term 'policy priesthood' has been used most commonly to describe the establishment in American foreign policy. Daniel Bell (1976) used the term 'priesthood' to describe the rise of a dominant professional technocratic elite.

References

Bell, D. (1976) *The coming of post-industrial society*, New York: Basic Books.

Harris, M. and Boyle, D. (2009) *The challenge of co-production*, London: nef/Nesta.

Nicolaus, M. (1968) *Fat-cat sociology: Remarks at the American Sociological Association Convention*, http://nicolaus.com/wp-content/uploads/writings/fatcat.pdf

Slater, T. (2016) 'The housing crisis in neoliberal Britain: free market think tanks and the production of ignorance', in S. Springer, K. Birch and J. MacLeavy (eds) *Handbook of Neoliberalism*, Abingdon: Routledge, pp 370–81.

38

A Magna Carta for learning disabled people

Kaliya Franklin and Gary Bourlet

The year 2015 marked the 800th anniversary of the Magna Carta, but we would argue that learning disabled people remain 'villeins', who are denied rights against arbitrary power. So what would a Magna Carta for look like for learning disabled people living in Britain today?

Who are the 'villeins' today?

> No free man shall be seized or imprisoned, or stripped of his rights or possessions, or outlawed or exiled, or deprived of his standing in any other way, nor will be proceed with force against him, or send others to do so, except by the lawful judgment of his equals or by the law of the land. To no one will we sell, to no one deny or delay right or justice.

Eight hundred years ago this set of freedoms was made law in England and, although Magna Carta is widely believed to have been the first 'Human Rights Act', it actually excluded most of the population. It did not apply to 'villeins' – the ordinary people. The Lords, Barons and 'free men' were granted the right to be judged by their own peers in courts of law. Most people were villeins and outside this new law.

Are people with learning disabilities our modern day villeins? The rights and positions of people with learning disabilities are not judged by juries of their peers but by systems where power is held by 'lords' – commissioners, social workers, service providers, psychiatrists, judges and politicians.

Social progress – but learning disabled people left behind

In Britain, the latter half of the 20th century was a time of social and economic change. The horrors of two global conflicts led to the breakdown of the formerly dominant class system in the UK, which had evolved from the earlier feudal system. The conditions imposed by combat affected all people, but the working classes realised that, having been essential to victory, they were now in a position to organise and achieve change.

The welfare state was introduced, healthcare was available to all, there was an ambition for homes for all. Employment was high, which meant that work was available to more people than before, including those people who had become disabled during conflict.

However, those born with their disabilities still tended to be excluded, often not even considered in this brave new world of freedoms. This group of people lived away from mainstream society, often in large buildings set just outside of towns, segregated from 'normal people'.

The 1960s and 1970s were also times of social change as groups still denied their freedoms fought for the rights everyone else had begun to take for granted – to live, love and work freely. This sense of radicalism penetrated the institutions in which disabled people lived. Disabled people fought to prove that everyone deserved the freedom to make their own choices over life, to be educated, and not forced to live away from mainstream communities.

This rights-based development is closely tied to the development of social security. Various allowances were introduced that enabled people to purchase some practical help. This new ability to get around independently meant that for the first time disabled people were able to travel, to shop, to socialise and for some enter higher education and plan careers.

However, one group of disabled people was left behind during this revolutionary time – those with learning disabilities. For learning disabled people, their long walk to freedom was to commence much later, and the abuses that had to be overcome are still occurring today. In the 1980s, community care policy meant the closure of large, long stay institutions in Britain. It was more about a political belief that it would be cheaper to keep people in their own flats than it was a desire to emancipate a disempowered group of people. For some learning disabled people community care freedoms were eagerly taken up. But for many more the reality of community care was being ripped away from the only homes and families they had ever known and sent to live isolated, unsupported lives.

Choosing where to live

In modern Britain, within the limits of financial resources, most of us expect to grow up and live in our own homes as adults. But even now, the options available to those with learning disabilities in adult life are severely restricted, and becoming ever more restricted as public sector funding cuts in Britain are felt in people's daily lives. Some people do live 'independently' – in a typical dwelling in the community. This option is only really available to those with learning disabilities who are the most able AND who have families supporting their right to live independently.

Independent living means having the support required to do so. But frequently those able to live independently with support do not reach the restrictive level of eligibility set for social care in Britain. Without supportive family or friends to ask for assistance this can threaten the person's ability to continue living independently.

What are the alternatives to independent living? Some people live with their families. Sometimes this is a positive choice which everyone in the family is happy about and sometimes it is a negative option where the adult with learning disabilities cannot leave the family home due to a lack of support or appropriate accommodation.

Another possibility is supported living, which may or may not be in an institutional environment. It usually implies a group of people more likely to qualify for support than those living independently. People might be supported in a typical flat or house either living alone, or live with someone else who requires a similar level of support who will be chosen for the person by the authorities.

Shared lives means living with a family, not your own family, to be supported towards gaining the skills and independence needed to move into supported or independent living, or it is sometimes a life-long arrangement.

Other learning disabled people still have no choice but to live in a residential environment – a nursing, care or group home. While a very small proportion of people do choose residential care for themselves, like all these options for living, they are mostly made 'for' people by family members or professionals.

The last place in which we find learning disabled people living are 'Assessment Treatment Units', often hidden away on the edges of industrial estates, and certainly far from typical communities, these are the modern equivalent of the old institutions. The British public only become vaguely aware of their existence when incidents like the torture and abuse at Winterbourne View unit in South Gloucestershire, England, reach their TV screens.

Free and equal citizenship denied

Even for those people with learning disabilities who have been sufficiently fortunate to be well supported to live independently, there are still many issues that restrict their freedoms and prevent full participation as citizens.

These range from things like exercising your right to vote, being able to get a job, to marry, to raise your children or even to live free from persecution of the state. Sadly the list of such examples is long and all too easy to find individuals who have had these rights removed. Two such cases are that of Kerry Robertson and Stephanie Bincliffe.

Kerry Robertson's case made headlines as social services had tried to prevent her marriage. Kerry and her husband Mark fled from their home country of Scotland in an attempt to escape their local authority's controlling approach to their lives. If there were truly issues surrounding consent and child protection, then of course the state has a duty to investigate, but given that Kerry and Mark have been deemed perfectly capable of parenting by another local authority social services department, it is difficult to see this as anything but a deliberate restriction of freedoms based solely on Kerry having a mild learning disability.

Kerry's experiences of having her freedoms restricted by the state are bad enough, but pale in comparison to that of Stephanie Bincliffe who had more significant learning disabilities and the label of 'challenging behaviour'.

'Challenging behaviour' can mean anything from a learning disabled person being uncooperative with the desires of other people, through to a whole spectrum of behaviours that are harmful to that individual or others. It is a label that is uniquely applied to those with learning disabilities, and is often punished or results in referral to an Assessment Treatment Unit.

For Stephanie, during the seven years of her detention by the state, freedom must have seemed so very far away. Stephanie was taken into an Assessment Treatment Unit at the age of 18. She was held in a 'safe room', which amounted to a padded cell with a tiny, bare patch of outdoor space; she slept on a beanbag and was fed through a hatch in the door to her 'room'. When Stephanie died, aged 25, still in that padded cell, it was due to the complications of morbid obesity.

What would Robin Hood do?

For the 2015 Magna Carta anniversary year we wanted to consider what a modern day British folk hero like Robin Hood would do about this situation. How could she help this excluded and often powerless group of modern villeins take up their power and gain their freedoms? This led us to questions about UK legislation – would a new Magna Carta aimed specifically at this group be effective, or would we need something entirely new?

We considered many options, but eventually concluded that these were the three priorities for gaining freedom and equality:

1. A fund that is specifically aimed at supporting people to live independently, where the money is contributed by those who earn over a certain amount and distributed fairly.
2. Support for people to build resilient communities where people look after each other, and ensure that nobody is hungry or isolated, bringing all classes of people together.
3. Taking action against the bullies who deprive learning disabled people of their freedoms and sometimes even their lives and seeking justice in partnership with those learning disabled people.

We asked the question 'how can people with learning disabilities take up their power and move away from being villeins or serfs?' The conclusion was that the most important part of this was about being accepted, and integrated into the community from the earliest ages.

To enable people to take up their rights, these kind of aspirations are not enough. Like the original Magna Carta, which for the first time limited the power of the king, legislation will be required to provide a clearer structure of legal freedoms and obligations.

We think that a new Magna Carta would be based on the United Nations Convention on the Rights of Persons with Disabilities, the UK Human Rights Act 1998 and Care Act 2014. The legal priorities would be being considered truly equal, the freedom from torture or cruel treatment, whether at the hands of the state or not, and the ability to live both freely and safely.

To enact these principles we believe there would have to be a statutory right to independent living and the support required to achieve it; a culture change to respect people's existing rights, such as ensuring those with learning disabilities are not denied their legal right to vote; and supporting people to have friends and relationships.

In addition to legislation we think that independent advocacy, joined up services and a culture of supportive enablement instead of deprivation of liberty at crisis points would be needed.

Finally, in considering our new future we needed to think about what freedom would be and how that might look. We decided that freedom would be:

> A world where you could wake up in a comfortable home and go to work being safe and valued. There would be no inequality or discrimination. There would be the right to sufficient financial support to feed, house and clothe yourself and your family. You could make your own choices about where you want to live and what support, if any, you would need. There would be free access to transport and free medical care. Education would be free and available for all. People would be free to love and befriend as they choose.

Acknowledgements

The original version of this article was published under a Creative Commons Attribution-NonCommercial 4.0 International licence as an openDemocracy.net blog: opendemocracy.net/ourkingdom/kaliya-franklin-and-gary-bourlet/magna-carta-for-learning-disabled-people

Many thanks to openDemocracy for granting permission to publish an edited version of the original blog here.

39

Pat's Petition: the emerging role of social media and the internet

Pat Onions and others

Pat's Petition is a group that campaigns about the 'perfect storm' of UK political and social policy changes impacting on disabled people and carers, concentrating particularly on so-called 'welfare reform' (Machin et al, 2014). It is a pioneer in a development that has international implications. Formed in 2011, it was set up originally to launch an e-petition on what was then a new UK government website to enable online petitions. Any petition raising 100,000 signatories would be debated in parliament. Although it was one of the most successful early campaigns, Pat's Petition did not reach the required number of signatories, but was awarded a debate in Parliament by the Labour Party. The group continue to campaign, occupying a unique position in taking a neutral political line and being inclusive of both disabled people and carers, consistently championing their cause and focusing on a 'safety net' of support.

Part of the impetus behind starting the e-petition came from the realisation that many disabled people and carers could not take part in demonstrations and marches or even get out easily to meet in groups. The internet opened up connections and made it possible to find people with comparable interests for peer support and community. This has been life changing for many disabled people and carers including Pat herself, who is blind, and previously could not communicate beyond a limited circle of friends. However, as she describes the difficulties of file formats, including on official websites, and the slow speed of hearing emails in comparison to other's speed reading, it is clear that difficulties of access for disabled people have not been completely overcome by electronic communication.

The new opportunities for contact through the internet soon moved on to people being able to join together to campaign. Discussions highlighted the similarity of concerns and that complaints are often dismissed one by one, year in and year out, in different areas, all over the country and internationally. Joining together on the web, enabled individuals who had previously been excluded from traditional campaigning to make themselves heard. As individuals, group members had years of experience of trying to get things changed, and had piles of paper with polite yet dismissive replies to prove it! The letters invariably explained that, because of lack of funding, nothing could be done to change things. The e-petition was the start of a long-lasting initiative to campaign by and for disabled people and carers.

Campaigning online was new to the group members. For the first few years, most of the group had never met each other in person, and for some that is still the case, and yet they have made strong connections through campaigning together: They have built up contacts and yet never meet face to face. They have created trust in each other, agreeing to disagree where necessary, but always focusing on their main aims, with members of the group contributing more or less as needed in relation to their personal circumstances. The commitment to democratic working ensured that everyone worked hard to reach a compromise that they could all agree on, so that if any one member felt strongly against a decision, the group would look for alternative solutions.

People becoming involved have been self taught when it comes to the skills required for blogs and social media, but over time, as a group, they gained the confidence with these new skills. They could see it was a much faster way, and easier, to grow the necessary contact list to give a level of engagement never known before: "a bit like the proverbial pebble in the water. You can post something online and depending on the interest it can go viral so quickly", such that

> 'I'll never forget that night when we each sat in our own homes watching the computer screen showing the numbers increasing until we hit our first 10,000 signatories. There was a tangible sense of a community, with each other and with all these other strangers who agreed with our ideas.'

The internet thus enabled the group to form and continue such that "obviously we wouldn't exist without the internet", but members emphasise that the internet is not always a positive force:

> 'The flip side to being open and able to make connections, is the amount of negativity that people can face, such that it can feel like people just want to vent and blog and post comments. That doesn't really make a conversation or encourage debate.'

Members of Pat's Petition with a longer history suggest that it has changed. In the early days, the joy of making contact with others with the same problem was intoxicating. The main feelings were of friendship and comradeship, and the internet was a liberation. But then it changed. Strands emerged that made it toxic and tribal, to the extent that members now question whether it is possible to operate in a tabloid and vengeful atmosphere where groups jostle for power, accusing each other of monopolising campaigning, yet not wanting to move in their different positions. They feel that they have seen the debates move from constructive criticism to something more destructive that wastes the time and energies of all involved, so that it can feel like organising and moving forward together will never work. Existing tribal political groups remain influential; existing vested interests like charities kill off new initiatives; independent groups that do get going may get dominated by one strong personality. And at the end of the day, the fundamental measure is improvements in the lives of disabled people and carers and whether the government of the day listens to and acts on the demands of campaigners.

This increasingly challenging online environment is not a problem particular to disability: it's a problem for all social media now and the providers and politicians are looking for solutions. It may perhaps be that the skills for campaigning together online are still being developed and that the internet may go on and fulfil the hopes of the early days. Or it may be a point in time where, as campaigners, we need to actively intervene and find ways to develop the skills to enable diverse groups to work together. As one member suggested, "I hear about the bullying, shouting and much swearing from others in groups. I keep away rather than put myself through it." Whereas another member said, "The only reason I am still here is because our group is closed and safe. Every time I step outside it gets harder and nastier."

Certainly, there are many differences among disabled people and carers, so that it is hard to unite such a disparate group to any one solution to a problem. The experience of Pat's Petition suggests that carers have found it easier to come together in online discussion groups because their charities are global whereas issues of disability are often divided by condition. But even here, there is a deep chasm between the campaign aims of pensioner carers and working age carers. Pat's Petition has also emphasised that there is a tension between campaigns against the new UK disability benefit Employment Support Allowance (ESA), splitting disabled people into groups who campaign for better inclusion and access to paid work and those who campaign for a safety net in the welfare system for those who may not be able to do paid work.

The internet is not going back into the bottle. It has been a life transforming development for people with limited mobility and opportunities for inclusion. Unfortunately it has more recently developed toxic tendencies. Pat's Petition feel that it would be tragic not to take internet campaigning forward and so it is imperative that we all get together and find ways of recovering friendly, co-operative ways of working together to achieve the aims of supporting all disabled people and carers.

References

Pat's Petition website: https://patspetition.wordpress.com/

Original e-petition: 'Stop and review the cuts to benefits and services which are falling disproportionately on disabled families, their carers and families', https://petition.parliament.uk/archived/petitions/20968

Machin, K., O'Neill, R., Onions, P. and all other group members (2014) 'Pat's Petition: A new approach to online campaigning', *Groupwork*, 24 (1), 9–25.

Part VII
Breaking down barriers

In Part VII we explore some of the barriers that have long operated in social policy, to exclude particular voices, perspectives and experience. We look at how these have developed and how they can be broken down. The first section focuses on overcoming divisions associated with people's different sexualities. The second makes clear that participatory social policy can and perhaps should mean much more than consulting with people or market researching them.

Section One: Inclusion and difference in the formulation and operation of social policy

For contributor Sue Sanders, her job as a teacher, her identity as a lesbian and her experiences of homophobic British government policy resulting in classroom discrimination and censorship propelled her to strategic equal rights campaigning for lesbian, gay and bisexual (LGB) people. In her opening chapter, she describes her involvement with establishing UK LGBT History month as a tactical way to support the implementation of new LGB and later, Trans★ (T) equality policies. Christine Burns' chapter tells the story of how a silenced, 'social pariah' group found a voice and challenged an absence of legislation and policy, which left them without rights or protections. She explores the fight for transgender recognition and rights in the UK, and her role in the campaign, characterised by visibility and voice often gained through strategic legal action.

Section Two: User-led approaches to social policy

Participation in public policy is often seen narrowly in terms of user involvement, partnerships and collaborations. These are still probably the most common approaches to participation in place and mainly mean service users' inputting their knowledge, experience and expertise into essentially traditional policy processes. However, some of the most effective and ground-breaking developments are 'user led' or 'user controlled' and these offer some of the most significant insights. It is this end of the spectrum of involvement that the contributors in this section are concerned with. Each of the three brings new insights to bear.

First, academic and educator Helen Casey discusses a newly coined international idea in professional education, pioneered in social work. It is called 'gap-mending'.

Its aim is to break down divisions and barriers between people as service users and service workers/learners. The focus is on doing it in a way that brings the people together, helps them to understand each other and highlights ourselves in our learning and education instead of reinforcing separations/differences/gaps between us.

Sam Barnett-Cormack then writes about the collective virtual disability activism and rapid mobilisation of the Spartacus Network and their work on producing and disseminating evidence to challenge UK government welfare benefit reforms, culminating in 'Responsible Reform: A Report on the proposed changes to Disability Living Allowance' – also known as the 'Spartacus report'. Finally, psychiatric system survivors Sarah Yiannoullou and Alison Faulkner report how a national service user network has collectively created national standards for involvement to enable coherent campaigning and effective participation and co-production in mental health policy and practice.

40

"LGBT History Month is a thing!"
The story of an equal rights campaign

Sue Sanders

Introduction

In 2016 someone said to me, "LGBT History Month is a thing!"

I agree. It is a vibrant, loving celebration of all things lesbian gay bisexual and trans (LGBT), across the UK every February. By 2016, it had been going for 11 years. There have been literally thousands of events up and down the country, from big conferences backed by local authorities, universities or unions, to exhibitions in libraries and museums, events in pubs, clubs theatres and churches. Many are organised like LGBT History Month itself is, by unpaid volunteers. Some are now embedded in institutions' zeitgeist, so are part of each year's calendar.

UK LGBT History Month: Origins

Prior to the establishment of LGBT History Month in 2005, positive media images of LGBT people were few and far between. Section 28 of the UK Local Government Act 1988 stated:

A local authority shall not—

(a) intentionally promote homosexuality or publish material with the intention of promoting homosexuality;
(b) promote the teaching in any maintained school of the acceptability of homosexuality as a pretended family relationship.

It had cast a long shadow. Though there were no prosecutions under Section 28 in England, Wales and Scotland, its censoring effect had been all-powerful, particularly in schools.

Censorship and self-censorship meant that children were denied information about the existence of LGBT people in the past or present. This constituted a denial, therefore, of the rich and various contributions made by them to society, here in Britain and round the world.

We had been 'invisibilised' consciously and unconsciously and we needed to change that. In 2003, Section 28 was repealed and Schools OUT could see that more laws were in the pipeline to promote human rights for LGBT people in the UK.

Laws are crucial in enabling groups who have been discriminated against to gain their rights, but that is only half the story. We LGBT folk had been vilified for years in the media. Some depicted us as child molesters or sexual fiends, if mentioned at all, thus enabling dangerous stereotypes to take root.

Founded in 1974 (and then known as the Gay Teachers group) Schools OUT (now known as Schools OUT UK) has been busy for years, providing resources and training to schools that challenge institutional homophobia. Our website has many unique resources that supported LGBT and heterosexual teachers to teach inclusive lessons and develop a whole school approach to make all their pupils safe.

We are aware that all too often we have been talking to the converted. We usually depended on one teacher in a school to initiate change. This was because in the 1990s and 2000s, many schools were not ready for a cultural shift.

A strategic approach to implementing equality policy

With the UK New Labour Government promoting a Single Equality Policy, including a Public Equality Duty in 2003, Schools OUT were heartened but knew that the resources for a proactive strategy were not in place.

Black History Month was a successful tool in schools that had legitimised and encouraged teachers to educate about black people and their history and to recognise the need to tackle racism.

In 2004, Co-Chair Paul Patrick and I, having seen the effect of Black History Month, discussed the potential of an LGBT History Month. With the support of the Schools OUT committee, we decided to initiate and promote it.

Our strategy was to gain as much publicity and credibility for an LGBT February as possible. If we were to challenge the dearth of coverage and the negative embedded status of LGBT people we needed to make a big splash and achieve the support of ethical and respected public figures.

We approached the UK Department for Education and Skills, asking them for a small grant to enable us to set up a website and, while they said 'Yes', written confirmation came after we had to announce it. We took this risk to enable the first LGBT History Month to take place in 2005.

So we were able to buy the website and pay a history lecturer and web technician, Gill Spraggs, to set it up. She designed a website that is both informative and interactive, as we wanted.

People and organisations could put the details of their LGBT History Month event on a calendar within the website. We could publicise their activities by promoting the website.

It included new resources about LGBT people through the ages, in all their diversity, and we provided links to other useful pre-existing websites.

Schools OUT was run by unpaid volunteers who could devote time to the work only after a doing a paid job, so this was a very ambitious project.

We attracted attention in both the press and the House of Commons, mostly negative. We were accused of telling 5-year-olds about gay sex, wasting public money and being achingly politically correct!

However, we struck the right note with many public and cultural institutions. Over the years we have had thousands of events on our calendar and we know there are many other events around the country that do not make it to the site.

We chose February, as we wanted to exploit the month when schools are relatively quiet, and as we expected that museums and libraries would be the first to use the half term break. This has proved true to this day. Teachers, parents and students can often see LGBT themed exhibitions, in such places as the British Museum, the Museum of London, the People's History Museum, Manchester, and libraries and other museums around the UK, that can give them both the confidence and resources to take the ideas back to their schools and classrooms.

Embedding LGBT anti-discrimination policy

The New Labour Government commissioned The Lawrence Report (Macpherson, 1999), which defined institutional racism and recognised the need to deal with hate crime. This raised newly awareness was one of the drivers for the equality legislation that followed. It supported the proliferation of equality training and equality posts in both the private and public sector. There was a recognition of both the moral and business need for the inclusion of all groups that had been marginalised and/or vilified.

As a Management Consultant I delivered equality training to members of the Criminal Justice System (CJS). As Co-Chair of Schools OUT, I sat on several Independent Advisory Groups set up to challenge institutional homophobia.

The CJS were keen to be seen to be supportive of LGBT History Month as they wanted to get the message across to a community they had neglected that they were now taking hate crime seriously.

Their opportunity came in supporting the high profile launches that we organise every November to remind people of the next LGBT History Month. The CJS and others advertise in the various LGBT History Month journals that have now sprung up.

We have wooed and involved both the movers and shakers in the public sector and the grassroots organisations of LGBT communities.

We want to make all our multiple identities within the LGBT community visible, so we promulgated intersectionality long before that term was coined.

"LGBT History Month is a thing." It is now celebrated in many schools, colleges and universities. Most libraries and many museums have not only held events in February but have looked at how they might make themselves inclusive of LGBT issues and themes throughout the year. Every year at the LGBT Trades Union Congress conference there are motions that include the promotion and involvement of LGBT History Month.

The month has evolved. We set a theme for every year, which enables us to promote our contributions in all areas. We link themes to the curriculum and produce classroom resources so that we make it as easy as possible for teachers to educate out prejudice. We also produce a badge for every year, which reflects the theme, which is designed by students as part of their course in design at University of Bedford. The money we raise for them is our one constant, other monies we raise are mainly from unions and supporters; as we have no core funding we function on a shoe string!

Conclusion

Changing cultural attitudes about a group of people is a complex affair. The amazing journey we have been on in Britain since 1967, when partial male homosexuality was partially decriminalised, has not been a straight line. Few would have guessed back then that we would have same-sex adoption in 2002 and same-sex marriage in 2010.

Laws do not always mean cultural change. In South Africa, which has one of the most advanced constitutions, with LGBT rights enshrined, we witness the unchecked corrective rape of lesbians; other countries water down their laws with the introduction of anti-propaganda laws.

Now, in 2016, the UK is embarking on a new venture, the extrication of the UK from the European Union and the European Court of Human Rights. The Court was responsible for making many aspects of discrimination against LGBT people illegal, in an effort to restore our rights. With that link gone we will need to be more vigilant, monitor government actions and encourage each other to get to know and value their diverse LGBT neighbours.

LGBT History Month, coming as it does from both inside and outside of the mainstream, provides a platform for educating all of us about a community and individuals who have been a crucial part of our history.

Theatre, film, art, poetry, music and sport have been the foci of past LGBT History Months. Outing the Past Festivals, our latest initiative, led by Jeff Evans, are hosted in cities throughout England. They broaden our scope by adding both academic and popular presentations of LGBT History. When we learn through the heart as well as the head understanding grows and we find what it takes to stand up to prejudice and ignorance, and to change policy so it changes society.

Reference

Macpherson, W. (1999) *The Stephen Lawrence Inquiry: Report of an inquiry*, Cm 4262-I, The Stationery Office.

41

Progressing gender recognition and trans rights in the UK

Christine Burns

Introduction

The UK House of Commons passed the Gender Recognition Bill by a majority of 355 votes to 46 at 7.11pm on Tuesday 25 May 2004. Having already been debated by the House of Lords, the new and virtually unamended legislation completed the remaining formalities quickly and received Royal Assent on 1 July 2004 (Burns, 2014: Foreword) The following spring, in April 2005, the new Act of Parliament came into full effect and several thousand British transsexual women and men began applying for legal recognition of their acquired gender.

Women became recognised as women, men as men – for all purposes in UK law. Successful applicants received replacement birth certificates to protect their privacy, and it became an offence for officials learning about a transsexual person's gender reassignment history to disclose that to a third party without consent (except in specifically defined instances). It also became possible for transsexual women to marry men (or enter a Civil Partnership with another woman) and vice versa for transsexual men. The new law provided a resolution to a nightmare that transsexual people had contended with for 34 years. While not the first law to be changed by their activism, the new Act was the prize that trans campaigners had fought to obtain for more than a dozen. And yet the most remarkable thing was that the whole legislative process had taken place with so little discourse in the conventional media-hosted sense. The reasons for that will become plain in this account.

The backstory

But first some background ... British transsexual people had experienced serious problems with the official view of their gender for 34 years. That was since a high stakes divorce case involving the former model April Ashley and her estranged husband Arthur Corbett led to all transsexual men and women being regarded forever as their birth gender for the purposes of marriage law (*Corbett v Corbett*, 1970). Thirteen years later that decision was widened through another case to dictate that transsexual women and men were to be regarded as their birth assigned gender for all purposes in law, not just marriage (*R v Tan*, 1983). The two decisions ended a period when transsexual people had hitherto enjoyed unofficial recognition in their new genders. The Register of Births would be annotated at the discretion of a sympathetic registrar and new certificates could be issued, permitting transsexual people to go about their lives with identification that matched their lived reality. Indeed, it was on that kind of 'grace and favour' basis that April Ashley, and others like her, had been able to marry. That all ended as a result of the court judgments though – underlining just what a precarious position it had been. And nobody was in any hurry to put that right.

Elsewhere in Europe several states passed legislation on the status of transsexual people (Sweden 1972; Germany 1980; Italy 1982; The Netherlands 1985; Turkey 1988). Reflecting concerns at the time, some of those early legislative provisions were quite brutally prescriptive in the conditions imposed. Several required absolute certainty of permanent sterility in return for recognising the applicant's acquired gender. Most also required applicants to be divorced or never to have married. Some excluded transsexual people who had parented children in their birth assigned gender. Legislation could be repealed with changes of government. Generally it was a pretty tough and uncompromising deal, reflecting the reluctance by states to be offering recognition in the first place (Will, 1993).

Meanwhile in Britain, there was very little taste for talking about the discrimination experienced by transsexual people, their medical needs, or social attitudes towards them. The travel writer Jan Morris famously completed her gender transition in 1972 and published a 1974 autobiography about her decade-long transition and eventual surgery in Casablanca (Morris, 1974). The media was scornful – lining Morris up to be challenged and criticised by everyone from feminists to politicians and church figures. Indeed, this then became the dominant mode for public treatment of others like her. The press became bent on pursuing and 'outing' transsexual people (relying on tip offs to find their victims). And when it wasn't 'outing' transsexual people in the tabloids, the weightier side of the press would be critiquing their existence – following a script developed within radical feminism in the late 1970s and throughout the 1980s.

Social pariahs

The toxic mix of 'outing' and feminist critique in the media served to ensure that, for over two decades, any grassroots transgender activity was focused on support and survival. Trans people got the message from society. The media weren't going to entertain any nuanced discussion about the problems in their lives. The received wisdom was that any problems were transsexual people's own fault for 'choosing' to transition. Politicians weren't going to touch such a toxic matter. Why would they? Nobody was highlighting problems. Culturally, trans people were considered beyond the pale. Courts had ruled. As a class, trans people were trussed and stuffed like turkeys with no apparent prospect of change and few allies anywhere to be seen. To add to the problem, the consequences for any trans person brave enough to stick their head above the parapet were dire. Case law had established that transsexual people weren't protected by the Sex Discrimination Act. Many, as a result, had insecure jobs, often working below their skill level if at all. And trans people were relatively rare too – geographically dispersed, closeted and lacking the means to organise nationally.

Throughout the 1970s and most of the 1980s transsexual people, therefore, were locked into an almost inescapable social prison: media coverage that cast them as social pariahs, to be blamed for their own pain – unemployed or unemployable through documents that continually 'outed' them, and legal interpretation which said they had no redress for dismissal – too poor and too isolated to organise politically or seek redress – viewed as toxic by politicians. Were this a game of chess you'd topple your pieces and resign.

The fightback begins

The impasse began to be broken eventually by two transsexual people – a man and a woman – who quite independently decided they had had enough and began the lengthy legal process to reach the European Court of Human Rights. The man, Mark Rees, was first. His case came to a conclusion at Strasbourg in 1986 (*Rees v United Kingdom*, 1986). He lost. The court noted that there was no settled view among contracting states on how to handle transsexuals, or why transsexual people existed. But, crucially, the door was left open to permit further cases that could keep the situation under review. The second case, Caroline Cossey, exploited that opening. In 1990 she too lost, but by a far smaller margin (*Cossey v United Kingdom*, 1990). And it is these two cases that showed a route by which transsexual people might campaign with a chance of success.

The crucial aspect of the Rees and Cossey cases were that they exposed the issues to a degree of legal debate in public. The evidence in both instances showed how often transsexual people were put into embarrassing or harmful situations by the inability to change their birth certificate details. Cossey (a successful model whose work and marriage prospects had been derailed by press 'outing') also illustrated an inability to marry (other than to another woman, where the law regarded her as a man). These and subsequent cases all appealed to Article 8 of the European Convention on Human Rights (the right to privacy and private life); to Article 12 (the right to marry and found a family); and Article 14 (the right to be free of discrimination).

The court cases led to some sympathetic discussion in the quality press, although there was also still the kind of opinion writing that criticised transsexuals for 'choosing' to transition and thereby put themselves in harm's way. More importantly, the legal arguments also pointed to the courts being perhaps the only place where the transsexual case could be objectively considered and where (maybe with further development) a winning argument might be constructed. And if the courts supported transsexual people then maybe the legislators would have to follow.

The basis for a campaign

This is how the mould for transsexual rights campaigning was cast. It was to be primarily a legal campaign, but with a focus also on winning over supporters in Parliament and the media (vital if the case for change was to be detoxified). It would draw on the assistance of young human rights lawyers willing to give their services on a contingency basis. It was hoped that gradually, if cases could be won in the domestic courts, the Human Rights Court in Strasbourg could be won over too – and then Parliamentarians would have to listen. The founding campaigners were advised by the Liberal Democrat Home Affairs spokesman, Sir Alex Carlile MP (their first political ally), to set up an organisation (Rees, 1996; Burns, 2013). He warned that the struggle could take ten years (in fact it took twelve). On 27 February 1992 Press for Change was born.

Press for Change was born in the same era as the gay rights lobby Stonewall, yet the two were very dissimilar. Stonewall was launched with vocal support from high profile gay and lesbian celebrities; it drew on an established tradition of gay activism; there was a gay press and venues where LGB people could read about the organisation and make donations. Being well funded from the outset, Stonewall could soon establish permanent offices and staff. It had the resources to lobby Westminster. It had the tacit backing of at least some commentators in the quality press. Press for Change had none of these benefits. It was founded by six activists – none with much money – who were still either living in so-called 'stealth' or dealing with regular discrimination where their trans background was known. There was no money. No offices. No phone. No high profile backing. And few sympathetic columnists to publicise their existence. Added to that, trans people weren't welcomed in LGB events such as Pride and even the gay press at the time (1992) was not a sympathetic outlet.

Faced with these obstacles – the sense of an almost impossible hill to climb – the founders of Press for Change ran a shoestring campaign from their spare bedrooms. The only capital they had to work with was their ingenuity and determination. The first major breakthrough was not until 1996, when the European Court of Justice ruled that employment discrimination against a transsexual woman ('P') fell within the ambit of the European Community's Equal Treatment Directive (*P v S and Cornwall County Council*, 1996). This ruling required states throughout the European Union to update their discrimination legislation if it was not compatible. In Britain the new Labour Government of 1997 chose to create new regulations to extend the Sex Discrimination Act 1975 – albeit with an attempt to water down the scope and effectiveness of the ruling. Press for Change mobilised a now substantial number of followers by post and a new email list server to help argue against the proposed exceptions to the law. This action brought the organisation belatedly to the attention of Ministers and Parliamentarians and opened the way for the group to conduct direct argumentation and lobbying (Burns, 2014: Chapters 2 and 3).

Press for Change relied on private individuals to bring forward the cases which it then exploited. It had a strategy for what it wanted to achieve (social equality and security supported by legal recognition) and a slowly widening circle of supporters. The quid pro quo for the litigants was the access to sympathetic lawyers and a sharing of know-how and case law that had already been developed. The campaign then made use of the legal outcomes to strengthen their lobby argument. This should be compared with other campaigns for social change which more typically engage in approaches such as direct action or bringing commentators on side in the press. Bringing transsexual people onto the streets was difficult, given that so many were wary of exposure and feared public hostility. And the press remained largely unhelpful. Indeed, the press reception to favourable legal judgments was often extremely hostile, as witnessed when the Court of Appeal ruled in 1999 that transsexual people couldn't be systematically denied NHS treatment for their condition (Burns, 2014: Chapter 8).

The final breakthrough for Press for Change occurred in 2002. The fourth in a succession of human rights cases that had begun with Mark Rees in 1986 was decided unanimously in favour of the two transsexual plaintiffs (*Goodwin & I v United Kingdom*, 2002) The Labour Government now turned to Press for Change (still a handful of unpaid activists working in their spare time) as the experts in how to draft legislation without it placing Ministers at risk. The result of two years of collaboration was the Gender Recognition Act 2004.

Not the end, but a beginning

The employment, health and privacy/marriage protections won by Press for Change did not of course end the discrimination faced by transsexual people, or the wider umbrella of people termed trans or intersex. These advances merely made some of the most egregious instances of discrimination unlawful or less likely to occur (by protecting people's privacy). Trans people still continued to be 'outed' by the press. They were still depicted in the crudest of ways on television and in film. Neither medical professionals nor NHS policy managers had any clue how to treat trans patients or staff with anything approaching respect or competent care. These challenges defined the objectives for trans campaigning after the Gender Recognition Act came into effect. They remained grassroots led. Initiatives either came from individuals or voluntary led organisations operating on much the same terms as Press for Change, because the key structural problems (marginalisation; lack of wider support; no access to funds) shaped the solutions considered possible by a new generation of trans activists.

The past two to three years have seen the beginnings of change. A new breed of activist has emerged with a more significant public profile. Typically these have begun as bloggers and progressed to paid commissions from the quality press. A concerted effort to win over support in the broadcast and print media has also paid dividends – leading to jobs for trans actors, plays and current affairs inclusion. Finally, having arrived at a place where trans topics are now regularly reported and featured, the gay rights organisation Stonewall took an historic decision to support trans causes too – bringing to bear the resources of a professional public relations and lobbying campaign to tackle problems that remain for trans people in areas such as bullying and hate crime.

References

Burns, C. (2013) *Pressing Matters*, Volume One, Manchester: Self-published eBook.

Burns, C. (2014) *Pressing Matters*, Volume Two, Manchester: Self-published eBook.

Morris, J. (1974) *Conundrum*, London: Faber & Faber.

Rees, M. (1996) *Dear Sir or Madam*, London: Cassell.

Will, M. (1993) *Legal Conditions of Sex Reassignment by Medical Intervention – Situation in Comparative Law*, Amsterdam: Proceedings of the Council of Europe's 23rd Colloquy on European Law.

Legal cases

Corbett v Corbett (1970) Family Division of the High Court, All England Law Reports, London.

R v Tan and others (1983) Court of Appeal Criminal Division, All England Law Reports, London.

Rees v United Kingdom (1986) European Court of Human Rights, Strasbourg.

Cossey v United Kingdom (1990) European Court of Human Rights, Strasbourg.

P v S and Cornwall County Council (1996) C-13/94, European Court of Human Rights, Strasbourg.

Goodwin & I v United Kingdom (2002) European Court of Human Rights, Strasbourg.

Section Two: User-led approaches to social policy

42

Transforming professional training and education – a gap mending approach: the PowerUs European partnership

Helen Casey

Introduction

The PowerUs European partnership was established in 2012 by social work lecturers from Lund University, Sweden, Lillehammer University, Norway and members of Shaping Our Lives, a national service user-led organisation in the UK.[1] It was formed in recognition of the introduction of 'gap mending' methods which were being developed to transform professional training and education. The concept of 'gap mending' is about promoting methods of inclusion within professional educational and practice contexts that result in more equal practice. As partners in learning and developing innovative projects, students, practitioners and service users can make a genuine contribution to research, knowledge and improving practice.

Some examples are provided of innovative projects with parents who have had their children removed, young people in the looked after system, and asylum seekers and refugees. Outcomes from these programmes have evidenced that, by creating a learning environment where people share their experiences and knowledge, traditional barriers that exist between people on the receiving end of professional support and those providing it can be removed. Further, these programmes, which began with social work students, have widened the professional context where this approach can apply.

Background

Service user and carer involvement has been formally recognised as an essential part of social worker training and education in the UK since the establishment of the social work degree in 2003 (Levin, 2004). Much has been written on this subject, including the historical context for service user and carer involvement and continuing challenges to ensure that participation is meaningful (for example, Forbes and Sashidharan, 1997; Beresford, 2005; Beresford and Carr, 2012). Since 2003, a wide range of ways have been developed in which people with experiences of receiving services contribute to social work education and training. The challenge for educators has been to widen the scope of involvement and promote dialogue as well as to increase participation between service users, carers and students. The effectiveness of this in terms of benefits to service users and carers and improving practice is less clear. Research that focused on how to make user involvement work (Branfield and Beresford, 2006) found that

> Big question marks remain about how much change has actually been achieved in line with what people say they want. How real is that change? How many people do actually get involved and do they reflect the diversity of the overall population they are part of?

Literature on the effectiveness of service user/carer involvement is limited and does not recognise more recent emerging 'gap mending' methods.

Current context

A definition of gap mending is provided by Cecelia Heule and Arne Kristiansen, who pioneered the gap mending approach at Lund University in 2005:

> The gap mending concept is not a specific model or method, but should be seen as an analytical approach that can be used in common efforts to resolve problems and prevent gaps. The analysis should highlight both problems and opportunities and illustrate power relationships. It can enable mutual learning and development, which contributes to awareness and changes of the binary and unequal roles which social workers and service users are maintaining in social work practice. It requires that people's needs are given priority and that both service users' experiences and knowledge are considered as valuable and necessary in order to improve practice. This also requires that the social workers abandon the role of experts and the service users abandon the client role. (Kristiansen and Heule, 2016: 38)

Kristiansen and Heule contributed to a book edited by a social work educator at Zurich University, Switzerland, who has been inspired to discover how a gap mending approach includes 'the service user as a partner in social work projects and education' (Chiapparini, 2016). This book provides an informative overview of the different courses with a gap mending approach in Europe. Contributions are made from six countries, providing the reader with a valuable insight into the different ways that the gap mending approach has been implemented to adapt to each country's current context in relation to education and society.

Notably, the uniqueness of the commitment to service user and carer involvement in social work education in the UK has been central to discussion among European PowerUs partners, who are working to achieve similar goals within their own governments.

Examples from the UK

The first gap mending programmes in the UK have been established at London Southbank University (LSBU) and New College Durham (NCD).

A summary is provided of the first gap mending programme I was involved with at NCD, which paved the way for subsequent programmes in diverse contexts. It is hoped that this brief overview will inspire those in professional education and practice to identify opportunities where a gap mending approach could be applied.

Pilot programme with parents

An opportunity to pilot this innovative approach was identified when students on work placement at a children's centre were excluded from parenting support groups by parents due to their negative experiences of professionals, as one parent later explained:

> 'When you hear the words 'social worker' it fills you with so much fear that you want to run a mile.' (Parent, 2014)

The aim of the programme was to mend the gap between parents who had lost or been separated from their children and student social workers. Following the first voluntary meeting to which parents were invited to discuss the barriers that existed with social workers, a series of planning meetings for piloting the gap mending programme were held. The content of the programme was mainly identified by parents' experience of health and social work support.

These meetings took place at the children's centre – an environment that parents were familiar with and felt comfortable in. The important point to emphasise about the planning process is how parents were supported to shape and develop this project. This was key to empowering them from the outset as, for the first time in their experience, they were not being invited to join in something that others had decided the content of. In this context, eight social work students and one community health nurse student would be recruited as co-participants. A balance of numbers was achieved with nine parents participating.

A central philosophy of the gap mending approach is for people to meet as *people* – therefore, the course began with an introductory activity to enable people to come together prior to teaching sessions. The themes of the eight weekly sessions were largely informed by the gaps identified by parents at the first meeting. However, what brought them to life were the discussions that involved sharing both experiences and learning together. Parents stated that they felt their voices were being heard for the first time.

Social work students said they would be better social workers as a direct result of working with parents.

The unanticipated outcomes were:

- the establishment of a creative writing group
- the development of parent-led support service – 'Parentkind'
- involvement in teaching sessions on a social work programme
- social workers from the children and families team became involved with the programme
- the local BBC radio station interviewed parents and an article about the project was published in the national press
- parents and students had a lot more confidence and spoke at social work conferences
- parents and students together held a workshop at the first PowerUs UK conference (Beresford, 2015).

The success of the first programme inspired Sunderland University to develop a gap mending programme with carers (Beresford, 2015).

The Higher Education Academy's interest and support for this approach continued and a funded event to explore how to mend the gap with young people led to the establishment of a gap mending programme with young people with experience of the looked after system. Mending the gap with young people has operated differently to the weekly scheduled programmes with adults as different events have been organised to promote action in response to gaps identified by young people; for example, a meeting was held with a local MP to explore gaps between young people and policymaking and social work support (NCD, 2015).

In 2016, two new programmes were delivered with refugees and asylum seekers, in collaboration with other universities and independent agencies. One of these programmes has been the biggest so far with 30 participants and a wider range of student involvement. Fifteen parent refugees and asylum seekers met over ten weeks with 15 students, mostly social work and occupational therapy and one student each of psychology, criminology and sociology. A significant difference with this programme has been the involvement of a lead professional within each session addressing a range of topics, including: crime, safeguarding, housing, mental health, learning difficulties, lesbian, gay, bi-sexual transgender (LGBT), domestic abuse, female genital mutilation (FGM) and disabilities. These topics have raised discussion around ethnicity and sexuality where participants have challenged each other to exchange perspectives based on different values and beliefs. Evaluation of this programme revealed how parents' views had changed to accept difference and an individual's right to live peacefully without judgement.

Key learning from this programme emphasises cultural knowledge exchange, challenging discrimination, improved understanding of key support systems and each other's roles.

As one student wrote in his feedback:

> These sessions suggest the absolute importance of conversation, of raising awareness, and of proper training for all involved. The importance of programs such as Mending the Gap, and organizations such as Investing in People and Culture (IPC), which act to place asylum seekers as active members of local communities, and facilitate mutual understanding between them and the service providers around them, cannot be overstated ... my experiences with this program so far have taught me the importance of learning outside the classroom, from discussing real, lived experience – a far too easy to overlook component of a well-rounded university education. (Student, 2016)

Key outcomes from the programme include closer links with the local authority and a new gap mending project being developed with young unaccompanied minors.

European context

While outcomes from gap mending programmes in the UK are relatively small scale, elsewhere in Europe where courses have been operating over ten years, we can see the scope for this approach to develop and transform professional training and education. At Lund University, Sweden, all participants gain university credits, which mends the gap between service users and education as for many this is their first experience of attending university. At Lillehammer University, Norway, course evaluations reveal positive long-term outcomes underpinned by challenges made through learning together around power, roles, oppression and stigma. At the Metropolitan University in Denmark, courses have been delivered to include social work and occupational therapy students where outcomes have led to improvements in welfare services (Chiapparini, 2016: pp 16, 20, 62).

Summary

PowerUs is a growing international network creating opportunities for service users, students, educators and practitioners to move forward on the road towards greater diversity and increased integration by challenging the traditional foundations of professional education. Gap mending programmes across Europe are transforming professional training and education. There is scope for wider application of this model globally and in diverse professional contexts.

Note

[1] www.powerus.eu

References

Beresford, P. (2005) 'Service user: regressive or liberatory terminology?' *Disability and Society*, 20 (4), 469–77.

Beresford, P. (2015) 'Mending the gap: A radically new approach to professional learning and academic teaching', Higher Education Academy blog, 6 July, www.heacademy.ac.uk/blog/mending-gap-radically-new-approach-professional-learning-and-academic-teaching

Beresford, P. and Carr, S. (2012) *Social care, service users and user involvement*, London: Jessica Kingsley.

Branfield, F. and Beresford, P. (2006) *Making user involvement work: Supporting service user networking and knowledge*, York: Joseph Rowntree Foundation.

Chiapparini, E. (ed) (2016) *The service user as a partner in social work projects and education: concepts and evaluations of courses with a gap-mending approach in Europe*, Zurich: Barbara Budrich Publishers.

Forbes, J. and Sashidharan, S.P. (1997) 'User 'nvolvement in services – incorporation or challenge?' *British Journal of Social Work*, 27 (4), 481–98.

Kristiansen, A. and Heule, C. (2016) 'Sweden: Power, Experiences and Mutual Development. Using the Concept of Gap-Mending in Social Work Education', in E. Chiapparini (ed) *The Service User as a Partner in Social Work Projects and education: Concepts and Evaluations of Courses with a Gap-Mending Approach in Europe*, Zurich: Barbara Budrich Publishers.

Levin E., (2004) *Involving service users and carers in social work education*, SCIE guide 4, Social Care Institute for Excellence.

NCD (2015) 'MP visit helps Mend the Gap with young people', www.newcollegedurham.ac.uk/news-events/latest-news/mp-visit-to-help-mend-the-gap-with-young-people/

43

Grassroots tackling policy: the making of the 'Spartacus Report'

Sam Barnett-Cormack

Introduction

In 2011, something new happened. Without an organisation or funding, disabled people and allies came together to challenge government policy, and the narrative accompanying it. They did this not by the time-honoured methods of protest and appealing to the public's sympathies, but by sitting down and demonstrating, with evidence, that the government was wrong.

In this chapter, we will explore the background behind the 'Spartacus Report', *Responsible Reform* (Campbell et al, 2012), a report put together by disabled people and allies to challenge proposed reforms to Disability Living Allowance (DLA).

Background

DLA was introduced in Britain in 1992, bringing together and expanding two existing benefits, Attendance Allowance and Mobility Allowance (Kennedy, 2011). DLA was available to children and working age adults, and to people over state pension age who were receiving it when they reached that age.

In February 2011, the British coalition government's Welfare Reform Act 2012 was introduced, following a White Paper on Universal Credit and a consultation on DLA in 2010. The Act replaced most means-tested welfare benefits with Universal Credit, and replaced DLA for working age claimants with Personal Independence Payments (PIP). That consultation received 5,500 responses from individuals and organisations, and was summarised and responded to in April 2011 (Department for Work and Pensions, 2011). The summary claimed a remarkably positive response to the consultation, which provoked a rather incredulous reaction from many disabled people and some of us set out to take apart the arguments for the proposed reforms.

The cast

Those responsible for the production and impact of the report would be hard to number, and many who were closely involved have chosen to remain anonymous because they did not wish public attention, or because they feared retaliation from the UK Government Department of Work and Pensions (DWP). Large and small contributions from many went into publicity, content, checking details and raising funds, along with some support from British social justice organisations like Ekklesia.

Key players who were identified included disability activists Sue Marsh, who acted as an organiser and clearing house for everyone's work, Kaliya Franklin, who provided valuable input throughout and worked directly on promotion, and those who directly contributed sections, including myself and fellow activist Declan Gaffney. The lead author was Sarah Campbell, a former academic mathematician who reluctantly left that career due to worsening health, who carried out most of the analysis of the information obtained under a UK Freedom of Information (FOI) Act request.

Process

As this was, to our knowledge, a new type of work, so the process emerged as we went along. We're used to seeing reports like this from think tanks or academics, but those involved in *Responsible Reform* did not have a lot of experience in that area. We will look at the process step by step, but first we considered the principles that underpinned the work.

Principles

Two key principles underpinned our work, and continued to be important in future work involving some of the contributors.

First, the work was driven by people who have direct experience of the subject. The report was driven by people with lived experience of disability and the associated parts of the British welfare system. This was important for the perspective it brought, and the passion it instilled.

The second principle is that of being solidly evidence-based. Claims were well-reasoned, with a firm evidence base. This helped to offset any real or perceived risk of bias due to the contributors' proximity to the issues in question.

The centrepiece: Freedom of Information data

As well as being the centrepiece of the report, this data was also the impetus for it. An anonymous disabled person was so aghast at the claims in the government's response to the consultation that they requested the contributions of organisations under the UK FOI Act, 2000.

The organisational responses to the consultation, coming from Disabled People's Organisations, charities, medical professional bodies and unions, among others (Department for Work and Pensions, 2011: 46–56), represented a lot of data. In order to challenge the government's presentation of the responses as broadly supportive, it was necessary to determine whether each of them was supportive of each proposal. Key points were outlined, particularly if omitted from the government's summary.

The additional material

Two other key sections were included, looking at the government's claims about the rate at which the DLA caseload had grown and at the claim of a 'DLA effect' on employment, both key arguments in the government's case for wholesale reform of DLA.

There was also a brief section on failures of the consultation process, and addenda concerning the Benefit Integrity Project of 1997–1999 and trends in mental health. All of these were contributed by different people, coordinated using various online communication platforms.

The social media campaign

While the content of the report was important, as was working directly with parliamentarians and support from organisations, I believe that the publicity obtained through social media also made a significant contribution to the report's impact.

This is where the 'Spartacus Report' sobriquet came in. When looking for a Twitter hashtag to promote the Responsible Reform report that would be catchy, and stir people's imaginations, this is what those working on promoting the report came up with – and they were clearly successful. The intent was to convey the sense of a largely powerless group standing up to the powerful, with the additional implication of both solidarity and anonymity, as many contributors, and even supporters, feared repercussions from the DWP. The UK government even took to Twitter using the same hashtag to defend itself (Butler, 2012).

Organiser Sue Marsh estimated that about 2,000 people were actively engaged through email groups in planning and preparing promotion, including about 300 constituency reps signed up to promote the report to their Member of Parliament (MP), 5,000 people actively engaged on social media before the launch, and 20,000 actively engaged on social media on the day of the launch (Marsh, 2016).

Crowdfunding, printing, distribution and promotion

For maximum impact, it was decided that the report should be printed and delivered to British MPs and Peers in the House of Lords. This would obviously cost money, which we did not have. Sue Marsh launched a crowdfunding campaign (Marsh, 2011a) asking for £3,500. It eventually raised over £7,000 (Marsh, 2011b), reflecting widespread engagement. This was used for printing, distribution and promotion.

It was also vital that people involved worked with the British press, MPs and Peers. This was not the work of slick professional lobbyists. It was the work of dedicated and passionate people who, with some advice from more experienced operatives, ventured into the unknown to let everyone know the flaws in the UK government's proposals and consultation.

The result

Interest in the report was at least as high as we dared hope, with mentions in parliament and national media, Sue Marsh appearing on the BBC Newsnight flagship current affairs programme, and with many crediting us with the government's defeats in the House of Lords over amendments to the Welfare Reform Bill – despite the defeats largely being related to Employment and Support Allowance, with an amendment calling for a pause in the implementation of PIP being defeated by the government.

Impact on the debate

While it is hard to trace the direct impact of the work on debates in the UK parliament, public debate was informed by the media coverage of the report (Egan, 2012; Butler, 2012; Moore, 2012) and its reference later in the ongoing debate over the replacement of DLA with PIP (Full Fact, 2012).

Responsible Reform, along with later reports, has been referred to in Parliament on several occasions: in the contributions of Barbara Keeley (HC Deb, 23 January 2012a) and Anne McGuire (HC Deb, 23 January 2012b) in oral questions on PIP; Liam Byrne, then shadow Secretary of State for Work and Pensions, in support of a motion criticising reforms to benefits and social care (HC Deb, 20 June 2012); John McDonnell in a Westminster Hall debate on welfare reform (HC Deb, 18 December 2012); and Baroness Grey-Thompson in a Lords debate on the regulations implementing PIP (HL Deb, 13 February 2013). It was also referenced in a letter from the chair of Parliament's Joint Committee on Human Rights, Hywel Francis (2012), to the then Minister for Disabled People in the coalition government, Maria Miller.

Impact on policy and implementation

The government's planned reforms to DLA went through much as intended. The qualifying period changed, as we and many others had called for. While the defeats in the Lords slowed things down, they had little impact on the legislation.

A specific point in the report concerned the qualifying period being increased from 3 months under DLA to 6 months under PIP. The eventual implementation did reduce this back to 3 months, though it can hardly be attributed solely or mainly to our report.

The great impact and true success of the report was in its impact on the disability movement going forward.

Importance for the disability movement and future work

The idea of 'Spartacus' captured the imagination of many disabled people online. As well as the sterling ongoing work of groups like Disabled People Against Cuts (DPAC) and Black Triangle, specialising in traditional campaigning and direct action, people saw that things could be achieved by the less emotional seeming act of sitting down and sorting through evidence, checking facts and references, and using those to back up your arguments. It is a tactic that is well-used in the world of non-governmental organisations (NGOs), and similar to the strategies of many think tanks, as well as being similar to academic engagement with policy.

People wanted to see more. The engagement of so many in the process of producing and promoting *Responsible Reform* (aka 'The Spartacus Report') meant that many felt that we had given them a voice. However, despite all our organising, there was no formal organisation to carry on; all the work had been focused on producing and promoting the report. However, many people felt that we had inadvertently created a recognisable social media brand, and should take advantage of it.

Later that year, I coordinated a community-based response (Barnett-Cormack et al, 2012) to the government's consultation on the assessment for PIP, using the Spartacus name. This response was quoted in the government's reply to the consultation, and seems to have had a modest impact on improving the assessment, even if it was, as one would expect, largely ignored. The next year, disabled campaigners and allies worked together to produce *Emergency Stop* (Young et al, 2013), a report on the effects of the reforms on the Motability scheme, which allows some recipients of DLA/PIP to lease cars or motorised wheelchairs using their benefits.

This has continued as people have felt the need to address an area of disability-related policy broadly following the principles established by *Responsible Reform*, including in 2016 in relation to changes to the handling of aids and appliances in the PIP assessment (Richardson et al, 2016). While they may not always be able to change the direction of policy, they can make it harder for governments to claim they were not aware of problems and objections.

Conclusion: lessons we learned

While the publication of *Responsible Reform* didn't have the influence on policy that was hoped, it did raise public awareness and influence the debate. Its much greater impact was to demonstrate that dedicated grassroots activists, even without reliable funding or organisational backing, can engage in policy debates and be heard by approaching the matter methodically, and by making thorough use of evidence.

That is not to say that traditional campaigning and direct action aren't needed. It is undeniable that direct action has an impact, but confrontation is not the only way to approach debate. It is possible to challenge the premise of proposed changes by engaging constructively to mitigate the harms in policy. This is an approach familiar in the world of NGOs, but the work of a loosely knit-group of grassroots campaigners and researchers on *Responsible Reform* and later reports demonstrates that it is not exclusive to institutional actors.

The Spartacus Report campaign also demonstrates the importance of active engagement with allies, and potential allies, in the world of politics and the press. While the viral social media campaign was vital, it stood alongside the work of promoting the report to press and parliament. Convincing those with influence is not merely a matter of volume. Shouting loudly can alienate some people, while others can be engaged, and credibility established, by working through appropriate channels. From there, a reputation can be built that makes such policy campaigning work easier in future.

References

Barnett-Cormack, S., Campbell, S., Morris, B., Nicholson, F., Stock, P., Sumpter, S. and Young, J. (2012) 'Together We Shout', The 'We are Spartacus' Community Submission to the Government Consultation on Assessments for Personal Independence Payments, https://janeyoung.me.uk/2012/05/01/together-we-shout/

Butler, P. (2012) 'How the Spartacus welfare cuts campaign went viral', *Guardian*, 17 January.

Campbell, S.J., Marsh, S., Franklin, K., Gaffney, D., Dixon, M., James, L., Barnett-Cormack, S., Fon-James, R. and Willis, D. (2012) *Responsible Reform*, http://www.ekklesia.co.uk/responsiblereformDLA

Department for Work and Pensions (2011) *Government's response to the consultation on Disability Living Allowance reform*, London: DWP

Egan, L. (2012) 'Welfare reform – why disabled people are worried', Channel 4 News, 11 January.

Francis, H. (2012) *Letter to Maria Miller*, 6 March (unpublished).

Full Fact (2012) 'Do Iain Duncan Smith's DLA claims ring true?', *Full Fact*, 14 May.

HC Deb (18 December 2012) vol 555 cc214–215WH.

HC Deb (20 June 2012) vol 546 cc893–894.

HC Deb (23 January 2012a) vol 539 c4.

HC Deb (23 January 2012b) vol 539 c5.

HL Deb (13 February 2013) vol 743 cc729–730.

Kennedy, S. (2011) *Disability Living Allowance reform*, House of Commons Library Standard Note SN/SP/5869, London.

Marsh, S. (2011a) 'Fighting fund', Diary of a benefit scrounger, 28 December, https://diaryofabenefitscrounger.blogspot.co.uk/2011/12/fighting-fund.html

Marsh, S. (2011b) 'Research fund – fighting disability cuts', https://www.gofundme.com/b9x7c

Marsh, S. (2016) Personal communication, 25–30 September 2016.

Moore, S. (2012) 'The Lords are the only decent politicians left', *Mail on Sunday*, 14 January.

Richardson, C., Benstead, S. and Nock, E. (2016) 'Crippling Choices', Spartacus Network, 29 January, https://spartacusnetwork.wordpress.com/2016/01/29/crippling-choices/

Young, J., Parsons, R., Morris, B. and Barnett-Cormack, S. (2013) *Emergency Stop*, We are Spartacus, www.centreforwelfarereform.org/uploads/attachment/412/emergency-stop.pdf

44

Involvement for influence: developing the 4Pi Involvement Standards

Sarah Yiannoullou and Alison Faulkner

Introduction

The 4Pi National Involvement Standards for England were developed by the National Involvement Partnership (NIP) project from 2012 until 2015. NIP was a partnership of organisations hosted by the independent user-led organisation for England, the National Survivor User Network (NSUN). NSUN is a national network bringing together individuals and groups with direct experience of mental distress to communicate, feel supported and empowered, and to have direct influence over their services and lives. One of the main aims of the NIP project was to establish the reality of involving service users and carers in the planning, delivery and evaluation of health and social care services.

Service user and carer involvement has been on the policy agenda for health and social care services in Britain for several decades. The UK 1990 NHS and Community Care Act introduced a focus on the 'consumer' and assumed that greater choice would mean that involvement would improve the relevance and quality of services for the consumer (or service user). More recently, the UK cross-government mental health outcomes strategy 'No Health without Mental Health' (2011) placed an emphasis on wellbeing and on outcomes for individuals, based on principles of 'freedom, fairness and responsibility'.

Over the years, many mental health organisations in Britain have addressed service user involvement in different ways, developed guidance and policies for better involving service users and carers, with the aim of improving individual care and services. However, much of the learning from progressive policy implementation programmes has been lost along the way. A particularly good example of this loss is the Making a Real Difference (MARD) programme developed under the UK New Labour government during the early 2000s. The MARD programme developed some excellent materials to support the involvement of service users and carers, all of which are now archived on the NSUN website.[1] MARD also supported the five-year Delivering Race Equality

(DRE) programme to improve services for people from Black and minority ethnic communities who experience discrimination and disadvantage.

When NSUN embarked upon this three-year UK government Department of Health funded work, our intention was to help to create a new platform for involvement that would encourage and promote more equitable participation. The main aims were to: develop a baseline for meaningful involvement, build an infrastructure that connects and coordinates involvement at a government level, ensure the direct independent voice of people is present at local and national policy level, strengthen systems and networks for involvement, increase capacity of service users and carers to engage and influence, share good practice and centralise resources. Crucial to this was embedding the work of Jayasree Kalathil on working in partnership with black and minority ethnic communities (Kalathil, 2011). Too often, involvement has meant primarily the involvement of white service users. We wanted to incorporate values and principles that would make the involvement framework significantly more inclusive than involvement has been in the past. We particularly wanted to build a framework that would include black and minority ethnic (BME) service users given that many racialised communities experience more oppressive forms of mental health services and treatments than their white counterparts.

The 4Pi framework is a kind of acronym that gives us the following core standards:

Principles	How do we relate to each other? Principles and values are the rules or beliefs that influence the way we relate to each other and work together.
Purpose	Why are we involving people? Why are we involved? The purpose for any involvement activity needs to be clearly stated and understood.
Presence	Who should be involved? We would like to see a diversity of service users and carers involved at all levels and at all stages of a project or organisation.
Process	How shall we involve people? The process of involvement needs to be carefully planned to make sure people can make the best possible contribution.
Impact	What difference will involvement make? Involvement needs to make a difference if it is not to be tokenistic. Involvement should improve the lives and/or the experiences of people using services or experiencing distress.

Ultimately, the core purpose of service user and carer involvement should be to improve people's lives. Developing good practice policies and procedures for involvement has no meaning if those policies and procedures do not reach the individual who is admitted to hospital today, tomorrow or next week.

Investigating how and where involvement happens

There has certainly been much rhetoric regarding service user involvement with a tacit acceptance that 'the service user voice' should be heard. A 4Pi companion document, 'Service User Involvement in Health and Social Care Policy and Legislation' (NSUN, 2015), charts developments chronologically from the British NHS and Community Care Act of 1990 up until 2015. There has been a formal requirement for service user involvement in service planning since the 1990 NHS and Community Care Act, but NSUN's members still report that tokenism remains the rule rather than the exception and, although they may sit on panels, be members of working groups and are encouraged to contribute, this is too often a matter of presence without influence. Developing good practice policies and procedures for involvement has no meaning if those policies and procedures do not reach the individual experience.

Led by people using services and carers, the development of the 4Pi Standards addressed the themes of power, diversity, change and tokenism, while working to tackle the gap between the rhetoric and reality – that is, the policy and practice. The work started with ten consultation events in 2012 gathering views from around the country about experiences and opinions around influencing services and support. People's experiences were recorded and explored in an effort to understand what motivates people to do involvement work and to establish what enables good involvement to happen. The report of these consultations formed the basis of further work in three pilot site areas across England (Newcastle, Leicester and London) and the early shaping of the 4Pi framework. Leadership training in each area enabled people to build their skills and confidence to influence and establish their own networks. Two examples of where this worked well emerged in the North East of England and in London. In both cases, a co-ordinated, supported and consistent approach to networking and leadership training led, first, to a well-established user-led network in the North East and, second, to the Making A Difference (MAD) Alliance of 32 service user and carer advisors to eight Clinical Commissioning Groups in London.

We found that if people are able to influence policy at both local and national level, it is very much a 'win–win' situation, with services and the professionals working in them benefiting from genuine partnership working and more efficient and effective responses.

When people are involved in their own care, self-esteem increases and service satisfaction improves as a result of genuine choice and control. Involvement at community, operational and strategic levels can produce positive 'social capital', which is associated with the wellbeing and resilience and improve relationships and outcomes.

Wider recognition: influencing policy and practice

Since the formal launch, the 4Pi National Involvement Standards have started to gain wide recognition. A range of voluntary and community groups, statutory organisations and academic institutions have signed up to the framework, using it to help shape their involvement strategies and develop implementation plans and indicators. It also has a mention in the NHS England Five Year Forward View for Mental Health, cited in Chapter One of the report ('Getting the Foundations Right') as a framework that will 'help ensure services or interventions are accessible and appropriate for people of all backgrounds, ages and experience' ((NHS England, 2016, p 25). 4Pi is also recommended as good practice for the English Care Quality Commission (CQC) to inspect 'the quality of co-production in individual care planning, carer involvement and in working in partnership with communities to develop and improve mental health services' in the *Monitoring the Mental Health Act in 2016/17* report (CQC, 2018). It remains the only initiative in the UK developed by people using services and carers to be included in the CQC plan.

Working with partners including the West London Collaborative and Engage Visually, and guided by the 4Pi quality assurance framework, NSUN established the MAD (Making a Difference) Alliance in West London. The 4Pi framework complemented values-based practice and peer-led experience based co-design (EBCD), a participatory action research method of designing experiences for staff, service users and carers as the foundation for a 'service user and carer alliance'. The aim was to ensure that the voice of people using services was central to commissioning and delivery across the work of eight Clinical Commissioning Groups in North West London. Through this process we were able to bring about a strategic re-focus on the aesthetics and feel of services, especially during times of change as well as to challenge the traditional means of knowledge production in services.

Conclusion

The 4Pi Involvement Standards' authenticity is its greatest strength. Having been developed by people who have been 'involved' in mental health and social care initiatives over many years and in many different circumstances, and being based on research evidence, it provides a simple and systematic way of really thinking about how to effectively involve service users to influence improvement and change, and to realign power in decision making.

Service users, their organisations and networks can help create positive change through the brokering and facilitating of opportunities to influence policy at a local and national level. Since the launch of 4Pi there has been a shift in practice, notably the direct involvement of people with experience of using services rather than by proxy. Following the publication of the 4Pi framework, NSUN produced the *Members Manifesto* (NSUN, 2015) using feedback from annual member surveys and events over the previous three years to structure and prioritise organisational activity. The Manifesto begins by asking: 'Make the principle of 'nothing about us without us' a reality through effective and meaningful involvement in all aspects of our lives'. The unique 4Pi Involvement Standards are instrumental for driving this effective and meaningful involvement.

Note
[1] www.nsun.org.uk

References and useful readings
Beresford, P. (2013) *Beyond the Usual Suspects*, London: Shaping Our Lives.

CQC (Care Quality Commission) (2018) *Monitoring the Mental Health Act in 2016/17*, London: Care Quality Commission.

Department of Health (2011) *No Health Without Mental Health: A cross-governmental mental health outcomes strategy for people of all ages*, London: Department of Health.

Gould, D. (2012) *Service users' experiences of recovery under the 2008 Care Programme Approach*, London: NSUN and the Mental Health Foundation.

Kalathil, J. (2008) *Dancing to Our Own Tunes: Reassessing black and minority ethnic mental health service user involvement*, London: NSUN/The Afiya Trust.

Kalathil, J. (2011) *Dancing to Our Own Tunes: Reassessing black and minority ethnic mental health service user involvement*, Reprint of the 2008 report with a review of work undertaken to take the recommendations forward, London: NSUN.

NHS England (2016) *The Five Year Forward View for Mental Health*. Available at: https://www.england.nhs.uk/wp-content/uploads/2016/02/Mental-Health-Taskforce-FYFV-final.pdf

NSUN (2015) *Involvement for Influence: the 4Pi standards for involvement*. Available at: https://www.nsun.org.uk/Handlers/Download.ashx?IDMF=995617f8-1cd7-40af-8128-5eaaf2953b8e

Wallcraft, J. with Read, J. and Sweeney, A. (2003) *On Our Own Terms: Users and survivors of mental health services working together for support and change*, London: Centre for Mental Health.

Part VIII
Participatory research and evaluation

If conventional social policy research can sometimes seem dry, dusty and irrelevant, largely restricted to peer-reviewed journals and academic texts with a very limited readership, the same is not true of participatory, particularly user controlled research. Its raison d'être is making change and it has increasingly grown out of the struggles of service user movements. Its primary concern is to articulate marginalised perspectives and support people's empowerment.

In the final part of the book, we explore research in relation to participatory social policy. Such research has developed to inform, evidence and evaluate participatory social policy. We critique the role and nature of participatory research, exploring both practicalities and methodological issues. This includes case studies of such research as well as providing insights into the realities of 'getting involved in research' and the impacts it can have – on research, the researcher, research participants and the policy process.

Michele Moore writes as both a senior academic and a service user. As she argues we may be, all of us, more than one thing. The issue is not just one of including lay people/service users in social policy as if they are separate groups, but of learning how to include all of ourselves. Like her we may be both researcher and service user. This chapter highlights this issue, the problems that may be encountered and offers ways of understanding and overcoming them. In her chapter, academic Charlotte Williams offers a case study of the use of participatory research methodologies to involve marginalised perspectives. She reports on a major state funded participatory research project where the focus was on minority ethnic participation. As we might expect it was a project beset with contradictions, competing agendas and political and organisational constraints. However, by bringing them out into the open, we can get a clearer idea of how to address and overcome them.

Next Mo Stewart, medically retired healthcare professional and disabled female war veteran, describes the journey that led her to undertake research and produce influential research publications. Her experience is part of a broader picture of disabled people and other service users acquiring research skills in order to create the crucial evidence (which mainstream researchers were not producing) needed to challenge prevailing exclusionary, anti-personal social policies. What she found out from her own experience was happening to many more people, and became the driver for her to get involved at research and policy levels.

Drawing on research findings, survivor researcher Alison Faulkner looks at how user controlled research can help to develop new and inclusive knowledge about the issues that particularly concern people facing exclusion and discrimination. She explores the particular barriers and challenges that such research faces, as well as the benefits it can bring, for example, in terms of added impact because of its commitment to change.

Diane Richardson and a research team of an anti-trafficking organisation, led by women with lived experience, academics and workers, explore a new agenda on post-trafficking in Nepal. This is gaining momentum through anti-trafficking collaborations based on co-producing knowledge with women who have returned from trafficking situations. In their chapter, the authors describe a collaborative research and policy partnership to change the way human trafficking is understood and addressed in Nepal with Shakti Samuha, an anti-trafficking campaigning and advocacy organisation founded in 1996 by women with experience of being trafficked.

Finally survivor researcher Jasna Russo asks, from her own long-term experience of activism in Europe, if and how survivors, their organisations and knowledge will become 'real protagonists in matters that directly affect our lives', rather than just being nominally involved. She considers the distance between the formal rights offered in official declarations and the continuing realities of 'treatment' regimes. She highlights 'the deep-rooted epistemic exclusion of people deemed mad'; the need for survivors to put forward their own inclusive agenda for change and what some key components of that are likely to be.

45

From expert to service user: challenging how lived experience is demeaned

Michele Moore

I'm learning a great deal through being a service user representative on a research project that aims to develop new forms of support for people with dissociative seizures. Dissociative seizures superficially resemble epileptic seizures. They are episodes of impaired functioning associated with a range of motor, sensory, neurological and psychological manifestations, which in my case last around 50 minutes and can cause transient loss of speech and cognisance. Other names for these phenomena include 'psychogenic non-epileptic seizures', 'Non-Epileptic Attack Disorder', 'non-epileptic seizures', 'functional seizures'. Usually I'm the principal investigator in charge of large research projects so being involved as a service user representative is a new experience. The opportunity has given me fresh insight into how the lived experience of service users can be diminished in research and I describe some of the ways in which this happens in this chapter.

Although I'm going to focus on the difficulties of being positioned as a service user representative rather than a research expert in a project, and am going to illustrate demeaning of service user input, I am keen to say that the trouble I've seen from the service user representative point of view is trouble I think well worth having for the purpose of critical reflection on how to create research that is more respectful of service users and our experience. I have not been personally offended by the demeaning of lived experience described in this chapter, disabling as it is; rather it fuels my interest in the polarity between service user and service provider perspectives in research projects, and in how to reduce the distance between people to produce better research outcomes. It is disappointing to witness the way in which service users are sometimes positioned and talked about in research being conducted by service providers who pride themselves on the services they provide. But being on the receiving end of shortcomings in respectful involvement offers the chance to think about potential for improving practice.

The research project

I was asked to take part as a service user representative in research management meetings of a UK study being conducted to trial new support services for people with dissociative seizures. My main motivation for agreeing to take part was to help drive forward new services, where few, if any, already exist. I should say at this point that my principal motivation for getting involved was not to receive a £30 shopping voucher – the significance of this becomes clear later. There was a demeaning query about whether I could be 'sufficiently objective', as a user of a service in a Centre that was to be involved in the trial, to be on the management group. Hearing this immediate reservation about my capacity as a service user to help manage the research project made plain that service providers frequently struggle to appreciate the input of service users; willingness to fully include service users in research management is far from well-established. I felt like a distrusted member of the team already, whose experiences would be de-valued rather than valued (Russo and Beresford, 2016).

Now appointed to the research management group, my role involves giving input on the running of a multi-centre randomised trial, particularly with reference to advice on how best to get people with dissociative seizures involved with the research, how to keep people involved, how best to run the trials in order to ensure the wellbeing of all people taking part in the study. I give input on recruitment to the study, whether the project is meeting its targets, budget, staffing, report writing and research dissemination issues. The research management group meets via telephone conference calls chaired from London to ensure inclusion of participants from across the UK.

Assumptions about service user representatives

The first surprise of my new experience of being a service user representative on a research project was to notice the difficulty research managers have accounting for people's different levels of knowledge and research experience. An assumption was made that service users as a group were unlikely to have research experience and two of us appointed as representatives for the research management group were provided with training that would explain to us 'what research is' and 'what it involves'. I realised that once seen as a service user, the defining element of my identity became personal experience of dissociative disorders seen through the eyes of a medical research community as so indicative of deficiency a level of professional qualification would not be anticipated. We were told by the research consultant providing training for our involvement in research management that she "wasn't expecting you would have a degree or a postgraduate qualification … that's very interesting". It cannot be beyond the bounds of imagination that service users drawn to involvement in research management of multi-centre randomised controlled trials might have some basic understanding of 'what research is'. The point here is that what a service user can bring to research should not be underestimated.

As service user representatives we bring to the project and its proceedings insider experience of the mental health issues that the research seeks to develop responses to, but the experience of service users is not solely defined by the reasons for their service use. The two of us who use services and stepped up to be representatives of the research management group are both able to engage in a robust way with research management as well as to bring insights from our experience of dissociative disorders. This has greatly surprised some service providers involved in the project. Service users bring more besides a particular experience of services we use. The focus of our training for involvement as service users in research management was predicated on well-meaning principles for maximising inclusion but diversity and equity issues should be addressed from service users' own starting points, not from a deficit view of service users that resides in the head of research trainers.

Likewise, it is legitimate to question an assumption that service providers involved in project management have relevant research experience. On the research team being described, some are new to research as the majority of their time is spent on clinical work. They have a great deal of clinical knowledge and expertise, but far less familiarity with the importance of collaborative enquiry or co-production with service users on research design and implementation. They are typically trained in principles of positivistic enquiry – exercised much more by the subtleties of control group constitution, for example, than service user perspectives – which is ironic when they then find themselves vexed about dropout rates or non-compliance. For some of the service providers on the project, this is their first experience of research management roles. Some are quite evidently bemused about service user input, occasionally having to apologise for forgetting service users are in the meeting:

> 'I didn't mean to be trivialising the condition of dissociative seizures
> ... [what I said] may seem glib and if it caused any offence I am truly
> apologetic.' (Hospital Consultant)

That service providers are mindful of the importance of respect for service user involvement in research is evidenced by the apology sincerely given above. Not only did members of the research management group trivialise our experience of dissociative seizures, however, they also completely misjudged our research expertise. Fortunately, the project's principal investigator is extremely good at spotting potential for belittling the contribution of service users and has excellent skills for respectful intervention which carefully challenge those providers who persist in seeing service user involvement research as at the bottom of their list of priorities and impossible to take seriously in terms of possible contribution to research management. For those who need to know more about improving inclusion of service users in mental health research, the report by Beresford et al (2016) suggests practical and straightforward strategies.

Diminishing service users

I notice a respectful view to inclusion of service user perspectives often depends on what we actually say. When our input chimes with the view of service providers, our contribution is celebrated and invested with the authority of our suddenly remembered research expertise. If what we are saying is at odds with the prevailing service provider viewpoint, then the response we get is likely to be dismissive, reverting back to an invariably demeaning recollection that here is a service user speaking. Even in a telephone conference call it is possible to hear interest in what you are saying fade away as people start to talk to others in the background. Shuffling of papers and clearing of throats can be heard, audible glazing over while one of the service users takes time to speak. It is possible to be resilient, determined to have an input and carry on but this is not an easy or comfortable process. Not everybody is dismissive, some people continue listening respectfully so you hope that gradually service user participation does have some kind of influence. But the volume is quite often noticeably turned down when service users contribute, so that our input is diminished, if not erased by some of the participants. Some, for example, remember they have 'another meeting' when discussion turns to service users' input and dip out of the conference call. At times like this there is great benefit in knowing another service user representative is alongside – even at a distance in a telephone conference call – because you know there will be someone with commitment to understanding of a point of view that you're making, or question that you're raising.

Sometimes as service user representatives we are asked to respond on behalf of service users as a group, which exposes a lack of respect for issues relating to diversity and difference. Much more needs to be considered about issues of diversity, equality and difference, which would cast light upon additional barriers service users face in taking part in research management and how to deal with that. Such a request also reveals an assumption that service users are familiar with other service users, which may or may not be the case. Moreover, when we are asked to respond on behalf of service users as a group the task at hand often becomes one of needing to resist deficit views of service users as a group.

A specific observation of undermining views of service users came to light in discussion of why some participants were failing to submit research diaries in a timely way. Negative views of service users were quickly and plainly expressed by some service providers. Two consultants seemed particularly exercised by what they saw as lack of commitment by service users to return their research diaries, prolonging discussion for an unusual length of time to insist failure to return research diaries confirms that service users are motivated to get involved in research solely to receive a shopping voucher and, once they receive such a voucher, they will shirk their obligation to contribute. It was very difficult to push back the view that receipt of a shopping voucher is the primary motivator for involvement in research and to assert any alternative explanation, including that pre-existing mental health issues (which are the focus of the research), are much more likely to account for unreturned or late research diaries than a 'grab a voucher and run' attitude that was being conjured up as common among service users. This discussion revealed a patronising view of service users among some members of the research management group. Exasperation over the presumed impoverishment and avarice of service users was not directly aimed at myself or the other service user on the management group, but it was immensely difficult to hear service users discussed in derogatory ways and the discussion injected a vein of distrust between service users and providers that it has been hard to dissipate.

In my experience the primary motivation of service users to be involved in research projects is to help improve access to treatment and support, rather than to get hold of token rewards. It is more than likely that service user involvement in design of the research diaries would have ironed out difficulties for completion, or service user involvement in scheduling the return of diaries could have improved timeliness. As many researchers have found, where the voices of service users are missing from control of mental health projects the quality of research is significantly undermined (Russo and Beresford, 2016; Beresford et al, 2016). Further illustration follows.

Erasure of service user experience

In one meeting we were addressing ideas service users put forward for their own support. A few respondents had raised the possibility of being issued with medi-alert jewellery in case of having seizures in public or emergency services being called. A consultant objected to this saying such jewellery constitutes "a kind of stigmata for serious medical illness that needs emergency medical treatment not appropriate for people with dissociative seizures". I mentioned carrying a card saying my diagnosis, explaining should I lose speech what other people should do. I started doing this after being helped off a train and left on the platform at Leeds because I could not explain I wished to stay on the train until Sheffield. The reply to this was "I agree cards would be better – *not least because we control the content*" (Consultant's emphasis). The important point is that service users may wish to control what is said about them themselves. Suggested wording may be helpful but a personalised card reminds a service user (and service providers who see it) that we are individuals and not simply a patient to be controlled by others. As difference of opinion surfaced in the discussion, it was settled service providers would take the matter for separate consideration as it was about treatment options rather than research management; thus a neat strategy was found for sidelining input of service users in research-led service development. This encounter shows how difficult it is for user-led application of ideas to impact on provider preferences, including in research discussions and on suggestions for research outcomes. Attaching primary importance to the voices of medical service providers in research to evolve mental health services recycles the dominance of medical thinking about practice and is always limiting. As a service user representative on a research management group I constantly see aspirations of service users overwritten in the course of research discussions as others have described (for example, Voronka et al, 2014).

The importance of service users' own voices coming through in research is made vivid in another example. Concern arose over the recording of 'adverse events' on a service user's records as such events were depleting the pool of service users eligible for recruitment to the study. Discussion was specifically focussed on 'deliberate self-harm' and questions of whether deliberate self-harm need not be recorded as an adverse event "because it is so common nowadays" (Registrar) which would mean many more people could be asked to take part in the study. Here, the voices of service users on the research management group were pivotal in preventing the normalisation and rendering invisible of experience. If whatever service providers were referring to as 'deliberate self-harm' was no longer to be recorded – not for clinical reasons, but to expedite research recruitment – then service users would find aspects of their experience eliminated from their treatment plan. As service users involved in research management of clinical trials, we know there are decisions for clinicians to make, but this example reaffirms the importance of optimising service user input to complement decision making. Similarly when concern was expressed by service providers about what service users might write in their research diaries, the use of checklists had to be resisted by service user representatives who immediately saw the production of a checklist putting service providers' own words into the mouths of service users.

Valuing service user representatives

Over a period of two years greater recognition and acceptance of the value of service user representatives in research management has been established. There are far fewer demeaning incidents, although moments requiring critical reflection still arise. There are structural opportunities to reduce undermining service user representatives that need to be addressed such as routine placing of service user perspectives last on the agenda. In the conference calls, typically two-thirds of those participating leave early so that service user perspectives are aired with the principal investigator and a small handful research assistants or team members who happen not to feel too busy to stay on the phone. Having our voices fixed as the last point of discussion is a signifier of minimal importance attached to service user perspectives – shifting agenda items for more respectful inclusion would be easy to do.

Conclusions

I greatly value involvement as a service user representative on the research management group of the project discussed in this chapter. When listening, sometimes cringing with frustration at topics or modes of engagement that are demeaning to service users, I look for scope for learning and development. A hallmark of quality commitment to co-production inspired by the principal investigator has been a qualitative study set up to raise seldom heard service user representative experiences of being involved in research management from which pointers for better practice can emerge.

I am keen to encourage service users to get involved in research representation despite encounters with humiliation and other criticisms of involvement described. Projects cannot be satisfactory if they neglect service user perspectives and optimising positive outcomes from funded projects is an important goal. Involving service users in research management is not a straightforward case of assigning places in a group, however. Ways of operationalising research business without demeaning the experience of service users requires careful, constant and collaborative attention so that complacency does not mean research processes and outputs are themselves demeaned.

References

Beresford, P., Perring, R., Nettle, M. and Wallcraft, J. (2016) *From Mental Illness to a Social Model of Madness and Distress*, London: Shaping Our Lives.

Russo, J. and Beresford, P. (2016) 'Supporting the sustainability of Mad Studies and preventing its co-option', *Disability & Society*, 31 (2), 270–74.

Voronka, J., Wise Harris, D., Grant, J., Komaroff, J., Boyle, D. and Kennedy, A. (2014) 'Un/helpful help and its discontents: peer researchers paying attention to street life narratives to inform social work policy and practice', *Social Work in Mental Health*, 12 (3), 249–79.

46

Participatory methodologies involving marginalised perspectives

Charlotte Williams

Introduction

In recent decades the imperative to achieve greater levels of engagement in public policymaking has given rise to a plethora of participatory methodologies aimed at reaching out to so called 'hard to reach groups' (Boag-Munroe and Evangelou, 2012; Brackertz, 2007). In all social policy fields, engaging under-represented groups in governance is driven by the need to design and deliver more responsive services, provide legitimacy for policy decisions, improve take up of services and communicate confidence that as citizens all will receive fair treatment from agencies and institutions. This ambition to include has meant that government bodies and associated organisations have turned their attention to specific groups that do not easily participate either as a result of socioeconomic, demographic, attitudinal and cultural barriers, or too often as a result of stigma and discrimination. Participation is fundamental to the notion of citizenship, encompassing issues of recognition, representation, consultation and the right to have one's voice heard and incorporated in decision making (Fishkin, 2011). Such participation points to the responsibility of governments to devise solutions to increase engagement and finding a balance with the bottom up solutions that emerge from among marginal groups in pressing for change. There are accordingly both formal and informal processes involved – political and infra-political realms to consider – that run their own multi-varied course in particular contexts.

This chapter focuses on minority ethnic participation in policymaking as an acknowledged marginalised perspective. The issues attendant on migrant or ethnic minority participation raise some very particular concerns in relation to participatory strategies not least because they defy the boundaries of what Wimmer and Glick Schiller (2002) call 'methodological nationalism' which characterises much social policymaking. Migrations of various kinds challenge the very frontiers of citizenship (Kastoryano and Schader, 2014).

This chapter opens by tussling with some of the known issues that proscribe ethnic minority participation, noting some of the good practice frameworks that exist to promote engagement. I then consider the challenges posed for minorities in sustaining involvement in social policy processes. My example involves attempts to engage with the policy agenda on health and social care in Wales, in particular attempting to highlight minority ethnic needs by contributing to the evidence base underpinning social policy priorities. Having been involved in a cross Wales research network for over six years that attempted to *mainstream* ethnicity in relation to health and social care evidence base for policy, I present this as a case study which highlights the issues of capacity building, attrition and specificity as they relate to engagement strategies. What this example will illustrate are the limitations of top-down bureaucratic forms of engagement that focus on the creation of opportunity structures for access at the expense of a focus on the *processes* needed to support effective engagement.

The minority paradox

On an international level, a regulatory and legal framework assists the efforts of governments in responding to ethnic minority inclusion, setting out key standards and practice for the political participation of minorities (Weller and Nobbs, 2010; Council for Europe, 2007). Such frameworks offer protective mechanisms for national minorities (for example, indigenous peoples) as well as distinct legal mandates for the inclusion and protection of other migrant minorities. The scope of the debate is considerable covering issues of representation, consultation, special issue participation, minority self-governance and the tricky issues of implementation in particular country contexts (see Weller and Nobbs, 2010); as well as the relationship between the existence of formalised opportunities for participation and non-institutionalised ethnic minority mobilisation (Kaya, 2013). The principle tools to share ownership and participation range from constitutional devolution, anti-discrimination and equality measures and rights to actual and procedural representation through to mechanisms of engagement such as standing councils for minority groups. The types and forums utilised in consultation and engagement processes, however, are neither neutral nor universal. What works in one situation may flounder in another and there is a need to avoid the attractiveness of 'best fit solutions' (Humphris, 2014; Marcaletti and Riniolo, 2015: 13). Nevertheless, genuine participation remains elusive. The barriers for ethnic minority groups are well rehearsed in the literature (Kastoryano and Schader, 2014). Opportunities to influence policy are constrained by a number of factors including linguistic, cultural and attitudinal issues, time paucity, legal status, prior experience, feelings of attachment and belonging, geographical and practical access issues, all of which are significantly constrained by socioeconomic circumstances, power and capacity and by racisms and discrimination. In addition, as Marcaletti and Riniolo (2015: 4) point out, however collaborative and participative the processes deployed are, there are issues associated with dealing with the 'relevant influence, resources and knowledge, asymmetries and imbalances'. It is not easy to get involved; it is not easy to have your voice heard and even if you do participate it is not easy to achieve tangible outcomes.

At the heart of strategies for ethnic group participation is the tricky notion of ethnic category. How people identify, associate and mobilise around issues that have salience for them will not simply be related to their ethnic status. Minority group engagement therefore presents what has been called the 'minority paradox' reflecting the tension between group based or issue based participation (Crowley, 2001). The Policy Exchange's (UK) most recent report *A Portrait of Modern Britain* (Sunak and Rajeswaran, 2016) maps considerable diversity between ethnic minority communities, challenging the view of them as a single political entity. What is more, even within ethnic categories there is huge diversity of experience, capital and capacity to get involved.

The minority participation discourse is also challenged in relation to *intersections* with 'other' forms of marginality including gender, sexuality, disability and more, which acknowledges both the need for specificity of tools relevant to ethnic minority engagement and the potential for transferable techniques across disadvantaged groups.

Such is the problem of ethnic category that there are arguments put forward to suggest a move away from minority ethnicity as a focus for participatory engagement. It is argued that it limits learning and cohesion across groupings; that it has essentialising tendencies that do not permit the emergence of new political identities and expression of identity claims; that it disregards intersectionalities of interest by prioritising and creating hierarchies and that it places policymakers in the arbiter position between competing claims – positing them as benign neutral arbiters. Others would argue it is not an either/or focus and that participatory mechanisms can expose participants to both specific and mainstreamed opportunities for voice and choice (Cameron and Grant-Smith, 2005). Specific arenas allow for protected and safe moments for expression of claims, for building solidarity and power base, for political learning and provide a complementary and ultimately transitionary function in the shift from community based participation to issue based participation. Involvement in broader forums can then expose participants to a range of views and processes of public deliberation.

Good practice guidance on ethnic minority engagement and examples of models in practice abound with reference to different projects and scales of activity (Intercultural Cities, 2013; Education, Audiovisual and Culture Executive Agency, 2013; Humphris, 2014; Marcaletti and Riniolo, 2015). Examples include using a variety of participatory methodologies including mainstreaming, rapid appraisal, participatory visual methods, digital activism, participatory planning, mentoring and shadowing schemes and establishing consultative fora for deliberation and debate (Humphris, 2014; Ramalingham, 2013). I (with Hong Baker, 2016) have recently written about consultation and engagement with minority groups in rural Wales and the challenges this poses in areas where ethnic minority mobilisation is weak. Rural areas often lack experience or service infrastructure to provide effectively for migrant populations or to involve them in service design. This particular study showed public bodies hampered by their reliance on traditional top down models of engagement and argued for more innovative and flexible strategies determined with the participants themselves. Using mixed methods, exploring flexible approaches, innovative participatory models such as participatory diagramming, utilising food and friends, multi-media techniques, activity based incentives, phone and electronic snowballing, piggybacking other events and offering training or other resources are all known strategies for building engagement. What is clear, however, is that people are not queueing up to participate. Fears of being overburdened, fears about representativeness, exhaustion and exploitation with few demonstrable results act as deterrent in themselves (Hong Baker and Williams, 2016). Developing engagement and participation relies on trust, partnership working, drawing sensitively on expertise and building positive relationships, experimentation and innovation, investments in time and resource to build meaningful and sustained channels of two way flow of communication (Fennema and Tillie, 2001; Marcaletti and Riniolo, 2015; Hong Baker and Williams, 2016). The challenges lie not simply in establishing the conditions for participation but working on the processes involved. This will inevitably include thinking about models that engage with questions of scale, degrees of influence, investment, asymmetries and knowledge transfer.

Much of the aforegoing discussion relates to the efforts, issues and dilemmas made by the state to include minorities in policy design and policymaking. Such top down mechanisms have a tendency to promote certain kinds of activity in certain terms, modifying opportunity structures within the frame of well-worn political patterns and agendas. Policy frameworks structure relations and mobilisations; indeed, they structure politics pushing some forms of expression out of the formal process (Kaya, 2013). The tension between top down and bottom up processes requires resolution for good collaborative practice. It is this tension that bedevils good outcomes in the following case study.

First hand: the case example of the Welsh Equality and Diversity in Health and Social Care Support Network (WEDHS)

The devolutionary project within the UK, itself a strategy of minority inclusion, offered a unique opportunity to track new democracies in the making and the infrastructure put in place to ensure inclusivity in what are essentially social policy bodies (see Williams and De Lima, 2006; Chaney, 2015). In post devolution Britain the issue of black and ethnic minority participation (BME) became foregrounded in elite political rhetoric in a way unprecedented on the sub-national public policymaking agenda. In Wales, the National Assembly (later the Welsh Government) designed a series of mechanisms to foster participation based on the principle of *mainstreaming* (Squires, 2005). These included the establishing and funding of a multi-tier consultative infrastructure within civil society, the use of equality impact assessment tools in all policy fields, a number of affirmative action schemes to boost capacity, representation and diversity of staffing within the administrative bodies and the establishment of a government Equality Committee to monitor progress. Chaney's overall review (2015: 324) concludes that developments have been 'disappointing' with by far the greatest inroad being at a symbolic level rather than any significant shift towards deepening ethnic minority participation in public life. His observation is that the Welsh Government has relied on a top-down expert-bureaucratic strategy in the model of mainstreaming deployed, rather than a participatory-democratic model.

The research and development agenda in Wales on BME health and social care issues must be placed in the context of this constitutional change. Prior to 1999, government policies and practices in Wales were largely driven by an assessment of priorities based on an England/UK wide perspectives. With devolution the impetus was to become 'a country that develops its policies on the basis of evidence, and that has mechanisms in place to improve the health and social care of the people of Wales' (WAG, 2002 – *A Health and Social Care Research and Development Strategic Framework for Wales*). By 2005 the Assembly had set out its policy course in *Designed for Life*, a ten-year strategy for change (WAG, 2005).

It is within the context of these constitutional and policy changes that a unique initiative to develop a national research and support framework for evaluating and responding to the health and social care needs of BME groups came to be established. The evidence base on the health and social care needs of the BME population is notably weak and patchy and it is well documented that there is an apparent lack of information on access to care for BME populations in Wales (Williams et al, 2015). This situation in itself would provide a strong rationale for the development of a BME specific initiative but this explanation in itself does not account for the government support of what would represent in total some seven years of direct sponsorship.

The Welsh Government, as part of a more generic push to respond to the lack of any systemised approach to the development of healthcare knowledge, needed to develop a strategy that would incorporate attention to its core cross cutting themes which underpinned all government policymaking– namely equality of opportunity, sustainability and social justice (inclusion). Thus arguably it was not so much a concern to address the information gaps regarding BME need that paved the way for the incorporation of these issues into the grand plan that would become the Clinical Research Collaboration Cymru (CRC) but a commitment to embed in the emerging infrastructure attention to equality issues.

In the lead up to the establishment of the CRC, the then Welsh Assembly Government (WAG) through its agency the Wales Office of Research and Development (WORD) put out a generically pitched tender for a number of such scoping studies that would assess the feasibility of a variety of thematic networks based on key health needs. A farsighted researcher from the University of Glamorgan, Dr Roiyah Saltus, capitalised on this opportunity to frame this commitment around a work plan specifically focused on the needs of the BME population. She proposed the scoping of a Health and Social Care Research and Development network covering BME groups. The aims, development and achievements of the initial scoping study have been documented elsewhere (Saltus, 2005; Williams et al, 2007). In sum the key selling points when the WAG sought to consider applications for continued funding within the proposed new R&D infrastructure were that such a network could add value to research per se in Wales by providing cross cutting expertise to all other areas of research activity, facilitating community engagement and other stakeholder partnerships across and beyond Wales, assist in mainstreaming minority needs and capitalise on extensive goodwill and identified research needs as established by the scoping study. The CRC was formally launched in July 2006 with strategic aims stated as: the development of policy and practice that is underpinned by evidence; the generation of evidence that is missing; the translation of findings into clinical practice; the improvement of recruitment and retention and for the benefit of patients and the public. The infrastructure initiated funded a coordinating centre which comprised a management unit and a patient and carer network; nine thematic networks based on particular fields of clinical practice such as mental health, older people or on conditions such as diabetes and epilepsy; two clinical trial units and a number of infrastructure collaborations which included those for minority ethnic groups and language awareness to ensure inclusive participation.[2] Accordingly the Wales Equality and Diversity in Health and Social Care Support Service Network (WEDHS) was established with funding in the first phase for three years 2005–08 and in the second phase extension funding from 2008–10. It simply comprised a small group of us as academics, largely from BME backgrounds, in a cross institutional collaboration. From the perspective of the CRC the WEDHS was designated an 'infrastructure group' and as such was expected to relate to and provide a support service for the entire delivery framework.

WEDHS planned activities included providing a gateway to all research in Wales specifically involving BME patients, service users and community groups; to establish a research support service that proactively promotes an equality agenda; to design and support high quality evidence based research that addresses the priorities of BME patients, service users and groups; and to identify, review and utilise research findings that will improve the health and wellbeing of BME populations in Wales.

In several respects this project was in its own terms evaluated as a success. It achieved against an ambitious agenda of work that included a number of research projects as driven bottom up by the BME stakeholders; a programme of community engagement activities based on a small grant scheme; the establishment and coordination of a number of research projects which brought together a critical mass of academics and practitioners interested in ethnicity research; the development of web based resources and a database and a regional and national conference and seminar programme to promote dissemination of research findings. In addition, from a small core membership, it made attempts to link strategically with the nine thematic networks of the CRC to influence its work plans. In effect WEDHS from its inception operated as both an infrastructural support service but also in seeking to meet the needs of its core constituency it also acted as a thematic network.

By the time of the call for applications for the third round of funding, however, a number of developments emanating from a more mature CRC meant that WORD, now renamed the National Institute of Social Care and Health Research (NISCHR) was communicating new top level objectives to its prospective bidders. The CRC framework in which the infrastructure services had been based was undergoing transformation and there were no guarantees of future funding.

The shifting agenda had been communicated to the WEDHS partnership in a number of review and evaluation meetings which took place across 2009. It became clear that expectations had changed and, while the WAG Executive indicated their satisfaction with the previous orientation and work programme of WEDHS, they sought evidence of 'the level of impact WEDHS had had on the thematic networks' as an indicator of success and evidence of what 'added value' the service brought to the CRC. These were not unreasonable questions to ask of an infrastructure support service group. However, the way in which they sought to assess the 'added value' was by evaluating whether any of the nine thematic groups had mentioned WEDHS in their progress reviews. It became clear that they had not and if specifically questioned in review meetings the overriding suggestion was that these networks had set up their own procedures for ethical review and did not therefore see the need the services of WEDHS. To compound issues, the WAG Executive also appeared to be assessing WEDHS research activity on the basis of the level of research grant income as a criterion of evaluation, which by any measure could not stand up to comparison with the specialist thematic networks. What is more, at the same time a startling paragraph appeared in the WAG-published Single Equality Scheme (2009), which suggested under the objective 'Promote equality and diversity in health and social care research and development in Wales' an action to

> carry out the following through Wales Office Research Development: monitor the effectiveness of the Wales Equality and Diversity in Health and Social Care Research and Support Service to ensure that researchers within the Clinical Research Collaboration for Wales are aware of all relevant equality and diversity issues and that patients and service users from minority groups are able to participate in appropriate Clinical Research Care Cymru trials and other well designed studies.

This, whether by malevolence or misunderstanding of the remit, suggested a much broader role for WEDHS in relation to '*all* relevant equality and diversity issues'. The WEDHS collaboration in turn responded within their grant application saying:

It is important to note WEDHS is not currently funded to undertake the above action point, not least because it covers all the equality strands. Moreover, that we would want the focus to be not on monitoring our effectiveness, but rather for there to be a monitoring of E & D *throughout* the research infrastructure, with WEDHS providing a supporting role. (WAG, 2009: 14)

This light rebuttal belied a deepening gulf opening up between the WEDHS grouping and their funders and revealed important issues that strike to the heart of the mainstreaming aspirations of the WAG discussed below.

The experience of working within the CRC was one of ongoing frustration. As a group we had little power to enforce the compliance or even the cooperation of the large and powerful thematic groups which were heavily clinically dominated. Despite being designated as a cross cutting infrastructural group, the reality was our position was marginal, isolated and unsustainable.

This tale ends in 2010 when WEDHS formulated an extensive bid that comprised an action plan pitched to the refreshed agenda of NISCHR.[1] The WEDHS bid graciously dropped its aspirations in terms of a stakeholder driven research agenda focused on BME need and designed a portfolio of work much more targeted at infrastructural support activities aimed at servicing the work of others in the collaboration. The bid was ostensibly successful but with a considerably reduced budget such that was effectively not feasible to deliver on the proposed objectives. WEDHS withdrew from the process with the decision that the expectations of the WAG had grown (and indeed changed) and that the funding offered was not commensurate with the tasks/effort involved.

Discussion: some lessons from WEDHS

A number of issues arise from the WEDHS story that are instructive to the notion of participative methodologies. This could simply be read as a story of mixed messages, competing agendas and expectations, mis-communication and the product of a rapidly changing policy environment. However, what this story demonstrates, for me as one of the minority participants, is a top down bureaucratic mode of engagement and participation in tension with the grassroots initiative that it exploited. The appearance of a dedicated infrastructure support group focused on the issue of diversity within the framework ostensibly addressed the mainstreaming requirements of the Welsh Government. Indeed it would have high rhetorical value given its formalised position within the CRC. However, making a reality of their relative influence in developing the evidence base and shaping true engagement in policy development in Wales would have required much more on the part of the commissioners. Opportunity does not confer empowerment. Creating the participatory conditions but neglecting participatory methods and content – the very processes of participation – would inevitably lead to a poor outcome.

The WEDHS collaboration, as a small group of academics working in ethnicity research, had clearly identified a programme of work based on scoped minority ethnicity concerns. While its name, WEDHS, signalled broad equality and diversity concerns this belied the specific focus on ethnicity. The group had proceeded on the rationale that ethnicity concerns were of importance in themselves but could also provide the driver for wider equality considerations. We argued that if we could mainstream these considerations then it would be axiomatic that other aspects of diversity would follow. The extent to which this was understood by the other participants in the collaboration is debatable, which raises interesting points about category formation and labelling. NISCHR, indeed the management committee of the collaboration itself, could have done more to signal and underscore the place of WEDHS, and communicate its role and function within the Wales wide research governance framework. Instead this was left to a rather marginalised group of people, working from a relatively weak power base, to manage in relation to the medical hierarchy.

There was therefore inevitably some ambiguity about WEDHS's aims and ambitions vis-à-vis the CRC which was increasingly felt across the life of WEDHS as the group struggled to make inroads into the work of the wider clinical collaboration. When asked within the NISCHR review and evaluation, the thematic groups response that equality considerations were part and parcel of their ethical review processes was evidently a misreading of what WEDHS aimed to offer to the partnership. In essence the mainstreaming efforts were wholly unsuccessful. The opportunity for whole system transformation was lost.

Their inability to acknowledge the 'added value' benefits WEDHS offered to their projects if they had been compelled to draw on this support service was evident everywhere; for example, access to ethnic minority community groups, individuals and community researchers, grassroots information/knowledges, the data base of existing research and research capacity, to name a few.

Beyond the issue of missed opportunities for mainstreaming, other enduring lessons relate to issues of capacity, specificity, attrition, investment and trust. Capacity issues on all fronts mean that race/ethnicity specific research and policy development in Wales will always be vulnerable to being little more than an interesting sideline. The strength of the caucus of researchers interested in these issues will always be self-limiting as will the capacity at grassroots level within civil society. This required nurturing if it were to be sustained. In addition, we constantly struggled in WEDHS to identify what it was that is Wales specific about the BME experience that we should communicate to policy actors. Diabetes, eye care, the incidence of certain conditions in the minority population may be factors irrespective of place but issues of access to services, discriminations, quality of service delivery would not. This was a difficult point to get across to our stakeholder groups who, in drawing up their agendas for research, might prioritise areas where evidence UK-wide was already established. The costs of poor strategies of inclusion and engagement on the investment expended by minority participants, their time, trouble and trust are high. Poor experiences of engagement can in themselves be a precursor to lack of future participation. No attempts were made to salvage the WEDHS products, profile, energy and commitment beyond the funding cycle or to evaluate and garner the relationships built within civil society.

The WEDHS story also illustrates many of the complexities of attempting to 'speak truth to power' from a marginal positioning and refracts with the wider issues incumbent on ethnic minority participation in policymaking in Wales. The translational issues of moving from evidence to policy including issues of 'discursive authority', skill in establishing a persuasive narrative and the communication of 'difficult truths' (Wetherell, 2008: 314) might procure their own frustrations but the processes of involvement and engagement themselves could have been seen to confer substantial benefits. As we become repeat players in the policy game so we become more proficient political actors.

Conclusion

Recognising difference in policymaking so that marginalised groups are targeted for specific engagement activities has become increasingly the norm. Interest in examining new forms of political and social participation on both national and supranational levels is growing apace, as is considering emerging patterns and implications of minority participation in national arenas (Humphris, 2014). This extends to looking at the ways in which opportunities offered by new technologies are enhancing such engagement nationally and transnationally – and the role of so called e-governance (Twitchen and Adams, 2011).

The barriers to genuine engagement for minority groups across national contexts are many. Opportunity structures will vary context to context. Racism and socioeconomic disadvantage on the basis of exclusions from the labour market are significant precursors to active citizenship. There are deep implications of the current widespread economic crisis for the situation of minority groups noting that the flagging economy reinforces socioeconomic inequality (EHRC, 2016). It has been observed that economic recession augments the social and economic vulnerability of groups and this will inevitably have impact on their ability to participate in policy arenas.

The search for a participatory logic and theoretical models to guide good participatory governance will always be limited. While general models are useful there is little to suggest their transferability from issue to issue, context to context. Marcaletti and Riniolo (2015) accordingly offer a 'contingency model of action' that looks to emergent theory building whereby innovative elements and solutions and lessons from the field can extend existing practice. Building from their work with Roma peoples in Italy, they argue that what is at stake in citizen engagement is not simply the participatory conditions and opportunities created but also the negotiated methodologies and contents, which they define as 'topics and issues over which the contribution of citizens involved in the decision making process make a difference and adds value' (Marcaletti and Riniolo, 2015: 14). Their plea is for greater clarity about the scale, level and degrees of influence citizens and their associations can expect to realise in the participatory flux between top down and bottom up streams, which requires a degree of openness on both sides about expectations at the outset. This requires interrogating the decision making process in terms of the spaces available for influence. It should be clear to me if I participate at what point, how and to what extent my input can shape decisions.

My conclusion is that we learn by doing. Participatory design activity in itself is an exercise in deliberative democracy which demands accommodations, shifts, negotiation as citizen building and citizen in the making processes.

Notes

[1]   The current infrastructure map for Wales R&D is available at www.healthandcareresearch.gov. wales/research-infrastructure-map/

[2]   The framework used in 2005 was accessible on the CRC website at the time, but see CRC, 2018 for the current structure.

References

Boag-Munroe, G. and Evangelou, M. (2012) 'From hard to reach to how to reach: A systematic review of the literature on hard-to-reach families', *Research Papers in Education*, 27 (2), 209–39, DOI: 10.1080/02671522.2010.509515

Brackertz, N. (2007) *Who is Hard to Reach and Why?*, http://library.bsl.org.au/jspui/bitstream/1/875/1/Whois_htr.pdf

Cameron, J. and Grant-Smith D. (2005) 'Building Citizens: Participatory Planning Practice and a Transformative Politics of Difference', *Urban Policy and Research*, 23(1), 21–36.

Chaney, P. (2015) 'Getting Involved: Public Policy Making and Political Life in Wales', in C. Williams, N. Evans and P. O'Leary (eds) (2015) *A Tolerant Nation? Revisiting Ethnic Diversity in Wales*, Cardiff, University of Wales Press.

Council for Europe Framework Convention for the Protection of National Minorities (2007) *Participation of Persons Belonging to National Minorities in Cultural, Social and Economic Life and in Public Affairs*, Council for Europe.

CRC (Clinical Research Collaboration Cymru) (2018) 'Clinical research networks in Wales', http://www.ukcrc.org/research-infrastructure/clinical-research-networks/clinical-research-networks-in-wales/

Crowley, J. (2001) 'The Political Participation of Ethnic Minorities', *International Political Science Review*, 22 (1), 99–121.

Education, Audiovisual and Culture Executive Agency (2013) 'MiStra – Migrant Inclusion Strategies in European Cities: Progress report', http://eacea.ec.europa.eu/LLP/project_reports/documents/ka4/2012/progress/KA4-KA4MP-531325_MiStra.pdf

Equality and Human Rights Commission (EHRC) (2016) *Race Report: Healing a divided Britain*, https://www.equalityhumanrights.com/en/race-report-healing-divided-britainwww.equalityhumanrights.com/en/race-report-healing-divided-britain

Fennema, M. and Tillie, J. (2001) 'Civic community, political participation and political trust of ethnic groups', *Connections*, 24, 26–41.

Fishkin, J.S. (2011) *When the People Speak: Deliberative Democracy and Public Consultation*, Oxford: Oxford University Press.

Hong Baker, T. and Williams, C. (2016) 'Consultation and Civic Engagement', in C. Williams and M.J. Graham (eds) *Social Work in a Diverse Society: Transformative Practice with black and minority ethnic individuals and communities*, Bristol: Policy Press.

Humphris, R. (2014) 'Integration practice in the European Union: Initiatives and innovations by institutions and civil society', University of Birmingham, IRiS working papers, No. 3/2014, www.birmingham.ac.uk/research/activity/superdiversity-institute/publications/working-paper-series.aspx

Intercultural Cities (2013) *Guidance for city policy-makers with good practice examples. Joint action of the Council of Europe and of the European Commission*, Brussels, Council of Europe.

Kastoryano, R. and Schader, M. (2014) 'A Comparative View of Ethnicity and Political Engagement', *Annual Review of Sociology*, 50, 240–61, http://www.annualreviews.org/doi/abs/10.1146/annurev-soc-071811-145421www.annualreviews.org/doi/abs/10.1146/annurev-soc-071811-145421

Kaya, C. (2013) 'Ethnic Minorities and Political Participation: Non-institutionalised participation of ethnic minorities', E-International Relations Students, http://www.e-ir.info/2013/05/20/ethnic-minorities-and-political-participation/www.e-ir.info/2013/05/20/ethnic-minorities-and-political-participation/

Marcaletti, F. and Riniolo, V. (2015) 'A Participatory Governance Model: Towards the Inclusion of Ethnic Minorities. An Action Research Experience in Italy', *Revue Interventions Économiques / Papers in Political Economy*, 53, https://interventionseconomiques.revues.org/2609

Ramalingham, V. (2013) *Integration: What Works? Research Report*, London, Institute of Strategic Dialogue.

Saltus, R. (2005) *Scoping Study to explore the feasibility of a Health and Social Care Research and Development network covering Black and minority ethnic groups in Wales. Final Report*, Pontypridd: University of Glamorgan.

Sunak, R. and Rajeswaran, S. (2016) *A Portrait of Modern Britain*, London: Policy Exchange.

Squires, J. (2005) 'Is Mainstreaming Transformative? Theorizing Mainstreaming in the Context of Diversity and Deliberation', *Social Politics*, 12 (3), 366–88.

Twitchen, C. and Adams, D. (2011) 'Increasing levels of public participation in planning using web 2.0 technology', School of Property, Construction and Planning, Birmingham City University Working Paper Series, no. 5.

WAG (Welsh Assembly Government) (2002) *A Health and Social Care Research and Development Strategic Framework for Wales*, Cardiff: Welsh Assembly Government.

WAG (2005) *Designed for Life: Creating World Class Health and Social Care for Wales in the 21st Century*, www.wales.nhs.uk/documents/designed-for-life-e.pdf

WAG (2009) *Single Equality Scheme 2009–12*. Cardiff: WAG.

Weller, M. and Nobbs, K. (2010) *Political Participation of Minorities: A Commentary on International Standards and Practice*, Oxford: Oxford University Press.

Wetherell, M. (2008) 'Speaking to power: Tony Blair, complex multicultures and fragile white English identities', *Critical Social Policy*, 28(3), 299–319.

Williams, C. and De Lima, P. (2006) 'Devolution, multicultural citizenship and race equality: from laissez-faire to nationally responsible policies', *Critical Social Policy*, 26 (3), 498–522.

Williams, C., Evans, N. and O'Leary, P. (eds) (2015) *A Tolerant Nation? Revisiting Ethnic Diversity in Wales*, Cardiff: University of Wales Press.

Williams, C., Merrell, J., Rance, J., Olumide, G., Saltus, R. and Hawthorne, K. (2007) 'A critical reflection on the research priorities for improving the health and social care to black and minority ethnic groups in Wales', *Diversity in Health and Social Care*, 4(3), 193–201.

Wimmer, A. and Glick Schiller, N. (2002) 'Methodological nationalism and beyond: nation state building, migration and the social sciences', *Global Networks*, 2 (4), 301–34.

47

Developing the evidence to challenge 'welfare reform': the road to 'Cash Not Care'

Mo Stewart

Introduction

Nine years ago I would not have described myself as a 'researcher'. Nine years ago I had no need to be a 'researcher'. That all changed in September 2008 when I was confronted by a staff member employed by a company generally known as 'Atos Healthcare'. They were under contract to the British government to conduct the Work Capability Assessment (WCA), introduced by the Department for Work and Pensions (DWP) to limit funding for the new Employment and Support Allowance (ESA) income replacement sickness benefit.

The Atos Healthcare visitor claimed to be a doctor, yet refused to offer any form of identity when he entered my home for what was meant to be a medical review of my War Pension. He behaved unethically, going out of his way to create tension; refused to offer eye contact when devoting all his attention to firing off meaningless questions and entering my answers in his laptop. When I attempted to hold a conversation, he unceremoniously dismissed me with an offensive wave of his hand.

A War Pension is not a benefit and, until April 2005, it was the medical pension provided for disabled personnel who were medically discharged from military service with a permanent and significant disability. It is unrelated to long-term sickness benefit funded by the DWP.

In December 2008 I hadn't heard of the WCA and I wasn't anticipating any problem with the War Pension review medical. I had no idea that the DWP had adopted a 'non-medical' assessment model, as influenced by the discredited corporate American healthcare insurance giant, UnumProvident Insurance, who were appointed as official government advisers for 'welfare claims management' in 1994 in order to reduce the future DWP welfare budget. The corporate giant

389

government advisers changed their name to Unum Insurance in 2007, following relentless legal challenges in America.[1, 2]

Regarding the War Pension review, the Atos Healthcare report was a work of fiction when using the WCA and claimed that I had no physical limitations, while disregarding all previously provided very detailed medical evidence. This claim challenged my integrity and I 'went to war' with the then Service Personnel and Veterans Agency (SPVA) to clear my name. I refused to permit some SPVA administrator to suggest that I was dishonest and this was eventually resolved when a consultant visited me on behalf of the Appeal Tribunal. His detailed and accurate medical report exonerated me and exposed the Atos Healthcare report as being 'preposterous'.

The journey to find justice took two years involving a protracted battle with the SPVA and thus began my personal 'voyage of research discovery', as I realised that the evidence I was uncovering for my own battle had implications for other chronically sick and disabled people who would eventually have to endure the WCA, which is based on the totally discredited biopsychosocial (BPS) model of assessment.[3]

From the personal to the political

While my increasing disability was belatedly acknowledged by the SPVA, and the War Pension was eventually increased and backdated, nevertheless, I faced a moral dilemma as the evidence I had discovered when challenging the Atos Healthcare WCA report clearly needed to be shared with other long-term sick and disabled people. Forewarned is forearmed.

I began sharing the research evidence with the new and growing number of Disabled People's Organisations (DPOs) and, by 2010, my first research report 'Atos Healthcare or Disability Denial Factories'[4] was published thanks to the kindness of my original webmaster, Mike Bach, who willingly shared his website at Why Wait Forever[5] to permit my research evidence to be published online. The research evidence was welcomed by DPOs and reproduced on a variety of websites, as claimants began offering the evidence to MPs who asked questions about the WCA in the House of Commons.

As my research continued I began sharing the evidence with members of the House of Lords (HoL) and, by 2011, I was invited to provide a research briefing for a welfare reform debate in the HoL. 'Welfare Reform – Redress for the Disabled'[6] was quoted by Baroness Tanni Grey-Thompson, exposing the influence of the American corporate giant Unum Insurance with the DWP welfare reforms, and the fact that Atos Healthcare was not registered with the health and social care regulator, the Care Quality Commission, so the general public had no protection from malpractice.

My early research reports were written for and on behalf of other long-term sick and disabled people. They were not intended as academic papers but straightforward reports, exposing a lot of information that could be understood by the lay public, when identifying the corporate influences behind the introduction of the WCA.

As a former healthcare professional, I had already established that the WCA was a bogus and dangerous assessment model. The WCA was described by the DWP as a 'functional assessment', which seemingly justified the fact that the appointed Atos Healthcare 'health professional' would conduct the WCA without access to the claimant's past medical history. The diagnosis and prognosis would be totally disregarded by basic grade DWP administrators who were given the title of 'Decision Makers' and, from this limited evidence, I knew that the WCA could cause preventable harm and that many ESA claimants were likely to die – as indeed they have. But I had to prove it, and little did I know that it would take almost seven years to complete my task. Over time, I was to become a very experienced researcher!

The lessons learned

Eventually, I approached academics at various universities, whose research tends to be published in peer reviewed academic journals that few people know of, and even fewer will have accessed due to the costs involved. I discovered that the cost of such access was prohibitive for me, so I nervously began to contact the academics to seek access from them. Without exception, all those I contacted willingly shared their research papers and encouraged my efforts. I was to learn the great value of detailed independent academic research, which was not funded by a discredited American corporate giant or commissioned by the DWP.

When conducting my research, the first thing I needed to learn was *persistence*. DWP administrators think that questions can be dismissed by a standard reply, while failing to answer a direct question with a direct answer. I also needed to adopt *patience* when requesting access to evidence from busy academics and other professionals. This coincided with the realisation that they were under no obligation to help me as I pursued the evidence with no budget, and without the academic qualifications to suggest that I was capable of conducting the research.

During what was to become six years of in-depth research, together with another 12 months needed to write the book – *Cash Not Care: The planned demolition of the UK welfare state* – no one I approached ever dismissed my request for help, and a handful of academics went the extra mile to help me, including promoting my book when it was released in September 2016.

I learned that human decency still exists, even from strangers whom I'll never meet, yet who did anything they could to help me to produce the book.

The research exposed the fact that the British welfare reforms were a duplicate of American designed welfare policies, as both nations had conducted simultaneous attacks on their most vulnerable citizens, jointly planned over 20 years ago.

Encountering and overcoming problems

Little did I know when I began the research what disturbing evidence I would often find. This produced frequent moral challenges, as I knew that some of the evidence could cause distress to readers who might already be very, very ill. I'm not certain I ever overcame the concern that something I wrote could cause distress to a vulnerable claimant, but I told myself that the evidence must be exposed.

The self-funded book *Cash Not Care: The planned demolition of the UK welfare state* was released by New Generation Publishing on 14 September 2016 and has enjoyed approval from academics, professionals and DPOs.[7] The national press refused to expose research evidence described as 'government funded tyranny'[8] claiming they 'would not risk'[9] exposing a corporate giant's influence with the UK government in fear of possible future litigation.

Cash Not Care is available online via Blackwell's books in Oxford who, to date, are the only bookseller to have stocked the book, which is of relevance to at least three million people in the UK. It is also available online via Waterstones, WH Smith and Amazon.

Conclusion

What began as an investigation into the unacceptable behaviour of a staff member from Atos Healthcare, who carried out a WCA instead of a War Pension review, became what I have termed my 'voyage of research discovery'.

The research opened the door to contact with some exceptional people, who have gone out of their way to encourage my efforts, to support my research and to use the evidence I reported. This includes other chronically sick and disabled people, with DPOs publishing my research on a variety of websites to inform their readers. I have benefitted from help from national charities, military charities, independent professionals and, especially, from academics who were very enthusiastic that their research findings, which were usually restricted to academic journals, would be cited and quoted in my book and accessed by a wider general public.

My research reports have been quoted during debate in both the HoL and the House of Commons, and a number of noble members appear to trust my judgement and consult me regarding my area of expertise.

What began as a personal battle to restore my integrity became, over time, a very long journey of research discovery that culminated in September 2016 with the publication of my book, *Cash Not Care*. From my 2008 Atos Healthcare assessment to the publication of the book involved a total of eight years of independent research. And the future seems promising, as I gave the keynote talk to the National Union of Disabled Students in April 2017, and I have been invited to take part in an academic seminar in September 2018. Whilst the book is complete, my voyage of research discovery continues.

Notes

[1] 'Insurer Unum Group reverses 42% of previously denied disability claims' https://attorneypages.com/hot/unum-group-reverses-denied-disability-claim.htm

[2] 'Unum Complaints', Online Lawyer Source, www.onlinelawyersource.com/unum/complaints/

[3] Shakespeare, T., Watson, N. and Abu Alghaib, O. (2016) 'Blaming the victim, all over again: Waddell and Aylward's biopsychosocial (BPS) model of disability', *Journal of Critical Social Policy*, 37 (1), 22–41, http://csp.sagepub.com/content/early/2016/05/25/0261018316649120

[4] 'Atos Healthcare or Disability Denial Factories: research summary', 25 June 2010, www.whywaitforever.com/dwpatosveteranssummary.html

[5] 'DWP ESA Medical Examinations', Why Wait Forever, www.whywaitforever.com/dwpatos.html

[6] 'Welfare Reform – Redress for the Disabled', research summary, September 2011, www.whywaitforever.com/dwpatosveterans.html#wres

[7] 'Disabled researcher's book exposes 'corporate demolition of welfare state'', Disability News Service, 15 September 2016, www.disabilitynewsservice.com/disabled-researchers-book-exposes-corporate-demolition-of-welfare-state/

[8] 'UK government refuses to accept responsibility for identified crimes against humanity – a report', https://www.researchgate.net/publication/263673446_UK_GOVERNMENT_REFUSES_TO_ACCEPT_RESPONSIBILITY_FOR_IDENTIFIED_CRIMES_AGAINST_HUMANITY_-a_report

[9] *Guardian* sub-editor personal telecom, October 2008.

48

Service user-controlled research for evidence-based policymaking

Alison Faulkner

In this chapter I explore the role and value of user-controlled research in relation to the development of social policy, drawing on the pioneering UK experience as a case study. The chapter turns our attention towards the different situations in which service users (disabled people, patients, members of the public) have seen the need to do their (our) own research rather than becoming involved in research directed by others. The focus here is on the value it has to those undertaking it and the potential impact it can have on people, services and social policy. User-controlled research has its origins in people's frustration with the services that fail to listen to them and the research that fails to explore issues of concern to them, as this chapter will demonstrate.

Together with other evidence, I will draw on a report that explored seven examples of user-controlled research: *Changing Our Worlds: Examples of user-controlled research in action* (Faulkner, 2010), funded by INVOLVE. INVOLVE is the arm of the UK National Institute for Health Research established to support active public involvement in NHS, public health and social care research. The report was commissioned in 2010 to explore the role and value of user-controlled research through a series of seven case studies.

What is user-controlled research?

The key piece of work to shed light on 'user-controlled research' was undertaken by Turner and Beresford (2005), funded by INVOLVE. In defining it, they align user-controlled research with both survivor and emancipatory disability research. At the heart of user-controlled research is the principle that service users hold the control of the research, but it is also allied with the notion of empowerment or liberation of service users and disabled people inherent in emancipatory research. Turner and Beresford (2005) suggest that control by service users is the key defining characteristic of user-controlled research, but that its central purpose is to bring about positive change to the lives or experiences of service users and disabled people. They further identify the aims in terms of:

- Empowerment – both through the process and the purpose of the research
- Being part of broader social and political change
- More equal relations of research production
- Being based on social models of understanding and interpretation.

In a later scoping review for the NIHR School for Social Care Research, Beresford and Croft (2012) refer to user-controlled research as 'research that is actively initiated, controlled, directed and managed by service users and their organisations, exploring subjects and questions that concern them'.

There are other terms sometimes used to refer to user-controlled research (although their meanings may be confusing and need to be explored within context). One of these is user-led research and, although this is often used to refer to user-controlled research, it is also a term used to refer to user-focused research or involvement in research; in other words, the control of the research may not be absolute. The term 'survivor research' is used to refer to user-controlled research carried out by mental health service users and survivors. Equally 'emancipatory disability research' is used to refer to user-controlled research carried out by disabled researchers.

The roots of user-controlled research

One of the strongest roots of user-controlled research lies within the disabled people's movement. The focus of emancipatory research is on researching disabling environments or a disabling society rather than the individual deficits of disabled people (Boxall and Beresford, 2013). Integral to the emancipatory paradigm is a challenge to academic or professional knowledge about disabled people, as is the accountability of researchers to organisations of disabled people; 'such research approaches are therefore openly partisan' (Boxall and Beresford, 2013: 592).

Research can seek to emancipate disabled people/service users through challenging traditional research methods, adopting an inclusive and participatory approach to research, and through describing people's individual or collective experience in their own terms. Survivor research (research by mental health service users/survivors) shares a common pathway with emancipatory research, in that it is controlled by mental health service users and has the aim of empowerment at its heart (Beresford and Wallcraft, 1997; Faulkner, 2004).

Another significant root of user-controlled research is research emerging from social movements such as feminism. Feminist research adopted a 'standpoint' approach (Harding, 1993; Rose, 2014; Burstow, 2015), which aimed to overturn the traditional roles of the researcher and the researched through sharing identity and understandings with research participants. This shares with user-controlled research and survivor research the value placed on experiential knowledge and on reducing the distance between researcher and researched (Beresford, 2005), an approach anathema to positivist research, which values the distance of an assumed objectivity.

Key to these approaches is a transparency about the identity, perspective and approach undertaken by the researcher. This is followed through in user-controlled research in the range of ways in which service users undertake and control research that amplifies certain aspects of their own lives and experience. It is fundamentally about power: the power to undertake the research that you want, to define yourself as you want, the power to become the 'knowers' and not the 'known' or pathologised (Boxall and Beresford, 2013; Jones and Brown, 2013).

Experiential knowledge

The foregrounding of experiential knowledge gained from direct personal experience of the issues under study also distinguishes user-controlled research (Beresford, 2005). Glasby and Beresford (2006) ask some fundamental questions about the nature of knowledge within a context based on evidence-based medicine and practice. They highlight the crucial contribution that 'experiential knowledge' has to bring to the evidence table, and Beresford (2005) highlights the value of *reducing* the distance between direct experience and its interpretation through user-controlled research. If traditional research is prepared to ignore abuse and discrimination in the interests of positivist methodology, then it can create a 'false and potentially dangerous view of the world' (Glasby and Beresford, 2006: 271). Russo (2012) emphasises the importance of imparting an insider perspective to research; for her, too, closeness to the subject of the research is beneficial to the research quality, enhancing its validity.

Involvement in research

To set user-controlled research in context, it is useful to look at the broader movement for user (or public) involvement in research in the UK and beyond. The establishment of the government body NIHR INVOLVE (formerly 'Consumers in NHS Research') in 1996 signified a turning point in public involvement in UK publicly funded research. It meant that policies were in place to support and promote the involvement of people directly affected by research in the production of research. The definition of involvement was then quite clearly about the active involvement of members of the public in research: deciding on topics, designing and planning research, carrying out and analysing research and disseminating research findings. In other words, involvement was envisaged as undertaking an active role.

INVOLVE initially proposed a continuum of involvement (Hanley et al, 2004) that runs from consultation through collaboration (involvement) to control. Most public involvement in research is concerned with the large and very mixed area in the middle of this continuum, where the research itself is largely controlled or initiated by (non-service user) academic researchers. In truth, the wide range of ways in which service users are involved in research is inadequately described by this continuum. Sweeney and Morgan (2009) developed this and describe four levels of involvement – consultation, contribution, collaboration and control – but even this masks the potential for variation in form, quality and inequalities at each level.

There are many examples of good practice in collaborative or involvement research (see, for example, Faulkner et al, 2008; Gillard et al, 2012) and growing evidence of its impact (Staley, 2009). However, the move to promote public involvement in research has not been without its difficulties. There have been, and continue to be, many examples of research involving service users or members of the public where their roles are far from active and their involvement is fundamentally tokenistic. Involvement in research brings with it many profound challenges (Russo, 2012; Beresford, 2005; Faulkner, 2004), not the least of which concerns the lack of power/authority to challenge the prevailing research paradigm. An awareness of these challenges was one of the drivers for developing user-controlled research (Glasby and Beresford, 2006). For many people coming from a service user/survivor perspective this approach is seen to 'embody inequalities of power which work to the disadvantage of service users' (Turner and Beresford, 2005: iv). Service users are often 'involved' at some point in the process too late to influence or challenge such fundamental assumptions, resulting in the marginalisation of their experiential knowledge (Russo, 2012).

Power and control

The capacity of user-controlled research to challenge the power and control inherent in social policy decision making with which it is in conflict is limited. By its very nature, user-controlled research embodies challenge (to conventional research methods and mainstream knowledge) and hence is unlikely to attract the resources or support to enable it to challenge the status quo. There are few user-controlled organisations with the resources to carry out significant research. However, as pointed out by Beresford and Croft (2012), collective action can be powerful. Service user and disabled people's organisations working together can effect change. There are some significant examples of user-controlled research challenging public policy with some success. One such example is the research undertaken by disabled researchers and their organisations to establish the evidence base for 'direct payments' (state funds made available to disabled people to purchase the kind of support of their choice; Zarb and Nadash, 1994). The projects featured in Changing Our Worlds (see below) also demonstrate the change that can be brought about on a small scale with limited resources.

Who is doing user-controlled research?

A study commissioned by NIHR INVOLVE tells us that there are many different groups of service users and disabled people engaged in user-controlled research in the UK (Faulkner, 2010). The seven case studies explored in this study were selected from a previous mapping study in which 45 examples of user-controlled research were identified. The research projects were carried out by people representing a wide range of different health and social care themes including people with physical and sensory impairments, older people, people with learning disabilities and mental health service users, young people and people with alcohol issues. The largest group of examples came from mental health service users and people with learning disabilities, which does not reflect the overall population of people who are social care users (Beresford and Croft, 2012).

Changing Our Worlds

'Changing Our Worlds' was commissioned by INVOLVE with the aim of enhancing understanding and awareness of user-controlled research (Faulkner, 2010). Through exploring a small number of projects in detail, the aim was to reach a better understanding of the role and value of user-controlled research. The seven projects selected are listed here.

- Deaf people's mental health pathways: Vision Sense, www.visionsense.co.uk
- Comparison of urine and blood tests for thyroid function: Thyroid UK, www.thyroiduk.org.uk
- Connect Works (what people with learning difficulties want from personal assistants), 2008/9: Connect in the North, www.citn.org.uk
- Disability Hate Crime, 2007: DITO (Disability Information Training Opportunity)
- The Rainbow Ripples report (needs and hopes of Lesbian, Gay and Bisexual disabled people in Leeds), 2006, supported by the Leeds Involvement Project (LIP)
- (1) Get the life you want (GLUW) Making the Lives of Young People in Care Better and (2) Have Your Say – How Looked After Children are involved in the Review Process, 2008/9: two projects supported by the National Youth Agency (NYA) Young Researcher Network
- Relationship Matters, 2008/9: Shaping Our Lives, www.shapingourlives.org.uk

---

People who are not recorded as carrying out user-controlled research in large numbers are service users and disabled people from black and minority ethnic (BME) communities, and older people. When the aforementioned NIHR INVOLVE study was being carried out, the paucity of BME research projects was of concern to the author and commissioners. Jayasree Kalathil (a Black survivor researcher involved in the original mapping project) suggested that these are concepts and modes of working that have developed within a survivor movement in which BME service users had very little role to play.

> 'Even today there are very few BME user researchers around, very little money to train/sustain BME user researchers. Very little opportunities for BME user researchers to find work, especially in "general" projects that are not in some way ghettoised ... I just feel there might be other definitions of how people see "control."' (Kalathil, personal communication)

There is also evidence of user-controlled and survivor-controlled research being carried out internationally (Russo, 2012) although the language used to describe it can be different. For example, Jones et al (2014) talk of 'community-owned research' as research that is genuinely based in, and controlled by, the community, in this case, of mental health service users/survivors.

Reasons for doing user-controlled research

Turner and Beresford (2005) point out that the motivation to make change happen is central to the purpose of user-controlled research. Very often the motivation of service users and disabled people to carry out research for themselves emerges out of frustration with existing research and research paradigms, and a desire to describe or change a situation for their communities (Faulkner, 2010). The Changing Our Worlds projects powerfully demonstrate the needs and priorities of groups frequently ignored or overlooked by mainstream society, some of whom face multiple sources of discrimination.

> 'Somebody needed to tell the story of our lives as LGB [lesbian, gay and bisexual] disabled people.' (service user quoted in Faulkner, 2010)

Through raising awareness of the experiences and needs arising out of their lived experience, groups like lesbian, gay and bisexual disabled people, young people in care, disabled people and Deaf people with mental health needs placed themselves on the map of human experience and were able to exert some influence on local and/or national service or policy development. Closely related to this, several of the projects were responding to a specific need identified by the group: an issue that no-one else would know about or be interested in if they did not have the relevant lived experience, but which could have life-changing implications. Sometimes then, this research shines light into the dark corners of our social care system. As an example, research funded by the Joseph Rowntree Foundation into risk (Faulkner, 2012) highlighted the risks to service users and disabled people of simply having contact with services, and the fear of losing their independence.

Ways of doing user-controlled research

As Beresford and Croft (2012) point out, user-controlled research is not associated with any particular research methods, although the issue of control is central. People very often adopt participatory and qualitative methods as befits the ethos of emancipatory research. Large scale research is rare due to the funding constraints on carrying out research from predominantly small user-led organisations. Some of the largest pieces of research have been based in non-user controlled organisations, which has its own challenges.

The methods used in the Changing Our World projects ranged from the more conventional use of questionnaires, interviews and focus groups through to more innovative and exploratory methods. For example, people with learning difficulties facilitated focus groups and used unconventional but necessarily accessible methods of recording and analysing the data. The Shaping Our Lives project (Relationship Matters) took perhaps the most innovative approach to the research. Through engaging people in five local events they explored people's experiences of the meaning of networking and relationships, 'gathering knowledge' from and with service users. DITO, Vision Sense, and Rainbow Ripples each engaged experienced researchers who shared key aspects of the group's identity to undertake the research on their behalf.

The issue of control needs to be seen within the context of public involvement in research, where service users and disabled people are often making a small contribution to the research but not determining the research direction or paradigm. In the Changing Our Worlds projects, absolute control over the research depended on service users having independent funding (and having control of that funding) as well as a user-controlled organisational base. Two of the projects originated from within non-user-controlled organisations and their control of the research was not absolute. These projects supported service users with no previous research experience, but ensured that they retained control of the majority of the work. People spoke passionately about the significance of having control. For some, this was linked to their commitment to the social model of disability and the importance of carrying out research within the context of this paradigm.

The benefits of user-controlled research

User-controlled research brings many benefits with it: to the researchers, the quality of the research and the communities of service users and disabled people with and for whom the research is undertaken.

Access and trust

For marginalised groups, it makes a significant impact when the research is carried out by someone who identifies as a member of that group. A shared identity between the researcher and participants means that trust can be established, particularly when conducting face-to-face interviews and focus groups, leading to improved access to participants and to open and honest accounts about the issue under investigation (Faulkner, 2010).

> '... when you're interviewed by an academic or someone you don't know you don't have the same level of trust because you don't know what they're doing with that information.' (Rainbow Ripples researcher quoted in Faulkner, 2010)

The value of having a shared identity is also demonstrated when it comes to assessing the quality of the research: the 'insider knowledge' can ensure that the research will address the 'right' questions, and be interpreted by people with an understanding of the nature of that lived experience.

Empowerment

User-controlled research can bring about empowerment for the service users and disabled people involved. People can learn new skills and gain in confidence, enabling them to take part in other activities beyond the research. In the example of Connect Works, some of the people with learning difficulties were enabled to carry out training of personal assistants and to choose their own personal assistants. Empowerment reached out beyond the research and into people's lives.

> 'I want to be able to choose who I want to look after me, rather than have others controlling me.' (Connect in the North researcher, quoted in Faulkner, 2010)

Making a difference

As mentioned earlier, a major motivation for user-controlled research is to make a difference for service users and disabled people. In the Changing Our Worlds research, one project started out with a close relationship with the commissioners which meant that they were able to inform the development of services for D/deaf people with mental health needs. Several of these projects obtained additional funding for disseminating and implementing their findings, and several were able to influence local or national policy (see below).

The challenges of user-controlled research

As mentioned earlier, user-controlled research cannot easily access the same level of resources that academic and mainstream research can. This inevitably has implications for the size and scope of projects, but also for their reach. A parallel challenge is the issue of credibility. The continued privileging of positivist research methods along with their values of 'objectivity' and 'distance' means that user-controlled research is called into question in the academic arena (Beresford and Croft, 2012). However, credibility within voluntary sector, service user and disabled people's communities has different criteria, and this is where user-controlled research more often has its impact. Arguably, for user-controlled research to make more of an impact on social policy the credibility goal posts may have to be moved.

A common factor across at least five of the groups featured in Changing Our Worlds was a strong commitment to a social model of disability, which supports one of the principles of user-controlled research identified by Turner and Beresford (2005). Beresford and Croft (2012) similarly describe user-controlled research as characterised by a commitment to social approaches. This is significant in relation to the potential to impact social policy, as this approach can be in conflict with the dominant paradigm, which places individual impairment or deficit at the centre.

Alongside credibility is the issue of discrimination. Many of the projects featured in Changing Our Worlds involved people facing multiple discrimination. For two researchers, this became a very real part of the research process. The Rainbow Ripples researcher received threatening emails in response to publicity about the research and the disabled researcher for DITO was verbally abused by a member of the public as he left one of the interviews. These experiences reflect the very issues that many of the projects were seeking to address, and powerfully emphasise the importance of planning in support for service user and disabled researchers, particularly for lone workers.

Sharing key aspects of personal identity or experience with research participants can give rise to dilemmas about identity and power as well as distress for researchers. Gaining people's trust through a shared identity can lead to discomfort about the power inherent in their (new) role as researcher.

> 'I want to get my research skills up, report writing and things but I am aware that I'm growing in power. I've only realised it recently because of getting into emancipatory research. It's like I'm being paid, but you [the interviewee] are the one who is still having to go through it.' (Deaf researcher quoted in Faulkner, 2010)

There is a wider challenge to the future of user-controlled research and its inclusivity. The only project in the selection for Changing Our Worlds to involve BME service users was Shaping Our Lives. The earlier mapping stage by INVOLVE identified no projects from BME communities. However, these modes of working within the research and academic worlds have developed within disability and survivor movements in which BME service users have had very little role to play (Kalathil, 2013). Service users from racialised communities face power imbalances from within service user and disability communities as well as from outside: marginalisation and discrimination based on race, ethnicity and culture. The involvement work of BME communities may look different and be assigned different terminology, but is no less valid. Kalathil (2013) points out that the mainstream definition of involvement excludes 'a lot of the work that people were doing on the ground, within their communities' (Kalathil, 2013: 128).

The impact of user-controlled research

A thread running throughout this chapter has been the importance to people doing user-controlled research of making a difference to the lives of service users and disabled people, to their own communities. The impact of research tends to be judged in ways that are problematic in relation to user-controlled research. Research impact is often assessed in academic terms in relation to the number of citations and articles in peer-reviewed journals. The impact of public involvement in research cannot be measured easily, although there are increasing attempts to do so in relation to research quality and outcomes (Staley, 2009).

The challenge is that the impacts valued by those undertaking user-controlled research tend to be seen in terms of changes to services, to social policy and changes to the lives of disabled people and service users (Beresford and Croft, 2012; Faulkner, 2010). These are harder to identify and quantify. Nevertheless, the impact of the projects in Changing Our Worlds was in many ways disproportionate to their size, funding and scale: in short, they 'punched above their weight'. This was largely due to a strong commitment to maintain a focus on implementation from the beginning, and a proactive approach to making use of significant allies and networks.

Nearly all of these projects achieved some degree of change within a local or national context. Some directed their findings towards people in decision making positions within local services with the aim of making changes through policy and service development. Some of the service users who became researchers in these projects talked passionately about gaining new skills, gaining in confidence and feeling empowered. Some had gone on to develop their skills further or to do more research. Many of the projects resulted in tangible outputs which aimed to extend their impact to their wider community of disabled people or service users. Examples of these include: training packs, information packs and a dedicated website, a training programme, DVDs and an improved pathway through mental health services.

Some of the projects managed to have an impact on national policy, whether by virtue of their efforts at disseminating the findings, or through support from their funding body.

Recommendations from the Rainbow Ripples report entered the Commission for Social Care Inspection guidelines. Connect Works, through dissemination via the Skills for Care website, may have had an impact on personalisation policy in relation to people with learning difficulties. The Young Researchers Network (YRN) projects were able to disseminate their findings at a national level through support from the NYA, including taking part in a House of Lords' debate. The YRN projects also had an impact locally: one made a DVD to be shown to children on entering foster care, and the other managed to get two of its recommendations taken up by local services.

Conclusions

In foregrounding experiential knowledge and democratising research relationships, user-controlled research has the potential to transform what we know and understand about social care and social policy. Some of the projects that fall under this umbrella have had life-changing consequences despite often being small in scale with limited resources.

The projects featured in Changing Our Worlds powerfully demonstrate what can be achieved by small organisations or groups of service users and disabled people on sometimes very small budgets. Most had found creative ways of ensuring that the findings reached the people that mattered, some through obtaining additional funding and some through their relationships with powerful allies. The projects were motivated by the desire for positive change: to improve the lives of service users; to improve services or influence policies that will affect the lives of service users. For the most part, they achieved just that. They highlighted the potential of user-controlled research to raise awareness of the needs of groups and people often ignored or overlooked by mainstream society, creating opportunities to describe and account for their lives, and to identify and explore specific needs not addressed by mainstream research. They further highlight the potential of user-controlled research to create the conditions for empowerment which closely accord with the concerns at the heart of the core methodological base of user-controlled research identified by Beresford and Croft (2012: 9).

Russo (2012) is clear that survivor-controlled research has the potential to produce different outcomes to those generated by conventional research and that such outcomes can fundamentally question mainstream practices. Nevertheless, she says 'despite its considerable progress, this research direction faces major barriers in the effort to gain acknowledgment and secure a future'. The future undoubtedly needs a greater commitment to the value of experiential knowledge and to the organisations that support this. It may seem weak to finish the chapter with a call for more funding, but in many ways that is the reality. Nevertheless, despite this reality, there is no doubt that the projects featured in this chapter are a testament to the power of people with passion and commitment to change their worlds.

References

Beresford, P. and Croft, S. (2012) *User Controlled Research: Scoping review*, London: NIHR School for Social Care Research.

Beresford, P. and Wallcraft, J. (1997) 'Psychiatric system survivors and emancipatory research: Issues, overlaps and differences', in C. Barnes and G. Mercer (eds) *Doing Disability Research*, Leeds: The Disability Press, pp 66–87.

Beresford, P. (2005) 'Developing the theoretical basis for service user/survivor-led research and equal involvement in research', *Epidemiologia e Psichiatria Sociale*, 14 (1), 4–9.

Boxall, K. and Beresford, P. (2013) 'Service user research in social work and disability studies in the United Kingdom', *Disability & Society*, 28 (5), 587–600.

Burstow, B. (2015) *Psychiatry and the Business of Madness: An Ethical and Epistemological Accounting*, New York: Palgrave Macmillan.

Faulkner, A. (2004) *The Ethics of Survivor Research: Guidelines for the ethical conduct of research carried out by mental health service users and survivors*, Bristol: Policy Press on behalf of the Joseph Rowntree Foundation.

Faulkner, A. (2010) *Changing Our Worlds: Examples of user-controlled research in action*, Eastleigh: INVOLVE.

Faulkner, A. (2012) 'The right to take risks: service users' views of risk in adult social care', *The Journal of Adult Protection*, 14 (6), 287–96. [Emerald Literati Highly Commended paper]

Faulkner, A., Gillespie, S., Imlack, S., Dhillon, K. and Crawford, M. (2008) 'Learning the lessons together', *Mental Health Today*, 8 (1), February, 24–5.

Gillard, S., Borschmann, R., Turner, K., Goodrich-Purnell, N., Lovell, K. and Chambers, M. (2012) 'Producing different analytical narratives, coproducing integrated analytical narrative: a qualitative study of UK detained mental health patient experience involving service user researchers', *International Journal of Social Research Methodology*, 15(3), 239–54.

Glasby, J. and Beresford, P. (2006) 'Who knows best? Evidence-based practice and the service user contribution', *Critical Social Policy*, 26 (1), 268–84.

Hanley, B., Bradburn, J., Barnes, M., Evans, C., Goodare, H., Kelson, M., Kent, A., Oliver, S., Thomas, S. and Wallcraft, J. (2004) *Involving the public in NHS, public health, and social care research: Briefing notes for researchers*, Eastleigh: INVOLVE.

Jones, N. and Brown, R.L. (2013) 'The absence of psychiatric C/S/X perspectives in academic discourse: consequences and implications', *Disability Studies Quarterly*, 33 (1).

Jones, N., Harrison, J., Aguiar, R. and Munro, L. (2014) 'Transforming research for transformative change in mental health: towards the future', in G. Nelson, B. Kloos and J. Ornelas (eds) *Community Psychology and Community Mental Health: Towards Transformative Change*, Oxford: Oxford University Press.

Kalathil, J. (2013) '"Hard to Reach"? Racialised groups and mental health service user involvement' in P. Staddon (ed) *Mental health service users in research: Critical sociological perspectives*, Bristol: Policy Press, pp 121–34.

Rose, D. (2014) 'Patient and public involvement in health research: Ethical imperative and/or radical challenge?', *Journal of Health Psychology*, 19 (1), 149–58.

Russo, J. (2012) 'Survivor-controlled research: a new foundation for thinking about psychiatry and mental health', *Forum: Qualitative Social Research*, 13 (1).

Staley K. (2009) *Exploring impact: Public involvement in NHS, public health and social care research*, Eastleigh: INVOLVE.

Sweeney, A. and Morgan, L. (2009) 'The levels and stages of service user/survivor involvement in research', in J. Wallcraft, B. Schrank and M. Amering (eds) *Handbook of service user involvement in mental health research*, West Sussex: Wiley-Blackwell, pp 25–35.

Turner, M. and Beresford, P. (2005) *User Controlled Research: Its meaning and potential*, Eastleigh: INVOLVE.

Zarb, G. and Nadash, P. (1994) *Cashing in on Independence*, Derby: British Council of Organisations of Disabled People.

49

Participatory citizenship, gender and human trafficking in Nepal

Diane Richardson, Nina Laurie, Meena Poudel, Shakti Samuha and
Janet Townsend

Introduction

Almost every country in the world is affected by human trafficking. It is a global phenomenon and a priority for many governments. Over the past two decades a concern with human trafficking has produced much research, most of which seeks to explain its causes and characteristics, in particular through attempts to quantify which groups of people and how many of them are trafficked, as well as documenting the process and geographical flows of trafficking. Despite this growth in the literature, human trafficking remains a contested concept. In addition to a lack of conceptual agreement on what trafficking is (and is not), the dominant approach to knowledge production and data collection on trafficking has itself also been criticised (Doezema, 2010; Zhang, 2009). Research has often been led by policy frameworks and NGO practices targeting the 'rescue' of people, especially women and children, experiencing diverse trafficking situations. In this chapter, we argue that, as a result, little empirical research has addressed post-trafficking. Consequently, scant attention has been given to the challenges post-trafficking scenarios raise for governments and (I)NGOs. What is also often missing in research that seeks to establish the 'facts' about trafficking are the voices, perspectives, and knowledge of those who have themselves been trafficked and are now attempting to establish new lives post-trafficking. This represents a significant gap in our understanding of trafficking and consequently the success, or not, of anti-trafficking initiatives and interventions.

Extensive debate exists on how marginal voices are included in policymaking following now well-established critiques of participatory development (Cooke and Kothari, 2001; Mohan, 2004). In this chapter we examine academic and activist collaboration through knowledge co-production as one aspect of participatory development. Co-production of knowledge is based on bringing different social worlds, in this case practitioners, academic, and community, together for a single goal.

In this chapter we examine how a new agenda on post-trafficking is gaining momentum through anti-trafficking collaborations based on co-producing knowledge with women who have returned from trafficking situations. This includes women who now consider themselves leading anti-trafficking advocates working through an increasingly high profile anti-trafficking organisation (Shakti Samuha, Nepal) which they themselves founded in 1996. Our analysis seeks to explore the importance of generating distinct types of co-produced knowledge through different spaces and at particular strategic moments. In this way, we reflect on the importance of planned and unplanned opportunities in long-term anti-trafficking advocacy by describing different knowledge production activities. Our analysis highlights their outcomes and teases out the roles of different actions, and reflective processes, in producing strategic engagements around knowledge exchange with policymakers, academics, and activists, as well as women who have experienced trafficking situations, some of whom identify as anti-trafficking activists. More broadly we aim to highlight how activist–academic forms of co-production on post-trafficking in the context of research in Nepal help to generate new understandings and agendas that, in turn, challenge the ways in which research on trafficking is conducted.

Understanding post-trafficking in Nepal

Broadly defined, the term 'post-trafficking' describes the processes and practices associated with returning 'home' from trafficking situations, for whatever purposes, whether this involves being trafficked internally in one's own country or elsewhere. The research we conducted sought to analyse the post-trafficking experiences of women. As mentioned above, the research was based on a collaborative partnership with Shakti Samuha, one of the first anti-trafficking organisations in the world to be founded and staffed by women who have experienced trafficking.[1] This partnership was important as not only are the issues faced by these women largely ignored, but also the stigmatisation and poverty which they typically encounter means that, even when women gain a voice through processes that transform identities from victims – survivors – to activists (as the work of Shakti Samuha indicates), these voices often go unheard in dominant policymaking discourses. Specifically, the research sought to create a space to make the voices of women who have experienced trafficking heard in policy development and implementation, through an investigation of how post-trafficking issues intersect with access to citizenship. Another partnership was also established with the International Organization for Migration (IOM) in Nepal once the funding had been awarded and provided further opportunities to influence the process by which knowledge could be co-produced, as explained in more detail later.

Nepal was chosen because it is one of the source countries for trafficked women in South Asia. Women are trafficked to India through the open border and also on to other countries, including those in Southeast Asia and the Middle East (Poudel, 2011). Although estimates are difficult to interpret, the US State Department TIP Report estimates that between 10,000 and 15,000 women and children are trafficked from Nepal to India and Gulf countries annually (US Department of State, 2012). Another reason for choosing Nepal is that women returning from trafficking situations, while representing one of the most stigmatised, vulnerable groups, are also beginning to organise around rights to livelihoods. This is a key aspect of the anti-trafficking work undertaken by Shakti Samuha. A further reason for the choice of Nepal is that it has undergone democratic reform through a constitutional process following a decade of civil war. Our project explored the intersections of sexuality, gender and citizenship in women's livelihood strategies as these new democratic processes, supported by national and transnational communities, unfolded (Richardson et al, 2016).

The research findings (see Laurie et al, 2015) established that the difficulties many women face on leaving trafficking situations present severe challenges to them in making new lives and forging sustainable livelihoods. Shakti Samuha and other anti-trafficking organisations have actively lobbied for rights to livelihoods and changes in citizenship rules that discriminate against women, who historically have needed a male relative to endorse their application for citizenship on reaching 16 years of age (Pant and Standing, 2011; Richardson et al, 2009). For many women returning from trafficking situations the stigma and family rejection they encounter makes this process formidable, often effectively making them stateless in their home country upon return.

These issues have fundamentally shaped the focus of our research, framing how, where, and why co-production occurred. Although our findings highlight an extreme case of discrimination, and draw on experiences taking place in a particular political context, our emphasis on co-production has implications for the approach to research on post-trafficking more generally. This includes in contexts where the discrimination may not be so obvious or where citizenship may be less central.

Methods and approach

Our study ran from November 2009 to April 2012.[2] In this chapter we draw and reflect on four sources of qualitative data which represent different levels and forms of collaboration and co-production. First, the overall framing of the discussion has been informed by the core data collection, which involved 37 interviews conducted with Nepalese women who had returned from diverse trafficking situations. Although we have not quoted directly from these data here, our interview analysis highlighted that professionalisation was an increasingly important issue for anti-trafficking groups in Nepal. It was therefore decided that a further subset of nine interviews would be conducted with women who had left trafficking situations and who identify as activists, in order to explore these issues in more depth. These interviews, which we draw on directly in this article, were carried out between October and November 2011. They took place midway between the study's two large co-hosted workshop activities (see below) and, in the case of senior long-serving Executive Committee members, sometimes became part of reflective learning processes in the ongoing dialogue among the research activist–academic partners. As a result, the new research theme and data source represented a more overt co-productive engagement with Shakti Samuha as research collaborator–participants, as do the third and fourth data sources.[3]

The third source of data was the two large co-hosted workshops: an activist workshop to debate emerging findings (February 2010) and a policy workshop 'Making Livelihoods Post Trafficking: Sexuality, Citizenship and Stigma' (November 2011), both of which took place in Kathmandu. The fourth set of data emerges from information collected by Shakti Samuha as a feature of the way they work with women who seek to become members of their organisation.

Specifically, this data collection relates to their understanding of trafficked identities not only as part of membership formation, but also in terms of raising public awareness about what a trafficked identity means and what being a trafficked activist involves. It is not the focus of this chapter to explore these issues and processes; rather here we explore what co-production means in practice through a reflective analysis of how a sample of this data was selected, with input from the research project team, for use in advocacy focused on the Constituent Assembly (CA). The opportunity for this advocacy moment arose directly from the co-hosted/co-produced activist workshop above (part of the third data source).

We draw on extensive participant observation in the co-hosted events and follow-up advocacy activities, as well as data from interviews with the Shakti Executive Committee, which included reflections upon these actions. The aim is to show the diverse ways in which collaboration and co-production were woven through the project at different levels, in order to ensure trafficked women's perspectives are made visible, and foregrounded in data production, analysis, and dissemination.

Collaboration, co-production, and a shared agenda

The collaborative partnership with Shakti Samuha shaped the research's focus on citizenship and livelihoods from the outset, prioritising in particular the situation of women returning from trafficking situations. Although founded in 1996, Shakti Samuha initially struggled to gain legal registration as an NGO because the founding members did not at that time hold citizenship cards. This lived reality sparked a longstanding interest in improving trafficked women's citizenship rights, which became a core focus of the research.

Growing from a small base, Shakti Samuha now provides solidarity in a number of ways for women who have left trafficking situations, through hostels, outreach programmes, and livelihoods training. Its work was recognised in 2013 by the Ramon Magsaysay Award, which celebrates courage in serving others and is widely understood to be Asia's Nobel Prize. While Shakti Samuha has grown significantly as an organisation in recent years, managing a number of projects funded by a range of international donors (Shakti Samuha, 2008); only women who have experienced trafficking can become members and serve on the Executive Committee.

As part of its increasingly diverse portfolio of advocacy activities the research project was Shakti Samuha's first move into academic research. At Shakti Samuha's request, research training became a central element of the research project's design, delivered through a two-year modularised programme for Executive Committee members. In this way, capacity building for knowledge co-production was emphasised from the outset. The training was conceptual and also involved practical skills.

Overall the training programme reflected a strong sense of the need for trafficked women to be authors of their own stories.

> 'Shakti has been doing research funded by other donors and recruiting researchers for us. But this is us doing research for ourselves and it is very important to analyse our social world from our perspective.' (Interview, Executive Committee Member, Charimaya Tamang, 2011)

In the feedback session after completing the first training module, the same Executive Committee member stated that the training would enable them to make informed decisions when dealing with the media and other researchers: "Now we know what to ask researchers/media interviewers and foreign researchers coming and taping our stories." This reflection indicates that engagement in knowledge exchange not only involved co-production but also knowledge sharing as part of 'grassroots attempts to operationalise empowerment' (Kabeer, 2004: 224).

Shakti Samuha argues that capacity building through research training for women who have experienced trafficking themselves is more likely to ensure that policy development is based on real not assumed needs. It highlighted this point with its presentation on the importance of research training ('A Reflection on the Journey from Trafficking Survivor to Social Researcher') at the policy workshop. In this presentation Executive Committee Member Laxmi Puri argued that: "Research conducted by survivors themselves would be more effective and help to identify the real status of trafficking survivors, identify their needs and make recommendations to stakeholders in order to fulfil their actual needs." This was a significant forum in which to make such a point, as this policy workshop (co-hosted by Shakti Samuha, the research team, and the IOM) attracted more than 100 participants, including senior policymakers, members of the Parliament Women's Caucus, and several CA members including members of the Fundamental Rights Committee. It was opened by the Minister for Women, Children and Social Welfare and chaired by the President of Shakti Samuha. The event served to highlight how policy development could be made more responsive to women's needs if building their research capacity is prioritised. Towards the end of its presentation Shakti Samuha outlined an agenda for future research and has since developed its own research proposal ('Access to Justice? Social impacts on women after filing legal cases against traffickers in post-trafficking situations').

Scaling up knowledge transfer and co-production

The research project's focus on the need to build capacity that enables trafficked women to become co-producers of knowledge on anti-trafficking was also scaled up through two additional training programmes taking advantage of moments when Shakti Samuha was playing a leadership role in national and international level anti-trafficking networks due to its growing profile. The first was during Shakti Samuha's period as chair of the Alliance Against Trafficking in Women and Children in Nepal, AATWIN (the national umbrella organisation for Nepal's anti-trafficking organisations). A two-day workshop (in November 2010) for AATWIN's 35 membership organisations promoted understanding of anti-trafficking's relationship with human rights. The second was a three-month research training programme (July–September 2012) jointly for AATWIN and the Global Alliance Against the Trafficking of Women (GAATW). Shakti Samuha was also a member of GAATW's board at the time. The training aimed to build capacity in generating baseline data on livelihood needs for future international lobbying around the UN optional (Palermo) protocol on trafficking, which the UN signed in 2000.

Another important feature of the emphasis on the co-production of knowledge with women who have returned from trafficking situations (including activists in Shakti Samuha) was the joint hosting of the activist workshop, in Kathmandu in February 2011. By reviewing NGO programmes' strategic development in the light of five core themes derived from research findings, the aim of the workshop was to generate co-produced advocacy-focused data with a wide group of anti-trafficking activists. This workshop was purposefully scheduled to coincide with the last stages of submission of the first drafts of various thematic committees to the CA writing the new constitution. This example highlights the importance of not only generating knowledge exchange opportunities that aim to co-produce new knowledge on anti-trafficking interventions, but also points to the way in which well-timed opportunities are able to take advantage of crossover interests around a specific issue such as citizenship. While women leaving trafficking situations experience citizenship in particular ways, some of the exclusions they face are also applicable to women in general. This is reflected in the alliances made through both the activist workshop and follow-up lobbying of the CA, as we elaborate below.

Activist workshop

Over 80 participants attended the activist workshop, including anti-trafficking NGOs, donors, 37 women who had experienced trafficking (some, but not all of whom, were members of Shakti Samuha), and high-level government representatives including members of the CA. The workshop acted as a catalyst in stimulating a chain of events that led to policy debate and political lobbying and, subsequently, to a number of recommendations on rights of citizenship being included in the draft Constitution and the National Plan of Action on Trafficking (MWCSW, 2012). The national action plan is currently being implemented and the draft constitution is currently in the hands of the new CA (see below).

The research methodology sought to bring trafficked women's perspectives into policy debates and responses. This had a direct effect on how some workshop participants started to envisage how democratic mechanisms could be used to support women in post-trafficking situations in specific local settings. For example, expressing a clear appreciation of what notions of active citizenship mean in practice, one participant from a grassroots NGO suggested that: "We should make each district and Village Development Committee [VDC – local government office] allocate a budget for women affected from trafficking and ask for their commitments on raising awareness on citizenship and livelihoods and establish rehabilitation centre" (Workshop evaluation feedback, February 2011). Another spoke about the need to follow up the workshop with strategic lobbying of the national CA process: "The issues raised should be collated and submitted to the Chairperson of the Constitutional Committee, for Shakti Samuha to take an initiation and a follow up, this will make change" (Workshop evaluation feedback, February 2011).

As a result, a number of demands concerning citizenship rights for trafficked women and their children came out of the workshop, which Shakti Samuha submitted to various bodies of the CA or constitution drafting committees (see the box below). These fed directly into debates on citizenship in the constitution writing process through ongoing dialogue with relevant subject committees of the CA and the Women's Caucus of the legislative parliament.

Shakti Samuha's proposal to change current citizenship provision in the new constitution
March 2011, Kathmandu

These points were raised in February's activist workshop, promoted through the media campaign, shared with anti-trafficking feminists, human rights activists and wider NGO communities and handed in to CA members/Fundamental Rights Committee Chair.

1 Citizenship to women and men should be granted based on birth, no parents' endorsement required.
2 Citizenship for children born abroad to the mothers who were sexually exploited abroad and now living in Nepal with their mothers should be granted based on state endorsement.
3 Considering the geopolitical location of Nepal and sensitivity attached to citizenship, our demand is to have a special provision. In regard to trafficked women, it should be the state formulating special provisions to grant citizenship to trafficked women and their children and it should be stated in the upcoming constitution.

4 Until radical changes are made, current provision must be amended in line of a provision to provide descent citizenship through mother as well.

5 The gender-based discrimination should be ended: marrying a foreigner, employment, giving citizenship rights to offspring, acquiring Naturalised citizenship should be based on Nepal's agreement with CEDAW[a] and other human rights commitments the country has signed/ratified.

6 Children special: The state should be responsible for providing citizenship to those whose parental detail or descent is unknown.

Note: [a] Convention on the Elimination of All Forms of Discrimination Against Women.

Lobbying the government and Constituent Assembly on anti-trafficking and citizenship

The process through which lobbying occurs illustrates how the co-production of knowledge for advocacy purposes operates on the ground, often through networks of trust and overlapping spaces of influence and jurisdiction. Such networks and opportunities can be the result of unanticipated alliances and opportunities, as well as more long-term strategic network building. Two examples illustrate these different contexts through which the co-production of knowledge generated by the research influenced attention to post-trafficking livelihoods and citizenship issues in policymaking in Nepal. The first example relates to the drafting process for the National Plan of Action on Trafficking. In her role as the IOM Nepal National Programme Advisor, team member Dr Poudel was invited to be a technical expert to the National Committee Controlling Human Trafficking (NCCHT) mandated to formulate, revise and implement the National Plan of Action on Trafficking. Shakti Samuha also served on this committee as a member representing women who had themselves experienced trafficking. While Dr Poudel's long-term relationship with Shakti Samuha pre-dated the research project, the partnership with the IOM did not. Rather this was established after the award of the research funding, as by this time she was employed by the IOM. Subsequently a partnership was formed and a sub-contractual arrangement negotiated between Newcastle University and the IOM in Nepal. This funder agreed because such an arrangement had the potential to influence policymaking at a high level.

The new partnership brought to the fore the need to think and work through positionality issues relating to insider/outsider status and more explicitly the knowledge of research teams members. The combination of Shakti Samuha's growing presence on the anti-trafficking scene in Nepal, combined with the wide reach and profile of IOM's UN networks, helped to ensure broad-ranging engagement with the project's dissemination activities and facilitated knowledge co-production with wider groups in the activist and policy workshops. The end result of the three-way collaboration influenced policy because in March 2012 the Cabinet endorsed the recommendations, informed by the research findings, for the provision of support for women post-trafficking through access to social rights of citizenship (such as housing, medical treatment, victim support fund, education, livelihoods; National Human Rights Commission, 2012).

The second example relates to lobbying the CA on citizenship following the activist workshop in February 2011. Immediately after attending the workshop, the Chair of the CA Fundamental Rights Committee, who had been an active and supportive participant in the research project, contacted Dr Poudel to solicit from Shakti Samuha case study examples of returnee trafficked women's exclusion from forms of citizenship, with a view to presenting them to the CA. They both went to the Shakti Samuha office the next day and while sitting in a room together with the founding members, including the current president, they leafed through compilations of the case histories which are part of the Shakti Samuha membership process.

The case study interviews create a fabric of common and diverse threads. Violence was explicit in the lives of many of the women in our research and this is reflected in the fact that violence against women featured explicitly in seven of the 13 case studies presented to the CA. In some it was the reason for failure to secure citizenship and be able to register a birth, as the following testimonial from one cases indicate.

> 'I fell in love with a boy when I was 21 and married him. I gave birth to a boy after one year. I started facing physical and psychological violence immediately after I became pregnant and later he left me … I started asking my husband to support in making my citizenship certificate and help in registering the baby's birth but he denied. I tried to make this from my maternal home but VDC secretary there also refused to do so. We both are in a big trouble because we don't have this essential document and we don't have our future.' (Case history 1)

In a number of other cases women also approached their VDC to process their citizenship applications without success.

While our research reveals how officials are often unsympathetic to women without citizenship, because they have been trafficked, the cases presented to the CA also suggests that this is a more generic problem for women who do not have the support of a husband or father, for whatever reason.

> 'At the age of 19, one of my friends showed me a man and requested and forced me to marry with him … later on I came to find that he already had two wives along with children. After a year, I also gave birth to a boy but I didn't get any kind of care and support from my husband. He started to abuse me verbally, emotionally and physically by beating and saying bad words to me … I couldn't stay with him … My father didn't agree to give endorsement for my citizenship …

and my husband also denied of giving me citizenship in his name. My son also doesn't have birth certificate.' (Case history 2)

A further and separate thread of deprivation of citizenship is woven for many women through inter-caste marriages. One woman in the case histories submitted to the CA was not accepted by her husband's family and in another case a woman's marriage was not accepted by her own parents. Our research indicates how bias against women in the processes of accessing citizenship is also compounded by the mutually re-enforcing links between poverty and trafficking (Laurie et al, 2010). Testimonial evidence in another case history submitted to the CA also makes this link very clear.

> 'Because I am from a very poor family and I am illiterate, I was lured to a fake marriage and trafficked to Kuwait as a domestic worker … I started to face a lot of domestic and sexual violence from my landlord. After my landlord found I was pregnant with his child, he snatched away all the documents and complained to the police that I was an illegal immigrant. At the custody I met Nepali woman who later helped me and my child to be rescued from there. We came to Nepal and started living with this woman … Later I met a social mobiliser who told me that this woman whom I was living with was also a broker and will potentially traffic me again.' (Case history 3)

In sum it seems likely from our analysis of the 13 cases documented by Shakti Samuha and selected by the Chair of the Fundamental Right's Committee to present to the CA, that in 11 cases simply having been trafficked and family reactions to this precluded women from citizenship. Each of the 13 cases represents a very real demand for the right to citizenship. In knowledge exchange terms these cases were translated and mobilised for advocacy through Shakti Samuha's membership archives providing mechanisms for knowledge storage, and the process of co-selecting cases serving as a form of knowledge brokerage.

Conclusion

Through Shakti Samuha's advocacy, trafficked women without citizenship are lobbying for new policies from a new CA in Nepal that will grant them citizenship in their own right. To this end, the research interviews, the activist workshop, letters to the different CA committees, and the 13 cases presented by the Chair of the Fundamental Rights Committee have been highly successful lobbying tools. The workshop in particular received extensive media coverage, including interviews on Nepali TV and radio stations, and print articles in the Nepali press. It also prompted follow-on events targeting the CA process organised by various NGOs, human rights groups, and media houses. In each of these events knowledge about trafficking continued to be co-produced through engagement between women who have experienced trafficking and identify to different degrees as anti-trafficking activists and leaders, and state and other civil society actors. Through these processes new understandings of anti-trafficking have been generated, setting a new agenda and parameters for the debate, as well as challenging the ways in which research on trafficking is traditionally conducted.

Engaging in research to help bring about change is never a straightforward, unilinear process. Nor is it easy to capture in a snapshot. Sometimes unexpected collaborations come about through changed circumstances, as we have tried to illustrate with the presentation and discussion of the four different kinds of co-produced data in this chapter. We have also suggested that for such circumstances to turn into opportunities, overlapping spaces of influence and jurisdiction need to be aligned through networks of trust built up over long periods of time. This, we would argue, is at the heart of a politically engaged understanding of collaboration that aims to raise the profile and listen to the voices of excluded and marginalised actors.

Notes

1 www.shaktisamuha.org.np
2 This work was supported by The Economic and Social Research Council (ESRC) [Res-062-23-1490].
3 A further 15 stakeholder interviews with activists, key personnel in NGOs and government were conducted.

References

Cooke, B. and Kothari, U. (eds) (2001) *Participation: the New Tyranny?* London: Zed Books.

Doezema, J. (2010) *Sex Slaves and Discourse Masters: The Construction of Trafficking,* London: Zed Books.

Kabeer, N. (2004) *Reversed Realities. Gender Hierarchies in Development Thought,* London: Verso.

Laurie, N., Poudel, M., Richardson, D. and Townsend, J.G. (2010) 'Sexual Trafficking, Poverty, Marginalization and Citizenship in Nepal', ESRC (Project Res-062-23-1490) Working Paper, http://research.ncl.ac.uk/posttraffickingnepal/publications/

Laurie, N., Richardson, D., Poudel, M. and Townsend, J.G. (2015) 'Post-Trafficking Bordering Practice: Marking and Stretching Borders', *Political Geography*, 48, 83–92.

Ministry of Women, Children and Social Welfare (MWCSW) (2012) *National Plan of Action Against Trafficking in Children and Women for Sexual and Labour Exploitation*, Kathmandu: Government of Nepal.

Mohan, G. (2004) *Beyond Participation Strategies for Deeper Empowerment*, London: Mendely.

National Human Rights Commission (2012) *Trafficking in Person Especially on Women and Children in Nepal. National Report 2011*, Lalitpur: Office of the Special Rapporteur on Trafficking in Women and Children.

Pant, B. and Standing, K. (2011) 'Citizenship Rights and Women's Roles in Development in Post-Conflict Nepal', *Gender and Development*, 19 (3), 409–21.

Poudel, M. (2011) *Dealing with Hidden Issues: Social Rejection Experienced by Trafficked Women in Nepal*, Saarbrucken: Lambert Academic Publishing.

Richardson, D., Poudel, M. and Laurie, N. (2009) 'Sexual Trafficking in Nepal: Constructing Citizenship and Livelihoods', *Gender, Place and Culture*, 16 (3), 257–78.

Richardson, D., Laurie, N., Poudel, M. and Townsend, J. (2016) 'Women and Citizenship Post-Trafficking: The Case of Nepal', *The Sociological Review*, 64 (2), 329–48.

Shakti Samuha (2008) *2008 Annual Report*, Kathmandu: Shakti Samuha.

United States Department of State (2012) *Trafficking in Persons Report* (TIP), www.state.gov/j/tip/rls/tiprpt/2012/

Zhang, S.X. (2009) 'Beyond the 'Natasha' Story – A Review and Critique of Current Research on Sex Trafficking', *Global Crime* 10 (3), 178–95.

50

Experiential knowledge in mental health policy and legislation: can we ever change the agenda?

Jasna Russo

The longstanding joint efforts of many disabled people's organisations as well as the committed work of individual activists resulted in the adoption of the United Nations Convention on the Rights of Persons with Disabilities (UN CRPD) in 2006. Signed and ratified by numerous countries along with the European Union, this unique international treaty also guarantees the fundamental rights of people with psychiatric diagnoses. Its Article 4 (3) stipulates that:

> [i]n the development and implementation of legislation and policies to implement the present Convention, and in other decision-making processes concerning issues relating to persons with disabilities, States Parties shall *closely consult with and actively involve* persons with disabilities, including children with disabilities, through their representative organisations. (emphasis added)

As clear and legally binding as this provision is, it cannot by itself reverse centuries of the exclusion and silencing of people labelled mad. Despite the latest discourses of personalisation, inclusion and co-production, the most important decisions about our lives continue to be made without us. Building on my long-time activism in the European movement of mental health service users and survivors of psychiatry as well as my research work, I want to explore how this happens and the prospects of us and our organisations becoming *real* instead of just declared protagonists in matters that directly affect our lives.

The United Nations Convention, reality and the great in-between

The advocacy and political work of many organisations of people who identify as mental health service users, psychiatric survivors or psychosocially disabled can be divided into the era before and after the UN CRPD. The injustices that our organisations have been protesting against for decades are now acknowledged as human rights violations (Russo and Shulkes, 2015). Our political demands are therefore no longer solely calls for what we hold to be just; they are guaranteed as rights and can be claimed as such. Despite this shift, the only right we seem to have in reality is the one to endlessly assert our rights; there has been no sign of those rights being implemented and taken forward in national legislation and/ or policy, let alone in our everyday lives and encounters with the webs of health and social services. In fact, the Convention has made hardly any difference in the individual lives of people with psychiatric diagnoses. If anything, things have become worse.

Among the many sensible provisions of the CRPD, the most exciting and long-awaited one for me and millions of others like me is the abolition of forced psychiatric treatment. It seems, however, that this change is also the hardest one to achieve. The end of forced treatment and substitute decision making is obviously terrifying not only for the psychiatric establishment but also for a number of mental health service users/consumers. Both groups seem unable even to imagine the possibility of support without coercive interventions (Steinert and Lepping, 2011; Plumb, 2015; Norvoll and Pedersen, 2016). And both invoke situations in which people's lives are at risk and need to be saved as the ultimate justification for a seemingly unavoidable and almost natural use of force. The problem with this argument is that while people's lives take place largely outside these extremes, the prospect of receiving unwanted treatment affects *everybody's* encounters with the mental health system. Further, physically saving someone's life at a particular moment is unfortunately not the same as truly saving their life. For the most part, the denial of our legal capacity happens in situations that are not at all life-threatening and preserves our status as second-class citizens. There is sufficient evidence to show that over the long term, a person's life is more likely to be ruined than saved by forced psychiatric interventions (Minkowitz and Dhanda, 2006; Campaign to Support CRPD Absolute Prohibition of Forced Treatment and Involuntary Commitment[1]). Elaborating on this point would exceed the scope of this chapter but I raise it here because the allowance of treatment against one's will remains the central distinguishing element of mental health systems around the world. This core issue cannot be set aside if we are to rethink the whole concept of support as the CRPD envisions and move towards *transforming* rather than endlessly reforming those systems. This is something that numerous inclusion initiatives for the 'mentally ill' and expensive anti-stigma campaigns completely ignore. The very availability of coercion, even when it is not applied, profoundly affects and limits what is possible not only in a helping relationship but also more broadly in the communities and societies in which we live. The UK survivor activist Peter Campbell (1996) summarises:

> That an individual can be compelled to receive psychiatric treatment affects each inpatient regardless of whether his stay is formal or

informal. It is hardly possible to be unaware that you are being cared for within a legal framework that allows for treatment against your will.

This was obviously written at a time when the UK did not have community treatment orders. Interestingly, that extension of forced psychiatric treatment was introduced in 2008, just one year after the UK signed the CRPD. There are other examples that highlight the contradiction between signing and ratifying the Convention on the one hand and adopting new laws and policies that not only enable business as usual but also extend coercion on the other. Six years after Germany ratified the CRPD, a mysterious decision made behind closed doors in Berlin authorised local community-based care providers to allocate 10% of their residential places to the involuntary admission of people with psychosocial and intellectual disabilities (Review Committee for Social Affairs Berlin, 2015). Similarly, when Canada ratified the CRPD in 2010, New Brunswick was one of two regions in the country that did not permit forced community treatment. Now, Community Treatment Orders (CTOs) are to be rolled out there as well (LeBlanc, 2016).[2] There are also countries where poverty means that coercion cannot be concealed and inflicted in 'friendlier' ways. Thus, despite Uganda's 2008 ratification of the CRPD, many Ugandans with psychosocial disabilities are still tied up with rope by family members and brought to psychiatric hospitals where they receive similar treatments (MDAC and MHU, 2014). These countries are increasingly the targets of 'aid' from global psychiatry initiatives that aim to 'educate' and 'humanise' by making psychiatric drugs more accessible.

Thus, despite the CRPD's potential to enact substantial changes, I have to agree with the sex worker activist and campaigner Toni Mac when she says "You can't legislate a better world into existence".[3] Even so, it seems to me that prohibiting, punishing or at least controlling psychiatric violence is a good first step. Legislation is certainly just one of the many areas where serious work is required. It could also be said that research and evidence cannot summon a better world into existence. Still, we need to start somewhere, or more precisely, we need to start everywhere. The question is therefore not so much where we start from but how we proceed. How do we enable and foster change?

What does it mean to be consulted?

The above examples show that there are many powerful ways that authorities can obstruct change even as they formally subscribe to it. This does not apply only at the level of legislation but also to official knowledge production and the use of evidence. It is clear that the abolition of something that has been at the core of a whole philosophy of 'care' for the 'mentally ill' for more than two centuries cannot happen by way of a single provision and isolated actions. The post-CRPD age is characterised by the rise of a new set of experts who are making our cause their agenda. The legal discourse is now interfering with and disrupting what has for too long been an almost exclusively medical realm. This creates new tensions and competition, not least around the issues of funding and authority to research the human rights of the psychiatrised. Due to their scarce resources, service user/survivor organisations fall far short of the requirements for even entering this competition on their own. The psychiatric profession remains the dominant player. With the generous help of public funds, it is now poised to take over a new research field, extending its clinical approach to inquiring into the human rights of its treatment subjects. Thus, for example, in the UK, a psychometrically validated scale has been developed to measure the stigma and discrimination experienced by the 'mentally ill' (Brohan et al, 2013). A similar situation can be seen in Germany, which was recently examined for the first time by the UN Committee on the Rights of Persons with Disabilities, the independent expert body in charge of monitoring implementation of the Convention. Expressing its concern about 'the widespread practice of involuntary placement in institutions of persons with psychosocial disabilities, the lack of protection of their privacy and the lack of data on their situation' (UN Committee on the Rights of Persons with Disabilities, 2015: 5), this Committee called on Germany to 'carry out an independent, human rights-based review of psychiatric services for persons with disabilities'. The German health ministry responded with a call for research proposals concerning the minimising of force in psychiatric institutions. One of the two winners is an exclusively psychiatric consortium led by a psychiatrist who is known to be pro-force. This consortium has, thus, received public funds to conduct an independent human rights-based inquiry into the current use of coercion and propose alternative solutions (BPE e.V., 2016). Turning back to the introduction of CTOs in New Brunswick, survivor activist Eugène LeBlanc (2016: 2) describes the real message of the related public consultation:

> We will bypass this important phase of participatory democracy, and ram the outcome down your throat. Now that we know that CTOs will be a reality, we are interested in your opinion on this important matter. How much tokenism can we bear?

These are just some examples that I happen to know of personally. In the UK and Canadian cases, service users were 'consulted', whatever that means. In Germany, the Federal Organisation of Service Users and Survivors of Psychiatry published an open letter to the Ministry of Health (BPE e.V., 2016) about the decision making process and so managed to draw some publicity to the entire case. But whether they occupied a pre-defined consultation role or held protests afterwards, in all these situations, those directly affected could not challenge the dominance of expert psychiatric knowledge.

Unfortunately, similar scenarios have also played out with legal experts. In its first inquiry into the situation of people with mental health problems and intellectual disabilities in the European Union, the EU's Fundamental Rights Agency (FRA) contracted a consortium which had a participatory approach and contained researchers from the 'target groups', myself included. People from the groups whose human rights and access to justice were being investigated and their representative organisations were substantially involved throughout the whole research process, including in the discussion of the outcomes and content of the final report. Nevertheless, that report was not accepted by the FRA, which held that it presented 'too dark' a picture and lacked best practice examples. Ultimately, our account of this unique international inquiry was broken up into several thematic reports that were then rewritten and released by the funder itself.[4]

This experience confirms Wilson and Beresford's analysis (1999) of how ideas of 'social responsibility' are constructed. These authors observe that in the area of mental health, taking social responsibility is rarely a joint undertaking with people with psychiatric diagnoses, who are not generally permitted to participate in related structures. They warn:

> By speaking *for* or acting *on behalf of* those deemed mentally ill they ('the socially responsible') also contribute to, and perpetuate notions of the 'dependency', 'passivity' and 'incompetence' of people with a mental illness diagnosis; *irrespective of whether or not this is their intention.* (Wilson and Beresford, 1999: 149, emphasis in original)

It is therefore unlikely that decision making processes dominated by professional expertise are up to the task of challenging the deep-rooted epistemic exclusion of people deemed mad. Top-down consultation and involvement activities are ill-suited to securing our fundamental rights and freedoms, as the CRPD demands. As Eugène LeBlanc (2016: 3) puts it:

> If the genesis of a process is unprincipled – then what follows after will sure be as well.

Moving towards leadership rather than participation

Unfortunately, I cannot offer any magic bullet to turn our devalued knowledges and experiential expertise into an integral part of research and policymaking on the issues that directly concern us. I would, however, reiterate that this is as our *right* under Article 4 (3) of the CRPD. In this final section, I will pull together some reflections from survivor authors on the nature of our potential contribution.

Building on work already done

In their excellent report 'Clearing a Path', one Canadian survivor research team writes:

> Perhaps the first consideration is the need for policy-makers to accept what psychiatric survivors have already built and use this as a foundation for change. (PDAC, 2015: 29)

I would suggest that this should also always be our first consideration. Rather than starting from scratch and only providing our individual opinions on given topics as many consultation and involvement activities foresee, we should ground our stances in the work that other users/survivors and their groups have already done. It is unlikely that our work ever starts from zero. Knowing our own history and drawing on contributions internationally will expand our thinking and make our positions stronger and better informed.

Developing our own agenda for change

Striving to develop and put forward our own agenda rather than working to one set by others is another important aspect of effecting change. This inevitably raises the questions of who our allies and partners are and how we are to protect our distinct interest, as Peter Campbell (2001) points out:

> There are underlying difficulties in being involved in work that is wrapped up in the seductive notions of common concerns or partnerships when we are the conspicuously less powerful partner, when others are always issuing the invitations and we are always the new arrivals at the party. ... But loss of control has been made more likely by our reluctance to have coherent, clear and well-communicated agendas of our own.

David Webb (2015: 166) from Australia notes that 'real change will only be possible if it's led by those directly affected by the urgent need for change'. This brings us to the question of leadership as opposed to participation. Mary O'Hagan (2009: 35) argues for the former:

> Part of the problem also lies with the concept of participation itself. To participate people have to rely on the goodwill and invitation of others. In the last decade some users and survivors have used a stronger concept, one that visualises users and survivors as equal to others, as the most informed about our needs, and able to take the initiative. This concept is leadership. Unlike participation, leadership assumes people with mental health problems have the power to set the agenda, make major decisions and control resources. Having said that, leadership of any sort must have boundaries; it should never be absolute and it needs to be shared.

In my opinion, the most important issue surrounding survivor leadership is how to ensure it is sensitive to and inclusive of all the other differences of race and ethnicity, class, gender, sexuality and physical ability that intersect with the psychiatrisation of our experiences. This question must be considered and dealt with carefully if we are to avoid focusing on one form of oppression while reproducing many other kinds. Or, as Audre Lorde (1984: 138) reminds us: 'There is no such thing as a single-issue struggle because we do not live single-issue lives.'

Detaching from biomedical psychiatry

Coming lastly to knowledge production and the question of how to approach madness and distress as full human experiences, I maintain it is essential that we leave biomedical psychiatry and its methods behind. Richard Ingram (2008) reflects on the need for Mad studies in this context:

> There is a problem with continuing to orient our thinking and practice around medicine, psychiatry, and other oppressive forces: the drawback of an excessive or exclusive focus on these oppressive forces is that we often unintentionally enable those forces to continue moulding our thinking and practice. ... Why not take a short-cut to a culture that breaks free of the old forces that once moulded it, and now hold back its development? Why not work on a power-knowledge formation (Disability studies, Deaf studies, Mad studies) that reflects this new-found confidence in not needing to persist in referring back to the forces that once constrained it?

These are just some ideas that may prove inspiring and helpful on the many future occasions when we face the question of how to work for change. As in life itself, our potential contribution depends on whether we follow the script offered to us or invest in developing and sustaining one of our own. Both approaches have their price; both are also subject to personal taste, political preferences and not least available resources. People with psychiatric histories do not represent a homogenous group in any way, including in our aspirations and the beliefs we subscribe to. The leadership versus participation question is probably never a matter of either/or. One thing is clear: while the scripts, invitations and resources are piling up for our role in participation-like activities (from consultation through to involvement and co-production), nobody is going to simply give up their position and enable us to take the lead. As we all know, that is not how emancipation happens. In my view, the question is, thus, not whether we should take the lead but rather how best to do this with the resources we have. I believe that in every situation, there are viable answers if we are only prepared to keep thinking in this direction. So much depends on whether, despite all the hardship involved, we can start to turn the question of how much tokenism we can bear into one of how much leadership we can provide.

Notes
[1]   Campaign to Support CRPD Absolute Prohibition of Forced Treatment and Involuntary Commitment, https://absoluteprohibition.wordpress.com/

2   At the time of this book going into print, CTOs have already come into force in New Brunswick (Bill 41: An Act Respecting the Mental Health Act, 1 November 2017, http://www.gnb.ca/legis/bill/FILE/58/3/Bill-41-e.htm).

3   Juno Mac, 'The laws that sex workers really want', TEDxEastEnd, January 2016, www.ted.com/talks/toni_mac_the_laws_that_sex_workers_really_want

4   Background information about the project along with the thematic reports themselves can be found on the website of the European Union Agency for Fundamental Rights: http://fra.europa.eu/en/project/2009/fundamental-rights-persons-intellectual-disabilities-and-persons-mental-health-problems

References

Brohan, E., Clement, S., Rose, D., Sartorius, N., Slade, M. and Thornicroft, G. (2013) 'Development and psychometric evaluation of the Discrimination and Stigma Scale (DISC)', *Psychiatry Research*, 208, 33–40.

Campbell, P. (1996) 'Challenging Loss of Power', in J. Read and J. Reynolds (eds) *Speaking Our Minds. An Anthology of Personal Experiences of Mental Distress and its Consequences,* London: Macmillan Press, pp 55–62.

Campbell, P. (2001) 'System survivors: is there anything we can do?', www.critpsynet.freeuk.com/PeterCampbell.htm

German Federal Organisation of Service Users and Survivors of Psychiatry (*Bundesverband Psychiatrie-Erfahrener e. V. – BPE e. V.*) (2016) 'Open letter to The Federal Ministry of Health', *Kerbe. Forum für Soziale Psychiatrie*, 03/2016, 41–3.

Ingram, R. (2008) 'From the Mad Movement to Mad Studies', www.academia.edu/15986428/From_the_Mad_movement_to_Mad_studies

LeBlanc, E. (2016) 'The Art of Hatching an Egg. Which came first: Community Treatment Orders OR Public Consultations?', *Our Voice: Viewpoints of the Psychiatrized since 1987,* 62, 1–4.

Lorde, A. (1984) *Sister Outsider,* Berkeley, CA: Crossing Press.

Mental Disability Advocacy Centre (MDAC) and Mental Health Uganda (MHU) (2014) *"They don't consider me as a person": Mental health and human rights in Ugandan communities,* www.mdac.org/sites/mdac.info/files/mental_health_human_rights_in_ugandan_communities.pdf

Minkowitz, T. and Dhanda, A. (2006) *First person stories on forced interventions and being deprived of legal capacity,* Pune: World Network of Users and Survivors of Psychiatry and BAPU Trust.

Norvoll, R. and Pedersen, R. (2016) 'Patients' moral views on coercion in mental healthcare', *Nursing Ethics,* OnlineFirst, 27 October.

O'Hagan, M. (2009) 'Leadership for empowerment and equality: a proposed model for mental health user/survivor leadership', *International Journal of Leadership in Public Services,* 5(4), 34–43.

Plumb, A. (2015) 'UN Convention on the Rights of Persons with Disabilities: out of the frying pan into the fire? Mental health service users and survivors aligning with the disability movement', in H. Spandler, J. Anderson and B. Sapey (eds) *Madness, Distress and the Politics of Disablement,* Bristol: Policy Press, pp 183–98.

Psychiatric Disabilities Anti-violence Coalition (PDAC) (2015) 'Clearing a path: A Psychiatric Survivor Anti-violence Framework', https://torontoantiviolencecoalition.wordpress.com/

Review Committee for Social Affairs Berlin *(Berliner Vertragskommission Soziales - Kommission 75)* (2015) Resolution Nr. 3/2015 *(Beschluss Nr. 3 / 2015),* https://webcache.googleusercontent.com/search?q=cache:mXKSDKDqYY0J: https://www.berlin.de/sen/soziales/_assets/vertraege/sgb-xii/kommission-75/ beschluesse/2015/beschluss2015_3_ergaenzung_lb_unterbringung_bgb. pdf+&cd=3&hl=de&ct=clnk&gl=de&client=firefox-b

Russo, J. and Shulkes, D. (2015) 'What we talk about when we talk about disability: Making sense of debates in the European user/survivor movement', in H. Spandler, J. Anderson and B. Sapey (eds) *Madness, Distress and the Politics of Disablement,* Bristol: Policy Press, pp 27–41.

Steinert, T. and Lepping, P. (2011) 'Is it possible to define a best practice standard for coercive treatment in psychiatry?', in T.W. Kallert, J.E. Mezzich and J. Monahan (eds) *Coercive treatment in psychiatry: Clinical, legal and ethical aspects,* West Sussex: Wiley-Blackwell, pp 49–56.

UN(United Nations) (2006) *Convention on the Rights of Persons with Disabilities* (CRPD), New York: United Nations.

UN Committee on the Rights of Persons with Disabilities (2015) Concluding observations on the initial report of Germany CRPD/C/DEU/CO/1, https://documents-dds-ny.un.org/doc/UNDOC/GEN/G15/096/31/PDF/ G1509631.pdf?OpenElement

Webb, D. (2015) 'The social model of disability and suicide prevention', in H. Spandler, J. Anderson and B. Sapey, (eds) *Madness, distress and the politics of disablement*, Bristol: Policy Press, pp 153–67.

Wilson, A. and Beresford, P. (1999) 'Surviving an abusive system', in H. Payne and B. Littlechild (eds) *Ethical practice and the abuse of power in social responsibility: Leave no stone unturned,* London: Jessica Kingsley, pp 145–74.

Conclusion

Editing this book has been a major project. Two things directly encouraged us to embark upon it. First, our own personal experience of the inadequacy of traditional social policies and services and second, our experience as activists that people's participation could make possible a more hopeful alternative. We felt both that conventional social policy has lost its way and that participatory social policy had something very helpful to offer instead. The work we have done in putting the book together, the contacts we have made and the developments we have discovered mean that our own understanding has expanded, rather than remained static. We have learned so much – especially internationally – and we hope that this book also offers that opportunity to readers. Editing it has opened our eyes to just how much is going on to advance participatory social work in theory and practice globally. It has confirmed our and other people's growing concerns that traditional social policy, whether of the political left or right, may be set on a road to nowhere, the two cancelling each other out. Proposals either continue to be prescriptive and therefore politically weak or backward looking, cutting welfare, turning to the market, deluding us that this offers a way forward.

In our view, the Grenfell Tower tragedy in the UK, in which so many died unnecessarily, is likely to have reverberations for social policy much more widely and for much longer than could ever have been imagined. It has given the lie to previously unchallengeable arguments that public spending is wasteful and damaging, that spending cuts are synonymous with 'efficiency savings' and that only the private sector can ensure that the 'consumer is king', rights and social responsibility secured and the voice of the citizen heard (Walker, 2017). Instead a hidden history has gained prominence, of local people and their organisations being disempowered and ignored as they have warned against hazardous and ultimately fatal policies being pursued. As Alison Cameron said in her chapter on housing, 'the focus on the provision of at best a *house* rather than a *home* ignores the impact lack of suitable housing can have on the human beings who are so often the recipients of the results of decisions made about them without them'.

However, if the Grenfell Tower tragedy offers a chilling warning of where the excesses of neoliberal ideology can lead, we cannot yet assume a politics or public opinion ready for something different. Jasna Russo's final chapter offers a thoughtful and critical but not necessarily optimistic last word from contributors to the book. We believe her realism and caution are justified. One of the themes emerging here is the scale of the challenges that participatory social policy faces. There is no question that our focus, participatory social policy, is still generally treated as marginal in academic and political social policy. Social policy has long

427

been a field of conflict, but the main one that tends to get identified in the 21st century is between right wing neoliberal and more traditional statist left of centre Fabian social policy. Yet both the latter are often experienced by people on the receiving end as arbitrary, patronising and controlling. They can feel like opposite sides of the same coin: imposed, prescriptive and too often unpleasant and demeaning.

As we have said, editing this book has confirmed our belief in and hopes for participatory social policy. It has highlighted for us the enormous body of work that there now is on the subject, both practical and theoretical, macro and micro, up-close and personal as well as structural. While its development is more advanced in some countries, settings and societies than in others, there is no question that we are now talking about a global phenomenon of participatory social policy.

We believe that the journey contributors to this book have taken us all on vindicates the view that participatory social policy has an increasingly important role to play globally and that it not only offers an effective alternative to the present residualising thrust of much policymaking but also a route out of it. However, you wouldn't really know this – unless it was brought to your attention or, like us, you were closely concerned with participatory policy.

So however much progress has been made on participatory social policy, this has yet to be more widely recognised and accepted. There is still a lack of fit between its importance and any more general political or policy acknowledgement of this. Mainstream discourses need to catch up and here is a big task for advocates of participatory social policy to advance. We can also see from contributors to this book, that there are key mainstream social policy commentators who 'get' these ideas and are supportive of them. At the same time, there are others who remain wary and suspicious of them. There is clearly still a big job to be done internationally to support many more to understand and be part of the project. Traditional social policy experts need to know that there is still a role for them, but a changed one; to support and enable broader involvement, rather than to lead or prescribe.

As contributors to the book emphasise, there are also many other challenges to be taken on. Thus, as Iain Ferguson and others highlight, participation can be a highly ambiguous and contradictory concept; used as much by neoliberals to obstruct people's empowerment as by citizens' and service user movements to secure it.

For example, there is increasing evidence to support the view that models, concepts and language originating with civil rights and social movements have been absorbed, co-opted and neutralised by government policymakers (see Beresford, 2016). This is exemplified for England and Wales when 'under the Coalition [government] key developments included a stated commitment to a much greater shared decision making and public engagement – [that was] summed up under the mantra of "no decision about me without me"' (Glasby, 2012: 140). This was the direct co-option of the disabled people's movement rallying cry 'Nothing about us without us' by UK government policymakers whose neoliberal politics undermined health, social care and welfare for disabled and older people and those who experience mental distress as problems – as several chapters in this book attest. 'No decision about me without me' was the title of a policy consultation document associated with the White Paper 'Liberating the NHS'. Ostensibly about patient empowerment in health, the policy has been widely regarded as a continued drive towards the privatisation of the NHS, something very few patient and health practitioner organisations in Britain support (BMA, 2016). As Walden observed in his book about the 'New Elites' in British politics, 'in an age when the abuse of power endured by the common man comes from his loudest champions he will need all the means of defence he can get' (Walden, 2006: 217).

While there are more and less deliberate attempts to subvert participation, for example, by adopting its language and rhetoric and paying lip-service to its principles, we have also seen that there can be less intentional difficulties in the way of its effective achievement. There can indeed be 'many a slip twixt cup and lip' in the practical undertaking of involvement. Many contributors report this in the book; for example, Nicola Yeates and Ana Amaya describe how professional and institutional agendas get in the way of participation, even when there might be a genuine preparedness to work with it. Because of this, it is important to be clear about the complexity of participation and the processes that make it up. We need to be explicit about them and not treat participation in the same superficial way that other ostensibly 'feel-good' concepts like 'community', 'caring' and 'neighbourhood' often seem to have been. Then their meaning is lost and they become a trigger for distrust rather than confidence building and engagement.

It also becomes clear that participatory social policy suffers when it comes to how much authority is conventionally invested in it. The evidence of this book is that this seems to be significantly less than for other kinds of social policy. That is perhaps not surprising since a key claim that academic social policy has long made is that it has the authority of professional 'expertise' and 'scientific' evidence. While we might attach authenticity to the first hand voices that participatory social policy includes, old habits die hard and to academic audiences this is not necessarily commensurate with authority. Furthermore, the introduction of experiential knowledge means that different values and principles apply, to which the same old legitimacy and 'scientific' authority are not necessarily attached. This issue emerges particularly strongly in relation to participatory and user-controlled research, which falls foul of traditional positivist values, but it extends to all aspects of participatory social policy. A key lesson perhaps to be learned from this book is that we should not be apologetic for advancing participatory social policy, as though it requires special pleading, but rather that we need constantly to be critiquing and developing its policy, practice and thinking. Such a process of constant evaluation is essential to safeguard the future of such social policy, but it is also essential that it is itself undertaken in an inclusive and diverse way. The book includes examples of such participatory evaluation and their helpfulness cannot be overestimated.

However, there are also likely to be obstacles in the way of such evaluation, as well as in the way of more participatory social policy more generally. This is because of continuing inequality in the allocation of resources. We perhaps have most evidence relating to this in the context of user-controlled research. Whatever the strengths of such research, we know that it still operates internationally at a relative disadvantage to more traditional research approaches. It faces continuing problems and inequalities accessing funding (Beresford and Croft, 2012). This goes for participatory social policy overall, and perhaps reflects the existing distribution of power and legitimacy that certainly advantages those at the top of the hierarchy, rather than service users, carers and face-to-face practitioners – whose voices still tend to be most marginalised.

We need to have a social policy as practice and discipline that is committed to and prioritises supporting these key stakeholders to have a voice, rather than imposing its own. Crucially the user-led organisations (ULOs) that provide a key basis for both personal empowerment and collective action are still globally denied anything like their fair cut of the cake. Even in countries like the UK where user involvement in public policy has been well advanced – to the degree of there being some requirements for it – service user organisations continue to be inadequately and insecurely funded. A strong network of such ULOs is critical to the ongoing development of more participatory social policy and is a key target to aim for.

We have tried to be honest about the scale of challenges facing more participatory social policy. However, what has struck us greatly about the contributions included in the book is not only the richness, depth and subtlety of what people bring to the subject, but also how much is already being achieved, despite people operating on some very unfertile ground. We organised the book into eight parts and it may be helpful to look at these in turn to explain what we mean.

Part I highlights for us what new and more traditional voices in social policy have to offer each other in developing new relationships between social policy and service users. Here we can see how the participatory project can be helped by theory building and the development of an overview in tune with its democratic and empowering principles. We also get a clearer picture of some of the key exclusions that continue to undermine social policy and serious insights into how to overcome them. In addition we can see how participatory social policy is as relevant in the global South as it is in the North, even though much more still has to be done to extend its reach. In Part II we revisited Beveridge's 'five giant evils' by exploring the views and experience of people who tend to be marginalised by social policy and face additional barriers and discrimination. What seems to emerge from this is less that the founding principles of the founding welfare state are outmoded, as their critics often suggest, but rather that implementing them without including and involving marginalised perspectives is likely to undermine them and be problematic.

In Part III we focused on the contribution that service users' 'experiential knowledge' may make to social policy. In her contribution Diana Rose offered a word of caution about changing understandings and welfare states. This has been taken up by other writers who have also warned against over-simplifying ideas like 'experiential knowledge' (Voronka, 2016). Certainly the diversity of service users means that their experience is unlikely to be either uniform or monolithic. All service users don't and can't know the same and diversity has to be acknowledged. This not an insurmountable problem, but rather a principle to be taken account of. At the same time, as the UK service user organisation Shaping Our Lives has highlighted, solidarity and diversity are not necessarily, as is sometimes assumed, antithetical to each other. Instead it reported that efforts to treat diversity with equality and work in inclusive ways had actually strengthened solidarity (Beresford and Branfield, 2012). Part IV, through the lens of a developmental life course approach, adds to the body of in-depth evidence included in the book which emphasises the importance of social policy involving people who face particular barriers and exclusions if it is not to add to these and the oppression they are subject to, even where that isn't the intention.

What we can learn from Parts V and VI of the book, which focus on campaigning and change, is that not only is social policy change possible but that participatory processes of change are likely to be most effective in achieving any improvement in social policy, as well as being the key route to making it more democratic and emancipatory. We hear over and over again of the gains from including the perspectives of people on the receiving end, as well as the increasing insights that they bring to bear about how to be effectively involved and involved in many different ways and at different levels. We also learn about new forms of campaigning that make possible collective action for individuals and groups who have previously been excluded from it.

Part VII of the book highlights as a theme an issue that actually runs right through the book and is crucial for taking forward more participatory social policy effectively: breaking down excluding barriers and developing effective and inclusive approaches to participation. Perhaps three of the most visible areas of exclusion relate to sexuality, ethnicity and indigenous peoples. The book addresses all of these. But as the earlier work of Shaping Our Lives around inclusive involvement, *Beyond the Usual Suspects*, highlighted, many groups of people still routinely face exclusion – even from participatory initiatives – and this must be challenged (Beresford, 2013). The final part of the book brings us back to research and evaluation. Contributors drill deep to show us the unique contributions of participatory research, as well as some of the rewards and costs of undertaking it. The message here, and perhaps the message of the whole book, is very much that we don't start from a blank page; complex issues surface and we are all likely to need support to take participation forward, whoever we are, but its value can no longer be crudely called into question.

We don't doubt that this book has many limitations, many omissions. We hope you will ascribe those to our shortcomings as editors rather than to the contributors, who we believe have brought an unbelievable range of insights, understandings, experience, analysis and evidence to this undertaking. But more than that, we hope you will see those any such gaps and failings as reasons to extend the focus on participatory social policy and make sure that it gains more and more traction and visibility.

Before we turn finally to proposals and actions for the future, it may be helpful to return to that critical point of departure for modern social policy: the Beveridge Report. In 1941, during the Second World War, William Emrys Williams, Secretary of the British Institute of Adult Education and active in the Workers Educational Association (WEA), set up the Army Bureau of Current Affairs (ABCA). The idea was to educate and encourage discussion about current affairs among men and women in the armed forces, to boost morale and later to focus on what sort of society they wanted to build after the war. Hansard, the official record of the UK parliament, from 2 February 1943 records a debate on controversies surrounding ABCA's summary of the Beveridge Report for discussion by these ordinary service men and women. It reveals an attitude to participatory social policy that persists today, and which this book's contributors challenge in theory and in practice. The Secretary of State for War deemed it too 'controversial' for ABCA participants to be able to access a summary of the Beveridge Report, which could inform and empower them to ask questions. His argument was that the information must be 'completely objective' and not raise expectations. Leading the resulting debate John Dugdale, Labour MP for West Bromwich, said:

> [851] The Gentleman's statement is that the people in the Army must wait until the Government have a definite settled policy and will not alter it; only then may they come forward and give their views. I do not believe this is the procedure to which this democratic country is accustomed. I feel it is most unusual. I would say that we need the opinion of these men and women on the Beveridge Report and on many other matters too. Who are they, these men and women who are not allowed to discuss the Beveridge Report in the only way in which they can discuss it? (HC Deb 2 February 1943 vol 386 cc848–60)

This passage succinctly describes the persistent tactic of, at best, only allowing service users and other citizens to be informed about and help implement social policy, rather than to influence and decide it directly, and in different ways. In their book *The Blunders of our Governments*, social scientists Anthony King and Ivor Crewe argue that this approach results in a cultural disconnect, which can cause policy disasters, 'when the assumptions that politicians and civil servants make … are radically wrong … when [they] unthinkingly project onto others values, attitudes and whole ways of life that are not remotely like their own' (King and Crewe, 2013: 244).

This is an important reminder that struggles over the control of social policy and pressures against participation have always been linked with power, the location of power and inequalities of power. Social policy is the arena where the individual's civic status can come into the sharpest collision with the meeting of their personal rights and needs; where having a say may be most important, but most uncertain and threatened.

In our view, now reinforced by the evidence, ideas and experience contained in this book, participatory social policy offers the best hope of offering an effective alternative to the old binary of state/market welfare. Even now, faced with fears of a neoliberal, automated future that minimises opportunities for employment, would-be progressive commentators are arguing for top-down prescriptions like 'basic income', regardless of already evident inadequacies. They are forgetting that we will need a new needs-led economics based on sustainability – perhaps the biggest issue now facing us as human beings – rather than 'growth' and consumption, and that participatory social policy committed to securing people's rights and needs can offer a route to achieve this. Clearly much more work has to be done supporting ULOs and groups, globally. They are universally under-resourced, although we know that the worst exclusions and disadvantage are in the South.

Finally, we want to return to those two questions with which we began this book and which grew out of its predecessor, *All Our Welfare*.

How should people look after each other in 21st century society?

and

Why and when did taking care of each other as human beings become contentious? (Beresford, 2016)

If we are to take these questions forward seriously then there are some clear but big steps that must be taken:

- Governments and corporations must stop imposing traditional Western approaches on developing countries and instead support them to develop their own participatory approaches.
- Black and minority ethnic communities and those from other oppressed perspectives such as disabled people and lesbian, gay, bisexual and transgender people facing marginalisation must be involved fully and equally in policy debates and decisions.
- The same support and involvement must be offered to indigenous peoples, that is to say ethnic groups who are descended from and identify with the original inhabitants of a given region, in contrast to groups that have settled, occupied or colonised the area subsequently.
- There must be pressure for a change in the distribution of support, learning opportunities, research and development funding so that service users and their organisations are prioritised rather than neglected.

Then a new truly inclusive 'we' may at last be in a position to advance truly *social* policy, based on and capable of securing the rights and needs of us all.

References

Beresford, P. (2013) *Beyond the Usual Suspects: Towards Inclusive User Involvement – Research Report*, London: Shaping Our Lives.

Beresford, P. (2016) *All Our Welfare: Towards participatory social policy*, Bristol: Policy Press.

Beresford, P. and Branfield, F. (2012) 'Building solidarity, ensuring diversity: lessons from service users' and disabled people's movements', in M. Barnes and P. Cotterell (eds) *Critical Perspectives on User Involvement*, Bristol, Policy Press, pp 33–45.

Beresford, P. and Croft, S. (2012) *User Controlled Research: Scoping Review*, London: NHS National Institute for Health Research (NIHR) School for Social Care Research and London School of Economics.

BMA (British Medical Association) (2016) *Privatisation and Independent Sector Provision of NHS Health Care*, London: British Medical Association.

Glasby, J. (2012) *Understanding Health and Social Care*, Bristol: Policy Press.

King, A. and Crewe, I. (2013) *The Blunders of our Governments*, London: OneWorld.

Voronka, J. (2016) 'The politics of "people with lived experience": experiential authority and the risks of strategic essentialism', *Philosophy, Psychiatry, & Psychology*, 23 (3/4), September/December, 189–201.

Walden, G. (2006) *The New Elites: A career in the masses*, London: Gibson Square.

Walker, P. (2017) 'Social housing crisis can no longer be ignored says housing chief', *Guardian*, 19 September, www.theguardian.com/society/2017/sep/19/social-housing-crisis-can-no-longer-be-ignored-says-housing-chief

Notes on contributors

Margaret Alston is Professor of Social Work at the University of Newcastle, Australia and an adjunct Professor of Social Work at Monash University, Melbourne, Australia. She heads the Gender, Leadership and Social Sustainability research unit (GLASS). She has undertaken a number of research projects across the Asia–Pacific region and within Australia on gender, climate change, and the impacts of environmental disasters on people and communities. She has published widely on gender equality issues, rural social issues, social work and environmental disasters, including several books.

Dr Ana B. Amaya was a research fellow on PRARI (2014–15). She is currently a Research Associate based at the UN University Institute for Comparative Regional Integration Studies (UNU-CRIS) in Belgium, where she has led participatory action research in collaboration with policy makers, public officials and civil society groups in South American and Southern African regional contexts.

Sam Barnett-Cormack became engaged in active campaigning around disability in response to the proposals of the coalition government which came to power in the UK in 2010. He has been closely involved in responding to proposed reforms to Disability Living Allowance, its successor benefit Personal Independence Payments, and the out-of-work benefit for sick and/or disabled people, Employment and Support Allowance. Sam's experience of disability derives mainly from living with several long-term conditions, which also led to his involvement as a lay member developing guidance on the care of adults with multiple long-term conditions for England's National Institute of Health and Care Excellence (NICE). Sam graduated from Lancaster University three times: with a BSc in Mathematics and Computer Science, an MSc in Advanced Computer Science, and an MA in Educational Research. He is currently self-employed providing computer-based services, and is a member of the Quaker Disability Equality Group committee.

Ruth Beresford is currently undertaking her PhD in the Department of Sociological Studies at the University of Sheffield. She has a BA in History and Politics, and an MA in Social Research. Her research addresses women's experiences of pornography in their everyday lives, and is being conducted within feminist epistemological and participatory methodological frameworks. She is interested more broadly in pornography studies and sexuality, and epistemological and methodological approaches which seek to democratise the production of knowledge.

Stella Black (Ngāi Tūhoe) is a research assistant in the School of Nursing at the University of Auckland and a member of the bi-cultural Te Ārai Palliative Care and End of life research group.

Gary Bourlet is a campaigner for people with learning difficulties, civil disability and human rights. He actively supports the rights of people with learning difficulties and promotes change. Gary's work began when he started to challenge day centres, supported by John Hersov of Mencap. Gary led on starting Learning Disability England, a national organisation of people with learning disabilities; their families and friends; and the organisations and people who work with them. He has been in the Self-Advocacy movement since 1984 and was a founder of the People First Movement in the UK when it began in September 1984. In the same year he set up People First London and Thames. During his early years of self-advocacy and activism, Gary was still on benefits but used his money to pay for envelopes, stamps and writing paper and hand-wrote over 400 letters, 4 pages long. He was determined to see other Self-Advocacy groups set up around the UK. Gary was then employed by People First, London and Thames as their first employee in 1988. Gary supported and set up People First, Norfolk in 1992 and then worked for Bristol and District People First 2000 as Training and Development Officer. Gary was also the television presenter of Life of Our Own for the BBC, a 10 part series about the lives of people with learning difficulties. He has also worked in partnership with local authorities being part of the Learning Disability Partnership Board to promote the objectives of Valuing People

Kathy Boxall is Professor of Social Work and Disability Studies at the South West regional campus of Edith Cowan University. She's from the UK and has been living in Australia for two years. Kathy feels very fortunate to live in the beautiful South West of Western Australia and to be working with such great people here.

Louca-Mai Brady is a researcher and trainer with longstanding interests in children and young people's participation and facilitating their involvement in research and in the development of policy and practice. She is currently a Research Associate at Kingston and St George's Joint Faculty of Health, Social Care and Education, alongside work as a freelance researcher consultant and trainer. Louca-Mai has a background in applied social research in the voluntary and public sectors, including as a senior researcher at the National Children's Bureau Research Centre, where she led the Centre's work on the involvement in children and young people in research and co-authored guidelines on research with children and young people. Her contribution to this book emerged from participative research with a healthcare organisation for her doctorate at the University of the West of England on 'embedding young people's participation in health services and research'.

Dr **Emmeline Burdett** gained her PhD from University College London in 2011, and is currently engaged in turning her thesis into a book. She is a board member of Disability Arts Online, and has had chapters in several other publications, including Colin Cameron's *Disability Studies: A Student's Guide* (London: Sage, 2013). She has recently completed the first draft of a translation (from Dutch into English) of a book about disabled Belgian veterans of the First World War.

Christine Burns MBE campaigned for a quarter of a century for the civil rights of transgender people. As an equalities consultant she also has more than a decade's experience of achieving positive equality outcomes in public sector organisations. She was a leading figure in 'Press for Change' for 15 years, building trans community self-awareness, and working on new employment legislation and the Gender Recognition Act. She wrote the first ever official guidance about trans health for the Department of Health. She also led for some years on challenging negative reporting in the media. As an independent diversity specialist she chaired the North West Equality and Diversity Group for many years and helped countless organisations develop equality plans, including a five-year stint as the Programme Manager for Equality, Inclusion and Human Rights at NHS North West. Her ebooks *Making Equality Work* and *Pressing Matters* (on trans activism in the UK) are both essential for practitioners interested in social policy development.

Alison Cameron is a graduate in Russian and Sovietologist who ran projects mainly in the countries affected by the Chernobyl disaster. Her career was cut short when she was diagnosed with Post Traumatic Stress Disorder after an accident in which her colleagues were killed. The consequences included homelessness, multiple admissions to hospital and identity loss. She resolved to put her experiences to good use and gradually started to reconnect with the assets that being a passive recipient of care had frozen. She advises NHS, housing and social care organisations on working in equal partnership with citizens. She regularly speaks at conferences and delivers training. In 2014 she was named by the *Health Service Journal* as one of 50 Inspirational Women in Health. She is currently working towards an MSc in Healthcare Leadership at the NHS Leadership Academy, having been offered a bursary as a 'non-standard candidate'. She is delighted to be considered 'non-standard'.

Colin Cameron is a senior lecturer in at Northumbria University, Newcastle upon Tyne. He teaches across areas including guidance and counselling, disability studies and health and social care. He has been active in the UK disabled people's movement since 1992 in various roles within organisations including Lothian Centre for Inclusive Living, Disability Arts Online and Shaping Our Lives. He is the editor of *Disability Studies: A Student's Guide*, published by Sage in 2014.

Caroline enjoys working in retail at Good Sammy's. She likes going swimming at beach, ten-pin bowling, and sailing with Sail into Life. Caroline also likes going to the movies and to coffee shops, and cooking pizza.

Helen Casey is Staff Tutor in Social Work at the Open University with a particular focus on user involvement. She was previously the course leader of the social work degree programme at New College Durham. She has over ten years' experience as a lecturer, and prior to this, ten years as a social worker with people with learning disabilities in hospital and community settings. In both education and practice Helen has promoted service user and carer involvement throughout her work. She has been developing gap-mending methods with adults and young people who feel most excluded from involvement in training and education. She has an international co-ordinator role within PowerUs and is currently undertaking research to explore the impact of service user and carer involvement in health and care professional education.

Professor **Colin Clark** teaches sociology and social policy at the University of the West of Scotland (UWS). His research is mainly located within the fields of Romani studies and Ethnic and Racial Studies, with a special interest in issues of identity, migration and citizenship. Colin has published widely in these areas and supervises a number of PhD students. Outside of UWS, Colin sits on the Board of Directors of the Glasgow-based anti-racist organisation the Coalition for Racial Equality and Rights, and he is also a Trustee of the Roma Rights group Friends of Romano Lav. Colin tweets as @profcolinclark

Lucy Costa is a systemic advocate in Canada's largest mental health and addiction hospital in Canada. Her work is focused on promoting the rights of mental health service users, as well as encouraging critical analysis about service user inclusion in the mental health sector. She sits on a number of advisories and has been involved with the consumer/psychiatric survivor community for over 20 years.

Suzy Croft has been a practising palliative care social worker for 26 years. Most recently she has been the social work and bereavement team leader at St John's Hospice, London. She has been a trustee of a number of social work and palliative care organisations and has written and researched widely in the field of participation, social work and beyond.

Michelle Daley is a British Black Disabled Woman, born to parents who moved from Jamaica in the late 1950s to live in the United Kingdom. She is the former member of United Kingdom Advisory Network on Disability Equality – Equality 2025 and the Independent Living Scrutiny Group. In 2013 Michelle made the online Disability News Service list as one of the most influential Disabled People in Britain. In 2010 she co-founded Sisters of Frida, a group committed to Disabled Women issues and is one of the directors. She is a trustee for Independent Living Alternative, a national personal assistant service for Disabled Peoples. Michelle also serves as a member of the National Co-Production Advisory Group who are working to promote co-production through health and social care organisations. She enjoys working at a grassroots level and says "this is where campaigning for political rights started". She works for Reaching Out East, a local Disabled Peoples' Organisation on independent living, at a senior level.

Anya de Iongh lives with several long-term health conditions, works as a self-management coach and a patient leader. She has made the journey from medical student at Cambridge University to patient-to-patient leader. Working as a self-management coach part time for an NHS service in Dorset, My Health My Way, Anya supports other people with long-term health conditions to develop the knowledge, confidence and skills, and to support the self-management movement at a national level. In addition to this, she lectures medical and healthcare students at a number of universities, supports patient and public involvement in research projects with Wessex CLAHRC, and chairs a patient and public engagement group within Dorset CCG. In June 2013, she was awarded the College of Medicine Self-Care Award for Individuals, acknowledging her personal and professional work, and was on both the HSJ Rising Stars and Patient Leaders lists in 2015. Blog: www.thepatientpatient2011.blogspot.co.uk; @anyadei

Rose Devereaux is a qualified social worker. She works for Person Shaped Support (PSS) in Liverpool and is seconded by them to Liverpool Hope University to facilitate service user engagement on their social work programmes.

Danny Dorling is the Halford Mackinder Professor of Geography at the University of Oxford. As well as *Injustice: Why social injustice still persists* (2015), his recent books include *The Equality Effect* (2017), *Peak Inequality* (2018) and, with colleagues, *The Human Atlas of Europe* (2016).

Clenton Farquharson MBE has held a life-long curiosity about why people and organisations do the things they do. Clenton acquired his disability many years ago and since then has come to use this event and his experiences to work towards a future, where people can thrive. Clenton is a Director of a Disabled People's User Led Organisation called Community Navigator Services CIC. He has 20 years' experience in working strategically to effect long-term attitudinal and major social systems change in relation to disabled people. He has worked extensively in the UK disabled people's movement; with the UK Government; with organisations like Think Local, Act Personal (TLAP) and The Coalition for Collaborative Care (C4CC), public bodies and the business community in their understanding of 'Social Justice, and Personalisation, Coproduction' as forces for living well for a better life.

Alison Faulkner is a freelance survivor researcher and trainer in mental health with over 25 years' experience of working in mental health research and consultancy. She has worked for most of the major UK mental health charities, including the Mental Health Foundation, NSUN (the National Survivor User Network), Mind and Together for Mental Wellbeing. She managed the user-led 'Strategies for Living' programme from 1997 to 2002, one of the first user-led research projects in the UK. Alison has personal experience of mental distress and of using mental health services, including inpatient care, medication, psychotherapy, A&E and crisis services. She is currently studying for her PhD at City University, London by prior publication, on the role and value of experiential knowledge in mental health research. Her lifetime goal is to transform adult inpatient care; so far she has made little, if any, progress.

Barbara Fawcett is Professor of Social Work (Adults and Communities), Co-Director of the Department of Social Policy and Social Work, and Director of Internationalisation in the College of Social Sciences at the University of Birmingham, UK. Previously she was Professor of Social Work and Policy Studies at the University of Sydney, Australia and the Head of School and Associate Dean (Research). Whilst at Sydney she was the co director of the Social Policy Research Network. Barbara spent 13 years in the field as a senior practitioner, manager, contract researcher and head of mental health services. Her work has a strong international dimension and she has produced nine books. She focuses particularly on mental health, disability studies, older age, research methodology, particularly participative researching, and postmodern feminism. Her work focuses strongly on the interface between theory, policy and practice, and she has a strong track record in the policy arena.

Before moving into social work education, **Iain Ferguson** worked for many years as a social worker and community worker in Glasgow. He is currently Honorary Professor of Social Work and Social Policy at the University of the West of Scotland. He is the author of many articles and several books including *Reclaiming Social Work: Challenging Neoliberalism and Promoting Social Justice* (Sage, 2008), *Radical Social Work in Practice* (Policy Press, 2009, with Rona Woodward) and *Global Social Work in a Political Context: Radical Perspectives* (Policy Press, 2017, with Michael Lavalette and Vasilios Ioakimidis). He is co-editor of *Critical and Radical Social Work: an International Journal*, and is a founder-member of the Social Work Action Network (SWAN).

Jennie Fleming is Co-Director of Practical Participation and Honorary Fellow at Nottingham Trent University, and is also Editor of the journal *Groupwork*. She has decades of professional experience working with groups as a youth worker, social worker, educator and researcher; as well as experience of being a member of groups in her personal life. She is continually inspired by what people acting together can achieve.

Tara Flood is a disability rights activist and has been the Director at the Alliance for Inclusive Education since April 2006. Tara has been involved with the disability rights movement at a grassroots level for many years, and she is committed to creating social and political change that will deliver equality for all disabled people at a local, regional, national, european and international level. The Alliance for Inclusive Education campaigns for the right of all Disabled pupils and students (including those with SEN) to be included in mainstream education and for the ending of segregation. Tara was involved in the discussions at the United Nations in the development of the UN Convention on the Rights of Persons with Disabilities and is now working to get the Convention fully implemented, particularly Article 24: the Right to Inclusive Education. Tara works with organisations led by disabled people, allied organisations, children's rights organisations, statutory agencies and Government departments, both in a personal and professional capacity, and is committed to the voices and experiences of ALL disabled people being at the heart of discussions and decision making about our lives. Tara is a disabled person and a 'special' school survivor.

Kaliya Franklin is an experienced disability rights campaigner, writer and speaker. She blogs at the 2012 Orwell Prize shortlisted blog Benefit Scrounging Scum, was voted one of the top 10 most influential users of Twitter in 2011, founded the lobbying group The Broken of Britain and was an author of the *Spartacus Report*. Kaliya currently works as co-development lead of People First England – a self-advocacy organisation set up to use new online media to complement traditional ways of campaigning, helping people with learning disabilities develop their own independent media presence and voice. Kaliya is a member of Labour's Taskforce on Disability and Poverty since 2007, recently acting as lead on sickness and disability issues. She is also an Ambassador for Brandon Trust, advocating for the people with learning disabilities supported by the charity. Kaliya was the co-creator of *Easy News* with the charity United Response, the first newspaper for people with learning disabilities written in easy-read format.

Jolie Goodman is an artist who has worked from a survivor perspective in the mental health sector for the over 15 years. She has worked in both voluntary and statutory organisations, with roles including the Interim Co-Director for Lambeth and Southwark Mind. After that she became Women's Development Worker at Southwark Mind, setting up the monthly Women's Forum group in 2001 which continues to meet to this day. She specialises in group facilitation and currently is Manager and Lead Facilitator for the Standing Together Project for the charity the Mental Health Foundation. Jolie facilitates weekly self-help groups, for tenants in later life, in extra care and retirement schemes, who experience mental health issues and loneliness.

Professor **Merryn Gott** is Professor of Health Sciences at the University of Auckland. She is the rangatira of the bi-cultural Te Ārai Palliative Care and End of life research group. Merryn has been conducting research with older people for over 20 years and has a particular interest in developing models of palliative and end of life care to meet the needs of ageing populations.

Marianne Grbin is a Master's student in the School of Population Health at the University of Auckland, NZ.

Joe Greener is Lecturer in Social Policy at the University of Liverpool in Singapore.

Whio Hansen (Ngāpuhi) is a senior Kaumātua for the Te Arai Palliative Care and End of life research group.

Dr **Michael Harris** is the co-founder of Guerilla Policy. He has worked in a wide range of sectors including planning and urban policy, social policy, innovation in public services and social enterprise, central and local government, and academia.

Felicity Hathway completed a mental health nursing degree in 2017 and now works in a Child and Adolescent Mental Health Service unit as a staff nurse. She has a background of lived experience of mental health services and an enduring interest in children and young people's participation. As a young advisor extensively involved in participation with organisations including Barnardos, YoungMinds and the Anna Freud Centre as a young participant. She also delivered training locally and nationally as well as offering consultation to NHS Employers to produce official guidance around involving children and young people in the recruitment process. Felicity's contribution to this book emerged from her involvement as a young advisor, alongside other young people with experience of participation in health services, in a project on embedding young people's participation in health services.

Adam Johnson is a PhD student at Edith Cowan University. His PhD project is exploring Bunbury's aspiration to become the Most Accessible Regional City in Australia (MARCIA). Adam used to work as the CEO of Advocacy South West and enjoyed playing indoor cricket with the Advocacy members.

George Julian is a freelance knowledge transfer consultant specialising in the application of research into practice. Her PhD looked at educational provision for profoundly disabled children, and since then she's worked in and around psychology, special education, early years education and social care. As a freelancer George works with researchers, policy makers, care providers and sector-led improvement organisations. George is an avid social media user, a blogger, tweeter and online activist. Most recently she has been involved in the #JusticeforLB campaign and was a specialist advisor to CQC's review of how the NHS investigates and learns from the death of patients in its care.

Frances Kelly is a carer for her adult son who has severe mental health disability. Frances worked for many years as a social statistician and researcher and hopes to bring this experience to campaigns. She was a founder member of CarerWatch and Pat's Petition and actively campaigns against the flaws in the ESA regime.

Shae Kermit used to go to Naval Cadets, where she met her partner Luke. She enjoys spending time with her grandmother and helping to clean her floors. She also loves camping and fishing and going to Busselton Jetty to fish. Shae says, "Hope you can come and visit Bunbury some time – it's a great place for a holiday!"

Navin Kikabhai is Chair of Alliance for Inclusive Education and campaigns for the end to segregated education. He has a varied teaching and research experience within the education sector. His early research interest relates to the experiences of young people permanently excluded from mainstream schools. He is also interested in informal and formal social networks, emancipatory and transformative research approaches, social justice and human rights. A more recent focus is within the area of disability and higher education participation, specifically with the way disabled people/students are institutionally disadvantaged from teaching and learning experiences.

Shuchi Kothari is a screenwriter and Associate Professor in Screen Production (Media and Communications) in the School of Social Sciences, Faculty of Arts at the University of Auckland. Her films (*Firaaq, Apron Strings, Coffee & Allah*) have garnered several awards and been screened at international festivals including Toronto, Telluride, Venice and Cannes. Shuchi and her colleague Dr Sarina Pearson devised and produced New Zealand's first prime-time Asian show titled *A Thousand Apologies*. Together they developed the DigitalStorytelling in the Pacific project to broaden the spectrum of amateur audio-visual production in the Pacific. Shuchi's creative work reflects her interest in issues related to migration, settlement, South Asian popular culture, food and identity, digital storytelling and the politics of difference.

Nicky Lambert is an Associate Professor (Practice) at Middlesex University, where she is Director of Teaching and Learning for Mental Health, Social Work and Integrative Medicine. She is registered as a Specialist Practitioner (NMC) and is a Senior Teaching Fellow (SFHEA). Nicky has worked across a range of mental health services both in the UK and internationally, supporting staff and practice development in acute and mental health trusts, councils, businesses and charities. She also works with the CQC as a Specialist Advisor and is a Trustee for West Hampstead Women's Centre. Nicky has a professional Twitter feed: https://twitter.com/niadla (@niadla) and is keen that all people with and interest in mental health engage together as a community to support good practice and challenge discrimination. She has teaching and research interests in women's health, physical and mental health, social media and health education.

Nina Laurie is Professor of Geography and Development in the Department of Geography and Sustainable Development, St Andrews University, UK. She is interested in how and what knowledge is produced about development and what role processes of professionalisation in NGOs and social movements play in this. This includes an interest in how social and advocacy movements generate and mobilise around diverse identity issues. Her books include *Working the Spaces of Neoliberalism* (2006) and *Indigenous Development in the Andes* (2009). With her co-authors, she has also published on post-trafficking in *Gender Place and Culture*, *Development in Practice* and *Political Geography*.

Michael Lavalette is Professor of Social Work and Social Policy at Liverpool Hope University. He is the national coordinator of the Social Work Action Network.

Sarah Lonbay is a Senior Lecturer in Advocacy and Engagement at Northumbria University and teaches across the pre- and post-qualified social work programmes, as well as the BA Guidance and Counselling degree for which she is the programme leader. Her research interests are broadly concerned with the engagement of service users and carers within health and social care contexts. Her interests also include older people, adult safeguarding, service user and carer participation, social policy, and advocacy.

Luke met his partner Shae at Naval Cadets. He used to do fund-raising for Advocacy South West and has been on holiday with them. Luke was sponsored to go on the *Leeuwin II* and the *Young Endeavour* (replica sailing ships), for ten days on each ship. He works part-time as a house re-stumper (read Chapter 13 to find out what this is). He likes fishing and has caught lots of fish – especially the ones like Trumpetfish that you can't eat. Luke says, "Come to Western Australia (if you don't live here already) – it's the best place!"

Karen Machin has campaigned around issues related to mental health for over 20 years from the perspective of personal experience of living with mental health problems and supporting family members through their own difficulties. She has first-hand experience of the impact of benefits and homelessness, which led to her becoming an active member of Pat's Petition. She now works freelance in mental health with a specific interest in the impact of technology on peer support.

Tina Minkowitz is founder and president of the Center of the Human Rights of Users and Survivors of Psychiatry. She was actively involved with the drafting, negotiation, interpretation and application of the Convention on the Rights of Persons with Disabilities, and represented the World Network of Users and Survivors of Psychiatry in this regard from 2002–15. She is a lawyer who works on theory and practice in international human rights law related to legal capacity, abolition of involuntary commitment and involuntary treatment, and on women's and lesbians' human rights.

Lawrence Mitting used to be on the Board of Advocacy South West and says it was a real privilege and a pleasure to help Advocacy out. He's a Freemantle Dockers (Aussie Rules Football) supporter and a member of the Cheer Squad, the Football Club and the South West Dockers Association. He's been going to Vineyard Church in Bunbury for many years and he's going to be baptised there in February 2017. Lawrence enjoys living in Australind, near Bunbury, and being involved with his local community. On Australia Day (26 January), he's going into Bunbury with a friend to watch the fireworks over the water from the barbeque in the park.

Dr **Tess Moeke-Maxwell** (Ngāi Tai and Ngāti Porou) is a research fellow in the School of Nursing at the University of Auckland and a member of the bi-cultural Te Ārai Palliative Care and End of life research group. She has been researching Māori palliative care and end of life issues since 2010.

Michele Moore is Professor of Inclusive Education at Northumbria University and Editor of the world leading international journal *Disability & Society*. She is also an Editor for *Medicine, Conflict & Survival*. She is a service user and member of the Management Board for Shaping Our Lives. She has carried out local, national and international research with disabled people, their families and representative organisations in schools and communities for over 25 years and has published widely in the field. All of her work is concerned with developing inclusion alongside those who feel or articulate they matter less than others.

Tessa Morgan is a research assistant in the School of Nursing at the University of Auckland and a member of the bi-cultural Te Ārai Palliative Care and End of life research group.

Dr **Deirdre O'Connor** is a lecturer and researcher in Resource Economics in the School of Agriculture and Food Science, University College Dublin (UCD), Ireland. Her research and teaching interests include agricultural, rural development and food policy analysis. She acted as Chair of the Healthy Food for All Initiative (a multi-agency initiative in Ireland addressing issues of food poverty and social exclusion in Ireland) from 2007–09 and was a member of its Board of Management until 2014. She has acted as the UCD Principal Investigator on a number of EU Framework-funded and nationally funded research projects related to agricultural/rural development policy, food security and food poverty. She has held visiting Professor positions at the University of Pisa, Italy and Senshu University, Japan.

Pat Onions is a founder member of Pat's Petition. She has personal experience of disability having lost her sight 30 years ago. She is also the full-time carer to her husband. With the addition of special computer software Pat finds she is able to communicate with others in her campaigns for all disabled and chronically sick people. Her first love is horticulture and she has created two award-winning gardens in Scotland. Armed with a few cuttings, several trees, two Border Collies and a container full of her usual exuberant enthusiasm, she and David recently moved to Tenerife to start a new chapter. Hopefully life will be a little quieter, though most unlikely, and the climate will help David.

Marilyn Palmer teaches social work at Edith Cowan University in Bunbury, Western Australia. Her doctoral thesis considered responses to domestic violence in light of a collapsing welfare state. Marilyn is actively engaged with an eco-social work practice group and a cross-disciplinary collaborative auto-ethnographic research team seeking to survive and thrive in the neoliberal university. Most recently she has been researching experiences and expectations of leadership in disaster recovery, with a focus on the rural community of Yarloop in Western Australia, devastated by a bushfire in 2016.

Dr **Sarina Pearson** is a Senior Lecturer in Media and Communications in the School of Social Sciences, Faculty of Arts at the University of Auckland. With Associate Professor Shuchi Kothari she has developed the Digital Storytelling Project, which gives voice to underrepresented communities in the Pacific. Together, they produced short films of international acclaim and for television, New Zealand's first prime-time Asian show titled *A Thousand Apologies*. Sarina's research interests include exploring how cultural production reflects dynamics of power, affect and subjectivity. In addition to her creative producing, she has published in *Media, Culture & Society, Camera Obscura, The Contemporary Pacific, Continuum* and *The Journal of the Polynesian Society*.

Meena Poudel has a PhD from Newcastle University and works on development and socially and politically marginalised groups in Asia. She has extensive experience on anti-trafficking and is the author of *Dealing with Hidden Issues: Social Rejection Experienced by Trafficked Women in Nepal* (2009).

Dr **Sweta Rajan-Rankin** is a senior lecturer at the School of Social Policy Sociology and Social Research, University of Kent. She trained as a social worker in India and then completed her PhD in social policy at the University of Oxford. Her research centres broadly on the sociology of race and ethnicity, with a focus on globalisation, transnationalism and embodied identities in the Global South. Her research tackles ways in which race, racialisation and embodied identities intersect with institutional processes and social construction of policy narratives. She is the co-convenor of the British Sociological Association (BSA) Race and Ethnicity Study Group.

Diane Richardson is Professor in the School of Geography, Politics, and Sociology, Newcastle University, UK. Her research on gender, sexuality and citizenship includes analyses of how stigma associated with being outwith sexual/gender norms can make accessing rights difficult or even impossible in some circumstances. Her books include *Contesting Recognition: Culture, Identity and Citizenship* (2011), *Sexuality, Equality and Diversity* (2012), *Introducing Gender and Women's Studies* (2015) and *Sexuality and Citizenship* (2017). Her recent research Transforming Citizenship: Sexuality, Gender and Citizenship Struggles was funded by a Leverhulme Major Research Fellowship.

Emily Roberts is now freelance after over 10 years with Barnardo's managing an innovative participation service with NHS children's community services in Bristol and South Gloucestershire. A social worker by background, Emily's passion in children's rights began in her safeguarding social care work. This led her to set up and lead a rights and participation service for and with children in care. Joining Barnardo's Emily advocated for participation with parents and younger children as part of one of the trailblazing Sure Start programmes. Contribution to this book followed Emily putting her service forward to feature as a case study in Louca-Mai Brady's research on 'embedding young people's participation in health services' where young people, NHS and Barnardo's staff worked together to identify and showcase 'what good participation looks like'.

Diana Rose has been a mental health service user all her adult life and has had two academic careers. The first was as a conventional social scientist but that came to a sticky end. She spent ten years 'living in the community' and became involved in the survivor movement. She came back into research and brought together her two identities as a 'service user researcher' 20 years ago. First she worked in an NGO developing peer evaluation of mental health services and then she went to King's College London where three years ago, much to her surprise, she was made Professor of User-Led Research.

Jasna Russo is based in Berlin, Germany where she works as an independent researcher. She is a long-term activist in the international user/survivor movement. Jasna has an MA in clinical psychology and has worked on both survivor-controlled and collaborative research projects, including several large-scale international studies. Her articles have been published in anthologies and journals in Germany and the UK. Together with Angela Sweeney, Jasna is the editor of *Searching for a Rose Garden: Challenging Psychiatry, Fostering Mad Studies* published by PCCS Books.

Sara Ryan is a research lead in the Health Experiences Research Group, University of Oxford. A sociologist by background, she has published widely in the area of autism, learning disability and broader health experiences. Sara's academic career was diverted in 2013 after the death of her son, Connor, and she became involved in the #JusticeforLB campaign to try to gain accountability for his death and raise awareness about the treatment of learning disabled people in the UK.

Shakti Samuha is the first organisation in Nepal to be established and run by survivors. Founded in 1996, it focuses on organising and empowering returning trafficking survivors by providing shelter, legal aid, vocational training, and counselling.

Sue Sanders is currently Chair of Schools OUT UK (www.schools-out.org.uk) and initiated LGBT History month in the UK (www.lgbthistorymonth.org) as well as www.the-classroom.org.uk, a suite of lessons that 'Usualise and Actualise' LGBT people in all their diversity across the curriculum and all age groups. She was a founding member of the LGBT advisory group to the

Metropolitan Police, an Independent Advisor to the London Criminal Justice Board, a member of the Southwark Anti Homophobic Forum and the National Union of Teachers LGBT working group and is still a member of the cross-government independent advisory group to the Hate Crime Board. She has spoken at many international conferences, is widely published, was made Professor Emeritus of the Harvey Milk Institute in 2016, and is the holder of other awards celebrating her long engagement in grass root political work in equality and diversity issues.

Hári Sewell has a wide range of operational and strategic leadership experience in health and social care. He is a social worker by background with over 20 years' experience. Recent projects include reviews of crisis resolution and home treatment teams; reviews of day hospitals for older people with mental health problems; delivery of a service specification and metrics for a primary care mental health liaison function and of a organisational staff engagement project in a large national charity. He has undertaken national research on race equality for the Department of Health. Hári has held a number of senior roles within social care and the NHS, most recently Executive Director for Organisational Development in an inner-city Mental Health NHS Foundation Trust. Previous to this Hári has held roles as Director of Substance Misuse Services, Director of Social Care, Business Link Inspector in Social Services Inspectorate, Regional Implementation for National Service Framework and Head of Strategic Planning in Housing and Social Service Directorate. Hári also led the Race Equality programme for the National Mental Health Development Unit up to the end of March 2011.

Kay Sheldon OBE: Following years of neglectful care from mental health services, Kay has spent the past 20 years working to improve the experiences of people who use health and social care services. She was involved in setting up a number of user-led initiatives including a mental health advocacy project, and has worked nationally with a wide range of public and not-for-profit organisations. A particular focus of Kay's work has been using regulation and inspection to improve the quality of care services. From 1998–2009, she was a Mental Health Act Commissioner visiting people detained under the Mental Health Act and also led an initiative to involve people with personal experience of detention in the work of the Mental Health Act Commission. In 2009 she was appointed to the board of the health and social care regulator, the Care Quality Commission (CQC). In 2011 she raised serious concerns about the leadership and approach of the CQC, which led her to give whistleblowing evidence to the Public Inquiry into the failings of the Mid Staffordshire NHS Trust. She then spent two years trying to get her concerns taken seriously and fending off many attempts to discredit her and remove her from the board of CQC. Ultimately she was vindicated and re-appointed to the board in 2013.

Peter James Simpson is Senior Technician and a Professional Teaching Fellow in Media and Communications in the School of Social Sciences, Faculty of the Arts at the University of Auckland. His area of interest lies in technological innovation in filmmaking such as visual effects techniques and virtual reality film making. He has also directed documentary for national broadcast and contributed to award-winning dramatic pieces.

Suzanne Simpson has chosen not to write a biography.

Mo Stewart is a former healthcare professional, a disabled veteran of the Women's Royal Air Force and, for the past nine years, has worked voluntarily as an independent disability studies researcher. Mo's research began in December 2008 when visited at home by an unethical young man from Atos Healthcare, for what was meant to be a review of her War Pension. The visitor claimed to be a doctor but refused to offer any ID, produced a bogus report following a Work Capability Assessment, and challenged Mo's integrity as the resulting decision by the Service Pensions and Veterans Agency (SPVA) was that there would be no increase in War Pension, and a very stern warning not to apply for any future pension reviews. Mo spent two years challenging the SPVA decision, and realised that the research evidence she was discovering would be of value to others. Mo's research reports have been shared with Disabled People's Organisations, politicians and academics and her research has been quoted during welfare reform debates in both the House of Commons and the House of Lords. Published in September 2016, Mo's book *Cash Not Care: The planned demolition of the UK welfare state* has attracted positive reviews.

Peter Taylor-Gooby is Research Professor of Social Policy at the University of Kent. He has directed a number of ESRC and EU research programmes, written extensively on comparative social policy, welfare state attitudes and the theory of welfare and chaired the Social Work and Social Policy panels in RAE2008 and REF2014. He is now seeking to present social policy ideas outside the policy community in his novels *The Baby Auction* and *Ardent Justice.*

Janet Townsend works with poor women in low income countries on poverty and self-empowerment. Her publications include *Women and Power* (1999), *Knowledge, Power and Development Agendas* (2002), and *NGOs and the State in the 21st Century* (2006).

Rawiri Wharemate (Ngāpuhi) is the Kaumātua for the Werry Centre for Child and Adolescent Mental Health in the Faculty of Medical and Health Sciences at the University of Auckland. He is also a senior Kaumātua for the Te Ārai Palliative Care and End of life research group.

Dr **Mary Wickenden** is a disability researcher, with a particular interest in inclusive and participatory research and in hearing the voices of adults and children with disabilities and their families, especially those living in the global south or in disadvantaged contexts. She initially trained as a speech/language therapist in the UK, working with families with children with severe disabilities. She subsequently trained in medical anthropology, her PhD focusing on issues around identity and agency for teenagers with severe disabilities and little or no speech. Being interested in cultural and social aspects of disabled people's experience, she has worked extensively on disability related research, intervention and training projects in South Asia, East and Southern Africa. She teaches about disability in global contexts, qualitative and participatory research methodologies and about children and childhoods. She believes strongly in the importance of inclusive approaches to international development and service provision and in the recognition of the equal rights of adults and children with disabilities globally. She works at the Institute for Global Health, University College London and the Institute for Development Studies, University of Sussex.

Charlotte Williams OBE is Professor and Deputy Dean Social Work at RMIT University, Melbourne, Australia. Charlotte is a professionally qualified social worker and has worked in a range of social services including housing, health and social development settings as well as statutory social work in the UK and internationally. She has over 25 years' experience in social work education. Her research is underpinned by an interdisciplinary body of theory drawing largely on critical social policy, social geography, social development and theories of migration and multiculturalism. She has extensively theorised issues of place, locality and nationhood as they impact on welfare practices particularly in relation to the racialisation of minoritised groups. Her most recent publications include: *Social Work in a Diverse Society: Transformatory practice with ethnic minority individuals and communities,* Policy Press, 2016 (with M. Graham); Special Issue of British Journal of Social Work entitled: *A World on the Move: Migration, Mobilities and Social Work* (2014) (with M. Graham); and *Social Work and The City: Urban Themes in 21st Century Social Work,* Palgrave Macmillan, 2016. In 2007 she was awarded an OBE in the Queen's New Year's Honours list for services to ethnic minorities and equal opportunities.

Dr **Lisa Williams** is a research fellow in the School of Nursing at the University of Auckland. She is a member of the Te Arai Palliative Care and End of life research group. Her interests are palliative care for the oldest old and developing innovative research methods for the dissemination of research findings.

Nicola Yeates is Professor of Social Policy in the Faculty of Arts and Social Sciences at The Open University. She was Principal Investigator of the ESRC-DfID PRARI project (2014-15), and has published widely on Social Policy in relation to globalisation, regional integration, social protection, health and migration. Her research publications can be accessed from Open Research Online (www.oro.open.ac.uk).

Sarah Yiannoullou has been the managing director of the National Survivor User Network (NSUN) since March 2009. Her previous experience has included work in the arts, learning disability services, youth services and mental health. Through both personal and professional experiences over the past 20 years, she has gained valuable insight into health, social and community services and issues. Sarah has been particularly active in service user and survivor led initiatives locally and nationally, and continues to promote the direct voice of individual and collective experience in the development of policy and service design from a rights based perspective. In 2017, she received the award of Doctor of the University by the Faculty of Professional and Social Sciences, Middlesex University London, in recognition of her national contributions to improving mental health services and the lives of mental health service users across England.

Jane Young is a disabled service user who writes on disability rights, equality and social care. She has worked in both the voluntary and statutory sectors, promoting equality for disabled people and advising on access to the built environment. Following her retirement from local government in 2009 she studied for a postgraduate certificate in disability studies, having originally graduated in law in the 1980s. In 2013 Jane was appointed to the First Tier Tribunal, Social Entitlement Chamber, where she sits as a disability qualified member.

Stefan Zwickl was a long-term member of the South West Self-Advocacy Network Group, which is where he met his wife Judith. He's also is a member of the West Coast Eagles Aussie Rules Football Club and has been to 11 home games. Stefan likes the Eagle's Club song: 'We're the big birds, kings of the big game. We're the Eagles, we're flying high!'

Judith Zwickl is a dancer and has passed all her dancing certificates. She enjoys going to the movies and swimming at the swimming pool and in the sea. Judith used to be a Board member for Advocacy South West. She got an Award for working at Hungry Jack's for 21 years, but she's finished work now because the Hungry Jack's shop where she worked has been sold.

Index

#107daysofaction 319
#JusticeforLB campaign 319–22, 320
  accountability of care providers 320–1
  apathy of large-scale charities 321, 322
  defensiveness of care providers 320–1
  and the media 321
  organic support 322
  social media 320
#LBBill 319

4Pi National Involvement Standards 362–6
  authenticity 365–6
  BME service users 363
  experience based co-design (EBCD) 365
  influencing policy and practice 365
  networks 364
  service user involvement 364
  standards 363, 364
  values-based practice 365

A

A2 countries 111
A8 countries 111
Aboriginal people 129
  discrimination against 262
  relationship with state agencies 268
  resistance to state closure policies 268,
    270–1, 272
    victory 272–3
  self-organisation 271–2
    non-violent approach 272
  threat of dispossession and displacement
    270–1, 272
  withdrawal of essential services for 268
abortion 181–2
academic knowledge 135
  risk of elitism 138
academic social policy 5–7
  authority 429
activation 27–8
activism 134, 149, 178
  approaches to 289
  interview 292–6
  local/grassroots 263, 269
  see also campaigning

Administration and Society (Brudney) 75
Adult Psychiatric Morbidity study (NHS
  Digital, 2016) 313
affordable housing 98
Age Concern 218
age-friendly cities 212
ageing population
  challenges 211
  citizenship 213–14
  and dementia 217
  dependency 217
  future projections 211
  lifespans 223
  older people
    accessibility issues 214
    construction of older age 215, 216–17
    diversity of 213, 217
    having a voice 214
    involvement 212
    social exclusion 214
    sub-optimal care 223
    taking control 212
    under-representation of 214
    unequal power relations 213
    viewed as problematic 211
  participatory approaches 213–18, 219
    activity of participation 217–18
    communication 217–18
    construction of ageing 216–17
    context 215
    gatekeepers' views 215
    jargon 218
    relationships 217
    Theatre of the Oppressed method 214
    training 218
    translating and interpreting services 218
    willingness 217
  retirement ages 216
  social policy
    adult safeguarding policy 212
    assigning categories 216
    dissatisfaction with 211–12
    expert-led 211, 212, 219
    neoliberal agenda 215, 219
agency 167
aid agencies 192

Aktion T4 4
All Our Welfare (Beresford) 3, 4, 433
Alliance Against Trafficking in Women and Children in Nepal (AATWIN) 411
Alliance for Inclusive Education (ALLFIE) 103–4, 105
Alternative for Germany (AfD) 30
Althusser, Louis 37
ambiguous agency 167
American dream 15
Amin, A. 37
Anderson, John 46
anti-assistentialism 279, 280, 286
anti-discrimination legislation 58
anti-immigrant chauvinism 25
anti-trafficking
  advocates 407
  collaborations 407
  organisations *see* Shakti Samuha
Arab Spring (2011) 19, 249
Army Bureau of Current Affairs (ABCA) 432
Arnstein, Sherry 244
Ashley, April 343–4
Assessment Treatment Units 329, 330
Asset Based Community Development (ABCD) Institute 295
assisted suicide 54
ATD Fourth World project viii, ix
Atos Healthcare 389, 390, 392
'Atos Healthcare or Disability Denial Factories' report 390
Attendance Allowance 355
Auschwitz 185
austerity 22–3, 25, 27, 28
  anti-austerity politics 28
  limited benefits for disabled people 267–8
  opposition by Greek workers 249
  research *see* RE-InVEST project
  in the UK 182, 185, 243, 247, 248
    impact on Black Disabled People 191
  and vulnerable groups 278
austerity snakes 280
Australia
  asylum seekers 267
  Census 122
  Centrelink 123
  disability
    Aboriginal people 129
    Disability Pension 122
    Disability Services Commission 123–4
    employment 125–6
    free birthday passes 123
    Fuel card 122–3
    government assistance 122
    housing 124–5
    Indigenous people 129
    Local Area Co-ordinators (LACs) 123–4

medicare and doctors 124
    National Disability Service Companion card 123
    transport 126–7
    TUSS vouchers 123
  election (2017) 272
  employers
    Coles New World 125
    Environmental Centre 126
    Good Sammy's (Good Samaritan Industries) 126
    Hungry Jack's 126
    Jobs4U 125, 126
    Kindy (Kindergarten) 126
    Woolworths 125
  governments 122
  land grab 268
  Medicare card 124
  Pensioner Concession card 122
  pensions 122
  voting 122
  welfare state 268–9
    attempts at preserving 268–9
    vulnerability of 268
  see also Aboriginal People; Bunbury
Australian Catholic Social Welfare Commission 46
Australind 120, 121

B

Bacchi, C. 270
Bach, Karl 258
Bach, Mike 390
Baggini, J. 18
Bangladesh 47–8
  cyclones 47
  early warning systems 47
  emergency response process 47
Barnardo's 64, 65, 66, 67
Barnett, Colin 272
Barton, E.L. 54
Beales, Anne 312
Begum et al. 190
Begum, Nasa 190
benefit scroungers 102
benefits
  case study 67
  characterisation of claimants 184–5
  cuts in 243
  for disabled people 25, 58, 86, 87
  income-replacement benefits 88, 89
  out-of-work 90, 92
  restrictions 28
  sanctions 88, 90, 110
  tightening of 111
Benefits Integrity Project 357

Benn, Tony 263, 265
Bennett, David 'Rocky' 208
Beresford, Peter 135, 138, 215, 396
Better Life Chances for Disabled People
  policy 293
Beveridge Report (1942) 102, 108
  ABCA's summary of 432
  modern interpretation 109
Beveridge, William 57
  'five giant evils' 14, 84, 108
  full employment goal 107, 111
Bhabh, H. 36
Bhopal disaster (1984) 266
Bill 51 (Katelynn Principle) 175
Bincliffe, Stephanie 330
biomedical psychiatry 424
biopsychosocial (BPS) model of assessment
  390
black and minority ethnic (BME) groups *see*
  BME groups
Black civil rights movement 58
Black Disabled People
  absence from political debate 190
  impact of austerity measures 191
  independent living 188–90
    direct payments 191, 192
    personal health budgets 191, 192
    quality of health and social care 191–2
      barriers accessing services 191
      diversity deficit 191
Black Disabled People's Movement 190, 191
Black History Month 339
Black Lives Matter Campaign 249, 325
Black, Stella 226
  influencing policy implementation 227
Black Triangle 248, 359
Blair, Tony 265
Blanchflower, Danny 114
bloggers 324–5
Blueprint approach 192
Blühdorn, I. 267
The Blunders of our Governments (King and
  Crewe) 432
Blunkett, David 110
BME groups
  health and social care issues 380
  Health and Social Care Research and
    Development network 380–1
  user researchers 398
  see also WEDHS
Boer War 57
Bouazizi, Tarek al-Tayeb Mohamed 19
Bourdieu, Pierre 216
Bovaird, T. and Loeffler, E. 77, 80
Brexit 3, 19, 30
BRICS 34
Bringing them Home report 273n1

Bristol Community Children's Health
  Partnership (CCHP) *see* CCHP
  (Bristol Community Children's Health
  Partnership)
British Museum 340
Brudney, J.L. 75, 79, 81
Brundtland Report (1990) 271
Buffalo Beach 121
Building Research Establishment 98–9
Bunbury 120–1
  beaches 121
  disability organisations 123
  disability services
    comparison to previous years 128–9
    complaints procedures 127
    cooking classes 127
    dance classes 127
    Day Activities Incorporated 127
    HACC fees (Home and Community Care
      fees) 127
    improvements 129
    NDIS (National Disability Insurance
      Scheme) 128
  kangaroos 120
  life in 121
  Multicultural Festival 121
  transport 121
  Bunbury Dance Studio 127
Burns, J. 17
Byrne, Liam 358

C

Cahn, Edgar 75–6, 77, 80, 81, 102
Cameron, David 105
Campaign for Women Only Psychiatric
  Wards (CWOPW) 316
campaigning 289, 293
  online 332–3
  tensions 334
  see also #JusticeforLB campaign
Campbell, Peter 419–20, 423
Campbell, Sarah 356
capabilities approach 278
Capay, Adam 177
capital
  complexity of 24
  strengthening of 25
Capra, F. 264
care
  inflexibility of 182, 183
  meeting users' needs 182, 183
  notion of, problematic 182
Care Act (2014) 98, 297, 298, 300–1, 302,
  331
  direct payments scheme 300
  influences on 300

opportunities for change 300–1
Care Quality Commission (CQC) *see* CQC
(Care Quality Commission)
carers 133
carers burden 133
Carlile, Sir Alex 346
Carr, Liz 185
Cash Not Care: The planned demolition of the
UK welfare state (Stewart) 391, 392
Castrilli, John 122
CCHP (Bristol Community Children's Health
Partnership) 62, 64–5
case study 65–9
benefits 67
children's participation in policy 66–7
children's participation in strategy
development 68–9
collaboration 68
diversity of children's backgrounds 66–7
findings 70
formal participation 67
linked documents 69
HYPE (Helping Young People to Engage)
65, 69
lessons 70
partnership 64
responsibilities of 64
censorship 339
Center for the Human Rights of Users and
Survivors of Psychiatry (CHRUSP) 261
Chamberlin, Judi 132
Changing Our Worlds: examples of user-controlled
research in action (Faulkner) 394
Changing Our Worlds project 397, 398, 399
control of service users 400
discrimination 402
impact of 403
methods 399–400
Changing Outcomes model 208
child protection laws 175
childcare 25, 26
services 176
childhood, sociology of 165
children 164–6
agency 167
ECCD policies and programmes 165
cost effectiveness 165
inclusion in policymaking and planning 165
inclusive education 166
life course approaches 164, 168
specific policies and initiatives 168
voices and rights 175–6
wellbeing 165
see also disabled children; young people,
mental health issues
children's participation 13, 62–3
boundaries and limits 70

in the CCHP *see* CCHP (Bristol
Community Children's Health
Partnership)
effectiveness of 70
in health policy and practice 63–4
in healthcare organisations 63
power and control 70
rights-based approach 63
theory and practice 70
children's rights 62–3, 70, 175–6
application of 63
denial of 164
Chomsky, Noam 211
citizenship 213–14
for learning disabled people 329–30
and older people 213–14
and participation 376
as a social right 213, 412–13, 414
civil rights movement 134
civil society organisations (CSOs) 325
class interests 24
class solidarity 27
classificatory politics 34, 39
Clegg, Nick 110
climate change 44
case studies
Australia 46, 48
Bangladesh 47–8
education, young people 238–9, 241
disproportionate impact on island nations
44
social and gendered impacts of 44
climate education 238–9
Clinical Commissioning Groups 364, 365
Clinical Research Collaboration Cymru
(CRC) 380, 381, 382, 383, 384
Clinton, Bill 265
co-production 13, 74–81, 294, 297
constraints of 300
definition 323
epochalist policy-making 78–9, 79, 80
in housing 101, 102
hybrid version 79–80
of knowledge 278–9, 406–7, 410, 411, 413
management consultancy model 79
ownership 74–7
Cahn, Edgar 75–6, 80, 81
Concordat policy 77
Du Gay, Paul 78, 80
NESTA 77–8
Ostrom, Elinor and Victor 74–5
professionals and leaders 79
think tanks 77, 78, 80, 81
and participation 75
and policymaking 324, 325, 326
purpose of 279
RE-InVEST project 277–9, 285

and service users 75, 76, 79, 80, 81
  for social policy 295
    UK 77–8
  values 76
  and wider social justice aims 75–6
Coalition of Disabled People 293
collaborative mode of participation 151, 156
collective action 17–20, 233
  from below 248
  vision of interdependence 248
  see also groups; groupwork
collegiate mode of participation 150, 151, 156
Collins, Patricia Hill 190, 192
colonialism
  ambivalence 36
  in contemporary policy 37
  moral basis for 37
Community-Based Participatory Research (CBPR) framework 225
Community Care (Direct Payments) Act (1996) 191
community-owned research 399
Community Treatment Orders (CTOs) 420, 421
compassion 17
compassionate communities 223
competitiveness 24–5
Connect Works 401, 403
conscientisation 280, 284
Consent and Capacity Board 176
Conservative Party
  reform of the welfare state 245
Constituency Assembly (CA) 409, 410
  lobbying of 414
    case studies 414–15
consultative mode of participation 151
contractual mode of participation 150, 151
Convention against Torture 259
Convention on the Rights of Persons with Disabilities (CRPD) 87, 104, 231–2, 331, 418
  abolition of forced psychiatric treatment 419
  Article 4 (3) 418, 422
  Article 24 104
  Article 27 88
  Article 28 88
  background 257–8
  breakdown 260
  Committee 260
  disability-based detention 259
  factors of success
    conceptual framework 260
    grassroots character 260
    legal capacity 260
    trust and cooperation 260

forced interventions 259
human rights and social development 257, 258
key advocacy issues 258–9
legal capacity 259
Optional Protocol 261
psychiatric diagnoses 418–19
  ignoring rights 419–20
  rights 419
ratification
  in Canada 420
  in Germany 420
  in Uganda 420
  in the UK 420
Working Group 258, 259, 260
Cook, D. 8
Copenhagen Conference (2009) 266
Corbett, Arthur 343–4
Corbyn, Jeremy 3, 185
core economy 76, 102
Cork Food Policy Council (CFPC), 200–1
Corrections Service Canada 177
Cossey, Caroline 345
Council of Europe
  Guidelines for Child Friendly Healthcare 63
CQC (Care Quality Commission) 64, 306, 307–10, 365, 390
  co-production 309
  confidentiality 308
  reform 309
  State of Health Care and Adult Social Care in England in 2015/16 report 309
  University Hospitals of Morecambe Bay Hospitals NHS Trust (UHMBT) 308–9
Crenshaw, K. 188–9
Criminal Justice System (CJS) 340
critical theory 135–7
Crosscare 199
Crossley, Nick 134
Crow, Liz 185, 187
crowdfunding 357–8
crowds, power of 16–17
cultural change 341

D

Darrow, Kim 259
Darrow, Sherry 259
de Saussure, Ferdinand 38
deaf people 134
Dean, H. 58–9
death 223
  advanced age 223
  end-of-life decisions 226
  lifespans 223
  palliative care 223

deinstitutionalisation 133
Delhi Metro 35–6
Delivering Race Equality (DRE) programme
206, 207, 208, 362–3
Champions 207
dementia 185–6, 187, 217
Department for International Development
(DfID) 156
Department for Work and Pensions (DWP)
110, 253, 357, 389
Decision Makers 391
non-medical assessment model 389
dependency 98, 189
culture of 90, 245
disability as 51, 90
older people 217
rejection of 279
Derrida, Jacques 37
Descartes, René 20
despair 15, 17, 19
developed countries 34
developing countries
globalisation and 35
post-colonial critique of social policy 36–9
critical questions 39–40
social policy in 34–6
arresting of 34
export-oriented employment 35
political and global factors 34–5
state policy and implementation 36
UN classification of 34, 39
see also Global South
Devereaux, Rose 278
Dhanda, Amita 259
Dhani, Jaspal 190
difference
acceptance and understanding 166, 181
in disability 58
study of 37–8, 39
digital storytelling (DST) 224–5, 228
community involvement 226–7
dissemination strategy 227
domestic violence in Nepal 227
implications for social policy research 224,
226–7
Maori 225–6
operating within a CBPR framework 225
providing an effective voice 224–5
structure 224
value of 224
women with eating disorders 227
direct payments 191, 192, 247, 300, 302, 397
disability 13
changing attitudes to 86–7
collective disability movement 243
definitions 52, 53, 54
dependency 51, 90

depersonalisation 182–3
and difference 58
and industrialisation 54, 55
and legislation 58–9
international and domestic law 87
medical model 52, 53, 54–5
as a negative experience 53
and oppression 59
and the Paralympics 181
Poor Law (1601) 55
and poverty 87–8
rights-based approach 166
social model 52–3, 55, 87
and social policy 51–9
early 56
see also Australia, disability; Bunbury,
disability services; impairments
Disability Arts Online 185
Disability Discrimination Act (1995) 58
Disability Movement 279
disability organisations 134
Disability Rights UK 189
Disability Services Commission 123–4
Disability Studies 181
theorists 54
disabled children 163–8
agency 167
choice and control 167
conceptual gap with non-disabled children
168
cultural influences 163
denial of rights 164
'developmentally faltering' 165–6
excluded and ignored 163, 164, 166, 168
inclusion 168
as invisible citizens 164
significantly disadvantaged 163–4
gender aspect 163
in the Global South 164
see also young people, mental health issues
disabled people 13
active involvement of 185–6
affordable housing 88
education 103–4
employment 86
barriers 86–7
discrepancies in earnings 87
individual placement and support 92
personal responsibility for 185
personalised support 91–2
right to work 88, 91–2
safer out-of-works benefits 90
specific needs 91
support for employers 92
supported employment 92
unsuitability 184
and the WCA 89–90

welfare to work policies 88, 90–1
welfare to work programmes 59, 91, 93
equality for 24–5, 87
fight for freedom 328
human rights 87
income-replacement benefits 88, 89
inequality 25, 54
interview 292–6
labels 293
leisure time 182–4
living expenses 87, 88
marginalisation and exclusion 51
objects of pity and horror 55
premature deaths of 54
removal from public sphere 56
rights of 328
separate education of 56
stress due to benefits cuts 243
violence and hostility towards 105
see also learning disabled people
Disabled People Against Cuts (DPAC) see
DPAC (Disabled People Against Cuts)
Disabled People's International 257
Disabled People's Movement 58, 190
Disabled People's Organisations (DPOs) 105,
260, 390, 392
Disabled Persons (Employment) Act (1944)
86
disassociative seizures 369
trial 370–5
discrimination 190
disease 84, 223
displacement 45
DITO 400, 402
diversity 58
DLA (Disability Living Allowance) 355, 357,
358
donor aid 34
Down's syndrome 181–2
DPAC (Disabled People Against Cuts) 248–9,
324, 359
drought 46, 48
Du Gay, Paul 78, 80
dualisation 24
Dublin Food Bank 199
Dufour, Dany-Robert 20
Dugdale, John 432

E

e-governance 385
e-petitions 332–3
early child care and development (ECCD)
policies and programmes 165
cost effectiveness 165
The Earth Charter 271
ecofeminism 269–70

ecojustice 263, 269–73
goals of the system
cultures of the First Nations people 271
intergenerational equity 271
maxims of permaculture 271
interventions 269–73
problem representations 270–1
promotion of 270
self-organisation 271–2
social and cultural paradigms 269–70
ecological crises 263, 266
Ecological Footprint 266
ecological system
ecological collapse
definition 266
post-ecologist turn 267–8
strategies of simulation 267
struggling welfare state 268–9
feedback loops 265
functioning of 265–6
overshoot 266
disproportionate consequences 266
unequal distribution of 266
replacement and absorption rates 265, 266
ecological systems theory 264
economic rationalism 264
education
black history 339
challenging institutional homophobia 339
climate change 238–9, 241
compulsory 56
of the oppressed 279
production for capitalism 56
separation of disabled and non-disabled
children 56
sex and relationship education (SRE) 146
see also inclusive education
education bloggers 324
educational divisions 14
Eight Minutes to Midnight (Benjamin) 262
Ekklesia 356
Elders Council 212
Elementary Education (Blind and Deaf
Children) Act (1893) 56
Elias, N. 56
elitism 14, 15, 17
Elliott, Larry 108–9
Ellis, Elizabeth Marrkilyi 272
emancipatory disability research 395
Emergency Stop (2013) 359
employment
disabled people in Australia 125–6
dualisation 24
export-oriented 35
full employment goal 107, 111
illegal immigrants 111
illegal working 111

and mental health problems 88, 89
  reserve army of labour 111
  unemployment rates (UK) 109
  working language barrier 107–8
  see also disabled people, employment
Employment and Support Allowance (ESA)
    89, 91, 334, 389
empowerment 66, 67, 243–9, 395, 401
  in PAR 149–50
  of professionals 295
Empowerment Council 177
Engage Visually 365
English Commission for Social Care and
    Inspection 191
entrepreneurial government 78
entrepreneurship 298
environmental disasters
  Australian case study 46, 48
  Bangladesh case study 47–8
  displacement 45
  human induced 44
  impact of 43
  increasing frequency of 43
    causes of 44
  and social policy 48
  social sustainability 45, 46
  social vulnerability 44, 45, 46
  vulnerability 43, 44–5
epistemology 12, 33, 137
  feminist 132, 142–6
  service user knowledge 132–9
    drawing on critical theory 135–7
    for social welfare practices 137–8
    standpoint epistemology 136
  see also knowledge
epochal change 78
equal opportunities 58–9
Equality 2025 policy 293
Equality Act (2010) 53, 58, 87
equality training 340
ESRC (Economic and Social Research
    Council) 148, 156
essentialism 136
ethnic minorities
  ethnic category 378
  minority paradox 378–9
  participation
    barriers to 377–8, 379, 385
    building engagement 379
    case study *see* WEDHS
    discourse 378
    good practice guidance 378
    methodologies 378
  policy design and policymaking 379
    top-down and bottom-up approaches 379
  regulatory and legal framework 377
  socioeconomic inequality 385

  see also BME groups
EU (European Union) 23
  funding rounds 285
  see also RE-InVEST project
eugenics 57–8
  policies 4
Eugenics Record Office 57
European Central Bank (ECB) 23, 28
European Court of Human Rights
    Article 8 345
European Court of Justice 346
euthanasia 4
Evans, Jeff 341
Excellence for All Children (DfES, 1997) 104
exclusion 12, 14, 14–15, 17
experience
  and feminism 135–6
  of individuals 135
  Scott's view 135
  tension 135
experience based co-design (EBCD) 365
experiential expertise 118–19, 145, 146
experiential knowledge 76, 115
  in mental health policy and legislation
    418–24
  superiority of 135
  and user-controlled research 395, 396
expertise viii–ix, 67, 84
  of academics 279
  disabled people's organisations (DPOs) 260
  from service user experiences 279
  individual 214
  professional 214, 252, 254
  social policy relating to older people
    211–12
  see also experiential knowledge; lived
    experience
experts 57, 80, 154, 223
  Fabianism 57
  problematic history within social policy 57
  professional 254, 420–1, 422
  service users 254
  top-down approaches 227
  young people 235
exploitation 269–70

F

Fabian Society 57
Fabianism 57
  approach 5
factory production 55
  migration of labour 56
Family Allowances Act (1945) 108
Far Beyond the Pale (Harling) 320
fascism 18

Federal Organisation of Service Users and
    Survivors of Psychiatry 421
feminism 58, 132–3, 135
    ecofeminism 269–70
    and experience 135–6
    and pornography 143
    standpoint approach 395
feminist epistemology 132
    researching pornography 142–6
Ferguson, H. 56
Figures project 185, 187
First Nations people 271
fitness for work 89–90
Food and Agriculture Organization (FAO)
    195
food and nutrition security (FNS) 196
Food Policy Councils 201
food poverty
    definition 195–6
    downstream approaches 198
    evolving debate on 195–6
    upstream approaches 198
food poverty in Ireland
    cost of healthy eating 197
    critiques of 198–9
        food assistance measures 198–9
    extent of 196–8
    food and nutrition security (FNS) 196
    issues effecting 196
    food banks 199
    interventions 198–9
        community and voluntary sector initiatives
            198–9, 201–2
        Crosscare 199
        downstream approach 198, 200
        in production 200
        upstream approach 200
    low income/minimum wage 197
    negative food experiences 197
    policy context 199–201
        agricultural sector 200
        Cork Food Policy Council (CFPC),
            200–1
        financial constraints 201
        Food Policy Councils 201
        Healthy Food for All (HFFA) 199, 200
        issues 201
        market mechanism 199–200
        School Meal Scheme 199
        state involvement 199–200
    sacrifices by women 197
    social inclusion/exclusion 197
    unhealthy foods 197
Food Safety Authority of Ireland 197
food security 195, 196
forced psychiatry 261
Foucault, Michel 37

France
    civil unrest (1968) 244
    interventionism 28
Francis, Hywel 358
Franklin, Kaliya 356
Freedom to Speak National Guardian 309
Freedom to Speak Up (Francis) 309
Freire, Paulo 38, 279–80
Front National 19, 30
Fundamental Rights Agency (FRA) 421, 422
Fundamental Rights Committee 410

G

Gaffney, Declan 356
gap mending 349, 350–1
    central philosophy 352
    definition 350
    in Europe 353
    NCD pilot programme 351–3
        unanticipated outcomes 352
    programmes across Europe 353–4
    refugees and asylum seekers programme
        352–3
gay activism 346
Gayle, Phil 321
gender
    practices in women's mental health 311–13
    and social vulnerability 45, 47
Gender, Leadership and Social Sustainability
    (GLASS) Research Unit 44
Gender Recognition Act (2004) 343, 347
Germany
    Federal Organisation of Service Users and
        Survivors of Psychiatry 421
    forced psychiatric treatment 420, 421
    review of rights-based psychiatric services
        421
Gig Buddies initiative 183–4, 185
Girlguiding 313
Give Youth a Voice 63
Glasgow Association for Mental Health
    (GAMH) 243
Glasgow City Council 243
Global Alliance Against the Trafficking of
    Women (GAATW) 411
Global Footprint Network 266
Global North 36
Global South 33, 34, 35
    see also developing countries
globalisation 24
    consequences of 35
    impact of 27
    and inclusion 167
    weakening of the nation state 35
    winners and losers 30
Goodley, Dan 320

Gosling, Ju 186
Gove, Michael viii
Grand Valley Institution for Women 177
Great Recession (2007-08) 22
Greece 19
greed 14, 15, 17
Grenfell Tower 427
Grey-Thompson, Baroness Tanni 358, 390
groups
  access to power 240
  commitment 241
  common concerns 234–5
  definition 233
  persistence of 240–1
  responsibility for group processes 238
  Young Advisers 236, 237, 238, 240
  young people
    gaining confidence 237, 238
    voicelessness of 237
  YOUNGO 237, 238–9
groupwork 233
  advantages of 235
  case studies
    climate change education 238–9, 241
    mosquito devices 234, 237, 240
    youth justice 236
  creating policy change 233–4
    international level 238–9
    local level 234
    national level 236
    new possibilities and opportunities 235
    success of 240–1
  diversity of views 235–6
  group action 239
  information sharing 237
  knowledge and skills 240
Guerilla Policy 323–6
guerilla policymakers 324

H

Hale, C. 92
Hall, Stuart 37, 38
Hansard 432
Haraway, Donna 136
Harding, Sarah 136
Harris, John 245
HBL (Harvey Brunswick Lions) 127
Headteachers' Roundtable 324
health and social care 64–5
  Black Disabled People 191–2
  BME groups 380
  co-production 77, 80–1
  older people 211–12, 214
  participation 244, 246
  power and control 79–80
Health Promoting Palliative Care 223

Healthwatch England 64
Healthy Food for All (HFFA) 199, 200
Heavy Load (band) 183
Heule, Cecelia 350
Higher Education Academy 352
Hill, Mildrette 190
Hogeweyk 185–6, 187
Hollande, President François 28
homelessness 98, 99
homophobia 338–9
hospice care 251
House of Lords 390
housing 98–102
  bed blockers 100
  bricks and mortar stock 102
  co-production 101, 102
  cost to the NHS 98–9
  decrepit 99–100
  definition 98
  disabled people in Australia 124–5
  safe 99, 100
  Turning Point project 100–1
  valuing of human assets 102
Howard League for Penal Reform 236, 240
human beings
  as social animals 248
human rights
  citizenship 412–13, 414
  disabled people 87, 328
  impact of austerity on 278
  of learning disabled people 327, 330–1
  of mobility 113
  of transsexual people 343, 346–7
  see also children's rights; CRPD (Convention
    on the Rights of Persons with Disabilities)
Human Rights Act (1998) 281, 285, 331
human trafficking 406–16
  research 406
  see also Nepal, case study; post-trafficking;
    Shakti Samuha
HYPE (Helping Young People to Engage)
  65, 69

I

ideologies 24, 27
idleness 84, 107–15, 110–14
  Beveridge Report 108
  see also employment
ignorance 84, 102, 103–5
  see also education
IMF (International Monetary Fund) 28, 35
Immigration Act (2016) 111
impairments 52, 53, 54, 55
  abortion of foetuses 181–2
  link to social problems 57
  overcoming 86

as part of the person 184
inclusion 166–7, 168
Inclusion International 259
inclusive education 103–5
 ALLFIE 103–4, 105
 emergence of 103
 individual approach adopted by governments
 104
 lack of commitment in the UK 104–5
income-replacement benefits 88, 89
Increasing Access to Talking Therapies
 programme 281
Independent Advisory Groups 340
independent living 188–90
 challenges to 191–2
 direct payments 191, 192
 independence, neoliberal view 248
 of learning disabled people 328–9
 personal health budgets 191, 192
Independent Living Movement 189, 248
Indigenous peoples 147, 162, 172, 175–6,
 270
 Aboriginal people *see* Aboriginal people
 Maori 224, 225–6
individual placement and support programme
 92
individualism 248
individuality 17–18
industrialisation 23, 24, 54
 economic survival 56
industriousness 55
inequality 12
 of Black Disabled People 192
 and injustice 14, 15
 in wealthy countries 15–16
*Informed Gender Practice: Mental health acute
 care that works for women* (NiMHE, 2008)
 311–13
Ingram, Richard 424
injustice 12, 14–20
 collective action against 17–20
 despair 15, 17, 19
 elitism 14, 15, 17
 exclusion 14–15, 17
 greed 15, 17
 power of crowds 16–17
 prejudice 15, 17
 in wealthy countries 15–16
Innovation Unit 78
inquiry 149–50
Institute for Public Policy Research (IPPR)
 114
institutional frameworks 24, 25
institutional racism 189, 192, 208, 209, 340
 administrative systems 192
Integration Alliance 103
intergenerational equity 271

Intergovernmental Panel on Climate Changes
 (IPCC) 44
International Classification of Impairments,
 Disabilities and Handicaps (ICIDH) 52
International Disability Alliance (IDA) 257,
 258
International Disability Caucus (IDC) 258
International Monetary Fund (IMF) 23
International Organization for Migration
 (IOM) 407, 410, 413
International Paralympic Committee 181
International Women's League for Peace and
 Freedom 269
internet 323
 e-petitions 332–3
 online campaigning 332–4
 toxic tendencies 334
 see also social media
intersectionality 135, 190, 191, 192, 341
 theory 188–9, 207
Investing in People and Culture (IPC) 353
INVOLVE 394, 396–7
 Changing Our Worlds project 397, 398,
 399–400, 402, 403
IQ tests 57
island nations 44

J

'Jack Project' initiative 172
Jobseeker's Allowance (JSA) 89
Joseph Rowntree Foundation 252, 399
Julian, George 319, 321
'Jungle' camp 249
jurisprudence 261

K

Kachaje, Rachel 51
Kalathil, Jayasree 363, 398, 402
Katelynn Principle 175, 176
Keating, Paul 265
Keeley, Barbara 358
Keynes, John Maynard 57
Keynesian economics 264
Kiribati 266
knowledge
 of marginalised groups 136
 partiality of 136
 privileged 132, 134, 136, 137
 see also academic knowledge; coproduction;
 experiential knowledge; service user
 knowledge
Kristiansen, Arne 350

L

labour market
  demand side 90–1
  policies 27–8
  supply side 90
labour movement interests 25
labour of language 110–14
Labour Party 3
  election victory (1945) 108
  legislative programme 108
  see also New Labour government
Ladder of Participation (Arnstein) 244
Landlord and Tenant (Rent Controlled) Act
  (1949) 108
Lane, Mary 269–70
language
  in mental health 312
Lansley, Andrew 307, 308
The Lawrence Report (1999) 340
Lawrence, Stephen 189
  The Lawrence Report (1999) 340
Leadbeater, Charles 78
learning disabled people 319–22, 327–31
  abuses of 328
  Assessment Treatment Units 329, 330
  community care policy 328
  conventional services 320–1
  denial of free and equal citizenship 329–30
  exclusion 328
  freedom and equality 330, 331
  independent living 328–9, 331
  legislation 330–1
  living with families 329
  residential environments 329
  rights of 327, 330–1
  shared living 329
  supported living 329
  as villeins 327, 330
  see also #JusticeforLB campaign
LeBlanc, Eugène 421, 422
left-wing parties 25, 30
Leschenault Conservation Park 121
Lewis, Dr Julian 317
LGBT History Month 338
  celebration of 341
  criticisms of 340
  education 341
  embedding anti-discrimination policy
    340–1
  origins 338–9
  Past Festivals 341
  support of the CJS 340
  website 339–40
LGBT Trades Union Congress conference
  341
liberal reforms 56–7

life course approach
  disability 181–7
  disabled children 163–8
  older age 213, 216, 217
Lillehammer University 349, 353
lived experience
  demeaning of 369–75
  of disabled people in Bunbury 120–30
  food poverty in Ireland 196–8
  health and housing policy 98–102
  patient leaders 95–7
  of pornography 142–6
  Roma communities 112–15
  value and expertise of 214
Liverpool Hope University 277
Living Fund 59
Local Area Co-ordinators (LACs) 123–4
Local Government Act (1988) 338–9
Localism Act (2011) 301
Locked Hexagon Model 206
London Southbank University (LSBU) 351
long-term health conditions 95–7
Lorde, Audre 424
Los Indignados 19
Lund University 349, 353

M

Mac, Toni 420
MacPherson Report 189–90
Mad Studies 135, 138, 172–3, 177–9
  activism 178
  burgeoning scholarship 178
  collaboration across disciplines 178
  people with psychiatric diagnoses 424
  representation 178
  risk of elitism 138
Magna Carta 327, 330–1
mainstreaming 379–80, 383, 384
Making A Difference (MAD) Alliance 364,
  365
Making a Real Difference (MARD)
  programme 362, 365
Mandela, Nelson 17, 105
Manifesto for the Core Economy (Cahn) 102
Maori digital stories 225–6
  distribution plan 227
  teaching tool 226
marginalisation
  participatory methodologies 376–86
  see also ethnic minorities
Marsh, Sue 356, 357
Martin, Serena 321
Marx, Karl 19, 248
maxims of permaculture 271
McDonald, M. 153
McDonnell, John 358

McGowan, Mark 272
McGuire, Anne 358
Medigold 308
Members Manifesto (NSUN, 2015) 365–6
Mental Deficiency Act (1913) 57
mental health
  cuts in benefits and support 281–3
  and employment 88, 89
  gendered practice 311–13
  impact of austerity 282
  *Informed Gender Practice: Mental health acute
    care that works for women* (NiMHE, 2008)
    311–13
  and language 312
  personal responsibility for 282
  social justice 311–12
  spending cuts 243
  toxic environment in England 284
  and the welfare to work approach 90–1
  of young people *see* young people, mental
    health issues
  see also people with psychiatric diagnoses
Mental Health Commission of Canada
  (MHCC) 172, 174
  Youth Council 174
  Youth Perspective document 174
mental health research 137
  Mad Studies 133, 138
Mental Health Resistance Network (MHRN)
  248
methodological nationalism 376
Metropolitan University 353
Mexico 257, 258
micro enterprise(s) 302–3
  comparison to larger providers 303
  constraints of 302
  flexibility of 302
  personalised approaches 303
  structure of 302
Mid-day Meal Scheme 36
Mid Staffordshire NHS Foundation Trust 307
Migrants' Rights Network 111
migration 112
millennium drought 46, 48
Miller, Maria 358
Mind 91, 317
minority groups *see* ethnic minorities
minority paradox 377–9
Mobile Creches 36
Mobility Allowance 355
Momentum 30
monetarism 264
Morecambe Bay Action Group 309
Morris, Jan 344
Morris, Isabel 318
Morris, Jenny 247
mosquito devices 234, 237, 240

Motability scheme 359
movements for change 19–20
Mulgan, Geoff 78
Museum of London 340
mutual learning 152
My Life My Choice 320
mydaftlife (blog) 319, 321, 322

N

National Assembly (Wales) 379
National Audit Office (NAO) 110, 307
National Committee Controlling Human
  Trafficking (NCCHT) 413
National Health Service Act (1946) 108
National Institute for Health Research
  (NIHR) 137
  School for Social Care Research 395
  see also INVOLVE
National Institute of Social Care and Health
  Research (NISCHR) 382, 383, 384
National Involvement Partnership (NIP) 362
National Mental Health Development Unit
  (NMHDU) 207
National Plan of Action on Trafficking 413
National Survivor User Network (NSUN)
  362, 363, 364, 365
  Members Manifesto (2015) 365–6
National Union of Disabled Students 392
natural realm 263, 269, 270
natural selection, Darwin's theory of 57
NDIS (National Disability Insurance Scheme)
  128
needs-led economics 433
Neilson, Saadia 190
neo-Keynesianism 22, 24, 27, 30
neoliberal welfare 4
neoliberalism 27, 29–30, 264
  advocates of 265
  call to action against 265
  co-option of disability rallying cry 428–9
  devaluing of eco-political values 267
  domination of public and private life 265
  failure of 248
  individualism and free choice 265
  policy interventions 264
  social policy 5
Nepal 227
  case study
    collaborative partnership with Shakti
      Samuha *see* Shakti Samuha
    democratic reform 408
    methods and approach 408–9
    post-trafficking 407–8
NESTA (National Endowment for Science
  Technology and the Arts) 77–8
New Brunswick 420, 421

New College Durham (NCD) 351–3
New Democrats 265
New Economics Foundation 77
New Generation Publishing 392
New Labour government 77, 78, 265
  Better Life Chances for Disabled People
    policy 293
  Equality 2025 policy 293
  The Lawrence Report (1999) 340
  Single Equality Policy 339
NHS and Community Care Act (1990) 245,
  362, 364
NHS England Five Year Forward View for
  Mental Health 365
NHS (National Health Service)
  co-production 79
  privatisation of 429
  White Paper 429
NHS Trusts 319–21
Nicolaus, Martin 323, 326
Nigeria 216
nimble-fingered hypothesis 35
No Country for Young Women (Young Women's
  Trust) 313
No More Throw-away People (Cahn) 76
non-being, state of 38
non-human species 269–70
normal self-consciousness 56
normalisation 55
normality, value of 58
North Bristol National Health Service Trust
  64

O

Occupy movement 19–20, 325
O'Hagan, Mary 423
older people *see* ageing population
Oliver, M. 103
Oliver, M. and Barnes, C. 53–4
ontology 12, 33
  participatory 36–9
OPEC oil crises 35
oppression 38, 59
  of Black Disabled People 192
  education of the oppressed 279
Ostrom, Elinor and Victor 74–5
'Other,' the 38, 39
Othering 38–9

P

palliative care 223, 251
  and the community 223
  and gender 224
  LGBTQ issues 224
  new public health approaches 223

underrepresentation of disabled people
  223–4
see also professional practice, participatory
  approach
PAR (participatory action research) 147–58
  agendas 156
  arguments for 151–2
  conscientisation 280, 284
  disassociative seizures trial 370–5
  distinction from conventional research 147,
    149, 151
  empowerment and social learning 149–50
  iterative participation 150
  knowledge for action 151–2
  methodologies involving marginalised
    perspectives 376–86
  modes of participation 150–1
  outcomes 150
  and policy development 157
  power, control and ownership 150–1
  practising 152–6
    capacity-building 154–5
    collective knowledge through partners
      154, 157
    competing priorities and common
      positions 154
    individual and community level risks and
      benefits 153
    pathways to impact 153
    policy monitoring systems 152–3
    power imbalances 153–4, 154
    scope for misunderstandings 155–6
    stability among stakeholders 154
    tensions 153, 154, 155
    trust-building 155
  PRARI project 152, 154, 156, 157
  RE-InVEST project 280–1, 286
  relevance of 147
  researchers
    affiliation and social background 155–6
    skills of 155, 156
  and social policymaking 148, 152, 157
  uses of 147–8
  see also user-controlled research
Paralympics 181
  Paralympians as role models 181
  problematic ethos and image 181
Parliament Women's Caucus 410
participation 22–30
  action against neoliberal capitalism 249
  beneficiaries of 244–5
  and citizenship 376
  and co-production 75
  complexities of 429
  demands 245
  problemitisation of 244

in research *see* PAR (participatory action research)

scepticism towards 244

tokenist gestures from leaders 244–5

see also welfare states (European)

participatory action research (PAR) *see* PAR (participatory action research)

participatory social policy 2, 138–9

approach 11

approaches to ageing populations 213–18

challenges and practicalities of 214–18

authenticity 429

authority 429

challenges 427–30

constant evaluation 429–30

definition 263

post-colonial critique 36–9

RE-InVEST project 277–86

sustainable 261–72

see also sustainable-participatory social policy; user-controlled research

paternalism 58, 183

Patient Advice and Liaison Services (PALS) 321

Patient and Public Involvement (PPI) 137, 138

patient leaders 95–7

patriarchy 132

Patrick, Paul 339

Pat's Petition 332–4

PCS (Public and Civil Servants) 249

people with disabilities *see* disabled people

people with psychiatric diagnoses 418

abolition of substitute decision-making 419

availability of coercion 419–20, 420

consultation 420–2

effecting change

building on existing work 422–3

detaching from biomedical psychiatry 424

developing own agendas 423–4

leadership 423–4, 424

forced treatment

abolition of 419

use of 420

legal experts 421–2

and legislation 420

professional experts 420–1, 422

dominance of 421

public funds for 421

rights under the CRPD 418–19

social responsibility 422

People's History Museum 340

person-centred support 252

Person Shaped Support (PSS) 278

personal health budgets 191, 192

Personal Independence Payments (PIP) 355, 358

personalisation health and social care policy 293–4

inconsistency of adoption 294

ownership of 294

personhood 267, 300

Pestoff, V. 80

Phillips, Sally 181–2, 187

Piercy, Liz 321

PLAN International 167

Podemos Party 20, 30

policing 74–5

policing bloggers 324

policy analysis 270

Policy Exchange 378

policy priesthood 324, 325, 326n2

policy research (PR) 148–9

see also PAR (participatory action research)

policymaking

alternative approaches 324–5

anti-participatory ideology 325

bloggers 324–5

co-production 324, 325, 326

coming disruption of 325–6

dialogue and coordination 152

improved understanding of policy process 152

methodological nationalism 376

mutual learning 152

policy priesthood 324, 325

promoting research uptake 152

undemocratic and unrepresentative 324

see also PAR (participatory action research)

politics of representation 37–8, 39

Poor Law (1601) 55

Poor Law Amendment Act (1834) 55

pornography 142–6

anti-pornography discourses 145

legislation on 143

men's use of 144

normalisation of 143

participatory research approach 145–6

research on 143, 144–5

sex and relationship education (SRE) 146

as social problem 143

women's experiences of 144–5

A Portrait of Modern Britain (Policy Exchange) 378

positivism 137

positivist research 395

post-colonial theories 36

post-ecologist turn 267–8

post-trafficking

collaborative partnership with Shakti Samuha *see* Shakti Samuha

definition 407

in Nepal 407–8

social rights of citizenship 414

voices of women 407
postmodernism 270
poststructural ecofeminism 269, 270
Poudel, Dr 413, 414
poverty viii–ix, 29
  Australian drought 46
  in Bangladesh 47
  and disability 87–8
  food poverty 195–6
  see also food poverty in Ireland
Poverty Reduction and Regional Integration
    (PRARI) project *see* PRARI project
PowerUs European partnership 349–54
PRARI project 148, 151, 156, 157, 158n1
  interaction and capacity building 154
  use of PAR 152, 154
prejudice 14, 15, 17
Press for Change 346–7
prisons
  segregation rooms 177
  solitary confinement 177
problem representations 270
productivity 76
professional practice, participatory approach
    251–6
  challenges of 252
  developing an agenda 253
  honesty and openness 253, 254–5
  inter-disciplinary working 255
  managing conflict 254
  Mercy (patient) 253–4
  Richard (patient) 251–2
  service users
    listening to 252–3
    partnership with 252
    recognising autonomy of 255
progressive social policy 6
progressivism 326
psychiatric diagnoses *see* people with
    psychiatric diagnoses
psychiatric drugs 420
psycho-compulsion 284
Psychologists Against Austerity (PAA) 284
Public Equity Duty (2003) 339
Public Health Services Ombudsman (PHSO)
    321
public services 75, 76, 77
  reform 78
Puri, Laxmi 410
Putting People First Concordat (2007) 77

R
race 37
  definition 205
  genetic differences 205
race equality policies

avoidance of racism
  challenges 206
  independent consultancy 209
  local services 208
  national policy implementation 207
  institutional racism 208, 209
  maintaining integrity
    challenges 206, 207, 208, 209
    independent consultancy 209
    local services 208
    national policy implementation 207
  paradox of 205
  system approaches
    challenges 206
    independent consultancy 209
    local services 208
    Locked Hexagon Model 206
    national policy implementation 207
Race Relations Act (1976) 58
racialisation 205
racism 15
  avoidance in race equality policies 206, 207,
    208
  institutional racism 189, 192, 208, 209, 340
  reproduced by the state 36–7
Rainbow Ripples 400, 402, 403
Randers, J. 266
RE-InVEST project 277–86
  action outcomes
    one-day conference 284
    photo exhibition 284
  aim of 277, 278
  assessment of claimants
    humiliation 282
    stigma 282
  austerity
    blame for 282
    economic hardship 281
    impact on human rights 278
    mental health problems 282
    reduction in support services 281–2
    social damage of 278
  capabilities approach 278, 285–6
  challenges
    capabilities approach 285–6
    service user involvement 284–5
    social policies 286
    time constraints 285
    vulnerable voices 285
  co-production 277–9, 285
  cuts to mental health services 281
    day centres 281
  key findings 281–4
    injustice and oppression 281–3
    resistance and survival 283–4
  mental health
    participation in service user groups 283

personal responsibility for 282–3
recognition by others 283
reduction in day centre care 281
reduction in services and financial assistance 282
safe and secure locations 283–4
stigma 282
therapeutic activities 283
PAR process 280–1, 286
austerity snakes 280
participative approach 278
recommendations
incorporating service users knowledge 286
increased funding 286
user-controlled research 286
theoretical framing 279–80
Under Occupancy Charge (the 'bedroom tax') 281
vulnerable groups 277–8
see also SUGAH (Service User Group At Hope)
Reagan, Ronald 264
reasonable adjustments 58, 87, 90
Rebuilding an Inclusive, Value based Europe of Solidarity and Trust through Social Investments (RE-InVEST) project see RE-InVEST project
Recovery Colleges 281–2
Rees, Mark 345, 347
Reflections (Begum et al.) 189
Reina, Maria Veronica 258
relativism 136
Removing Barriers to Achievement (DfES) 104
representation, politics of 37–8
research
independent academic, value of 391
see also PAR (participatory action research); user-controlled research
Responsible Reform see Spartacus Report
Rider, Gill 308
'Right by You' campaign 172
Right to Request programme 301
right to work 88
respecting 91–2
right-wing parties 25, 30
rights see human rights
Robertson, Kerry 329–30
Roma communities 107, 110
discrimination against 112, 113
employment 112–13
English language 111
escaping discrimination and attacks 111
first-hand accounts 110–11, 112, 112–13, 114
in Glasgow 112–14
insecurity post-Brexit 114
integration support 114
mobility rights 113
Rudd, Prime Minister Kevin 273n1
Runswick-Cole, Katherine 320
Russell, Cormac 295
Ryan, Sara 319, 321, 322

S

Saathi Nepal 227
Salamanca Statement (UNESCO, 1994) 104, 166
Saltus, Dr Roiyah 380–1
same-sex adoption 341
same-sex marriage 341
Sampson, Katelynn 175–6
Sanders, Bernie 249
Saunders, Dame Cicely 251
scaffolding 280
scandal 306, 310
school attendance 165
Schools OUT 339, 340
science 136
democratisation of 138
scientific determinism 173
Scottish referendum (2014) 249
Scottish Youth Parliament 233
SDGs (Sustainable Development Goals) 166, 167, 168
Section 28 (Local Government Act, 1988) 338–9
segregation 190
self-censorship 339
self-organisation 271–2
self-sufficiency 55
Service Personnel and Veterans Agency (SPVA) 390
service providers
assumptions about service users 370–1
attitude to service users 372–4
research experience 371
service user knowledge 132–9
double nature 137
service user organisations 6, 133–4
cultural and political change 134
deinstitutionalisation 133
inadequate funding 430
leadership 133
solidarity 133–4
tensions within 133
service user participation 245–7
direct payments policy and practice 247
market-driven agenda 246
privatisation of health and social services 246–7
abuse of residents 247
tokenism 246

transformation of policy 245–6
voluntary/third sector organisations 246
service user researchers 137–8
service users 80
  contributions of 7–8
  demand for control 244
  demeaning of lived experience 369–75
  experience of current social policy 3–4, 4, 6
  meeting the needs of 252
  participation in social workers education
    349, 350, 351
  participatory approaches 213–18
  participatory change 11
  patronising view of 373
  person-centred support 252
  personalised cards 373
  representatives, valuing 374
  research
    disassociative seizures trial 370–5
    involvement in 373
    service providers' assumptions about
      370–1
    voice of 374
  and social policy 12–13
    historic relationship 12
  telling their story 253
  views of 372–4
  voice for 138–9
  see also co-production; PAR (participatory
    action research); user-controlled research
Settlement Movement 298
sex and relationship education (SRE) 146
Sex Discrimination Act (1975) 58, 346
sexuality 213
Shakti Samuha 407, 408
  activist workshop 411–13
    citizenship rights 412–13
    research methodology 412
  anti-trafficking work 408, 411, 413–14
  capacity building 410, 411
  co-production of knowledge 406–7, 410,
    411, 413
  Executive Committee 410
  founding of 409
  lobbying 413–15
    Constituency Assembly (CA) 414–15
    Nepal government 413–14
  policy workshop 410–11
  Ramon Magsaysay Award 409
  research training 410
  rights to livelihoods 408
  social rights of citizenship 414
  solidarity for women 409
  training programmes 410, 411
Shaping Our Lives project 249, 349, 400, 402
Sherry, Mark 319–20
signifier-signified process 38

Silence Speaks 227
Silent Spring (Carson) 263
simulation, strategies of 267
Single Equality Policy 339
single sex wards 314–18
Smith, Ashley 176–7
social bricoleurs 299
social capital 364
social care 77, 86, 303
  choice of provision and funding 191
  financial cuts 243
  personalisation policy 79
  private sector 246
  provision and funding 191
  see also health and social care
Social Care Institute for Excellence (SCIE)
  297
social change 297, 299
social cleansing 18
social constructionists 299
social engineers 299
Social Enterprise Unit 301
social enterprise(s) 301–2
  in the arts 302
  community involvement 302
  opportunities 302
  and social work 302
social entrepreneurs 298
  perceptions of 299
social entrepreneurship 298–300
  benefits of 299
  characteristics of 299
  constraints of 299–300
  definition 298, 301
  in the USA 298–9
social groups
  differences between 136
  knowledge of 136
  marginalised 136
social housing 98, 100, 101
  residents of 101–2
social innovation 298, 299
social intrapreneurs 299
social intrapreneurship 298
  definition 299
social justice 311–12
social learning 149–50
social location 38, 39
social media 95–6, 97, 310
  #JusticeforLB campaign 319, 320
  challenges of 334
  and policymaking 324, 325
  Spartacus Report 357
  see also internet
social movements 134
social policy
  academic 5–7

conventional/traditional
  approach 10
  associations with 4–5
  characteristics of 3, 4
  domination of 5
definitions 48
eugenicists and 57–8
field of conflict 428
historical analysis of 2
historical foundations of 4
non-participatory approaches 4–5
political influences 34–5
prevailing, problems of 3–5
rationale and aim of 4
scope of 51
and service users 12–13
shaping of 51–2
and social change 297
subjects of 1
taken-for-granted assumptions 33
technical knowledge 2
understanding of 263
see also participatory social policy
social policymaking 376
social problems 57
Beverage's 'five giant evils' 84
social responsibility 422
social security 27
  development of 328
  individualised and pre-defined behaviour
    109–10
  reforms 28
  UK (United Kingdom) 86–93, 109
  see also benefits
social sustainability 43, 45, 46, 267
social value 299
Social Value Act (2013) 301
social vulnerability 44, 45, 46
Social Work Action Network 249
social work business 245
social workers
  engagement in policy debates 48
  gap mending 349, 350–1
    NCD pilot programme 351–3
  training and education 349
  service user and carer involvement 350
Society for the Study of Social Problems 320
solidarity 12, 22–30
  weakening of 24, 27
solitary confinement 177
Solnit, R. 1
South Africa 341
South-Self model 35
Southern African Development Community
  (SADC) 148, 152
Southern Cross 247

Southern Health NHS Foundation Trust
  (SHFT) 319, 320
Sparrowhawk, Connor (Laughing Boy)
  319–22
Spartacus 324
Spartacus Report (2012) 355–60
  crowdfunding campaign 357–8
  debate 358
  freedom of information data 356–7
  impact on policy and implementation
    358–9
  importance for disability movement 359
  lessons learned 359–60
  principles 356
  social media campaign 357
Spearmint Rhinos 144
Special Rapporteur on Torture 259
Spraggs, Gill 340
squalor 84, 98, 101
St Joseph's London 251
Standards We Expect project 252
standpoint epistemology 136, 395
state policy provision 36
state welfare 23–4
Stay Up Late (organisation) 183, 184, 186
Stephen Lawrence Inquiry (1999) 189
  The Lawrence Report (1999) 340
Stonewall 346, 348
strategic essentialism 37
Stuart, Dr Ossie 190
Student Companion to Social Policy (Alcock et
  al.) 3–4
SUGAH (Service User Group At Hope) 277,
  278
  difficulties accessing talking therapies 281
  experience of members 278
  Recovery Colleges 281–2
suicide 172, 173
Sunderland University 352
Support Groups 89
supported employment programme 92
*Supporting People: Towards a person-centred
  approach* (Beresford et al.) 252
Survey on Income and Living Conditions
  (SILC) 196
survivor-controlled research 395, 399, 403
Survivors History Group 134
sustainability
  needs-led economics 433
  social sustainability 45, 46
  and vulnerability 44–5
  see also environmental disasters
sustainable-participatory social policy 261–72
  ecojustice 263, 269–73
  ecological collapse 265–9
    post-ecologist turn 267–8
  environmentalism 263–4

goals of the system 270–1
  cultures of the First Nations people 271
  intergenerational equity 271
  maxims of permaculture 271
  neoliberalism 264–5
  self-organisation 271–2
  social and cultural paradigms 269–70
sustainable social policy 263
symbolic power 216
Syriza 19, 30

T

The Tale of Laughing Boy (film) 320
Thatcher, Margaret 264
think tanks 77, 78, 80, 81
  alternative kinds of 324–5, 326
  health 79
  ideology and interests 324
tolerance 108, 109
Townsend, Peter 133
trafficking *see* human trafficking
TRANSMANGO project 196, 200
transsexual people
  activists 347–8
  Article 14 345
  background 343–4
  birth gender 343–4
  fightback 345–6
  hostile press 347
  legal campaigning 345–7
    Goodwin & I v United Kingdom (2002) 347
  legislation in European states 344
  outing of 344, 347
  Press for Change campaign 346–7
  Register of Births 344
  rights 343
    campaign for 346–7
  social pariahs 344–5
Treaty on Stability, Coordination and
  Governance (2013) 22
Tromel, Stefan 258
Trump, President Donald viii, 3, 15
trust 400–1
The Turning Point (Capra) 264
Turning Point housing project 100–1
Tuvalu 266
Twitter 95–6

U

U R Boss project 236, 237, 238, 240
Uganda
  forced psychiatric treatment 420
UK (United Kingdom)
  immigration and asylum policies 111
  inequalities 109

psychiatric treatment
  forced 420
  psychometrically validated scale 421
social security 86–93, 109
  tightening of benefits 111
  tolerance of marginalised and minority
    groups 108, 109
  welfare transformation 280
UKIP (UK Independence Party) 30
UN Committee on the Rights of Persons
  with Disabilities 421
UN Convention on the Rights of Persons
  with Disabilities (CRPD) *see* CRPD
  (Convention on the Rights of Persons
  with Disabilities)
UN Framework Convention on Climate
  Change 238
Under Occupancy Charge (the 'bedroom
  tax') 281
Union of South American Nations
  (UNASUR) 148, 152
Union of the Physically Impaired Against
  Segregation 133
United Nations Convention on the Rights of
  the Child (UNCRC) 62
Universal Credit 355
University of Morecambe Bay Hospitals NHS
  Trust (UHMBT) 308–9
UnumProvident Insurance (later Unum
  Insurance) 389–90, 390
user-controlled research 92, 286, 395
  aims of 394–5
  benefits
    access and trust 400–1
    empowerment 401
    making a difference 401
  challenges of 401–2
    credibility 401–2
    discrimination 402
  Changing Our Worlds project 397, 398,
    399–400, 402
  definition 394
  effectiveness of 350
  emancipatory research 395
  empowerment 394, 395
  and experiential knowledge 396
  feminist standpoint approach 395
  impact of 402–3
  inequalities accessing funding 430
  involvement in 396–7
  origins 394
  power and control 397, 400
  reasons for doing 399
  roots of 395–6
  shared identity 400, 402
  survivor research 395
  ways of doing 399–400

user-focused research 395
user-led organisations (ULOs) 430, 433
user-led research *see* user-controlled research
user-related research *see* user-controlled research

V

Victorian City Chambers 243
Village Development Committee (VDC) 412, 414
villeins 327
Vincentian Partnership for Social Justice 197
Vision Sense 400
vulnerability 43
  definition 44, 278
  and gender 45
  social vulnerability 44, 45, 46
  and sustainability 44–5
Vygotsky, Lev 280

W

Walden, G. 429
Wales
  BME health and social care issues 380
  Clinical Research Collaboration Cymru (CRC) 380, 381, 382, 383, 384
  Equality Committee 380
  mainstreaming 379–80, 383, 384
    top-down approach 380
  National Assembly 379, 380
    Designed for Life policy discourse 380
  Wales Office of Research and Development (WORD) 380, 382
  Welsh Assembly Government (WAG) 380, 381, 382
    Single Equality Scheme (2009) 382
  see also WEDHS
want 84, 86, 87
War Pension 389, 390
Ward, Daisy 272
Webb, Beatrice and Sidney 57
Webb, David 423
Weber, Max 4
WEDHS
  achievements 381–2
  aims and ambitions 384
  assessment of added value 382, 384
  capacity issues 384
  establishment of 381
  grant application 382–3
  investment 384
  lessons from 383–5
  minority ethnicity concerns 384
  planned activities 381
  proposed broader role for 382

specificity issues 384
structure of 381
trust 384–5
withdrawal from bid process 383
welfare recipients *see* service users
welfare reform 84, 105, 243, 324, 332, 389–92
Welfare Reform Act (2012) 355, 358
welfare state
  in Australia 268–9
  dis-emergence 34, 39
welfare state (UK)
  attempted dismantling of 108
  austerity programme 182, 185
  characteristics of 4, 58
  compensatory approach 58
  conditionality 109
  dependency culture 245
  dual function of 58
  expansion of 58
  foundations of 108
  individualised forms of welfare 245
  introduction of 328
  reform of 245
welfare states (European) 25
  activation 27–8
  current settlement 22–3
  emergence of 22, 24
  ideologies 24, 27
  industrialisation 23, 24
  institutional frameworks 24, 25
  interests 24, 26
  international context 23, 24–5
  interventionism 28
  life-stage risks 26
  'new politics' of welfare 26–7
  outcomes 27–9, 30
  poverty 29
  social provision
    accountability/responsibility 28
    austerity 27, 28
  social risks 25–6, 28
  spending 23, 26, 27, 28
    Finland 28
    new welfare 28
    older people 28–9
    Sweden 28
welfare to work policies 88, 90–1
welfare to work programmes 59, 91, 93
wellbeing 302, 303, 362
Welsh Assembly Government (WAG) 380, 381, 382
  Single Equality Scheme (2009) 382
Welsh Equality and Diversity in Health and Social Care Support Network (WEDHS) *see* WEDHS
West London Collaborative 365

whistleblowing 307–10
  legal protection 309
Whittaker, Joe 103
Why Wait Forever website 390
Wilkinson, R. and Pickett, K. 18–19
Williams, Dame Jo 308
Williams, Sir William Emrys 432
Windrush-era immigration 111
Winterbourne View 247
WNUSP (World Network of Users and
    Survivors of Psychiatry) 227, 231, 257
  Ad Hoc Committee 258
women
  as carers 133
  and eating disorders 227
  equality for 24–5
  inequality 25
  and pornography 144–5
  sacrifices by 197
  solidarity for 409
  voices of 407
  vulnerability after disasters 45, 47
Woodley, Michael 271
WORD (Wales Office of Research and
    Development) 380, 382
Work by Agenda (2016) 313
Work Capability Assessment (WCA) 89, 90,
    278, 282, 389, 390
  bogus and dangerous model 391
  corporate influences 391
  failings of 89–90
Work Capability Test 243
work-related activity groups (WRAGs) 89
workhouses 55
working classes 327–8
working from home 96
World Bank 35
World Blind Union 257
World Federation of the Deaf 257
World Federation of the Deafblind 257
World Health Organization (WHO) 52
  Adolescent Friendly Health Services: an Agenda
    for Change 63
World Network of Users and Survivors
    of Psychiatry (WNUSP) see WNUSP
    (World Network of Users and Survivors of
    Psychiatry)

Y

Yellen, Janet 15
Young Advisers group 236, 237, 238, 240
Young, Iris 59
young people
  voicelessness of 237
young people, mental health issues 172
  Ashley Smith 176–7

biomedicine and psychologisms 173–4
  childhood illnesses 174
  Consent and Capacity Board 176
  imprisonment 177
  'Jack Project' initiative 172
  Katelynn Sampson 175–6
  Mary (case study) 173–5
  policies 174–5
  preventative measures 174
  'Right by You' campaign 172
  role of Mad Studies 177–9
    curbing anti-intellectualism 178
    engaging young people 178–9
  social factors 174
  see also children; disabled children; Mental
    Health Commission of Canada (MHCC)
Young Researchers Network (YRN) projects
    403
YOUNGO 237, 238–9, 240
  accountability 239
  annual meetings 238
  consensus model 239
  daily meetings 239
  virtual environment 238
Youth Forum 64
Youth Friendly Hospital Program 63
youth justice 236

Z

Zone of Proximal Development (ZPD) 280